Commercial Insurance

Commercial Insurance

1st Edition • 1st Printing

The Institutes
720 Providence Road, Suite 100
Malvern, Pennsylvania 19355-3433

1st Edition • 1st Printing • May 2016

ISBN 978-0-89463-889-3

Foreword

The Institutes are the trusted leader in delivering proven knowledge solutions that drive powerful business results for the risk management and property-casualty insurance industry. For more than 100 years, The Institutes have been meeting the industry's changing professional development needs with customer-driven products and services.

In conjunction with industry experts and members of the academic community, our Knowledge Resources Department develops our course and program content, including Institutes study materials. Practical and technical knowledge gained from Institutes courses enhances qualifications, improves performance, and contributes to professional growth—all of which drive results.

The Institutes' proven knowledge helps individuals and organizations achieve powerful results with a variety of flexible, customer-focused options:

Recognized Credentials—The Institutes offer an unmatched range of widely recognized and industry-respected specialty credentials. The Institutes' Chartered Property Casualty Underwriter (CPCU®) professional designation is designed to provide a broad understanding of the property-casualty insurance industry. Depending on professional needs, CPCU students may select either a commercial insurance focus or a personal risk management and insurance focus and may choose from a variety of electives.

In addition, The Institutes offer certificate or designation programs in a variety of disciplines, including these:

- Claims
- Commercial underwriting
- Fidelity and surety bonding
- General insurance
- Insurance accounting and finance
- Insurance information technology
- Insurance production and agency management
- Insurance regulation and compliance

- Management
- Marine insurance
- Personal insurance
- Premium auditing
- Quality insurance services
- Reinsurance
- Risk management
- Surplus lines

Ethics—Ethical behavior is crucial to preserving not only the trust on which insurance transactions are based, but also the public's trust in our industry as a whole. All Institutes designations now have an ethics requirement, which is delivered online and free of charge. The ethics requirement content is designed specifically for insurance practitioners and uses insurance-based case studies to outline an ethical framework. More information is available in the Programs section of our website, TheInstitutes.org.

Flexible Online Learning—The Institutes have an unmatched variety of technical insurance content covering topics from accounting to underwriting, which we now deliver through hundreds of online courses. These cost-effective self-study courses are a convenient way to fill gaps in technical knowledge in a matter of hours without ever leaving the office.

Continuing Education—A majority of The Institutes' courses are filed for CE credit in most states. We also deliver quality, affordable, online CE courses quickly and conveniently through CEU. Visit CEU.com to learn more. CEU is powered by The Institutes.

College Credits—Most Institutes courses carry college credit recommendations from the American Council on Education. A variety of courses also qualify for credits toward certain associate, bachelor's, and master's degrees at several prestigious colleges and universities. More information is available in the Student Services section of our website, TheInstitutes.org.

Custom Applications—The Institutes collaborate with corporate customers to use our trusted course content and flexible delivery options in developing customized solutions that help them achieve their unique organizational goals.

Insightful Analysis—Our Insurance Research Council (IRC) division conducts public policy research on important contemporary issues in property-casualty insurance and risk management. Visit www.insurance-research.org to learn more or purchase its most recent studies.

The Institutes look forward to serving the risk management and property-casualty insurance industry for another 100 years. We welcome comments from our students and course leaders; your feedback helps us continue to improve the quality of our study materials.

Peter L. Miller, CPCU
President and CEO
The Institutes

Contents

Overview of Commercial Insurance

Educational Objectives

After learning the content of this assignment, you should be able to:

▸ Explain how insurance can be viewed as one of several risk management techniques that can be applied through the risk management process.

▸ Describe the key characteristics and advantages of the following forms of business organizations:

- Corporations

- Partnerships

- Joint ventures

- Limited liability companies (LLCs)

- Unincorporated associations

▸ Summarize the purpose of and exposures addressed by each of the various lines of commercial insurance.

▸ Describe the components of the Insurance Services Office (ISO) Commercial Package Policy (CPP), including the following:

- Common Policy Declarations

- Common Policy Conditions

- Coverage parts

▸ Describe how commercial insurance premiums are determined, including the purpose and application of package modification factors to the ISO CPP program.

Overview of Commercial Insurance

INSURANCE AS A RISK MANAGEMENT TECHNIQUE

Insurance enables a person or an organization (called "the policyholder" or "the insured") to transfer the financial consequences of a loss to an insurer. In exchange for premiums paid, the insurer agrees to pay for covered losses, whose costs are distributed among all policyholders.

Commercial insurance is insurance that covers for-profit businesses and not-for-profit organizations against the adverse financial effects of property and liability losses. Insurance is just one technique that organizations use as part of an overall process known as risk management, which entails identifying, analyzing, and managing loss exposures in such a way that allows them to meet their objectives.

Loss Exposures

A **loss exposure** (or, simply, exposure) is any condition or situation that presents a possibility of loss, regardless of whether loss actually occurs. That is, if an organization could suffer a particular loss, it is exposed to that type of loss. For example, buildings in the midwestern United States are exposed to tornado damage and thus have a tornado loss exposure. Conversely, buildings in west coast states have little tornado loss exposure.

The loss exposures to which commercial insurance responds include property loss exposures, liability loss exposures, and personal loss exposures:

- A property loss exposure is the possibility that a person or an organization will sustain a financial loss as the result of the damaging, destruction, taking, or loss of use of property in which that person or organization has a financial interest. The previously discussed possibility of tornado damage is an example of a property loss exposure.

- A liability loss exposure is the possibility that a person or an organization will sustain a financial loss as the result of a claim by someone seeking monetary damages or some other legal remedy. An example of a liability loss exposure is the possibility that a restaurant will be sued by one of its customers who has slipped and fallen because of a water spill on its floor.

- The term "personal loss exposure" describes the possibility of financial loss to a person that is caused by injury, sickness, or death. For example, anyone who could be injured on the job or in an auto accident has a per-

Commercial insurance
Insurance that covers for-profit businesses or not-for-profit organizations against the adverse financial effects of property and liability losses.

Loss exposure
Any condition or situation that presents a possibility of loss, whether or not an actual loss occurs.

sonal loss exposure. (An accident victim often can sue or otherwise make a liability claim against the responsible party, who then may also incur a liability loss.)

Risk Management Process

Property and liability and personal loss exposures can be identified and treated through the risk management process. The risk management process consists of six steps:

1. Identifying loss exposures
2. Analyzing loss exposures
3. Examining the feasibility of risk management techniques
4. Selecting the appropriate risk management techniques
5. Implementing the selected risk management techniques
6. Monitoring results and revising the risk management program

Other Risk Management Techniques

Insurance is only one of several risk management techniques and is almost always used in combination with other techniques, such as these:

*   Avoidance—An organization uses this risk management technique when it avoids an identified loss exposure by choosing not to own a particular item of property or not to engage in a particular activity. For example, by not manufacturing a new and potentially dangerous product, a manufacturer avoids the potential liability for injuries resulting from the new product. Successful avoidance reduces the probability of loss to zero.

*   Loss control—Loss control includes any measure to prevent losses from occurring (such as storing gasoline in sealed, approved containers) or to reduce the size of losses that do occur (such as installing an automatic sprinkler system in a building).

*   Retention—An organization that pays all or part of its own losses is said to retain, or self-insure, its losses. For example, a business may choose to retain certain exposures entirely or to purchase insurance policies with large deductibles. When an organization has the financial ability to absorb some or all of its own losses, its long-run cost of retention is frequently less than the cost of buying insurance to cover them.

*   Noninsurance transfer—Noninsurance transfer occurs when an organization (such as a building owner) obtains the promise of a second, noninsurance organization (such as a remodeling contractor) to pay for certain losses for which the first organization would otherwise be responsible. Also known as hold-harmless agreements or indemnity agreements, noninsurance transfers are commonly included in a wide variety of contracts, such as leases, construction contracts, and purchase agreements.

FORMS OF BUSINESS ORGANIZATIONS

In an insurance context, the form of ownership is important because it affects the insurability of the business. It determines who the owner is; that is, who has the legal responsibility for the organization's decisions and its employees' actions. Form of ownership also determines, to some extent, exactly how the named insured should be identified in the policy.

Organizations eligible for commercial insurance use various forms of ownership, including sole proprietorships, corporations, partnerships, joint ventures, limited liability companies, and unincorporated associations.

Any individual can conduct a business as a sole proprietor. Corporations have a legal existence that is separate from their owners or managers. Partnerships enable individuals to combine their efforts and resources for a business purpose. A joint venture is a business association formed by agreement of two or more parties to accomplish a particular project, such as the construction of a building. Limited liability companies combine some features of both corporations and partnerships. Unincorporated associations are a less complicated form of ownership that is often used to bring individuals together for a common purpose.

Corporations

The three main types of **corporations** are:

- For-profit business corporations
- Charitable or not-for-profit corporations, such as colleges, universities, hospitals, and religious institutions
- Governmental corporations, such as cities, counties, and states

A corporation is a separate, legally recognized entity that can sue, be sued, own property, hire employees, and enter into contracts in its own name, based on its separate legal identity.

The primary advantage of incorporation is that it limits the owners' liability for the corporations' contracts and torts. For example, if the corporation goes bankrupt or if a tort claim consumes both the corporation's available insurance and its assets, the stockholders (the corporation's owners) are generally not liable for the remaining debt.

Corporation

An entity organized under law and entitled to the same rights as a person, distinct from its owners.

Partnerships

A **partnership** is a for-profit business entity jointly owned by two or more persons who share ownership and profits (or losses), although not necessarily on an equal basis.

Partners are legally responsible for the partnership's torts and contracts. A key advantage of a partnership is that income flows to each partner and is

Partnership

A for-profit business entity jointly owned by two or more persons who share ownership and profits (or losses), although not necessarily on an equal basis.

taxable at that individual's rate, rather than at a rate that would apply to a corporation.

Joint Ventures

Joint venture

A business association formed by an express or implied agreement of two or more persons (including corporations) to accomplish a particular project, such as the construction of a building.

A **joint venture** is a business association formed by an express or implied agreement of two or more persons (including corporations) to accomplish a particular project, such as the construction of a building. Once the project is completed, the joint venture is dissolved. Profits or losses are shared by the members of the joint venture. In the U.S., joint ventures are governed by state laws on partnerships. Similarly, a joint venture is regarded as a partnership for federal income tax purposes. Advantages of joint ventures are that they can be formed quickly, and participants can pool resources in order to preempt competitors while sharing the risks of an undertaking. Joint ventures are often used as an expedited means to enter new markets, especially foreign markets.

Limited Liability Companies

Limited liability company (LLC)

A form of business entity that provides its owners the limited liability of a corporation and the tax advantages of a partnership.

A **limited liability company (LLC)** is a form of business entity that provides its owners the limited liability of a corporation and the tax advantages of a partnership. The owners of the LLC are known as members. The members appoint managers, who conduct the LLC's operations. (Members may also serve as managers.) This form of organization is appealing to real estate firms, start-up companies in the technology sector, and other entrepreneurial businesses that have small numbers of active investors.

Unincorporated Associations

Unincorporated association

A voluntary association of individuals acting together under a common name to accomplish a lawful purpose.

An **unincorporated association** is a voluntary association of individuals acting together under a common name to accomplish a lawful purpose. An association can be for-profit or not-for-profit. Its form and organization resemble a corporation's. However, because an association is not a legal entity like a corporation, its members can be held individually liable for the association's activities.

Associations are a common organizational form assumed by not-for-profit institutions. The primary advantages of unincorporated associations are that they can be easily formed and are not subject to many of the taxes commonly levied on corporations.

LINES OF COMMERCIAL INSURANCE

Line of business

A general classification of insurance, such as commercial property, commercial general liability, commercial crime, or commercial auto.

A **line of business**, or simply a line, is a general classification of insurance, such as commercial property, commercial general liability, commercial crime, or commercial auto.

The divisions used to identify lines of business depend on the purpose for which the lines are being identified. For example, the lines of business listed in the annual statement form that insurers use to report financial data to state insurance regulators differ from the line of business distinctions commonly used by insurers and practitioners in their everyday operations. The exhibit lists the lines of business this section discusses. These lines conform generally to those used by insurers in their everyday operations. See the exhibit "Lines of Commercial Insurance."

Lines of Commercial Insurance

- Commercial property insurance
- Business income insurance
- Crime insurance
- Equipment breakdown (boiler and machinery) insurance
- Inland and ocean marine insurance
- Commercial general liability insurance
- Commercial auto insurance
- Businessowners insurance
- Farm insurance
- Workers compensation and employers liability insurance
- Excess and umbrella liability insurance
- Professional liability insurance
- Management liability insurance
- Aircraft insurance
- Environmental insurance
- Surety bonds

[DA02420]

Commercial Property Insurance

In general, commercial property insurance refers to any type of commercial insurance that covers loss to property. In this sense, several of the lines of business are commercial property insurance (as opposed to commercial liability insurance). In a narrower sense, the term "commercial property insurance" describes insurance covering commercial buildings and their contents against loss caused by fire, windstorm, and many other causes of loss, or perils. Commercial property insurance (in its narrower meaning) provides little, if any, coverage for property while it is in transit or otherwise away from the insured location. Commercial property insurance omits most crime-related perils as well as mechanical or electrical breakdown or steam boiler explosion. Most references to commercial property insurance in this discussion pertain to the narrower concept of the commercial property line of business rather than to the broader concept of all insurance covering property loss exposures.

Business Income Insurance

When property is physically damaged, the owner suffers a financial loss equal to the reduction in the property's value. Damage to property can also result in lost income and increased expenses. Though sometimes called an "indirect" loss, the loss of income or the increased expenses needed to continue operations can have a devastating financial effect. Business income insurance provides organizations with protection against this possibility. Although generally included within the commercial property line, business income insurance differs significantly from insurance against physical loss to buildings and contents and is therefore discussed separately.

Crime Insurance

Commercial crime insurance covers property and perils not covered by most commercial property policies. For example, money and securities are generally excluded types of property, and employee dishonesty is almost always an excluded cause of loss in commercial property policies. Various commercial crime coverages are available to insure (1) money and securities against a wide range of perils (not limited to crime perils) and (2) property other than money and securities against various crime perils, such as employee theft, burglary, robbery, theft, and extortion.

Equipment Breakdown Insurance

Equipment breakdown insurance (traditionally known as boiler and machinery insurance) is another type of insurance that fills a gap in commercial property policies. Mechanical breakdown, electrical injury (other than lightning), and steam boiler explosion are causes of loss that are typically excluded from commercial property policies. Equipment breakdown insurance can be used to cover damage to property resulting from these perils, as well as resulting business income losses.

If, for example, a store lost business income because its air conditioning system suffered a mechanical breakdown during the hottest week of the summer, a properly arranged equipment breakdown policy would cover both the physical damage and the resulting loss of business income.

Inland and Ocean Marine Insurance

Outside the United States, marine insurance principally means insurance on vessels and their cargoes. In the U.S., marine insurance is divided into ocean marine and inland marine insurance. Ocean marine insurance conforms to the international meaning of marine insurance, whereas inland marine insurance includes a wide variety of risks that in the U.S. were first insured by marine underwriters. These risks include property in domestic transit, mobile equipment, buildings in the course of construction, property essential to transportation or communication (such as bridges, tunnels, and radio and television towers), and many other classes of property that typically involve an element of transportation.

Commercial General Liability Insurance

Every business, even one that has little or no property exposed to loss, faces the threat of claims and lawsuits for damages arising from its acts or omissions in conducting its operations. The basic protection for this exposure is commercial general liability (CGL) insurance. CGL insurance covers an organization against liability for bodily injury or property damage arising from its premises and operations, its products, or its completed work. CGL insurance also covers the insured's liability for various "personal and advertising injury" offenses, such as libel, slander, false arrest, and invasion of privacy.

Commercial Auto Insurance

Commercial property insurance does not cover physical damage to automobiles. Moreover, CGL insurance excludes liability arising out of the ownership, maintenance, or use of autos in most circumstances. Both auto physical damage insurance and auto liability insurance are available under a commercial auto insurance policy. Various coverages for personal loss exposures can be added to an auto policy by endorsement, such as auto medical payments coverage and uninsured/underinsured motorists coverage. Commercial auto insurance also encompasses specialized forms for trucking firms and auto dealers.

Businessowners Insurance

The businessowners policy combines, in a simplified manner, most of the property and liability coverages, other than auto and workers compensation, needed by small and medium-sized businesses such as stores, offices, and apartment buildings. Smaller organizations can thus avoid the more complex structure of a policy containing many separate forms providing these various coverages. Several optional coverages printed in the businessowners policy form can be activated by the insured's payment of an additional premium, and a limited number of other optional coverages can be added to the policy by endorsement.

Farm Insurance

Because many farmers and ranchers live and work on their own land, they need a combination of personal insurance and commercial insurance. Farm insurance provides this blend of coverages. The personal insurance aspect is similar to a homeowners policy, covering the farmer's home and household property. The commercial insurance aspect is similar to commercial property and inland marine coverage, covering property used in farming operations, including livestock, mobile equipment and machinery, and farm structures such as barns and outbuildings. Farm insurance also covers liability arising out of either personal or farming activities. When farm insurance is written for an agribusiness organization, the personal coverages are omitted from the policy.

Workers Compensation and Employers Liability Insurance

Workers compensation laws, which apply throughout the U.S., obligate employers to pay specified medical, disability (lost wages), rehabilitation, and death benefits for their employees' job-related injuries and diseases. The obligation to pay these benefits exists regardless of whether the employer or the employee was in any way at fault. In theory, employees are precluded from suing their employers for injuries or diseases covered by the applicable workers compensation law. However, in some cases employees are permitted to sue their employers for work-related accidents. Accordingly, workers compensation and employers liability insurance provides coverage for benefits the insured employer is obligated to pay under workers compensation laws and coverage for employee injury claims made against the insured employer that are not covered by workers compensation laws.

Excess and Umbrella Liability Insurance

Many commercial insureds want higher coverage limits than they can obtain in their primary liability coverages, such as CGL and commercial auto liability. For instance, the general liability and commercial auto insurer may not be willing to provide liability limits above $1 million for each accident or occurrence. The insured can obtain additional coverage limits through excess liability policies. A common type of excess liability policy is the umbrella liability policy, which not only provides excess limits above primary policy limits but also "drops down" to cover some claims that are not covered by the insured's primary policies. For example, an umbrella liability policy might provide an extra $4 million of liability coverage in addition to the $1 million limit provided by the insured's primary policies.

Professional Liability Insurance

Traditionally, the term "professional liability insurance" has referred to policies covering professionals such as doctors, lawyers, and engineers against liability arising out of their rendering, or failing to render, professional services. Today, the term is used to describe policies written to protect a much broader spectrum of occupations.

Management Liability Insurance

Although sometimes included in the definition of professional liability insurance, the coverages such as directors and officers liability, employment practices liability, and fiduciary liability are commonly called management liability insurance.

Aircraft Insurance

CGL insurance excludes liability for aircraft, and commercial property insurance excludes physical damage to aircraft owned or used by the insured. Insureds that own or operate aircraft can obtain aircraft insurance policies that provide aircraft liability coverage, aircraft physical damage coverage, and other aircraft coverages.

Environmental Insurance

Injury, damage, or cleanup costs resulting from the release of pollutants are largely excluded under most commercial insurance policies. Organizations that wish to insure their pollution loss exposures can obtain various types of environmental insurance.

Surety Bonds

A surety bond is an agreement by one party (the surety) to answer for the failure of another (the principal) to perform as the principal has promised. Most surety bonds are provided by insurers, and surety bonding is regulated in the same manner as insurance. For example, contract surety bonds are widely used to guarantee that a contractor (the principal) will complete a building project according to specifications and within a stated time frame, that the contractor will pay certain bills for labor and materials, and that the contractor's work will be free from defects for a specified period. Commercial surety bonds provide a wide range of other guarantees in any number of situations.

ISO COMMERCIAL PACKAGE POLICY PROGRAM

This section focuses primarily on the policy forms developed by Insurance Services Office (ISO), an advisory organization that serves United States insurers. Some insurers use similar policy forms developed by the American Association of Insurance Services (AAIS), an advisory organization similar to ISO.

The National Council on Compensation Insurance, Inc. (NCCI) has developed policy forms for workers compensation and employers liability insurance for use in many states. (Some states have their own system for workers compensation insurance.) Like ISO and the AAIS, the NCCI is an advisory organization serving member insurers.

Advisory service forms are not available for all lines of business. An insurer that wishes to underwrite a line for which no form exists must develop its own. Even when a standard policy form exists, many insurers develop their own forms or endorsements to ISO forms, often to broaden coverage relative to their competitors.

A commercial insurance policy can be either a monoline policy or a package policy. A **monoline policy** is a policy that covers only one line of business. A **package policy** is a policy that covers two or more lines of business. In practice, most organizations have a package policy that provides most or all of their needed coverages. In addition to their package policies, many organizations also have one or more monoline policies from other insurers providing coverages that the package insurer either does not write or is unwilling to provide to the insured.

For example, an architect's office may have an insurance program that consists of three policies:

- A package policy covering commercial property, commercial crime, commercial inland marine, commercial general liability, and commercial auto lines
- A monoline workers compensation and employers liability policy
- A monoline architects professional liability policy

A **Commercial Package Policy (CPP)** is a policy that covers two or more lines of business by combining ISO's commercial lines coverage parts. Under the rules and forms developed by ISO and used by many insurers, a CPP includes three components:

- Common Policy Declarations
- Common Policy Conditions
- Two or more coverage parts

A policy that contains declarations and conditions but only one coverage part is a monoline policy. The exhibit depicts examples of these coverages. See the exhibit "Components of a Commercial Package Policy (CPP)."

Monoline policy

Policy that covers only one line of business.

Package policy

Policy that covers two or more lines of business.

Commercial package policy (CPP)

Policy that covers two or more lines of business by combining ISO's commercial lines coverage parts.

Components of a Commercial Package Policy (CPP)

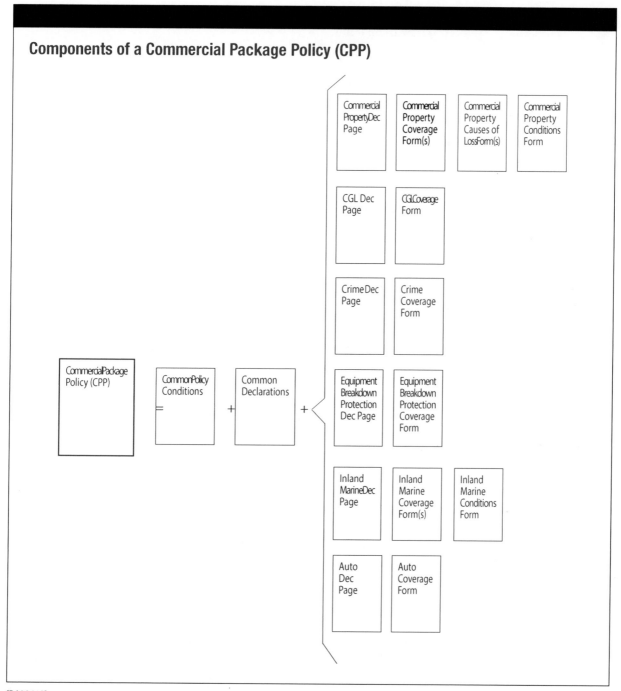

[DA02419]

Common Policy Declarations

Common Policy Declarations is a required CPP component that provides basic information about the insurer, the policyholder, and the insurance provided. This component is often called the common "dec" page. The Common

Common Policy
Declarations

A required CPP component
that provides basic
information about the
insurer, the policyholder, and
the insurance provided.

Policy Declarations are printed on one or more pages at the front of the policy and show these items:

- Policy number
- Names of the insurer and the producer
- Name, address, and business description of the named insured
- Effective date and expiration date of the policy
- Premium for each coverage part included in the policy
- Total premium

The Common Policy Declarations also includes a general statement, known as the "in consideration" clause. In this clause, the insurer agrees with the named insured to provide the insurance as stated in the policy in return for the payment of premium and subject to all the policy terms.

Common Policy Conditions

Common Policy Conditions

A required CPP component that contains six conditions applicable to all coverage parts unless a coverage part states otherwise.

The **Common Policy Conditions** are contained in a separate form attached to the policy. This approach alleviates the need to repeat them in each coverage part. These are the six conditions in the form:

- Cancellation
- Changes
- Examination of Your Books and Records
- Inspections and Surveys
- Premiums
- Transfer of Your Rights and Duties Under This Policy

Cancellation

The insured may cancel the policy at any time by mailing or delivering written notice of cancellation to the insurer. If two or more insureds are listed in the declarations, only the one listed first ("the first named insured") can request cancellation.

The insurer can cancel the policy by mailing or delivering written notice of cancellation to the first named insured. To provide reasonable time for the insured to obtain other insurance, the insurer is required to give advance notice of cancellation. Notice of cancellation must be mailed or delivered to the insured at least ten days before the date of cancellation if the cancellation is for nonpayment of premium or at least thirty days before the date of cancellation for any other reason.

If the notice of cancellation is mailed, the insurer is not required to prove that the insured actually received the notice. The insurer is required to prove only that the notice was mailed to the first named insured at the mailing address shown on the policy.

If the cancellation results in a return premium, the refund will be sent to the first named insured. In effect, the first named insured is designated as the agent who can act on behalf of all other insureds for all transactions related to cancellation of the policy.

In almost every state, the Cancellation condition is superseded by state law, and a state-specific cancellation endorsement is added to the policy. That endorsement modifies the Cancellation condition to conform with the applicable law. The state laws commonly address permissible reasons for cancellation and the advance notification period.

Changes

The Common Policy Conditions include a clause concerning changes in the policy. This clause states that the policy constitutes the entire contract between the parties. The policy can be changed only by a written endorsement issued by the insurer. Such changes may be made, with the insurer's consent, upon the request of the first named insured. Only the first named insured has the authority to request policy changes, and the insurer is authorized to make changes upon the request of the first named insured without specific permission of any other insured.

Examination of Books and Records

The insurer reserves the right to examine and audit the insured's books and records related to the policy at any time during the policy period and for up to three years after the termination of the policy. This provision is included because many commercial insurance policies are issued with estimated premiums. The final premium is determined after the policy expires, based on reported values of the insured property, the amount of the insured's sales or payrolls, or some other variable on which the premium charge is based.

The insured is required to report the final figures to the insurer, and the insurer may accept the insured's reports without verification. However, this provision permits the insurer to make an on-site verification as it deems necessary. The insurer's rights under this condition may also be exercised during the loss adjustment process.

Inspections and Surveys

The insurer has the right, but not the obligation, to inspect the insured's premises and operations at any reasonable time during the policy period.

The inspections may be made by the insurer's own personnel or by another organization acting on behalf of the insurer. Such inspections are important in determining the insurability of the insured's property and operations, in setting proper insurance rates, and in making loss control recommendations.

The insurer *may* inform the insured of the results of such inspections and may recommend changes. However, it does not have a duty to do either.

The Inspections and Surveys condition clarifies that the insurer does not make safety inspections, does not guarantee that conditions are safe or healthful, and does not guarantee that the insured is in compliance with safety or health regulations. These disclaimer clauses protect the insurer against suits by persons who allege injury as a result of the insurer's failure to detect a hazardous condition or against a suit by the insured alleging that the insurer failed to detect a violation of laws or regulations, with a resulting fine or other penalty against the insured.

Premiums

The first named insured is responsible for paying the premium under the policy. The insurer must also pay any return premium under the policy to the first named insured.

Transfer of Rights and Duties Under the Policy

The insured cannot transfer any rights or duties under the policy to any other person or organization without the written consent of the insurer. For example, if the insured sells the property covered by the policy, the coverage cannot be transferred to the new owner without the insurer's written consent. Such a transfer of coverage is generally referred to as an assignment of the policy, but that terminology is not used in the Common Policy Conditions.

The transfer of rights and duties condition also provides specifically for the automatic transfer of coverage upon the death of an individual named insured. Upon death, the insured's rights and duties under the policy are automatically transferred to the insured's legal representative, or, if the insured's legal representative has not yet been appointed, to any person having proper temporary custody of the insured property.

Coverage Parts

Coverage part
A component of a CPP or a monoline policy that contains the policy provisions relating to a particular line of business, such as commercial property or commercial general liability; consists of the coverage part's declarations page, one or more coverage forms, applicable endorsements, and in some cases a general provisions form.

A **coverage part** is a component of a CPP or monoline policy that contains the policy provisions relating to a particular line of business, such as commercial property or commercial general liability. Each coverage part consists of three elements:

- A declarations page that pertains only to that coverage part
- One or more coverage forms, which contain insuring agreements, exclusions, and other policy provisions
- Applicable endorsements, which modify the terms of the coverage form(s) to fit an insured's needs

Some coverage parts include a conditions form containing general provisions that could apply to any of the coverage forms included in the coverage part. Other coverage parts use coverage forms that include all the applicable general provisions and therefore do not need a conditions form.

The coverage parts that may be included in a CPP correspond generally to the lines of business. Examples of coverage parts include these:

- Commercial property
- Commercial crime
- Equipment breakdown
- Commercial inland marine
- Commercial general liability
- Commercial auto

DETERMINING COMMERCIAL INSURANCE PREMIUMS

Ideally, an insurance premium should be commensurate with the risks the corresponding policy insures. For example, a roofer is more likely to make a workers compensation claim than an accountant. Therefore, insurers expect the total cost of workers compensation losses for a given number of roofers to exceed the cost of losses for the same number of accountants. As a result, an insurer charges roofers a higher premium for such coverage than it charges accountants. Different premium charges for different classes of insureds are determined in the rating process.

Rating Fundamentals

Rating is the process of applying a **rate** to a particular exposure and performing any other necessary calculations to determine an appropriate policy premium. In this context, the exposure, or exposure basis, is a measure of susceptibility to loss (distinct from the meaning of "loss exposure"). If $0.50 per $100 of property insurance coverage is provided for a building, the exposure basis is the value of the property insured, expressed in units of hundreds of dollars. The exposure basis varies by line of business and can vary within a particular line of business by business classification.

Rate

The price per exposure unit for insurance coverage.

As a simplified example, if the applicable rate for a particular coverage is $0.50 per $100 of insurance and the amount of insurance is $100,000, the premium for the coverage can be calculated in this manner:

$$\frac{\$0.50}{\$100} \times \$100,000 = \$500$$

Another way to reach the same result is to establish the number of exposure units by dividing the amount of insurance by the unit amount, and then multiplying the number of units by the rate:

$$\frac{\$100,000}{\$100} \times \$0.50 = \$500$$

In reality, rating is usually more complicated; additional calculations are often needed. For example, the rate or the premium must often be multiplied by additional factors to account for territorial differences, to reduce the premium when the insured has selected a higher deductible, to increase the premium when a coverage option has been added, and so forth.

The primary source of information for rating ISO coverages is the **Commercial Lines Manual (CLM)** (Similar information is provided by the AAIS on behalf of its member companies for rating its coverage forms.) The CLM contains eighteen divisions, encompassing most of the lines of commercial insurance shown in the exhibit, plus others. See the exhibit "Lines of Commercial Insurance."

Commercial Lines Manual (CLM)

An ISO publication that includes rules and rating procedures for several major lines of commercial insurance.

Lines of Commercial Insurance

- Commercial property insurance
- Business income insurance
- Crime insurance
- Equipment breakdown (boiler and machinery) insurance
- Inland and ocean marine insurance
- Commercial general liability insurance
- Commercial auto insurance
- Businessowners insurance
- Farm insurance
- Workers compensation and employers liability insurance
- Excess and umbrella liability insurance
- Professional liability insurance
- Management liability insurance
- Aircraft insurance
- Environmental insurance
- Surety bonds

[DA02420]

The CLM contains rating procedures and loss costs. Loss costs are the portion of the rate that covers projected claim payments and loss adjusting expenses. To convert loss costs to complete rates that can be used to rate a policy, each insurer calculates a loss cost multiplier to cover other expenses that it will incur (such as underwriting, marketing, and taxes). In addition, a charge is usually added to allow for possible errors in the insurer's predictions. An allowance for insurer profit may also be added.

Package Modification Factors

An important element of the CPP program is the package discount the insured may receive. The premium for a CPP is initially determined as if each coverage part were being issued as a monoline policy. If, as is commonly the case, a CPP includes both property coverage and liability coverage, the premiums for certain coverage parts are multiplied by **package modification factors**. The resulting discounts are justified by the greater efficiency of issuing a single package policy instead of several monoline policies for an insured.

The package discount is determined by applying the appropriate package modification factors to the premiums for the eligible coverage parts included in the policy. The package modification factors reflect the type of business (apartment, office, mercantile, and so forth), the particular coverage part being rated, and other eligibility requirements. A package modification factor of 0.75, for example, means that the premium for that coverage part will be three-fourths of the premium that would apply if the coverage part were issued in a monoline policy. The factors vary from state to state, and a particular insurer may develop its own package modification factors instead of using those shown in the *CLM*. See the exhibit "Example of Package Modification Factor."

Package modification factors

Factors that are applied to the regular policy premiums for certain coverage parts of a CPP that includes both property and liability coverages, resulting in premium discounts for those coverage parts.

Example of Package Modification Factor

Premium for general liability coverage part (if rated as a monoline policy)	$25,220
Package modification factor	× 0.80
Discounted CPP premium for general liability coverage part	$20,176

[DA02463]

SUMMARY

Commercial insurance is property and liability insurance for businesses and other organizations such as schools and churches. Commercial insurance is one of several techniques used in risk management, which is the process of identifying, analyzing, and managing loss exposures so that an organization can meet its objectives. Other risk management techniques often used in combination with insurance include avoidance, loss control, retention, and noninsurance transfer.

Organizations can have different forms of ownership, including sole proprietorships, corporations, partnerships, joint ventures, limited liability companies, and unincorporated associations.

Commercial insurance is divided into several lines of business, or distinct coverages. Lines of commercial insurance include commercial property insurance, business income insurance, crime insurance, equipment breakdown (boiler and machinery) insurance, inland and ocean marine insurance, commercial general liability insurance, commercial auto insurance, businessowners insurance, farm insurance, workers compensation and employers liability insurance, excess and umbrella liability insurance, professional liability insurance, management liability insurance, aircraft insurance, environmental insurance, and surety bonds.

Commercial insurance is often provided in a package policy, which is a policy that covers two or more lines of business. In some cases, a policyholder may need to obtain additional coverages under monoline policies. A monoline policy is a policy that provides only one line of coverage, such as a workers compensation and employers liability policy.

Under the Insurance Services Office (ISO) Commercial Package Policy (CPP) program, a package policy consists of Common Policy Declarations, Common Policy Conditions, and two or more coverage parts. The Common Policy Declarations page contains essential information about the policyholder and the coverages being provided. The Common Policy Conditions form contains six basic conditions that apply to all coverage parts included in the policy. Each coverage part consists of a declarations page for that coverage part; one or more coverage forms; and, for some coverage parts, a separate conditions form.

Commercial insurance premiums are calculated by multiplying the rate by the exposure. The premium for a CPP is often lower than if the same coverages in the CPP were issued in separate monoline policies. This premium reduction results because some coverage parts in a CPP qualify for a discount based on the advantages to an insurer of issuing a single package policy rather than several monoline policies. The discount is determined by multiplying the monoline premium by a package modification factor (such as 0.80).

Direct Your Learning ▶▶

Introduction to Commercial Liability Insurance

Educational Objectives

After learning the content of this assignment, you should be able to:

▷ Explain how each of the following can be the basis for legal liability:

- Torts
- Contracts
- Statutes

▷ Describe the legal foundations and the general scope of each of the following commercial liability loss exposures:

- Premises and operations liability
- Products and completed operations liability
- Automobile liability
- Workers compensation and employers liability

▷ Explain how organizations use each of the following to manage loss exposures, claims, and potential claims:

- Risk control techniques
- General concepts of commercial liability risk control

▷ Explain how organizations can use commercial liability risk control to manage the following loss exposures:

- Premises liability
- Off-premises operations
- Products-completed operations
- Motor vehicle liability
- Workers compensation and employers liability
- Technology and communication

Introduction to Commercial Liability Insurance

LEGAL LIABILITY: TORTS, CONTRACTS, AND STATUTES

Every person and all organizations are exposed to liability loss. The possibility of a liability loss is a **liability loss** exposure. To be able to identify, analyze, and properly handle an organization's liability loss exposures, one must understand the concept of **legal liability** and the common sources of liability loss exposures.

Anyone who wishes to evaluate an organization's liability loss exposures must understand the various ways in which the organization may become legally liable. Legal liability imposed by civil law can be based on torts, contracts, or statutes.

A liability insurance policy typically obligates the insurer to defend the insured against allegations that, if true, would be covered under the policy. Therefore, an organization can experience a liability loss even as a result of a suit in which it is not legally held liable. In addition, the policy obligates the insurer to pay damages for which the insured is legally liable. In most liability claims in which the insurer believes that its insured is legally liable, it attempts to settle the claim (by offering to pay a certain amount of damages to the claimant) in order to avoid the additional expense of a court proceeding.

Civil Law and Criminal Law

Legal liability can be imposed by **civil law**, **criminal law**, or both. Liability insurance responds to liability imposed by civil law. Insurance for criminal liability is prohibited by law.

In some instances, a single act can constitute both a civil wrong and a crime. For example, if a driver causes the death of a pedestrian, law enforcement authorities may charge the driver with vehicular homicide, a criminal act. The driver may also be subject to a civil action by the estate of the deceased pedestrian for medical bills, funeral expenses, loss of support, and other damages that the law allows. Insurance coverage would not respond to the criminal charges. It could, however, provide payment for the civil claims.

Civil liability can be based on torts, contracts, or statutes. See the exhibit "Bases for Legal Liability."

Liability loss

Any loss that a person or an organization sustains as a result of a claim or suit against that person or organization by someone seeking damages or some other remedy permitted by law.

Legal liability

The legally enforceable obligation of a person or an organization to pay a sum of money (called damages) to another person or organization.

Civil law

A classification of law that applies to legal matters not governed by criminal law and that protects rights and provides remedies for breaches of duties owed to others.

Criminal law

The branch of the law that imposes penalties for wrongs against society.

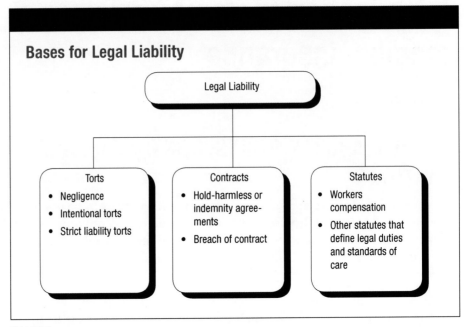

Bases for Legal Liability

[DA02515]

Legal Liability Based on Torts

Tort

A wrongful act or an omission, other than a crime or a breach of contract, that invades a legally protected right.

Torts may be civil wrongs or private wrongs. Most of the claims covered by liability insurance are based on tort law, which protects the rights of individuals. These rights originally included the rights to security of person, property, and reputation. Over the years, legal changes have established other rights of individuals, such as the right to privacy. Where a right exists, others have a corresponding duty to respect it and to refrain from any act or omission that would impair or damage it. Any wrongful invasion of legally protected rights entitles the injured party to bring an action against the wrongdoer for damages.

The numerous types of torts fall into three broad categories:

- Negligence
- Intentional torts
- Strict liability torts

Negligence

The failure to exercise the degree of care that a reasonable person in a similar situation would exercise to avoid harming others.

Negligence is based on four elements:

- A duty owed to another person
- A breach of that duty
- A close causal connection between the negligent act (breach of duty) and the resulting harm
- The occurrence of actual loss or damage of a type recognized by law and measurable in monetary terms

For example, a motorist who drives at an unsafe and excessive speed and, as a result, causes an accident that injures another motorist has committed the tort of negligence.

An **intentional tort** is a tort committed by a person who foresees (or should be able to foresee) that his or her act will harm another person. The act does not necessarily have to be performed with malicious or hostile intent. An example of an intentional tort is libel, the publication of a false statement that damages a person's reputation.

> **Intentional tort**
> A tort committed by a person who foresees (or should be able to foresee) that his or her act will harm another person.

Strict liability (or absolute liability) is liability that is imposed even though the defendant acted neither negligently nor with intent to cause harm. Common examples of strict liability include liability for abnormally dangerous instrumentalities (such as wild animals), ultrahazardous activities (such as blasting), and dangerously defective products (such as malfunctioning smoke detectors).

> **Strict liability (absolute liability)**
> Liability imposed by a court or by a statute in the absence of fault when harm results from activities or conditions that are extremely dangerous, unnatural, ultrahazardous, extraordinary, abnormal, or inappropriate.

Strict liability is also used to describe liability imposed by certain statutes, such as workers compensation laws.

Legal Liability Based on Contracts

In addition to torts, **contracts** also impose legal liability. If one party fails to honor the promise, the other may go to court to enforce the contract. Liability based on contracts can arise out of either a breach of contract or an agreement one party has made to assume the liability of another party.

> **Contract**
> A legally enforceable agreement between two or more parties in which each party makes some promise to the other.

Breach of contract is a failure to fulfill one's contractual promise. A common type of breach of contract involves the promise (called a warranty) made by a seller regarding its product. If the product fails to fulfill its promise, the warranty has been breached, and the buyer can make claim against the seller. The warranty may be either expressly stated or implied by law. For example, the law implies a warranty that every product is fit for the particular purpose for which it is sold. If the product is unfit for its intended purpose and the buyer is injured as a result, the seller may be held legally liable for damages.

> **Breach of contract**
> The failure, without legal excuse, to fulfill a contractual promise.

Liability for injury or damage resulting from a seller's breach of warranty is commonly insurable. Other consequences of breach of contract are not insurable. For example, if a builder fails to complete a new store by the promised date, the store owner's claim for loss of revenue is normally not insurable under the builder's general liability insurance.

A **hold-harmless agreement (or indemnity agreement)** typically requires one party to "hold harmless and indemnify" the other party against liability arising from the activity or product that is the subject of the contract.

> **Hold-harmless agreement (or indemnity agreement)**
> A contractual provision that obligates one of the parties to assume the legal liability of another party.

For example, a building's lease may obligate the tenant to hold the landlord harmless against any liability claims made by any person injured on the leased premises. The tenant, in this case, is agreeing by contract to pay claims for which the tenant would not otherwise have been legally liable. Construction

Contractual liability

Liability assumed through a hold-harmless agreement.

contracts and other types of agreements also often contain hold-harmless agreements. **Contractual liability** is liability assumed through a hold-harmless agreement and is commonly covered under liability insurance policies.

Legal Liability Based on Statutes

Statute

A written law passed by a legislative body, at either the federal or state level.

In addition to torts and contracts, statutes are a third major basis for imposing legal liability. A **statute** is a written law passed by a legislative body, at either the federal or state level. Written laws at the local level are usually referred to as ordinances. Statutes and ordinances can modify the duties that persons owe to others. Thus, the duties imposed by statute or ordinance may be used as evidence of a person's duty of care in a tort action. A statute can also impose legal liability on certain persons or organizations regardless of whether they acted negligently, committed any tort, or assumed liability under a contract.

A statute can give certain persons or organizations an absolute legal obligation to compensate other persons if certain events occur. This type of obligation is a form of strict liability, like that previously discussed, except that it is based entirely on requirements imposed by statute rather than on tort law. An important example of liability imposed by statute is the workers compensation system, which requires employers to pay prescribed benefits for occupational injuries or illness of their employees. The employer must pay these benefits even if an employee's injury or illness did not result from the employer's negligence.

COMMERCIAL LIABILITY LOSS EXPOSURES

Commercial liability loss exposures are potential losses that can arise when an organization is held to be financially responsible to another individual or organization for bodily injury or property damage.

Commercial liability loss exposures can be categorized in many ways, depending in part on the purpose of the categorization. The exhibit depicts a broad categorization that reflects insurance practices. See the exhibit "Major Categories of Commercial Liability Loss Exposures."

Several of the primary exposures are discussed here:

- Premises and operations liability
- Products and completed operations liability
- Automobile liability
- Workers compensation and employers liability

Premises and Operations Liability Loss Exposure

The premises and operations liability loss exposure relates to liability arising from bodily injury or property damage caused either by an accident that

Major Categories of Commercial Liability Loss Exposures

- Premises and operations liability
- Products and completed operations liability
- Automobile liability
- Workers compensation and employers liability
- Management liability
- Professional liability
- Environmental liability
- Marine liability
- Aircraft liability

[DA04739]

occurs on an organization's owned, leased, or rented premises or by an accident that arises out of the organization's ongoing (as opposed to completed) operations but occurs away from the premises. An organization's liability for such accidents is usually based on negligence—that is, the organization's failure to exercise the appropriate degree of care owed to some person under the circumstances.

Under the common law, owners and occupiers of land owe different duties of care to others on the premises, depending on their reasons for being on the premises. For example, an owner or occupier would owe a greater degree of care to a business guest or a customer than to an adult trespasser. Many jurisdictions have abandoned these common-law rules in favor of a reasonable care standard for owners and occupiers that applies under the circumstances to anyone who might be on the premises.

In some cases, premises and operations liability can be based on strict liability. For example, a blasting contractor could be held strictly liable for unintentional damage to buildings near the blasting operations. It can also apply to liability assumed by a land owner or occupier under hold-harmless agreements in contracts such as leases of premises, maintenance agreements, and construction contracts.

The premises and operations liability loss exposure includes bodily injury or property damage claims arising out of the use of mobile equipment (such as bulldozers and cranes). However, liability arising from the ownership, maintenance, or use of automobiles is treated as a distinct loss exposure, as is watercraft (vessel) liability and aircraft liability. Liability for employee injury or illness, whether based on obligations under workers compensation laws or based on common-law principles, is also regarded as a distinct loss exposure.

Products and Completed Operations Liability Loss Exposure

Liability for products and liability for completed operations are often treated as components of one loss exposure. However, products liability and completed operations liability each have distinguishing characteristics.

Products Liability

Products liability arises out of the manufacture, distribution, or sale of an unsafe, dangerous, or defective product and the failure of the manufacturer, distributor, or retailer to meet its legal duties to the user or consumer of the product.

Products liability lawsuits may be based on a variety of recovery theories, including negligence, misrepresentation, fraud, deceit, and breach of warranty. In actions for products liability, the plaintiff must prove that the defendant failed to take reasonable care in the design, manufacture, distribution, or sale of the article that caused the injury.

Since the 1960s, many products liability lawsuits have been based on strict liability in tort. In contrast to negligence actions, under strict liability in tort, the conduct of the manufacturer, distributor, or retailer is irrelevant, and the focus is on the safety of the product itself. The plaintiff must prove three elements:

- The product was defective when it left the manufacturer's or supplier's custody or control.
- The defective condition made the product unreasonably dangerous.
- The defective product was the proximate cause of the plaintiff's injury.

Although products liability actions based on strict liability in tort are typically directed at the manufacturer of the defective product, the plaintiff can seek damages from any entity that qualifies as a seller, including a distributor or retailer.

Completed Operations Liability

Completed operations liability is the legal responsibility of a contractor, repairer, or other entity for bodily injury or property damage arising out of the entity's completed work, as in these examples:

- Several months after a heating contractor installed a new boiler in an apartment building, the boiler exploded because the contractor had installed it negligently. The explosion damaged the apartment building and injured a tenant. Both the building owner and the tenant sued the contractor for damages.

- A family was hosting a picnic in their backyard. A wooden deck completed a few weeks earlier by a contractor collapsed under some guests, who were injured. They sued the decking contractor for damages.

- A repair shop overhauled a production machine belonging to a manufacturer. After the machine was returned to service, it malfunctioned and injured an employee of the manufacturer. The employee sued the repair shop for damages.

Under the common-law accepted work doctrine, a contractor could not be held liable for negligent performance of completed work once the owner had accepted the work. Over time, courts formulated several exceptions to this doctrine, holding contractors liable even after the work was accepted if the contractor knew of a danger or deliberately concealed a defect in the completed work. Eventually, many courts abandoned the accepted work doctrine altogether and permitted a right of action to anyone injured through the contractor's negligence. Some courts have even applied the strict liability in tort rule in much the same way as in holding the product manufacturer liable to the ultimate consumer or user.

Automobile Liability Loss Exposure

Automobile liability is legal responsibility for bodily injury or property damage arising out of the ownership, maintenance, or use of automobiles.

Under the common law, ownership of an auto does not in itself make the owner liable for injury or damage caused by someone else's negligent operation of the vehicle. Several states have passed laws making an auto owner liable for damages arising from any person's operation of the auto with the owner's express or implied permission.

Auto liability loss can also arise from negligent maintenance of a commercial auto. For example, negligent servicing of brakes, tires, or steering apparatus may be the proximate cause of a truck's running into another vehicle.

Anyone who is injured or whose property is damaged as a result of the negligent use of an auto has a right of action against the operator. In addition, any person or organization legally responsible for the operator's conduct can be held jointly liable. For example, an employer can be held jointly liable for its employee's negligent operation of an auto during the course of employment. However, when an employee substantially deviates from the scope of employment, the employer is not usually liable. For example, if a truck driver deviates from a prescribed route in order to spend the night at the home of a relative, the employer would not be responsible for an accident that occurs while the driver is on the way to the relative's home.

Liability for Operation by Others

A person who negligently furnishes a defective auto to another person may be held liable to a third person injured as a proximate result of the defect. Some courts have recognized an exception to the general rule in cases involving a used auto sold "as is," on the theory that the buyer understands (or can reasonably be expected to understand) that the used auto has not been inspected for defects and should be inspected by the buyer before being put into use.

Similarly, a person who negligently entrusts an auto to a person who is unskilled in its operation or otherwise incompetent to operate it may be held directly liable for resulting injuries. To establish liability for negligent entrustment, the plaintiff must show that the party entrusting the vehicle knew or should have known of the driver's incompetence, inexperience, or reckless tendencies.

Auto No-Fault Laws

The goal of auto no-fault laws is to provide stated benefits for all persons injured in auto accidents without a need to prove fault. In the United States, nearly half the states have some form of no-fault system in operation.

Provisions in the no-fault laws vary widely. About half of the no-fault states preserve the tort system but require insurers to offer, or require all auto registrants to purchase, personal injury protection (PIP) insurance that provides specified first-party benefits for medical expenses, loss of income, or death resulting from auto accidents. These states are said to have "add-on" no-fault plans.

The remaining states have "modified" no-fault plans that restrict the right to sue for torts in motor vehicle cases and require all auto registrants to purchase specified PIP benefits. Some of the states in this category have a "verbal threshold" that defines the seriousness of the injuries (for example, total or partial loss of a bodily member or bodily function, permanent disability or disfigurement, or death) beyond which the right to sue is allowed. The remaining states with modified no-fault plans set a monetary damages threshold that, if exceeded, allows auto accident victims to sue.

A few of the no-fault states give auto owners the choice to either retain the right to sue or to accept some limitations on their right to sue. Those who accept limitations on their right to sue are charged lower auto liability insurance premiums.

Because the right to sue is not entirely eliminated, organizations that use autos still should obtain auto liability insurance or adopt some other risk management technique for handling their auto liability loss exposure. In addition, each state has either an auto financial responsibility law or a compulsory liability insurance law requiring motorists to carry minimum amounts of auto liability insurance.

Workers Compensation and Employers Liability Loss Exposure

An employer's responsibility to pay claims under workers compensation statutes is a common example of liability imposed by statute. In the context of this discussion, the term "workers compensation statutes" includes the various state workers compensation statutes as well as federal statutes, such as the U.S. Longshore and Harbor Workers' Compensation Act, that have essentially the same effect as the state laws with regard to certain classes of employees.

In addition to payments required by workers compensation statutes, an employer may also be held liable for occupational injuries or illnesses of its employees as a result of either tort suits or hold-harmless agreements to which the employer is a party.

Employees' Tort Suits Against Employers

The typical workers compensation statute is intended to provide an "exclusive remedy" for occupational injury or illness to all employees subject to the law. Exclusive remedy means that the only remedy available to an injured employee under workers compensation is to recover, on a no-fault basis, the benefits required by the applicable statute.

In practice, various exceptions, such as these, allow a covered employee (or a spouse or family members) to make a tort claim against the employer:

- Claims for employee injury caused intentionally by the employer
- Claims by the employee's spouse for loss of consortium as a result of employee injury caused by the employer's negligence or other torts
- Claims for injury resulting from the employer's negligence or torts while acting in some capacity other than employer

Workers compensation statutes exempt some types of employees—for example, farm workers, domestic workers, occasional laborers, real estate agents, and employees who are members of the employer's own family. These employees retain the right to make tort claims against their employers for occupational injury or illness resulting from the employer's wrongful acts or omissions.

Hold-Harmless Agreements

An employer's liability for the injuries of employees can also be assumed under contract. An employer who agrees to indemnify another party against certain types of claims may be agreeing (sometimes unknowingly) to indemnify the other party for claims made by the employer's own employees against the other party. See the exhibit "Liability for Employee Injury Assumed Under Contract."

> ### Liability for Employee Injury Assumed Under Contract
>
> Miguel, a building contractor, agreed in his construction contract with Emma to indemnify her for any bodily injury or property damage claims made against her in connection with his work at her premises.
>
> Carl, one of Miguel's employees, was injured because of a dangerous condition at the building site for which Emma was responsible. Although he was eligible for workers compensation benefits, Carl made a negligence claim against Emma because he believed that the damages recoverable in a tort suit would be greater than workers compensation benefits. Workers compensation statutes do not prohibit covered employees from suing persons other than their employers for occupational injuries or diseases.
>
> Apart from his regular workers compensation obligations, Miguel was legally obligated by contract to indemnify Emma for damages resulting from Carl's suit. This case illustrates how an employer (or the employer's insurer) can end up paying for injury to the insured's own employee despite the fact that workers compensation is considered to be the exclusive remedy for on-the-job injuries of employees.

[DA04741]

USING COMMERCIAL LIABILITY RISK CONTROL

Organizations can reduce operational costs and reputational risk through accident prevention. If accidents do occur, the resultant damages or injuries can be mitigated. The risk control techniques used to prevent accidents and mitigate losses help organizations achieve their missions.

An organization can employ many strategies to address a liability loss along the continuum of its "life," from exposure to hazard to accident to litigation. Action may be taken at any point along the continuum.

Risk control techniques alter the nature of risk. These techniques can decrease the probability of an accident (loss prevention) and diminish the financial loss potential (loss reduction).

Claim management can provide another dimension to risk control, extending it beyond its traditional scope. Claim management is an effective and necessary component of an organization's **risk management** program, but it occurs far along the continuum of the liability loss.

Because claim management takes place after an accident has occurred, it may appear disconnected from the traditional concept of risk control. Yet, if the loss is viewed from the perspective of a continuum, claim management becomes both an extension and an integral part of an organization's risk control program. See the exhibit "The Continuum of a Loss Exposure."

Risk control

A conscious act or decision not to act that reduces the frequency and/or severity of losses or makes losses more predictable.

Risk management

The process of making and implementing decisions that will minimize the adverse effects of accidental losses on an organization.

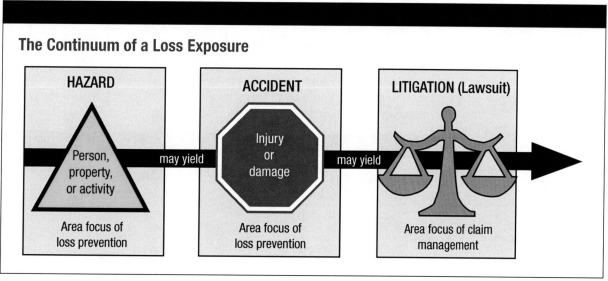

The Continuum of a Loss Exposure

HAZARD — Person, property, or activity — Area focus of loss prevention

may yield

ACCIDENT — Injury or damage — Area focus of loss prevention

may yield

LITIGATION (Lawsuit) — Area focus of claim management

[DA06783]

Basic Risk Control Techniques

There are several compelling and fundamental tenets to support a risk control program.

First, the liability exposures presented by the products and activities of many organizations have the potential to cause serious harm, injury, or death to employees, bystanders, and those who use their products.

Second, exposures that develop along the loss continuum can result in significant financial consequences for an organization.

Third, poor safety records, documented by published fines or penalties, and serious accidents can cause reputational damage for an organization that can undermine its potential and even its existence as a going concern. An example of serious harm, financial consequences, and reputational damage to organizations can be seen in the aftermath of the 2010 *Deepwater Horizon* oil rig explosion in the Gulf of Mexico.

The Foundation

As with any other major activity or project, it is important for an organization to set a strong foundation on which to build a successful risk control program. Almost all organizations have risk control programs, but not all of them are successful at actually controlling risk.

Management support is vital to success. Studies of both history and human nature reveal that the most effective program is one in which management exhibits consistent and vibrant support. For example, management's attendance at health and safety committee meetings gives credibility to risk control activities among the staff.

Risk control should be a dimension equal to other organizational areas such as marketing, finance, quality control, and human resources. Risk control analysis and techniques should be integrated into the overall mix of inputs that are processed in the development and production of an organization's products. This integration of risk control into the decision-making process will yield a more efficient and safer operation. See the exhibit "Risk Control in the Decision-Making Process."

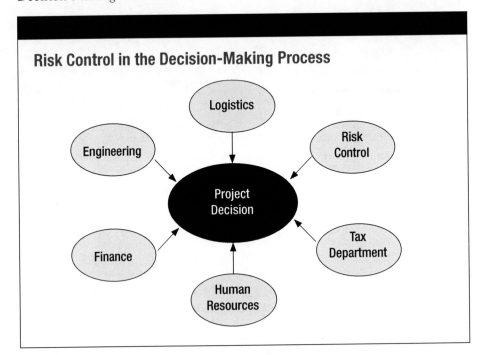

Risk Control in the Decision-Making Process

[DA06784]

Because human behavior is responsible for 85 to 95 percent of accidents, depending on the study referenced, it is vital that employees be given a sense of ownership in the risk control program. Staff needs to actively participate in formulating ideas, as doing so energizes them. Additionally, if management invites a "grass roots" perception of the issues, the underlying reasons for accidents (**root causes**) and obstacles to following established policies can be determined more readily. Practical solutions are often formulated, and procedures that are more readily followed are developed, because of the input of the employees who perform the operations.

Root cause

The event or circumstance that directly leads to an occurrence.

Pre-Accident Techniques

Once a foundation has been set, risk control techniques can be used to build a successful program. These techniques are used in a variety of combinations, depending on the specific loss exposure. However, several general considerations need to be evaluated in the development of any risk control technique:

- The cost-effectiveness of any technique needs to be considered, which involves evaluating the cost of the measure against the benefit to be derived. For example, the cost of global positioning systems in an automobile fleet to monitor driving behavior must be measured against the potential for decreased cost of risk and improved operating efficiencies.

- Legal requirements must be considered in developing and implementing all risk control techniques. Certain techniques are required by local building ordinances, fire department regulations, and Occupational Safety and Health Administration (OSHA) standards. For example, several states' building codes now require automatic fire sprinklers in new residential construction.

- Another important consideration includes the requirements and recommendations of the organization's insurers. For example, an underwriter may require the installation of safety guards or warning devices on machinery before accepting a manufacturer's application for insurance.

- The image of a company is increasingly exposed and subject to public scrutiny due to the extensive global use of the Internet and other communication media. The public perception of an organization can be enhanced via high-quality risk control programs in which sincere concern is shown for the safety of workers and customers. An example is the positive publicity from a pharmaceutical company's voluntary recall of a product that even appears to pose a safety risk to the public.

- The degree of risk aversion of an organization's senior management is also a consideration for risk control techniques. The degree of risk aversion and the corresponding risk control techniques often reflect the nature and operations of an organization. For example, a pharmaceutical company may be more risk-averse than manufacturers of other types of products because of the potential harm to users of the products along with the potential for financial and reputational damage to the company. Therefore, a pharmaceutical organization may expend greater resources on risk control techniques, such as research protocols, quality control procedures, and training, than less risk-averse organizations.

Loss prevention is the optimum risk control technique. This technique disrupts the events on the loss continuum that may lead to an accident. As a result, the probability of an accident is reduced. These are examples of loss prevention measures:

Loss prevention
A risk control technique that reduces the frequency of a particular loss.

- Back-up alarms (beepers) installed on new box trucks create awareness on the part of pedestrians.

- Electrical equipment used in accordance with the National Electrical Code (NEC) and installed in a flammable liquid mixing area eliminates an ignition source in the presence of a flammable vapor.

- Markings on full glass doors or windows help prevent persons from walking into the glass.
- Adhesive packing material (versus staples) minimizes the chance of cuts sustained by customers who open a company's product packaging.
- An overhead cage protects a forklift operator from falling debris.
- Safety glasses, worn by employees and visitors in a machine shop area, prevent eye injuries from debris.

Loss reduction

A risk control technique that reduces the severity of a particular loss.

The technique of **loss reduction** limits the damage or injury resulting from accidents that occur despite loss prevention efforts. Examples of loss reduction measures include these:

- Smoke detectors in a hotel alert occupants to a fire.
- Sprinkler systems in shopping malls reduce damage and injury from fire.
- Seat belts in automobiles can reduce the severity of injuries to drivers and passengers by curbing the forces of inertia during an accident.
- Portable showers in manufacturing areas can reduce the severity of accidental exposure to a caustic material.

The technique of separation is theoretically possible but rarely practiced for liability exposures. This strategy involves separating loss exposures to reduce frequency or severity or both.

For example, a transportation organization could consider using two seven-passenger vans instead of one fifteen-passenger van. This separation of passengers into two vans would reduce the potential number of passenger injuries, as well as the cost of those injuries, in the event of an accident involving one of the vans, thereby reducing potential severity.

It is also possible that the smaller vans may be more maneuverable and help to reduce the number of accidents, thereby decreasing potential frequency. However, the cost of doubling an organization's fleet and drivers would likely outweigh any risk control benefit.

Avoidance

A risk control technique that involves ceasing or never undertaking an activity so that the possibility of a future loss occurring from that activity is eliminated.

Another risk control strategy is **avoidance**. Although an organization cannot avoid performing core business operations, it may be possible to avoid other operations. For example, manufacturing of sodium azide (an explosive material used in deploying automobile airbags) can be performed by an organization other than the automobile manufacturer.

A technique similar to avoidance is noninsurance risk transfer. This technique transfers the exposure to a third party. Typically, this occurs in a contractual transfer, such as hold-harmless or indemnification agreements. Compared with the other risk control techniques, neither avoidance nor noninsurance risk transfer alters the risk profile, but those techniques do change the potential financial impact associated with the transferred risks.

Post-Accident Techniques

Claim management is the technique of mitigating the effects of losses after they occur. A loss can have many different effects on different parties. Effective claim management measures at each stage along the post-accident loss continuum can result in significantly improved outcomes.

Using the analogy of a horse leaving a barn, loss prevention efforts (such as locking the barn door) preclude the horse from escaping. Loss reduction—in this scenario, fencing the area outside the barn—limits the injuries and damages that occur if the horse escapes despite the loss prevention efforts. Claim management reduces the costs of any damages and injuries that occur as a result of the horse's escape.

These are examples of claim management techniques:

- Following a child's foot injury caused by a lift truck in a home improvement store, the general manager compassionately and expediently responded to the injury, assisting the family in obtaining prompt medical treatment for their child. The manager then followed up with the child's parents for feedback, demonstrating continuing concern. The child's injury was treated successfully, and the parents expressed gratitude to the manager for assisting in obtaining medical treatment and offering compassion.

- At a jewelry store, a claimant bombastically demanded to see the manager and reported that he was injured the previous night, after hours, when he slipped on the pavement outside the store. The manager checked the tapes from the surveillance video camera and found no indication of a slip or fall. The claimant did not appear to be injured. The manager reported these findings to the insurer's claim representative, who undertook a full investigation. This investigation revealed that the claimant had a long history of filing slip-and-fall claims, and the claim representative successfully denied the claim.

Another important aspect of claim management in a risk control program is the information provided by the investigation after accidents (including close calls) that can be used in determining the root causes of accidents. Determining such root causes based on claim information helps to direct future loss prevention and loss reduction techniques.

CONTROLLING LIABILITY LOSSES

Risk control techniques can assist organizations in preventing or mitigating losses associated with a variety of liability loss exposures.

The context for commercial liability is formed by two tenets:

- Organizations, as well as individuals, must respect others' rights. These rights are varied and numerous. Some of them are contained in the

Common-law system

A legal system in which the body of law is derived more from court decisions as opposed to statutes or constitutions.

Tort law

The branch of civil law that deals with civil wrongs other than breaches of contract.

Statutory law

The formal laws, or statutes, enacted by federal, state, or local legislative bodies.

United States Constitution and state constitutions. Rights are shaped by court cases over time. These court decisions become **common law** and create varied duties, such as the duty to allow one to enjoy his or her property without trespass and the duty to preserve another's rightful reputation. The degree of such duties ranges from the low level of care that is required in relation to a trespasser to the high degree of care expected from a professional who is dispensing services. The relevance of this tenet to commercial liability is mostly encompassed by **tort law**.

- Government at all levels, from federal to township, creates laws and regulations that impose responsibilities on some entities and confer rights on others. This **statutory law**, in conjunction with tort law, fashions a labyrinth of legal principles that demands vigilance from an organization. These laws include state workers compensation laws (mandating benefits for injured workers on a no-fault basis) and federal and state environmental laws (regulating disposal, storage, and cleanup of hazardous wastes).

Legal duties imposed on organizations continuously evolve because of the passage of new statutory laws by governments and the numerous legal cases that modify laws and precedents. A creative approach to risk control may best be summarized by posing this question for all of an organization's activities: "What grounds for liability could a plaintiff's attorney assert?" When evaluating a proposed operation, decision, product, or service, this critical-thinking exercise reveals potential legal pitfalls that will then become risk control challenges.

Organizations can use commercial liability risk control to manage these loss exposures:

- Premises liability
- Off-premises operations
- Products-completed operations
- Motor vehicle liability
- Workers compensation and employers liability
- Technology and communication

Premises Liability

Ownership or use of property mandates responsibility to others such as guests, customers, and vendors, and even to some degree to trespassers (as counterintuitive as that may sound). Commercial liability risk control can provide safeguards in these ways:

- Regular inspections—One of the cornerstones of a risk control program is evaluation of the premises to ensure that it is safely maintained. Typically, a form is used to guide a complete assessment and proper documentation. Areas inspected include walkways, stairs, and elevators for tripping or pinching hazards; fire protection and security systems such as smoke detectors, sprinkler systems, and fire extinguishers; means of egress for clearly marked, accessible, and lighted routes in the event of an emergency evacuation; storage areas conforming to height restrictions and general housekeeping standards; and safety procedures, proper housekeeping, and protective features for special hazard areas, such as paint spray booths, chemical mixing areas, and storage racks.

- Maintenance programs—A systematic, preventive program for the building, machinery, heating, and electrical infrastructure reduces the chance of an accidental event and maximizes reliable operation.

- Policies and procedures—These procedures include the response required in the event of snow to maintain clear, ice-free pavements; the staff response to a robbery to protect customers; and the preservation of sensitive customer information such as credit card records and Social Security numbers.

- Protection—In addition to meeting statutory requirements, fire protection and security systems are effective methods of safeguarding a building's occupants. These systems include automatic sprinkler protection, smoke detection, video surveillance, and perimeter intrusion detection that are coordinated with an alarm system to notify a central station.

The focus of the risk control program will depend on the organization's operation. A manufacturing operation will not have the same level of customer exposure as a retail establishment. Therefore, while a primary focus at a retail grocery store may be to keep the floor dry and clear in the produce aisle to prevent customers from slipping, the focus at a manufacturer may be to reduce the slipping hazard for employees in the dyeing area under the yarn-knitting machines. See the exhibit "Sample Portion of On-Premises Inspection Form."

Off-Premises Operations

Off-premises operations present the inherent challenge of liability hazards that are more difficult to control than those that arise on an organization's own premises. Although an organization is liable for losses that occur as a result of its operations away from its own premises, the organization does not have control over many aspects of other premises.

For example, a beverage supplier can use risk control methods in its warehouse to prevent accidents resulting from lift truck collisions with employees or vendors. However, the organization has no control over customers' premises where its employees make deliveries. A crowded store area could result in a delivery representative hitting someone with a handtruck and causing serious injury.

Construction contractors, unlike firms that operate predominantly from fixed locations, may be confronted with somewhat different hazards at every job site. Additionally, as construction of a building or another project progresses, the hazards at the job site change. Operation of mobile equipment at such job

Sample Portion of On-Premises Inspection Form

Interior/Exterior Buildings and Grounds	Yes	No
1. Are the walkways, sidewalks, and parking areas even, dry, and free of debris?	☐	☐
2. Are there adequate secured floor coverings, minimal wear and tear?	☐	☐
3. Are the balcony railings secured?	☐	☐
4. Are large expanses of glass protected with proper markings?	☐	☐
5. Are the hallways and buildings adequately lighted?	☐	☐
6. Are the trees, plants, and shrubs protruding or soil divots?	☐	☐
7. Are the compounded area(s) fenced and lighted?	☐	☐
8. Does the lawn need to be cut/snow shoveled?	☐	☐
9. Is the equipment and furniture in good repair (list broken items, remove if safety issue)	☐	☐
10. Is the hot water temperature within the guidelines?	☐	☐
11. Is the exterior in good condition (i.e. no trash, broken windows, downed gutters, any missing screens or storm windows, etc.)	☐	☐
12. Any furniture repairs needed within the facility?	☐	☐

Life Safety	Yes	No
1. Are all exits marked and illuminated?	☐	☐
2. Are all exit ways accessible?	☐	☐
3. Are doors that are not exits clearly marked "NOT AN EXIT"?	☐	☐
4. Do exit doors swing outward?	☐	☐
5. Are there ample exits?	☐	☐
6. Any keyed locks on any exits (excluding staff rooms)?	☐	☐
7. Are panic hardware unchained and unlocked?	☐	☐
8. Is emergency lighting functioning/tested?	☐	☐
9. Are operable flashlights/lanterns onhand?	☐	☐
10. Are emergency response plans current?	☐	☐
11. Are evacuation procedures and floor plans posted?	☐	☐
12. Evacuation drill last conducted on : _____ (date)		
13. Are fire alarms tested? Last fire alarm test: _____	☐	☐
14. Is first-aid kit fully stocked and accessible?	☐	☐
15. Are there sleeping bags under everyone's bed?	☐	☐

[DA06729]

sites should be a focus of risk control efforts. For example, a contractor that uses backhoes or other excavating equipment should be careful to determine, before digging starts, the location of underground telephone and electrical cables and oil or natural gas pipelines.

Products-Completed Operations

Products loss exposures arise from products or services that are provided by an organization. Virtually any organization that manufactures or sells products or provides services has a products liability loss exposure. For example, a pharmaceutical product could be found to have side effects that result in illness or death. A consultant who assisted in the development of the pharmaceutical product could also have liability related to the services provided. The goal of products liability risk control is to prevent or reduce liability losses arising out of the organization's products or services.

The potential liability loss exposures of a product may not be obvious. For example, products-completed operations losses arose when a man died of a heart attack while starting a lawnmower with a manual pull start. It appeared to be an unfortunate event with no liability implications for the manufacturer, but the plaintiff's attorney noted the amount of torque required to pull the starter cord on an eight-horsepower engine. The court concluded that objective measurement indicated the effort required posed a hazard for some classes of users and required cautionary labeling and instructions that were not provided by the manufacturer. The result was a large-dollar verdict for the plaintiff and a warning for the manufacturers of lawn mowers.

Creating products that satisfy varied legal requirements (such as those of the Consumer Products Safety Commission), do not present any undue danger to various users, and are also marketable presents significant challenges that require a commitment to these risk control practices:

- Research, testing, and development of the materials to be used
- Quality control of the raw materials
- A manufacturing process with precise specifications and quality control
- Strict adherence to procedures in manufacturing processes
- Clear and explicit instructions for employees and users of the product
- The design of proper packaging
- Storage of the product in a controlled environment (as needed)
- Documentation of product test results
- Documentation of product lots to provide tracking in the event of a need to determine the origination of an alleged defective product and/or plan a recall of the product

These risk control strategies entail detailed and sophisticated engineering and design. Additionally, a manufacturer should consider risk control evaluation of these potential areas for concern:

- The unpredictable behavior of the product's consumers, who could unwittingly defeat a safety feature and/or misinterpret instructions, requiring a new standard of product safety
- The high liability standard that applies to products liability—strict liability, which focuses on the inherent safety of the product itself rather than on the conduct of the manufacturer or others in the chain of distribution
- Evolving statutes and regulatory requirements
- The catastrophic consequence of having a batch of products found defective, resulting in injury to numerous consumers and a class action lawsuit involving multiple claimants

Construction, electrical, plumbing, and related contracting operations are examples of completed operations liability exposures. During such operations, if someone is injured, the incident would represent an off-premises exposure. After the completion of the project, however, liability persists.

If someone is injured due to a defective installation, the injury would come within the scope of the completed operations hazard. As an example, three people sustain serious injuries caused by a fire that was later determined to have been caused by electrical arcing in a switchgear installation. The electrician had carelessly pulled through electrical cable, stripping insulation, which resulted in the arcing.

A contractor can have a completed operations exposure for many years after the original installation. High-quality workmanship, reliable materials, and independent inspections of the work product are essential loss prevention practices for these types of operations.

Motor Vehicle Liability

Perhaps in no other type of activity does risk control play a more significant role in reducing accidents than in the operation of a motor vehicle. This is so because we have a high level of control over how we drive. It does not mean that we are fully in control of our circumstances on the highway. It does mean, however, that we make decisions that can reduce or create liability. When we strictly adhere to traffic signs, such as slowing down in school zones, we reduce the liability exposure. When we read or send text messages on cellular devices while driving, we increase the liability exposure.

Organizations should be proactive in managing their motor vehicle liability by exercising care in hiring and training those persons who will drive their vehicles. These are examples of commercial driver risk control techniques:

- A comprehensive, written safe-driver policy that is communicated to all staff
- Driver selection criteria based on each individual's driving record and the results of the physical examination required by the Federal Motor Carrier Safety Administration (FMCSA)
- Training of the staff at orientation, in campaigns (for example, "Prevent Rear-End Collisions!"), and annually in both classroom and over-the-road venues
- Substance abuse testing that follows at least the minimum guidelines required by the FMCSA
- Consistent disciplinary procedures for unsafe driving practices

Workers Compensation and Employers Liability

Many organizations dedicate more of their risk control resources to workers compensation and employers liability loss exposures than to any other category. For many organizations, workers compensation loss exposures represent their highest-cost liability. For example, a construction contractor may have greater exposure to workers compensation losses than to other types of liability. Also, state and federal laws may require certain risk control activities for worker safety. Additionally, organizations may experience significant decreases in productivity as a result of workers compensation injuries. Most states require employers with more than a specified number of employees (often one employee in construction and three in other types of organizations) to purchase workers compensation insurance. Large employers may choose to qualify with one or more states to retain the risk rather than transfer it through insurance.

The same risk control concepts that apply to commercial general liability apply to workers compensation and employers liability. The distinguishing elements of workers compensation include the injured person involved (employee) and the law that applies (statutory workers compensation).

A result of these distinguishing elements of workers compensation is that the employee usually has a more personal relationship with the employer because they typically share the same working environment and a common goal. An injury to an employee in an organization caused by a fall strikes a different chord, for example, than an injury to a vacationing child caused by the collision of a horse-drawn carriage with a taxicab whose driver was careless. The former situation presents the potential for amicable resolution within a collegial environment, whereas the latter is more likely to result in emotional and difficult litigation.

Another significant difference between workers compensation liability and commercial general liability is that workers compensation provides no-fault coverage to employees for most types of occupational injury and illness. For example, if an inexperienced employee loses her right hand as a result of improper operation of a fabric cutter, negligence on the part of the employee would not eliminate or reduce the employer's liability. However, in exchange for receiving prompt payment of benefits for medical treatment and lost wages, the employee in most cases has no right to sue the employer in tort for damages such as pain and suffering. This is the doctrine of exclusive remedy, under which workers compensation benefits, as described in the applicable state or federal statute, are the exclusive remedy available from the injured worker's employer.

Exceptions to the doctrine of exclusive remedy are often covered under Part Two—Employers Liability Insurance of the workers compensation policy, which, unlike Part One—Workers Compensation Insurance, has an applicable dollar limit. Exceptions typically arise because of one of these situations:

- The employer's liability for the injury rises to a level at which the governing statutes or common law permit employees to sue their employers for occupational injuries. In some states, if an employee's injury is found by a court to result from his or her employer's gross negligence, the employee may be permitted to sue. In other states, if a court finds that the employer's actions were substantially certain to cause injury, the employee may be permitted to sue. For example, if an employer removes a safety guard from machinery to speed up production and an employee loses several fingers because of the removal, the employee may be permitted to sue the employer.

- The employer is operating in a dual capacity both as the employer of an injured employee and as the manufacturer of the product that injures the employee. For example, an employee is severely injured while working on a machine manufactured by the employer, as a result of a defect in the machine. The employee may be permitted to sue the organization in its role as the manufacturer of the machine.

As with general liability exposures, it is important for risk control tenets and techniques to be applied in all decisions and operations that affect employees. It is important for management to develop a safety culture within the organization. The ideal culture is one in which employees are not only concerned for their own safety but also for that of their co-workers. A proactive risk control practice is to apply the techniques of loss prevention and loss control to a job analysis of each type of position within the organization. Consideration should be given to activities that can cause repetitive injury, such as operation of a machine over a period of years, in addition to activities that can cause sudden injury, such as working on construction scaffolds.

Post-accident claim management is important following workers compensation injuries. Although workers compensation provides no-fault benefits to employees, litigation can occur regarding coverage and benefits. In most states the litigation takes place in administrative forums, although in a few states workers compensation cases are brought to the same courts as other types of liability cases. As with general liability claims, litigation usually adds significantly to the cost of a claim and may also result in the organization's loss of a productive employee during prolonged litigation. A good employment relationship without litigation can often be maintained through effective claim management techniques.

Care should be taken in the delivery of medical and disability benefits. Supervisors should contact an employee who is unable to work in an effort to demonstrate sincere compassion and provide encouragement. A transitional duty program provides an opportunity for an injured worker to return to work within a temporary restricted capacity in which the employee benefits from interaction with colleagues and involvement in productive activity.

As with general liability claims, a thorough investigation can mitigate certain losses. Post-accident drug and alcohol testing, for example, can determine whether an accident was caused by an employee's intoxication. In some states, a positive post-accident drug or alcohol test may disqualify a workers compensation claim. Additionally, such testing can also identify an employee who represents a safety risk to the organization. "Red flags," such as an unwitnessed accident to a short-term employee with a significant prior claim history, a Monday morning report of an unwitnessed Friday injury, and a supervisor's suspicions about the claim, should trigger additional investigation.

Technology and Communication

Communication media, including the Internet, represent a significant and rapidly growing dimension for most organizations. The rapid growth of new communication technologies has created a new category of liability. Insurers have responded by excluding certain exposures from commercial general liability coverage forms and by creating new cyber-risk liability coverage forms. The new communication technology exposures require innovative and knowledgeable risk control techniques. These are examples of risk control techniques for organizations that conduct business over the Internet:

- The establishment of firewalls and antivirus software can mitigate the possibility of intrusion into an organization's computer network by a third party. An intrusion could include the extrication of sensitive information and create a liability exposure for the organization if the perpetrator reveals or uses private customer or patient information. The information can also be held for ransom (cyberterrorism) when a financial demand is made in exchange for the release of the information.

- Policies and procedures are essential for employees who use portable devices, such as laptop computers and certain cellular telephones, with access to confidential information. There have been many instances of stolen portable devices resulting in significant liability exposures.

- Risk control includes a preconceived and measured response after sabotage or another infiltration that jeopardizes the confidentiality of client information. Those who may have had their confidentiality compromised need to be notified. In addition to being good business practice, this notification may be mandated by a number of state statutes.

- Web sites present information to the world. Text, trademarks, and ideas may represent an infringement of another's rights. Regular, critical reviews of Web site content can minimize the chance of such infringement.

In addition to exposures resulting from use of the Internet, organizations face varied loss exposures for personal and advertising injury from traditional operations. These loss exposures include injury, including but not limited to bodily injury, resulting from false arrest or detention, wrongful eviction or entry, slander, libel, oral or written publication in any manner of material that violates a person's right of privacy, and copyright or trademark infringement. Injury other than bodily injury includes mental anguish or injury, fright, shock, humiliation, and loss of reputation, but it is not limited to them.

Risk control techniques for these exposures begin with an assessment of an organization's exposures and include the development of appropriate policies and procedures and employee training. Retail organizations, for example, face significant crime loss exposures from shoplifting. However, methods to deter shoplifting can create false arrest and detention exposures, such as a store security guard falsely accusing a customer of theft. Apartment complexes have loss exposures from fire if tenants use unsafe appliances, such as certain types of heaters. However, the apartment management also may face loss exposures from wrongful entry and invasion of privacy. A comprehensive risk control program will address and balance the various types of loss exposures, including those arising from loss control programs.

SUMMARY

A liability loss exposure is the possibility of experiencing a liability loss. A liability loss includes all costs to an organization as the result of a specific legal claim or suit against that organization. The person making claim or suit against the organization (the claimant) ordinarily attempts to prove that the organization is legally liable to pay damages.

Anyone who wishes to evaluate an organization's liability loss exposures must understand the various ways in which the organization could become legally liable. Broadly speaking, civil liability (in contrast with criminal liability) can be based on torts, contracts, or statutes.

Liability loss exposures can be categorized in many ways that reflect insurance practices. Such categories include these:

- Premises and operations liability
- Products and completed operations liability

- Automobile liability
- Workers compensation and employers liability

Regardless of the type of organization, good business practice demands a sound risk management program. Liability exposure can be reduced and mitigated by the employment of various risk control strategies:

- Loss prevention
- Loss reduction
- Claim management

Judicious employment of these measures will ultimately yield decreased operating costs, enhanced public reputation, and the achievement of company goals.

Liability exposure is rooted in a responsibility imposed by society or government. The financial cost of commercial liability includes the costs of both defense and damages to a third party. Additional costs include the suffering of injured parties and their families and the damage to an organization's reputation. There are many different types of commercial liability loss exposures arising from an organization's premises, off-premises operations, products-completed operations, motor vehicles, workers compensation and employers liability, and technology and communication. Risk control techniques can prevent or mitigate losses arising from these exposures.

3

Commercial General Liability Insurance, Part I

Educational Objectives

After learning the content of this assignment, you should be able to:

▷ Analyze the conditions of the insuring agreement for Coverage A— Bodily Injury and Property Damage Liability of the Commercial General Liability Coverage Form (occurrence version) that must be satisfied in order for a claim to be covered under this insuring agreement.

▷ Describe the exclusions, and specific exceptions to the exclusions, applicable to Coverage A of the Commercial General Liability Coverage Form, and endorsements that modify the form.

▷ Explain whether Coverage A of the Commercial General Liability Coverage Form would cover a described claim.

Commercial General Liability Insurance, Part I

CGL COVERAGE FORM: INSURING AGREEMENT FOR COVERAGE A—BODILY INJURY AND PROPERTY DAMAGE LIABILITY

Organizations of all types purchase general liability insurance to cover their premises and operations liability loss exposures and their products and completed operations liability loss exposures. Because general liability insurance covers a wide range of liability loss exposures, it is the foundation for most organizations' liability insurance programs.

The form most commonly used to provide general liability insurance is the **Commercial General Liability Coverage Form** (CGL coverage form) developed by Insurance Services Office, Inc. (ISO). The American Association of Insurance Services (AAIS) has also developed CGL coverage forms, and some insurers use their own independently developed forms.

ISO maintains two versions of the CGL coverage form: the occurrence version (CG 00 01), which is more commonly used, and the claims-made version (CG 00 02). The claims-made version is used only in cases in which the possibility of long-tail claims is a major underwriting concern. In most ways, the two versions of the CGL coverage form are the same, and they include these coverages:

- Coverage A—Bodily Injury and Property Damage Liability
- Coverage B—Personal and Advertising Injury Liability
- Coverage C—Medical Payments

This discussion addresses the December 2007 version of each form.

The Coverage A insuring agreement states two distinct duties of the insurer: a duty to pay damages on behalf of the insured and a duty to defend the insured against suits seeking damages covered under the policy.

Insurer's Duty to Pay Damages

The Coverage A insuring agreement states the insurer's duty to pay damages on behalf of the insured: "We will pay those sums that the insured becomes legally obligated to pay as damages because of 'bodily injury' or 'property damage' to which this insurance applies."[1] See the exhibit "Distinction Between "You" and the "Insured"."

Commercial General Liability Coverage Form

A coverage form commonly used for insuring an organization's premises and operations liability loss exposures and products and completed operations liability loss exposures.

> ## Distinction Between "You" and the "Insured"
>
> Understanding the distinction between "you" and "the insured" is important because these terms are used throughout the CGL policy. The distinction can be summarized in this manner:
>
> - "You" means the named insured shown in the declarations.
>
> - "The insured" (or, for that matter, "an insured" or "any insured") includes either the named insured or any other person or organization that qualifies as an insured under the "Who Is an Insured" section of the policy. Employees of the named insured, for example, are insureds even though they are not individually named in the policy.
>
> The distinction can be crucial. For example, an exclusion of damage to property in the custody of the insured would apply to property in the custody of the person or organization qualifying as the insured and against whom a claim is made. In contrast, an exclusion of damage to property in "your" (the named insured's) custody would apply only to property in the custody of the named insured.

[DA04750]

This sentence imposes these conditions:

- The insured must be legally obligated to pay damages.
- The damages must result from bodily injury or property damage.
- The policy must apply to the bodily injury or property damage.

Further provisions of the insuring agreement impose several additional conditions:

- The bodily injury or property damage must be caused by an occurrence.
- The occurrence must take place in the coverage territory.
- The bodily injury or property damage must occur during the policy period.
- Before the policy period began, the bodily injury or property damage must not have been known, in whole or in part, to the named insured or to certain other persons who qualify as insureds.

Legally Obligated to Pay Damages

Coverage applies only when the insured is legally obligated to pay damages, which may be the proximate result of any type of legal wrong for which the civil law provides a remedy in the form of a suit for damages. Such wrongs include the occurrence of a tort, a breach of a contractual obligation, or any other wrong for which damages are payable. However, the policy does not cover all legal obligations to pay damages; it covers only the kinds of obligations that are within the scope of the insuring agreement and are not excluded elsewhere in the policy. The wrong may have been committed by the insured or by another person for whose conduct the insured is vicariously liable.

Either a court (such as when a plaintiff wins a judgment against the insured) or the insurer's investigation of a claim can determine whether the insured is legally obligated to pay damages. In many cases, the insurer's investigation reveals that the insured is legally liable. If the insurer also believes that the policy covers the claim, the insurer usually tries to negotiate with the third-party claimant and arrange an out-of-court settlement, thus avoiding the expense and inconvenience of a trial.

To permit the insurer to investigate and settle claims, the insuring agreement states that the insurer may, at its discretion, investigate any occurrence and settle any resulting claim or suit. (The CGL coverage form defines "suit" to include not only formal lawsuits but also informal civil proceedings and arbitration proceedings.) In some cases, insurers will settle a claim to avoid the higher costs of defending against the claim, even though the plaintiff's case may be weak. Although the insured might prefer to see the insurer defend against the claim or suit, the insurer has the sole right to decide whether it will settle or defend.

The damages that a court may impose can take the form of special damages for such out-of-pocket costs as loss of earnings and medical expenses; general damages for pain and suffering; and, in many jurisdictions, punitive damages awarded to punish or make an example of the wrongdoer. Although the CGL obligates the insurer to pay all damages for which the insured is liable, many states do not permit courts to award punitive damages that are compensable under the policy when the insured is directly liable, and some states do not permit insurers to pay punitive damages on behalf of an insured when the insured is vicariously liable. Even in states that do allow insurers to pay punitive damages, insurers are not likely to pay them in an out-of-court settlement.

Damages for Bodily Injury or Property Damage

Coverage A applies only to damages for bodily injury or property damage as those terms are defined in the coverage form. The CGL defines **bodily injury** as "bodily injury, sickness or disease sustained by a person, including death resulting from any of these at any time." Because bodily injury is defined in part simply as bodily injury, the meaning of that term is open to judicial interpretation. For example, some courts have held that mental injury or emotional distress is bodily injury even in the absence of physical bodily harm. In its usual sense, bodily injury means hurt or harm to the human body by contact of some force and any resulting pain and suffering, sickness or disease, or death. The Coverage A insuring agreement specifies that damages because of bodily injury include damages for care, loss of services, or death.

Bodily injury
Physical injury to a person, including sickness, disease, and death.

The policy definition of **property damage** contains two parts:

- Physical injury to tangible property, including resulting loss of use of that property. An example of physical injury is the destruction of a customer's building by fire resulting from a contractor's negligence. Damages for

Property damage
Physical injury to, destruction of, or loss of use of tangible property.

"resulting loss of use" would include the loss of income sustained by the customer until the building could be rebuilt.

- Loss of use of tangible property that is not physically injured. An example is the loss of use of a stock brokerage's telephones and computers as a result of telephone and power lines being severed by a negligent contractor. Even though the firm's property did not sustain any physical injury, the firm nevertheless suffered loss of business income as a result of being unable to use its telephones and computers. The loss of use of the undamaged telephones and computers qualifies as property damage.

The definition of property damage also states that, within the CGL coverage form, "electronic data is not tangible property." Thus, the CGL coverage form (unless modified by endorsement) does not cover the insured's liability for causing damage to electronic data.

The position of most insurers is that electronic data are intangible property and therefore are not covered by the CGL coverage form because the policy definition of property damage includes damage to tangible property only and not to intangible property. To avoid the possibility of having to pay claims for loss of electronic data under the CGL coverage form, ISO clarified the definition of property damage and also added an exclusion of electronic data to Coverage A.

For an additional premium, many insurers are willing to cover the insured's liability for loss of electronic data under either a CGL endorsement (Electronic Data Liability, CG 04 37) or a separate coverage form (Electronic Data Liability Coverage Form, CG 00 65).

Injury or Damage to Which the Insurance Applies

Coverage A insures only bodily injury or property damage "to which this insurance applies." Consequently, the insurer is not obligated to pay damages if one or more of the Coverage A exclusions apply to the claim or if for any other reason the claim is not covered.

Caused by an Occurrence

Occurrence

An accident, including continuous or repeated exposure to substantially the same general harmful conditions.

To be insured under Coverage A, bodily injury or property damage must be caused by an **occurrence**, which is defined in the policy. The purpose of this definition is to provide coverage for any adverse condition that continues over a long period and eventually results in bodily injury or property damage, as well as to provide coverage for an event that happens suddenly and results in immediate bodily injury or property damage. In either case, the bodily injury or property damage would be caused by an occurrence.

The fact that the policy defines occurrence as "an accident" does not mean that bodily injury or property damage resulting from any intentional act is therefore excluded. In many cases, the accident covered by a CGL policy is the unintended result of an intentional act. For example, in using a propane torch with the intent to thaw out a customer's frozen water pipe (intentional act), a plumber may accidentally set the building on fire. In such a case, although the fire resulted from an intentional act, setting the building on fire was an accident. Consequently, the plumber's CGL policy would cover the customer's claim against the plumber for fire damage to the customer's building.

The CGL coverage form contains an exclusion of bodily injury or property damage intended by the insured. (If the plumber had purposely set the building on fire, the plumber's CGL policy would not have covered the customer's claim.) The difference between an intentional act and intentional injury or damage, though perhaps a subtle distinction, can be extremely important.

Occurrence in the Coverage Territory

Coverage A applies only to an occurrence that takes place in the "coverage territory," as defined in the coverage form. The coverage territory that applies to most claims is the United States (including its territories and possessions), Puerto Rico, and Canada. In some cases, a broader coverage territory applies, including international waters and international airspace, if injury or damage occurs in the course of travel or transportation between any of the following places: the U.S., its territories and possessions, Puerto Rico, and Canada.

The coverage territory also includes "all parts of the world" when the circumstances of the occurrence meet two carefully defined conditions (see "Coverage Territory" in the CGL Form, Section V—Definitions). The first condition for worldwide coverage is that the injury or damage must arise out of goods or products sold in the U.S., its territories and possessions, Puerto Rico, or Canada; the activities of a person whose home is in those locations but who is away for a short time on the named insured's business; or personal and advertising injury offenses that occur through the Internet or similar electronic communications.

The second condition for worldwide coverage is that the insured's liability for damages must be determined in either a settlement to which the insurer agrees or a suit "on the merits" filed in the U.S., its territories or possessions, Puerto Rico, or Canada. A suit on the merits is a suit that is based on facts and legal grounds as opposed to extraneous or technical points such as rules of legal procedure.

Worldwide products coverage applies to products made or sold by the named insured in the U.S., its territories or possessions, Puerto Rico, or Canada. The CGL form therefore covers injury arising out of a product made in one of those jurisdictions but sold abroad, as long as the suit is also filed in one of those jurisdictions.

Although U.S. courts will hear original suits based on occurrences in other countries, not all foreign plaintiffs file their suits in the U.S. To obtain coverage for products liability suits filed in other countries, some organizations obtain products liability coverage that specifically covers such suits.

In contrast with the CGL's worldwide products liability coverage, the coverage territory for injury or damage arising from completed operations is usually limited to the U.S., its territories and possessions, Puerto Rico, and Canada. For example, a completed operations liability claim involving a building that the insured has constructed in Mexico would not be covered under the insured's CGL policy.

However, the coverage territory includes international waters or airspace in the course of transportation between places in the U.S., its territories or possessions, Puerto Rico, or Canada. In some cases, this portion of the coverage territory could provide coverage for completed operations claims based on accidents occurring in international waters or airspace. For example, work performed by a ship repairer or an aircraft repairer might malfunction in international waters or airspace during a voyage or flight between two places within the basic coverage territory (such as Florida and Puerto Rico or California and Hawaii). Bodily injury or property damage occurring under such circumstances would be within the coverage territory. See the exhibit "Worldwide Products Coverage."

Worldwide Products Coverage

Before going on vacation to Australia, Joan bought some medicine made by a pharmaceutical firm headquartered in the U.S. After arriving in Australia, Joan took the medicine and became ill from impurities in the medicine. After curtailing her trip and returning home, Joan sued the pharmaceutical firm for damages arising out of her bodily injury.

Question: Will the pharmaceutical firm's CGL policy cover Joan's claim?

Answer: Because the firm sold the medicine in the U.S. and the claimant made suit in the U.S., the firm's CGL insurer is obligated to defend against Joan's suit and pay damages for which the firm may be held liable.

[DA04751]

Injury or Damage During the Policy Period

For a claim to be covered under the occurrence version of the CGL coverage form, the bodily injury or property damage must occur during the policy period. Thus, the policy that applies to a particular claim is the one that is in effect when the bodily injury or property damage occurs. This is the case even if the claim is not made until many years after the policy period ends.

Assuming that no exclusions or conditions eliminate coverage, the claim will be covered under the policy that was in effect when the bodily injury or property damage occurred, not under the policy in effect when the claim is made. The occurrence of bodily injury or property damage during the policy period is the event that triggers coverage under the occurrence coverage form and is therefore called the occurrence coverage trigger. See the exhibit "Occurrence Coverage Trigger."

Occurrence Coverage Trigger

Since it was founded, Atley Company has been continuously insured under the occurrence version of the CGL coverage form. Insurer X provided coverage during Year 1, Insurer Y provided coverage during Year 2, and Insurer Z provided coverage during Year 3. In Year 3, Atley Company received first notice of claim from an Atley customer who alleged that he had been injured by a defective Atley product in Year 2. The particular product causing the injury was negligently manufactured in Year 1. These events are depicted on the following timeline:

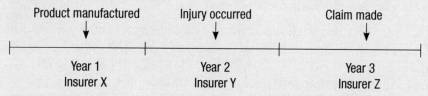

Product manufactured	Injury occurred	Claim made
Year 1	Year 2	Year 3
Insurer X	Insurer Y	Insurer Z

Question: Assuming that CGL coverage applies to the claim, which insurer—X, Y, or Z—would be obligated to provide a defense for Atley and possibly to pay the claimant's damages?

Answer: The injury occurred in Year 2, when Insurer Y's policy was in effect. Thus, Insurer Y would respond to the claim.

[DA04752]

The occurrence coverage trigger is easy to understand and apply to claims resulting from accidents that occur at a definite time, such as a motor vehicle accident, a drowning accident, or a slip-and-fall accident. However, applying the occurrence coverage trigger in other cases can sometimes be problematic.

Claims for disease resulting from prolonged exposure to asbestos are a classic example. Some courts have adopted a "continuous trigger theory," holding that bodily injury occurred continuously from the time the claimant was first exposed to asbestos until disease actually manifested, perhaps twenty or more years later. Consequently, all occurrence liability policies in effect during those years were triggered and their limits "stacked." Stacking refers to a situation in which the insured can collect multiples of the policy limit. If, for example, bodily injury is considered to have occurred over a twenty-year period, the insured might recover the sum of the policy limits in effect during each of the twenty years.

In 1986, to address this problem, as well as other problems inherent in insuring long-tail liability loss exposures with the occurrence coverage trigger, insurers introduced the claims-made CGL coverage form. In contrast with the occurrence form, the claims-made form basically requires that the claim must be made during the policy period. Thus, in its purest form, a claims-made policy will not cover any claims made after the policy period ends. In practice, however, claims-made policies usually give the named insured the option to purchase an extended reporting period. An extended reporting period, often called "tail coverage," covers claims made after the end of the policy period for injury or damage that occurred before the policy expired.

Injury or Damage Not Known Before the Policy Period

The occurrence version of the CGL coverage form contains wording aimed at eliminating coverage for bodily injury or property damage that was known, by designated insureds or by designated employees of the insured, to have occurred in whole or in part before the policy's inception date. The designated insureds are those described in the CGL coverage form under paragraph 1. of Section II—Who Is an Insured. The designated employees are those who are authorized by the named insured to give or receive notice of an occurrence or a claim, such as the named insured's risk manager.

This policy wording is known as the Montrose language, taking its name from the 1995 California case of *Montrose Chemical Corp. v. Admiral Insurance Co.*[2] In this case, the court rejected the "known loss" rule of policy interpretation, which states that an insurer is not liable for injury or damage that is known and in progress before the policy period begins. The basic intent behind the Montrose language is to eliminate coverage for progressive injury or damage that spans multiple policy periods if the named insured or certain other insureds knew of the original injury or damage before the current policy period began. (Progressive injury or damage is injury or damage that occurs over a period of time, which could encompass more than one policy period.) If courts give the Montrose language its intended effect, the only coverage that an insured will have for progressive injury or damage claims will be under policies that went into effect before the insured first knew about the injury or damage. Stacking of policy limits is thereby avoided for all subsequent policy periods in which continuing injury or damage occurs.[3]

Challenges to the Montrose language by insurance industry commentators led to ISO's inclusion of an amendment to the Coverage A insuring agreement clarifying known injury or damage, which was later incorporated into the 2001 edition of the CGL policy. Often called "anti-Montrose policy language," this provision clarifies that insureds can become aware of these losses "by any means" but fails to specify whether (1) liability must be established prior to the knowledge or (2) the proof of loss for a known loss or a loss in progress must follow (a) an objective standard (the insured knew or had reason to know of the loss before policy inception) or (b) a subjective standard (the insured had not yet been held liable for the loss but it had actual knowledge that a loss was probable). Most states are undecided, but the majority of states that have taken a position adopted the subjective standard position.[4]

Insurer's Duty to Defend

In addition to stating the insurer's duty to pay damages, the Coverage A insuring agreement expresses the insurer's right and duty to defend the insured against any suit seeking damages for bodily injury or property damage to which the insurance applies.

Courts have consistently held that the insurer's duty to defend is broader than its duty to pay damages. Even if a suit is later found to be groundless, false, or fraudulent, the insurer must defend an insured if the plaintiff alleges facts that could conceivably fall within policy coverage.

In determining whether the insurer has a duty to defend, some courts have based their findings solely on the allegations expressed in the plaintiff's complaint. Other courts have looked beyond the allegations and considered the facts, the reasonable expectations of the plaintiff, or both. In 1996, ISO amended the Coverage A insuring agreement to state that the insurer has no duty to defend the insured against any suit seeking damages for injury or damage to which the insurance does not apply. According to ISO, the purpose of the change was to relieve the insurer of the duty to defend when none of the allegations made against the insured would be covered under the policy. In most states, the insurer is obligated to defend the insured if at least one of the claimant's allegations would be covered, even if the other allegations are not covered.

The costs of defending the insured against covered suits or claims are payable in addition to the applicable limits of insurance. However, the insurer's duty to defend is stated to end when the applicable limit of insurance has been exhausted in paying damages for judgments or settlements.

EXCLUSIONS APPLICABLE TO COVERAGE A

The Insurance Services Office, Inc. (ISO) Commercial General Liability (CGL) Coverage Form can take you on a journey with unexpected twists and turns, especially when negotiating the exclusions section. Many of the exclusions contain exceptions, creating hairpin turns in what is excluded or not. The purpose of the journey is to determine how coverage is provided under the form.

As the Coverage A exclusions of the CGL are examined, it will be apparent that sometimes coverage is excluded and then is immediately provided by an exception to the exclusion. Before the study of exclusions begins, these are some thoughts to ponder:

- When a business prices its products/services, it first must determine the underlying cost component. The primary cost component for the insurance business is claims cost, which is mainly driven by the level of coverage provided. Exclusions are used to contour such cost estimates by clarifying the types of claims covered by the policy. This entails eliminating claims considered uninsurable (criminal acts) or catastrophic (war), or that are covered under other policies (automobiles).

- The comprehensive approach to determining whether coverage is provided for a loss involves a systematic examination of the insuring agreement, exclusions, and definitions.

The seventeen basic exclusions under Coverage A—Bodily Injury and Property Damage Liability of the CGL coverage form (CG 00 01 12 07) can be classified in a myriad of ways—for example, by primary type of exposure (such as premises/operations or products/completed operations) or by whether there is an exception to the exclusion. In this discussion, the exclusions are categorized in the latter fashion.

Exclusions With Exceptions

It may appear counterintuitive, yet coverage can exist within the Coverage A exclusions. Coverage exists through exceptions to the exclusions. Endorsements are also available to modify the exclusions, either by broadening or restricting coverage. Some of the available endorsements are noted within the discussion of each exclusion. These are the CGL exclusions that contain exceptions:

- Expected or Intended Injury
- Contractual Liability
- Liquor Liability
- Employers Liability
- Pollution
- Aircraft, Auto, or Watercraft
- Mobile Equipment
- Damage to Property
- Damage to Your Product and Damage to Your Work
- Damage to Impaired Property and Property Not Physically Injured
- Recall of Products, Work, or Impaired Property

Expected or Intended Injury

This exclusion defines a type of loss that is excluded because the bodily injury or property damage was expected or intended from the insured's standpoint. However, there is an exception for bodily injury resulting from the use of reasonable force to protect persons or property.

For example, Marco is an employee of Animal Farm, a children's recreational restaurant. Marco restrained a belligerent trespasser who threatened Charlie Coyote, who was entertaining the children, and frightened the children. As a result of the restraint, the trespasser fell backwards and sprained his ankle. Marco used reasonable force to restrain the trespasser and did not intend to harm him. Rather, Marco was attempting to protect Charlie and the children from harm. The exclusion would not apply to coverage for the trespasser's bodily injury because it resulted from the use of reasonable force to protect persons or property.

Conversely, if Charlie mistook the trespasser for someone who owed him money and punched him, the exclusion would apply because Charlie intended to cause injury.

Contractual Liability

Because of its exceptions and definitions, this exclusion can be challenging to interpret. The exclusion clearly states that coverage is excluded for bodily injury or property damage for which the insured is obligated to pay damages because of the assumption of liability in a contract or an agreement.

The challenge associated with interpreting this exclusion relates to its exception—or when coverage may apply. The exception covers these types of contractual liability:

• Liability the insured would have in the absence of the agreement

• Liability assumed within an insured contract—a defined term under the policy

The first exception essentially states that the purpose of the Contractual Liability exclusion is not to preclude coverage for what otherwise is the basic intent of the policy— to cover bodily injury or property damage liability of the insured. If the agreement in question does not extend the insured's liability beyond that which is otherwise covered by the CGL, then the exclusion does not apply.

Evaluating the second exception requires examining the definition of "insured contract." The coverage form provides a definition that includes several types of contracts. It is important to note that any insured contract must have been executed before the occurrence of the bodily injury or property damage. These are the types of insured contracts in the CGL coverage form:

• A contract for lease of premises—Leases are one of the more common agreements of a business. However, the portion of a lease that indemnifies any person or organization for damage by fire to premises while rented to you or temporarily occupied by you with permission of the owner is not an insured contract. A typical lease contains an indemnification provision in favor of the landlord wherein the tenant agrees to protect and reimburse the landlord for bodily injury and property damage arising from the use of the premises. However, fire damage is not included in the definition of an insured contract when it occurs to the portion of the premises rented to or occupied by the insured.

• A sidetrack agreement—Businesses may operate more efficiently if a railroad can transport goods onto or off their premises via a sidetrack. Therefore, certain manufacturing and distribution operations have sidetrack agreements with railroads. In exchange for offering this service, the railroad will contractually require that the business hold the railroad harmless for the ownership, maintenance, or use of the sidetrack. Such a stipulation may also require that the business be responsible for damage to the railroad's property.

- Any easement or license agreement, except in connection with construction or demolition operations on or within fifty feet of a railroad—An easement or a license agreement entitles another party to the restricted use of one's property. As an example, a public utility may have an easement to an underground pipe that feeds through A's property to B's property. This easement may contain an indemnification in favor of the property owners that protects them in the event of damage or injury caused by the utility's use of the property to maintain the underground pipe. Such assumption of liability by the utility would be covered by this definition. The Contractual Liability—Railroads endorsement (CG 2417) is available to provide coverage for liability assumed in an easement or license agreement in connection with operations within fifty feet of a railroad.

- An obligation, as required by ordinance, to indemnify a municipality, except in connection with work for a municipality—As part of the permit process with a municipality, a business may need to indemnify the municipality, such as for a sign permit. The municipality will typically expect that the business will be fully responsible and protect the municipality from damages arising from the use or maintenance of the sign. This exception, however, does not extend coverage to a contractor who agrees to indemnify a municipality under a maintenance or construction contract, as that constitutes "work for a municipality." That particular type of contractual liability is covered under a different type of insured contract.

- An elevator maintenance agreement—If a business has an elevator, it is legally required to maintain it. Liability assumed under a maintenance agreement with a licensed elevator contractor is a covered type of insured contract.

- That part of any other contract or agreement pertaining to your business (including an indemnification of a municipality in connection with work performed for a municipality) under which you assume the tort liability of another party to pay for bodily injury or property damage to a third person or organization—This aspect of the definition of "insured contract" effectively creates blanket **contractual liability coverage** for contracts including construction, sales, or service contracts. A few limits and exclusions apply:

- This assumed obligation is for tort liability—liability that would be imposed by law rather than solely by contract. For instance, a warranty for product performance would not qualify as an insured contract because the warranty itself creates liability rather than the law. For example, in a sales contract, a company sells a gas generator with a service contract to a restaurant and agrees in the sales contract to assume tort liability for the generator. If the generator explodes and causes injury to the restaurant's customers, this contractual tort liability would be covered. However, if the sales contract also included a warranty on the performance of the genera-

Contractual liability coverage

Coverage for liability that the insured has assumed under an insured contract.

tor and the generator failed to perform after a power outage, resulting in spoilage of food, this loss would not be covered. Contracts that indemnify a railroad for bodily injury or property damage arising out of construction or demolition operations—within fifty feet of any railroad property and affecting any railroad bridge or trestle, tracks, roadbeds, tunnel, underpass, or crossing—are excluded (the Contractual Liability—Railroads endorsement can add this coverage).

- Contracts that indemnify an architect, an engineer, or a surveyor for injury or damage arising out of various professional services are excluded. In addition, liability for professional service assumed under any contract made by an insured who is an architect, an engineer, or a surveyor is excluded.

This discussion of contractual liability coverage provided by exceptions to the exclusion focuses on the liability assumed—namely, damages in the form of bodily injury and/or property damage. However, what about defense costs and related legal fees? These costs are covered if such costs are assumed within the agreement and relate to allegations that would be covered under the terms of the policy. Defense costs are considered damages and are, therefore, part of the limit of liability. When a lawsuit is brought against both the insured and the indemnitee, such defense costs are covered in addition to the limit of liability.

The broadest level of indemnification occurs when one party protects another for liability, even if caused solely by the other party. Courts are typically not favorable toward such language within a contract. In some cases, a court could reform the contract, rendering it meaningless. Courts of certain jurisdictions consider such contracts wholly inequitable and therefore illegal. Insurance underwriters could restrict coverage under the contractual liability coverage by the attachment of the **Amendment of Insured Contract Definition endorsement** (CG 2426). This endorsement modifies the definition so that it applies to circumstances under which the insured caused the liability "in whole or in part." This modification effectively precludes coverage for situations in which the insured is obligating itself to protect another party who is solely responsible for an accident. See the exhibit "Navigating the CGL Contractual Liability Exclusion, Exceptions, and Endorsements."

Liquor Liability Exclusion

There is an exclusion for bodily injury or property damage for which any insured may be held liable by causing or contributing to the intoxication of any person; by furnishing alcoholic beverages to a person under the legal drinking age or under the influence of alcohol; or through any statute, ordinance, or regulation relating to the distribution or use of alcoholic beverages.

However, a significant exception exists. The Liquor Liability exclusion applies only if the insured is in the business of manufacturing, distributing, selling, serving, or furnishing alcoholic beverages. This exception is primarily intended to provide **host liquor liability coverage** for the tangential serving of liquor, such as after a board meeting or another special occasion.

Amendment of Insured Contract Definition endorsement

The endorsement that modifies the CGL coverage form so that subpart f. of the insured contract definition will not include bodily injury or property damage caused solely by an indemnitee of the named insured.

Host liquor liability coverage

Coverage for a person or an organization that serves alcoholic beverages to others but is not in the alcoholic beverage business; it covers the insured host against liability for accidents caused by persons who become intoxicated as a result of the insured's serving of alcoholic beverages.

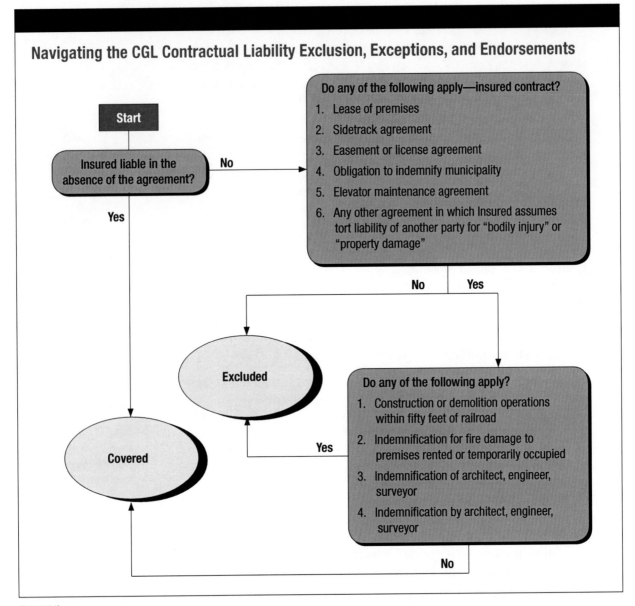

Navigating the CGL Contractual Liability Exclusion, Exceptions, and Endorsements

Start

Insured liable in the absence of the agreement?

No → Do any of the following apply—insured contract?
1. Lease of premises
2. Sidetrack agreement
3. Easement or license agreement
4. Obligation to indemnify municipality
5. Elevator maintenance agreement
6. Any other agreement in which Insured assumes tort liability of another party for "bodily injury" or "property damage"

Yes

No / Yes

Excluded

Covered

Do any of the following apply?
1. Construction or demolition operations within fifty feet of railroad
2. Indemnification for fire damage to premises rented or temporarily occupied
3. Indemnification of architect, engineer, surveyor
4. Indemnification by architect, engineer, surveyor

Yes

No

[DA06780]

The pivotal aspect to this exclusion is the exception language. Complexity is added by case law, in addition to state statutes governing liquor licenses, regarding what constitutes "being in the business of …alcoholic beverages." For example, in Pennsylvania, a "beef and beer" event requires a liquor license, even if it is held for a charitable purpose. Depending on the operations of the insured, underwriters may attach the Amendment of Liquor Liability Exclusion endorsement (CG 21 50). This endorsement adds coverage for events at which the insured sells or furnishes alcoholic beverages for a charge or at which a license is required for such activities. Special coverage forms are available to provide coverage for organizations, such as restaurants, that serve alcoholic beverages as a regular part of their business operations.

Employers Liability Exclusion

Although workers compensation is considered the **exclusive remedy** in most cases for an employee who is injured in the course and scope of employment, there is potential for actions against an employer based on other legal theories. The Employers Liability exclusion applies if the insured is liable in another capacity, such as one of these:

- **Dual-capacity doctrine**—The employee may have an additional relationship with an organization other than the employer-employee relationship. For example, if Hobbs, a salesperson for an appliance store, is involved in a work-related accident while demonstrating a used stove repaired by his employer, he could claim that the accident was caused by negligence in repair of the stove and establish a consumer relationship with the store. Coverage for the store for any tort suit claiming the dual capacity is excluded under the CGL. Coverage would be provided by the store's Coverage B—Employers Liability Coverage in the workers compensation policy.

- **Third-party-over action**—Continuing the preceding example, the employee might file suit against the manufacturer of the stove instead of against his employer. The manufacturer might then sue the store for negligence in repairing the stove. If the store were found by the court to be liable to the appliance manufacturer, the exclusion would bar coverage for that liability. Any coverage would be provided by Coverage B of the workers compensation policy.

This exclusion contains an exception for liability assumed by the insured under an insured contract. In the foregoing example, if the store had a contract with the appliance manufacturer to indemnify the manufacturer for any injury resulting from the repair of appliances and involving negligence on the part of the store, the CGL policy would provide coverage.

Pollution Exclusion

Pollution liability and cleanup claims are the subject of a separate type of insurance, and the Pollution exclusion eliminates coverage under the CGL for most pollution exposures. These exceptions apply:

- Coverage is provided for bodily injury caused by smoke, fumes, vapor, or soot emanating from cooling, heating, or dehumidifying equipment. For example, a natural-gas-fired boiler in the basement of a hospital fires improperly, causing the accumulation of carbon monoxide that emanates throughout a section of the building. This results in illness among a dozen patients. Any resulting claims would be covered by this provision.

- Coverage is provided for bodily injury or property damage if the insured is a contractor and the owner of the premises is named as an additional insured regarding the premises on which the insured is conducting operations. The caveat is that such premises are not, and never were, owned, occupied by, or rented to any insured other than the additional insured.

Exclusive remedy

The workers compensation law grants benefits as the employee's sole source of recovery against the employer, so employees lose the right to sue their employers for injuries covered by workers compensation.

Dual-capacity doctrine

A legal doctrine giving the employee the right to sue the employer when the employer acts in a capacity other than that of employer.

Third-party-over action

A separate legal action, brought by a defendant in a lawsuit, against a third party that might be liable to the defendant for all or part of the plaintiff's claim in the original lawsuit.

As an example, CBA Enterprises is an excavating contractor that was engaged by Plastics Corp. to assist in the construction of a new building within a chemical plant complex. Plastics Corp. is named as an additional insured on CBA's CGL policy. One of CBA's equipment operators accidentally severs a pipeline, resulting in the spillage of sulfuric acid and causing illness to several onlookers. CBA does not have and never had an interest in these premises. Plastics Corp. is an additional insured, and coverage would be available to Plastics Corp. as well as to CBA.

- Coverage is provided for bodily injury or property damage resulting from a hostile fire spewing smoke, particulates, and other "pollutants" into the surrounding area.

- Coverage is provided for bodily injury or property damage resulting from the escape of fluids needed to perform normal functions of mobile equipment operation—for example, a transmission fluid leak from a cracked gear box.

- Coverage is provided for bodily injury or property damage that occurs within a building and is caused by the release of gases, fumes, or vapors that emanate from materials (not pollutants) brought onto the premises by the insured (or on the insured's behalf) for its operations.

These exceptions can provide a limited amount of coverage for pollution in various circumstances that typically have a narrow scope of time and place. See the exhibit "Practice Exercise—Pollution Exclusion and Exceptions."

Practice Exercise—Pollution Exclusion and Exceptions

ABC Carpet, Inc. is a carpet installer that has been contracted to install carpeting in the executive area of Atom Industries. It installs the carpet with an inappropriate adhesive in excessive amounts. Fumes from the adhesive pervade the area. A major client of Atom Industries becomes ill from the fumes and is taken to the hospital.

Question

Does ABC's CGL policy cover ABC for a claim from Atom's client?

Answer

ABC's CGL policy would provide coverage under the exception for release of fumes within a building from materials brought onto the premises by an insured for its operations. ABC brought the adhesive into the building, and fumes from the adhesive caused Atom's client to become ill.

[DA06638]

Despite the exceptions, the Pollution exclusion eliminates coverage for a broad range of pollution incidents. Every organization should assess its pollution liability loss exposures carefully, compare them against the Pollution exclusion and exceptions in the CGL, and decide whether additional pollution liability coverage is required. See the exhibit "Navigating the Pollution Exclusion and Exceptions."

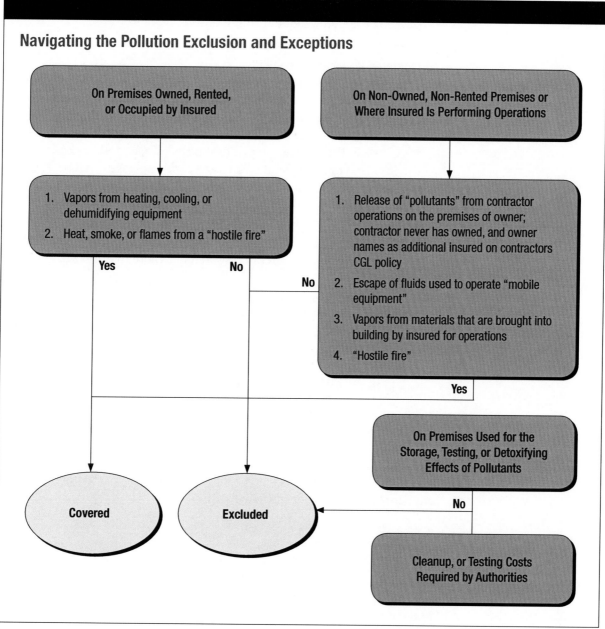

Navigating the Pollution Exclusion and Exceptions

[DA06781]

Aircraft, Auto, or Watercraft

Coverage is excluded under the CGL for bodily injury or property damage arising out of the ownership, maintenance, use, entrustment to others, loading, or unloading of any aircraft, auto, or watercraft owned, operated by, rented, or loaned to any insured.

The purpose of this exclusion is primarily to defer to other insuring forms that are more appropriate, particularly the commercial automobile coverage form. The exceptions to this exclusion include these:

- Owned or rented watercraft that is ashore.
- Non-owned watercraft less than twenty-six feet long and not used to carry people or property for a charge.
- Parking a non-owned or non-rented auto adjacent to the insured premises. This coverage applies to damage to a third party's property and/or bodily injury only. There is no coverage for damage to the vehicle being driven. This would require garagekeepers legal liability coverage, designed to cover liability for damage to autos in the care, custody, or control of the insured. For example, if a valet at a parking garage hits a pedestrian or another vehicle while parking a car, there would be coverage for injury to the pedestrian or to the other vehicle, but there would not be coverage under the CGL for damage to the vehicle being driven by the valet.
- The assumption of liability under an insured contract for the ownership, maintenance, or use of aircraft or watercraft (note that this does not refer to autos).
- The operation of machinery or equipment attached to what otherwise would be considered an auto. Although an insecticide-spraying machine may be attached to a vehicle subject to motor vehicle insurance law, the liability originating from the operation of the sprayer would be covered under the CGL. The operation of the vehicle transporting the sprayer would be the subject of commercial auto insurance.

The definition of "auto" is significant. The more challenging aspect of the "auto" definition is any land vehicle that is "subject to a compulsory or financial responsibility law." It is important, therefore, to understand the state requirements for various vehicles because the requirement may change across state lines. What may be considered mobile equipment in one state may be considered an auto in a neighboring state.

Mobile Equipment

The only CGL exclusion that specifically applies to mobile equipment is exclusion h, which applies to liability arising out of the ownership, maintenance, or use of mobile equipment. The exclusion eliminates coverage for: (1) the transportation of mobile equipment by an auto that is owned, operated, rented, or borrowed by an insured; or (2) the use of mobile equipment in a prearranged racing, speed, or demolition contest or in a stunt activity. However, claims arising from the operation of mobile equipment are covered under the CGL as long as they are not excluded by the provisions of h and as long as any mobile equipment involved meets the CGL definition of "**mobile equipment**."

Mobile equipment

Various types of vehicles designed for use principally off public roads, such as bulldozers and cranes.

Damage to Property

Some interesting claim scenarios are rooted in the exclusion for damage to property. A key theme to remember is that this exclusion is concerned mainly with property damage that occurs while the insured has possession of the damaged property or is working on it. This exclusion has four parts:

1. The insured's property—Coverage is excluded for damage to property the named insured owns, rents, or occupies. However, there is an exception for property damage (other than damage by fire) to premises, including their contents, rented to the named insured for a period of seven or fewer consecutive days. Damage by fire to rented premises is addressed in a different section of the exclusions. There is also an exception for property loaned to the insured or otherwise in the care, custody, or control of the insured for a period of seven or fewer consecutive days.

2. Coverage for property damage to a building that has been sold or given away to another party—This was formerly called the alienated premises exclusion. The insured seller of a building would not be covered under the CGL policy if the buyer asserted that a collapse of the newly purchased building's roof in a snowstorm was caused by a latent defect that the insured should have known about.

3. Property damage to the particular part of real property on which the named insured, or any contractors or subcontractors working on the insured's behalf, are performing operations—This has importance primarily for the construction industry. The reference to the particular part of real property where the insured is working is significant. If there is damage to the portion of real property on which the insured is working, then there is no liability coverage for such damage. By exception, however, there is coverage for the other portions of a building that may have been damaged as a result of the insured's operations, including areas where the insured previously completed construction.

4. Work that was incorrectly performed—If a contractor's work needs to be restored, repaired, or replaced because the insured's work was not performed correctly, coverage is excluded. There is an exception for liability under a sidetrack agreement and property damage included in the products-completed operations hazard.

The exception for property damage included in the products-completed operations hazard depends on the CGL's definition of a products-completed operations hazard. According to the definition, bodily injury or property damage is included under the products-completed operations hazard if three requirements are met. First, the injury or damage must arise out of the insured's product or work. Second, the injury or damage must occur away from premises owned or rented by the named insured. Third, the product causing the injury or damage must not be in the named insured's physical possession when the injury or damage occurs. In the case of a completed operations liability claim, the work must be completed or abandoned when the injury or damage occurs. For example, if a contractor completes a building and the building subsequently collapses, the resulting injury and property damage would be covered under the definition of the products-completed operations hazard, which has a separate limit.

However, certain operations, such as restaurants, have a products liability exposure on their premises. For example, a restaurant's cherries jubilee, while being heated, could cause damage to a patron's coat or injury to a patron. For the premises exposure, coverage can be obtained with the Products-Completed Operations Hazard Redefined endorsement (CG 24 07). See the exhibit "Navigating the Property Damage Exclusion and Exceptions."

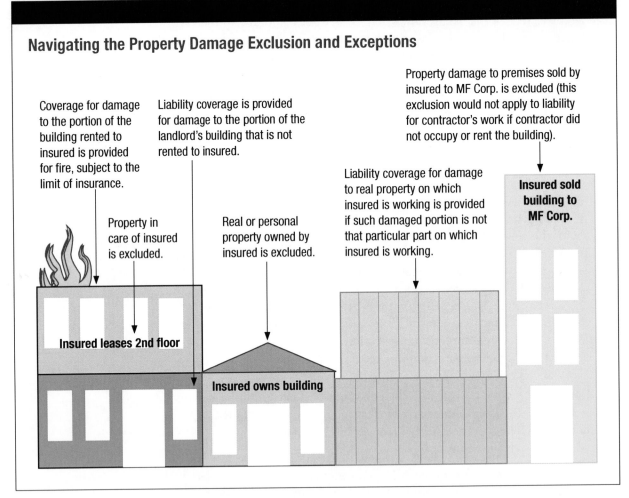

Navigating the Property Damage Exclusion and Exceptions

Coverage for damage to the portion of the building rented to insured is provided for fire, subject to the limit of insurance.

Liability coverage is provided for damage to the portion of the landlord's building that is not rented to insured.

Property damage to premises sold by insured to MF Corp. is excluded (this exclusion would not apply to liability for contractor's work if contractor did not occupy or rent the building).

Property in care of insured is excluded.

Real or personal property owned by insured is excluded.

Liability coverage for damage to real property on which insured is working is provided if such damaged portion is not that particular part on which insured is working.

Insured sold building to MF Corp.

Insured leases 2nd floor

Insured owns building

[DA06782]

Damage to Your Product and Damage to Your Work

The two exclusions for damage to the insured's product and damage to the insured's work are closely related. These two exclusions are similar to several of the prior exclusions that eliminate coverage for damage to the insured's own property. The purpose of both of these exclusions is to prevent the insurer from having to pay for repairing or replacing a product that was incorrectly designed or defectively produced—a business risk that is not normally insurable. The exclusion applies only to the product itself, not to any damage or injury caused by the product.

For example, if a hair dryer is defective and does not produce warm air, there is no coverage for the product defect. However, if the defect in the hair dryer causes it to catch fire and results in property damage to a customer's property, coverage would exist for that property damage.

There is an exception to the exclusion for damage to the insured's work, and this exception helps to explain the distinction between these two exclusions. The exception for damage to the insured's work applies if the damaged work, or the work that caused the damage, was performed on behalf of the insured by a subcontractor. The damage to work exclusion applies primarily to construction work, and, therefore, the exception for work performed by a subcontractor is important. However, this exception applies to work that has been completed, not to work in progress. The exclusions discussed for property owned by an insured would eliminate coverage for most property owned by an insured while work is being performed.

For example, if a general contractor completes a building that is found to have a defect in the electrical wiring that requires the wiring to be replaced, coverage may exist under the exception if the wiring was installed by a subcontractor. This exception can be deleted by the Damage To Work Performed by Subcontractors On Your Behalf endorsement (CG 22 94).

Damage to Impaired Property or Property Not Physically Injured

In the course of commerce—in particular, manufacturing—a host of businesses produce various components used to make a final product. If one of those components fails to operate in accordance with design parameters, the cost of replacing such a failed or an inadequately performing component is not covered by the CGL because of the exclusion for damage to impaired property or property not physically injured. As an example, if a capacitor for a television were deficient because of improper temperature tolerances and this deficiency resulted in a need to replace the capacitors in 100,000 televisions, coverage would not exist under the CGL for the replacement costs.

The policy definition for "impaired property" defines impaired property as tangible property (other than the insured's product or work) that cannot be used or is less useful because it includes a product of the insured's that is defective—if the property could be restored to use by the repair, replacement, or removal of the insured's product. Under this definition, property that is impaired because of a defect in the insured's product is excluded. However, the definition and the exclusion's title imply that if the insured's product does cause physical injury to another party's property, there would be coverage. To continue the preceding example, if the insured's capacitor caused the television to overheat and melted essential components beyond repair, there would be coverage for the damage to the television but not to the capacitor.

There is an exception to this exclusion. The exclusion does not apply to the loss of use of other property arising out of sudden and accidental physical injury to the insured's product or work after it has been put to its intended use. If a contractor improperly wires a heating unit and it catches fire, the claim by the building owner for loss of use of the building while the unit is being repaired or replaced would be covered.

Recall of Products, Work, or Impaired Property

To slightly revise the example in the previous section regarding the television capacitor, if the television manufacturer needed to recall the 100,000 televisions, the capacitor manufacturer would not be covered under the CGL for recall or replacement costs, and neither would the television manufacturer, because of the same exclusion. Coverage for product recall expense is available through the Limited Product Withdrawal Expense Endorsement (CG 04 36) or the Product Withdrawal Coverage Form (CG 00 66). See the exhibit "Practice Exercise—Property Damage Exclusions and Exceptions."

Practice Exercise—Property Damage Exclusions and Exceptions

Water Cooler Manufacturer (WCM), a water cooler manufacturer, recently discovered that 10,000 of its water coolers (the H2O 9000 model) leak due to defective seals. These seals were manufactured by Manufacturing Company. WCM discovered the problem when one of its customers complained about a leak after her area rug was damaged by water leaking from the cooler. She requested that WCM cover the cost of $800 to replace her rug. The cost of recalling the units and making the necessary repairs is $120,000. WCM asks Manufacturing Co. to cover all of these costs. There was no indemnification clause in the contract between WCM and Manufacturing Co.

Question

Will Manufacturing Company's CGL policy provide coverage?

Answer

Manufacturing Company's CGL policy will most likely provide coverage for the damaged rug if the leak was caused by Manufacturing Company's seal. However, because of the exclusion for costs incurred by the insured or others for recall of products, the CGL policy will not cover the recall costs unless there was an endorsement added to provide this coverage.

[DA06654]

Exclusions Without Exceptions

These CGL Coverage A exclusions do not contain exceptions:

- Worker's Compensation
- War
- Personal and Advertising Injury
- Electronic Data
- Distribution of Material in Violation of Statues

Workers Compensation

The CGL coverage form excludes coverage for liability of the insured under any workers compensation, disability benefits, unemployment compensation, or similar law. The purpose of the exclusion is to eliminate duplication between the CGL coverage form and other policies specifically designed to provide protection for employees.

Coverage for injuries to the employees of third parties that result from the products or operations of the insured can be complex. Workers compensation is primary coverage, and the workers compensation policy of the employer whose employee is injured in the course and scope of employment should respond. However, if the insured's product or operations caused the injury, the employee may have a cause of action, apart from workers compensation, against the insured. The workers compensation insurer may have a subrogation claim against any recovery by the employee for both past and future benefits provided. Additionally, the employer and/or the workers compensation insurer may have a cause of action to recover the amount of benefits paid against the CGL insured. See the exhibit "Workers Compensation and the CGL."

War

The 2001 edition and several prior editions of the CGL coverage form contained a war exclusion that provided an exception if the insured had assumed liability related to acts of war under a contract. In 2002, ISO introduced a mandatory CGL endorsement that excluded bodily injury or property damage arising directly or indirectly out of war, regardless of whether the insured had assumed such liability under a contract. This change was necessitated by a legal environment in which insureds could be sued directly for war-related losses. When ISO revised the CGL coverage form in 2004, the new war exclusion, without an exception, was added to the form. The same exclusion was retained in the 2007 edition of the CGL coverage form.

This exclusion does not apply to acts of terrorism. Coverage is provided for many commercial loss exposures through the Terrorism Risk Insurance Act (TRIA).

Workers Compensation and the CGL

✓ **Reality Check**

The majority of employers are required by state law to have workers compensation insurance, and this requirement cannot be met by the CGL. It is important, even in economically difficult times, for employers to have workers compensation coverage. It is also important to understand that even when there seems to be duplicate coverage, the insurance principle that a loss should never result in a profit (or "double dipping") still applies. This example illustrates how coverage under a workers compensation policy may intersect with coverage under a third-party CGL policy.

Leif, an employee who is unloading a floral arrangement from a Fresh Flowers delivery van outside an office complex, is struck by a steel girder dropped from Heron's crane. Leif sustains severe head and spinal cord injuries. Fresh Flowers' workers compensation insurer, WCI, pays $1,273,000 in medical benefits and $57,450 in indemnity benefits over a three-year period for Leif's injuries. Heron has an each occurrence CGL limit of $1 million. Leif files suit against Heron for damages, including pain and suffering. WCI files a subrogation lien with the court of jurisdiction for Leif's suit against Heron. Heron's commercial general liability insurer offers the policy limits of $1 million to settle Leif's suit, and Leif agrees to the settlement. WCI, rather than proceed to a court hearing on distribution of Leif's settlement, negotiates a lien settlement with Leif's attorney for $527,000. Although Heron and its CGL insurer have resolved all of their financial responsibility for this claim through the settlement, WCI remains responsible for Leif's future medical and indemnity benefits.

[DA06655]

Personal and Advertising Injury

An exclusion for bodily injury arising out of personal and advertising injury applies to Coverage A of the CGL coverage form. The purpose of this exclusion is to eliminate duplicate coverage under Coverage A for bodily injury that might result from an offense covered under Coverage B—Personal and Advertising Injury. Bodily injury resulting from any of the offenses, such as false arrest or wrongful eviction, included in the policy definition of "personal and advertising injury" is covered under Coverage B and subject to the Coverage B limit of insurance rather than the each occurrence limit that applies to Coverage A.

Electronic Data

The definition of "property damage" in the CGL is limited to tangible property, and the definition states that electronic data are not considered tangible property. The electronic data exclusion was added to the CGL coverage form in 2004 to reinforce the definition that electronic data are not considered tangible property. Limited coverage for liability for the electronic data loss exposure can be added by the Electronic Data Liability endorsement (CG

04 37). Broader coverage can be provided by the Electronic Data Liability Coverage Form (CG 00 65).

Distribution of Material in Violation of Statutes

The CGL excludes bodily injury or property damage resulting from violation of the Telephone Consumer Protection Act (TCPA); the CAN-SPAM Act of 2003; or any other statute, ordinance, or regulation that "prohibits or limits the sending, transmitting, communicating or distribution of material or information." The TCPA and the CAN-SPAM Act are federal laws that restrict the use of telephones, fax machines, and computers for transmitting unsolicited advertisements or e-mail messages. The exclusion also applies to similar state or local laws. For example, if a company sends an unsolicited electronic communication containing a code that causes damage to the computers of the recipients, coverage for the damage to the computers is excluded.

Fire Legal Liability Coverage

At the end of the section containing the Coverage A exclusions is an exception that applies to most of the Coverage A exclusions. This exception creates a coverage known as **fire legal liability coverage**. A separate limit of insurance is specified in the policy limits section for this coverage.

Tenants often agree to indemnify their landlords for fire damage to the leased premises. Although the CGL definition of "insured contract" states that such agreements are not insured contracts, the exclusion for contractual liability provides an exception for liability that the insured would have in the absence of the contract or agreement. Whether or not a tenant agrees to indemnify a landlord for fire damage, the CGL policy covers legal liability for fire damage. Therefore, if fire damage results from an insured's negligence, the CGL fire legal liability coverage still applies.

However, this exception does not apply if the only reason the insured becomes liable for fire damage is because of an indemnification agreement. For example, if a fire starts because a building is struck by lightning, coverage would be excluded.

Fire legal liability coverage
Coverage for the insured's liability for fire damage to premises rented to or temporarily occupied by the named insured.

COMMERCIAL GENERAL LIABILITY CASE STUDIES

An organization must be able to rely on its insurance program. Because the Insurance Services Office, Inc. (ISO) Commercial General Liability (CGL) Coverage Form is a key aspect of many organizations' insurance programs, a fundamental understanding of the coverage the CGL does or does not provide is vital for risk management and insurance professionals.

Case studies present an opportunity to see how the CGL form works in practical application. For insurance and risk management professionals, case studies can hone the skills required to determine whether the CGL form provides the appropriate insurance coverage for the liability exposures of an organization or whether the CGL provides coverage after a liability loss.

Painting, Inc., Case Study

Painting, Inc., is a mid-sized painting contractor. Painting's CGL coverage form changed from a claims-made form to an occurrence-based form on the renewal date of July 1, 20X1.

On May 2, 20X1, Painting contracted to paint the exterior walls of a warehouse owned by Pet Supplies Co. On June 23, 20X1, three of the walls were completed. A four-day delay in the completion of the project due to wind and the possibility of overspray ensued, after which the foreman opted to complete the project on Friday, June 27. Because of the delay, the paint was remixed in a slightly different composition.

Unfortunately, it was still windy enough on June 27 to cause overspray on the vehicles in the parking lot. These autos were owned by customers and employees of Pet Supplies. One of the customers was Pamela, the owner of several pet stores in the area, whose 1930s roadster had its original finish marred by the overspray. In all, nine autos were damaged.

Case Facts

On August 1, 20X1, Pet Supplies filed these claims with Painting:

- Each auto owner pursued damages for auto repair due to the overspray. The total cost was $18,000. Pet Supplies paid the auto owners to maintain good relationships with its customers and demanded reimbursement from Painting.
- Pet Supplies pursued damages for mismatched color of the paint on the final wall.
- Pet Supplies pursued damages from Painting for the loss of profit on Pamela's account, which had since been canceled.

Painting had an occurrence-based Commercial General Liability Coverage Form (CG 00 01 12 07). See the exhibit "Painting's CGL Limits."

Painting's limits were similar in the previous claims-made coverage form with a $500,000 per claim limit instead of a per occurrence limit. There was no deductible for either policy. The basic extended reporting period was in effect following the claims-made policy's expiration.

Painting's CGL Limits

•	$1,000,000	General Aggregate
•	$1,000,000	Products-Completed Operations Aggregate
•	$500,000	Per Occurrence Bodily Injury and Property Damage
•	$500,000	Personal and Advertising Injury
•	$100,000	Damage to Rented Premises
•	$10,000	Medical Payments

[DA06723]

Case Analysis Tools

An analysis of coverage involves applying the policy to the case facts. There are four key aspects of the policy to consider:

- Whether there was coverage for the insured at the location and date of the loss
- Whether there was coverage for the type of loss
- Whether there are any conditions that apply
- Whether there are any exclusions or endorsements that apply

After coverage is determined, the policy limits need to be evaluated to determine whether, and how much, the insurer will pay.

Coverage Analysis

The first question that must be answered is whether there is coverage under either the claims-made form or the occurrence form. Under the insuring agreement of the occurrence form, the occurrence must take place during the policy period stated in the declarations. The occurrence form was effective July 1. The overspray occurred on June 27, prior to the inception date of the occurrence form. Therefore, there was no coverage under the occurrence form.

The claim was reported during this extended reporting period for an occurrence that took place during the policy period. Therefore, there was coverage under the claims-made form for the date of loss.

The auto damages were covered by the CGL form because the property damage to the autos caused by the overspray resulted from Painting's negligence in spraying paint during windy conditions. There are no exclusions for this loss in the CGL.

Pet Supplies's claim for mismatched paint could not be considered "property damage," as defined in the CGL. Rather, it was an inherent defect or inadequacy in the "work" performed by Painting. The exclusion for damage to impaired property or property not physically injured can be applied to the claim for mismatched paint. The warehouse was not physically injured, and the exclusion barred coverage for impaired property arising out of a defect, deficiency, or inadequacy from the insured's work.

Pet Supplies's claim for the loss of profits due to the cancellation of Pamela's account was causally related to the negligence of Painting. The definition of "property damage" in Painting's CGL policy notably includes physical damage to tangible property including the loss of use of such property. If the damage to Pamela's vehicle resulted in loss of use of her vehicle, this would be covered under the CGL. The consequential economic loss suffered by Pet Supplies, however, does not come within the scope of this definition. Any proper cause of action Pet Supplies may have against Painting would not be covered under Painting's CGL policy.

The only loss covered by Painting's CGL was the auto damage. Because there was no deductible in Painting's policy, the full amount of damages for the covered auto loss was payable by the insurer and below the per-claim limit. Painting had only one prior claim for $7,002 for the policy period, and therefore the $18,000 damages were within the aggregate limit.

Faux Stone Enterprises Case Study

In 20X1, Faux Stone Enterprises installed stone facades for exterior commercial office buildings. Faux Stone contracted with Carnation Real Estate to apply a stone facade to the Downtown Office Complex.

In 20X5, the owners of Faux Stone sold their company to Vincent's Veneer Corp., which retained it as a wholly-owned subsidiary. Vincent's risk manager never formally added Faux Stone to Vincent's CGL policy.

Case Facts

In 20X7, Mary was struck by a piece of the stone facade that fell from the Downtown Office Complex. Subsequently, several other pieces fell (indicating a problem with the adhesive), although without resulting in any injury or damage other than to the building's exterior.

Mary sustained serious head, neck, and back injuries that required several surgeries. She sued Carnation Real Estate, owner of the Downtown Office Complex, for $2 million—$300,000 in special damages, including loss of income and medical expenses, and $1.7 million in general damages, including pain and suffering. Carnation Real Estate, in turn, brought Faux Stone into the suit, alleging that it was Faux Stone's negligence that caused the piece of stone facade to fall.

Carnation Real Estate also sued Faux Stone for $500,000 for the cost of replacing the facade.

Both Carnation and Vincent's Veneer filed claims under their respective occurrence CGL coverage forms. See the exhibit "Carnation and Vincent's Veneer CGL Limits."

Carnation and Vincent's Veneer CGL Limits

These were Vincent's Veneer's CGL limits:

•	$4,000,000	General Aggregate
•	$2,000,000	Products-Completed Operations Aggregate
•	$2,000,000	Per Occurrence Bodily Injury and Property Damage
•	$500,000	Personal and Advertising Injury
•	$100,000	Damage to Rented Premises
•	$5,000	Medical Payments

These were Carnation's CGL limits:

•	$10,000,000	General Aggregate
•	$1,000,000	Products-Completed Operations Aggregate
•	$5,000,000	Per Occurrence Bodily Injury and Property Damage
•	$500,000	Personal and Advertising Injury
•	$100,000	Damage to Rented Premises
•	$10,000	Medical Payments

[DA06724]

There were no deductibles for either policy. According to the agreements executed when Vincent's Veneer acquired Faux Stone, Vincent's Veneer agreed to assume all of Faux Stone's liability.

Case Analysis Tools

Key elements of the policy—declarations, insuring agreement, conditions, exclusions, and endorsements—are reviewed to determine if coverage applies to the facts of the case. After coverage is determined, the policy limits are reviewed to determine how much the insurer will pay for covered damages.

Coverage Analysis

Because the injury and damage were caused after Faux Stone completed the project, this was a completed operations claim. One danger of the completed operations exposure is the lengthy time period that persists for a given project. The claim representative for Vincent's Veneer's insurer was unable to obtain a copy of Faux Stone's policy at the time of installation. The occurrences resulting in the claims for injury and property damage took place within the policy period for both Vincent's Veneer and Carnation. However, it is not certain that either policy provided coverage.

Because the agreement between Vincent's Veneer and Faux Stone met the definition of an insured contract in the CGL coverage form, if all of the other conditions for coverage were met, the exception to the exclusion for contractual liability provided coverage in this case.

Concerning Mary's injury, the injuries occurred because of a problem with the installation of the stone facade by Vincent's Veneer's subsidiary, Faux Stone. Therefore, Vincent's Veneer is liable. No exclusions eliminated or limited coverage for Mary's injuries.

Carnation's claim for the costs to replace the stone facade is not covered because there was no coverage afforded for replacing the defective facade explicit under the exclusion for damage to the work of the insured.

Because there was coverage under Vincent's Veneer's policy, and because Faux Stone, a subsidiary of Vincent's Veneer, had liability and sufficient limits to meet Mary's claim, coverage for Mary's claim would not be needed under Carnation's CGL. There was no coverage for the replacement of the facade under Carnation's CGL form because of the exclusion for damages to the insured's own property. However, there would likely be coverage under Carnation's commercial property coverage form. Carnation's insurer would have subrogation potential against the manufacturer of the adhesive used by Faux Stone to apply the stone facade.

Mary's claim was settled for $1.3 million. Carnation's CGL form did not cover the cost to replace the facade, but its commercial property coverage form did.

Confections, Inc., Case Study

Confections, Inc., a candy manufacturer, leased 12,000 square feet of storage and office in a 27,000 square-foot building owned by Market Street, LLC. The lease contained a provision that the tenant would be responsible for any and all damage to the landlord's property arising from or related to the tenant's use of the premises.

Confections packaged some of its candy in decorative boxes for Valentine's Day and maintained these boxes on the premises. These boxes were supplied by a customer, Gianetti's Candies.

Case Facts

On September 22, 20X2, a fire started in the premises occupied by Confections. The fire spread into adjoining areas of the building before being extinguished. The fire marshal determined that the cause of the fire was heat from the molasses machine that the operator forgot to turn off at the end of the second shift.

Market Street claimed $1.2 million in damages to the building plus the loss of rent of $125,000 for the period of time required to reconstruct. The damage to the leased portion of the building was $650,000; the rest of the building sustained damages of $550,000.

In addition, Gianetti's Candies claimed $12,000 in damages for the replacement of its candy boxes.

Confections promptly notified its insurer of the claims by Market Street and Gianetti's Candies. Confections had an occurrence CGL coverage form effective for one year from July 1, 20X2, with no deductible. See the exhibit "Confections' CGL Coverage Limits."

Confections' CGL Coverage Limits

•	$3,000,000	General Aggregate
•	$3,000,000	Products-Completed Operations Aggregate
•	$2,000,000	Per Occurrence Bodily Injury and Property Damage
•	$500,000	Personal and Advertising Injury
•	$1,000,000	Damage to Rented Premises
•	$5,000	Medical Payments

[DA06726]

Case Analysis Tools

After a review of the policy to determine whether and how coverage applies, the policy limits are analyzed to determine how much the insurer will pay for covered damages.

Coverage Analysis

The CGL form was in effect on the date of the occurrence and was a form triggered by occurrence. Confections was negligent by leaving a machine turned on, and this negligence caused the fire. There was an exclusion for fire damage to rented premises; however, coverage was provided by the provision at the end of the CGL Coverage A exclusions for fire damage legal liability.

The exclusion, which stipulates that there is no coverage for liability resulting from fire damage to rented premises, does not apply to exclusions c through n. This constitutes the fire damage legal liability coverage.

Market Street's loss of rent was covered under the definition of property damage in the CGL form, which included the resulting loss of use of that property.

Gianetti Candies's boxes were personal property of others within the custody of the insured, and therefore coverage was excluded by exclusion j, Damage To Property, subsection (4).

There was a separate limit for the damage to premises rented to the insured. Because Confections had a $1 million limit, the loss of $650,000 was fully covered.

The damage to the balance of the landlord's building was recoverable under the CGL without the restrictions of the fire legal liability coverage carve-out. The amount paid under the separate limit for damage to premises rented to the insured applied to the occurrence and aggregate limits. There was a $2 million occurrence limit with $1.35 million available after the damages to the insured's portion of the premises. Therefore, the $550,000 in damages to the remainder of the building was fully covered. The $125,000 in loss of rent was also fully covered. See the exhibit "Market Street, LLC v. Confections."

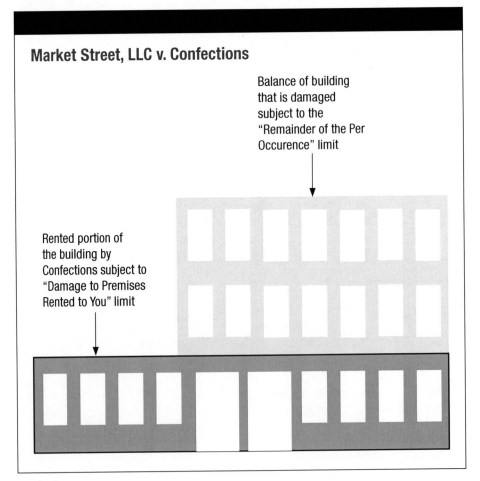

Market Street, LLC v. Confections

Balance of building that is damaged subject to the "Remainder of the Per Occurence" limit

Rented portion of the building by Confections subject to "Damage to Premises Rented to You" limit

[DA06727]

Coverage Determination and Amounts Payable for Cases

Case	Claim	Coverage Determination	Amount Payable
Painting, Inc.	Damage to autos $18,000	This claim for property damage that results from the insured's negligence is covered under the extended reporting period of the claims-made coverage form.	$18,000
	Mismatched paint	This claim is not covered because of the exclusion for work performed by the insured.	N/A
	Loss of business	This claim is not covered because the loss of business did not result from loss of use as the result of property damage.	N/A
Faux Stone Enterprises	Injury to Mary $2,000,000 (Settled for $1,300,000)	This claim is covered under the definition of an insured contract that provides coverage to Vincent's Veneer for Faux Stone's liability.	$1,300,000
	Replacement of stone facade $500,000	This claim is not covered because of the exclusion for work performed by the insured. (However, there was coverage under the insured's property coverage form.)	N/A
Confections	Fire damage to Market Street's building $1,200,000	This claim is covered under the exception to exclusions for fire legal liability damage to rented premises.	$1,200,000
	Market Street's loss of rental income $125,000	This claim is covered because the loss of income results from the damage caused by the insured's liability.	$125,000
	Loss of Gianetti's candy boxes $12,000	This claim is excluded because the boxes were property in the care, custody, and control of the insured.	N/A

[DA06728]

SUMMARY

The CGL coverage form is commonly used to insure a wide range of liability loss exposures faced by most organizations. Coverage A of the CGL coverage form protects the insured against liability for bodily injury and property damage arising out of premises and operations liability loss exposures and products and completed operations liability loss exposures.

The question of whether a claim is covered under Coverage A of the CGL coverage form can be answered by determining whether any of the exclusions apply to the claim. If any of the exclusions apply, the claim is not covered. However, many exclusions contain one or more exceptions, and these exceptions can, in turn, contain exclusions. Endorsements can be added to a CGL coverage form to remove, limit, or expand an exclusion or exception. Properly interpreting the exclusions, exceptions, and exclusions to the exceptions requires a thorough analysis of the language of each exclusion in the context of other policy provisions, including endorsements, and the facts of the claim.

It is important for insurance and risk management professionals to understand when and how coverage applies under the CGL coverage form. Some organizations will require endorsements, specialized coverage forms, or other options to address their loss exposures. Analyzing how the CGL coverage form responds to a claim develops the necessary skills to avoid coverage gaps and make appropriate claim decisions.

ASSIGNMENT NOTES

1. Copyright, ISO Properties, Inc., 2006.
2. 10 Cal. 4th 645 (1995).
3. For an in-depth description and evaluation of Montrose exclusionary language, see "Progressive Injury Exclusions," *Malecki on Insurance*, vol. 9, no. 6 (April 2000), pp. 1–10.
4. International Risk Management Institute, "Known Loss/Loss in Progress Doctrines," September 2008, www.irmi.com/online/pci/ch05/1105g000.aspx (accessed November 12, 2010).

4

Commercial General Liability Insurance, Part II

Educational Objectives

After learning the content of this assignment, you should be able to:

▷ Describe the insuring agreements, coverage limits, and exclusions applicable to each of the following commercial general liability (CGL) coverages:

- Coverage B—Personal and Advertising Injury Liability

- Coverage C—Medical Payments

▷ Describe the supplementary payments provided by the CGL coverage form.

▷ Identify the persons and organizations insured by the CGL coverage form.

▷ Explain how the CGL limits of insurance are applied.

▷ Describe the claims-made provisions of ISO coverage forms and endorsements.

▷ Describe the general categories of endorsements for the CGL coverage form.

▷ Given a case, determine whether, and for what amount, the Commercial General Liability Coverage Form (occurrence version) covers a described claim.

▷ Explain why an organization may want each of the following coverage forms available in ISO's commercial general liability program:

- Electronic Data Liability Coverage Form

- Owners and Contractors Protective Liability Coverage Form

- Railroad Protective Liability Coverage Form

- Liquor Liability Coverage Form

Commercial General Liability Insurance, Part II

4

COMMERCIAL GENERAL LIABILITY COVERAGE

In addition to providing coverage for bodily injury and property damage liability loss exposures, the Commercial General Liability (CGL) Coverage Form is also designed to provide coverage for various other types of liability loss exposures. Additionally, the CGL contains coverage provisions designed both to provide medical treatment to injured persons and to prevent litigation.

The operations of various types of organizations present liability loss exposures that have the potential to cause injuries or damages other than bodily injury or property damage. Retail operations present the risk of security personnel falsely detaining a customer for shoplifting. Apartment building and mall owners face the risk of allegations of improper entry into a tenant's premises or wrongful eviction of a tenant. Increasingly, almost all organizations have various loss exposures resulting from the use of the Internet. The CGL form provides coverage for many of these exposures under Coverage B—Personal and Advertising Injury Liability.

All organizations—and their insurers—face exposure from litigation by persons who claim injury as a result of the organization's activities. Litigation can be costly. Organizations, even if they have insurance coverage, can be bankrupt as a result of one liability verdict in which awarded damages exceed policy limits. Insurers are often required to pay defense costs in addition to policy limits. Litigation can sometimes be avoided by paying for an injured person's medical treatment after an accident without admitting liability. The CGL form provides this option under Coverage C—Medical Payments.

Coverage B—Personal and Advertising Injury Liability

The CGL coverage form includes **personal and advertising injury** liability coverage as Coverage B. When the insurer does not want to provide Coverage B or the insured does not want to pay for it, it can be excluded by endorsement.

Personal and advertising injury

Injury that is covered by Coverage B of the CGL and includes injury resulting from numerous offenses, such as false detention, malicious prosecution, wrongful eviction, slander, libel, use of another's advertising idea, and copyright infringement.

Insuring Agreement

The Coverage B insuring agreement parallels the Coverage A insuring agreement in these ways:

- The insurer agrees to pay those sums that the insured becomes legally obligated to pay as damages.
- The insurer agrees to defend the insured against any suit seeking such damages.

Coverage B applies to personal and advertising injury caused by an offense arising out of the named insured's business if the offense is committed in the CGL coverage territory. The CGL defines personal and advertising injury as injury, including "consequential 'bodily injury'," arising out of one or more of these offenses:

- False arrest, detention, or imprisonment
- Malicious prosecution
- The wrongful eviction from, wrongful entry into, or invasion of the right of private occupancy of a room, dwelling, or premises that a person occupies, committed by or on behalf of its owner, landlord, or lessor
- Oral or written publication, in any manner, of material that slanders or libels a person or organization or disparages a person's or organization's goods, products, or services
- Oral or written publication, in any manner, of material that violates a person's right of privacy
- The use of another's advertising idea in one's advertisement
- Infringing upon another's copyright, trade dress, or slogan in one's advertisement

The CGL definition of personal and advertising injury includes, but is not limited to, bodily injury. Although the policy does not define other-than-bodily injury, *Black's Law Dictionary* (9th ed.) defines injury as "[t]he violation of another's legal right, for which the law provides a remedy; a wrong or injustice," or simply as "harm or damage." For example, injury includes mental anguish or injury, fright, shock, humiliation, and loss of reputation, but it is not limited to them. "Consequential 'bodily injury'" that results from personal and advertising injury, such as bodily injury resulting from the false detention and imprisonment of a store customer by a security guard, is covered under Coverage B and excluded under Coverage A. Thus, the Coverage B limit applies to the entire claim for personal and advertising injury, including consequential bodily injury.

Limits Applicable to Coverage B

The most that the insurer will pay for damages under Coverage B for any one person or organization is the personal and advertising injury limit shown in the policy, subject also to the general aggregate limit. Defense costs are covered in addition to the limits, and the insurer's duty to defend ends only when the insurer has paid the personal and advertising injury limit or the general aggregate limit.

Coverage Triggers Applicable to Coverage B

In the occurrence version of the CGL coverage form, the coverage trigger for Coverage B is a personal and advertising injury offense committed during the policy period. That is, the policy in effect when the insured is alleged to have committed a covered offense is the policy that covers any defense costs and/or damages resulting from that offense. This would be true even if the claim for resulting injury were made after the policy period ended.

In the claims-made version of the CGL coverage form, Coverage B, like Coverage A, is subject to a claims-made coverage trigger. See the exhibit "Exclusions Applicable to Coverage B."

Coverage for E-Commerce Loss Exposures

Conducting business over the Internet has become an increasingly important component of the operations of many different organizations. Online retail sales, according to the Internal Revenue Service (IRS), increased by 243 percent during the period between 2000 and 2004. The CGL provides limited coverage for certain e-commerce exposures of organizations whose primary business is not related to advertising or Internet services.

Exclusions Applicable to Coverage B

POLICY LANGUAGE	COMMENTS
• Knowing Violation of Rights of Another • Material Published With Knowledge of Falsity	Although Coverage B covers certain offenses that arise out of intentional acts, such as publishing defamatory information, these exclusions are intended to eliminate coverage in cases when the insured knowingly commits an offense.
• Material Published Prior to Policy Period	The purpose of this exclusion is to limit coverage for progressive injury claims to the policy period in effect when the first offense occurs. In the claims-made form, this exclusion applies to publication taking place before the policy retroactive date, if any.
• Criminal Acts	This exclusion may eliminate coverage for any act that could be prosecuted through a criminal proceeding.
• Contractual Liability	Coverage B does not provide coverage for liability assumed under an insured contract. However, the Limited Contractual Liability Coverage for Personal and Advertising Injury endorsement (CG 2274) can be added to cover contractual liability for false arrest, detention, or imprisonment if such liability is assumed under a designated contract, such as insureds who hire contractors to provide security services.
• Breach of Contract • Quality of Performance of Goods—Failure to Conform to Statements • Wrong Description of Prices	These exclusions are for so-called business risks for which insurance is not readily available.
• Infringement of Copyright, Patent, Trademark or Trade Secret—this exclusion does not apply to infringement, in your "advertisement", of copyright, trade dress or slogan	There is an exception contained in this exclusion that preserves coverage for infringement of copyright, trade dress (the total image of a product or service that distinguishes it from the competition), or slogan in the named insured's advertisement.
• Insureds in Media and Internet Type Businesses—this exclusion does not apply to the definitions of "personal and advertising injury" that relate to false arrest or detention; malicious prosecution; or wrongful eviction, wrongful entry, or invasion of private occupancy	The exclusion eliminates coverage for businesses that are highly exposed to advertising and personal injury liability and are usually insured under media errors and omissions liability policies. However, this exclusion does not apply to a firm only because it engages in common e-commerce activities and is not in the business of advertising, broadcasting, publishing, or telecasting.

POLICY LANGUAGE	COMMENTS
• Electronic Chatrooms or Bulletin Boards • Unauthorized Use of Another's Name or Product	These exclusions eliminate coverage for e-commerce loss exposures that most insurers are unwilling to cover except under specialized e-commerce policies.
• Pollution • Pollution-Related	These exclusions are worded to exclude any conceivable claim for personal or advertising injury arising out of any type of pollution incident, including cleanup costs. Unlike the pollution exclusion that applies to Coverage A, the Coverage B pollution exclusions have no exceptions and are intended to be absolute.
• War	Same as the War exclusion in Coverage A.
• Distribution of Material in Violation of Statutes	Same as the Distribution of Material exclusion in Coverage A.

Includes copyrighted material of Insurance Services Office, Inc., with its permission, Copyright, ISO Properties, Inc., 2007. [DA04780]

E-commerce can be broadly defined as conducting business activities on the Internet. E-commerce therefore includes acts such as these:

- Accepting online orders for products or services through an organization's Web site.

- Disseminating information about an organization or its products or services through the organization's Web site.

- Using e-mail to communicate directly with employees, customers, vendors, contractors, regulators, or other parties.

- Coverage B contains several provisions that clarify its applicability to personal and advertising injury arising out of e-commerce. Some e-commerce loss exposures are covered, and others are excluded.

- The policy definition of "advertisement" states that material placed on the Internet can qualify as an advertisement. Coverage B therefore covers liability arising out of advertisements that appear on the Internet, subject to the following restriction: "only that part of a Web site that is about your goods, products or services for the purposes of attracting customers or supporters is considered an advertisement." Historical information about the company, for example, would not be considered an advertisement simply because it is included on the company's Web site. Coverage is excluded for liability arising out of the unauthorized use of another's name or product in the named insured's e-mail address, domain name (the address of a Web site), or metatag (a searchable hidden code embedded in the source code of a Web page). Coverage is also excluded for liability arising out of an electronic chatroom or bulletin board that the insured hosts.

E-Commerce Exposure Example

An Internet retailer, J&S Shoes, does its own Internet advertising. J&S Shoes pays a search engine organization to have J&S Shoes's advertisement displayed when users search for the words "shoes," "sneakers," and the names of several famous brands of sneakers. Joe, the partner of J&S Shoes who manages the advertising, inadvertently designates one of the famous sneaker brand names as a dynamic key word. As a result of the dynamic key word insertion (code embedded into the copy of the online ad), the brand name appears in the banner of J&S Shoes's ad that appears when users type the brand name in the search engine.

J&S Shoes did not have permission from the manufacturer to use the brand name in advertising. The manufacturer sues J&S Shoes. Joe and Steve, the partners who own J&S Shoes, are surprised to learn that their CGL policy does not cover the lawsuit because of the exclusion for the unauthorized use of another's name or product.

A cyber-risk or cyber-liability policy is an option available to organizations that conduct business on the Internet to provide broader protection for these exposures than the CGL coverage form offers.

[DA06556]

Coverage B does not cover insureds, such as a Web site designer or an Internet search or service provider, that provide Internet-related services to others. This type of firm, which can be highly exposed to personal and advertising injury liability, can insure this loss exposure under an errors and omissions or a professional liability policy designed for providers of Internet-related services.

Although the CGL coverage territory is limited to the United States, its territories or possessions, Puerto Rico, and Canada for most occurrences, the coverage territory is worldwide for personal and advertising injury offenses that occur through the Internet or similar electronic means of communication.

Coverage C—Medical Payments

Medical payments coverage

Coverage that pays necessary medical expenses incurred within a specified period by a claimant (and in certain policies, by an insured) for a covered injury, regardless of whether the insured was at fault.

Coverage C provides **medical payments coverage**. Because it pays regardless of whether the insured is legally liable, medical payments coverage is not liability insurance. However, many liability policies include medical payments coverage as a way to settle minor injury cases without a determination of legal liability. In such cases, the insurer can make prompt settlements with claimants and possibly avoid larger liability claims. When the insured does not want medical payments coverage, it can be excluded by endorsement.

The insurer agrees to pay medical expenses for bodily injury caused by an accident occurring on or on ways next to premises that the insured owns or rents. Bodily injury caused by an accident that occurs away from the insured's premises (for example, at a job site where the insured is working) is covered if the accident results from the named insured's operations.

The accident must take place in the CGL coverage territory and during the policy period. The medical expenses must be incurred and reported to the insurer within one year after the date of the accident.

Covered medical expenses include these services:

- First aid administered at the time of an accident
- Necessary medical, surgical, X-ray, and dental services, including prosthetic devices
- Necessary ambulance, hospital, professional nursing, and funeral services

These expenses are payable up to the medical expense limit shown in the policy. Consistent with the purpose of medical payments coverage—settling minor bodily injury claims on a no-fault basis to avoid possibly larger liability claims—the basic limit for medical payments coverage in the ISO *Commercial Lines Manual* (CLM) is $5,000 per person. All medical expenses paid by the insurer are also applied to the each-occurrence limit along with damages payable under Coverage A for the same occurrence.

The injured person who wishes to receive medical payments coverage must submit to examination, at the insurer's request, by physicians of the insurer's choice as often as the insurer reasonably requires. This provision allows the insurer to verify the nature and severity of any injury being claimed. See the exhibit "Exclusions Applicable to Coverage C."

Exclusions Applicable to Coverage C

EXCLUSION	COMMENTS
• Any Insured	Many people can qualify as insureds, including the named insured's employees and partners. None of these persons can receive medical payments coverage. The only exception is the named insured's volunteer workers.
• Hired Person	This excludes any person hired to do work for or on behalf of any insured or a tenant of any insured, such as a contractor.
• Injury on Normally Occupied Premises	This exclusion applies primarily to a tenant who is injured in the unit the person normally occupies. The exclusion would not apply to a tenant who is injured on another part of the premises, such as a sidewalk.
• Workers Compensation and Similar Laws	This exclusion applies to any person injured in the course and scope of employment, regardless of whether the person is an employee of the insured.
• Athletics Activities	This exclusion was reworded in 2004 and is now broadly stated to apply not only to athletics or sports, but also to any exercise or fitness activities.
• Products-Completed Hazard	Any injury is excluded that occurs away from premises owned or rented by the insured and results from any work of the insured that has been completed.
• Coverage A Exclusions	All of the exclusions that apply to Coverage A also apply under Coverage C.

CGL SUPPLEMENTARY PAYMENTS

The Commercial General Liability Coverage Form (CGL coverage form) contains sections relating to supplementary payments.

The Supplementary Payments section of the CGL coverage form specifies the costs that the insurer will pay as part of any claim the insurer investigates or settles or any suit the insurer defends against under either Coverage A or Coverage B. Any such costs paid by the insurer do not reduce the policy's limits of insurance.

These are the costs covered as supplementary payments:

- All expenses incurred by the insurer, such as the fees charged by outside defense counsel.

- Up to $250 for the cost of bail bonds required because of accidents or traffic law violations arising out of the use of any vehicle (such as mobile equipment being driven on a public street) to which the bodily injury liability coverage applies. The insurer does not agree to provide these bonds, only to pay for them.

- The cost of bonds to release attachments, but only for bond amounts that do not exceed the applicable limit of insurance. The insurer is not obligated to provide such bonds—only to pay their cost. A bond to release attachments is a surety bond that the insured might have to provide before a court would order the release of property (such as a piece of the insured's mobile equipment) that a plaintiff has legally seized (attached) as part of litigation against the insured.

- All reasonable expenses incurred by the insured at the insurer's request to assist the insurer in investigating or defending claims or suits. Actual loss of earnings resulting from time away from work is covered up to $250 per day.

- All court costs taxed (assessed) against the insured in the suit.

- Prejudgment interest awarded against the insured on that part of the judgment that the insurer pays.

- Interest on the full amount of any judgment that accrues after entry of the judgment and before the insurer has paid (or offered to pay) that part of the judgment that is within the applicable limit of insurance

The Supplementary Payments section also contains provisions concerning the insurer's duty to defend indemnitees of the insured. The insurer agrees to defend an indemnitee of the insured, but only if specific conditions are met. The indemnitee and the insured must both be named as defendants in the same suit, and the insured must have assumed the obligation to defend the indemnitee under an insured contract.

In addition, the insured and the indemnitee must ask the insurer to conduct and control the defense. Finally, the indemnitee must cooperate with the insurer in the defense and perform essentially the same duties as any other insured would have to perform.

Like the other supplementary payments, this one is payable in addition to the limits of insurance, but the insurer's duty to defend ends when either the insurer has paid (toward damages) the applicable limit of insurance or the conditions outlined previously are no longer met.

Another provision of the Supplementary Payments section covers the insured's liability for defense costs that the insured has assumed in an insured contract (regardless of whether the insured is named in the suit against the indemnitee).

CGL FORM: WHO IS AN INSURED

Section II—Who Is an Insured identifies the persons and organizations that qualify as insureds under the Commercial General Liability (CGL) Coverage Form.

Any person or organization listed in the CGL coverage form declarations as a named insured (referred to as "you" in the policy) is an insured, but Who Is an Insured includes many other categories of insured persons and organizations.

Persons Who Receive Insured Status Through the Named Insured

Various persons are insured under the CGL coverage form because of a family or business relationship to a named insured. If the named insured is designated in the declarations as an individual, the named insured and the named insured's spouse are insureds, but only with respect to the conduct of a business of which the named insured is sole owner.

If the named insured is designated in the declarations as a partnership or joint venture, the designated partnership or joint venture is an insured. Partners of the designated partnership, members of the designated joint venture, and the spouses of either are also insureds, but only with respect to the conduct of the named insured's business. Partnerships and joint ventures are similar in that each type of organization consists of two or more persons who are engaged in business together. However, a partnership is usually an ongoing business, whereas a joint venture is usually formed to accomplish a single defined project.

If the named insured is a limited liability company (an entity that in some ways resembles a partnership and in other ways resembles a corporation), the named company is insured, and so are these individuals:

- The members of the limited liability company (the persons who receive the company's income), but only with respect to the conduct of the named insured's business
- The managers of the limited liability company, but only with respect to their duties as managers of the named insured

If the named insured is designated in the declarations as an organization other than a partnership, joint venture, or limited liability company (such as a corporation or an association), the designated organization is an insured. In addition, executive officers and directors are insureds, but only with respect to their duties as the named insured's officers or directors. The policy defines "executive officer" as a person holding any of the officer positions created by the named insured's charter, constitution, or similar governing document. Stockholders are also insureds, but only with respect to their liability as stockholders.

If the named insured is a trust (a legal entity created for the benefit of designated beneficiaries), the named trust is an insured. The named insured's trustees are also insureds, but only with respect to their duties as trustees.

Employees and Volunteer Workers of the Named Insured

Employees of the named insured are insured for acts within the scope of their employment by the named insured or while performing duties related to the conduct of the named insured's business. This provision is subject to the policy definitions of employee and executive officer and also to several exclusions.

The term "employee" takes its common, everyday meaning. A "leased worker," as defined in the CGL definitions, qualifies as an insured just as any other regular employee of the named insured. However, the "temporary worker" definition clarifies that temporary workers are not employees under the CGL (even though temporary workers might otherwise qualify as employees).

Executive officers of an organization other than a partnership, joint venture, or limited liability company are also not covered under this provision regarding employees. If the named insured is a corporation, the named insured's executive officers are covered, but only with respect to their duties as such.

The scope of an executive officer's duties may be narrower or broader in some cases than the duties of an employee. Similarly, the managers of a limited liability company are not covered under this provision regarding employees.

Like corporate executive officers, the managers of a limited liability company are covered under one of the provisions discussed previously, but only with respect to their duties as managers.

The named insured's volunteer workers are also insureds, but only while performing duties related to the conduct of the named insured's business. The CGL coverage form defines "volunteer worker" as someone who is not the named insured's employee but works under the named insured's direction for no compensation.

The named insured's employees and volunteer workers are not protected as insureds in every situation, because of various exclusions.

Co-Employee and Related Exclusions

Traditionally, liability insurance policies have contained a co-employee exclusion, excluding claims made by one of the named insured's employees against another of the named insured's employees. This exclusion is intended to avoid duplication of workers compensation insurance.

The Who Is an Insured provisions regarding employees contain a co-employee exclusion as well as some related exclusions. Accordingly, the CGL coverage form does not cover an employee or a volunteer as an insured for injury to these parties:

- The named insured
- A partner or member of the named insured (if the named insured is a partnership, joint venture, or limited liability company)
- A co-employee while in the course of his or her employment or while performing duties related to the conduct of the named insured's business
- Any of the named insured's other volunteer workers while performing duties related to the conduct of the named insured's business
- The spouse, child, parent, brother, or sister of a co-employee or volunteer worker

Medical Professional Liability Exclusion

Employees are not insured for bodily injury or personal injury arising out of their providing or failing to provide professional healthcare services. So, for example, an employee of the named insured who is a registered nurse would not be covered by the named insured's CGL policy against professional liability claims.

The exclusion applies only to employees. Consequently, the exclusion does not apply to the named insured's liability for an employee's professional acts.

Moreover, the exclusion applies only to an employee's professional healthcare services. If the employee who administers first aid is not a medical professional, coverage applies to both the employee and the employer. These aspects of CGL coverage are often called "incidental medical malpractice coverage."

When a CGL policy is issued to a clinic, a hospital, or some other organization whose main purpose is to provide healthcare services, the insurer usually endorses the policy to exclude professional liability for rendering or failing to render healthcare services. In such a case, the incidental medical malpractice coverage is eliminated. Healthcare providers and professionals ordinarily buy professional liability insurance to cover the loss exposure.

Exclusion of Named Insured's, Employees', or Partners' Property

No employee or volunteer worker is an insured for damage to property owned, occupied, or used by the named insured, by any of the named insured's employees or volunteer workers, or by any partner or member. The exclusion also applies to property rented to these persons or in their care, custody, or control.

If, for example, a warehouse employee negligently ran a forklift into merchandise owned by the named insured, the employer's CGL policy would not cover a claim for damages made by the named insured against the employee.

Similarly, if the employee had run the forklift into another employee's car in the warehouse parking lot, the policy would not cover the other employee's claim for damages against the forklift driver.

Real Estate Managers

Also qualifying as an insured is any person or organization (other than an employee or a volunteer worker of the named insured) while acting as a real estate manager for the named insured. The policy does not define "real estate manager." The phrase presumably includes any person or organization that manages the real property (buildings and grounds) of the named insured. A real estate manager's duties could involve maintaining the premises, making minor repairs, collecting rents, advertising for prospective tenants, filling vacancies, and answering complaints.

Legal Representatives

When a CGL policy covers one or more individuals (as opposed to organizations) as named insureds, any person or organization having proper temporary custody of the named insured's property following the named insured's death is an insured. However, this person or organization is an insured only for liability arising out of the maintenance or use of that property, and only until the named insured's legal representative has been appointed.

The named insured's legal representative is an insured with respect to his or her duties as such and has all of the named insured's rights and duties under the CGL coverage form.

Newly Acquired or Formed Organizations

Any organization—other than a partnership, joint venture, or limited liability company—that the named insured acquires or forms is automatically covered as a named insured. This coverage continues until the new organization is specifically added to the policy or for ninety days, whichever period is shorter.

If the new organization is not added to the policy by the ninetieth day (or by the end of the policy period if it comes first), the new organization is no longer covered.

For such new organizations, Coverage A does not apply to bodily injury or property damage that occurred before the named insured acquired or formed the organization. Similarly, Coverage B does not apply to personal and advertising injury arising out of an offense committed before the named insured acquired or formed the organization.

Unnamed Partnerships, Joint Ventures, or Limited Liability Companies

The CGL coverage form does not include as an insured any person or organization involved in any current or past partnership, joint venture, or limited liability company that is not listed as a named insured. If the named insured wants to cover current or past partnerships, joint ventures, or limited liability companies, they must be specifically declared and named in the policy. The insurer will usually charge an additional premium for covering the added loss exposure. See the exhibit "The Importance of Naming Past Partnerships, Joint Ventures, or Limited Liability Companies."

The Importance of Naming Past Partnerships, Joint Ventures, or Limited Liability Companies

Why would an organization want or need to list a past partnership, joint venture, or limited liability company as a named insured in its CGL policy? Assume that Canston Construction Corporation formed a joint venture with another building contractor two years ago to construct a high-rise office building. The joint venture terminated one year ago, when the building was completed.

Although the joint venture has terminated, Canston could still be sued, as a member of that joint venture, for bodily injury or property damage arising out of the joint venture's construction operations. Assuming that Canston had an occurrence-basis CGL policy in effect during the construction period and that this policy named the joint venture, injuries that occurred during the construction phase would be covered under that policy even if claim was made at some point in the current policy period.

What if Canston were sued for injury, arising out of completed operations at the high-rise building, that occurred during a later policy period? This claim would not be covered under the policy in effect during the course of construction. It would be covered under the subsequent occurrence type policy that was in effect when the injury actually occurred—but only if the past joint venture were still listed as a named insured in this policy.

As this illustration demonstrates, a member of a past joint venture that could be subject to products or completed operations claims would be well advised to have the joint venture listed in all policies, beginning with the one that was in effect from the time the joint venture was formed.

[DA05294]

Individuals who began their businesses as sole proprietors and subsequently incorporated can have problems similar to those encountered by unnamed partnerships or joint ventures. The CGL policy issued in the name of the corporation will not cover the former sole proprietor (who is a current executive officer or director) who is sued in his or her personal capacity as an individual for injury arising out of work completed when the business was a sole proprietorship.

Unless modified by endorsement, the CGL policy covers executive officers and directors of the insured corporation only with respect to their duties as such for the corporation—not for an earlier proprietorship. Thus, the CGL policy for the corporation must be endorsed to maintain coverage for the past sole proprietorship as well.

LIMITS OF INSURANCE

The amount an insurer is obligated to pay for a covered claim is subject to the applicable limits of insurance stated in the Commercial General Liability (CGL) Coverage Form.

CGL coverage forms contain two types of **aggregate limits**: a general aggregate limit and a products-completed/operations aggregate limit. The CGL coverage form also contains a limit for each covered occurrence. The dollar amounts of the limits are shown in the policy declarations, and the provisions under Section III—Limits of Insurance explain how the limits apply.

Aggregate limit
The maximum amount an insurer will pay for all covered losses during the covered policy period.

The Limits and How They Apply

The each occurrence limit is the most the insurer will pay for any one occurrence, including all damages under Coverage A and all medical payments under Coverage C. Because Coverage C is often subject to a relatively low limit (such as $5,000 per person), the each occurrence limit is principally concerned with limiting damages under Coverage A. A typical each occurrence limit is $1 million. Defense costs do not apply to each occurrence limit. However, if the each occurrence limit is paid, the insurer has no further duty to defend or pay claims. Additional insurance for each occurrence is commonly provided through **excess liability insurance** or an **umbrella liability policy**.

The **personal and advertising injury limit** is the most the insurer will pay under Coverage B for damages because of personal and advertising injury to any one person or organization. Under Insurance Services Office (ISO) *Commercial Lines Manual (CLM)* rules, this limit is set at the same amount as the policy's each occurrence limit, but it is possible for a different amount to be used.

Excess liability insurance
Insurance coverage for losses that exceed the limits of underlying insurance coverage or a retention amount.

Umbrella liability policy
A liability policy that provides excess coverage above underlying policies and may also provide coverage not available in the underlying policies, subject to a self-insured retention.

Personal and advertising injury limit
The most the insurer will pay under Coverage B for the sum of all personal and advertising injury to one person or organization.

The damage to premises rented to you limit is the most the insurer will pay under Coverage A for damage to any one premises while rented to the named insured or, in the case of fire damage, while rented to or temporarily occupied by the named insured. Under *CLM* rules, the basic amount for the damage to premises rented to you limit is $100,000, adjustable by agreement for an adjustment in premium.

The medical expense limit is the most the insurer will pay under Coverage C to any one person. Under *CLM* rules, the basic amount for the medical expense limit is $5,000, and this limit can be increased by agreement for an additional premium. See the exhibit "Each Occurrence, Damage to Premises Rented to You, and Medical Expense Limits."

The CGL coverage form also has these two aggregate limits:

- A general aggregate limit
- A products-completed operations aggregate limit

The purpose of an aggregate limit (regardless of whether it is the general aggregate limit or the products-completed operations aggregate limit) is to cap the total amount of damages that the insurer will pay for the entire policy period. Defense costs do not apply to the aggregate limit.

For example, a policy has an each occurrence limit of $1 million and an aggregate limit of $2 million. Under these limits, the insurer will pay up to $1 million in damages for each covered occurrence, but after payments for all covered occurrences during the policy period total $2 million, the insurer will no longer have an obligation to pay claims or defend against suits. An excess or umbrella liability policy is often purchased to provide coverage after an aggregate limit has been exhausted. See the exhibit "Aggregate Limits."

The general aggregate limit of the CGL coverage form is the most that the insurer will pay during the policy period for the sum of these values:

- Damages under Coverage A, except those that arise out of the products-completed operations hazard
- Damages under Coverage B
- Medical expenses under Coverage C

The products-completed operations aggregate limit is the most the insurer will pay during the policy period under Coverage A for damages arising out of the products-completed operations hazard.

Products-Completed Operations Classifications

The policy definition of the products-completed operations hazard (P/CO hazard) is important to the application of aggregate limits. The effects of the definition on application of the aggregate limits can be summarized in this manner:

- The products-completed operations aggregate limit (P/CO aggregate limit) is reduced by any damages the insurer pays for bodily injury or property damage arising out of the P/CO hazard.
- The general aggregate limit is reduced by any damages the insurer pays for bodily injury or property damage that does not fall within the P/CO hazard.

However, the definition of the P/CO hazard contains a provision that can change the normal application of the aggregate limits. This provision (Provision b.3) states that the P/CO hazard does not include bodily injury or

Each Occurrence, Damage to Premises Rented to You, and Medical Expense Limits

Discount Appliance Store (DAS) has a CGL policy with the following limits:

General aggregate	$2,000,000
Products-completed operations aggregate	$2,000,000
Each occurrence	$1,000,000
Damage to premises rented to you	$500,000
Medical expense	$5,000

During the current policy period, a fire occurred at DAS as a result of negligence by a DAS employee. In the ensuing panic, several store customers were injured, and the store building, which DAS leases, was damaged. These claims were made against DAS as a result of the fire (considered to be one occurrence):

1. Eight customers who were treated at a hospital emergency room for minor injuries asked DAS to pay their medical bills of $2,000 each, and DAS asked the insurer to pay this claim under medical payments coverage.

2. A customer sued DAS for $1 million. Disputing the amount of damages, the insurer contested the claim in court and incurred $25,000 in defense costs. The court awarded the customer $200,000 in damages.

3. The building owner demanded that DAS pay for the $600,000 in fire damage to the building.

4. A customer sued DAS for $900,000. The insurer defended, at a cost of $10,000. The customer won a $300,000 judgment against DAS.

Question: How much will the insurer pay for each of these claims, and how would each claim payment affect the each occurrence limit? Assume that the claims were paid in the order shown and that no other claims had been paid during that policy period.

Answers:

Claim	Amount Claimed	Type of Claim	Amount of Claim Paid by DAS's CGL Policy	Effect on Each Occurrence Limit
1	$2,000 for each of eight persons	Medical payments	$16,000 Medical expense limit applies per person, not per occurrence.	$1,000,000 − $16,000 = $984,000.
2	$1,000,000	Premises/ operations liability	$200,000 CGL pays only the amount for which DAS was held liable, plus defense costs.	$984,000 − $200,000 = $784,000. Defense costs do not reduce the limit.
3	$600,000	Fire legal liability	$500,000 This is the policy limit for damage to premises.	$784,000 − $500,000 = $284,000.
4	$900,000	Premises/ operations liability	$284,000 This is all that remains of the each occurrence limit. Defense costs are payable in addition.	$284,000 − $284,000 = $0. Insurer has no further duty to defend or pay claims resulting from the fire.

Aggregate Limits

Moray Manufacturing Corporation (MMC) has a CGL policy with the following limits:

General aggregate	$2,000,000
Products-completed operations (P/CO) aggregate	$2,000,000
Each occurrence	$1,000,000
Personal and advertising injury	$1,000,000

MMC was liable for the following damages resulting from seven different liability claims that were, disregarding the applicable limits of insurance, covered under MMC's CGL policy.

Claim	Damages Awarded	Type of Claim
1	$700,000	Premises/operations liability
2	$1,100,000	Products liability
3	$500,000	Personal and advertising injury liability
4	$900,000	Premises/operations liability
5	$400,000	Products liability
6	$800,000	Products liability
7	$3,000	Medical payments

Question: How much would MMC's CGL insurer pay for each claim listed, and how would that payment affect the applicable aggregate limit? Assume that the claims were paid in the order listed and that no other claims were received during the same policy period.

Answers:

Claim	Damages Awarded	Type of Claim	Amount of Claim Paid by MMC's CGL Policy	Effect on Aggregate Limit
1	$700,000	Premises/operations liability	$700,000	General aggregate $2,000,000 − $700,000 = $1,300,000.
2	$1,100,000	Products liability	$1,000,000	P/CO aggregate $2,000,000 − $1,000,000 = $1,000,000.
3	$500,000	Personal and advertising injury liability	$500,000	General aggregate $1,300,000 − $500,000 = $800,000.
4	$900,000	Premises/operations liability	$800,000 This is all that remains of the general aggregate limit.	General aggregate $800,000 − $800,000 = $0.
5	$400,000	Products liability	$400,000	P/CO aggregate $1,000,000 − $400,000 = $600,000.
6	$800,000	Products liability	$600,000 This is all that remains of the P/CO aggregate limit.	P/CO aggregate $600,000 − $600,000 = $0.
7	$3,000	Medical payments	$0	General aggregate limit was used up before this claim was made.

property damage arising out of products or operations classified in the declarations or in a policy schedule as subject to the general aggregate limit.

This provision pertains to certain business classifications that have only incidental products or completed operations liability exposures. The Classification Table of the *CLM* shows the notation "Products/Completed Operations Incl." (P/CO Incl.) for any business classifications subject to this approach. Previous editions of the ISO Classification Table indicated these classifications with a plus sign (+) or a dagger sign (†). Consequently, some insurance practitioners and reference publications still refer to these classifications as the "plus or dagger sign classifications." Examples of these businesses include salons, funeral homes, insurance agents, Internet access providers, kennels, nursing homes, daycare centers, and financial firms. The *CLM* provides only a premises-operations rate for these classifications, instead of both a premises-operations rate and a P/CO rate, as is the case for other classifications.

A CGL policy issued to an insured who has only P/CO Incl. classifications often does not show a P/CO aggregate limit. Such a policy covers P/CO liability claims. However, all damages that the insurer pays on behalf of the insured for P/CO liability claims reduce the general aggregate limit.

In some policies covering a P/CO Incl. classification, the insurer will include a dollar amount for the P/CO aggregate limit. This could be done because the insured's current or future operations may include one or more other classifications that are not subject to the P/CO Incl. notation. In this case, the P/CO aggregate limit applies to these other classifications. The P/CO aggregate limit shown in the policy does not apply to claims arising out of a P/CO Incl. classification; these claims remain subject to the general aggregate limit.

In some cases, insurers add an exclusion of the P/CO hazard (CG 21 04) to CGL policies covering one or more P/CO Incl. classifications. This exclusion does not eliminate P/CO coverage with respect to the P/CO Incl. classifications. However, a policy that contains exclusion CG 21 04 will not cover P/CO claims resulting from any new operations arising during the policy period that are subject to a separate premium charge for P/CO. Insureds should therefore seek to have exclusion CG 21 04 eliminated if there is any possibility that they might acquire or begin new operations that would be classified as P/CO during the policy period.

ISO CLAIMS-MADE PROVISIONS

Because it sometimes takes time for bodily injury or property damage to become known, a claim could be made today for something that occurred forty years ago. Thus, a claim could be covered under an occurrence policy that was in effect many years in the past and possibly under other policies during the intervening years. A problem posed for insurers by these long-tailed claims is that their ultimate cost cannot be accurately predicted when the insurer determines the policy premium. The claims-made coverage form addresses this problem.

A liability policy with an occurrence coverage trigger covers injury or damage that occurs during its policy period, regardless of when claim is made. In the 1970s, a liability insurance crisis developed because of litigation in several areas of liability—professional liability (medical malpractice); pollution; and environmental exposures, such as asbestos. Some insurance companies became insolvent as a result of claims made many years after policies were written. Insurance coverage became unavailable for certain types of liability exposures.

Insurance Services Office (ISO) developed various policy innovations to provide a tool for both insurers and insureds to address the issues arising from **long-tail claims**. Exclusions were developed in occurrence forms for certain hazards, such as pollution. Another innovation was the claims-made coverage form.

Long-tail claim

A claim that is characterized by an extended delay between the claim's triggering event and the reporting of the event to the insurer.

Instead of covering injury that occurs during its policy period regardless of when claim is made, a claims-made policy covers only claims first made against the insured during its policy period. A claim made after the policy expires is not covered by that policy, unless the claim is made during an extended reporting period.

Although claims-made forms can benefit insurers by controlling the long-tail problem, they are not widely used outside of specialty types of coverage. The claims-made version of the commercial general liability (CGL) coverage form is rarely used except for businesses that are known to pose long-tail claim problems. Unless insurers insist on using claims-made forms, as they often do for difficult long-tail exposures, insureds usually select policies that have an occurrence coverage trigger. Typical exposures insured by claims-made forms include medical malpractice, directors and officers (D & O), and pollution.

ISO has developed claims-made versions of several of its liability coverage forms. The provisions of the ISO forms can differ substantially from those developed by individual insurers. See the exhibit "ISO Claims-Made Coverage Forms."

ISO claims-made liability coverage forms include various versions of these provisions:

- Retroactive dates
- Extended reporting periods

Retroactive Dates

The basic requirement of the ISO claims-made coverage trigger is that the claim for the covered event must be first made against any insured during either the policy period or an extended reporting period provided by the policy. An additional requirement is that the covered event (such as bodily

ISO Claims-Made Coverage Forms

These ISO coverage forms provide both occurrence and claims-made versions:

- Commercial General Liability Coverage Form (CG 00 02)
- Liquor Liability Coverage Form (CG 00 34)
- Products/Completed Operations Liability Coverage Form (CG 00 38)

These ISO coverage forms provide only claims-made versions:

- Pollution Liability Coverage Form (CG 00 39) and Pollution Liability Limited Coverage Form (CG 00 40)
- Underground Storage Tank Coverage Form (CG 00 42)
- Electronic Data Liability Coverage Form (CG 00 65)
- Employee Benefits Liability Coverage (CG 04 35)

[DA06569]

injury, property damage, or personal/advertising injury) must not have occurred before the policy's retroactive date, if any, or after the end of the policy period. Thus, the claims-made policy in effect when a claim is first made against the insured is the policy that covers the claim.

An ISO claims-made policy may contain no retroactive date, a retroactive date that is the same as the policy inception date, or a retroactive date that precedes the policy inception date. The retroactive date, if any, is shown in the policy declarations.

- If the policy has no retroactive date, it will cover claims first made during the policy period regardless of when the injury, damage, or other insured event occurred.
- If the policy has a retroactive date, it will cover claims first made during the policy period only if the injury, damage, or other insured event occurred on or after the retroactive date.

After a retroactive date has been established, *Commercial Lines Manual* (CLM) rules state that the insurer may not advance the retroactive date without the insured's consent, and then only if at least one of these events has occurred:

- The insured has changed insurers.
- The insured's operations have changed substantially, with a resulting increase in loss exposure.
- The insured failed to provide the insurer with material information.
- The insured has requested the change.

If a retroactive date is advanced in a new or renewal policy, the new policy will not cover claims made during the new policy period if the injury occurred before the retroactive date shown in the new policy. However, a claim may be covered under the extended reporting period provisions of an earlier claims-made policy.

Extended Reporting Periods

To be covered under an ISO claims-made liability form, a claim must be first made against any insured during the policy period or an extended reporting period. An extended reporting period is an additional period (also called a "tail") following the expiration of a claims-made policy. The expired policy covers claims first made against any insured during this additional period, if the injury, damage, or other insured event occurred on or after the retroactive date, if any, and before policy expiration. The ISO claims-made forms differ considerably in the extended reporting periods they provide.

Some of the ISO claims-made forms automatically provide, for no additional premium, a basic extended reporting period and, under certain conditions, also give the insured the right to purchase a supplemental extended reporting period as an endorsement. Other ISO claims-made forms do not automatically provide a basic extended reporting period, but they give the named insured the right to purchase an optional extended reporting period through an endorsement. CLM rules apply caps, or ceilings, on the amount that the insurer can charge for a supplemental or optional extended reporting period. These caps are expressed in percentages or multiples of the premium for the expiring coverage form to which the endorsement applies.

The ISO claims-made forms make their extended reporting periods available to the named insured when any one of these scenarios occurs:

- The insurer renews or replaces the current coverage with claims-made coverage that has a retroactive date later than that applying to the current coverage.
- The insurer renews or replaces the current coverage with coverage that does not apply on a claims-made basis.
- The coverage form is either canceled or nonrenewed.

These three criteria limit the availability of extended reporting periods to situations in which the insured has no other means of obtaining coverage for claims first made after the end of the expired policy period for events occurring before the policy expired.

If an insurer cancels its claims-made policy or does not offer to renew it, the insured will need an extended reporting period, unless replacement coverage can be obtained with a retroactive period sufficient to cover claims reported after expiration of the previous policy.

MODIFYING THE CGL COVERAGE FORM

More than 200 endorsements are available for modifying the Insurance Services Office (ISO) Commercial General Liability (CGL) Coverage Form to meet the requirements of both insureds and insurers.

ISO organizes Commercial General Liability (CGL) endorsements into categories that describe the purpose of the endorsements. Each category is identified by the two digits following the "CG" prefix in the form number that ISO assigns to each endorsement. It is important to note that some insurers draft additional endorsements for various purposes.

Deductible Endorsements (CG 03 __)

This category consists of one endorsement for use with the CGL coverage form, the Deductible Liability Insurance endorsement (CG 03 00). The CGL coverage form does not provide for a deductible, but this endorsement can be used to add either of these types of deductibles for bodily injury liability, property damage liability, or both:

- A per-claim deductible applies to all damages sustained by any one person or organization as a result of any one occurrence. For example, if five persons make claims against the insured for injuries received in one occurrence, a per-claim deductible will apply separately to each person's claim.

- A per-occurrence deductible applies only once to the total of all claims paid arising out of one occurrence.

Additional Coverage Endorsements (CG 04 __)

This category includes endorsements for adding various coverages to the CGL coverage form. Several of the endorsements in this category provide broadened pollution coverage by adding exceptions to the CGL pollution exclusion. Others provide options for covering additional loss exposures that would not otherwise be covered under the CGL coverage form. Two examples of such endorsements are those covering employee benefits liability and electronic data liability.

Employee Benefits Liability Coverage (CG 04 35)

This endorsement, unlike the CGL coverage form, does not provide coverage for bodily injury or property damage. Instead, it provides coverage for damages resulting from negligent acts, errors, or omissions in administering the named insured's benefits program. Typical benefits programs include retirement and group health, dental, life, and disability insurance.

The coverage provided by the endorsement applies to damages only if the act, error, or omission is negligently committed in the administration of the named insured's employee benefits program. Claims based on legal grounds other than negligence, such as intentional torts or breach of contract, are not covered. A number of exclusions are typically included in this endorsement that reinforce the limitation of coverage to negligence in administration of the insured's benefits plans.

The Employee Benefits Liability (EBL) endorsement usually has a claims-made coverage trigger. However, some insurers offer this endorsement with an occurrence coverage trigger. Defense costs are paid in addition to the applicable limit. The applicable limits under the EBL endorsement include an aggregate limit and an each-employee limit (the most the insurer will pay for all damages sustained by any one employee, including that employee's dependents and beneficiaries). An each-employee deductible applies that does not reduce the limits of insurance.

Electronic Data Liability Endorsement (CG 04 37)

The CGL excludes coverage for loss of electronic data. However, limited coverage for loss of electronic data can be added by the Electronic Data Liability endorsement. The endorsement provides coverage for loss or loss of use of electronic data resulting from physical injury to tangible property. The coverage is subject to a specific limit stated in the endorsement.

Additional Insured Endorsements (CG 20 __)

Nearly forty different endorsements are available for providing additional insured status, in a variety of situations, to individuals or organizations that are not already covered under the "Who Is an Insured" provisions of the CGL coverage form. See the exhibit "Examples of Additional Insured Relationships."

Examples of Additional Insured Relationships

Named Insured of CGL Policy	Additional Insured
Contractor performing operations for the property owner	Property owner
Subcontractor performing operations for the general contractor	General contractor
Manufacturer	Vendors (such as retail stores) selling the named insured's products
Franchisee	Grantor of franchise
Organization leasing the equipment	Lessor of leased equipment
Club	Club members
Church	Church members and officers

[DA04795]

Additional Insured—Owners, Lessees, or Contractors—Scheduled Person or Organization (CG 20 10)

Endorsement CG 20 10 is typically used for naming property owners, lessees, or contractors as additional insureds under the CGL policies of organizations that are entering into contracts with any of those parties. For example, when a property owner enters into a construction agreement with a general contractor, the property owner often asks the general contractor to make the property owner an additional insured under the general contractor's CGL policy.

This endorsement provides coverage only if the injury or damage is caused, in whole or in part, by the acts or omissions of the named insured at the designated location of operations. The additional insured is not included in the definition of "named insured." For example, an organization hired a contractor to build an addition to an office complex. The organization required the contractor to add the organization as an additional insured on the contractor's CGL policy, and the contractor added a CG 20 10 endorsement. The contractor's endorsed CGL will cover only the organization's liability for damages that result from the contractor's work on the office complex addition.

This endorsement is subject to two exclusions in addition to those in the CGL coverage form. These exclusions eliminate coverage for bodily injury or property damage occurring after the work at the location of the covered operations has been completed or arising out of a portion of the work that has been put to its intended use.

Additional Insured—Owners, Lessees, or Contractors—Automatic Status When Required in Construction Agreement (CG 20 33)

This endorsement provides coverage in construction agreements for an additional insured without the requirement to name the additional insured or specify the location of the covered operations. These two conditions must be met for the endorsement to apply:

- The named insured must be performing operations for the person or organization that has requested additional insured status under the named insured's policy.
- The named insured and the person or organization requesting additional insured status must have agreed in a written contract or agreement that the person or organization be added as an additional insured in the named insured's policy.

The endorsement provides coverage for the liability of the additional insured only for damage arising from the named insured's performance of operations for the additional insured. The same exclusions for completed work that apply to the CG 20 10 also apply to this endorsement. Additionally, there is an exclusion that eliminates coverage for any injury or damage arising from professional architectural, engineering, or surveying services.

Certificates of Insurance

A certificate of insurance is a brief description of insurance coverage prepared by an insurer or a producer that is used by an insured to provide evidence of insurance. A certificate of insurance (COI) is usually provided to organizations that ask to be named as additional insureds on the policies of contracting firms.

The certificate is not a policy endorsement. A typical COI contains a disclaimer that it confers no rights upon the certificate holder and does not amend, extend, or alter the coverage afforded by the listed policies. The COI also typically includes a statement that the issuing insurer will endeavor to notify certificate holders of policy cancellations, but failure to do so will not impose any obligation or liability.

Exclusion Endorsements (CG 21 __)

The endorsements in this category are used for adding exclusions to the CGL coverage form or other general liability coverage forms. Most of these exclusion endorsements are optional and are added only if the insurer and the insured agree to add them. See the exhibit "Examples of Exclusion Endorsements."

Other exclusion endorsements are required by *Commercial Lines Manual* (CLM) rules in all CGL coverage forms.

Nuclear Energy Liability Exclusion Endorsement (IL 00 21)

Under CLM rules, the Nuclear Energy Liability Exclusion Endorsement (IL 00 21) is added to any policy containing a commercial liability coverage part. This exclusion eliminates coverage for bodily injury or property damage resulting in any way (whether in peace or war) from the hazards of nuclear material. Nuclear energy liability policies are available to cover organizations that have significant nuclear energy loss exposures.

Employment-Related Practices Exclusion Endorsement (CG 21 47)

The Employment-Related Practices Exclusion endorsement (CG 21 47) is required by CLM rules for CGL insureds with employment practices liability (EPL) policies and is optional for CGL insureds without EPL policies. In practice, however, many insurers add this exclusion to every CGL coverage form.

This exclusion eliminates coverage for bodily injury or personal and advertising injury to a person arising out of any employment-related practice, policy, act, or omission.

Examples of Exclusion Endorsements

Name and Number	Purpose
Exclusion—Products/ Completed Operations Hazard (CG 21 04)	To exclude bodily injury or property damage arising from the products-completed operations hazard
Exclusion—Coverage C— Medical Payments (CG 21 35)	To omit Coverage C—Medical Payments
Exclusion—Personal and Advertising Injury (CG 21 38)	To omit Coverage B—Personal and Advertising Injury Liability
Exclusion—Explosion, Collapse, and Underground Property Damage (Specified Operations) (CG 21 42)	To exclude coverage at the described location for the explosion, collapse, and underground ("X, C, U") hazards as defined in the endorsement
Exclusion—Financial Services (CG 21 52)	To exclude coverage, under CGL policies for financial institutions, for injury or damage resulting from the insured's rendering or failing to render any of several financial services
Exclusion—Volunteer Workers (CG 21 66)	To eliminate insured status for the named insured's volunteer workers

[DA04796]

Classification Endorsements (CG 22 __)

The endorsements in this category are designed for particular classifications of insureds. Many of the endorsements are exclusions, while others broaden CGL coverage to meet special needs. See the exhibit "Examples of Classification Endorsements."

Miscellaneous Coverage Amendment Endorsements (CG 24 __)

This category contains several endorsements that, in most cases, broaden CGL coverage to accommodate a particular insured's coverage needs. For example, the liquor liability coverage endorsement eliminates the liquor liability exclusion and provides coverage for organizations in the business of selling or serving alcoholic beverages. Another example is the endorsement that expands the coverage territory to provide worldwide coverage, with the exception of any country or jurisdiction subject to trade sanction or another economic sanction or embargo by the United States.

Examples of Classification Endorsements

Name and Number	Type of Insured and Purpose
Exclusion—Corporal Punishment (CG 22 30)	Intended for schools to exclude coverage for injury to any student resulting from corporal punishment
Exclusion—Construction Management Errors and Omissions (CG 22 34)	Intended for contractors involved in construction management, such as design-build projects and to exclude injury or damage arising out of several activities that are usually covered by an architects and engineers professional liability policy
Exclusion—Public Utilities—Failure To Supply (CG 22 50)	Intended for public utilities, including governmental subdivisions that produce gas, oil, water, electricity, or steam for sale and to exclude injury or damage resulting from the failure of the insured to supply the services described in the endorsement
Misdelivery of Liquid Products Coverage (CG 22 66)	Intended for fuel oil dealers and other businesses that deliver liquid products and to cover injury or damage resulting from (1) the delivery of a liquid product into the wrong receptacle or (2) the erroneous delivery of one liquid product for another by an auto—if the injury or damage occurs after the delivery has been completed
Operation of Customers' Autos on Particular Premises (CG 22 68)	Intended for auto repair shops, car washes, gasoline stations, and tire dealers and covers injury or damage resulting from operating customers' autos on the insured premises and adjoining ways

[DA04797]

Endorsements for Amending Limits (CG 25 __)

This category includes three endorsements for amending the limits of insurance under the CGL coverage form:

- Amendment of Limits of Insurance (CG 25 02) replaces the limits shown in the policy declarations.
- Designated Construction Project(s) General Aggregate Limit (CG 25 03) provides a separate general aggregate limit for each construction project designated in the endorsement's schedule.
- Designated Locations(s) General Aggregate Limit (CG 25 04) provides a separate general aggregate limit for each location designated in the endorsement's schedule.

Claims-Made Endorsements (CG 27 __)

This category contains endorsements for providing extended reporting periods for the claims-made version of the CGL coverage form and the Employee Benefits Liability Coverage endorsement. Two of the endorsements in this category are the Supplemental Extended Reporting Period Endorsement (CG 27 01) and the Supplemental Extended Reporting Period Endorsement for Employee Benefits Liability Coverage (CG 27 15).

CGL COVERAGE FORM CASE STUDY

Commercial general liability insurance covers the majority of liability loss exposures for many organizations. These exposures are significant—businesses of all sizes and types can become bankrupt as a result of one or more liability lawsuits.

The Commercial General Liability Coverage Form is the principal form used to provide commercial general liability (CGL) insurance. A case study will assist risk and insurance professionals in understanding how this form provides—and excludes—coverage for commercial liability loss exposures.

Case Facts

Excavating Contractor, Inc. (ECI) is insured under a commercial package policy that includes the occurrence version of the Commercial General Liability Coverage Form. The policy inception date for ECI's annual policy period is January 1, 20X1, and the applicable limits of CGL coverage are as shown. See the exhibit "ECI's CGL Limits."

ECI's CGL Limits

	Limits
Each occurrence	$ 1,000,000
Damage to rented premises (each occurrence)	$ 100,000
Medical expense (any one person)	$ 5,000
Personal and advertising injury (any one person or organization)	$ 1,000,000
General aggregate limit	$ 2,000,000
Products/completed operations aggregate limit	$ 2,000,000

[DA06498]

On July 2, 20X1, ECI was performing operations as the excavation subcontractor at a building construction site in the United States. An ECI employee, while operating a backhoe/excavator owned by ECI at the job site, punctured a mobile storage tank containing several hundred gallons of fuel. The operator's error resulted in a fire that caused these losses:

- The backhoe/excavator, valued at $40,000, was destroyed.
- The fuel and fuel tank, both owned by General Contractor (GC), were destroyed. Their combined value was $2,400.
- An office trailer and its contents, all owned by GC, were destroyed. The value of this property was $125,000.

The insurer's claim representative investigated the claim, verified the losses, and established these facts, which none of the concerned parties disputed:

- The damage resulted from the ECI equipment operator's negligence in operating the backhoe attached to the backhoe/excavator unit. As the operator's employer, ECI is vicariously liable for injury or damage sustained by others because of the operator's negligent acts or omissions committed in the course of his employment with ECI.
- The operator's error and the resulting fire were an accident, and the ECI employee had no intent to cause the losses.
- The backhoe/excavator was not subject to a motor vehicle insurance law in the state in which it was principally garaged, and thus it did not meet the CGL definition of "auto."
- ECI was working under a contract that did not contain any hold-harmless agreements.

The accident resulted in these claims:

- Claim 1—ECI asked its insurer to pay for its total loss of the backhoe/excavator.
- Claim 2—GC demanded that ECI pay damages for the loss of its fuel tank, fuel, and office trailer and its contents.

It must be determined whether each of these claims would be covered under ECI's CGL policy and, if so, for what amount.

Case Analysis Tools

Required Reference Material

You will need to have a copy of the Commercial General Liability Coverage Form (CG 00 01 12 07) available for reference while working on this coverage case.

Relevant Questions

The answers to these questions will help determine whether and for what amount each of the described claims is covered by the CGL coverage form:

- Does the claim meet the conditions imposed by a CGL insuring agreement?
- Do any exclusions apply to the claim?
- Do any supplementary payments apply?
- Do the circumstances of the claim meet applicable policy conditions?
- What is the amount payable for the claim?

Determination of Coverage

Does the Claim Meet the Conditions Imposed by a CGL Insuring Agreement?

The only applicable insuring agreement in ECI's CGL is Coverage A—Bodily Injury and Property Damage Liability. Therefore, it is not necessary for the claim representative to consider whether any of the claims would be covered under the insuring agreements for Coverage B—Personal and Advertising Injury Liability or Coverage C—Medical Payments. To be covered under Coverage A, a claim must meet several conditions:

- The insured must be legally liable to pay damages. Because one cannot be held legally liable to pay damages to oneself, ECI is not legally liable to pay damages for property damage to its own property, the subject of Claim 1. Therefore, Claim 1 is not given further consideration for coverage under ECI's CGL. However, ECI's insurer will determine whether Claim 1 is covered under a contractors equipment coverage form included in the inland marine coverage part of ECI's commercial package policy. According to the claim investigation, the insured, ECI, is legally liable for the damages sustained by others because of the accident caused by the ECI employee. Therefore, ECI is legally liable to pay the damages alleged in Claim 2.

- The damages must result from bodily injury or property damage. The damages alleged in Claim 2 resulted from property damage.

- The damage must be covered under ECI's CGL. Determination of whether the claim satisfies this condition must wait until the exclusions and other policy conditions are analyzed.

- The damage must be caused by an occurrence. The claim investigation found that the backhoe's striking the tank, and the resulting fire, was an accident. Because the policy definition of "occurrence" is "an accident," this condition is met.

- The occurrence must take place in the coverage territory. The occurrence took place at a work site in the U.S., which is in the CGL's coverage territory.
- The damage must occur during the policy period. ECI's policy period began on January 1, 20X1, and the accident occurred on July 2, 20X1. Therefore, the damage occurred during the policy period.
- The damage must not have been known to the named insured or others before the policy period began. Because the bodily injury and property damage occurred several months into the policy period, this condition does not apply to any of the claims made against ECI.

In summary, Claim 1 does not meet all of the conditions imposed by the Coverage A insuring agreement and is therefore not covered under the CGL. Because Claim 2 meets all of the conditions of the Coverage A insuring agreement (disregarding, for now, the requirement that the damage be covered), the next step is to determine whether any of the Coverage A exclusions apply to this claim.

Do Any Exclusions Apply to the Claim?

To determine whether any of the Coverage A exclusions apply, Sean, the insurer's claim representative, will consider each claim separately. If one or more exclusions apply to a claim, it is not covered.

1. Claim 1

Because Claim 1 does not meet the conditions imposed by the Coverage A insuring agreement, it is not necessary to review the exclusions to determine whether any of the Coverage A exclusions apply.

2. Claim 2

Claim 2 was made against ECI by GC, seeking damages for property damage to GC's fuel tank, fuel, and office trailer and its contents. Each Coverage A exclusion is considered separately in relation to the facts of this claim.

Sean quickly determines that several exclusions do not apply to this claim, including those for liquor liability, workers compensation and similar laws, employers liability, war, personal and advertising injury, electronic data, and distribution of material in violation of a state statute. Sean carefully considers relevant exclusions to determine whether they might apply to this claim.

Sean determines that the exclusion for expected or intended injury does not apply because the investigation determined that there was no intent to injure on the part of ECI or the ECI employee.

His review of the contract between ECI and GC leads Sean to decide that the exclusion for contractual liability does not apply because no hold-harmless agreements were in effect.

Sean considers the exclusion for pollution because the fuel that burned in the accident could meet the CGL definition of "pollutants" if supported by state law. The relevant part of the pollution exclusion applies to the release of pollutants at any location where the insured is performing operations, but only if the pollutants are brought to the location by the insured or a contractor or subcontractor working on behalf of the insured. In this case, the fuel was brought to the work site by GC, not by ECI. GC, as the general contractor, was not a contractor or subcontractor working on the insured's behalf. Therefore, Sean decides that this exclusion does not apply.

Sean decides that the exclusions regarding auto and mobile equipment do not apply to the claim. The claim investigation revealed that ECI's backhoe/excavator was not subject to a motor vehicle insurance law at the time of the accident and, therefore, not excluded as an "auto." Because the backhoe/excavator was not being transported by an "auto" at the time of the accident, the mobile equipment exclusion does not apply.

The exclusion for damage to property raises an important consideration: Was GC's fuel tank, fuel, or office trailer and its contents "personal property in the care, custody, or control of the insured"? If so, damage to such property would be excluded. Because the claim investigation revealed that none of these items of GC's property were in ECI's care, custody, or control, Sean determines that this exclusion does not apply.

Sean also determines that the exclusions for damage to your product and damage to your work do not apply to Claim 2. Both of these exclusions apply only to property damage included within the products-completed operations hazard as defined in the CGL. The property damage alleged in Claim 2, because it occurred while ECI was actively conducting operations, does not fall within the products-completed operations hazard.

Sean concludes that none of the Coverage A exclusions apply to Claim 2.

Do Any Supplementary Payments Apply?

Assuming that the insurer settles the claims out of court, most of the supplementary payments available under the CGL (such as court costs and prejudgment interest) will not be needed. However, supplementary payment a., "All expenses we incur," clarifies that the insurer will pay all the costs it incurs in investigating and settling the claims made against ECI. These expenses paid by the insurer do not reduce the applicable limits of insurance.

Do the Circumstances of the Claim Meet Applicable Policy Conditions?

In addition to meeting the conditions imposed by the Coverage A insuring agreement, the circumstances of the claim must meet all other applicable policy conditions contained in the Commercial General Liability Conditions section of the CGL or in the Common Policy Conditions. The Duties in the Event of Occurrence, Offense, Claim or Suit section in the Commercial General Liability Conditions section applies to any claim scenario. ECI satisfactorily performed all the duties as described in that condition, and no other conditions raise any issues with regard to the claims made against ECI.

Determination of Amounts Payable

Claim 1 is not covered under ECI's CGL. (It may be covered under the inland marine coverage part in ECI's commercial package policy.) Claim 2 meets all the conditions of the Coverage A insuring agreement and is not subject to any of the Coverage A exclusions. No policy conditions apply that would invalidate or reduce the amount payable. Therefore, Sean determines that the insurer will pay all sums that ECI is legally liable to pay as damages because of bodily injury or property damage caused by the covered occurrence involving ECI's backhoe/excavator, subject to any further provisions that could limit the amount payable.

Although some CGL policies are subject to a deductible added by endorsement, ECI's policy does not include any deductible. Moreover, the Other Insurance condition is inapplicable because no other insurance applies to the claims made against ECI. However, Section III—Limits of Insurance states that the amount payable may not exceed the applicable limits of insurance shown in the declarations.

The limits of insurance apply only to damages for which ECI is liable. The limits do not apply to any of the costs payable as supplementary payments, such as costs the insurer incurred to investigate and settle the claims against ECI.

ECI's insurer paid a previous CGL claim for an occurrence in the current policy period. This claim totaled $155,000 in damages for bodily injury arising out of ECI's ongoing operations at another work site. The claim payment reduced ECI's $2 million general aggregate limit to $1,845,000, an amount greater than the damages claimed for this occurrence. Therefore, ECI's general aggregate limit does not reduce the amount payable for the current claims.

ECI's each occurrence limit of $1 million is also sufficient to cover the damages payable for the current claims. If the damages arising out of the current occurrence had exceeded $1 million, the excess amount would not have been covered under ECI's CGL, but could have been payable under an umbrella liability policy carried by ECI.

None of the other limits of insurance under ECI's CGL apply to the two covered claims. Therefore, the amount payable as damages for the claims made against ECI is the total of the damages claimed by GC in Claim 2. GC claimed $2,400 for the tank and fuel plus $125,000 for the trailer and its contents. Therefore, Sean concludes that the total of $127,400 claimed by GC is the amount payable.

Correct Answer to ECI CGL Coverage Case

- Does the claim meet the conditions imposed by a CGL insuring agreement?

  Claim 1, for ECI's property damage, does not meet the conditions imposed by the CGL insuring agreement. Claim 2, for GC's property damage, does meet the conditions imposed by the CGL insuring agreement.

- Do any exclusions apply to the claim?

  Because Claim 1 does not meet the conditions imposed by the CGL insuring agreement, it is not necessary to evaluate whether there are any exclusions applicable to Claim 1. There are no exclusions that apply to Claim 2.

- Do any supplementary payments apply?

  There are no applicable supplementary payments. Because the insurer will pay GC's property damage claim in full, it is unlikely that there will be litigation costs.

- Do the circumstances of the claim meet applicable policy conditions?

  The circumstances of the claim meet the applicable policy conditions.

- What is the amount payable for the claim?

  The amount payable for the claim is $127,400 payable to GC.

[DA06499]

OTHER GENERAL LIABILITY COVERAGE FORMS

Although the ISO (Insurance Services Office) Commercial General Liability (CGL) Coverage Form is adaptable with endorsements, both insureds and insurers may prefer other ISO coverage forms for special liability loss exposures.

There are liability exposures that are different from the exposures typically covered by the CGL coverage form. The ISO commercial general liability program provides coverage forms to address the special exposures that arise from using electronic data, having projects performed by contractors, performing contracts on or near railroads, and serving alcoholic beverages.

Electronic Data Liability Coverage Form

Electronic data has become increasingly important to individuals and organizations. However, liability loss exposures for electronic data are excluded in the CGL coverage form. The Electronic Data Liability Endorsement (CG 04 37) can be added to the CGL form. However, this endorsement applies only to electronic data losses that result from physical injury to tangible property.

If, for example, an electrical company's employee, while working on a customer's property, accidentally caused a fire that damaged the company's mainframe computer containing all of the company's electronic data, the endorsement could provide coverage for the loss of the data. However, if the employee instead accidentally caused a power surge that resulted in destruction of the data without causing any physical property damage, the endorsement could not provide coverage for that loss.

The ISO Electronic Data Liability (EDL) Coverage Form (CG 00 65) provides broader coverage for an insured's liability for loss of electronic data caused by an "electronic data incident." The EDL coverage form defines "electronic data incident" as "an accident, or a negligent act, error or omission, or a series of causally related accidents, negligent acts, or errors or omissions, which results in loss of electronic data." Because of this definition, the EDL coverage form encompasses a broader range of causes of loss than the endorsement. The EDL coverage form applies on a claims-made basis. The EDL coverage form could provide coverage for the loss caused by the power surge in the previous example.

Owners and Contractors Protective Liability Coverage Form

Traditionally, the common law did not hold a principal vicariously liable for the negligent acts of its independent contractor. However, over time, courts allowed certain exceptions to that rule, and there are now many situations in which a principal can be held vicariously liable for injury to others resulting from the negligence of its general contractor. A principal can also be held directly liable for injury to others that results from the principal's failure to properly supervise its independent contractor's work.

A regular CGL policy covers these types of loss exposures. However, some property owners prefer that the contractor pay the cost of obtaining a separate insurance policy protecting the property owner against these loss exposures for the duration of the work that the independent contractor performs.

Owners and contractors protective (OCP) liability insurance, purchased by the independent contractor and listing the property owner as the named insured, was designed for such situations. OCP coverage can also be purchased by a subcontractor to protect the general contractor who has employed them. The policy provisions discussed here are those of the ISO Owners and Contractors Protective Liability Coverage Form—Coverage for Operations of Designated Contractor (CG 00 09).

Insuring Agreement

The named insured listed in an OCP policy is the project owner (or general contractor) for whom the contractor (or subcontractor) has purchased the insurance. The contractor who bought the insurance is shown as the designated contractor in the policy declarations. The OCP form has an occurrence coverage trigger. ISO has not developed a claims-made version of the form.

The insuring agreement of the OCP coverage form expresses the insurer's promise to pay damages that the named insured becomes legally obligated to pay because of bodily injury or property damage arising out of either of these:

- Operations performed for the named insured by the designated contractor at the location specified in the policy
- The named insured's own acts or omissions in connection with the "general supervision" of such operations

The OCP form does not cover the named insured for liability arising out of any other operations, acts, or omissions other than those listed previously. For example, an OCP policy would not cover the named insured's day-to-day business operations. Unfortunately, however, the OCP form does not define "general supervision," so the meaning of this term can lead to coverage disputes.

Exclusions

Most of the exclusions found in the OCP coverage form are similar or identical to exclusions contained in Coverage A (Bodily Injury and Property Damage Liability) of the CGL policy. Two of the exclusions in the OCP coverage form are unique to that form, and two others contain significant variations from their counterparts in the CGL form. See the exhibit "OCP Coverage Form Exclusions."

Limits of Insurance

The OCP form is subject to a general aggregate limit and an each occurrence limit. The OCP form does not need limits for personal injury and advertising injury, medical payments, damage to rented premises, or products and completed operations, because it does not provide those coverages.

Other Insurance

The OCP other insurance condition states that the coverage is primary insurance and that the insurer will not seek contribution from any other insurance available to the named insured unless the other insurance is provided by another contractor working at the designated site.

Alternatives to OCP Insurance

A project owner's CGL policy will cover the loss exposures covered by OCP insurance. An OCP policy merely transfers the cost of insuring these exposures to the contractor. OCP insurance is not the only way to achieve that transfer.

The owner could instead require the contractor to add the owner as an additional insured under the contractor's CGL policy. A drawback to this method, compared to the OCP, is that an additional insured usually does not

OCP Coverage Form Exclusions

Exclusion	Description
Completed Operations	This exclusion, unique to the form, applies to bodily injury or property damage that occurs after the designated contractor has completed the project (or a portion of the project that has been put to its intended use), other than service, maintenance, or repairs.
Acts or Omissions of the Insured Except for General Supervision of the Contractor's Work	This exclusion, also unique to the form, applies to injury or damage arising out of any act or omission of the named insured, or an employee of the named insured, other than general supervision of work performed by the contractor.
Damage to Property	This exclusion is a modified version of the CGL exclusion and applies only to property owned, rented to, loaned to, or occupied by the named insured; personal property in any insured's care, custody, or control; or work that the contractor performs for the named insured.
Contractual Liability	This exclusion is the same as the CGL version except that the definition of insured contract does not include the CGL provision concerning "that part of any other contract or agreement" in which the named insured assumes tort liability of another party.

[DA06567]

receive notice of cancellation from the insurer. Another potential drawback to this method is that an additional insured must share coverage limits with the named insured. However, in practice, the actual limits are usually high enough to trigger an umbrella or excess policy.

Another alternative to the OCP is a hold-harmless and indemnification agreement in the construction contract. If the liability is assumed by the contractor under an insured contract, as defined in the contractor's CGL policy, the contractor's CGL policy will cover the liability up to the applicable limits. This method also presents the drawback that the project owner will not receive notice if the contractor's CGL policy is canceled.

Construction Project Management Endorsement

ISO developed the Construction Project Management Protective Liability Coverage endorsement (CG 31 15) to modify the OCP coverage form to insure not only a project owner but also a designated contractor, architect, engineer, surveyor, or construction manager.

This endorsement broadens the insuring agreement of the OCP to include not only operations performed by the contractor, but also operations performed for the contractor in connection with the designated construction project. The endorsement also covers acts or omissions in connection with any insured's general supervision of the work performed by others, rather than the more limited OCP coverage for the owner's supervision.

Railroad Protective Liability Coverage Form

A railroad owner typically requires any contractor working on, over, under, or adjacent to the railroad owner's property to provide insurance protecting the railroad owner against liability arising out of the work performed by the contractor. This insurance is called railroad protective liability insurance. It serves essentially the same purpose as owners and contractors protective liability insurance but is designed specifically for insuring railroad owners.

The coverage is for the sole benefit of the railroad owner, who is the named insured. The premium is paid by the contractor or by an entity for which the work is being performed, such as a municipality that wants to construct a roadway that will pass over railroad tracks. The coverage is often provided by the same insurer that provides the contractor's or project owner's CGL insurance.

The Railroad Protective Liability (RPL) Coverage Form (CG 00 35) contains two coverage agreements. Coverage A applies to bodily injury and property damage liability. Coverage B applies to physical damage to property owned by or leased or entrusted to the railroad.

In either insuring agreement, the injury or damage must arise out of acts or omissions at the job site that are related to the work the contractor performs. The coverage applies to injury or damage that occurs during the policy period. ISO does not offer a claims-made version of this form.

Coverage A—Bodily Injury and Property Damage Liability

Coverage A of the RPL coverage form is similar to Coverage A in the CGL. There are, however, additional exclusions and exceptions that apply.

The only insureds under this coverage form are the named railroad owner, its executive officers and directors, its stockholders, and any railroad operating over the named insured's tracks. The designated contractor is not an insured.

The RPL contractual liability exclusion eliminates coverage for liability assumed under any contract other than a "covered contract," which is "any contract to carry a person or property for a charge or any interchange contract respecting motive power, or rolling stock equipment." Thus, contract liability is limited to contracts between the railroad owner and those using its wheeled vehicles for transportation.

Like the OCP, the RPL contains a completed work exclusion that eliminates coverage for injury or damage occurring after the contractor's work is completed.

Also like the OCP, the RPL contains an exclusion for injury or damage caused solely by acts or omissions of any insured, except for any designated employees of the insured. Designated employees include any supervisory employee who is at the job location, any employee who is loaned to the designated contractor, or any employee who is operating equipment assigned to the contractor.

The RPL provides coverage for injury or damage sustained at the job location by employees of the designated contractor, employees of the "governmental authority," and any other contracting party (other than the railroad owner) specified in the declarations.

There is an exception to the exclusion for workers compensation and similar laws in the RPL form. The RPL exclusion does not apply to any obligation of the insured under the Federal Employers' Liability Act (FELA). FELA permits employees of interstate railroads (or intrastate railroads that connect to interstate railroads) to sue their employers for occupational injuries resulting from the employer's negligence. The RPL form provides coverage for FELA suits relating to covered injuries sustained by employees of the insured railroad.

There are exceptions to the pollution exclusion for bodily injury or property damage arising out of the escape of fuels or lubricants from equipment used at the job site or arising out of heat, smoke, or fumes from a hostile fire.

There is an exclusion for damage to property owned by or leased or entrusted to the named insured. This exclusion eliminates any duplication of Coverage B of the RPL form.

Coverage B—Physical Damage to Property

Coverage B of the RPL coverage form provides first-party physical damage insurance on these types of property owned by, leased, or entrusted to the named insured:

- Rolling stock and their contents
- Mechanical construction equipment or motive power equipment
- Railroad tracks
- Roadbeds
- Catenaries (overhead transmission lines)
- Signals
- Bridges
- Buildings

There are four exclusions under Coverage B, similar to those under Coverage A, for completed work, acts or omissions of the insured, nuclear incidents or conditions, and pollution. See the exhibit "Railroad Protective Liability Coverage."

Railroad Protective Liability Coverage

River City hired Argot Construction Company to construct an elevated walkway over railroad tracks. In order to receive the railroad owner's permission to work on its property, Argot was required to provide railroad protective liability coverage for the railroad owner. This coverage was arranged using the RPL coverage form of ISO.

During the course of construction, the elevated walkway collapsed. The falling debris injured a boy who was watching the work, and it also damaged the railroad tracks and roadbed below. The boy's family sued both the contractor and the railroad owner. The railroad owner incurred expenses to repair the roadbed and replace its tracks.

Coverage A—Bodily Injury and Property Damage Liability of the RPL form would provide the railroad owner with defense coverage against the boy's suit and pay any damages for which the railroad owner might be held liable. Coverage B—Physical Damage to Property would pay the railroad owner for the damage to the tracks and roadbed. The RPL form would not provide any coverage for Argot, because Argot is not an insured under the policy, even though it paid for the policy.

[DA06568]

Limits of Insurance

Coverages A and B of the RPL coverage form are subject to an aggregate limit and an each occurrence limit. Payment under Coverage B is also limited to the lesser of these two values:

- The actual cash value of the property immediately before the physical damage occurred
- The cost to repair or replace the property with other property of like kind or quality

Liquor Liability Coverage Form

Bars, restaurants, liquor stores, and any other organizations that serve or sell alcoholic beverages are exposed to liquor liability. Liquor liability may be based on the common law or on state statutes known as alcoholic beverage control acts or **dram shop acts.**

Dram shop laws ordinarily do not allow the intoxicated person to recover damages from the person or organization that served or sold the alcohol; only the people who have been injured by the intoxicated person may recover damages. However, under common law in some jurisdictions, an injured

Dram shop acts
Statutes holding establishments that serve alcoholic beverages responsible for harm that results from serving patrons alcohol in violation of statutes.

intoxicated person may be able to recover damages from a provider who continued to serve the person after he or she became intoxicated.

The CGL coverage form excludes liquor liability if the insured is "in the business of manufacturing, distributing, selling, serving or furnishing alcoholic beverages." However, the exposure can be insured by deleting the exclusion.

Either an insured or an insurer, or both, may prefer to provide coverage for liquor liability under a form designed for these exposures. The ISO Liquor Liability Coverage Form is available for providing this type of insurance. The Liquor Liability Coverage Form comes in either an occurrence version (CG 00 33) or a claims-made version (CG 00 34). In either form, the insurer agrees to pay those sums that the insured becomes legally obligated to pay as damages because of bodily injury or property damage resulting from the selling, serving, or furnishing of any alcoholic beverage.

Exclusions

The Liquor Liability Coverage Form contains four exclusions of the CGL form for expected or intended injury, workers compensation and similar laws, employers liability, and war. In addition, the coverage form provides several exclusions that apply only to liquor liability exposures.

The Liquor Liability Coverage Form excludes injury arising out of any alcoholic beverage sold, served, or furnished while any required license is not in effect. Most states require licenses for the different types of organizations that sell liquor. For example, a different license may be required for a store to sell packaged liquor than the license required for a restaurant to serve alcoholic beverages to patrons.

Another exclusion in the Liquor Liability Coverage Form eliminates coverage for injury arising out of the named insured's products. This form is not intended to cover, for example, bodily injury resulting from choking on a foreign object in a beer bottle. However, the exclusion contains an exception clarifying that the exclusion does not eliminate all coverage for liability resulting from the alcoholic product.

The Liquor Liability Coverage Form does not exclude liability arising out of the use of an auto, aircraft, watercraft, or mobile equipment. Consequently, the form covers the liquor liability of the insured if the intoxicated person was operating an auto, aircraft, watercraft, or piece of mobile equipment at the time of the injury. However, another exclusion, titled "Other Insurance," eliminates coverage for any injury to which other insurance applies, or would apply, if its limits of insurance were not exhausted. If, for example, an auto accident caused by an intoxicated person is covered under the insured's auto liability insurance, any resulting injuries would be excluded under the Liquor Liability Coverage Form.

Limits of Insurance

The Liquor Liability Coverage Form is subject to an aggregate limit and an each common cause limit. The each common cause limit is the most the insurer will pay for all injury sustained by one or more people as the result of the selling or serving of any alcoholic beverage to any one person. If, for example, a drunk driver injures five people in five separate incidents after leaving Joe's Bar, the most that Joe's Liquor Liability Coverage Form will pay for the claims of all five people is the each common cause limit.

SUMMARY

In addition to bodily injury and property damage liability insurance (Coverage A), the CGL coverage form provides personal and advertising injury liability insurance (Coverage B) for a variety of loss exposures, including false detention, wrongful eviction, slander, and libel. The definition of "advertising" includes various e-commerce loss exposures, although there are also several exclusions that apply to use of the Internet. The CGL also provides coverage, other than liability insurance, for medical treatment of injuries (Coverage C) resulting from minor accidents on the insured's premises or as a result of the insured's operations.

The Supplementary Payments section of the CGL coverage form specifies the supplemental costs that the insurer will pay as part of any claim the insurer investigates or settles or any suit the insurer defends against under either Coverage A or Coverage B.

In addition to the named insured, a wide range of persons and organizations qualify as insureds under the CGL coverage form, subject to various conditions and exclusions.

Various limits of insurance cap the amount payable by the insurer. These limits include the general aggregate limit, the products-completed operations aggregate limit, the each occurrence limit, the personal and advertising injury limit, the damage to premises rented to you limit, and the medical expense limit.

ISO claims-made liability coverage forms address problems arising out of long-tail liability claims. A claims-made form covers claims first made during the policy period or an extended reporting period. The covered event must have occurred on or after the retroactive date, if any, shown in the policy. Some claims-made forms automatically provide a basic extended reporting period, with an option to purchase a supplemental extended reporting period. Other claims-made forms do not provide an extended reporting period automatically but give the named insured the right to purchase one.

Endorsements are available for modifying the CGL coverage form for purposes such as adding a deductible, providing additional coverages, specifying additional insureds, adding exclusions, addressing loss exposures of a particular category of insureds, changing how limits apply, and adding extended reporting periods under a claims-made form.

To determine whether, and for what amount, the Commercial General Liability Coverage Form covers a described claim, one must answer these questions by applying the relevant policy provisions to the facts of the claim:

- Does the claim meet the conditions imposed by a CGL insuring agreement?
- Do any exclusions apply to the claim?
- Do any supplementary payments apply?
- Do the circumstances of the claim meet applicable policy conditions?
- What is the amount payable for the claim?

The ISO Commercial General Liability Coverage Form includes special coverage forms for these loss exposures:

- Electronic data liability
- Owners and contractors liability
- Railroad owners and contractors liability
- Liquor liability

These coverage forms contain similar provisions to the CGL form and also contain features specially designed for the characteristics that each of these exposures present to insureds and insurers.

Direct Your Learning ▶▶

Business Auto Insurance

Educational Objectives

After learning the content of this assignment, you should be able to:

▸ Describe the property, liability, and personal loss exposures that arise from the ownership, maintenance, and use of commercial autos.

▸ Describe the symbols and the symbol system used to activate coverage under the Business Auto Coverage Form.

▸ Describe what is covered and what is excluded by the liability and physical damage coverages of the Business Auto Coverage Form.

▸ Describe the conditions contained in the Business Auto Coverage Form.

▸ Describe the purpose and provisions of common Business Auto Coverage Form endorsements.

▸ Explain whether the Business Auto Coverage Form and applicable endorsements would cover a described claim and, if so, for how much.

Business Auto Insurance

COMMERCIAL AUTO LOSS EXPOSURES

Because most organizations own, lease, rent, or otherwise use automobiles, liability arising out of the ownership, maintenance, or use of autos is a common loss exposure. Even after doing all it can to prevent or reduce its auto liability losses through risk control programs, an organization usually is required by law to obtain auto liability insurance. Auto liability insurance is therefore a basic need of most organizations.

A commonly used standard form for providing commercial auto liability insurance is the Insurance Services Office's (ISO'S) Business Auto Coverage form.

Property Exposures

The main consequences of damage to or destruction of an auto are these:

- Decrease in or loss of the auto's value
- Loss of use of the auto until it can be repaired or replaced

Auto physical damage insurance can cover damage to or destruction of an auto. Ordinarily, the insurer pays the cost of repairing the vehicle or its actual cash value, whichever is less.

To a limited extent, loss of use of an auto is insurable under a rental reimbursement endorsement to auto physical damage insurance. If a covered auto is destroyed, stolen, or disabled by a covered cause of loss, the insurer will reimburse the insured, up to a stated limit, for the cost to rent a substitute vehicle. This allows the insured to continue operations and avoid loss of income.

Automobiles are subject to many of the same causes of loss that can damage property at a fixed location, such as fire, hail, windstorm, and vandalism. Because autos are mobile, they are highly susceptible to some additional perils, such as collision, overturn, and theft. However, their mobility also makes them less susceptible than fixed property to certain other perils. For example, a car can often be quickly driven away from rising floodwaters, an approaching forest fire, or other perils that could destroy stationary property.

Liability Exposures

Liability can arise from the use of owned, hired, or borrowed autos or even from employees' operation of their own autos on behalf of the business. Furthermore, one organization can assume the auto liability of another organization by contract.

Owned Autos

Perhaps the most likely way a business can incur auto liability is when an employee of the business, while operating an auto owned by the business, negligently injures other persons or damages their property. As long as the employee operates the vehicle within the scope of his or her employment, the liability for resulting injuries and damage ordinarily falls on the employer as well as the employee. This rule of placing liability on the employer, known as the doctrine of *respondeat superior* ("let the employer answer"), is based on the fact that the employee was acting on behalf of the employer at the time of loss. The employer's liability in this situation is also referred to as vicarious liability.

Under the common law (the law that is made and applied by court decisions), the owner of an auto is not liable for negligent operation of the vehicle by someone who is not acting on behalf of the owner.

To illustrate, suppose that John's Garage allows a customer to borrow one of John's business vehicles as a loaner while the customer's car is being serviced. If the customer injures another person by negligently operating John's vehicle, John should not have any liability for resulting damages.

This common-law principle does not apply in all states, however. Many states have enacted laws that make the owner of an auto liable for injuries arising out of the use of the auto by those that borrow it. Commercial auto insurance covers liability of the insured that arises out of the "ownership, maintenance, or use" of a covered auto. The insured's liability in any of these situations would be covered by commercial auto insurance, assuming the owned auto is a covered auto.

Hired and Borrowed Autos

In several situations, an organization can become liable for injury or damage to others that results from the use of autos it does not own. An organization may hire autos from others for terms ranging from a few hours to a number of years. A rental period of six months or longer is usually referred to as a lease, and shorter rental periods are typically called rentals. In either case, the organization hiring the auto can be held legally liable for injury that results from the vehicle's operation. Similarly, the person or organization that borrows an auto from another can be held liable for injury arising from its operation.

An organization that hires or borrows autos can also become liable for damage to the hired or borrowed auto itself. This liability may be based either on user negligence or on a contractual duty to return the auto in the same condition as when hired, normal wear and tear excepted. These exposures are typically insured by purchasing auto physical damage insurance on hired autos.

Liability Assumed Under Contract

An auto rental agreement or lease may contain a hold-harmless agreement in which the renter, or lessee, agrees to indemnify the owner for the owner's liability to others arising out of use of the hired auto. The lessee is normally liable for damage resulting from use of the vehicle, even in the absence of the contract. However, the hold-harmless agreement also could obligate the lessee to reimburse the owner for amounts the owner is required to pay for injury to others arising out of the owner's faulty maintenance of the auto. Subject to certain restrictions, commercial auto insurance covers auto liability assumed by the insured under contracts, including auto rental agreements and leases.

Employers Nonownership Liability

Some employees use their own auto in performing job duties. A sales representative, for example, may use his or her own car to drive to customers' offices. In such cases, because the auto is being used to further the employer's business, the employer is exposed to liability. **Employers nonownership liability** is an employer's liability for its employees' operation of their autos in the employer's business. All three of the commercial auto forms provide insurance for this exposure.

Employers nonownership liability

An employer's liability for its employees' operation of their autos in the employer's business.

Bailee Loss Exposures

Any business that services, repairs, or otherwise attends to customers' autos can become liable for damage to cars temporarily left in its custody. Such businesses are said to face bailee loss exposures. A bailee is legally liable for damage to customers' property only if the damage occurs as a result of the bailee's negligence. However, in order to maintain good customer relations, many bailees choose to make "goodwill" payments for customers' losses even when not legally obligated to do so.

The Garage Coverage Form contains optional garagekeepers coverage for insuring loss to customers' autos while the autos are in the custody of the insured auto or trailer dealer. Nondealer auto service businesses, which are no longer eligible for coverage under the Garage Coverage Form, can insure their bailee loss exposures under a separate garagekeepers endorsement to the Business Auto Coverage Form.

Personal Loss Exposures

Anyone who could suffer injury in an auto accident—either while occupying an auto or as a pedestrian—has a personal loss exposure. In many cases, an auto accident victim can sue or otherwise make a liability claim against the responsible party, in which case the responsible party may also incur a liability loss.

In other cases, an auto accident victim may not be able or willing to sue the responsible party (typically an at-fault driver or the at-fault driver's employer).

For example, the injured person may also have caused the accident. Similarly, the injured person may be a family member or friend of the at-fault driver and unwilling to sue. In other cases, the injured party may be willing but unable to sue because the at-fault driver cannot be identified or may have no insurance or other assets with which to pay a judgment. In each of these instances, the injured person is exposed to loss for the costs of his or her injuries and perhaps resulting loss of income if temporarily or permanently disabled.

Various commercial auto coverages cover personal loss exposures that arise from auto accidents. These coverages include auto medical payments coverage, personal injury protection (PIP) coverage, and uninsured motorists (UM) coverage. Some states require auto owners to maintain certain amounts of PIP coverage and/or UM coverage to ensure that auto accident victims are compensated through insurance.

THE BUSINESS AUTO COVERAGE FORM

The Insurance Services Office, Inc. (ISO) Business Auto Coverage Form (CA 00 01) is a flexible coverage form used for insuring a wide variety of loss exposures for all types of organizations other than auto dealers and motor carriers.

Business Auto Coverage Form

A coverage form, filed by ISO, that covers liability arising out of the ownership, maintenance, or use of autos and physical damage to autos owned, leased, or hired by the named insured.

The 2010 version of the **Business Auto Coverage Form,** along with business auto declarations and any applicable endorsements, can be included in a commercial package policy or issued as a monoline policy. The form's declarations are longer and more detailed than the declarations for most other coverage forms. In addition to the usual information contained in any declarations form, the business auto declarations form includes various schedules for recording applicable coverages, covered autos, limits, deductibles, premiums, and rating and classification information.

The Business Auto Coverage Form consists of five sections:

- Section I—Covered Autos
- Section II—Liability Coverage
- Section III—Physical Damage Coverage
- Section IV—Business Auto Conditions
- Section V—Definitions

The Business Auto Coverage Form allows great flexibility in designating covered autos for its various coverages. A coverage chosen by the named insured need not apply to all covered autos. For example, the insured might want to provide liability coverage for all autos and physical damage coverage only for specifically described autos.

Coverage Symbols

The ten commercial auto **coverage symbols** are defined in Section I of the coverage form. The appropriate symbol or symbols appear beside each coverage in the schedule of coverages and covered autos in the declarations. See the exhibit "Symbols in Personal Auto."

Coverage symbols

Numeric symbols used in a commercial auto policy to indicate which autos are covered for particular coverages.

Symbols in Personal Auto

The term "symbol" is used differently in personal auto insurance. To help determine the rate for physical damage coverage (such as collision) on a personal auto policy, insurers assign every vehicle a symbol that roughly corresponds to its list price. The use of the term "symbol" in personal auto is unrelated to its use in commercial auto.

[DA02618]

The exhibit illustrates how the schedule might be completed. See the exhibit "Schedule of Coverages and Covered Autos."

This is the Business Auto Coverage Form definition of "auto":

> 1. A land motor vehicle, "trailer" or semitrailer designed for travel on public roads; or 2. Any other land vehicle that is subject to a compulsory or financial responsibility law or other motor vehicle insurance law where it is licensed or principally garaged. However, "auto" does not include "mobile equipment".[1]

The policy definition of "mobile equipment" is the same as that in the Commercial General Liability (CGL) Coverage Form. Consequently, mobile equipment (generally covered under the CGL coverage form) is excluded under the business auto form unless it is subject to motor vehicle or financial responsibility laws. A semitrailer, one of the terms used in the definition of "auto," is a trailer that, because it has no front axle, relies on its power unit (truck tractor) to support its forward weight. A semitrailer often has legs that can be lowered to support the front end when it is disengaged from the truck tractor.

The exhibit describes each of the commercial auto policy coverage symbols. See the exhibit "Descriptions of Covered Auto Designation Symbols."

Symbol 1—Any Auto

If symbol 1 is entered for a coverage, that coverage is provided for any auto, including autos owned by the named insured, autos the named insured hires or borrows from others, and other nonowned autos used in the insured's business. Symbol 1 provides the best protection for the insured. Ordinarily, this symbol is used for liability coverage only. Sometimes insurers are unwilling to use symbol 1 because of the all-encompassing coverage it triggers.

Schedule of Coverages and Covered Autos

ITEM TWO
Schedule Of Coverages And Covered Autos

This policy provides only those coverages where a charge is shown in the premium column below. Each of these coverages will apply only to those "autos" shown as covered "autos". **"Autos" are shown as covered "autos" for a particular coverage by the entry of one or more of the symbols from the Covered Autos Section of the Business Auto Coverage Form next to the name of the coverage.**

Coverages	Covered Autos	Limit	Premium
Liability	1	$	$
Personal Injury Protection (Or Equivalent No-fault Coverage)	5	Separately Stated In Each Personal Injury Protection Endorsement Minus $ Deductible	$
Added Personal Injury Protection (Or Equivalent Added No-fault Coverage)	5	Separately Stated In Each Added Personal Injury Protection Endorsement	$
Property Protection Insurance (Michigan Only)		Separately Stated In The Property Protection Insurance Endorsement Minus $ Deductible For Each Accident	$
Auto Medical Payments		$	$
Medical Expense And Income Loss Benefits (Virginia Only)		Separately Stated In The Medical Expense And Income Loss Benefits Endorsement	$
Uninsured Motorists	6	$	$
Underinsured Motorists (When Not Included In Uninsured Motorists Coverage)	6	$	$

© Insurance Services Office, Inc., 2009   CA DS 03 03 10   ▫

ITEM TWO
Schedule Of Coverages And Covered Autos (Cont'd)

Coverages	Covered Autos	Limit	Premium
Physical Damage Comprehensive Coverage	7, 8	Actual Cash Value Or Cost Of Repair, Whichever Is Less, Minus $ Deductible For Each Covered Auto, But No Deductible Applies To Loss Caused By Fire Or Lightning See Item Four for Hired or Borrowed Autos.	$
Physical Damage Specified Causes Of Loss Coverage		Actual Cash Value Or Cost Of Repair, Whichever Is Less, Minus $ Deductible For Each Covered Auto For Loss Caused By Mischief Or Vandalism See Item Four for Hired or Borrowed Autos.	$
Physical Damage Collision Coverage	7, 8	Actual Cash Value Or Cost Of Repair, Whichever Is Less, Minus $ Deductible For Each Covered Auto See Item Four for Hired or Borrowed Autos.	$
Physical Damage Towing And Labor		$ For Each Disablement Of A Private Passenger Auto	$
			$
		Premium For Endorsements	$
		Estimated Total Premium*	$

*This policy may be subject to final audit.

Descriptions of Covered Auto Designation Symbols

Symbol	Description of Covered Auto Designation Symbols	
1	Any "Auto"	
2	Owned "Autos" Only	Only those "autos" you own (and for Liability Coverage any "trailers" you don't own while attached to power units you own). This includes those "autos" you acquire ownership of after the policy begins.
3	Owned Private Passenger "Autos" Only	Only the private passenger "autos" you own. This includes those private passenger "autos" you acquire ownership of after the policy begins.
4	Owned "Autos" Other Than Private Passenger "Autos" Only	Only those "autos" you own that are not of the private passenger type (and for Liability Coverage any "trailers" you don't own while attached to power units you own). This includes those "autos" not of the private passenger type you acquire ownership of after the policy begins.
5	Owned "Autos" Subject To No-fault	Only those "autos" you own that are required to have no-fault benefits in the state where they are licensed or principally garaged. This includes those "autos" you acquire ownership of after the policy begins provided they are required to have no-fault benefits in the state where they are licensed or principally garaged.
6	Owned "Autos" Subject To A Compulsory Uninsured Motorists Law	Only those "autos" you own that because of the law in the state where they are licensed or principally garaged are required to have and cannot reject Uninsured Motorists Coverage. This includes those "autos" you acquire ownership of after the policy begins provided they are subject to the same state uninsured motorists requirement.
7	Specifically Described "Autos"	Only those "autos" described in Item Nine of the Declarations for which a premium charge is shown (and for Liability Coverage any "trailers" you don't own while attached to a power unit described in Item Nine).
8	Hired "Autos" Only	Only those "autos" you lease, hire, rent or borrow. This does not include any "auto" you lease, hire, rent or borrow from any of your "employees", partners (if you are a partnership), members (if you are a limited liability company) or members of their households.
9	Non-owned "Autos" Only	Only those "autos" you do not own, lease, hire, rent or borrow that are used in connection with your business. This includes "autos" owned by your "employees," partners (if you are a partnership), members (if you are a limited liability company) or members of their households but only while used in your business or your personal affairs.
19	Mobile Equipment Subject To Compulsory Or Financial Responsibility Or Other Motor Vehicle Insurance Law Only	Only those "autos" that are land vehicles and that would qualify under the definition of "mobile equipment" under this policy if they were not subject to a compulsory or financial responsibility law or other motor vehicle insurance law where they are licensed or principally garaged.

[DA06765]

Symbol 2—Owned Autos Only

If symbol 2 is entered for a coverage, that coverage applies to all autos owned by the named insured. When symbol 2 is used to signal liability coverage, it also includes trailers (or semi-trailers) the named insured does not own while attached to power units owned by the named insured. For liability insurance only, coverage is also provided for a nonowned trailer while it is attached to a power unit owned by the named insured. ("Power unit" is not defined in the coverage form, but the term refers to a truck tractor used to pull a semitrailer. "Trailer," defined in the coverage form, includes, but is not limited to, a semi-trailer.) Symbol 2 does not cover hired or borrowed autos or other autos the named insured does not own. It is also used for physical damage and medical payments coverages. If symbol 2 is used for signaling liability coverage, symbols 8 and 9 must also be shown for liability coverage in order to cover hired and nonowned autos. Because symbol 1 covers owned, hired, and nonowned autos, showing symbol 1 for liability coverage has essentially the same result as showing symbols 2, 8, and 9. However, symbol 2 might be used for liability coverage if the insured does not want to cover either hired autos or nonowned autos. If, for example, the insured wanted to cover liability for all owned autos and nonowned autos but not hired autos, symbols 2 and 9 would be shown for liability coverage.

Symbol 3—Owned Private Passenger Autos Only

Symbol 3 entered for a coverage indicates that coverage is provided only for private passenger autos owned by the named insured. This symbol does not include trucks or buses owned by the named insured or any kind of auto not owned by the named insured.

Symbol 4—Owned Autos Other Than Private Passenger Autos Only

Symbol 4 entered for a coverage indicates that coverage is provided for all autos owned by the named insured except private passenger autos.

Symbol 5—Owned Autos Subject to No-Fault

Symbol 5 is normally entered only on the personal injury protection (PIP) or added PIP line of the declarations. It provides PIP coverage only for those autos that are required by law to have it.

Symbol 6—Owned Autos Subject to a Compulsory Uninsured Motorists Law

Symbol 6 normally is used only for uninsured motorists coverage. It indicates that coverage is provided only for autos that are required by law to have uninsured motorists coverage.

Symbol 7—Specifically Described Autos

If symbol 7 is used, coverage applies only to those autos specifically described in the policy and for which a premium is shown in the policy. It also includes, for liability coverage only, any trailer not owned by the insured while it is attached to one of the covered power units.

Symbol 8—Hired Autos Only

Symbol 8 provides coverage only for autos leased, hired, rented, or borrowed by the named insured. It does not cover autos leased, hired, rented, or borrowed from the named insured's employees or family members.

Symbol 9—Nonowned Autos Only

Symbol 9 provides coverage only for autos not owned, leased, hired, or borrowed by the named insured while such autos are used in connection with the named insured's business. Symbol 9 includes autos owned by the named insured's employees or members of their households but only while used in the named insured's business or personal affairs. Symbols 8 and 9 are normally used only for liability coverage. If symbol 1 is used for liability coverage, then symbols 8 and 9 do not need to be shown in order to provide coverage for hired and nonowned autos; symbol 1 includes such coverage. If another symbol is shown for liability coverage—for example, symbol 2 or 7—most insureds should add symbols 8 and 9 to obtain hired and nonowned autos coverage.

Symbol 19—Mobile Equipment Subject to Compulsory or Financial Responsibility or Other Motor Vehicle Insurance Law Only

Symbol 19 indicates coverage only for land vehicles that would otherwise qualify under the policy's definition of mobile equipment if they were not subject to a compulsory or financial responsibility law or other motor vehicle insurance law in the state in which they are licensed or principally garaged.

Coverage for Newly Acquired Autos

If any of symbols 1 through 6, or 19, is shown for a coverage, that coverage applies to vehicles of the type indicated by the symbol if such vehicles are acquired during the policy term. Coverage for newly acquired vehicles of the type indicated by the symbol is automatic, without any requirement that the insurer be notified of the acquisition. (The insurer typically discovers any newly acquired autos when it audits the insured at the end of the policy period.) Likewise, a premium auditor will determine the actual nonowned and hired auto exposure. The insured must then pay an additional premium for the actual exposures covered during the policy period. However, many insurers do not audit policies that generate smaller premiums.

If symbol 7 is shown for a coverage, autos acquired during the policy term are covered from the time of acquisition only if both of these conditions are met:

- The insurer insures all autos owned by the named insured, or the newly acquired auto replaces a covered auto.

- The named insured asks the insurer to cover the newly acquired auto within thirty days of the acquisition.

Other Covered Items

If the coverage form provides liability insurance, trailers with a load capacity of 2,000 pounds or less are covered automatically for liability insurance. Mobile equipment is automatically covered for liability while being carried or towed by an auto that has liability coverage. An auto used as a temporary substitute for a covered auto that is out of service because of its breakdown, repair, service, loss, or destruction is also covered for liability insurance only.

LIABILITY AND PHYSICAL DAMAGE COVERAGES OF THE BUSINESS AUTO COVERAGE FORM

The Business Auto Coverage Form, which provides liability and physical damage coverages, can be included in a commercial package policy or issued in a monoline policy.

The Business Auto Coverage Form, filed by Insurance Services Office (ISO), covers liability arising out of the ownership, maintenance, or use of autos and physical damage to autos owned, leased, or hired by the named insured.

Section II of the form contains the liability coverage provisions, which include a coverage agreement, a definition of who is insured, coverage extensions, exclusions, and a limit of insurance provision.

Section III of the form provides auto physical damage coverage, which insures loss of or damage to autos owned by the insured. However, coverage can also be arranged for autos hired or borrowed by the insured.

Section II—Liability Coverage

The business auto form includes these liability coverage provisions:

- A coverage agreement
- A definition of who is insured
- Coverage extensions

- Exclusions
- A limit of insurance provision

Coverage Agreement

In the liability coverage agreement, the insurer expresses three distinct duties:

- A duty to pay damages
- A duty to pay "covered pollution cost or expense"
- A duty to defend the insured

The insurer agrees to pay all sums an "insured" must legally pay as damages because of "bodily injury" (BI) or "property damage" (PD) to which the insurance applies, caused by an "accident" and resulting from the ownership, maintenance, or use of a covered auto.

The terms in quotation marks are defined in Section V of the coverage form. See the exhibit "Definitions From Section V, Business Auto Form."

Definitions From Section V, Business Auto Form

"Insured" means any person or organization qualifying as an insured in the Who Is An Insured provision of the applicable coverage. . . .

"Bodily injury" means bodily injury, sickness or disease sustained by a person including death resulting from any of these.

"Property damage" means damage to or loss of use of tangible property.

"Accident" includes continuous or repeated exposure to the same conditions resulting in "bodily injury" or "property damage".

CA 00 01 03 10, Copyright, ISO Properties, Inc., 2010. [DA02613]

The insurer's obligation to "pay all sums" is governed not only by these definitions but also by exclusions, policy limits, and other conditions.

The business auto form is subject to a broad pollution exclusion that eliminates almost all coverage for bodily injury or property damage resulting from the escape of pollutants being transported by a covered auto. However, the form covers certain pollution costs and expenses, such as those resulting from the escape of fuel or other fluids needed for the normal running of the covered auto.

In the event of an incident that produces pollution, damages for bodily injury and property damage are not the only consequences for which the insured can be held liable. The insured can incur various costs and expenses for cleaning up or otherwise dealing with the effects of pollutants in response to demands by governmental authorities or private citizens.

To address this exposure, the insurer agrees to pay all sums the insured must legally pay as "covered pollution cost or expense." To be covered, pollution cost or expense must be caused by an accident and must result from the ownership, maintenance, or use of a covered auto. In addition, the same accident that causes the pollution cost or expense must also result in bodily injury or property damage covered by the policy. Cleanup costs for any incident excluded by the pollution exclusion are not covered.

Unlike defense costs, covered pollution cost or expense is not paid in addition to the stated limit of liability. All payments for covered pollution cost or expense reduce the applicable limit.

The insurer's duty to defend the insured applies to any claim or suit against any insured alleging damages that would be covered under the policy. The claim or suit need only allege damages that would be covered. Hence, the insurer must defend against even false or fraudulent claims or suits as long as they allege covered damages.

The coverage form defines "suit" to include not only a civil proceeding but also an arbitration proceeding or any other alternative dispute resolution proceeding to which the insured must submit or does submit with the insurer's consent. The duty to defend ends when the insurer has paid its applicable policy limit in full or partial settlement of the claim. The costs of defending the claim are payable in addition to the limit of insurance.

Who Is an Insured

The business auto form's liability insurance agreement may cover many persons in addition to the named insured, depending on the circumstances of the accident.

The named insured is an insured for any covered auto. If, for example, symbol 1 is shown for liability coverage, the named insured is an insured for any auto. If only symbol 7 is shown for liability coverage, the named insured is an insured only for specifically described autos.

Anyone other than the named insured is an insured while using—with the named insured's permission—a covered auto owned, hired, or borrowed by the named insured. However, these restrictions apply:

- The owner or anyone else from whom the named insured hires or borrows a covered auto is not an insured, unless the covered auto is a trailer connected to a covered auto owned by the named insured. If, for example, ABC Company hires a car from A-1 Auto Rentals, A-1 will not be an insured under ABC's business auto liability coverage.

- An employee of the named insured is not an insured if the covered auto is owned by the employee or a member of the employee's household. For example, Sue is not an insured under her employer's business auto liability coverage while operating her car on an errand for her employer. (Sue's employer, however, is insured for this use of Sue's car if the policy includes either symbol 1 or symbol 9 for liability coverage.)

- A person using a covered auto while working in the business of selling, servicing, repairing, or parking autos is not an insured unless that business is the named insured's. For example, a mechanic of Bob's Brake Shop is not an insured under ABC's business auto liability coverage while test-driving ABC's car.
- Anyone other than the named insured's employees or partners, or a lessee or borrower of a covered auto or any of their employees, is not an insured while moving property to or from a covered auto. If, for example, employees of Jones Warehouse are unloading ABC Company's truck, the Jones employees are not covered under ABC's business auto liability coverage.
- If the named insured is a partnership, a partner of the named insured is not an insured for a covered auto owned by that partner or by someone residing in that partner's household.
- If the named insured is a limited liability company, a member of the named insured's company is not an insured for a covered auto owned by that member or by someone residing in that member's household.

Any person or organization (other than those previously noted as excluded) held liable for the conduct of an "insured" is also an insured. For example, assume that an employee of XYZ Corporation operates an auto covered under ABC's business auto insurance and causes an accident for which XYZ is held to be liable. This provision stipulates that XYZ will be an insured under ABC's auto insurance. (XYZ's employee also will be an insured because of the earlier provision relating to "anyone else" other than the named insured.)

Coverage Extensions

The business auto liability provisions include coverage extensions for supplementary payments and for increased protection while a covered auto is out of the state in which it is licensed.

Business auto liability coverage provides six supplementary payments that are similar in most respects to those provided in the Commercial General Liability (CGL) Coverage Form. As with the CGL coverage form, these supplementary payments are payable in addition to the limit of insurance.

If a covered auto is outside the state in which it is licensed, the limit of insurance is, if necessary, increased on that auto to the minimum required by the outside jurisdiction in which the auto is being operated. Also, if the outside jurisdiction requires a different type of coverage, the policy provides such coverage automatically.

For example, assume that a business auto policy has a $50,000 limit for liability insurance and that a covered auto is driven out of state through two other states. If the first outside state requires a minimum limit of $100,000, the limit is increased automatically to $100,000 while the auto is in that state. If the second outside state requires no-fault coverage, the insured's policy will automatically provide no-fault coverage while the auto is in that state.

Exclusions

The exclusions that appear in the liability coverage section impose several limitations on the liability coverage agreement. See the exhibit "Titles of Exclusions That Apply to Business Auto Liability Coverage."

Titles of Exclusions That Apply to Business Auto Liability Coverage

- Expected or Intended Injury
- Contractual Liability
- Workers' Compensation
- Employee Indemnification and Employer's Liability
- Fellow Employee
- Care, Custody or Control
- Handling of Property
- Movement of Property by Mechanical Device
- Operations
- Completed Operations
- Pollution
- War
- Racing

[DA06715]

Under the Expected or Intended Injury exclusion, bodily injury or property damage expected or intended from the standpoint of the insured is excluded.

Under the Contractual Liability exclusion, liability assumed by contract or agreement is excluded, but the exclusion does not apply in two instances:

- Liability the insured would have in the absence of the contract
- Damages assumed in an "insured contract," provided the injury or damage occurs after the contract has been executed

Section V's definition of "insured contract" lists the types of contracts in which an assumption of liability is covered. This definition resembles the definition of "insured contract" in the CGL coverage form.

For example, both definitions include leases of premises. The business auto form covers liability assumed under a lease of premises only if the liability being assumed arises out of the ownership, maintenance, or use of an auto; the CGL form covers liability assumed under a lease of premises if the liability being assumed does not arise out of the ownership, maintenance, or use of an auto. The same distinction applies to the other types of insured contracts.

Under the Workers' Compensation exclusion, the business auto form, like the CGL form, excludes any liability under a workers compensation, a disability benefits, or an unemployment compensation law.

The Employee Indemnification and Employer's Liability exclusion is also nearly identical to one found in the CGL coverage form. It effectively eliminates, subject to two exceptions, coverage for bodily injury to employees of the insured that should be covered under workers compensation and employers liability insurance. The two exceptions that allow coverage for employee injury are injury to domestic employees not entitled to workers compensation and liability assumed by the insured under an insured contract.

The Fellow Employee exclusion in the business auto form excludes bodily injury to any fellow employee of any insured that arises in the course of the fellow employee's employment. It also excludes injury to fellow employees' family members. If, for example, one of ABC's drivers negligently strikes another ABC employee with a truck while at work, ABC's business auto coverage will not protect the driver against any legal action the injured employee may bring against the driver. By endorsement (for an additional premium), the fellow employee exclusion can be deleted entirely or modified so that it does not apply to specified employees, job titles, or positions.

Under the Care, Custody or Control exclusion, no coverage exists for property owned by the insured or in the care, custody, or control of the insured. Property owned by the insured can be covered under an appropriate form of property insurance. Property of others in the care, custody, or control of the insured is frequently insured under inland marine coverage. For example, motor truck cargo insurance covers property of others that is being transported by the insured.

The Handling of Property exclusion helps define the scope of coverage for accidents that occur during the loading or unloading of autos. The exclusion eliminates coverage for bodily injury or property damage resulting from the handling of property under these conditions:

- Before property is moved from the place where it has been accepted by the insured for movement into a covered auto
- After it has been moved from a covered auto to the place where it is finally delivered by the insured

Consequently, the exclusion does not apply to—and thus coverage exists for—accidents that occur while property is being moved into a covered auto from the place where the insured has accepted the property or from a covered auto to the place where the property is finally delivered.

If, for example, two employees of an appliance store damage a hallway wall while moving a clothes washer from their delivery truck to a second-floor apartment, the store's business auto insurance will cover the damage to the wall, because the property damage occurred before the washer was moved to the place of final delivery.

The CGL coverage form excludes "loading and unloading" and uses the same definition of the term as that in the business auto form, thus avoiding duplication of business auto coverage. The CGL form covers the exposures that exist in connection with property before loading begins or after unloading is completed.

The Movement of Property by Mechanical Device exclusion in the business auto form excludes bodily injury or property damage resulting from movement of property by a mechanical device unless the device is attached to the covered auto or is a hand truck. For example, movement of property by a mechanical hoist attached to a flatbed truck is covered; movement of property by a conveyor belt not attached to the truck is excluded by the business auto form (but covered by the CGL form).

The Operations exclusion eliminates coverage for the operation of several specified types of equipment attached to covered autos. The specified types of equipment are "cherry pickers" and similar devices used to raise or lower workers; air compressors, pumps, or generators; equipment used for spraying, welding, building cleaning, geophysical exploration, lighting, or well servicing; and machinery or equipment that is part of, or attached to, a land vehicle that would qualify as "mobile equipment" if it were not subject to a compulsory or financial responsibility law or other motor vehicle insurance law in the state in which it is licensed or principally garaged. See the exhibit "Mobile Equipment Under CGL and Business Auto Coverages."

In the absence of this exclusion, the business auto form might be considered to cover the operation of such equipment because the equipment is attached to a covered auto. The CGL policy covers the operation of such equipment regardless of whether it is attached to an auto.

For example, assume C&D Electric has a service truck on which a cherry picker is mounted. If the driver of the truck causes an accident while driving to a work site, the resulting liability is covered under C&D's business auto insurance. If, after the truck reaches its work site, a passerby is injured as a result of C&D's operation of the cherry picker, the resulting liability is excluded by C&D's business auto insurance and covered by C&D's CGL insurance. The Completed Operations exclusion clarifies that the business auto form provides no insurance for completed operations performed with the insured's autos. For example, injury resulting from allegedly negligent snowplowing performed (and completed) by the insured would not be covered.

The business auto Pollution exclusion eliminates, with few exceptions, coverage for bodily injury or property damage resulting from the discharge of any pollutants being transported or stored in, or moved to or from, a covered auto. By a specific exception, the exclusion does not apply to the escape of fuels, lubricants, fluids, exhaust gases, or other similar pollutants needed for the functioning of the covered auto. If, for example, gasoline leaks from the fuel tank of a covered auto after a collision, liability for the spill is covered. See the exhibit "Pollution Exclusion."

Mobile Equipment Under CGL and Business Auto Coverages

The CGL form and the Business Auto Coverage Form both contain the same definition of "mobile equipment." In general, the CGL excludes auto liability coverage but covers liability arising from the ownership, maintenance, or use of mobile equipment, and the business auto form covers auto liability but excludes mobile equipment liability. Typically, in states that require motor vehicle registration of certain types of mobile equipment, such as backhoes, these vehicles can be added to the business auto form for coverages available under that form. However, the business auto form would not cover liability losses resulting from the operation of any machinery that is attached to or part of those vehicles. In other words, liability coverage for the operation of the mobile equipment would still revert to the CGL.

This is the definition of mobile equipment in the Business Auto Coverage Form:

K. "Mobile equipment" means any of the following types of land vehicles, including any attached machinery or equipment:

   1. Bulldozers, farm machinery, forklifts and other vehicles designed for use principally off public roads;

   2. Vehicles maintained for use solely on or next to premises you own or rent;

   3. Vehicles that travel on crawler treads;

   4. Vehicles, whether self-propelled or not, maintained primarily to provide mobility to permanently mounted:

      a. Power cranes, shovels, loaders, diggers or drills; or

      b. Road construction or resurfacing equipment such as graders, scrapers or rollers.

   5. Vehicles not described in Paragraph 1., 2., 3. or 4. above that are not self-propelled and are maintained primarily to provide mobility to permanently attached equipment of the following types:

      a. Air compressors, pumps and generators, including spraying, welding, building cleaning, geophysical exploration, lighting and well-servicing equipment; or

      b. Cherry pickers and similar devices used to raise or lower workers; or

   6. Vehicles not described in Paragraph 1., 2., 3., or 4. above maintained primarily for purposes other than the transportation of persons or cargo. However, self-propelled vehicles with the following types of permanently attached equipment are not "mobile equipment" but will be considered "autos":

      a. Equipment designed primarily for:

         (1) Snow removal;

         (2) Road maintenance, but not construction or resurfacing; or

         (3) Street cleaning;

      b. Cherry pickers and similar devices mounted on automobile or truck chassis and used to raise or lower workers; and

      c. Air compressors, pumps and generators, including spraying, welding, building cleaning, geophysical exploration, lighting or well-servicing equipment.

However, "mobile equipment" does not include land vehicles that are subject to a compulsory or financial responsibility law or other motor vehicle insurance law where it is licensed or principally garaged. Land vehicles subject to a compulsory or financial responsibility law or other motor vehicle insurance law are considered "autos".

Business Auto Coverage Form (CA 00 01 03 10), Copyright, ISO Properties, Inc., 2010. [DA06766]

Pollution Exclusion

Jack, an employee of Landscaping Service, was carrying a load of topsoil in a dump truck covered under Landscaping's Business Auto Coverage Form. Jack fell asleep at the wheel and veered into the path of an oncoming tanker truck carrying a load of fuel oil. The tanker swerved off the road and overturned. The tank ruptured, resulting in a large spill that entered the basement of a nearby house, causing extensive property damage. The owners of the house made claim against Landscaping Service for their loss, which included both physical damage and loss of use.

Question: Would the Pollution exclusion in Landscaping's Business Auto Coverage Form eliminate coverage for this loss?

Answer: No. The loss is covered. Although the oil was a pollutant, it was not being transported (or otherwise handled) by or on behalf of Landscaping Service. The exclusion therefore does not apply.

[DA06718]

The business auto form's War exclusion excludes liability for damage caused by war, warlike actions, civil war, insurrection, rebellion, or revolution.

The form's Racing exclusion is similar to that in the CGL coverage form. While the CGL excludes racing of mobile equipment, the business auto form excludes covered autos while they are used in organized races or demolition contests. Practice or preparation for such activities is also excluded.

Limit of Insurance

Business auto liability coverage is subject to a combined single limit of insurance applicable to all bodily injury, property damage, and covered pollution cost or expense arising from a single accident. No annual aggregate limit applies. The single limit is the maximum amount the insurer will pay for all claims arising from a single accident regardless of the number of vehicles, the number of drivers, or the number of claimants involved.

Repeated exposure to essentially the same circumstances is considered to be a single accident. For example, if a truck is driven across the sidewalk repeatedly over several months, all of the damage it causes to the sidewalk would be considered a single accident.

An endorsement is available to provide split BI/PD limits of insurance. The endorsement shows a per person limit and a per accident limit for bodily injury and a per accident limit for property damage.

Section III—Physical Damage Coverage

Section III of the business auto form provides auto physical damage insurance. The primary purpose of the coverage is to insure loss of or damage to autos owned by the insured. However, coverage can also be arranged to cover autos hired or borrowed by the insured.

Available Coverages

The insured may choose from three basic physical damage coverages:

- Collision coverage
- Comprehensive coverage
- Specified causes of loss coverage

Any of these coverages can be purchased individually. Usually, however, the named insured selects either collision and comprehensive coverage or collision and specified causes of loss coverage. Because comprehensive coverage encompasses all of the specified causes of loss (and more), those two coverages are never purchased on the same auto.

In addition to these basic physical damage coverages, the business auto form includes provisions for optional towing and labor coverage, an extension covering transportation expenses, and an extension covering loss of use of rental autos.

Collision coverage covers loss resulting from collision or from overturn of a vehicle. The coverage form defines loss as direct and accidental loss or damage. The form does not define collision or overturn. Collision is generally understood to mean a striking together with violent impact. Overturn is generally considered to include any incident in which a vehicle loses its equilibrium; the vehicle need not turn over completely.

Comprehensive coverage covers loss from causes other than collision or overturn. This is essentially the same approach to defining covered perils as is used in a special form, which covers unnamed, unanticipated perils as long as they are not specifically excluded.

Glass breakage, damage resulting from hitting an animal, and damage caused by falling objects or missiles, although they might otherwise be considered losses caused by collision, are paid under comprehensive coverage. This provision usually benefits the insured because most insureds carry lower deductibles on comprehensive than on collision coverage.

If glass breakage is caused by collision, however, the insured can choose to have it covered by collision coverage rather than comprehensive coverage. By doing so, the insured can avoid paying a deductible for the glass breakage and another deductible for the other damage resulting from the collision.

A somewhat less expensive alternative to comprehensive coverage is **specified causes of loss coverage**.

Towing and labor coverage applies to expenses that arise from a vehicle's disablement. To be covered, the labor must be performed at the place of disablement. The limit for this coverage, selected by the insured, is the most that the insurer will pay for each disablement.

Transportation expenses apply when a private passenger vehicle has been stolen. The insurer agrees to pay costs of substitute transportation actually

Collision coverage

Coverage for direct and accidental loss or damage to a covered auto caused by collision with another object or by overturn.

Comprehensive coverage

Coverage for direct and accidental loss or damage to a covered auto by any peril except collision or overturn or a peril specifically excluded.

Specified causes of loss coverage

Coverage for direct and accidental loss caused by fire, lightning, explosion, theft, windstorm, hail, earthquake, flood, mischief, vandalism, or loss resulting from the sinking, burning, collision, or derailment of a conveyance transporting the covered auto.

Towing and labor coverage

Coverage for necessary towing and labor costs (for labor performed at the place of disablement) due to the disablement of a covered private passenger auto.

Transportation expenses

Coverage extension for substitute transportation costs incurred when a private passenger type auto has been stolen.

incurred by the named insured, subject to a daily limit of $20 and a total limit of $600. Payments begin forty-eight hours after the theft and end when the insured auto is returned to use or when the insurer pays for the auto. Such payments may extend beyond the expiration of the policy.

Insureds who want broader coverage can add the Rental Reimbursement Coverage endorsement. It covers the cost of renting a substitute auto for a designated auto of any type that has sustained a loss due to any covered peril, subject to maximum daily and aggregate limits.

Loss of use expenses apply to rental vehicles. When the insured rents an auto, the rental agreement may obligate the insured to pay for physical damage to the auto that occurs during the rental period, as well as resulting loss of use of the auto, regardless of whether the insured is at fault. Although an organization can buy physical damage insurance on hired autos (through symbol 8), such coverage applies only to the physical loss and not to the resulting loss of use. The coverage extension for loss of use expenses provides up to $20 per day, to a maximum of $600, to cover that exposure. These limits can be increased by endorsement.

Loss of use expenses
Coverage extension that pays for loss of use of a rental auto when an insured becomes contractually obligated to make such payments.

Exclusions

Auto physical damage insurance is subject to relatively few exclusions. Like virtually any other type of property insurance, it excludes nuclear hazards and war or military action. Notably, however, auto physical damage insurance does not exclude earthquake or flood or other water damage.

Business auto physical damage insurance excludes certain types of losses that are likely to occur as a normal consequence of prolonged use of the vehicle or the owner's neglect. Thus, loss "due and confined to" wear and tear, freezing, mechanical or electrical failure, and road damage to tires is excluded unless it results from other loss insured by the coverage form. For example, an auto with comprehensive coverage may be stolen. If the auto sustains a mechanical breakdown and tire damage resulting from abusive driving by the thief, that damage would not be excluded, because the proximate cause of the loss is a covered peril (theft).

The business auto form excludes many, but not all, types of electronic equipment in a covered auto. In fact, the drafters of the form have taken great care to specify exactly which types of electronic equipment are excluded and which are covered. These exclusions have been redrafted several times in recent years to keep up with technological change.

The insurer will not pay for loss to these types of equipment:

- Tapes, records, discs, or similar devices
- Radar detectors, laser detectors, and similar devices
- Any electronic equipment—regardless of whether it is permanently installed in the vehicle—that reproduces, receives, or transmits audio, visual, or data signals
- Any accessories used with the previously described equipment

If the insured would like to insure such equipment, coverage can usually be added to the business auto form by endorsement.

A detailed exception to this exclusion reinstates coverage for all electronic equipment that reproduces, receives, or transmits audio, visual, or data signals. (Before 2010, this exception applied only to equipment that reproduces audio signals.) The exception applies only if the equipment is designed to be powered solely by the vehicle's electrical system and if it also has either of these qualities:

- It is either permanently installed in or on the vehicle or removable from or an integral part of a permanently installed housing unit.
- It is necessary for the auto's normal operation or for monitoring the auto's operation.

Like business auto liability coverage, the physical damage section excludes coverage for autos while used in organized races or demolition contests, including practice or preparation for such activities.

Finally, the physical damage section excludes "diminution in value," which the form defines as "the actual or perceived loss in market value" resulting from a covered auto being repaired.

Limit of Insurance

The most the insurer will pay for a physical damage loss is the lesser of two amounts:

- The actual cash value of the property at the time of loss
- The cost of repairing or replacing the property with other property of like kind or quality

The policy sets a separate limit of $1,000 for loss to electronic equipment that is not excluded by the policy.

Deductible

The insurer's payment for each covered auto is reduced by any applicable deductible shown in the declarations. Thus, if two of the insured's vehicles collide, two deductibles will apply.

The deductible applicable to comprehensive coverage does not apply to loss by fire or lightning. This exception can be of considerable value to an owner of a fleet of autos that are garaged at the same location and therefore susceptible to total loss by fire. In the absence of this exemption, the insured would have to bear a portion of the loss equal to the amount of the deductible multiplied by the total number of cars destroyed.

BUSINESS AUTO COVERAGE FORM CONDITIONS

Section IV of the Business Auto Coverage Form, Business Auto Conditions, contains all conditions that apply to all coverages under the business auto form.

Some of the conditions in the Business Auto Coverage Form are similar to those found in the CGL form; others are specific to auto insurance. The conditions can be categorized as loss conditions or general conditions.

Loss Conditions

The first five conditions of Section IV of the Business Auto Coverage Form, Business Auto Conditions, are loss conditions:

- Appraisal for Physical Damage Losses
- Duties in the Event of an Accident, Claim, Suit or Loss
- Legal Action Against the Insurer
- Loss Payment—Physical Damage Coverages
- Transfer of Rights Against Others

Appraisal for Physical Damage Losses

If the named insured and the insurer cannot agree on the amount of a covered loss, either may call for an appraisal. Each will then appoint an appraiser, and the appraisers will appoint a "competent and impartial" umpire.

The appraisers then determine actual cash value and the amount of loss payment. Any item on which the appraisers cannot agree is submitted to the umpire, and an award in writing, signed by any two of the three, binds both parties.

Each party pays its own appraiser, and both parties share the cost of the umpire. This procedure applies only to disagreements about the amount of loss, not to coverage disagreements.

Duties in the Event of an Accident, Claim, Suit or Loss

The insured's duties after loss are essentially the same as those imposed by the CGL policy. The named insured must give prompt notice of accident or loss to the insurer or its agent and assist the insurer in obtaining the names of injured persons or witnesses. Also, both the named insured and any other person who seeks liability coverage under the policy (for example, the driver of an insured vehicle) must take these actions:

- Cooperate with the insurer in its investigation and defense of the accident or loss
- Immediately send to the insurer copies of any notices or legal papers received in connection with the accident or loss
- Submit to physical examinations by physicians selected and paid by the insurer as often as the insurer may reasonably request
- Authorize the insurer to obtain medical reports and other medical information

Moreover, no insured can commit the insurer to make any payment either for damages or expenses.

If the claim is for loss or damage to a covered auto, the named insured must take these actions:

- Promptly notify the police if the insured auto or any of its equipment is stolen
- Do what is reasonably necessary to preserve the property from further loss
- Permit the insurer to inspect and appraise the damaged vehicle before it is repaired
- Agree to be examined under oath at the insurer's request and give a signed statement

Legal Action Against the Insurer

No legal action can be brought against the insurer under any coverage until the named insured and the insured bringing the action, if different, have complied with all provisions of the coverage form.

In addition, under the liability coverage, no action can be brought against the insurer until either a court has determined that the insured is liable for the loss or the insurer has agreed in writing that the insured is liable for the loss.

Loss Payment—Physical Damage Coverages

The insurer has three options with regard to damaged or stolen property:

1. Pay to repair or replace the property
2. Return the property at the expense of the insurer and repair any damage caused by theft
3. Keep all of the property and pay an agreed or appraised value

Transfer of Rights Against Others

The insured may have a right to recover a loss from some other party, usually because the other party caused the loss.

If the insurer pays the loss, it is entitled, under this condition, to take over the insured's right of recovery from the other party. This right is referred to as subrogation. The insured must not do anything to impair the insurer's right of recovery and must do everything reasonably necessary to secure and preserve that right.

General Conditions

The last eight conditions of Section IV of the Business Auto Coverage Form, Business Auto Conditions, are general conditions:

- Bankruptcy
- Concealment, Misrepresentation, or Fraud
- Liberalization
- No Benefit to Bailee—Physical Damage Insurance Only
- Other Insurance
- Premium Audit
- Policy Period, Coverage Territory
- Two or More Coverage Forms or Policies Issued by the Insurer

Bankruptcy

Bankruptcy or insolvency of the insured does not relieve the insurer of any of its obligations under the policy.

If the insured is relieved through bankruptcy of any obligation to pay a liability claim, the insurer is still obligated to make payment just as it would have been had the insured remained solvent.

Concealment, Misrepresentation, or Fraud

In the case of fraud by the named insured relative to business auto coverage, the coverage is void.

It is also void if any insured intentionally conceals or misrepresents a material fact about the coverage form, any autos covered, the insured's interest in any covered auto, or a claim under the coverage form.

A material fact is one that would have changed the underwriting decision in some way.

Liberalization

If, during the policy term, the insurer revises the Business Auto Coverage Form to provide more coverage at no increase in premium, the insured's policy will provide that additional coverage, automatically, as of the date the revision becomes effective in the insured's state.

That is, the policy is liberalized (by providing more coverage at no extra cost) when the insurer's revised business auto form becomes effective, rather than on the policy renewal date.

No Benefit to Bailee—Physical Damage Insurance Only

Railroads and other transporters of property sometimes try to gain the benefit of the property owner's insurance by inserting a provision in their bill of lading stating that they are not liable for any loss for which the shipper is reimbursed by insurance. This provision in the bill of lading could invalidate the insurer's right of subrogation against the transporting company. Accordingly, the "no benefit to bailee" condition attempts to preserve the insurer's subrogation rights by stating that the insurer does not recognize any assignment of coverage or any other grant of coverage to any person or organization that holds, stores, or transports property for a fee.

Other Insurance

Business auto coverage may be either primary or excess, depending on the circumstances of the accident or loss.

For any covered vehicle owned by the named insured, the coverage is primary.

For any covered auto not owned by the named insured, the coverage is excess, and the insurance, if any, carried by the owner of the auto is primary.

For purposes of hired auto (symbol 8) physical damage coverage, any auto the named insured leases, hires, rents, or borrows is deemed to be a covered auto owned by the named insured. Such an auto is therefore covered on a primary basis. However, no coverage exists for an auto that is hired or borrowed with a driver.

Coverage for trailers follows the autos to which they are attached. Thus, coverage is excess for a trailer attached to an auto not owned by the named insured, and coverage is primary for a trailer attached to an auto owned by the named insured. The coverage is primary for a covered trailer owned by the named insured when it is not attached to any auto.

Regardless of these provisions, business auto liability coverage is primary for any liability assumed under an insured contract.

If two or more policies of the same level (either excess or primary) apply to the same loss, each policy contributes to the loss in the proportion that its limit bears to the total limits of all policies of its level. See the exhibit "Illustration of Other Insurance Provisions."

Premium Audit

The premium shown on the declarations, which the insured pays at policy inception, is an estimate. The actual premium is determined by a premium audit and based on actual exposures at the end of the policy period.

> ### Illustration of Other Insurance Provisions
>
> To illustrate the Other Insurance provision when two primary policies apply to the same claim, assume that Policy A has a $100,000 limit and Policy B has a $300,000 limit. If the covered amount of the claim was $40,000, Policy A, which has one-fourth of the total limits, would pay $10,000, and Policy B, which has three-fourths of the total limits, would pay $30,000.

[DA02611]

If the final premium is less than the estimate, the named insured gets a refund. If the final premium is greater than the estimate, the named insured must pay the difference.

Policy Period, Coverage Territory

Accidents and losses are covered if they occur during the policy period shown on the declarations and occur within the coverage territory. The coverage territory includes the United States, its territories and possessions, Puerto Rico, and Canada. Losses and accidents involving a covered auto while it is being transported between the covered territories are also covered.

A worldwide coverage territory applies to covered autos of the private passenger type that are leased, hired, rented, or borrowed without a driver for a period of thirty days or less. The insured's liability for damages must be determined in a suit in the U.S., its territories and possessions, Puerto Rico, or Canada, or in a settlement to which the insurer agrees.

Two or More Coverage Forms or Policies Issued by the Insurer

When an accident or a loss is covered by two or more policies issued by the same insurer or affiliated insurers, the maximum amount the insurer or affiliated insurers will be required to pay is the highest limit provided under any one policy.

However, this does not apply to any coverage specifically purchased as excess over business auto coverage, such as a commercial umbrella liability policy.

BUSINESS AUTO COVERAGE FORM ENDORSEMENTS

Insurers use the Business Auto Coverage Form to insure the auto loss exposures of any type of organization other than auto or trailer dealers and motor carriers (businesses that transport the property of others). In addition to providing liability insurance, the Business Auto Coverage Form includes optional provisions.

The liability and physical damage provisions contained in the Business Auto Coverage Form do not meet the needs of all policyholders. In some states, personal injury protection (PIP) (no-fault coverage) or uninsured/underinsured motorists coverage is mandatory. Regardless of legal requirements, many insureds may want to add an optional coverage such as medical payments insurance or may need coverage modifications to tailor coverage to their particular needs.

Any of these optional endorsements can be attached to the Business Auto Coverage Form:

- Employees as Insureds endorsement
- Employee Hired Autos endorsement
- Rental Reimbursement Coverage endorsement
- Stated Amount Insurance endorsement
- Uninsured and underinsured motorists coverage endorsements
- PIP (no-fault) endorsements
- Auto Medical Payments Coverage endorsement
- Individual Named Insured endorsement
- Drive Other Car—Broadened Coverage for Named Individuals endorsement

Employees as Insureds Endorsement

A business auto policy can be extended by endorsement to include employees as insureds while using their own autos on the named insured's behalf. The Employees as Insureds endorsement (CA 99 33) covers any employee of the named insured while using any covered auto that the named insured does not own, hire, or borrow in the named insured's business or personal affairs. (A similar endorsement, Social Service Agencies—Volunteers as Insureds [CA 99 34] is available for covering volunteers of social service agencies.) These endorsements pay in excess of what the employee (or volunteer) can collect under his or her own auto liability insurance. When the endorsement is requested, the insurer often requires the named insured to present evidence that each insured employee (or volunteer) has auto liability insurance in effect with certain minimum limits of insurance.

Employee Hired Autos Endorsement

In many cases, employees rent cars in their own names and use such autos to conduct their employers' business. For example, an employee may rent a car after flying to a distant city to attend a business meeting or convention. Although some insurers might interpret the Business Auto Coverage Form to provide liability coverage for employees while using such autos (as long as the policy includes symbol 1 or 8), other insurers may not, because the auto is rented in the name of the employee and not in the name of the named insured.

An employer that wants to make certain that its employees will be covered when renting autos in their own names to conduct the employer's business can ask the insurer to attach the Employee Hired Autos endorsement (CA 20 54). This endorsement states that an employee of the named insured is an insured while operating an auto rented in that employee's name, with the named insured's permission. However, the employee is covered only while performing duties related to the conduct of the named insured's business. Consequently, if the employee is planning to use the vehicle for strictly personal use, the employee should either have personal auto coverage of his or her own or obtain temporary insurance from the rental company.

Rental Reimbursement Coverage Endorsement

By endorsement, rental reimbursement coverage can be added to the Business Auto Coverage Form. The Rental Reimbursement Coverage endorsement (CA 99 23) pays the cost to rent a temporary substitute auto when a covered auto has been damaged by any covered cause of loss—not just theft. A daily limit and a maximum limit (expressed in terms of both days and money) are selected by the insured and shown in the declarations. Rental reimbursement coverage begins to pay twenty-four hours after the auto was damaged. Reimbursement ends (regardless of when the policy expires) when the lesser of these periods is reached:

- The number of days reasonably required to repair or replace the covered auto
- The number of days shown in the schedule of the endorsement

The amount of payment is limited to the lesser of the necessary expenses actually incurred or the monetary limit applicable to any one day or any one period of disablement.

Stated Amount Insurance Endorsement

In some cases, auto physical damage insurance is modified by endorsement to apply on a stated amount basis. When the Stated Amount Insurance endorsement (CA 99 28) is attached to the policy, the insurer's liability for physical damage loss is the least of these values:

- The actual cash value of the damaged or stolen property as of the time of the loss
- The cost of repairing or replacing the damaged or stolen property with other property of like kind and quality
- The limit of insurance shown for the covered auto in the endorsement's schedule

That is, if the stated amount is less than the amounts described in the first or second item, the insurer will pay no more than the stated amount. This endorsement is mainly used on high-valued, specialized types of vehicles whose cost when new (and actual cash value) may increase over time. The stated amount approach should not be confused with valued coverage, for which the insurer is obligated to pay the agreed value of the property in the event of a total loss.

Uninsured and Underinsured Motorists Coverage Endorsements

Uninsured motorists (UM) coverage provides a source of recovery for occupants of a covered auto or for pedestrians who are injured in an accident caused by an at-fault motorist who does not have bodily injury liability insurance or by a hit-and-run driver. Underinsured motorists coverage (UIM) extends the coverage to situations in which the at-fault motorist has insurance but it is inadequate to pay all of the insured's damages. In many cases, UM coverage and UIM coverage are combined in a single endorsement. In some states, UM coverage also pays for property damage to a covered auto caused by an uninsured motorist.

Subject to the policy limits, the insurer providing UM and/or UIM coverage basically agrees to put its insured in the same position that he or she would have been in if the motorist responsible for the accident had carried adequate auto liability insurance or (in the case of a hit-and-run driver) if the motorist could have been identified. UM/UIM motorists coverage applies only if the uninsured or underinsured motorist is legally liable for the covered person's damages.

The provisions for the UM/UIM endorsements used with the Business Auto Coverage Form differ from state to state. Typically, the coverage applies in excess of what the injured person can collect under a workers compensation law. Nevertheless, organizations frequently purchase the coverage for these reasons:

- Even when workers compensation benefits are payable, they do not always pay all of an injured employee's damages. UM/UIM coverage can provide needed excess coverage for these employees.

- Employees may be injured by an uninsured motorist while driving a company auto for personal use or under other circumstances that do not qualify for workers compensation.

- Executive officers or other employees who are provided with company cars for personal use may have no other auto insurance and therefore want UM/UIM coverage for themselves, their family members, and other persons who occupy such autos.

- The insured organization may transport customers or other persons who are not covered by workers compensation.
- The named insured may be a sole proprietor who has chosen not to be covered by workers compensation.

Some states make UM/UIM coverage compulsory, while others make only UM coverage compulsory.

Personal Injury Protection (No-Fault) Endorsements

Many states either require auto owners to carry PIP coverage or require insurers to offer the coverage to all motorists, who may either buy it or reject it. PIP varies from state to state but typically provides first-party benefits for medical expense, loss of income, loss of services, and funeral expenses resulting from bodily injury to occupants of a covered auto because of an auto accident. PIP is also called no-fault coverage because it pays regardless of which party was at fault in the accident.

The Business Auto Coverage Form contains no coverage provisions for PIP. In states where no-fault insurance applies, a state-specific endorsement is used to add the coverage to a policy, and appropriate symbols should be selected on the Business Auto Coverage Form for PIP coverage.

Auto Medical Payments Coverage Endorsement

The Auto Medical Payments Coverage endorsement (CA 99 03) provides a prompt source of medical expense reimbursement for the named insured and other persons injured in auto accidents. Auto medical payments coverage applies regardless of who is at fault in an accident and is subject to a relatively low limit of insurance.

Auto medical payments coverage is provided for the benefit of the named insured (if an individual) and his or her family members while occupying any auto or when struck by an auto as pedestrians. Auto medical payments coverage also applies to anyone else occupying a covered auto or a temporary substitute for a covered auto.

Many organizations purchase auto medical payments coverage on private passenger autos furnished to the organization's executives or key employees, as well as on autos used to transport customers of the organization and other persons who are not employees of the named insured.

Auto medical payments coverage can also be signaled by entering the appropriate symbol or symbols (such as 2, 3, or 7) next to "Auto Medical Payments" in the Business Auto Declarations. Most insurers do not permit symbols 1 or 9 to be used for auto medical payments coverage.

Individual Named Insured Endorsement

When the named insured under a Business Auto Coverage Form is a sole proprietor, the policy can be amended by endorsement to provide coverages that the named insured and his or her family members would have if they were covered under the Personal Auto Policy. More specifically, the Individual Named Insured endorsement (CA 99 17) performs these functions:

- If the policy provides liability coverage on a private passenger auto owned by the named insured, the endorsement will extend liability coverage to (1) resident relatives while using any auto the named insured owns of the private passenger type that is a covered auto for liability coverage and (2) the named insured and resident relatives while using autos that are not owned by them or furnished or available for their regular use.

- If the policy provides physical damage coverage on a private passenger auto owned by the named insured, the endorsement will also cover, for purposes of physical damage coverage, a "non-owned auto," defined as a private passenger auto that is not owned by or furnished or available for the regular use of the named insured or any resident relative while such auto is in the custody of or being operated by the named insured or any family member. If, for example, the named insured's spouse borrows a neighbor's car and damages the car in a collision, the policy will cover the loss—assuming the policy provides collision coverage on a private passenger auto owned by the named insured.

- The endorsement eliminates the Fellow Employee exclusion regarding bodily injury to fellow employees of the named insured or any resident relatives of the named insured.

Drive Other Car—Broadened Coverage for Named Individuals Endorsement

Many employers provide company cars to their executive officers or other employees. As long as these cars are covered autos under the employer's business auto insurance, that insurance will cover the officers and employees and their family members while driving these cars for business or personal use.

A problem that sometimes arises with such arrangements is that an officer or employee with a company car does not own a car and therefore does not carry any personal auto insurance of his or her own. If the officer or employee (or one of his or her family members) drives a car that is not covered under the employer's policy, he or she will not be covered while driving that other car.

For example, assume that Anne normally drives a company car provided by her employer and has no other auto insurance. If Anne borrows a neighbor's car for personal use, her employer's policy will not cover her while she uses that car. If the owner of the car carries no insurance (or an inadequate amount of insurance), Anne would be uninsured (or underinsured) for an accident resulting from her use of the car.

The Drive Other Car—Broadened Coverage for Named Individuals endorsement (CA 99 10) addresses this problem. The endorsement provides liability insurance for the individual named in the endorsement and his or her spouse while using autos that they do not own. For additional premium amounts, the endorsement can be extended to provide medical payments; comprehensive coverage and/or collision coverage, subject to the deductible(s) stated in the endorsement Schedule; uninsured motorists coverage; and underinsured motorists coverage on such autos.

In some states that have no-fault auto laws, a broadened PIP coverage endorsement may be added. These endorsements provide first-party coverage for the individual(s) named in the endorsement; therefore, coverage would be provided when a named individual drives a car owned by another.

The Individual Named Insured endorsement and the Drive Other Car— Broadened Coverage for Named Individuals endorsement are commonly confused with each other and with the Employees as Insureds and Employee Hired Autos endorsements. The exhibit provides a comparison of these four endorsements that may be helpful in distinguishing among them. See the exhibit "Comparison of Four Commonly Confused Business Auto Endorsements."

Comparison of Four Commonly Confused Business Auto Endorsements

Endorsement	Persons Covered	Why Needed	Coverages Affected
Employees as Insureds CA 99 33	Employees of the named insured	To cover employees while driving their own cars on the named insured's business	Liability only
Employee Hired Autos CA 20 54	Employees of the named insured	To cover employees while operating autos rented in the employees' names while on the named insured's business	Liability Physical damage
Individual Named Insured CA 99 17	Individual named insureds and their resident relatives	To supplement business auto coverage with coverages comparable to those of the Personal Auto Policy	Liability Physical damage
Drive Other Car— Broadened Coverage for Named Individuals CA 99 10	Executive officers or other employees of the named insured who have been provided with company cars and who are named in the endorsement	To cover these persons (and their spouses) while they are driving autos they rent or borrow from others (other than the covered autos they are provided by their employer)	Liability Physical damage Medical payments Uninsured motorists Underinsured motorists

[DA04826]

With the 2010 revision of the Business Auto Coverage Form, ISO also introduced some new endorsements. See the exhibit "Noteworthy Endorsements Introduced With the 2010 ISO Business Auto Coverage Form."

Noteworthy Endorsements Introduced With the 2010 ISO Business Auto Coverage Form

CA 04 44 Waiver of Subrogation—This endorsement amends the subrogation condition so that it does not apply to the entity listed in the endorsement if subrogation is waived before the accident or loss under a contract with the entity.

CA 23 98 Trailer Interchange Coverage—This endorsement allows trailer interchange coverage to be added to the Business Auto Coverage Form for a private carrier that enters into trailer interchange agreements and wants to obtain this coverage.

CA 04 45 Golf Carts and Low–Speed Vehicles—This endorsement allows coverage for golf carts and other low-speed vehicles that are not subject to financial responsibility or other motor vehicle insurance laws and thus would not otherwise meet the definition of "auto" in ISO commercial auto forms.

[DA06609]

BUSINESS AUTO COVERAGE FORM CASE STUDY

Owning and operating commercial vehicles creates exposures to losses that are potentially severe and unavoidable for most commercial businesses. Knowing how to apply commercial auto insurance coverages to address these exposures is a necessary skill for an insurance professional. That skill can be taught through the use of a case study.

The Business Auto Coverage Form (BAC) is the principal form used to provide organizations with business auto insurance. A case study will assist insurance professionals in understanding how this form provides and excludes coverages for commercial auto loss exposures.

Case Facts

Quipson is a corporation that is a wholesaler of eye care products. It operates in most of the United States and Canada and has a large fleet that is used in the delivery of its products. Quipson and its fleet are insured under a BAC that was renewed two months ago. See the exhibit "Relevant Provisions of Quipson's Declarations Pages."

Relevant Provisions of Quipson's Declarations Pages

Coverages	Covered Auto Designation Symbols	Description of Covered Auto Designation Symbols	Limits or Deductibles
Liability	1	Any "Auto"	$500,000 limit
Physical Damage Collision Coverage	7, 8	7. Specifically described "Autos"— Only those "autos" described in Item Three of the Declarations for which a premium charge is shown (and for Liability Coverage any "trailers" you don't own while attached to any power unit described in Item Three).	$1,000 deductible
		8. Hired Autos" Only— Only those "autos" you lease, hire, rent or borrow. This does not include any "auto" you lease, hire, rent or borrow from any of your "employees", partners (if you are a partnership), members (if you are a limited liability company) or members of their households.	

[DA06787]

Within the first two months of the inception date of the policy, a box truck owned and operated by Quipson was involved in a serious accident. At the time of the accident, the truck was listed on the policy schedule and was transporting $12,000 worth of contact lens inventory in Toronto. While on his cell phone, the employee driver for Quipson failed to negotiate a curve, resulting in an overturn of the vehicle.

Assuming compliance with all relevant Canadian laws, these claims resulted:

- $23,000 in damages to the truck.
- $100,000 in liability for damage to a public fire hydrant and related municipal property.
- $200,000 in liability for bodily injury sustained by an employee passenger. The employee passenger sued both Quipson and the driver.
- $7,500 in damages to the inventory on the truck.
- $2,200 in cleanup costs related to spillage of the truck's fuel.

The employee driver promptly reported the accident to the insurance and risk manager of the corporation, who reported it to the BAC insurer in a timely manner. The employee has been cooperative in the insurer's investigation of the accident.

Case Analysis Tools

As with the declarations pages of most policy types, the BAC declarations pages indicate the named insured, the effective dates of the policy, the limits of liability, and the deductibles. The BAC declarations pages also include covered auto designation symbols that state which autos (for example, owned or nonowned) are covered for which coverage (for instance, liability or physical damage). The symbol can determine whether a particular claim is covered.

The unendorsed BAC is the primary reference tool for coverage determination. Certain portions of the policy are highlighted in the Determination of Coverage section to better address the application of the policy to the circumstances of each claim.

The answers to these questions will help determine whether each of the described claims in the case is covered by the BAC and, if so, for what amount:

- Do the declarations pages confirm that coverage applies to the accident, which includes addressing issues such as whether the accident occurred during the policy period and whether it involved a covered auto?
- Is coverage triggered by one or more of the BAC insuring agreements?
- Do the circumstances of each claim meet applicable policy conditions?
- Do any exclusions apply that would limit or eliminate coverage for a claim?
- What is the amount payable for each claim?

Determination of Coverage

This case presents several coverage concerns. One concern is that the truck was operating outside the U.S. The BAC was written in the U.S., and may have a territorial limitation that suspends coverage when a covered auto is operated in another country.

Another concern is the damage to the truck. The policy should be examined to determine if the covered auto symbol for collision coverage includes the truck. Damage to the goods that were being transported in the truck raises another concern as coverage for this loss may be excluded. The cleanup of pollutants is discussed in the insuring agreement of Section II—Liability Coverage and Section V—Definitions.

Finally, two parties are involved in lawsuits brought by the employee passenger. The lawsuits may be covered by a workers compensation policy and therefore excluded in the BAC.

Do the Declarations Pages Confirm That Coverage Applies to the Accident?

The accident occurred within the first two months of coverage, as confirmed by review of the declarations pages, meaning that the policy was in effect at the time of the loss. Also, the BAC declarations pages should show the vehicle in question (the box truck) on the vehicle schedule; therefore, it is covered by symbol 7 for collision damage as a specifically described auto. For liability purposes, symbol 1 is noted for any auto, whether owned or scheduled or not.

In view of the lawsuits that have been asserted, the liability limit is a concern as it may be too low. The $500,000 limit of liability, as noted in the declarations pages, is available.

Is Coverage Triggered by One or More of the BAC Insuring Agreements?

The insuring agreements of the physical damage (collision) and liability coverages need to be reviewed.

The physical damage portion covers a "loss" to a "covered auto," but not the contents in the auto. Therefore, coverage will not be provided for the $7,500 in damages to the inventory that was in the truck. Inland marine coverage is one example of coverage that would have provided protection for the contents of the truck.

In the liability portion of the policy, the insurer agrees to be responsible for the insured's legal liability, including defense costs resulting from an accident involving bodily injury and property damage. Also under the liability portion, coverage exists for "covered pollution cost or expense" to pay for the fuel that escaped the truck and caused pollution. That phrase is clarified in the definitions section of the BAC to both exclude and grant some coverages. The section states that "'Covered pollution cost or expense' does not include any costs or expense arising out of the actual, alleged or threatened discharge, dispersal, seepage, migration, release or escape of 'pollutants'."

This language would exclude coverage for the spilled fuel. However, later in the same section there is an exception to the exclusion which states the "... above does not apply to fuels, lubricants, fluids, exhaust gases or other similar 'pollutants' that are needed for or result from the normal electrical, hydraulic, or mechanical functioning of the covered 'auto' or its parts...."

Another definition that plays a key role in the assessment of coverage in this case is the one for "coverage territory." Its definition includes not only the U.S., but also Canada. Therefore, the fact that the truck was operating in Toronto at the time of the loss does not prohibit coverage under the BAC.

Do the Circumstances of Each Claim Meet Applicable Policy Conditions?

The case facts indicate that the employee driver and Quipson have complied with the relevant policy conditions to date by promptly reporting the accident to the insurance and risk manager of Quipson, who, in turn, notified the BAC insurer without delay. The employee driver has also cooperated in the insurer's investigation of the accident. There is no indication that any policy conditions have not been met.

Do Any Exclusions Apply That Would Limit or Eliminate Coverage for a Claim?

The liability exclusions section contains an exclusion for suits brought against a fellow employee; therefore, the suit brought against the employee driver by the employee passenger is excluded. There are also exclusive remedy statutes that are intended to preclude the ability of an employee who is collecting workers compensation benefits from suing his employer and/or another employee. Some states, however, permit such fellow employee actions. In those states, the Fellow Employee Coverage (CA 20 55) may be of value.

There is also an Employers Liability exclusion in Section II that eliminates coverage for employee-related suits due to the exclusive remedy statutes. In addition, the employer would have employers liability insurance under its workers compensation policy for those rare tort actions that succeed against an employer, either directly or indirectly.

An important definition in Section V relates to the pollution cleanup. The definition explains that the exclusion, which is referenced within the definition, does not apply (in other words, coverage is provided) to the spillage of fuel that is needed to operate the vehicle if the spillage arises from an accident.

Determination of Amounts Payable

These are the amounts payable by the BAC insurer for each claim:

- $23,000 in damages to the truck. This loss is covered under the physical damage section of the BAC, as the truck was a covered auto driven by an insured and was involved in an accident. However, the collision coverage has a $1,000 deductible. Therefore, the amount payable to the named insured for the physical damage to the truck is $22,000.

- $100,000 in liability for damage to a public fire hydrant and related municipal property. This is covered under the liability section of the BAC, which has a $500,000 limit of liability. This limit is more than enough to pay this claim in full, including defense costs, if needed.

- $200,000 in liability for bodily injury sustained by an employee passenger. The employee passenger sued both Quipson and the driver. The BAC excludes coverage for a suit by one employee against a fellow employee and for damages that should be paid by workers compensation. Therefore, the BAC will not pay for this loss or defend the suit.

- $7,500 in damages to the inventory on the truck. Per the insuring agreement of Section III—Physical Damage Coverage, this is not covered, so no damages are payable for this claim under the policy.

- $2,200 in cleanup costs related to spillage of the truck's fuel. Pollution is generally excluded from coverage; however, there is an exception to the exclusion that allows this claim to be paid from Section II—Liability Coverage, which has a $500,000 limit of liability. Even with the $100,000 claim for damage to a public fire hydrant and related municipal property—also payable from this same $500,000 limit—enough of the limit remains to pay this claim in full.

Correct Answers to Quipson BAC Coverage Case

- The collision damage to the truck is covered: $23,000 minus $1,000 deductible, or $22,000 payable.

- The $100,000 in property damage liability, plus legal defense, is covered.

- The suit brought by the employee passenger against the employee driver and Quipson is excluded.

- The damage to the inventory on the truck is excluded.

- The $2,200 in cleanup costs for the truck's fuel spill is covered because the spill resulted from the accident.

[DA06740]

SUMMARY

Commercial property and general liability forms exclude auto loss exposures. Depending on the business type, commercial auto loss exposures can be covered under ISO's Business Auto Coverage Form, Garage Coverage Form, or Motor Carrier Coverage Form.

The auto liability exposure is the possibility that the organization may have to defend itself against, and perhaps pay damages as a result of, suits alleging negligent ownership, maintenance, or use of autos. Liability can arise from owned autos, hired or borrowed autos, or employees' autos operated on behalf of the organization. In addition, one organization may assume by contract the auto liability of another organization. Some auto businesses, such as dealers and repair shops, have a bailee liability exposure for customers' autos.

The Business Auto Coverage Form, together with business auto declarations and any applicable endorsements, can be included in a commercial package policy or issued in a monoline policy. The business auto form contains five sections. Section I contains ten descriptions of covered auto symbols. These symbols are entered in a schedule in the declarations to indicate which autos are covered for each coverage selected.

Section II of the Business Auto Coverage Form contains the provisions for auto liability insurance, including a coverage agreement, a definition of who is insured, coverage extensions, exclusions, and a limit of insurance provision.

Section III of the Business Auto Coverage Form contains four optional insuring agreements for auto physical damage insurance: collision, comprehensive, specified causes of loss, and towing and labor. Other provisions of Section III include coverage extensions, exclusions, a limit of insurance clause, and a deductible clause.

Section IV of the Business Auto Coverage Form, Business Auto Conditions, contains all conditions that apply to all coverages under the Business Auto Form. These can be categorized as loss conditions and general conditions.

The Business Auto Coverage Form can be modified by these common endorsements:

- Employees as Insureds endorsement
- Employee Hired Autos endorsement
- Rental Reimbursement Coverage endorsement
- Stated Amount Insurance endorsement
- Uninsured and underinsured motorists coverage endorsements
- Personal injury protection (PIP) (no-fault) endorsements
- Auto Medical Payments Coverage endorsement
- Individual Named Insured endorsement
- Drive Other Car—Broadened Coverage for Named Individuals endorsement

Taking a systematic approach to reviewing the Business Auto Coverage Form will lead to a more consistent and accurate determination of coverage in claim situations. Such an approach can require answering questions such as these:

- Do the declarations pages confirm that coverage applies to the accident? This includes addressing issues such as whether the accident occurred during the policy period and whether it involved a covered auto.
- Is coverage triggered by one or more of the BAC insuring agreements?
- Do the circumstances of each claim meet applicable policy conditions?
- Do any exclusions apply that would limit or eliminate coverage for a claim?
- What is the amount payable for each claim?

These questions will help focus the review of the facts and the policy on the relevant issues.

ASSIGNMENT NOTE

1.   Copyright, Insurance Services Office, Inc., 2009.

Direct Your Learning ▶▶

Garage and Motor Carrier Insurance

Educational Objectives

After learning the content of this assignment, you should be able to:

▷ Identify the types of businesses that are eligible for the Garage Coverage Form under ISO Commercial Lines Manual rules.

▷ Explain what is covered and what is excluded by each of the following sections of the Garage Coverage Form:

- Liability

- Garagekeepers

- Physical damage

▷ Summarize the provisions of each of the following endorsements or options of the Garage Coverage Form:

- Broad Form Products Coverage

- Broadened Coverage—Garages

- Garage Locations and Operations Medical Payments Coverage

- Garagekeepers Direct Coverage Options

- False Pretense Coverage

- Dealers Driveaway Collision Coverage

- Audio, Visual and Data Electronic Equipment Coverage Added Limits

▷ Explain whether, and for how much, the Garage Coverage Form and related endorsements would cover a described claim.

▷ Explain how the Motor Carrier Coverage Form differs from the Business Auto Coverage Form.

Garage and Motor Carrier Insurance

GARAGE COVERAGE FORM

Although the Business Auto Coverage Form meets the auto insurance needs of most organizations, some businesses have such unique auto insurance needs that separate forms have been developed for insuring them. One such form, developed by Insurance Services Office, Inc. (ISO), is the Garage Coverage Form.

General liability and auto liability exposures of auto dealers are closely interrelated and sometimes difficult to separate because these businesses involve the sale and servicing of autos. Accordingly, the **Garage Coverage Form** (CA 00 05) provides the equivalent of commercial general liability insurance and business auto insurance in a single coverage form, an approach that prevents coverage gaps and disputes that might occur if an auto dealer had separate general liability and auto policies.

In addition to combining general liability and auto coverages, the Garage Coverage Form includes provisions that address loss exposures of auto dealers.

Examples of such provisions include these:

- Garagekeepers coverage, which insures loss to customers' autos in the care, custody, or control of the insured
- Value reporting provisions for determining premiums for physical damage coverage on an auto dealer's fluctuating inventory of autos

These and other ways in which the Garage Coverage Form (2010 edition) differs from the Business Auto Coverage Form and the Commercial General Liability Coverage Form may be examined in the context of the three main coverages of the Garage Coverage Form:

- Liability Coverage
- Garagekeepers Coverage
- Physical Damage Coverage

Under ISO *Commercial Lines Manual* (CLM) rules, the only organizations that are eligible for the Garage Coverage Form are franchised and nonfranchised auto and trailer dealers. A franchised dealer is a dealer that is authorized by one or more auto manufacturers (through a franchise agreement) to sell their autos under the manufacturers' names and trademarks. A nonfranchised dealer, in contrast, has no franchise agreement with an auto manufacturer and typically sells used vehicles. The term "auto and trailer dealers" is interpreted

Garage Coverage Form
The coverage form, filed by ISO, that covers the commercial auto and general liability exposures of auto and trailer dealers.

broadly for eligibility purposes. All of these ISO classification descriptions are eligible for the Garage Coverage Form:

- Franchised private passenger auto dealer
- Franchised truck or truck-tractor dealer
- Franchised motorcycle dealer, including all two-wheeled cycle vehicles
- Franchised recreational vehicle dealer
- Other franchised self-propelled land motor vehicle dealer
- Nonfranchised dealer
- Franchised and nonfranchised residence trailer dealers
- Franchised and nonfranchised commercial trailer dealers

Before ISO changed the eligibility rule for the Garage Coverage Form in 2002, auto service businesses (such as repair shops, service stations, auto detailing shops, parking lots, and other garage businesses) were also eligible for this form.

AUTO COVERAGE UNDER THE GARAGE COVERAGE FORM

The exposures of general liability, bailee liability, and auto liability are often intertwined in organizations that sell, service, park, and/or store autos. Their products, services, and inventory are mobile—they often move between the business premises and public streets. In addition to an organization's employees driving its autos, a customer may drive an auto owned by the organization or an employee may drive an auto owned by a customer. Also, bailee exposure for the vehicles in the care, custody, or control of the organization while being serviced by it should be insured.

In 1978, to meet the increasing liability needs auto dealers, trailer dealers, and auto service operations face, Insurance Services Office (ISO) introduced its garage policy, which included three coverages under one form:

- Liability Coverage
- Garagekeepers Coverage (covering damage to customers' autos in the insured's care, custody, or control)
- Physical Damage Coverage (with a reporting form option for auto dealers' inventories)

ISO's Garage Coverage Form covers the commercial auto and the general liability exposures of auto and trailer dealers using a modular format that allows it to be written as either a monoline policy or part of a commercial package policy. Auto and trailer dealers include repair shops, service stations, storage garages, public parking facilities, and tow truck operators.

Effective July 2002, ISO removed auto service operations from the eligibility rules. As a result, insurers that use ISO forms and rules insure only auto and trailer dealers under the Garage Coverage Form. They use the Commercial General Liability (CGL) Coverage and Business Auto Coverage forms to insure auto service operations. Eligible auto and trailer dealers may be either franchised (for example, an authorized dealer by the manufacturer) or non-franchised (such as a used car dealer).

This discussion focuses on ISO's Garage Coverage Form, edition CA 00 05 03 10, and the unique aspects of its six sections in relationship to the CGL and business auto forms:

- Section I—Covered Autos
- Section II—Liability Coverage
- Section III—Garagekeepers Coverage
- Section IV—Physical Damage Coverage
- Section V—Garage Conditions
- Section VI—Definitions

Section I—Covered Autos

As in the business auto policy, the garage form uses numerical symbols to describe the coverage provided. The symbol indicates the type of auto being covered. For each coverage purchased, the insured selects the appropriate symbol or symbols—more than one symbol can be included on the declarations page. If there is no symbol shown for the coverage, the coverage does not apply.

There are eleven symbols for the garage form. Symbols 21 through 29 are similar to the business auto policy symbols 1 through 9. Symbols 30 and 31 are unique to the garage form. See the exhibit "Garage Coverage Symbols."

Garage Coverage Symbols

21	Any "Auto"	Broadest coverage—includes owned, nonowned, private passenger, commercial, and newly acquired
22	Owned "Autos" Only	Includes owned private passenger, commercial, and newly acquired, but does not include nonowned autos
23	Owned Private Passenger "Autos" Only	Includes owned private passenger and newly acquired private passenger, but does not include owned commercial and nonowned autos
24	Owned "Autos" Other Than Private Passenger "Autos" Only	Includes owned commercial and newly acquired commercial, but does not include owned private passenger and nonowned autos
25	Owned "Autos" Subject to No-fault	Includes owned private passenger, commercial and newly acquired autos that are required by law to have no-fault coverage, but does not include nonowned autos
26	Owned "Autos" Subject To A Compulsory Uninsured Motorist Law	Includes owned private passenger, commercial and newly acquired autos that are required by law to have uninsured motorist coverage, but does not include nonowned autos
27	Specifically Described "Autos"	Each auto separately listed on the declarations page
28	Hired "Autos" Only	Includes leased, hired, rented, or borrowed autos; does not include autos of employees, partners, members, or household members
29	Nonowned "Autos" Used In Your Garage Business	Includes autos not owned, leased, hired, rented, or borrowed; includes autos owned by employees, partners, members, or household members
30	"Autos" Left With You For Service, Repair, Storage Or Safekeeping	Includes customers' autos, which includes autos of employees and household members who pay for services performed
31	Dealers "Autos" (Physical Damage Coverages)	Any autos and interests in autos described on declarations page

[DA_06721]

Section II—Liability Coverage

The garage form contains two distinct liability insuring agreements: Garage Operations—Other Than Covered Autos and Garage Operations—Covered Autos. These agreements relate to two different aspects of "garage operations" as defined in the form:

- The first insuring agreement covers damages and related defense costs for bodily injury and property damage liability arising out of garage operations other than the ownership, maintenance, or use of covered autos.

- The second insuring agreement covers liability arising out of garage operations involving covered autos and covers both damages for bodily injury and property damage and "covered pollution cost or expense" arising out of the ownership, maintenance, or use of covered autos. The agreement also covers the cost of defending the insured against suits alleging bodily injury, property damage, or pollution costs covered under the policy.

The first agreement is comparable to but not as broad as in the CGL form (occurrence version). Under the Garage Operations—Other Than Covered Autos insuring agreement, coverage is not provided for bodily injury or property damage for which the insured is legally responsible arising from the ownership, maintenance, or use of covered autos. As in the CGL, a per occurrence limit and an aggregate limit apply.

The second agreement is comparable to the agreement in the business auto form and includes a per occurrence limit, with no aggregate limit.

The garage form addresses customers, as listed under Who Is An Insured. Different descriptions apply to each of the two insuring agreements. A wider range of persons and organizations is insured for garage operations involving covered autos than for garage operations other than covered autos. A customer's limits of insurance under either form will not exceed the minimum limits required by the state. A customer who has no other available insurance is only covered up to the limit required by the state's compulsory insurance or financial responsibility law, even if that is less than the garage liability limit.

When a customer has insurance with limits that are less than those required by the state's compulsory insurance or financial responsibility law, under the garage form, even if the customer's limits are less than the garage liability limit, the customer will only receive the difference in limits. For an additional premium, insureds can cover customers for the full limit of insurance. In all cases, the garage business insured will have the full limits of insurance available for their liability in an accident involving a customer.

Garage liability coverage is restricted to liability arising out of "garage operations." If the insured opens a new business that is not a garage and is not incidental to the existing garage business, it will not be covered by garage liability coverage. In contrast, the CGL coverage form automatically covers any additional type of business that the insured may enter into during the policy period.

Garage liability coverage for products is virtually identical to that provided under the CGL coverage form, provided the product was made or sold in a garage business. In most states, the auto is considered a dangerous instrument, and the entity that releases it into the stream of commerce last is responsible. Therefore, an auto dealer who has done nothing to the vehicle except sell it can be brought into a lawsuit alone or with the manufacturer.

Garage liability coverage provides completed operations insurance, subject to a $100 deductible. For example, a garage repaired the brakes on Charlie's auto but did so improperly. Three days later, while Charlie was driving the vehicle, the brakes failed, resulting in damage to Charlie's vehicle, bodily injury to Charlie, and damage to a homeowner's fence and yard. The costs for the bodily injury, the fence, the yard, and the repairs to Charlie's car, minus the cost of the brakes, would be covered, subject to a $100 deductible.

The garage liability section contains an auto liability coverage exclusion not found in the business auto form that eliminates liability coverage for any covered auto while leased or rented to others. An exception to the exclusion allows coverage when the auto is rented to a customer for use while the customer has left an auto with the insured for service. The named insured can purchase an endorsement to provide coverage for autos it rents to persons other than customers.

The exclusion for damages arising from watercraft and aircraft has only one exception and that is for watercraft while on shore at the premises where the garage operations are conducted. No restrictions apply to craft or motor size. This differs from the CGL exclusion.

Section III—Garagekeepers Coverage

Garagekeepers Coverage covers the insured's bailee liability for damage by a covered cause of loss to autos and their equipment while left in the insured's care, custody, or control while the insured is attending, servicing, repairing, parking, or storing the autos in the garage operation. Section II—Liability Coverage has a specific exclusion for damage to autos in the insured's care, custody, or control. This coverage fills that gap.

The coverages for customers' autos from which the insured may select include these:

- Comprehensive
- Specified causes of loss (only three causes)
- Fire, lightning, or explosion
- Theft
- Mischief or vandalism
- Collision

As with other types of liability insurance, Garagekeepers Coverage also pays the cost of defending the insured against suits alleging covered losses. For the coverage to apply, the insured must be legally liable for the damages. For example, a customer parked his auto next to the garage's service area after hours, to be serviced the next day, and he dropped his keys into the appropriate lock box. During the night, lightning struck the building in the service area causing a large fire that destroyed the building, as well as eight customers' autos inside and the customer's auto parked next to the service area. The garage was not responsible for the lightning and resulting fire that damaged the customer's auto; therefore, it is not legally responsible and the customer's damages would not be paid under this coverage.

For an additional premium, Garagekeepers Coverage can be extended to cover loss to customers' autos regardless of whether the insured is legally liable. This coverage is known as direct coverage. It allows a garage business to preserve customer goodwill by compensating its customers for their losses even if the garage has no legal obligation to do so. No endorsement is required. The insured marks a box in the garage declarations form to make its election. Two options are available: direct excess and direct primary.

The direct excess coverage option contains a two-tiered approach. Under the first approach, coverage applies, based on legal liability for any collectible insurance applicable to the auto. Under the second approach, excess coverage applies after payment of any other collectible insurance, with no regard for legal liability for the damages.

For example, Bob took his auto to ABC Dealer for servicing. ABC Dealer has garagekeepers liability comprehensive coverage. Bob has a personal auto policy with a $500 other-than-collision deductible. While the auto is at ABC, lightning strikes the service building, resulting in a significant fire. Bob's auto sustains $1,200 in damages. ABC is not legally liable for the damages, so Bob's auto policy pays $700 ($1,200 in damages minus $500 deductible), leaving $500 uncollectible from Bob's policy. The second tier of the direct excess coverage ignores legal liability, so ABC's garagekeepers policy pays the remaining $500. If Bob did not have collectible insurance, then the entire loss would have been covered under the second tier.

The direct primary coverage option applies without regard to legal liability and on a primary basis, not as excess coverage. In Bob's lightning damage case, had ABC Dealer elected direct primary coverage, its policy would have paid all of Bob's fire damages and Bob would not have placed a claim with his insurer.

This coverage has a minimum deductible of $100 and a maximum deductible per occurrence. When the insurer makes full payment to the customer, the insurer is entitled to promptly collect the deductible from the named insured.

This coverage excludes losses resulting from theft or conversion by the insured, employees, or shareholders; defective parts or materials; and faulty work of the insured. Also excluded are tapes, records, and sound reproducing devices not permanently installed or attached. This exposure can be addressed by endorsement; however, devices that detect auto speeds (such as radar detectors) are not covered. Losses resulting from war and other military actions are excluded.

Garagekeepers Coverage is appropriate for nondealer auto service operations and some restaurants, hospitals, or other organizations that offer valet parking to customers or patients. Although these types of organizations are not eligible for the garage coverage form, they can obtain Garagekeepers Coverage by endorsement to the business auto form.

Section IV—Physical Damage Coverage

Garage physical damage insurance provides the collision and comprehensive or specified causes of loss coverages that are available under the business auto form. These specified causes of loss are more extensive than the causes of loss under the Garagekeepers Coverage:

- Fire, lightning, or explosion
- Theft
- Windstorm, hail, or earthquake
- Flood
- Mischief or vandalism
- Sinking, burning, collision, or derailment of any conveyance transporting the covered "auto"

Garage physical damage insurance is subject to many of the same provisions as business auto physical damage insurance; however, no towing coverage is included and, under the coverage extension, no transportation expenses are included. Garage operations often have their own towing equipment and have many vehicles; therefore, they have no need for these two coverages.

Values

Because a dealer turns over its inventory rapidly, it is impractical to individually rate each auto held for sale. Autos held for sale by a dealer are insured in the aggregate, subject to a single overall limit. Physical damage premiums are based on the total value of covered autos. The insurer makes entries in a designated section of the garage declarations to indicate the types of autos (new, used, or demonstrator) covered and the interests covered (owned, financed, or consignment).

The value of the vehicles on a dealer's lot may fluctuate widely from month to month. To assist dealers in obtaining appropriate amounts of insurance, the garage form offers a reporting provision on a quarterly or monthly basis. The advantage is that the premium is based on actual values rather than an overall limit. The disadvantage is that reports must be submitted to the insurer on a timely basis to avoid penalties for non-reporting or under-reporting values.

A dealer can elect a non-reporting premium basis. The advantage is that no reports are required. But the limit selected must be high enough to cover the highest inventory for any day of the year, or penalties will apply. Therefore, the disadvantage is that the dealer can overpay for the coverage based on the values actually at risk on any given day.

A deductible may apply to loss caused by any covered peril or only to loss caused by theft, vandalism, or mischief. The insured may also elect a maximum deductible per occurrence.

Exclusions

Garage physical damage insurance contains several exclusions that are not found in the business auto form.

Loss to a covered auto that is leased or rented to others is excluded, except if the covered auto is rented to a customer whose auto is being serviced or repaired. This resembles an exclusion in Section II—Liability Coverage.

The false pretense exclusion eliminates coverage for loss to a covered auto resulting from someone causing the named insured to voluntarily part with the auto by trick, scheme, or other false pretense. For example, a person comes to a dealership to buy an auto and takes one for a test drive but never returns it. The dealer has voluntarily allowed the person to drive the auto off the premises. Because of the dealer's voluntary actions, the auto is not considered stolen under the law and cannot be reported to the police as a theft. If a salesperson had accompanied the customer on the test drive and the customer had pushed the salesperson out of the car and taken off with it, it would be considered a stolen auto and the false pretense exclusion would not apply because the dealer did not voluntarily part with the vehicle. This exclusion encourages the dealer to establish proper procedures, verifications, and loss control measures.

A second part of the false pretense exclusion eliminates coverage for an auto that the insured has acquired from a seller who did not have legal title. When the rightful owner makes claim for the auto, the insured cannot recover for the loss under Physical Damage Coverage.

The named insured's expected profit is excluded from coverage, including loss of market or resale value, and diminution in value. Expected profit can be a factor when the dealer repairs damage to the covered autos. For new vehicles, each state has disclosure rules concerning vehicle repairs. When repairs to a new vehicle are required to be disclosed, the sale value of the vehicle may be reduced.

Loss to any auto displayed or stored at a location not shown in the declarations is excluded, if the loss occurs more than forty-five days after the named insured began using that location. Consequently, a dealer can take autos to an auto show in the local mall or display them at a charity event, as long as the autos are returned to a location stated in the declarations page in less than forty-five days.

Another exclusion eliminates collision coverage for any covered auto while it is being driven or transported from the point of purchase or distribution to its destination, if the two locations are more than fifty road miles apart. Because this exposure can be significant by today's standards, insurers do not cover such collision without assessing the risk and charging an appropriate additional premium. The coverage may be added by attaching an endorsement.

Section V—Garage Conditions

The conditions of the garage form are virtually identical to those of the business auto form. The garage form contains five Loss Conditions that apply in addition to the Common Policy Conditions and eight General Conditions. The wording and provisions of these conditions is consistent with policy conditions in other property and liability coverage forms. See the exhibit "Garage Form Conditions."

Garage Form Conditions

Loss Conditions

- Appraisal
- Insured's duties in the event of accident, claim, suit, or loss
- Legal action against the insurer
- Loss payment for physical damage coverages
- Transfer of rights of recovery (subrogation)

General Conditions

- Bankruptcy
- Concealment, misrepresentation, or fraud
- Liberalization
- No benefit to bailee for physical damage coverages
- Other insurance provisions
- Premium audit provisions
- Policy period, coverage territory
- Two or more coverage forms or policies issued by the insurer

---

Includes copyrighted material of Insurance Services Office, Inc., with its permission. Copyright, ISO Properties, Inc., 2009. [DA06684]

Section VI—Definitions

Because the Definitions section gives meaning to the words in quotes within the policy, insurance professionals may need to review it first, even though it is the last section of the policy.

The garage form contains most of the definitions provided in the business auto form and includes some definitions from the CGL form to facilitate its combination of general liability and auto liability coverage. For example, the garage form contains definitions for "products" and "work you performed" with wording similar to comparable terms in the CGL. It also expands the definition of "insured contract" to include the same types of contracts that are covered in the CGL.

In the garage form, the definition of "auto" implicitly includes mobile equipment. "Mobile equipment" is specifically excluded in the "auto" definition in the business auto form and the CGL form, and "mobile equipment" definitions are included to delineate which policy responds to each mobile equipment liability loss type. Because the garage form is a hybrid of the business auto and the CGL forms, no definition for mobile equipment is needed.

In the garage form, the definition of "loss" is extended to include resulting loss of use for Garagekeepers Coverage only.

Two definitions are unique to the garage form, "garage operations" and "customers' auto."

> H. "Garage operations" means the ownership, maintenance or use of locations for garage business and that portion of the roads or other accesses that adjoin these locations. "Garage operations" includes the ownership, maintenance or use of the "autos" indicated in Section I of this coverage form as covered "autos". "Garage operations" also include all operations necessary or incidental to a garage business.

> E. "Customer's auto" means a land motor vehicle, "trailer" or semitrailer lawfully within your possession for service, repair, storage or safekeeping, with or without the vehicle owner's knowledge or consent. A "customer's auto" also includes any such vehicle left in your care by your "employees" and members of their households, who pay for services performed.[1]

The garage form wording for "customer's auto" was revised with the 2010 edition to expressly provide coverage when an auto comes under the care, custody, or control of the garage and the owner of the auto may not have given permission. For example, the police have the garage tow and store a car from a no parking zone. Because the policy requires that the auto be possessed by the insured in accordance with the law, coverage would exist under the 2010 edition.

GARAGE FORM: ENDORSEMENTS AND OPTIONS

Although the Insurance Services Office, Inc. (ISO) Garage Coverage Form is designed to meet the specialized needs of auto dealers, it contains provisions that restrict coverage. Some of these restrictions can be removed or expanded by the addition of endorsements and other options.

Most auto dealers have two different business operations—selling and servicing vehicles. Some of the distinct loss exposures of auto dealers from these operations are excluded or restricted by the basic Garage Coverage Form.

For example, the business of selling vehicles entails the acceptance of customers' vehicles as trade-ins and the resale of those vehicles. Loss exposures, excluded in the basic coverage form, arise from the transfer of title to these vehicles. In an auto dealer's service business, various parts are installed in vehicles. Loss exposures, restricted in the basic coverage form, arise if any of these parts are defective.

Auto dealers can receive coverage for these and additional exposures through various ISO endorsements and coverage options.

Broad Form Products Coverage Endorsement

The Broad Form Products Coverage endorsement (CA 25 01) can be used to delete the Garage Coverage Form exclusion for defective products. Subject to a $250 deductible, this endorsement covers the named insured's liability for property damage to the named insured's products resulting from defects in those products. This approach is unavailable by standard endorsements to the Commercial General Liability (CGL) policy. However, this exposure is intrinsic to many auto dealers' operations because service to vehicles routinely entails the use of various parts. Insurers usually agree to provide this coverage by endorsement because many auto parts sold or supplied by garage businesses are inexpensive and fall totally or largely within the deductible. Moreover, defects in products sold by a garage business are often the ultimate responsibility of their manufacturer. Therefore, an insurer that pays on behalf of a garage business to replace a defective product may be able to obtain a subrogation recovery from the manufacturer.

Broadened Coverage—Garages Endorsement

A package of additional liability coverages can be added to the Garage Coverage Form through the Broadened Coverage—Garages endorsement (CA 25 14). The endorsement provides these coverages:

- Personal and advertising injury liability coverage—This coverage is comparable to the personal and advertising injury liability coverage provided under Coverage B of the CGL form. Exclusions to this endorsement were modified in 2010. The exclusion for employment practices was expanded to exclude malicious prosecution and to exclude employment-related claims for personal injury occurring before or after, as well as during, employment. As auto dealers increasingly conduct business over the Internet, the coverage provided or excluded by the Garage Coverage Form and its endorsements should be carefully evaluated when placing coverage.

- Host liquor liability coverage—This coverage duplicates the effect of the exception to the liquor liability exclusion of the CGL form. As long as the named insured is not engaged in an alcoholic beverage business, coverage applies to bodily injury or property damage arising out of the serving of alcoholic beverages at functions incidental to the garage business. Because the 2006 Garage Coverage Form does not contain a liquor liability exclusion, it covers liquor liability even if the Broadened Coverage—Garages endorsement is not attached to the policy.

- Damage to rented premises—This extension, formerly titled Fire Legal Liability coverage, provides coverage comparable to the legal liability coverage of the CGL form for fire damage to rented premises, not including contents. In 2010, coverage was expanded to include damage resulting from causes other than fire to premises rented for fewer than seven days. The limit of insurance is set at $100,000 unless another limit is shown in the endorsement schedule. This coverage can also be provided by the Damage to Rented Premises Liability Coverage—Garages endorsement, formerly titled the Fire Legal Liability Coverage—Garages endorsement (CA 25 10).

- Incidental medical malpractice liability coverage—This coverage expands the definition of bodily injury to include injury resulting from providing or failing to provide any medical or professional healthcare services, furnishing food or drink in connection with such services, or furnishing or dispensing drugs or medical supplies. However, the coverage excludes any insured in the business or occupation of providing any of the listed services or goods. Consequently, coverage applies only to those insureds who are not engaged in such a business or occupation. For example, this provision would provide coverage if an employee of a garage rendered emergency CPR to a customer.

- Nonowned watercraft coverage—This extension provides coverage for a watercraft less than twenty-six feet long that is not owned by the named insured or being used to carry persons or property for a charge. For example, this provision would provide liability coverage for a watercraft on a trailer attached to a customer's vehicle.

- Additional persons insured—If the named insured is a partnership, this provision grants insured status to the spouse of any partner of the named insured.

- Automatic liability coverage for newly acquired garage businesses—This provision automatically grants named insured status to any garage business that is acquired or formed by the named insured, and over which the named insured maintains ownership or majority interest. However, because this automatic coverage expires after ninety days, it should only be viewed as providing a reasonable period in which to ask the insurer to add the new organization to the policy as a named insured.

- Limited worldwide liability coverage—This provision broadens the Garage Coverage Form's coverage territory to include injury or damage that occurs anywhere in the world if caused by an insured who resides within the United States, its territories or possessions, Puerto Rico, or Canada, but is temporarily outside any of those places. To be covered, the original suit must be brought within the U.S., one of its territories or possessions, Puerto Rico, or Canada.

Garage Locations and Operations Medical Payments Coverage

Auto medical payments coverage can be added to the Garage Coverage Form by the same endorsement (CA 99 03) used to add medical payments coverage to the Business Auto Coverage Form. Alternatively, coverage similar to medical payments coverage in the CGL form can be added to the Garage Coverage Form by the Garage Locations and Operations Medical Payments Coverage endorsement (CA 25 05). This endorsement may be appropriate for most garage businesses because customers are ordinarily on their premises, either shopping for autos or waiting for repair or maintenance work to be completed.

Garagekeepers Direct Coverage Options

Garagekeepers coverage can be modified to apply on a direct coverage basis instead of a legal liability basis. Two direct coverage options are available. Either option is activated by marking the box beside the option chosen. See the exhibit "Garagekeepers Direct Coverage Options."

Both of the direct coverage options modify garagekeepers coverage so that it will apply regardless of whether the insured is legally liable for a loss. However, for the loss to be covered, it must still meet all other conditions of garagekeepers coverage. For example, the loss must be caused by a covered peril; the damaged property must be a covered auto; and the auto must be left in the insured's care while the insured is attending, servicing, repairing, parking, or storing the auto. The difference between the two direct coverage options is that one provides excess coverage, while the other provides primary coverage.

The direct excess option does not eliminate the basic garagekeepers legal liability coverage, which applies as primary insurance. This is made clear in the wording of the direct excess coverage option in the Garage Declarations. Consequently, if the insured who has purchased direct excess coverage is legally liable for damage to a customer's auto (and assuming all other conditions of coverage are met), the garagekeepers insurance will still apply on a

Garagekeepers Direct Coverage Options

DIRECT COVERAGE OPTIONS

Indicate below with an "X" which, if any, Direct Coverage Option is selected.

☐ **EXCESS INSURANCE**

If this box is checked, Garagekeepers Coverage remains applicable on a legal liability basis. However, coverage also applies without regard to your or any other "insured's" legal liability for "loss" to a "customer's auto" on an excess basis over any other collectible insurance regardless of whether the other insurance covers your or any other "insured's" interest or the interest of the "customer's auto's" owner.

☐ **PRIMARY INSURANCE**

If this box is checked, Garagekeepers Coverage is changed to apply without regard to your or another "insured's" legal liability for "loss" to a "customer's auto" and is primary insurance.

Includes copyrighted material of Insurance Services Office, Inc., with its permission. Copyright, ISO Properties, Inc., 2005. [DA04851]

primary basis, regardless of any physical damage insurance that the customer might have on the auto.

The benefit that the insured receives by purchasing direct excess coverage is that the insurer will also pay for damage to customers' autos when the insured is not legally liable. However, in such cases, the additional direct excess coverage applies as excess over any other collectible insurance regardless of whether the other insurance covers the insured or the owner of the auto.

Because auto physical damage insurance ordinarily pays up to the vehicle's actual cash value, direct excess coverage (when the insured is not legally liable) will usually only be needed to pay the deductible under the owner's insurance plus any covered loss of use. If there is no collectible physical damage insurance on the auto, the direct excess coverage will pay the entire loss as if it were primary.

When the direct primary option is chosen, garagekeepers coverage will pay the whole loss, subject to the applicable garagekeepers coverage limit and deductibles, even though other collectible insurance on the auto may exist. The direct primary option provides better customer goodwill protection than direct excess coverage because direct primary coverage is not contingent on the customer's insurance paying first.

False Pretense Coverage Endorsement

Coverage for losses excluded by the false pretense exclusion can be arranged by adding the False Pretense Coverage endorsement (CA 25 03). The endorsement deletes the false pretense exclusion and states that the insurer will pay for loss of any covered auto under these circumstances:

- Someone causes the named insured to voluntarily part with a covered auto by false pretenses.
- The named insured acquires an auto from a seller who did not have legal title.

The False Pretense Coverage endorsement contains an exclusion that applies only to a loss resulting from someone causing the named insured to voluntarily part with a covered auto. The exclusion states that coverage does not apply unless the named insured had legal title to, or consignment papers for, the covered auto before the loss occurred; also, the insured must make every effort to recover the covered auto when it is located. The legal title requirement does not apply if the named insured acquired an auto from a seller who did not have legal title.

There is an exclusion in this endorsement for any loss that results from the failure of a bank or other drawee to pay funds for any reason. For example, the exclusion would eliminate coverage for an auto dealer's loss resulting from the dealer's acceptance of a worthless check from a customer.

The limit of insurance for false pretense coverage is $25,000 per loss caused by any one person within any one year of the policy period, unless another limit is shown in the policy.

Dealers Driveaway Collision Coverage Endorsement

Garage physical damage coverage does not cover collision damage to any covered auto while being driven or transported from a point of purchase or distribution to its destination if such points are more than fifty road miles apart. The point of purchase or distribution can be either the insured's own lot, if the insured is delivering a car to a customer, or some other location, if the insured takes possession of a car at a manufacturer or another dealer.

This exclusion can be deleted by attaching the Dealers Driveaway Collision Coverage endorsement (CA 25 02). The endorsement requires the named insured to include, in its monthly or quarterly reports of values, a statement of the point of origin, the destination, and the factory price for each of the covered autos for delivery trips in excess of fifty road miles. Premiums for driveaway coverage are charged on the basis of these reports. To encourage accurate reporting of driveaway values, the endorsement also contains a full reporting clause similar to the clause that applies to the dealer's physical damage reporting provisions.

Audio, Visual and Data Electronic Equipment Coverage Added Limits

In 2010, the Garage Coverage Form was modified to provide coverage for all types of electronic equipment that are permanently installed in covered autos. The limit of coverage is $1,000. The Audio, Visual and Data Electronic Equipment Coverage Added Limits (CA 99 61) can increase the coverage limits for an additional premium.

GARAGE COVERAGE FORM CLAIMS CASE STUDY

Part of the challenge of being a risk management or insurance professional is assessing the nuances of different insuring forms, as well as the underlying risks which they cover. The Garage Coverage Form covers general liability and automobile coverage in one form, but the challenge is in discerning some of its idiosyncrasies. This case study is intended to augment an insurance professional's ability to discern some of those idiosyncrasies and assess the primary attributes of the Garage Coverage Form.

In this case study, an event resulting in several losses will occur at an automobile dealership that is insured by the Garage Coverage Form. The resulting claims will have insurance coverage ramifications that will warrant assessment. An insurance professional should determine whether the event is covered and, if so, for what amount.

Case Facts

Binoco Brothers is a successful car dealership that sells new and used cars and repairs and services autos.

Despite the fact that Binoco Brothers is a successful car dealership, negative events sometimes affect it.

Six customer-owned vehicles were parked along the rear wall of the service building. On May 10, a hailstorm impacted the area. Golf ball-sized hail caused damage to three customer vehicles.

- Bob's vehicle sustained $3,500 in damage. Bob had personal automobile comprehensive coverage subject to a $250 deductible.

- William's vehicle sustained $5,000 in damage; however, he had only liability insurance on his vehicle.

- Bonnie's vehicle suffered $7,000 in damage. She had comprehensive coverage subject to a $250 deductible.

The hail also caused widespread damage to the new and used car inventory of Binoco Brothers. Seventy-six of the vehicles were damaged at a cost of $1 million. At the time of the damage, there was a total of $12 million in inventory values. The last reported value for April 30 was $10 million. A review of the records revealed that, as of April 30, the values were $10 million.

Binoco Brothers is insured under an Insurance Services Office (ISO) Garage Coverage Form, which includes coverage for customer's vehicles under Section III—Garagekeeper's Coverage and coverage for the new and used car inventory of the Binoco Brothers under Section IV—Physical Damage Coverage. See the exhibit "Excerpt from Item Two, Schedule of Coverages and Covered Autos, in Binoco Brothers' Declarations."

Excerpt from Item Two, Schedule of Coverages and Covered Autos, in Binoco Brothers' Declarations

Coverages	Covered Autos	Limit of Insurance	Deductible
Garagekeepers Comprehensive Coverage	30	$250,000	$250 for All Perils for Each Customer's Auto $1,000 Maximum Deductible for All Loss In Any One Event
Physical Damage Coverage— Comprehensive	31	$10,000,000	$1,000 Deductible for All Perils for Each Covered Auto $5,000 Maximum Deductible for All Loss In Any One Event

[DA06788]

Case Analysis Tools

The insurance professional will need to have a copy of the Garage Coverage Form (CA 00 05 03 10) available for reference while working on this coverage case. Several unique policy provisions of a garage coverage policy will be provided.

The answers to these questions will help determine whether and for what amount each of the described claims is covered by the Garage Coverage Form:

- Is coverage indicated by the declarations pages?
- Is coverage triggered by the insuring agreement?
- Do the circumstances of the claim meet applicable policy conditions?
- Do any exclusions apply?
- What is the amount payable for each claim?

Determination of Coverage

Any coverage analysis should start with studying the declarations page to gain a proper context for the application of coverage. The dates on the declarations page indicate the hailstorm occurred during the policy period. The page further shows the dealership is covered at the location of the hail storm and is the named insured on the policy. The insuring agreements of the sections of the policy that are needed to respond to the damages incurred by the customers' vehicles and the dealership's inventory of new and used cars have been triggered.

The dealership also promptly reported the hail losses to the insurer, and its personnel cooperated in the insurer's investigation of the hail damage. All other policy conditions that affect whether coverage applies have been complied with. A review of the policy terms reveals that no exclusions apply that would eliminate or reduce coverage for the reported hail losses.

Referring specifically to the damage to the customers' vehicles, such damage involves a section of the multifaceted garage form, specifically, Section III—Garagekeeper's Coverage. For the damage to the customers' vehicles it is noted under the garagekeeper's section of the declarations page that covered auto symbol 30 is applicable. Symbol 30 applies coverage to autos left with the dealership for the purpose of service, repair, storage, or safekeeping. The insurer's investigation reveals each of the three customers who had their autos damaged in the hailstorm had left their autos with the dealership for one or more of these purposes.

Review of the coverage form for this section of the policy shows hail, because it is not excluded, is considered a comprehensive peril when damage to customers' cars results. Please refer to page 9 of 17 of ISO's Garage Coverage Form (CA 00 05 03 10).

Coverage analysis of the claims from the dealership's customers for the hail damage to their autos has determined that they are payable under the terms of the policy, which includes the limit of insurance, deductible, and maximum deductible for the event.

Regarding the damage to the dealership's inventory of cars, another section of the coverage form, specifically, Section IV—Physical Damage Coverage, is involved. The declarations page for the section lists covered auto symbol 31, which indicates the dealer's autos are covered for physical damage.

The dealer's autos are also covered on a monthly reporting basis. The basis requires the Binoco Brothers to accurately report their inventory values to their insurer by the 15th of every month. The reports must contain the total value of their inventory they had on the last business day of the preceding month. Failure to comply with this policy provision has some implications under the conditions section that do not affect the coverage decision of whether the loss is payable. However, they may affect what amount is to be paid.

Coverage analysis of the claim for hail damage to the dealership's inventory of cars has determined that it is payable under the terms of the policy, which includes the limit of insurance, deductible, and maximum deductible for the event. That is fortunate for the dealership because it has hail damage of $1 million.

Determination of Amounts Payable

In the claims presented, there were no serious implications involving the limits of insurance. Rather, deductibles played a role in shaping the ultimate coverage.

Regarding the amounts payable for the damage to the dealership's customers' autos, there is a limit of $250,000 for comprehensive peril subject to a $250 deductible for each customer's auto and also subject to a maximum deductible in any one event of $1,000 (stipulated by the declarations page for Section III—Garagekeeper's Coverage). The maximum deductible will have no effect because only three customers' vehicles were affected ($750 total).

Review of the policy indicates that coverage is provided on a direct and an excess basis. Direct basis means that there is no need for the dealership to be considered legally liable for coverage to apply (the goodwill coverage). Because coverage is on an excess basis, however, it must be determined whether each customer with a hail-damaged auto had his or her own automobile physical damage coverage—specifically comprehensive coverage. (Note that it is open to question whether the dealership would have been legally liable in this circumstance, as it originated as an "act of god." It would depend on the facts of the case.)

In two of the claims, the customers did have comprehensive coverage; this will apply first before the dealership's policy, which is meant to be excess. Therefore, the customer would be expected to use his or her own insurance first to pay for repair of the damage. However, the reality is the dealership wants to retain its customers, so the dealership would pay out-of-pocket the $250 deductible for each claim. Alternatively, if the customer had a $1,000 deductible, then the $1,000 would be paid as follows: the dealership would pay out of pocket for $250 for each auto, and the dealership's garage form would pay for the $750 balance of the $1,000 deductible for each auto.

William did not have any automobile physical damage coverage. Therefore, the dealership's garage form will satisfy the total damage subject to the dealership's responsibility for the $250 deductible.

Regarding the amount payable for the damage to the dealership's inventory of cars, the declarations page for Section IV—Physical Damage Coverage stipulates that there is a limit of $10 million, which is more than enough to satisfy this $1 million claim. The deductible for each auto is $1,000, subject to a maximum deductible of $5,000. Because seventy-six autos were damaged, $5,000 will be the maximum responsibility for the dealership. However, the value of the inventory as reported to the insurer by the dealership did not match the actual value at the time of the loss.

There is a conditional issue relative to the monthly reporting form. In this case, the dealership reported that there was $10 million of inventory at the end of April (the month before the loss). This report was not late, having arrived on May 5. More important, this $10 million figure matched the actual value, which was determined on the last day of the month. On the day of the loss, however, the total values were $12 million. Please refer to page 12 of 17 of ISO's Garage Coverage Form (CA 00 05 03 10).

If the insurance carrier were to assert that the $12 million exceeds the $10 million that was reported, how would that affect the amount payable? The inventory values fluctuate, and the dealership was honest in its reporting. As discussed earlier regarding monthly reporting basis, the central point is a comparison of the reported values on the last day of the month versus the actual values on the last day of the month—not the values at the time of the loss.

Use of the reporting form is equitable, although it requires some administrative work because it develops a premium that is more commensurate with the exposure. As long as the insured is abiding by the "honesty" clause, there are no implications except for the limit of insurance.

(Reported values divided by actual values) × amount of loss = claim payment

($10,000,000 divided by $10,000,000) × $1,000,000 = $1,000,000

Applying the deductibles, the maximum deductible is $5,000, despite the fact that a host of vehicles were involved in this episode. Thus, the $1 million in damages would be diminished by the $5,000, yielding a total claim payable of $995,000. See the exhibit "Correct Answer to Binoco Brothers Garage Coverage Case."

Correct Answer to Binoco Brothers Garage Coverage Case

For the claims involving the customers' vehicles, Binoco Brothers are responsible for the $250 per auto deductible for Bob's and Bonnie's autos. The insurance protection will have application, however, for William's auto for $4,750 ($5,000 minus the $250 deductible).

For the damage to the seventy-six cars in Binoco Brothers' inventory, the insurer will remit the $995,000 in loss to the hail-damaged autos ($1,000,000 minus $5,000 maximum deductible).

[DA06790]

MOTOR CARRIER COVERAGE FORM

Motor Carrier
Coverage Form

The coverage form filed
by ISO that can be used
to insure a person or an
organization providing
transportation by auto in the
furtherance of a commercial
enterprise.

Insurance Services Office (ISO) has developed the **Motor Carrier Coverage Form** (MCCF; CA 00 20) for insuring individuals or organizations in the business of transporting property of others for hire, owned property, or people. Previously, the Truckers Coverage Form (TCF) was available as an alternative to the MCCF and covered the auto loss exposures of individuals and organizations in the business of transporting property for others. ISO has withdrawn the TCF because of changes in motor carrier regulation.

This discussion focuses on the Motor Carrier Coverage Form (2010 edition). Coverages are indicated in the Motor Carrier Coverage Form (MCCF) by adding coverage symbols to a schedule of coverages and covered autos in the policy declarations. These coverage symbols, which are similar to those used in the Business Auto Coverage Form and the Garage Coverage Form, are shown in the exhibit. See the exhibit "Description of Covered Auto Designation Symbols for Motor Carrier Coverage Form."

The Motor Carrier Coverage Form differs from Business Auto coverage in these areas:

- Eligibility
- Motor carriers' use of owner-operators
- Trailer interchange coverage
- Trailer interchange exclusion
- MCS 90 endorsement

Eligibility

Under *Commercial Lines Manual* (CLM) rules, any motor carrier is eligible for the Motor Carrier Coverage Form. The CLM defines "motor carrier" to include any person or organization providing transportation by auto in the furtherance of a commercial enterprise. This definition is broad enough to include trucking companies that transport the property of others, as well as firms that transport their own property.

Motor Carriers' Use of Owner-Operators

The Motor Carrier Coverage Form is a modified version of the Business Auto Coverage Form designed to meet the special needs of motor carriers.

Understanding why the Motor Carrier Coverage Form contains modifications requires a basic understanding of the trucking business itself, particularly motor carriers' widespread practice of using independent contractors, called **owner-operators**, to do some or all of their actual hauling.

Owner-operators

Individuals who lease
themselves and their owned
trucks to motor carriers to
transport property for the
motor carrier.

Owner-operators furnish their own truck-tractors (also called "power units" or simply "rigs") to haul cargo in trailers provided by either the owner-operator

Description of Covered Auto Designation Symbols for Motor Carrier Coverage Form

Symbol		Description of Covered Auto Designation Symbols
61	Any "Auto"	
62	Owned "Autos" Only	Only the "autos" you own (and for Liability Coverage any "trailers" you don't own while connected to a power unit you own). This includes those "autos" you acquire ownership of after the policy begins.
63	Owned Private Passenger Type "Autos" Only	Only the "private passenger type" "autos" you own. This includes those "private passenger type" "autos" that you acquire ownership of after the policy begins.
64	Owned Commercial "Autos" Only	Only those trucks, tractors and "trailers" you own (and for Liability Coverage any "trailers" you don't own while connected to a power unit you own). This includes those trucks, tractors and "trailers" you acquire ownership of after the policy begins.
65	Owned "Autos" Subject To No-Fault	Only those "autos" you own that are required to have No-Fault benefits in the state where they are licensed or principally garaged. This includes those "autos" you acquire ownership of after the policy begins provided they are subject to the No-Fault law in the state where they are licensed or principally garaged.
66	Owned "Autos" Subject To A Compulsory Uninsured Motorists Law	Only those "autos" you own that, because of the law in the state where they are licensed or principally garaged, are required to have and cannot reject Uninsured Motorists Coverage. This includes those "autos" you acquire ownership of after the policy begins provided they are subject to the same uninsured motorists requirement.
67	Specifically Described "Autos"	Only those "autos" described in Item Three of the Declarations for which a premium charge is shown (and for Liability Coverage any "trailers" you don't own while attached to any power unit described in Item Three).
68	Hired "Autos" Only	Only those "autos" you lease, hire, rent or borrow. This does not include any "private passenger type" "auto" you lease, hire, rent or borrow from any member of your house-hold, any of your "employees", partners (if you are a partnership), members (if you are a limited liability company), or agents or members of their households.
69	"Trailers" In Your Possession Under A Written Trailer Or Equipment Interchange Agreement	Only those "trailers" you do not own while in your possession under a written "trailer" or equipment interchange agreement in which you assume liability for "loss" to the "trailers" while in your possession.
70	Your "Trailers" In The Possession Of Anyone Else Under A Written Trailer Interchange Agreement	Only those "trailers" you own or hire while in the possession of anyone else under a written "trailer" interchange agreement. When Symbol "70" is entered next to a Physical Damage Coverage in Item Two of the Declarations, the Physical Damage Coverage exclusion relating to "loss" to a "trailer" in the possession of anyone else does not apply to that coverage.
71	Nonowned "Autos" Only	Only those "autos" you do not own, lease, hire, rent or borrow that are used in connection with your business. This includes "private passenger type" "autos" owned by your "employees" or partners (if you are a partnership), members (if you are a limited liability company) or members of their households but only while used in your business or your personal affairs.
79	Mobile Equipment Subject To Compulsory Or Financial Responsibility or Other Motor Vehicle Insurance Law Only	Only those "autos" that are land vehicles and that would qualify under the definition of "mobile equipment" under this policy if they were not subject to a compulsory or financial responsibility law or other motor vehicle insurance law where they are licensed or principally garaged.

or the motor carrier. Owner-operators operate their vehicles under lease to motor carriers that need their transportation services. The terms and conditions between the owner-operator (the lessor) and the motor carrier (the lessee) are usually contained in a written lease. The lease period can be for a single trip or for a specified period of time.

The terms of a lease can include hold-harmless agreements and other provisions that affect insurance needs. Consequently, both the motor carrier and the owner-operator must understand their responsibilities under the lease.

Liability for the owner-operator's negligence can be imputed to the motor carrier whenever the owner-operator is held to have been acting within the terms of the lease. Conversely, if the responsibility for an act or omission is not imputed to the motor carrier, the owner-operator may be held accountable. Customarily, the auto liability insurance of motor carriers covers owner-operators while hauling for the insured motor carrier. See the exhibit "Coverage for Owner-Operators."

Coverage for Owner-Operators

The Motor Carrier Coverage Form automatically covers owners and lessors of autos hired by the named insured, subject to some conditions. These conditions differ depending on whether the hired auto is a trailer.

The owner or anyone else from whom the named insured hires or borrows a covered trailer is an insured while the trailer is connected to a power unit that is a covered auto or while the trailer is not connected to a power unit but is being used exclusively in the named insured's business.

When the covered auto that is leased to the named insured is a power unit, the owner-operator, as well as any employee, agent, or driver of the owner-operator, is an insured under the lessee's Motor Carrier Coverage Form if both of these conditions are met:

- The vehicle must be leased to the named insured under a written agreement that does not require the lessor (owner-operator) to hold the named insured (motor carrier) harmless.

- The lessor is covered only while the leased auto is used in the named insured's business as a motor carrier for hire.

When these two conditions are met, the owner-operator is insured on a primary basis under the motor carrier's auto liability insurance. In some cases, a lease may require the motor carrier to hold the owner-operator harmless while the owner-operator is hauling for the carrier. To insure the motor carrier against such contractual liability loss exposures, the Motor Carrier Coverage Form's definition of "insured contract" includes such liability assumed by the named insured.

[DA06610]

In many cases, motor carriers hire owner-operators to transport cargo on a one-way basis. During such a one-way trip, the motor carrier can be held legally responsible for the owner-operator's conduct. After the shipment is delivered, the owner-operator has at least two alternative courses of action:

- The owner-operator can return home without a load. Returning with an empty trailer is referred to as "deadheading." Operating without a trailer is referred to as "bobtailing."
- The owner-operator can enter into a trip lease with another motor carrier to haul a return load, a practice known as "backhauling." In this instance, the owner-operator should be protected by the insurance of the motor carrier that hires the owner-operator for the backhaul and not by the insurance of the motor carrier that hired the owner-operator for the initial trip.

When backhauling, the owner-operator should remove all identification of the first motor carrier from the truck and replace it with that of the second motor carrier. Ignoring such a precaution could make the first carrier legally liable if an accident occurs in the course of the return trip.

Trailer Interchange Coverage

In addition to the use of owner-operators, another unique feature of the trucking business is the common use of **trailer interchange agreements**. Normally, each carrier agrees to indemnify the other for any damage that occurs to the other's trailer while in the borrowing carrier's possession.

> **Trailer interchange agreement**
>
> A contract under which two motor carriers agree to swap trailers and to indemnify each other for any damage that occurs to the other's trailer while it is in the borrowing motor carrier's possession.

Although trailer interchanges can solve logistical problems for motor carriers, they can also present risk management problems if not handled correctly. For example, if Carrier A was involved in an accident while conveying Carrier B's loaded trailer, the liability insurance in Carrier A's policy would provide no coverage for damage to Carrier B's trailer (because of the Care, Custody, or Control exclusion in Carrier A's policy). Nevertheless, Carrier A would be legally obligated by the interchange agreement to pay for the damage to the trailer.

A motor carrier can cover its liability for damage to trailers in its possession under written trailer interchange agreements by purchasing **trailer interchange coverage**. Provisions for trailer interchange coverage are included in the Motor Carrier Coverage Form and can be activated in the policy declarations by marking symbol 69 beside whichever of these coverages are desired:

> **Trailer interchange coverage**
>
> Coverage for a motor carrier's liability for damage to trailers in its possession under a written trailer interchange agreement.

- Trailer interchange comprehensive coverage
- Trailer interchange specified causes of loss coverage
- Trailer interchange collision coverage

Trailer Interchange Exclusion

Another difference between the Business Auto Coverage Form and the Motor Carrier Coverage Form is that physical damage coverage under the Motor

Carrier Coverage Form excludes loss to a covered auto while in someone else's possession under a written trailer interchange agreement.

In the previously described accident (damage to Carrier B's trailer while in Carrier A's possession under a written trailer interchange agreement), Carrier B would have no coverage under its own policy for damage to its trailer even though the trailer was otherwise a covered auto under Carrier B's policy. In theory, Carrier A should have trailer interchange coverage, and, therefore, Carrier B should not need to have its own physical damage coverage apply to the trailer while in Carrier A's possession. For these reasons, Carrier B may want to have the exclusion of interchanged trailers eliminated. The exclusion can be deleted, for an additional premium, by marking symbol 70 in the policy declarations beside the chosen physical damage coverages. See the exhibit "Determining Coverage During Trailer Interchange."

Determining Coverage During Trailer Interchange

MCC is a common carrier whose operating territory is east of the Mississippi. To get its cargo delivered west of the Mississippi, MCC has an arrangement with another common carrier, named DSM, to meet and exchange trailers in St. Louis, Missouri. Each company has agreed in writing to be responsible for damage or destruction of the nonowned trailers in its possession.

Question: DSM's owner-operator negligently caused a collision while hauling an MCC trailer. The accident resulted in (1) damage to the cargo, (2) destruction of the trailer, and (3) bodily injury to other motorists and property damage to their cars. To what extent would the respective motor carrier policies of MCC and DSM cover the consequences of this accident?

Answer: MCC's cargo would not be covered under either of the policies because the policies exclude damage to property in the care, custody, or control of the insured. Motor truck cargo insurance is needed to cover a carrier's liability for cargo damage.

The destruction of MCC's trailer would be covered under DSM's policy if that policy provided trailer interchange collision coverage with symbol 69. If DSM's policy did not show symbol 69, MCC's policy would cover damage to the trailer if the trailer was a covered auto under MCC's policy and MCC's policy showed symbol 70 for physical damage collision coverage.

The liability of the owner-operator for bodily injury and property damage to other motorists should be covered by DSM's policy.

[DA04859]

MCS 90 endorsement

The commercial auto endorsement required by the Motor Carrier Act of 1980, in which the insurer agrees to pay, up to specified limits, damages that the insured becomes legally obligated to pay for liability resulting from negligence in the operation, maintenance, or use of any motor vehicle subject to that law.

MCS 90 Endorsement

Various endorsements in addition to those already discussed are available for modifying the Motor Carrier Coverage Form to meet the needs of policyholders and underwriters. One of the more important endorsements, required of any carrier subject to the Motor Carrier Act of 1980, is known as the **MCS 90 endorsement**. Its full name is "Endorsement for Motor Carrier Policy of

Insurance for Public Liability under Sections 29 and 30 of the Motor Carrier Act of 1980."

The Motor Carrier Act of 1980 requires that certain minimum liability insurance limits be maintained on these vehicles:

- All trucks of 10,000 pounds or more gross weight used to transport certain hazardous cargoes in bulk
- Trucks for hire used for interstate transportation of any type of material
- All trucks that transport hazardous cargo in bulk that do not come within item two in this list

What constitutes hazardous cargo can be determined by obtaining a list from the federal government. The list contains thousands of substances considered hazardous.

When the MCS 90 endorsement is attached to a commercial auto policy, the insurer agrees to pay, up to the limits shown in the endorsement, damages that the insured becomes legally obligated to pay for liability resulting from negligence in the operation, maintenance, or use of any motor vehicle subject to this law, whether described in the policy or not. No provisions of the applicable auto coverage form can relieve the insurer from payment. In effect, the insurer's obligation under the MCS 90 endorsement is nearly absolute, subject to the limits as specified in the endorsement. However, the insurer has the right to proceed against its own insured for reimbursement of damages paid solely because of the endorsement.

SUMMARY

The Garage Coverage Form is designed to meet the insurance needs of certain types of businesses for which the Business Auto Coverage Form might be inadequate.

ISO's Garage Coverage Form covers the commercial auto and the general liability exposures of auto and trailer dealers using a modular format including six sections.

The Definitions section clarifies definitions of important terms. The Covered Auto section enables the insured to select coverages using numerical symbols that indicate the type of auto being covered. The Liability Coverage section has two insuring agreements for garage operations, one that includes covered autos and one that does not. Garagekeepers Coverage covers the insured's bailee liability. The Physical Damage Coverage provides collision and comprehensive or specified causes of loss coverages. The Garage Conditions section contains five Loss Conditions that apply in addition to the Common Policy Conditions and eight General Conditions.

These endorsements or options can be used to broaden or modify the coverage provided by the Garage Coverage Form:

- The Broad Form Products Coverage endorsement (CA 25 01)
- The Broadened Coverage—Garages (CA 25 14)
- Garage Locations and Operations Medical Payments Coverage endorsement (CA 25 05)
- Garagekeepers Direct Coverage Options
- False Pretense Coverage endorsement (CA 25 03)
- Dealers Driveaway Collision Coverage endorsement (CA 25 02)
- Audio, Visual and Data Electronic Equipment Coverage Added Limits (CA 99 61)

To determine whether, and for what amount, the Garage Coverage Form covers a specific claim, an insurance professional must answer questions that apply the relevant portions of the policy to the facts of the claim.

The Motor Carrier Coverage Form (MCCF) is available to meet the auto insurance needs of any motor carrier, defined as any person or organization providing transportation by auto in the furtherance of a commercial enterprise. The Motor Carrier Coverage Form is a modified version of the Business Auto Coverage Form designed to meet the special needs of motor carriers.

ASSIGNMENT NOTE

1. Copyright, Insurance Services Office, Inc, 2009.

Direct Your Learning ▶▶

Commercial Property Insurance, Part I

Educational Objectives

After learning the content of this assignment, you should be able to:

▸ Describe commercial property insurance in terms of these elements:

- The major categories of loss exposures that can be covered
- The components of a commercial property coverage part

▸ Determine whether a described item of property qualifies as Covered Property under one or more of these categories in the Building and Personal Property Coverage Form:

- Building
- Your Business Personal Property
- Personal Property of Others

▸ Determine which of the additional coverages and coverage extensions of the Building and Personal Property Coverage Form apply to a described loss.

▸ Determine whether the cause of a described loss is a covered cause of loss under either the Causes of Loss—Basic Form or the Causes of Loss—Broad Form.

▸ Determine whether the cause of a described loss is a Covered Cause of Loss under the Causes of Loss—Special Form.

▸ Apply the Limits of Insurance and Deductible provisions of the Building and Personal Property Coverage Form to a described loss.

Commercial Property Insurance, Part I

OVERVIEW OF COMMERCIAL PROPERTY INSURANCE

Almost all businesses, including not-for-profit and governmental organizations, face potentially devastating losses associated with commercial property ownership. Purchase of a commercial package policy's commercial property coverage is one method businesses may use to transfer the risks associated with such potential losses.

Commercial property loss exposures may be analyzed according to three components:

- Types of property
- Causes of loss to property
- Financial consequences of property losses

The commercial property coverage part is a common example of insurance policy provisions that cover commercial property loss exposures.

Commercial Property Loss Exposures

The three components used to analyze property loss exposures allow for identification of the exposures in specific terms. For example, they may refer to a building exposure (type of property), a windstorm exposure (cause of loss), or a loss of business income exposure (financial consequence). Similarly, they could identify a property loss exposure in terms of two or even all three of these elements, such as a building fire exposure or loss of business income resulting from breakdown of a production machine.

Types of Property

Property is any item with value. Individuals, families, and organizations own and use property, depend on it as a source of income or services, and rely on its value. Property can decline in value—or even become worthless—if it is lost, damaged, or destroyed. Any item of property can be classified as either **real property** or **personal property**.

Examples of real property, in addition to land, are buildings, driveways, sidewalks, underground piping, and radio transmission towers. Property that is permanently attached to a structure, such as built-in appliances or paneling,

Real property (realty)
Tangible property consisting of land, all structures permanently attached to the land, and whatever is growing on the land.

Personal property
All tangible or intangible property that is not real property.

is also generally considered part of the structure. For example, most buildings also include plumbing, wiring, and heating and air conditioning equipment. Similarly, a high-rise building usually has elevators and may have specially designed platforms, hoists, and tracks used by window washers. Such equipment is considered part of the building.

All property that is not real property is personal property. Examples of personal property include vehicles, merchandise, furniture, tools, clothing, and oil while being transported through an underground pipeline. For insurance purposes, personal property falls into these classifications:

- Contents—Property insurance policies typically use the term "personal property" to refer to the contents of a building (for example, office furniture, machinery and equipment, and stock such as completed products in inventory), rather than "contents," because the property often is covered even when it is not literally contained in the building. Policies generally use the term "business personal property" to refer to the contents of a commercial building. Contents also include personal property of others that is in the insured's care, custody, or control; this property is covered by the Personal Property of Others provision in commercial property coverage forms.

- Property in transit—Most businesses ship property to others (such as merchandise) or receive property from others (such as raw materials or supplies). Property in transit can be transported by a variety of means, for any length of time, and over various distances on the owner's own vehicles or by a transportation company. A commercial property policy may provide some coverage for property in transit, but it is often inadequate for insureds with significant transit exposures. A firm that needs broader coverage for property in transit can purchase separate cargo insurance.

- Property in the possession of others—In many situations, an organization may place its property in the temporary possession of others for processing, cleaning, repairing, adjusting, storing, exhibiting, or selling. Because the probability of loss at the temporary location could differ greatly from the probability of loss at the owner's location, building and contents insurance policies usually provide only a nominal amount of insurance for property at other locations. Like property in transit, property in the possession of others can be insured for its full value under specialized policies designed for that purpose.

- "Floating" property—Many businesses own property that normally does not remain at a fixed work site or that is in transit between work sites (for example, a wedding photographer's cameras and a building contractor's tools and mobile equipment). Such property is often referred to as "floating" property. Insurance for floating property is available under specialized inland marine policies called "floaters."

Causes of Loss to Property

The potential causes of loss to property are another important aspect of property loss exposures. A cause of loss (for example, fire or vandalism) adversely affects property and leaves it in an altered state. Some causes of loss do not alter the property itself but do affect a person's ability to possess or use the property. For example, property lost or stolen may still be used, but not by its rightful owner.

Buildings and personal property are subject to many potential causes of loss. For most insureds, fire is the cause of loss that poses the greatest risk of a large or even total property loss. Windstorms, such as hurricanes and tornadoes; flood; earthquake; terrorism; and war also pose potentially catastrophic exposures for insurers and insureds.

Financial Consequences of Property Losses

Financial consequences are the third and final important aspect of property loss exposures. The adverse financial consequences of a property loss may include a reduction in the value of the property, lost income, and/or extra expenses.

When a property loss occurs, the property's value is reduced. This reduction in value can be measured in different ways. Property that must be replaced has no remaining worth, unless some salvageable items can be sold. If the property can be repaired or restored, the reduction in value can be measured by the cost of the repair or restoration. For example, if a fence worth $7,000 is damaged by a falling tree and the fence owner has to pay $2,000 to have the damage repaired, the fence owner has incurred a partial loss that reduces the value of the fence by $2,000.

A business may lose income as a result of a property loss. When property is damaged, income might be lost because the property cannot be used until it is repaired, restored, or replaced. For example, when a business suffers a serious fire, it might have to close until repairs to the building are made and personal property is replaced. The resulting loss of income occurs over time. As another example, the owner of a rental property faces rental income loss if the property is damaged and temporarily unavailable for rent. The owner would probably continue to incur some expenses, such as mortgage payments and taxes, but would not receive the rent that helped pay those expenses.

For a business to determine the extent of a property loss exposure, it must consider the extra expenses that the loss of the property would require. When property is damaged, the property itself declines in value, and the owner or other affected party suffers a corresponding loss. In addition, the owner or other user of that property might incur extra expenses in acquiring a temporary substitute or in temporarily maintaining the damaged property in a usable condition. For example, when a store's premises are damaged, the owners might have to rent temporary space at considerably greater expense than their normal rent.

Components of a Commercial Property Coverage Part

Commercial property coverage part

Commercial package policy (CPP) coverage component that provides a broad range of coverages to "middle-market" or larger firms to insure buildings and business personal property.

Commercial property loss exposures can be insured under a **commercial property coverage part**, which consists of five components:

- Commercial property declarations
- One or more commercial property coverage forms
- One or more causes of loss forms
- Commercial Property Conditions
- Any applicable endorsements

The commercial property coverage part is a component of the commercial package policy (CPP) program of Insurance Services Office (ISO). A commercial property coverage part can be one of the two or more coverage parts included in a CPP. It can also be the single coverage part included in a monoline policy under ISO procedures.

An important element of the CPP program is the package discount the insured may receive. The premium for a CPP is initially determined as if each coverage part were being issued as a monoline policy. If a CPP includes both property coverage and liability coverage, the premiums for certain coverage parts are multiplied by package modification factors, resulting in premium discounts. These discounts are justified by the greater efficiency of issuing a single package policy instead of several monoline policies.

Commercial Property Declarations

Commercial property declarations page

A required commercial property coverage part component that provides basic information about the policyholder and the insurance provided.

A **commercial property declarations page** contains information that pertains specifically to property insurance:

- A description of the property insured
- The kinds and amounts of coverage provided and the covered causes of loss (basic, broad, or special)
- A list of mortgagees, if any
- The deductible amount
- A list of the property coverage forms and endorsements attached to the policy
- The applicable coinsurance percentage(s)
- Any optional coverages

Supplemental declarations can be added as needed on a separate page. For example, if an insured fast-food franchise cannot list all of its locations on the declarations page, it may add a supplemental schedule to show them.

Commercial Property Coverage Forms

The CPP program includes several different **commercial property coverage forms**. A commercial property coverage form typically contains these elements:

- Insuring agreement
- Delineation of the property covered and not covered
- Additional coverages and coverage extensions
- Provisions and definitions that apply only to that coverage form

A commercial property coverage part often includes more than one commercial property coverage form. Typically, one coverage form insures the insured's buildings and/or personal property, and another coverage form insures business income and/or extra expense.

A commonly used commercial property coverage form is the Building and Personal Property Coverage Form, also referred to as the BPP, which can be used to insure buildings, business personal property of the insured, and personal property of others in the insured's custody. Additional personal property coverage forms are available for insuring buildings and/or personal property in several special situations, such as buildings under construction, condominium association property, and condominium commercial unit owners' property. Commercial property coverage forms are also available for insuring loss of business income and/or extra expense.

Causes of Loss Forms

The three types of **causes of loss forms**—basic, broad, and special—allow the insured to select, or the underwriter to offer, a range of covered perils.

A commercial property coverage part may contain more than one causes of loss form. One causes of loss form (such as the special form) may apply to buildings, while another (such as the broad form) may apply to personal property.

The commercial property declarations indicate which form applies to each type of property at each location. It is generally the underwriter's reluctance to provide the broader coverages for certain types of property that results in the use of different causes of loss forms in the same policy. Such instances are infrequent, however.

Commercial Property Conditions

The **Commercial Property Conditions** are a required component of the commercial property coverage part that contains conditions applicable to all commercial property coverage forms. They are printed as a separate form and apply to all coverage forms included in a commercial property coverage part unless a coverage form contains a condition to the contrary. Like the

Commercial property coverage form

A Commercial Property Coverage Part component that can be any of several commercial property forms containing an insuring agreement and related provisions.

Causes of loss form

A required component of the Commercial Property Coverage Part that specifies perils covered.

Commercial Property Conditions

A required component of the commercial property coverage part that contains conditions applicable to all commercial property coverage forms.

Common Policy Conditions, the Commercial Property Conditions do not require reiteration in each coverage form.

Endorsements

Many endorsements are available to tailor commercial property coverage to meet the specialized needs of particular insureds or to eliminate exposures that underwriters are not willing to insure.

BPP COVERED PROPERTY

The main insuring agreement of the Building and Personal Property Coverage Form (BPP) states that the insurer will pay for direct physical loss of or damage to Covered Property at the described premises caused by or resulting from any Covered Cause of Loss. Determining whether property qualifies as Covered Property is therefore an essential step in deciding whether the BPP covers a loss.

The BPP can cover any combination of three broad categories of property:

- Building
- Your Business Personal Property
- Personal Property of Others

Coverage can be provided on any combination of these categories. The insured's selection of categories is indicated on the commercial property declarations page by entering a limit of insurance for each chosen category of covered property. If there is no entry for one of the categories of covered property (for example, Building), then no coverage applies to that category, even if the insured owns property fitting that category. The Property Not Covered section of the BPP specifies property that is not covered and therefore works in tandem with the Covered Property section to describe what property is covered by the BPP.

Categories of Covered Property

Understanding how the BPP defines each of the three categories of Covered Property is essential to determining whether it covers a particular loss.

Building

The policy covers buildings or structures listed and described in the declarations. The BPP's definition of Building also includes these elements:

- Completed additions to covered buildings
- Fixtures (including outdoor fixtures)

- Permanently installed machinery and equipment
- Personal property owned by the insured and used to maintain or service the building or its premises (for example, fire extinguishing equipment; outdoor furniture; floor coverings; and equipment for refrigeration, ventilation, cooking, dishwashing, or laundering)

In addition, if they are not otherwise insured, the building description covers additions, alterations, or repairs in progress, including materials, equipment, and supplies used in connection with such work. However, such materials, equipment, and supplies are covered only if they are located within 100 feet of the described premises.

Fixtures are items attached to a building or to the land, usually in such a way that they cannot easily be removed, such as plumbing and electrical fixtures. Outdoor fixtures include items outside the building but attached to the land, such as light poles and flagpoles. Fixtures are real property. The term "fixtures" is broad enough to include fences and outdoor signs, but coverage for these items is specifically excluded or limited.

Your Business Personal Property

Your Business Personal Property covers personal property owned by the insured and used in the insured's business. Except for an extension that provides limited coverage for property while away from the insured premises, coverage applies only when the property is located in or on the described Building or in the open (or in a vehicle) within 100 feet of the described premises. Your Business Personal Property includes furniture and fixtures, machinery and equipment, stock, and all other personal property owned by the insured and used in the insured's business, except those items excluded under the Property Not Covered section. The form defines stock as "merchandise held in storage or for sale, raw materials and in-process or finished goods, including supplies used in their packing or shipping." Your Business Personal Property also includes labor, materials, or services furnished by the insured on personal property of others.

The insured's interest in **improvements and betterments** is also insured as Your Business Personal Property, even though improvements and betterments are actually a part of the building and are technically real property. For example, a restaurant that rents space in a commercial building might install elaborate wall and ceiling treatments that could not be removed when the lease is terminated. It is common for some commercial tenants to spend $1 million or more upgrading their premises. It is important to consider the insurable value of improvements and betterments when setting the amount of insurance that a tenant should carry; ignoring improvements and betterments can result in severe underinsurance difficulties when a loss occurs.

Your Business Personal Property also includes leased personal property for which the named insured has a contractual responsibility to procure coverage. An example of such property is phone or computer equipment leased by the

Improvements and betterments

Alterations or additions made to the building at the expense of an insured who does not own the building and who cannot legally remove them.

insured under an agreement requiring the insured to purchase insurance on the equipment.

Personal Property of Others

This coverage is designed to protect the insured against loss of or damage to the personal property of others while such property is in the custody of the insured. It is an important coverage for businesses (bailees) that have customers' property in their custody, such as laundries, dry cleaners, appliance repair shops, and furniture upholstery shops. The BPP covers such property only while it is in the insured's care, custody, or control and in or on the building described in the declarations or within 100 feet of the described premises. Coverage applies regardless of whether the insured is legally responsible for the damage.

Even if the insured does not buy coverage for personal property of others (as indicated by an amount of insurance being shown for that category on the declarations page), the BPP still provides a coverage extension for personal property of others, which is limited to $2,500 at each insured location.

Property Not Covered

The BPP's Property Not Covered section lists several classes of property or kinds of property losses that do not qualify as covered property. Therefore, the Covered Property section and the Property Not Covered section must be read together when determining whether a specific kind of property is insured.

There are several reasons for excluding some kinds of property from coverage:

- Some kinds of property, such as smuggled goods being held for sale, are illegal to insure.
- Some property may be much less susceptible to loss by most of the perils insured against. Examples include building foundations below the lowest basement floor or the surface of the ground, retaining walls that are not part of a building, and underground pipes.
- Some kinds of property are excluded because they can be insured more advantageously under other forms. For example, insurers generally prefer to cover money, securities, automobiles, and aircraft under other policies.

By endorsement, insurance can be made available for almost all of the items listed in the Property Not Covered section. Only contraband or property in the course of illegal transportation or trade is totally uninsurable.

Property otherwise insured is not totally excluded. The BPP covers such property, but only in excess of the other insurance. For example, assume that a computer system valued at $150,000 is insured under the general category of business personal property in a BPP and is also insured for $100,000 under a separate electronic data processing (EDP) equipment policy issued by a different insurer. If the computer system is totally destroyed by fire, a cause of loss insured under both policies, the insurer that issued the EDP policy must pay its limit ($100,000). The insurer that issued the BPP would then pay the difference between the limit of the EDP policy and the amount of loss otherwise payable under the BPP.

Exceptions provide coverage under certain circumstances for some types of property not covered. For example, animals are not covered unless they are owned by others and boarded by the insured or held as stock, as in a pet shop. Similarly, some coverage is provided for vehicles or self-propelled machines.

Apply Your Knowledge

A business owns an office building and insures it under a BPP covering only the Building as defined in the policy. Would equipment that the business owns and uses to clean and maintain the building be Covered Property under its BPP?

Feedback: Yes, the equipment would be Covered Property under the BPP, because the definition of Building includes personal property owned by the insured and used to maintain or service the building or its premises.

A business owns a building insured under a BPP, with coverage indicated for the Building and Your Business Personal Property as defined in the policy. Would merchandise that the business owns and displays at a trade show held in a different city qualify as Covered Property under its BPP?

Feedback: No. The insured's merchandise meets the BPP's definition of stock, and stock is one of the types of property listed under Your Business Personal Property. However, while located in another city, the merchandise does not meet the requirement that the property must be located in or on the described building or in the open (or in a vehicle) within 100 feet of the described premises. Therefore, the merchandise is not Covered Property while located at the trade show.

BPP ADDITIONAL COVERAGES AND COVERAGE EXTENSIONS

The Building and Personal Property Coverage Form, also referred to as the BPP, includes additional coverages and coverage extensions that provide several enhancements of the basic coverage provided by the BPP.

The BPP provides several supplemental coverages in addition to the basic coverages for buildings, the insured's business personal property, and the property of others. These supplemental coverages are described under two subheadings: Additional Coverages and Coverage Extensions. See the exhibit "BPP Additional Coverages and Coverage Extensions: Special Limits."

BPP Additional Coverages and Coverage Extensions: Special Limits

All of the BPP's additional coverages and coverage extensions, except Preservation of Property, are subject to special dollar limits. In many cases, these limits result in insufficient coverage. For example, the limit for the Pollutant Cleanup and Removal additional coverage is $10,000 per policy year. Because losses related to pollutant cleanup can be extensive, this limit often proves inadequate for policyholders. Similarly, the Electronic Data additional coverage limit is $2,500 per policy year, a limit that does not adequately address the potentially catastrophic effects of losses related to electronic data.

The limits for many of the BPP's additional coverages and coverage extensions can be increased by showing a higher limit in the declarations, adding an appropriate coverage endorsement, or buying another type of policy to supplement the BPP. However, many insurers will not provide higher limits under the BPP for the Pollutant Cleanup and Removal or the Electronic Data additional coverages.

[DA07809]

Additional Coverages

These are the six additional coverages in the BPP:

- Debris Removal
- Preservation of Property
- Fire Department Service Charge
- Pollutant Cleanup and Removal
- Increased Cost of Construction
- Electronic Data

Debris Removal

Following a loss, large amounts of debris may remain on the premises, and the cost of removing the debris may be substantial. The Debris Removal additional coverage covers the cost of removing debris of covered property resulting from a covered cause of loss during the policy period. It would not, for example, pay to remove the debris resulting from a flood if flood is not a covered cause of loss or to remove the debris of a tenant's property or the insured's licensed automobiles, because they are not covered property.

The Debris Removal additional coverage includes the cost to clean up pollution at the insured's premises caused by an insured peril. For example, if a building is shown as covered property, the cost to clean up debris from a fire that causes the release of toxic chemicals onto the floor of the insured's building would be covered. However, the Debris Removal provision does not apply to costs for cleanup or removal of pollutants from land or water. Limited coverage for these costs is available under the provisions of another additional coverage. No coverage is provided for cleanup of off-premises pollution even when it results from a covered loss.

Preservation of Property

It is sometimes necessary to move covered property to another location to protect it. The Preservation of Property additional coverage extends the policy to protect covered property while it is being moved and for up to thirty days at the new location. This coverage is broader than the normal coverage under the policy. It protects against "any direct physical loss or damage" and is not limited to either the covered causes of loss or locations stipulated in the coverage form. The protection provided under this additional coverage is subject to the limits of insurance stated in the declarations. Consequently, the additional coverage provides no protection if the applicable limit of insurance is exhausted by payment for the physical loss.

Fire Department Service Charge

In some localities, the fire department may make a charge for its services in controlling or extinguishing a fire. The Fire Department Service Charge additional coverage pays fire department charges up to the specified limit if they are required by local ordinance or are assumed by contract before the loss occurs.

Pollutant Cleanup and Removal

The Pollutant Cleanup and Removal additional coverage provides limited coverage for the cleanup and removal of pollutants from land or water at the described premises. This additional coverage pays the insured's expenses to extract pollutants from land or water at the described premises if the release, discharge, dispersal, seepage, migration, or escape of the pollutants is the result of a covered cause of loss that occurs during the policy period.

Increased Cost of Construction

The Ordinance or Law exclusion contained in the causes of loss forms that can be attached to the BPP excludes the increased cost to comply with ordinances or laws regulating the repair, rebuilding, or replacement of covered buildings. The Increased Cost of Construction additional coverage provides a small amount of insurance to cover this loss exposure. The amount of insurance is equal to 5 percent of the amount of insurance or $10,000, whichever is less. It is paid in addition to the policy limit. This additional coverage applies only if the Replacement Cost optional coverage has been selected.

The Increased Cost of Construction additional coverage provides no coverage for these items:

- Loss to any undamaged portion of the building that an ordinance or law does not permit to remain in use
- The cost to demolish the undamaged portion of the structure and remove its debris

Electronic Data

Because of businesses' growing dependence on electronic data and the widespread belief that the exposure could better be treated by other forms of insurance, the BPP excludes electronic data except as provided by the Electronic Data additional coverage. This additional coverage is subject to a limit that is too low to provide meaningful coverage for most businesses and is the most that the insurer will pay per policy year, regardless of the number of occurrences or locations covered. All electronic data damage is deemed to have been sustained in the policy year that an occurrence began, even if the damage continues or results in additional loss or damage in a subsequent policy year.

Coverage Extensions

The BPP coverage extensions apply only if at least 80 percent coinsurance or a value reporting period symbol is shown in the declarations. The amounts payable under the coverage extensions are payable in addition to the overall limits of insurance stated in the declarations, subject to the special limits that apply to the coverage extensions. These are the six BPP coverage extensions:

- Newly Acquired or Constructed Property
- Personal Effects and Property of Others
- Valuable Papers and Records (Other Than Electronic Data)
- Property Off-Premises
- Outdoor Property
- Non-Owned Detached Trailers

Newly Acquired or Constructed Property

If the policy covers a building, the Newly Acquired or Constructed Property extension provides automatic coverage for a new building being constructed at the premises described in the declarations. Automatic coverage is also provided for newly acquired buildings at other locations, provided the purpose of the newly acquired building is similar to the use of the building described in the declarations or the newly acquired building will be used as a warehouse. The coverage extension states a maximum amount of coverage that applies to each building.

If the policy covers business personal property, the extension also provides automatic coverage for these types of property:

- Business personal property at any newly acquired location other than fairs, trade shows, or exhibitions
- Business personal property located at newly constructed or acquired buildings at the location described in the declarations
- Newly acquired business personal property at the described premises

A stated amount of coverage applies to loss of business personal property at each building.

The coverage for buildings and business personal property provided by this extension is temporary. It terminates automatically at the earliest of three dates:

- The expiration date of the policy
- Thirty days after the acquisition of the new location or the start of construction of the new building
- The date the insured notifies the insurer of the new location or new building

Personal Effects and Property of Others

The Personal Effects and Property of Others extension provides a limited amount of coverage for personal effects (such as a coat or jewelry) owned by an individual insured or a partner, a member, an officer, a manager, or an employee of the insured while on the premises described in the declarations. Personal effects are not covered for loss by theft. The extension also covers property of others in the care, custody, or control of the insured.

Valuable Papers and Records (Other Than Electronic Data)

Valuable papers and records (such as records of accounts receivable, mailing lists, legal documents, medical records, specifications, and drawings) are covered as business personal property, but only for the cost of blank records plus the labor to transcribe or copy duplicate information. This extension does not apply to electronic data; previous versions of the BPP did cover the cost of reconstructing electronic data.

Property Off-Premises

The Property Off-Premises extension provides coverage for covered property while it is away from the described premises. In addition to property temporarily at locations that the insured does not own, lease, or operate, the extension also covers property in storage at a location leased after the inception of the current policy and property at any fair, trade show, or exhibition. This extension does not apply to property in or on a vehicle or in the custody of the insured's salespersons unless the property in custody is at a fair, trade show, or exhibition.

Outdoor Property

The Outdoor Property extension covers loss to outdoor fences; radio and television antennas (including satellite dishes); and trees, shrubs, and plants. Unlike the other coverage extensions, the Outdoor Property extension has its own list of covered causes of loss. It covers only loss by fire, lightning, explosion, riot or civil commotion, and aircraft. Some of the more likely causes of loss to outdoor property—windstorm, vehicles, and vandalism—are not covered.

Non-Owned Detached Trailers

Insureds frequently lease trailers to expand office space or to provide additional storage or work areas at their own premises. The Non-Owned Detached Trailers extension permits the insured to extend Your Business Personal Property to include such trailers. The trailer must be used in the insured's business and be in the insured's care, custody, or control at the described premises. Moreover, the insured must have a contractual responsibility to pay for loss or damage to the trailer.

The coverage does not apply while the trailer is attached to any motor vehicle or motorized conveyance, whether or not it is in motion. Nor does it apply during hitching or unhitching operations or when a trailer becomes accidentally unhitched from a motor vehicle or conveyance.

Apply Your Knowledge

A business insures its building under a BPP that has 80 percent coinsurance. As the business grows, it acquires another building for use as a distribution warehouse. Two weeks after the insured acquires the building, a lightning strike on the warehouse premises damages the building and an outdoor security fence. At the time of the lightning strike, the insured has not reported the new building to the insurer. Identify the coverage extensions that would apply to this loss.

Feedback: The Newly Acquired or Constructed Property and the Outdoor Property coverage extensions would apply to this loss. The Newly Acquired or Constructed Property coverage extension applies because the purpose of the business's newly acquired building was for it to be used as a warehouse and because the business acquired the warehouse less than thirty days before the loss. The Outdoor Property coverage extension applies to the loss because lightning is a covered cause of loss and the outdoor fence is specifically covered.

Fire damages a business's office complex, which is covered under a BPP. The blaze destroys one of the complex's two buildings, which the business intends to rebuild. The cost of rebuilding the destroyed building will be increased because of building code changes that have taken place since it was constructed. The other building sustained only minor damage, but fire-damaged covered property will need to be hauled away before repairs can begin. Identify the additional coverages that would apply to this loss.

Feedback: The Increased Cost of Construction and the Debris Removal additional coverages would apply to this loss. The Increased Cost of Construction additional coverage applies because it provides coverage for the increased cost to comply with ordinances or laws regulating the repair, rebuilding, or replacement of covered buildings. The Debris Removal additional coverage applies because it covers the cost of removing debris of covered property resulting from a covered cause of loss during the policy period.

CAUSES OF LOSS—BASIC FORM AND BROAD FORM

The perils covered in an Insurance Services Office (ISO) commercial property policy are specified in any of three causes of loss forms.

The Causes of Loss—Basic Form and the Causes of Loss—Broad Form, two of the three causes of loss forms available for use in the ISO commercial property coverage part, are nearly identical. The coverage provided by the third causes of loss form, the Causes of Loss—Special Form, differs from the other two forms. This discussion focuses on three sections of the Basic Form and the Broad Form, noting instances where the two forms diverge:

- Covered Causes of Loss
- Exclusions
- Additional Coverages

Covered Causes of Loss

The Basic Form and the Broad Form both explicitly name the policy's covered causes of loss. This is known as a "named perils" approach. The Broad Form covers all of the perils covered in the Basic Form but also includes three additional perils that the Basic Form does not cover. Although the Broad Form is slightly more expensive than the Basic Form, most insureds choose it over the Basic Form. See the exhibit "Covered Causes of Loss in the Basic Form and Broad Form."

Exclusions

Both forms contain several exclusions that further define or limit the covered causes of loss. See the exhibit "Anti-Concurrent Causation Wording."

Ordinance or Law

To promote public welfare and safety, municipalities enact and regularly upgrade the building codes that set the standards for new construction or significant remodeling. For example, a building code might require that new buildings in a certain area be fire resistive. If an existing building in that area does not comply with the code and sustains damage by fire or another peril, the building code may require that its restoration meet the standards for

Covered Causes of Loss in the Basic Form and Broad Form

Covered Cause of Loss	Description
Fire	For most insureds, fire is the peril that poses the greatest risk of a large or total property loss.
Lightning	Lightning is a naturally occurring electrical discharge between clouds or between a cloud and the earth.
Explosion	The explosion peril includes the explosion of gases or fuel in a furnace or flue (called "combustion explosion" or "furnace explosion").
Windstorm or hail	Hurricanes and tornadoes are both examples of windstorms, although less severe windstorms can cause property damage and also fall within the coverage. Damage by rain, snow, sand, or dust to the interior of a building or to property inside the building is not covered unless the building first sustains exterior damage by wind, and the rain, snow, sand, or dust enters through the damaged part of the building.
Smoke	For smoke damage to be covered, it must be sudden and accidental. No coverage exists for damage by smoke from industrial operations or agricultural smudging (the intentional production of smoke to protect crops from frost damage).
Aircraft or vehicles	Damage caused by aircraft must result from actual physical contact with the aircraft or objects falling from it. Vehicle damage must result from accidental physical contact with a vehicle or an object thrown by the vehicle (such as a pebble propelled by a truck's tire). There is no coverage for damage caused by vehicles owned by the insured or operated in the insured's business.
Riot or civil commotion	In most states, a riot is defined by law as a violent public disturbance by three or more persons. However, the riot or civil commotion peril includes acts by striking workers while occupying the insured premises as well as looting occurring at the time and place of a riot or civil commotion.
Vandalism	Vandalism means the willful and malicious damage to or destruction of property. Although the vandalism peril does not cover loss by theft, it does cover damage to the building caused by the entry or exit of burglars.
Sprinkler leakage	Sprinkler leakage means the escape of any substance (water, carbon dioxide, or any other extinguishing agent) from an automatic fire protection or extinguishing system. The collapse of a tank constituting a part of such a system is covered, as is the cost of repairing damage to the system if the damage results in the sprinkler leakage or if the damage is caused by freezing. The cost to tear out and replace any part of the building or structure to repair damage to the automatic sprinkler system is also covered.

new buildings. In some cases, a building ordinance or law may require that a partially damaged building be totally demolished, changing what would have been a partial loss to a total loss. The Ordinance or Law exclusion eliminates coverage for consequential losses that result from the enforcement of building ordinances or laws. Some coverage for this exposure is provided by the Increased Cost of Construction additional coverage. Broader coverage for the excluded losses can be provided by an endorsement for an additional premium.

Sinkhole collapse	Sinkholes result from underground water dissolving limestone or dolomite and creating an empty space or cavern under the ground. When the roof of the cavern gets too close to the ground surface, the surface collapses, causing damage to buildings or other property located over or near the resulting sinkhole. This peril insures resulting damage to covered property (buildings or business personal property), but not the cost of filling the sinkhole. Loss caused by the collapse of land into man-made underground cavities, such as mineshafts, is not covered by this peril.
Volcanic action	The volcanic action peril covers damage caused by lava flow, ash, dust, particulate matter, airborne volcanic blast, or airborne shock waves resulting from a volcanic eruption. The earthquake damage that often accompanies a volcanic eruption is excluded by one of the exclusions discussed subsequently. Because such losses may occur over a relatively long period of time, both forms stipulate that all eruptions that occur within any 168-hour period are considered a single occurrence and are thus subject to only one deductible and policy limit.
Falling objects (Broad Form only)	The coverage for falling objects does not include damage to personal property in the open or to damage inside a building unless the roof or an outside wall is first damaged by the falling object.
Weight of ice, snow, or sleet (Broad Form only)	Does not cover damage to personal property in the open.
Water damage (Broad Form only)	Despite its name, the water damage peril is not intended to cover flooding, rainfall, sewer backup, and similar causes of water damage. Instead, it is limited to covering loss caused by water or steam leakage resulting from the breaking apart or cracking of a plumbing, heating, air conditioning, or other system or appliance that is located on the described premises. If the building is covered property, the form also covers the cost to tear out and replace any part of the building to repair damage to the appliance or system that leaked. The water damage peril is subject to several exclusions, including the cost to repair any defect that caused the loss or damage and the cost to repair any gradual damage that occurs over a period of fourteen days or more.

[DA07824]

Anti-Concurrent Causation Wording

The introductory language to the first group of eight exclusions provides that losses caused directly or indirectly by any of those perils are not covered, even if another covered cause contributed to the loss, regardless of the sequence in which the causes of events occur, unless the exclusion specifically provides otherwise. This wording was developed to eliminate claims based on the concurrent causation doctrine and is therefore referred to as "anti-concurrent causation wording." The concurrent causation doctrine holds that a loss is covered when caused by two or more independent, concurrent perils if only one of the perils is covered—even if the other peril or perils are clearly excluded.

[DA07825]

Earth Movement

Coverage is not provided for damage caused by earth movement, other than sinkhole collapse. Earth movement includes earthquake, landslide, mine subsidence, and similar movements. The exclusion does not apply to damage by fire or explosion caused by earth movement. Earthquake coverage can be added for an additional premium.

Governmental Action

Seizure or destruction of property by governmental action is not covered. This exclusion does not apply to the destruction of property by governmental order to stop the spread of a covered fire.

Nuclear Hazard

Loss caused by nuclear reaction, radiation, or radioactive contamination is excluded. However, the exclusion does not apply to loss by fire resulting from these causes.

Utility Services

Loss caused by power failure or failure of other utility service is excluded if the failure originates away from the described premises. For example, if electrical power to the described premises is interrupted because of lightning damage to an overhead power line situated away from the described premises, the exclusion will eliminate coverage for any loss caused by the resulting power failure.

The exclusion also applies if the utility failure originates at the described premises, but only if the failure involves equipment that supplies utility service to the described premises from a source away from the described premises. For example, if lightning takes out an overhead power line on the described premises, the exclusion will apply to any loss caused by the resulting power failure.

The exclusion does not apply to loss from a covered peril resulting from power failure. If, for example, loss of electrical power causes a natural gas leak that results in an explosion (a covered cause of loss), the Utility Services exclusion would not apply to the damage caused by the explosion.

War and Military Action

The War and Military Action exclusion eliminates coverage for loss caused by war, revolution, insurrection, or similar actions. The current insurance industry consensus is that the War and Military Action exclusion does not apply to acts of terrorism such as the terrorist attacks of September 11, 2001. Instead, insurers attach separate terrorism exclusion endorsements unless the insured purchases terrorism coverage.

Water

Flood-related loss is difficult to insure because of the potential for a large and concentrated loss. Insurers therefore exclude flood losses from commercial property forms.

The Water exclusion eliminates coverage for damage caused by these:

- Flood, surface water, tides, and tidal waves
- Mudslide or mudflow
- Backing up of sewers, drains, or sumps
- Underground water pressing on or flowing or seeping through foundations, walls, floors, basements, doors, windows, or other openings

The exclusion does not apply to damage by fire, explosion, or sprinkler leakage caused by any of the foregoing. The Water exclusion applies regardless of whether the loss event results in widespread damage or affects a substantial area.

"Fungus," Wet Rot, Dry Rot, and Bacteria

In recent years, mold claims have disrupted the homeowners insurance markets in some states and posed a similar problem for commercial property insurance. To mitigate this problem, ISO added a "Fungus," Wet Rot, Dry Rot, and Bacteria exclusion to the commercial property causes of loss forms. Fungus is defined to include mold or mildew and any mycotoxins, spores, scents, or by-products produced or released by fungi.

The exclusion does not apply when the fungus, wet rot, dry rot, and bacteria result from fire or lightning, but it is one of the exclusions subject to the anti-concurrent causation wording.

In addition to the foregoing exclusion, each of the causes of loss forms contains an additional coverage titled Limited Coverage for "Fungus," Wet Rot, Dry Rot, and Bacteria, which provides a modest amount of insurance for such losses.

Other Exclusions

The Basic Form and the Broad Form also contain a set of exclusions that are not subject to the anti-concurrent causation wording. These exclusions eliminate coverage for loss or damage caused by any of these:

- Electrical, magnetic, or electromagnetic energy that damages or otherwise interferes with any electrical or electronic wires or devices, including devices, appliances, systems, or networks using cellular or satellite technology. However, if a fire results, the resulting fire damage is covered.
- Rupture or bursting of water pipes, unless caused by a covered cause of loss. This exclusion does not apply to sprinkler leakage and is included only in the Basic Form.

- Leakage of water or steam from any part of an appliance or system containing water or steam (other than an automatic sprinkler system), unless caused by a covered cause of loss.

- Explosion of steam boilers, steam pipes, steam turbines, or steam engines owned by, leased to, or operated by the insured. However, if such an explosion causes a fire or a combustion explosion, the damage caused by fire or combustion explosion is covered.

- Mechanical breakdown, including rupture or bursting caused by centrifugal force.

- Loss resulting from the neglect of the insured to use all reasonable means to save and preserve property at and after the time of loss. This exclusion reinforces the insured's duty to protect covered property after a loss.

Finally, several additional exclusions apply only to certain commercial property coverage forms, such as ones that provide business income and extra expense coverage. These exclusions do not apply to the Building and Personal Property Coverage Form, also referred to as the BPP.

Additional Coverages

The Basic Form and the Broad Form both provide an additional coverage titled Limited Coverage for "Fungus," Wet Rot, Dry Rot, and Bacteria. The additional coverage is limited in dollar amount ($15,000 in the aggregate for any one twelve-month policy period) and scope of coverage.

The Broad Form also provides an additional coverage for collapse. Under this additional coverage, the insurer agrees to pay for loss resulting from collapse of a building or any part of a building if the collapse is caused by one or more of these:

- Any of the covered causes of loss.

- Hidden decay, unless such decay is known to an insured before the collapse occurs.

- Hidden insect or vermin damage, unless such damage is known to an insured before the collapse occurs.

- Weight of people or personal property.

- Weight of rain that collects on a roof.

- Use of defective materials or construction methods if the abrupt collapse occurs during the course of construction. (Collapse of a completed building caused by defective materials or construction is covered only if it is caused in part by any of the causes of loss listed here.)

Collapse is specifically and narrowly defined. It means an abrupt falling down or caving in of a building or part of a building that, as a result, can no longer be occupied for its intended purpose. It does not include a building that is in danger of falling down or caving in, nor one that is standing but shows evidence of cracking, bulging, sagging, bending, leaning, settling, shrinking, or expanding. A part of a building that is standing is not considered to be in a state of collapse even if it has separated from another part of the building.

The additional coverage for collapse also covers loss to property caused by the collapse of personal property inside a building (such as storage racks in a warehouse) if the collapse is a result of one of the causes listed previously.

Apply Your Knowledge

Assuming that each of these losses involved covered property, indicate whether each loss would be covered by the Broad Form:

Leaking natural gas accumulated in the insured's storage room and exploded.

Feedback: This loss would be covered under the Broad Form's explosion peril.

Vandals break several windows in the insured building.

Feedback: This loss would be covered under the Broad Form's vandalism peril.

A tree branch falls and damages the roof of the insured's store.

Feedback: This loss would be covered under the Broad Form's falling objects peril.

An earthquake damages an insured building.

Feedback: The loss would not be covered under the Broad Form, because earthquake is not a covered cause of loss (and is excluded by the Earth Movement exclusion).

CAUSES OF LOSS—SPECIAL FORM

Because it is the broadest option for covered causes of loss, the Insurance Services Office (ISO) commercial property policy's Causes of Loss—Special Form is the most frequently selected of the three causes of loss forms.

The Causes of Loss—Special Form (the Special Form) states that it covers "risks of direct physical loss," subject to the form's exclusions and limitations, instead of listing the perils covered. Use of the term "risks" means that loss or damage must be accidental and unforeseen by the insured in order to be covered. The Special Form is designed to cover any loss that would be covered by the Basic and Broad Forms. In addition, the Special Form covers perils that are not specified in the Basic and Broad Forms.

The Special Form offers these advantages to the insured:

- Certain causes of loss that are omitted or excluded under the Broad Form are not excluded—and are therefore covered—under the Special Form. Most significantly, the Special Form covers theft of covered property under a wide variety of circumstances, subject to some exclusions and limitations. The Basic and Broad Forms cover theft by looting at the time of a riot or civil commotion, but in no other circumstances.

- By covering any risk of loss other than those that are specifically excluded, the Special Form covers losses that the insured might not have anticipated.

- The Special Form shifts the "burden of proof" from the insured to the insurer. Under a named perils form, such as the Basic or Broad Form, the insured must prove that the loss was caused by a covered cause. Under the Special Form, an accidental loss to covered property is presumed to be covered unless the insurer can prove that it was caused by an excluded peril.

Exclusions and Limitations

The Special Form contains most of the exclusions of the Basic and Broad Forms, including many (but not all) of the limitations expressed in the descriptions of the basic and broad covered causes of loss. In those instances in which the Special Form does not contain an exclusion or a limitation equivalent to any of those contained in the Basic and Broad Forms, it provides broader coverage, as in these examples:

- The vehicle peril in both the Basic and Broad Forms excludes loss or damage caused by or resulting from vehicles owned by the named insured or operated in the course of the named insured's business. The Special Form, in contrast, does not contain such an exclusion. For example, the Special Form covers loss or damage to an insured building when an employee accidentally drives a truck owned by the insured into the building's garage wall.

- The windstorm peril in the Basic and Broad Forms excludes damage to the interior of a building by rain, snow, sleet, ice, sand, or dust, unless the roof or walls of the building are first damaged by a Covered Cause of Loss. The Special Form contains the same exclusion, but with an additional exception—the Special Form exclusion does not apply if loss results from the melting of ice, sleet, or snow on the building or structure. Therefore, unlike the Basic and Broad Forms, the Special Form covers water damage that occurs when water backs up under roof shingles because roof gutters are clogged with ice, a phenomenon known as ice damming.

Exclusions and Limitations Unique to the Special Form

Because the Special Form covers more causes of loss than the Broad Form, it contains some exclusions and limitations that are not needed in the Broad Form. The Special Form covers any risks of loss other than those that are specifically excluded. Thus, many difficult-to-insure perils that are not covered under the Basic and Broad Forms (because they are not named as covered causes of loss in those forms) must be specifically excluded in the Special Form. Examples of perils that the Special Form specifically excludes are these:

- Wear and tear
- Rust, corrosion, decay, deterioration, or hidden or latent defect
- Smog
- Settling, cracking, shrinking, or expansion
- Infestations and waste products of insects, birds, rodents, or other animals
- Mechanical breakdown
- Damage to personal property by dampness or dryness of atmosphere, changes or extremes in temperatures, or marring or scratching

However, the insurer will pay losses caused by a "specified cause of loss" that results from the excluded peril. The Special Form defines "specified causes of loss" to include all of the causes of loss insured under the Broad Form. For example, a basement wall of an insured building might crack because soil has settled beneath the foundation. The Special Form excludes such cracking damage. However, if the settling and cracking cause a natural gas pipe in the building to rupture, resulting in an explosion (a "specified cause of loss"), the resulting explosion damage will be covered even though the Special Form excludes the initial cause of loss (settling).

The Special Form also excludes loss caused by these:

- Weather conditions that contribute to other excluded causes of loss. If, for example, covered property is damaged by flood waters that were driven in part by high winds, the flood damage will not be covered even though windstorm is not otherwise excluded.

- Acts or decisions, including the failure to act or decide, of any person, group, organization, or governmental body. Thus, for example, if flooding occurs because municipal authorities fail to take proper flood control measures, the flood exclusion cannot be overcome by the insured's claim that the municipality's failure to act was the cause of the loss.

- Faulty or inadequate planning, zoning, surveying, siting, design, specifications, workmanship, repair, construction, renovation, remodeling, grading, compaction, materials, or maintenance.

If one of these excluded causes of loss results in a Covered Cause of Loss, the insurer will pay the loss resulting from the covered cause. For example, the failure of a city's fire department to take necessary measures might allow a fire to spread and burn down several row houses adjoining the insured's building. Even though the fire department's failure to act contributed to the destruction of the adjoining row houses, they were destroyed by fire, a Covered Cause of Loss. Thus, fire damage to the insured's building would be covered.

The Loss or Damage to Products exclusion eliminates coverage for damage to merchandise, goods, or other products resulting from production errors, such as adding wrong ingredients or measuring ingredients incorrectly. Many insurers believe that damage to products resulting from errors in the production process is a business risk that should not be insurable under commercial property policies. However, the exclusion specifically does not apply to loss or damage caused by a Covered Cause of Loss that results from an error or omission in the production process. If, for example, an error in the production process results in an explosion, the explosion damage will be covered.

Another noteworthy exclusion that is unique to the Special Form eliminates coverage for the release, discharge, or dispersal of pollutants. However, the exclusion does not apply to any release of pollutants caused by any of the specified causes of loss, nor does it apply to glass damaged by chemicals applied to the glass.

Loss to these kinds of property is covered only if it is caused by specified causes of loss:

- Valuable papers and records
- Animals, and then only in the event of their death
- Fragile articles if broken, such as glassware, statuary, marble, chinaware, and porcelain (but not including building glass and containers of property held for sale)
- Builders' machinery and equipment owned or held by the insured unless on or within 100 feet of the described premises

Theft-Related Exclusions and Limitations

The Special Form does not contain an absolute exclusion of theft, and thus it covers any theft of covered property that is not specifically excluded. Several theft-related exclusions and limitations define the scope of theft coverage under the Special Form.

The Special Form excludes dishonest acts of the insured or of partners, members, officers, managers, directors, or employees of the insured, but the exclusion does not apply to acts of destruction by employees. For example, if Fred vandalizes his employer's property in response to being demoted, the vandalism damage is covered. If, however, Fred steals money from his employer, this dishonest act is subject to the exclusion. Losses resulting from the excluded types of dishonest acts can be covered under separate crime coverage forms.

The Special Form also excludes the voluntary surrendering of property as the result of a fraudulent scheme or trickery. If, for example, a thief posing as an honest customer tricks the insured's salesperson into voluntarily allowing the thief to remove merchandise from the insured's store, the resulting theft loss will not be covered. Similarly, the Special Form excludes loss of property transferred outside the described premises on the basis of unauthorized instructions.

Loss by theft of construction materials not attached as part of the building is excluded unless the materials are held for sale by the named insured. Moreover, the Special Form excludes loss of property that is simply missing without explanation or that is evidenced only by an inventory shortage.

The Special Form imposes special limits on theft loss of certain kinds of property that are especially attractive to thieves, such as furs, jewelry, precious metals, and tickets. Such property can be insured for higher limits under separate crime or inland marine forms.

A theft exclusion endorsement can be attached to the policy to eliminate theft coverage entirely when the underwriter feels that the risk is unacceptable or when the insured wants to reduce the policy premium.

Additional Coverages and Coverage Extensions

The Special Form includes the same additional coverages for collapse and fungus as the Broad Form. It also contains three coverage extensions that insure certain losses not otherwise covered.

Property in Transit

The Property in Transit extension provides up to $5,000 of additional protection for loss to the insured's property in transit. The property must be in or on a motor vehicle owned, leased, or operated by the insured and cannot be in the custody of the insured's sales personnel. It covers only those losses that occur within the coverage territory.

The transit extension does not provide special form coverage. The perils insured against are fire, lightning, explosion, windstorm, hail, riot, civil commotion, vandalism, upset or overturn of the conveying vehicle, collision of the conveying vehicle with another vehicle or an object other than the roadbed, and theft. The coverage for theft is limited to theft of an entire bale, case, or package by forced entry into a securely locked body or compartment of the vehicle, evidenced by marks of the forced entry.

Because the transit extension has a low coverage limit and restricted covered perils, insureds who have property in transit should consider covering such property under an inland marine or ocean marine policy.

Water Damage, Other Liquids, Powder or Molten Material Damage

The Water Damage, Other Liquids, Powder or Molten Material Damage extension covers the cost to tear out and replace any part of a building necessary to repair an appliance or a system from which water or another liquid—or even powder fire-extinguishing agents or molten materials—has escaped. The extension does not pay for the repair of any defect that resulted in the leakage. It does pay for repairs to fire extinguishing equipment if the damage results in the discharge of any substance from an automatic fire protection system or is directly caused by freezing.

Glass

The Glass extension covers the expenses of installing temporary glass plates or boarding up openings when repair or replacement of damaged glass has been delayed. The insurer will also pay for the cost to clear obstructions (but not window displays) that prevent replacement of the glass. While the Basic, Broad, and Special Forms all insure glass breakage by a Covered Cause of Loss, only the Special Form includes this Glass coverage extension.

Apply Your Knowledge

A soft-drink producer is insured under the Building and Personal Property Coverage Form, also referred to as the BPP, with special form coverage. A mistake during the production process for one of its diet sodas causes too much artificial sweetener to be added to a large quantity of the beverage, forcing the soft drink producer to dispose of the entire batch. Would the cause of this loss be covered under the soft drink producer's Special Form?

Feedback: No, the cause of the loss would not be covered under the soft drink producer's Special Form, because the Loss or Damage to Products exclusion eliminates coverage for damage to merchandise, goods, or other products resulting from production errors, such as adding wrong ingredients or measuring ingredients incorrectly.

An office building is insured under the BPP with special form coverage. Firefighters' efforts to extinguish a fire caused extensive water damage to the insured building. In addition, several windows were broken by the intense heat of the fire. Would the cause of these losses be covered under the Special Form? Additionally, would the Special Form cover the cost of boarding up the windows?

Feedback: Yes, the Special Form would cover the cause of this loss, which was fire, because the Special Form does not exclude fire or any of the consequences of the fire.

BPP LIMITS OF INSURANCE AND DEDUCTIBLE

The dollar amount that the insurer is obligated to pay for a loss covered under the Building and Personal Property Coverage Form, also referred to as the BPP, is largely determined by the Limits of Insurance and Deductible provisions of the BPP.

The BPP's Limits of Insurance section contains provisions explaining how the insurer will apply the limit(s) of insurance to covered losses. The amount that the insurer will pay for a covered loss is also affected by the BPP's Deductible provision, which provides the rules for applying the deductible shown in the declarations.

Limits of Insurance

The Insurance Services Office (ISO) BPP's Limits of Insurance section states that the most the insurer is obligated to pay for a loss in any one occurrence is the applicable limit of insurance shown in the declarations. Total commercial property losses are rare, and the forms contain other limitations that reduce the amount the insurer pays. Therefore, the amount that the insurer pays for a loss covered under the BPP is generally less than the applicable limit of insurance. However, payments under all of the BPP's coverage extensions and under most of the additional coverages are paid in addition to the limit of insurance, which makes it possible for the total payment for one loss to exceed the limit of insurance.

A BPP can be subject to one or more limits, which can be either specific or blanket limits. When specific limits are used, the declarations show separate limits of insurance for each covered building and for personal property at each location. For example, a BPP's declarations could show these limits for the insured location:

- $1,000,000 for a Building
- $800,000 for Your Business Personal Property
- $50,000 for Personal Property of Others

A blanket limit is the alternative to specific limits. A blanket limit can apply one amount of insurance to all property covered by the policy. If the property described in the previous example was insured on a blanket basis, then the declarations would state that $1,850,000 blanket coverage is available on the Building, Your Business Personal Property, and Personal Property of Others at the address.

Property at different locations can also be covered on a blanket basis, in which case one limit of insurance can apply to all covered property at all locations. Alternatively, one blanket limit could apply to all of the insured's buildings (at one or more locations) and another blanket limit could apply to all the insured's business personal property (at one or more locations).

Deductible

An insurer is not obligated to pay anything to the insured unless the loss exceeds the deductible shown in the policy declarations. The limit of insurance then applies to the loss in excess of the deductible. That is, the deductible is subtracted from the loss, not from the limit of insurance. For example, under a policy that has a $100,000 limit on a building and a $1,000 deductible, an insurer's payment would be calculated as shown:

Amount of Loss	Insurer's Payment
$500	No payment (loss is less than deductible)
$100,000	$99,000 ($100,000 – $1,000 deductible)
$110,000	$100,000 ($110,000 – $1,000 deductible exceeds limit of insurance)

Unless a BPP is written for a single blanket limit, it typically covers two or more categories of property (such as two buildings, or a building and business personal property) with a separate limit applying to each category. How the deductible applies in such situations is determined by this passage in the Deductible provision:

> When the occurrence involves loss to more than one item of Covered Property and separate Limits of Insurance apply, the losses will not be combined in determining application of the Deductible. But the deductible will be applied only once per occurrence.

For example, a BPP covers five buildings at one location, each building is insured for a separate limit, and a $5,000 deductible applies. A windstorm (one occurrence) causes less than $5,000 damage to each of the buildings, but the combined total is $10,000 of damage. As stated in the Deductible provision, the losses will not be combined for purposes of applying the deductible. Therefore, because the insurer is not obligated to pay anything to the insured unless the loss on at least one building exceeds the deductible, the insurer will pay nothing for this loss.

If, instead, the amount of loss on one of the buildings is $6,000, the insurer will pay the $1,000 amount of loss on this building that exceeds the $5,000 deductible. And, because the deductible has now been applied (and "the deductible will be applied only once per occurrence"), the insurer will also pay the amount of loss on each of the other buildings even if it does not exceed the deductible amount.

If the Coinsurance condition or the Agreed Value optional coverage applies, the amount of the loss is first reduced by any penalty imposed by those provisions before applying the deductible.

Under ISO *Commercial Lines Manual* (CLM) rules, the standard deductible is $500. This may be reduced to $250 for an additional premium or increased to a higher amount that reduces the premium. A $1,000 or $5,000 deductible is common for middle-market insureds. The savings for higher deductibles are seldom attractive to smaller firms, but underwriters tend to prefer higher deductibles because they save the insurer the expense of handling small claims. In some cases, an underwriter may require a higher deductible before agreeing to provide coverage for an insured with frequent small losses.

Apply Your Knowledge

The owners of a restaurant are insured under a BPP coverage form that covers their building for a $400,000 limit and their business personal property for a $200,000 limit. The policy has a $1,000 deductible. A covered cause of loss results in $100,000 worth of damage to the building and a $50,000 loss of business personal property. Assuming that no coinsurance penalty applies, apply the policy's limits and deductible to this loss to determine the amount payable.

Feedback: In accordance with the Deductible provision, the $1,000 deductible is subtracted from the building loss before applying the building limit: $100,000 - $1,000 = $99,000. Because this amount is less than the $400,000 building limit, the insurer will pay $99,000 for the building loss. Because the deductible applies only once per occurrence and has already been applied to the building loss, it does not apply to the business personal property loss. Moreover, the business personal property loss does not exceed the applicable $200,000 limit. Therefore, the insurer will pay the $50,000 business personal property loss in full. The insurer's total payment will be calculated as $99,000 + $50,000 = $149,000.

A business office is insured under a BPP coverage form that specifies a $2 million limit of insurance on the office building and a $900,000 limit of insurance on business personal property at the building's address. The policy has a $5,000 deductible. A covered cause of loss results in $2.2 million worth of damage to the building and a $300,000 loss of business personal property. Two shrubs are destroyed, resulting in a $500 loss fully covered by the BPP coverage form's Outdoor Property coverage extension. Assuming that no coinsurance penalty applies, apply the policy's limits and deductible to this loss to determine the amount payable.

Feedback: The $5,000 deductible is subtracted from the amount of the building loss before applying the building limit: $2,200,000 - $5,000 = $2,195,000. Because this amount exceeds the applicable limit of insurance, the insurer will pay the full $2 million limit of insurance for the building loss. The deductible applies only once per occurrence and has already been applied to the building loss; therefore, it does not apply to the business personal property loss. Moreover, because the business personal property loss does not exceed the applicable $900,000 limit of insurance, the insurer will pay the $300,000 business personal property loss in full. Finally, the $500 payment for the shrubs under the Outdoor Property coverage extension is payable in addition to the limits of insurance. Therefore, the insurer will pay a total of $2,300,500, calculated as $2,000,000 + $300,000 + $500.

SUMMARY

Three important aspects of commercial property loss exposures are the types of property that might be exposed to loss, damage, or destruction; the causes of loss that might result in property being lost, damaged, or destroyed; and the financial consequences of a property loss. Many of the basic property coverages an organization needs are commonly provided under a commercial property coverage part, which consists of commercial property declarations, one or more commercial property coverage forms, one or more causes of loss forms, Commercial Property Conditions, and any applicable endorsements.

The BPP can be used to insure buildings; business personal property of the named insured; and personal property of others in the named insured's care, custody, or control. With only minor exceptions, property is covered only while located on or within 100 feet of the insured premises. The Property Not Covered section lists the various types of property that are not covered by the BPP. However, most types of property not covered can be insured by adding optional coverage endorsements to the BPP.

The BPP's additional coverages and coverage extensions cover loss exposures that would not otherwise be covered by the BPP's basic coverages. However, in some cases, the special limits that apply to these supplemental coverages are inadequate for many businesses. The limits stated in the form can often be increased by showing a higher limit in the declarations, adding an appropriate coverage endorsement, or buying another type of policy to supplement the BPP.

The perils covered in an ISO commercial property coverage part are specified in any of three causes of loss forms. The Causes of Loss—Basic Form and the Causes of Loss—Broad Form include nearly all of the same covered perils, but the Broad Form covers three additional perils, including collapse. This additional coverage makes The Broad Form the choice of most insureds over the Basic Form.

The most frequently selected of the three causes of loss forms, the Causes of Loss—Special Form is designed to cover any loss that would be covered by the Basic and Broad Forms. In addition, the Special Form provides coverages not found in the Basic and Broad Forms. The Special Form offers several advantages to the insured, including coverage for certain causes of loss that are omitted or excluded under the Broad Form, coverage for losses the insured might not have anticipated, and the placement of the "burden of proof" on the insurer as opposed to the insured.

Under the ISO BPP, the most the insurer is obligated to pay for loss in any one occurrence is the applicable limit of insurance shown in the declarations. The insurer is not obligated to pay anything to the insured unless the loss exceeds the deductible; the limit of insurance then applies to the loss in excess of the deductible.

Direct Your Learning ▶▶

8

Commercial Property Insurance, Part II

Educational Objectives

After learning the content of this assignment, you should be able to:

▷ Explain how each of the Loss Conditions and Additional Conditions affects coverage under the Building and Personal Property Coverage Form.

▷ Explain how each of the following optional coverages described in the BPP modifies the basic coverage of the BPP:
- Agreed Value
- Inflation Guard
- Replacement Cost
- Extension of Replacement Cost to Personal Property of Others

▷ Summarize each of the Commercial Property Conditions.

▷ Explain how each of the conditions contained in the Common Policy Conditions affects coverage under a commercial property coverage part.

▷ Explain how each of these documents modifies the Building and Personal Property Coverage Form:
- Ordinance or Law Coverage endorsement
- Spoilage Coverage endorsement
- Flood Coverage endorsement
- Earthquake and Volcanic Eruption Coverage endorsement
- Peak Season Limit of Insurance endorsement
- Value Reporting Form

▷ Identify the factors that affect commercial property insurance premiums.

▷ Given a case, determine whether, and for what amount, a described loss would be covered by a commercial property coverage part that includes the Building and Personal Property Coverage Form and any of the three causes of loss forms.

Commercial Property Insurance, Part II

BPP LOSS CONDITIONS AND ADDITIONAL CONDITIONS

The Building and Personal Property Coverage Form, also referred to as the BPP, requires both the insurer and the insured to perform certain duties and follow certain procedures in connection with any claim made under the BPP.

The Loss Conditions section of the BPP stipulates the duties of the insured and the insurer after a loss has occurred and establishes procedures for adjusting claims. It also includes an explanation of methods for establishing the value of damaged property. The BPP's Additional Conditions deal with coinsurance and the interests of a mortgageholder (mortgagee).

Abandonment

The Abandonment condition prohibits the insured from abandoning damaged property to the insurer for repair or disposal. Although the Loss Payment condition permits the insurer, at its option, to take all or any part of damaged property at an agreed or appraised value, the Abandonment condition clarifies that making arrangements for the repair or disposal of covered property is the insured's responsibility, unless the insurer chooses to exercise its option under the Loss Payment condition.

Appraisal

The Appraisal condition establishes a method for the insurer and the insured to resolve disputes about the insured property's value or amount of loss. It does not apply to policy coverage disputes. If the insured and the insurer cannot agree on the value of the property or the amount of loss, either party may issue a written demand for an appraisal. When either party demands an appraisal, the appraisal process described in the BPP must be followed.

Duties in the Event of Loss or Damage

The BPP imposes several duties on the insured when a loss occurs. If the insured fails to perform any of them, the insurer may not have to pay for the loss. When a loss occurs, the insured must take several actions:

- Notify the police if the loss appears to have resulted from a violation of law, such as vandalism, arson, or theft.
- Give the insurer prompt notice of the loss, including a description of the property damaged. Prompt notice is generally held to mean as soon as feasible under the circumstances.
- Provide information as to how, when, and where the loss occurred.
- Take all reasonable steps to protect the property from further loss.
- At the insurer's request, furnish the insurer with inventories of the damaged and undamaged property and permit the insurer to inspect the property and records.
- Submit to examination under oath regarding any matter related to the loss.
- Cooperate with the insurer in the adjustment of the loss.
- Send a signed, sworn **proof of loss** to the insurer within sixty days after the insurer's request for one.

Proof of loss

A statement of facts about a loss for which the insured is making a claim.

Loss Payment

If loss or damage is covered, the insurer has four loss payment options:

- Pay the amount of the loss or damage
- Pay the cost of repairing or replacing the damaged property (does not include any increased cost attributable to enforcement of ordinances or laws regulating the construction, use, or repair of the property)
- Take over all or any part of the property and pay its agreed or appraised value
- Repair, rebuild, or replace the damaged property with other property of like kind and quality

Insurers seldom exercise the last option because it may cause the insurer to become a guarantor of the repaired or replaced property. If the repaired or replaced property proves to be unsatisfactory, the insurer might be required to make it satisfactory, even if the cost of doing so exceeds the applicable limit of insurance.

The Loss Payment clause also states that regardless of the value of the loss, the insurer will pay no more than the insured's financial interest in the covered property.

The insurer is required to notify the insured of its intent either to pay the claim or to deny payment within thirty days after receipt of a satisfactory proof of loss. The insurer may, for example, deny payment because of lack of coverage under the policy or failure of the insured to comply with one or more of the policy conditions. Actual payment is due within thirty days after the parties have agreed on the amount of loss or an appraisal has been completed.

Recovered Property

If either the insurer or the insured recovers property, such as stolen merchandise, for which the insurer has paid a loss, the party that makes the recovery is obligated to promptly notify the other party. The insured has the option of taking the recovered property and refunding the loss payment to the insurer. The insurer would then pay the cost of recovering the property and the cost, if any, of repairing it. If the insured elects not to take the recovered property, the insurer may dispose of the property as it sees fit.

Vacancy

If the building where a loss occurs has been vacant for more than sixty consecutive days before the loss occurs, the insurer will not pay if the loss is caused by vandalism, sprinkler leakage (unless the sprinkler system was protected against freezing), breakage of building glass, water damage, theft, or attempted theft. If any other covered peril causes the loss, loss payment will be reduced by 15 percent.

The vacancy conditions apply differently for a building's tenant than for its owner or general lessee. A general lessee is an entity that leases the entire building and subleases portions of the building to others. In the case of a tenant, a vacant "building" means the unit or suite rented or leased to the tenant. A building is vacant when it does not contain enough business personal property to conduct customary operations.

If the policy covers a building owner or general lessee, "building" means the entire building, and it is considered vacant unless at least 31 percent of its total square footage is rented to a lessee or sub-lessee and is used by that party to conduct its customary operations or by the building owner to conduct its customary operations. Buildings under construction or renovation are not considered to be vacant.

Because of the differing definitions for tenants and building owners, when the building does not meet the 31 percent standard, the loss payment to the building owner may be reduced or eliminated, but a tenant may be able to collect in full. Similarly, if the building meets the 31 percent standard, the building owner may have full coverage, but a tenant may be penalized when its premises do not contain enough business personal property to conduct the tenant's customary operations.

Valuation

Actual cash value (ACV)

Cost to replace property with new property of like kind and quality less depreciation.

The Valuation condition sets forth rules for establishing the value of insured property. Subject to the exceptions summarized in the exhibit, the insured property is valued at its **actual cash value (ACV)**. ACV valuation can be changed to replacement cost valuation by activating the BPP's optional coverages for replacement cost, which are printed in the BPP. See the exhibit "BPP Valuation Provisions."

BPP Valuation Provisions

Property Type	Valuation Basis
Property other than that specifically listed	Actual cash value
Building damage of $2,500 or less	Replacement cost except for awnings, floor coverings, appliances, and outdoor equipment or furniture
Stock sold but not delivered	Selling price less discounts and unincurred costs
Glass	Replacement cost for safety glazing if required by law
Improvements and betterments:	
(a) replaced by other than the insured	Not covered
(b) replaced by insured	Actual cash value
(c) not replaced	Percentage of cost based on remaining life of lease
Valuable papers and records (excluding electronic data)	Cost of blank media and cost of transcription or copying ($2,500 coverage extension to replace or restore lost information)
Electronic data	(Covered only under additional coverage with a $2,500 annual aggregate limit)
If replaced	Cost to replace or restore electronic data that have been destroyed or corrupted by a covered cause of loss
If not replaced	Cost to replace the media with blank media of substantially identical type

[DA02466]

Coinsurance

The Coinsurance condition requires the insured to carry insurance equal to at least a specified percentage of the covered property's ACV (or replacement cost, if that optional valuation approach is in effect). The coinsurance percentage is shown in the declarations. If the amount of insurance carried is equal to or greater than the required percentage, the insurer will pay covered losses in full (subject to any applicable deductible) up to the limit of insurance. If the amount of insurance carried is less than the required percentage, loss payments are reduced proportionately.

If the amount of insurance carried does not meet the coinsurance requirement, the amount the insurer will pay (subject always to the limit of insurance) is calculated by this formula:

$$\text{Loss payment} = \left(\frac{\text{Amount of insurance carried}}{\text{Amount of insurance required}} \times \text{Loss} \right) - \text{Deductible}$$

The amount of insurance required is the property's ACV (or replacement cost, if that option has been chosen) immediately before the loss occurred multiplied by the coinsurance percentage. The deductible is subtracted after the coinsurance penalty has been calculated. The example in the exhibit illustrates this calculation. See the exhibit "Coinsurance Example."

Coinsurance Example

ACV of covered building at time of loss	$200,000
Limit of insurance	$140,000
Coinsurance percentage	80%
Amount of loss	$40,000
Deductible	$500

Amount of insurance required = 0.80 × $200,000 = $160,000

$$\text{Loss payment} = \left(\frac{140,000}{160,000} \times \$40,000 \right)$$

$$= \left(0.875 \times 40,000 \right) - 500$$

$$= 35,000 - 500$$

$$= 34,500.$$

If the amount of insurance carried had been $160,000 or more, the insurer would have paid $39,500, the amount of loss less the deductible.

[DA02468]

Mortgageholder

If a mortgageholder (such as a bank that has made a mortgage loan to the named insured) is shown in the declarations, the insurer is obligated to include the mortgageholder in any payment for loss to the mortgaged property. In practice, the loss payment check or draft is usually made payable jointly to the insured and all mortgageholders so that they can agree on the division of the payment. In most cases, the loss payment is used to repair or rebuild the mortgaged property, and the mortgages continue in force as before.

Any act or default of the insured does not impair the rights of the mortgageholder, provided the mortgageholder pays any premium due that the insured has not paid, submits a proof of loss if requested, and has notified the insurer of any change in ownership, occupancy, or substantial increase in risk of which the mortgageholder is aware. Consequently, the insurer is sometimes obligated to make a loss payment to the mortgageholder even though it has denied coverage, for example, to an insured who has committed arson. In such cases, the insurer, at its option, can take either of these actions:

- Take over the rights of the mortgageholder to the extent of such payment and collect the amount of payment from the insured
- Pay off the outstanding balance of the mortgage and take over all of the rights of the mortgageholder

If the insurer cancels the policy because the insured failed to pay the premium or if the insurer does not renew the policy for any reason, it must notify the mortgageholder ten days before the termination of coverage. If the insurer cancels the policy for any reason other than nonpayment of premium, it must give thirty days' advance notice to the mortgageholder. If the insurer fails to give the required notice to the mortgageholder, the policy remains in force for the protection of the mortgageholder even though it may not provide any protection for the insured.

BPP: OPTIONAL COVERAGES

The Optional Coverages section of the BPP contains provisions for four optional coverages:

- Agreed Value
- Inflation Guard
- Replacement Cost
- Extension of Replacement Cost to Personal Property of Others

The optional coverages apply only when an appropriate notation is made on the declarations page. Agreed Value, Inflation Guard, and Replacement Cost may be used for buildings only, personal property only, or both buildings and personal property.

Agreed Value

Agreed Value optional coverage

Optional coverage that suspends the Coinsurance condition if the insured carries the amount of insurance agreed to by the insurer and insured.

To activate the **Agreed Value optional coverage**, an amount is entered under the Agreed Value heading in the declarations for each category of property (building, personal property, or both) to which the option applies. This option enables the insured to remove the uncertainty as to whether the amount of insurance carried complies with the Coinsurance condition. With the option in force, the insurer and the insured have agreed in advance that the amount stated in the declarations—the agreed value—is adequate for coinsurance purposes. Because most losses are partial, insureds are often tempted to underinsure, knowing they will not suffer a coinsurance penalty when the agreed value option is in effect. Therefore, insurers underwrite agreed value carefully, requiring proof of value before providing agreed value coverage. At the very least, the insured ordinarily must submit a signed statement of values. Insurance Services Office, (ISO) Form CP 16 15, Statement of Values, can be used for this purpose.

The BPP Coinsurance condition does not apply to property insured under the agreed value option. However, it is replaced by a provision that, while not called coinsurance, is the practical equivalent of 100 percent coinsurance based on the agreed value. The agreed value option provides that if the limit of insurance equals or exceeds the agreed value stated in the declarations, losses will be paid in full up to the limit of insurance. If the limit of insurance is less than the agreed value, the amount of loss payment is calculated by this equation:

$$\text{Loss payment} = \left(\frac{\text{Limit of insurance}}{\text{Agreed value}} \times \text{Loss} \right) - \text{Deductible}$$

Coverage under this option extends until the agreed value expiration date shown on the declarations or the expiration date of the policy, whichever occurs first. If the coverage option is not renewed, the Coinsurance condition is reinstated.

Inflation Guard

Inflation Guard optional coverage is coverage for the effects of inflation that automatically increases the limit of insurance by the percentage of annual increase shown in the declarations. This percentage is applied on a pro rata basis, from the date the limit of insurance became effective to the date of the loss, before the loss payment is computed. The percentage of annual increase is shown separately for buildings and personal property.

Replacement Cost

The **Replacement Cost optional coverage** replaces the phrase "actual cash value" with "replacement cost" in the BPP Valuation condition. As a result, the insurer is obligated to pay the cost to replace the damaged or destroyed property with new property of like kind and quality without any deduction for depreciation or obsolescence.

Inflation Guard optional coverage

Coverage for the effects of inflation that automatically increases the limit of insurance by the percentage of annual increase shown in the declarations.

Replacement Cost optional coverage

Coverage for losses to most types of property on a replacement cost basis (with no deduction for depreciation or obsolescence) instead of on an actual cash value basis.

The insurer is not obligated to pay replacement cost until the property has been repaired or replaced, and then only if such repair or replacement is completed in a reasonable time. If repair or replacement is not completed in a reasonable time, the loss payment is based on the ACV at the time of loss.

The insured may make a claim on the basis of ACV, with the difference between ACV and replacement cost to be paid upon completion of repair or reconstruction. The insurer must be notified within 180 days after the occurrence of loss that a claim will be made for replacement cost.

If the replacement cost option is activated, the Coinsurance condition continues to apply, but with one important difference. The amount of insurance required by the Coinsurance condition is calculated by multiplying replacement cost by the coinsurance percentage if the claim is made on a replacement cost basis. If the insured makes a claim on an ACV basis, coinsurance is also calculated on an ACV basis.

If the replacement cost option is selected, tenants' improvements and betterments are also valued at replacement cost if the tenant actually repairs or replaces them, at its own cost, as soon as reasonably possible after the loss.

The replacement cost option does not apply to property of others; contents of a residence; manuscripts; or works of art, antiques, or rare articles. It also does not apply to "stock" unless the declarations indicate that the replacement cost option includes stock. The BPP defines stock to mean merchandise, raw materials, goods in process, and finished goods.

Extension of Replacement Cost to Personal Property of Others

Insureds frequently lease photocopiers, computers, phone systems, and other equipment. These leases or agreements may make the insured responsible for the replacement cost of these items in the event they are damaged. To cover this loss exposure, insureds who have selected the replacement cost option may also elect to have the personal property of others valued at replacement cost. In such cases, the amount of the loss is calculated according to the written agreement between the insured and the owner of the property, but cannot exceed the replacement cost of the property or the applicable limit of insurance.

COMMERCIAL PROPERTY CONDITIONS

Even if an insurance policy would otherwise cover an insured's loss, an insurer may deny coverage if the policy's conditions have not been met.

The Building and Personal Property Coverage Form and the other coverage forms that can be included in a commercial property coverage part each contain several conditions specific to those forms. In addition, the Commercial Property Conditions Form contains nine conditions that apply to any of the

Commercial Property Coverage Forms to which they are attached. These nine conditions are titled as shown:

- Concealment, Misrepresentation, or Fraud
- Control of Property
- Insurance Under Two or More Coverages
- Legal Action Against Us
- Liberalization
- Transfer of Rights of Recovery Against Others to Us
- No Benefit to Bailee
- Other Insurance
- Policy Period, Coverage Territory

Concealment, Misrepresentation, or Fraud

The commercial property coverage part is void if the insured commits any fraudulent act related to the coverage or conceals or misrepresents any material fact pertaining to the coverage part, the covered property, or the insured's interest in the covered property. Concealment and misrepresentation are related but distinct acts:

- A misrepresentation is an active, deliberate misstatement of fact. For example, assume that John Doe, who has previously been convicted of arson, applies for fire insurance. If the application asks whether the applicant has ever been convicted of arson, and Doe responds that he has not, his answer is a misrepresentation.
- Concealment does not involve a misstatement of fact, but instead is an intentional failure to disclose a material fact. In the John Doe example, if the application does not ask about past convictions for arson, and Doe does not offer information about his conviction, some courts might consider Doe's action to be concealment.

Misrepresentation or concealment does not always void coverage: Only material misrepresentation or concealment voids coverage. A fact is material if knowledge of it would cause the insurer to charge a higher premium or decline to write the coverage. For example, an insured might state that his or her building is painted red when in fact it is painted yellow. This misstatement would have no bearing on the insurance and is therefore not material.

Control of Property

The Control of Property condition consists of two parts. The first part states that coverage under the policy will not be affected by acts or omissions of persons other than the insured if those persons are not acting under the direction or control of the insured. The second part of the condition states that violation of a policy condition at one location will not affect coverage at any other location.

To illustrate how this clause might apply, assume that a liquor store's policy is endorsed, requiring the store's burglar alarm system to be maintained in working order at all insured locations. Assume also that the insured leases these locations from other parties. The first part of the clause would protect the insured if the alarm system was disconnected by a building owner, provided that the owner was not under the insured's control.

The second part of the Control of Property condition would be important in this example if the liquor store's policy provides coverage at more than one location. In the absence of this part of the condition, the insured's failure to maintain the alarm system at one location might suspend coverage at all locations, even if the alarm systems are properly maintained at the other locations. Under the second part of the condition, only coverage at the location with the deficient alarm system would be affected.

Insurance Under Two or More Coverages

This policy condition is necessary because some property might be covered under two or more coverage parts that can be included in a single commercial package policy (such as commercial property and commercial inland marine). The Insurance Under Two or More Coverages condition prevents double recovery by the insured in such instances. The total payment under all applicable coverage parts is limited to the actual amount of the loss. Duplication, or "stacking," of the limits is avoided.

Legal Action Against Us

This condition spells out two requirements the insured must meet before legal action can be brought against the insurer ("Us") to enforce the policy. First, the insured must have complied with all conditions of the policy, including those in the coverage part and the Common Policy Conditions, as well as the applicable Loss Conditions. Second, the action must be brought within two years after the date on which the direct physical loss occurred.

Liberalization

If the insurer adopts any revision that would broaden coverage under the commercial property coverage part and for which there is no additional premium charge, the broader coverage is extended automatically to policies already in effect. This automatic coverage applies only if the broadening amendment is adopted during the policy term or within forty-five days before the effective date of the policy. Liberalization applies only to amendments that broaden coverage, not to those that restrict coverage.

Transfer of Rights of Recovery Against Others to Us

Subrogation is a term commonly used by insurance practitioners but not used in Insurance Services Office (ISO) commercial property forms. If the insured takes any action that eliminates the insurer's right of recovery (other than one specifically authorized by this condition), the insurer may not be required to pay the loss. This condition specifically permits the insured to waive the right of recovery against any other party, provided the waiver is made in writing and before the loss occurs. A waiver of recovery may be given by the insured after loss only to another party insured under the same policy, a parent or subsidiary company, or a tenant of the insured property. Any other waiver given by the insured after loss has occurred may impair the insured's right to collect from the insurer for the loss.

Subrogation

The process by which an insurer can, after it has paid a loss under the policy, recover the amount paid from any party (other than the insured) who caused the loss or is otherwise legally liable for the loss.

 **Reality Check**

Subrogation

The importance of subrogation to insurers and their insureds can be illustrated by this hypothetical case. The insured's building and its contents, valued at $600,000, were destroyed by a fire that was covered under the insured's commercial property insurance. While investigating the claim, the insurer's claim representative discovered that the fire was caused by faulty electrical wiring that had been installed in the building only a few months before the loss. After paying its insured's loss in full, minus the policy's $1,000 deductible, the insurer exercised its subrogation rights against the contractor that did the faulty work and was legally liable for the resulting damage. The contractor's liability insurer paid the entire $600,000 loss to the commercial property insurer. Out of this subrogation recovery, the commercial property insurer reimbursed its insured for the $1,000 deductible and recovered the entire amount that the insurer had paid its insured for the loss.

[DA07822]

No Benefit to Bailee

A bailee is a person or business organization that has temporary custody of the property of another. Examples are dry cleaners, television repair shops, laundries, and fur-storage firms. Bailees may become legally liable to bailors (the owners of the property) for damage to the property they hold. Bailees sometimes try to limit their liability with contractual provisions stating that the bailee is not liable for damage if the damage is recoverable under insurance carried by the bailor. The No Benefit to Bailee condition is intended to defeat such provisions in the bailment contract and to reinforce the insurer's right of subrogation against the bailee.

Other Insurance

An insured may have more than one policy covering a given loss. In keeping with the principle of indemnity, the Other Insurance condition limits the total recovery from all applicable insurance to an amount not in excess of the actual loss sustained.

If the other insurance is provided by an additional policy subject to the same plan, terms, and conditions, then each policy pays in relation to all applicable policies. If the other insurance is not subject to all of the conditions of the commercial property coverage part, then the policy subject to the commercial property coverage part is considered excess coverage and pays only the covered loss amount that exceeds what is due from the other policy.

Policy Period, Coverage Territory

This condition states that coverage begins on the effective date and ends on the expiration date shown in the declarations. The declarations state that the beginning and ending time is 12:01 a.m., determined by standard time at the insured's mailing address as shown in the declarations, even though some or all of the insured property may be located in a different time zone. The insured property is covered only while it is located within the United States (including its territories and possessions), Puerto Rico, or Canada.

COMMON POLICY CONDITIONS

The Insurance Services Office (ISO) *Commercial Lines Manual* (CLM) requires that a common policy conditions form be attached to every Commercial Package Policy (CPP) or monoline policy. The Common Policy Conditions (IL 00 17) form contains six conditions, which apply to all coverage parts in the policy unless a particular coverage part states otherwise. This approach avoids the need to repeat these common conditions in each coverage part. These are the six conditions contained in the form:

- Cancellation
- Changes
- Examination of Books and Records
- Inspections and Surveys
- Premiums
- Transfer of Rights and Duties Under This Policy

Cancellation

The insured may cancel the policy at any time by mailing or delivering written notice of cancellation to the insurer. If two or more insureds are listed in the declarations, only the one listed first (called the first named insured) can request cancellation.

The insurer can cancel the policy by mailing or delivering written notice of cancellation to the first named insured. To provide time for the insured to obtain other insurance, the insurer is required to give advance notice of cancellation. The notice must be mailed or delivered to the insured at least ten days before the date of cancellation if the cancellation is for nonpayment of premium. The notice must be mailed at least thirty days before the date of cancellation for any other reason. If the cancellation results in a return premium, the insurer will send the refund to the first named insured.

In almost every state, the Cancellation condition is superseded by state law and an endorsement is added to the policy. The endorsement modifies the cancellation provisions to conform with the applicable law.

The state laws commonly address permissible reasons for cancellation and a longer advance notification period if the cancellation occurs for a reason other than nonpayment of premium.

Changes

The Changes condition states that the policy constitutes the entire contract between the insurer and the named insured, and that the policy can be changed only by a written endorsement issued by the insurer.

In practice, changes are often first made by verbal communication and confirmed afterwards in writing. In most states, such verbal changes are binding because an authorized agent of the insurer is viewed as having the power to waive the written endorsement requirement. Such changes may be made, with the insurer's consent, upon the request of the first named insured.

Only the first named insured has the authority to request policy changes, and the insurer is authorized to make changes upon the request of the first named insured without specific permission of any other insured.

Examination of Books and Records

The insurer reserves the right to examine and audit the insured's books and records related to the policy at any time during the policy period and for up to three years after the policy's termination. This provision is included because many commercial insurance policies are issued with estimated premiums. The final premium is determined after the policy expires, based on reported values of the insured property, the amount of the insured's sales or payroll, or some other variable premium base. The insured is required to report the final figures to the insurer, and the insurer may accept the insured's reports without verification.

However, if the insurer prefers to verify the reports by making an on-site inspection of the insured's books and records, the condition permits the insurer to do that. An insurer may also choose to exercise its rights under this condition in the process of investigating a claimed loss.

Inspections and Surveys

The insurer has the right, but not the obligation, to inspect the insured's premises and operations at any reasonable time during the policy period.

The inspections may be made by the insurer's own personnel or by another organization acting on the insurer's behalf. Such inspections are important in determining the insurability of the insured's property and operations, in setting proper insurance rates, and in making risk control recommendations.

The insurer may inform the insured of the results of such inspections and may recommend changes. However, it does not have a duty to do either. The condition makes it clear that the insurer does not make safety inspections, does not guarantee that conditions are safe or healthful, and does not guarantee that the insured is in compliance with safety or health regulations.

These disclaimer clauses have been included in the policy to protect the insurer against suits made by persons who allege that their injuries would not have occurred but for the insurer's failure to detect a hazardous condition or a violation of laws or regulations, and that the insurer is therefore responsible for the resulting damages, fines, or penalties assessed against the insured.

Premiums

The first named insured is responsible for paying the policy premium. If the insurer owes a return premium, it will make payment only to the first named insured.

Transfer of Rights and Duties Under This Policy

The insured cannot transfer any rights or duties under the policy to any other person or organization without the insurer's written consent. For example, if the insured sells a building covered by the policy, the insurance cannot be transferred to the new owner of the property without the insurer's written consent.

Such a transfer of insurance is generally referred to as assignment of the policy. The condition also provides specifically for the automatic transfer of coverage if an individual named insured dies. (An individual named insured is a person whose name is listed on the "Named Insured" line in the policy declarations.) In that case, the insured's rights and duties under the policy are automatically transferred to the insured's legal representatives or, if the insured's legal representatives have not yet been appointed, to any person having proper temporary custody of the insured property.

COMMERCIAL PROPERTY ENDORSEMENTS

The Building and Personal Property Coverage Form, also referred to as the BPP, can be modified by a variety of endorsements.

The BPP's endorsements are useful for these tasks:

- Providing coverage enhancements that some insureds may want but that others either do not believe they need or cannot afford
- Eliminating coverage for certain exposures, enabling underwriters to accept applications that they would otherwise decline
- Changing policy provisions to match the specific characteristics of certain industries or insureds
- Amending the policy to comply with state insurance regulations

The Insurance Services Office (ISO) portfolio of commercial property forms contains more than 100 multistate forms and endorsements and an even greater number of state-specific endorsements. In addition, many insurers use independently developed endorsements or draft manuscript endorsements to accommodate special requirements. This selection of endorsements illustrates their diversity:

- Ordinance or Law Coverage Endorsement
- Spoilage Coverage Endorsement
- Flood Coverage Endorsement
- Earthquake and Volcanic Eruption Coverage Endorsement
- Peak Season Limit of Insurance Endorsement
- Value Reporting Form

Ordinance or Law Coverage

The Ordinance or Law Coverage endorsement provides three coverages for losses resulting from the enforcement of building ordinances or laws:

- Coverage A covers the value of the undamaged portion of a building that must be demolished. For example, an entire structure may have to be totally demolished if it is a frame building in an area where only fire-resistive construction is currently permitted. Demolishing the undamaged parts of the building changes what would have been a partial loss to a total loss.
- Coverage B covers the cost to demolish the undamaged portion of a building and remove its debris when demolition is required by the building code.
- Coverage C covers the increased cost to repair or rebuild the property resulting from the enforcement of a building, zoning, or land use law. Building codes may require that reconstruction of damaged property meet higher standards, such as heavier electrical service, elevators to upper floors, and fire-resistive stairwells. Coverage C pays the added expense for these improvements.

Coverages B and C can be provided under one blanket limit. The unendorsed commercial property coverage forms exclude these losses except for the additional coverage for increased cost of construction, which adds a small amount of coverage for the types of loss insured by Coverage C of the endorsement.

Spoilage Coverage

The Spoilage Coverage endorsement covers damage to perishable stock due to power outages; on-premises breakdown; or contamination of the insured's refrigerating, cooling, or humidity control equipment. The power outage must be caused by conditions beyond the insured's control. The coverage is not subject to coinsurance and cannot be provided under a blanket limit.

Flood Coverage

In the United States, losses from flooding accompany hurricanes, heavy rains, and melting snow. Collapsing dams can also cause floods. Any of these events can cause catastrophic losses. Because of the movable nature of the property they insure, auto physical damage insurance and many inland marine forms include flood as an insured peril. However, insurers are reluctant to write flood insurance on property at fixed locations, such as buildings and their contents. Therefore, all three of the causes of loss forms exclude flood.

Flood insurance for buildings and their contents is available, though, in two ways.

The National Flood Insurance Program (NFIP) is a federal government resource that provides insurance for properties located in eligible communities. The NFIP is administered by the Federal Insurance Administration, part of the Federal Emergency Management Agency (FEMA). For commercial properties, the maximum NFIP limit is $500,000 per building and $500,000 for the contents of a building. Although the demand for flood insurance is greatest from insureds in the most hazardous flood zones, NFIP provides coverage in all areas of eligible communities. National flood insurance is sold through private insurers and agents and is backed by the U.S. government.

The other source for flood insurance on buildings and contents is private insurers without federal participation. Most private insurers are unwilling to provide flood coverage for commercial properties located in zones that have more than a once-in-100-years flooding probability risk (shown in NFIP flood maps as Zone A). For properties located outside the high-hazard flood zones, private insurers often write flood coverage by endorsement to the insured's commercial property policy, subject to a substantial deductible (often $25,000 or more). The ISO commercial property program includes a Flood Coverage endorsement for use with the ISO commercial property coverage forms. In some cases, insurers will provide only excess flood coverage that applies in addition to the maximum limit available from NFIP.

Earthquake and Volcanic Eruption Coverage

Earthquake and volcanic eruption, like flooding, present potentially catastrophic loss exposures. Consequently, earthquake insurance is expensive and limited in availability in areas with a high probability of severe earthquake damage, principally in parts of California and locations near the New Madrid Fault, which extends into portions of Arkansas, Illinois, Indiana, Kentucky, Mississippi, Missouri, and Tennessee.

In other areas, earthquake insurance is generally available but is often overlooked. Overlooking the earthquake exposure can be a costly mistake. In the past 100 years, earthquakes have occurred in thirty-nine of the fifty states.[1] One of the most severe earthquakes in U.S. history was centered in Charleston, South Carolina.

Insurers can use either of two ISO endorsements to add earthquake and volcanic eruption as covered perils under a commercial property coverage part. Independently filed earthquake endorsements are also available from some insurers. The two ISO endorsements are these:

- Earthquake and Volcanic Eruption Endorsement
- Earthquake and Volcanic Eruption Endorsement (Sub-Limit Form)

Both endorsements extend commercial property coverage to include earthquake and volcanic eruption. The first endorsement includes coverage for the full policy limit and contains a coinsurance condition. The second endorsement includes earthquake and volcanic eruption coverage subject to a sublimit that is lower than the regular policy limit, and it does not contain a coinsurance condition.

Peak Season Limit of Insurance Endorsement

Many organizations experience wide fluctuations (increases and decreases) in personal property values, especially the value of goods held for sale. The BPP does not provide a totally satisfactory method to cover fluctuating values. If the insured organization carries high enough limits to cover the maximum value, it is overinsured for much of the year and pays too much in premiums. If it carries less than the maximum value, it is underinsured during its peak inventory period. Continually amending the amount of insurance to correspond to changes in value would be an administrative burden on the insured and the insurer.

The Peak Season Limit of Insurance endorsement covers the fluctuating values of business personal property by providing differing amounts of insurance for certain time frames during the policy period. For example, a toy store may have a policy providing $100,000 of coverage on personal property with a peak season endorsement increasing coverage to $200,000 from October 1 to December 31, when the store expects to have higher inventory values.

Using this endorsement would have exactly the same effect as endorsing the policy on October 1 to increase the coverage and endorsing it again on December 31 to reduce the coverage. The peak season endorsement eliminates the need for these extra transactions and the possibility that they may be overlooked.

The peak season endorsement is usually attached when the policy is issued (although it may be added midterm), and a pro rata premium is charged for the period during which the limit is increased.

Value Reporting Form

Unlike the peak season endorsement, which actually modifies the limit of insurance, the Value Reporting Form covers the fluctuating values of business personal property by providing insurance for the insured's maximum expected values and requiring the insured to periodically report property values to the insurer. The insurer calculates the final policy premium based on the reported values instead of the limit of insurance. In this way, the insured has an adequate limit to cover maximum personal property values but pays a premium based on the reported property values.

Under the Value Reporting Form, the insured is required to report the value of the insured business personal property to the insurer periodically during the policy period. The frequency of reporting is indicated by a symbol entered in the declarations. For example, MR, the most common choice, calls for reporting values on hand on the last day of the month, with the report due within thirty days after the end of the month. Daily, weekly, quarterly, and annual periods can also be selected as a basis for reports by entering other codes in the declarations.

As long as the insured reports values accurately and on time, the insurer will pay the full amount of any loss that occurs (but not more than the policy limit), even if the values on hand at the time of the loss are greater than those last reported to the insurer.

 Reality Check

Value Reporting Form

A wholesaler insures its business personal property under a Value Reporting Form subject to a limit of $1 million for its single warehouse location. Its last monthly report of values was made on time and accurately showed the full value of business personal property—$800,000—as of the date of the report. Three weeks later, a fire destroyed the warehouse and its contents. Even though the value of covered personal property had increased to $900,000 since the last report, the loss is covered in full (minus the deductible).

[DA07816]

To encourage accurate and timely reports, the Value Reporting Form specifies penalties for failure to comply with its reporting requirements. Separate rules apply when no report is made (loss payment is reduced to 75 percent of the otherwise collectible loss), one or more reports are past due after the initial report (loss payment is limited to the last reported values), and reports are inaccurate (the loss is reduced by the proportion that the value reported bears to the correct value).

The insured pays an advance premium at the inception of the policy. The advance premium is based on 75 percent of the limit of insurance. The final premium is determined after the policy anniversary, based on the reported values. The premium is based on the values reported, even if the values reported exceed the policy limit. However, the insurer is not obligated to pay more than the policy limit in the event of loss, even if the reported values are higher. Thus, care should be taken to set the limit high enough to cover any possible increase in value.

Although the Value Reporting Form can more effectively match coverage to exposures than the Peak Season Limit of Insurance endorsement, many smaller firms do not have accounting systems of sufficient sophistication to generate the required reports accurately and on time. Furthermore, many insurers would decline to issue a Value Reporting Form for a smaller insured because the premium may not be large enough to warrant the added expense of processing the reports and calculating the final premium.

FACTORS AFFECTING COMMERCIAL PROPERTY PREMIUMS

The factors that affect commercial property premiums are information that the producer often needs to transmit to the underwriter. Understanding these factors is also fundamental to reducing the cost of insurance, since many of the factors are within the insured's control.

Commercial property rating procedures are numerous and complex. Therefore, this discussion focuses on the rating factors that principally affect the premiums for commercial property coverage on buildings and business personal property, not on the actual mechanics of rating. Some of the factors affecting commercial property premiums are certain aspects of coverage provided by the commercial property coverage part. Other factors—such as type of building construction and type of business occupying the building—exist independently of the coverage being provided.

Rating Fundamentals

Rating is the process of applying a rate to a particular exposure and performing any other necessary calculations to determine an appropriate policy premium. As a simplified example, if the applicable rate for commercial property coverage on a building is $0.50 per $100 of insurance and the amount of insurance is $100,000, the premium for the coverage can be calculated in this manner:

$$\frac{\$0.50}{\$100} \times \$100,000 = \$500$$

Another way to reach the same result is to establish the number of exposure units by dividing the amount of insurance by the unit amount, and then multiplying the number of units by the rate:

$$\frac{\$100,000}{\$100} \times \$0.50 = \$500$$

In reality, rating is usually more complicated; additional calculations are often needed. For example, the rate or the premium must often be multiplied by additional factors to account for territorial differences, to reduce the premium when the insured has selected a higher deductible, to increase the premium when a coverage option has been added, and so forth.

In the past, every commercial building was inspected individually, and building and contents rates reflecting the exposure to loss of a particular business were published by rating bureaus. This approach to developing rates is known as specific rating, which bases a building's property insurance rate on inspecting and evaluating that particular building.

As the methods used to collect loss statistics became more sophisticated, insurers were better able to generalize about the probabilities of loss within large groups of similar risks and to formulate rates that reflected the average probability of loss for businesses within these groups. Class rating is a rating approach that uses rates reflecting the average probability of loss for businesses within large groups of similar risks. Class rating allows a building and its contents to be rated without inspecting the building and developing a specific rate.

Large businesses, as well as certain other businesses with operations involving unusual or increased exposures to loss, are still specifically rated. However, class rating is used to rate the majority of commercial insureds.

Aspects of Coverage Affecting Premiums

Certain aspects of the coverage provided affect premiums. For example, higher limits result in higher premiums, and Special Form coverage involves a higher rate than Broad Form coverage, which in turn is higher than Basic Form coverage. Likewise, the applicable coinsurance percentage, the amount of the deductible, and any optional coverages that apply to the commercial property coverage part all affect the amount of the premium.

Limit of Insurance

The limit of insurance applicable to the coverage is an important component of the final premium because it represents the exposure against which the applicable rate is multiplied to calculate the premium. In addition, many insurers use a rating system for commercial property that varies the rate depending on the amount of insurance selected. This approach, called limit of insurance (LOI) rating, is based on the observation that most commercial property losses are partial, as opposed to total, and property losses do not increase proportionately with the value of the insured property. LOI rating recognizes this observation by using rates that decrease as the insured value increases. Thus, even though the owner of a high-value property still pays a higher premium than the owner of a low-value property of the same type, the high-value owner is charged a lower property rate (cost of insurance per each $100 of coverage).

Covered Causes of Loss

The rate for the Causes of Loss—Basic Form consists of a Group I rate (for fire, lightning, explosion, vandalism, and sprinkler leakage) and a Group II rate (for all other causes of loss covered under the Basic Form). If the policy provides Broad Form coverage, an additional rate is added to the Basic Form rates (Group I and Group II) for the cost of covering the additional perils of the Broad Form. The same approach is used with the Special Form except that the additional rate is higher than the Broad Form additional rate. The premium is determined by multiplying the applicable rate times the amount of insurance.

Coinsurance Percentage

The rates ordinarily used for insuring buildings and personal property are calculated with the assumption that they will be used with an 80 percent coinsurance clause in the policy. These rates are therefore called the "80 percent coinsurance rates." When a policy requires a higher coinsurance percentage, the 80 percent coinsurance rate is reduced, both to reflect the reduced likelihood that a loss will reach the insured amount and also to encourage the purchase of higher limits. Thus, with 90 or 100 percent coinsurance, the insured must buy a greater amount of insurance to comply with the coinsurance requirement, but the rate is reduced. When the coinsurance requirement is less than 80 percent, the rate is increased.

Deductible Amount

Commercial property rates are developed with the assumption that the policy will be subject to a $500 deductible. Many policyholders are willing and able to retain a larger deductible that may make the risk more desirable to underwriters (small claims are disproportionately expensive for insurers to handle). Rates are reduced in return for the insured's acceptance of a higher deductible, because raising the deductible reduces the insurer's loss payments. If the deductible is reduced to $250, rates are increased.

Optional Coverages

Adding optional coverages to the Building and Personal Property Coverage Form, also referred to as the BPP, or another coverage form ordinarily increases the policy premium. In some cases, the optional coverage increases the premium only because the limit of insurance must be increased to cover the additional property values being insured. For example, replacement cost insurance does not involve a higher rate, but the amount of insurance needed to meet the coinsurance requirement on a replacement cost basis may be considerably higher than the amount needed on an actual cash value basis. In other cases, the charge for a coverage option is a separate rate applied to the amount of insurance. For example, a grocery store that wishes to buy optional spoilage coverage will pay an additional premium calculated by applying a rate for that coverage to the amount of insurance.

Other Factors Affecting Premiums

Apart from the terms of coverage, factors that affect commercial property premiums are the building's construction, occupancy, protection, external exposure, and location. The first four factors are often referred to by the acronym COPE. To a large extent, the COPE factors relate to fire, which is often the most significant cause of loss in a commercial property policy.

Construction

Some types of buildings resist fire more effectively than others, thereby reducing the fire risk for both the buildings and their contents. Although buildings can be classified in many ways, the system used to classify buildings for purposes of rating commercial property insurance is based on their ability to resist fire. The six construction classes used for purposes of rating commercial property insurance are these:

- Frame
- Joisted masonry
- Noncombustible
- Masonry noncombustible
- Modified fire resistive
- Fire resistive

Frame construction, which uses wood or other combustible material in the exterior walls of a building (even if covered by brick veneer or stucco), is the most susceptible to fire damage. Fire-resistive construction uses materials with a fire-resistance rating of at least two hours and is the least susceptible to fire damage.

Occupancy

Occupancy refers to the type of activity conducted inside the building. Some occupancies are riskier than others. To cite an extreme example, a building used for manufacturing fireworks will face a greater explosion and fire risk than if it were used for storing bottled water. Accordingly, commercial property rates are higher for buildings with more hazardous occupancies.

Protection

Fire protection can be either internal (such as a sprinkler system) or external (the local fire department). For rating purposes, external protection is graded on a scale of one (the best protection) to ten (the worst), indicating the availability of fire-fighting personnel and equipment. For internal protection, buildings classified as "sprinklered" receive rate reductions. In contrast, buildings that have certain fire hazards (such as unsafe heating or cooking devices or inadequate electrical wiring) are charged higher premiums.

External Exposure

External exposure is another factor that can affect a commercial property premium. In addition to hazards arising from a building's construction, occupancy, and protection, other properties adjacent to the building can increase the probability of loss to the insured building and its contents. For example, a fire or explosion in the previously described fireworks plant could damage an adjacent building and its contents. Insurers include a charge for external exposure only when a specific rate is calculated for a particular location. Even if external exposure is not a factor in calculating the rate, underwriters consider external exposure when deciding whether to accept a particular submission.

External exposure

A property outside the area owned or controlled by the insured that increases the probability of loss to the insured's building and its contents.

Location

The risk of loss caused by windstorm, theft, earthquake, and other perils varies depending on the location of the insured property. For example, buildings along the coastline of the southeastern United States are more exposed to hurricane damage than buildings in other areas; tornadoes and hailstorms occur more frequently in parts of the midwestern U.S. Thus, different rates apply to different areas, or the rates are modified by territorial multipliers that account for the differences.

DETERMINING WHETHER THE BPP COVERS A LOSS

Knowing how to apply the commercial property coverage provided by the Insurance Services Office (ISO) Building and Personal Property Coverage Form, also referred to as the BPP, to the facts of a case is an important skill.

This case study will help you make the transition from knowing policy language to applying policy language to losses to determine whether coverage applies. As you progress through the case study, you can check your understanding of the coverage provided by answering the Knowledge to Action questions.

Case Facts

Jim owns a building in a beach town on the New Jersey coast. During the tourist season, the building had been occupied by a surfing-supply retailer to whom Jim rented the premises. At the end of the tourist season, on September 15, 20X1, the retailer vacated the building and relocated to Florida, leaving it empty. Jim was unable to find a new tenant, so the building remained vacant.

A tropical storm struck just north of the New Jersey beach town on October 25, 20X1. The storm's precipitation did not reach Jim's area, but strong wind associated with the storm ripped shingles from the building's roof and shattered several windows with flying debris. A storm surge from the ocean caused salt water to enter Jim's building, causing extensive damage to its interior. See the exhibit "Damage Estimates."

Damage Estimates

Item	Description	Replacement Cost	Actual Cash Value
Wind damage to building	Destroyed roof shingles and broken windows	$20,000	$12,000
Water damage to building	Damage to walls, floors, and fixtures	$95,000	$76,000
Water damage to maintenance equipment	Total loss to a lawnmower, an electric hedge trimmer, and a vacuum cleaner stored on the first floor	$750	$375
Total		$115,750	$88,375

[DA07841]

Jim has a commercial package policy (CPP) that includes a BPP and a Causes of Loss—Broad Form covering the building. The CPP's Common Policy Declarations form indicates that the policy's coverage period is one year. The policy does not contain any endorsements.

Given the facts presented in the case, will the claim for damage related to the storm be covered? If so, what amount will the insurer pay for the claim? When answering the questions in this case-based activity, consider only the information provided as part of this case.

Necessary Reference Materials

To determine whether the BPP provides coverage for the losses associated with the storm, you need to consult the relevant portions of the declarations page and any policy provisions that apply to the loss.

Overview of Steps

When examining policy forms to determine whether coverage applies to a loss, you can apply the four steps of the DICE method. Next, you can determine the amount payable for the loss under the applicable policy or policies. Doing this involves applying the limit(s) of insurance and any deductibles that apply. It also involves determining whether more than one policy provides coverage for the same loss.

Determination of Coverage

Determining whether the BPP applies to this loss involves analyzing the relevant portions of the policy and determining whether any information found at each step in the DICE process precludes coverage at the time of the loss. You should also examine other categories of policy provisions, such as the insured's duties, general provisions, endorsements (if applicable), and terms defined in the policy in relation to the declarations, insuring agreement, conditions, and exclusions.

DICE Analysis Step 1: Declarations

The first DICE step is to review the declarations page. In this case, the review will determine whether Jim and the building were covered by the BPP when the storm struck. See the exhibit "Excerpt of Declarations Page."

Knowledge to Action

Action Task: Review the relevant portion of the declarations in Jim's policy.

According to your analysis of the excerpt of the declarations page, is coverage applicable for Jim and his building during the coverage period?

Feedback: The declarations page confirms Jim as the insured for the premises damaged. The loss occurred during the policy period.

Excerpt of Declarations Page

POLICY NO. SP 0001   **EFFECTIVE DATE**   07 / 01 / 20X1   ☐ "X" If Supplemental
                                                                              Declarations Is Attached

NAMED INSURED

Jim Smith

DESCRIPTION OF PREMISES

Prem. No.	Bldg. No.	Location, Construction And Occupancy
001	001	100 Beach View Blvd., Jersey Shore Town, NJ 08000
		Joisted Masonry
		Retail Store

COVERAGES PROVIDED   **Insurance At The Described Premises Applies Only For Coverages For Which A Limit Of Insurance Is Shown**

Prem. No.	Bldg. No.	Coverage	Limit Of Insurance	Covered Causes Of Loss	Coinsurance*	Rates
001	001	Building	$1,000,000	Broad	80%	

*If Extra Expense Coverage, Limits On Loss Payment

OPTIONAL COVERAGES   **Applicable Only When Entries Are Made In The Schedule Below**

Prem. No.	Bldg. No.	Agreed Value			Replacement Cost (X)		
		Expiration Date	Cov.	Amount	Building	Pers. Prop.	Including "Stock"
001	001				X		

	Inflation Guard (%)	*Monthly Limit Of	Maximum Period	*Extended Period
	Bldg. Pers. Prop.	Indemnity (Fraction)	Of Indemnity (X)	Of Indemnity (Days)

*Applies to Business Income Only

MORTGAGEHOLDERS

Prem. No.	Bldg. No.	Mortgageholder Name And Mailing Address

DEDUCTIBLE

$500. Exceptions:

[DA07842]

DICE Analysis Step 2: Insuring Agreement

The second DICE step is to review the insuring agreement to determine whether it is applicable to the described loss. Specifically, it must be determined whether each item of damaged property qualifies as Covered Property under the Building description. For the purposes of this case, assume that none of the property damaged is Property Not Covered. Also assume that none of the additional coverages or coverage extensions apply.

▶▶

An analysis of whether the insuring agreement is applicable to a loss requires not only determining whether the damaged property qualifies as Covered Property, but also whether the damage was caused by a Covered Cause of Loss and whether any exclusions apply to coverage. These two items will be considered in Step 4. The relevant excerpt of the BPP insuring agreement indicates the types of Building property that qualify as covered property:

> 1. Covered Property
>
> Covered Property, as used in this Coverage Part, means the type of property described in this section, A.1., and limited in A.2., Property Not Covered, if a Limit of Insurance is shown in the Declarations for that type of property.
>
> a. Building, meaning the building or structure described in the Declarations, including:
>
> (1) Completed additions;
>
> (2) Fixtures, including outdoor fixtures;
>
> (3) Permanently installed:
>
> (a) Machinery and
>
> (b) Equipment;
>
> (4) Personal property owned by you that is used to maintain or service the building or structure or its premises, including:
>
> (a) Fire extinguishing equipment;
>
> (b) Outdoor furniture;
>
> (c) Floor coverings; and
>
> (d) Appliances used for refrigerating, ventilating, cooking, dishwashing or laundering;

Knowledge to Action

Action Task: Review the relevant portions of the BPP insuring agreement.

According to your analysis of the excerpt of the insuring agreement, does the definition of Covered Property in Jim's BPP include the damaged walls, floors, and fixtures, the destroyed roof shingles, and the broken windows?

Feedback: Yes, the definition of Covered Property in Jim's BPP includes all of these items because the walls, floors, roof shingles, and windows are parts of the building described in the declarations, and the Building description specifically includes fixtures.

According to your analysis of the excerpt of the insuring agreement, does the definition of Covered Property in Jim's BPP include the water-damaged maintenance equipment?

Feedback: Yes, the definition of Covered Property in Jim's BPP includes the water-damaged maintenance equipment because the Building definition includes "personal property owned by you that is used to maintain or service the building or structure or its premises."

DICE Analysis Step 3: Conditions

The third DICE step is to review the policy conditions to determine whether they affect coverage at the time of the loss. Jim protected the covered property from further loss by covering the damaged roof with a tarp, sent the insurer the required proof of loss, and fulfilled the other duties required of him after a loss. However, it is necessary to consider that Jim's building was vacant between September 15, 20X1, and October 25, 20X1, possibly making the Vacancy condition applicable to this loss. The Coinsurance condition also needs to be considered. If Jim does not have an amount of insurance that meets the Coinsurance requirement, a Coinsurance penalty will apply.

Knowledge to Action

Action Task: According to your analysis of the Vacancy condition, does it apply in this case? If so, how will it affect coverage?

Feedback: Part a. (Description Of Terms) of the Vacancy condition defines a building owned by the insured as being vacant "unless at least 31% of its total square footage is: (i) Rented to a lessee or sub-lessee and used by the lessee or sub-lessee to conduct its customary operations; and/or (ii) Used by the building owner to conduct customary operations." Because none of the building was being used by a lessee or sub-lessee or by Jim to conduct customary operations at the time of the loss, the building meets the definition of being vacant.

It is therefore necessary to consider Part b. (Vacancy Provisions) of the condition, which states that if "the building where loss or damage occurs has been vacant for more than 60 consecutive days before that loss or damage occurs," the insurer will not pay anything for loss caused by certain listed causes of loss and will reduce by 15 percent the amount that would otherwise be payable for loss caused by any other covered cause of loss.

Because Jim's building had been vacant for less than sixty days at the time of loss, neither the full exclusion of coverage nor the 15 percent reduction of loss payment applies. However, if another loss were to occur more than sixty days after the building became vacant, either of those consequences could apply, depending on the cause of the loss. To protect against that possibility in a future loss, Jim's insurance agent can ask the insurer to add (for an additional premium) a Vacancy Permit endorsement that suspends the Vacancy condition during a specified period while Jim's building is vacant.

Action Task: According to your analysis of the Coinsurance condition in relation to the facts in Jim's loss, does the amount of insurance carried by Jim satisfy the Coinsurance condition?

Feedback: The Coinsurance condition states that the insurer "will not pay the full amount of any loss if the value of Covered Property at the time of loss times the Coinsurance percentage shown for it in the declarations is greater than the Limit of Insurance for the property." The insurer determines that the value of Covered Property at the time of loss was $1,200,000. The declarations in Jim's policy show the Coinsurance percentage as 80 percent and the limit of insurance for the building as $1,000,000. Eighty percent of the value of the Covered Property ($1,200,000) at the time of loss is $960,000, which is less than the $1,000,000 limit of insurance. Therefore, the limit satisfies the Coinsurance condition and no coinsurance penalty applies.

DICE Analysis Step 4: Exclusions

The fourth DICE step is to determine whether the causes of loss are covered and, if so, if any exclusions affect coverage. In this case, it must be determined whether the windstorm that damaged the shingles and the windows and the water from the storm surge that damaged the building's interior are Covered Causes of Loss. The Causes of Loss—Broad Form indicates that windstorm is a Covered Cause of Loss. However, the Water exclusion may preclude coverage for losses related to the storm surge:

g. Water

(1) Flood, surface water, waves, tides, tidal waves, overflow of any body of water, or their spray, all whether driven by wind or not;

(2) Mudslide or mudflow;

(3) Water that backs up or overflows from a sewer, drain or sump; or

(4) Water under the ground surface pressing on, or flowing or seeping through:

(a) Foundations, walls, floors or paved surfaces;

(b) Basements, whether paved or not; or

(c) Doors, windows or other openings.

But if Water, as described in g.(1) through g.(4) above, results in fire, explosion or sprinkler leakage, we will pay for the loss or damage caused by that fire, explosion or sprinkler leakage.

Knowledge to Action

Action Task: Refer to the Causes of Loss—Broad Form Water exclusion.

According to your analysis of the Water exclusion, is the water damage to the building from the storm surge covered?

Feedback: Because the Water exclusion specifies that flood and waves, "whether driven by wind or not," are not Covered Causes of Loss, the Water exclusion eliminates coverage for the water damage caused by the storm surge, even though it resulted from the windstorm. (If Jim had purchased a flood endorsement to the BPP or other applicable flood coverage, this damage would have been covered elsewhere.)

Because Jim's building did not require demolition of undamaged portions of the structure or entail increased construction costs, the Ordinance or Law exclusion is not applicable in this case.

Determination of Amount Payable

Now that you have completed the DICE analysis, you can determine the amount payable. Doing this involves applying the limit(s) of insurance available to pay for the loss and any applicable deductibles and conditions. In this case, the DICE analysis has revealed that the wind damage to the building will be covered under the policy but that the water damage to the building and the maintenance equipment will not be covered.

In this case, the first step in calculating the amount payable is to determine whether the policy's coverage applies on a replacement cost or an actual cash value basis. A review of the BPP's Valuation condition reveals that none of the alternative valuation methods described in that condition (such as selling price valuation for "stock") apply to Jim's loss.

Knowledge to Action

Action Task: Review the relevant portion of the commercial property declarations in Jim's policy to determine the valuation method applicable to Jim's building.

According to your analysis of the declarations page, does Jim's coverage apply on a replacement cost or an actual cash value basis?

Feedback: Jim's coverage applies on a replacement cost basis, as indicated by the check mark below Replacement Cost in the Optional Coverages section of the declarations page.

The next step in the calculation is to determine how the BPP's limit of insurance and deductible affect the amount payable for the covered losses.

Knowledge to Action

Action Task: Review the relevant portion of the declarations page in Jim's policy to determine the policy limit and deductible that will be used to calculate the amount payable.

According to your analysis of the declarations page, what are the relevant policy limits and deductible that will be used to calculate coverage?

Feedback: The declarations page shows a $1,000,000 limit of insurance for the covered Building and a $500 deductible.

Action Task: Review the Damage Estimate exhibit to determine the amount claimed for each of the three categories of damaged items.

Given the information you have developed thus far, what is the amount payable for each of the three categories of damaged items?

Feedback: The amount payable for the wind damage to the building, which is a Covered Cause of Loss to Covered Property, is $20,000, the full amount claimed. Jim will not recover for the water damage to the first floor and to the maintenance equipment, both of which are excluded despite being Covered Property because they were not caused by a Covered Cause of Loss. Therefore, before accounting for any applicable deductible, the total amount payable is $20,000.

Action Task: Review the policy's deductible as shown on the commercial property declarations page. Accounting for the deductible, what is the total amount payable?

Feedback: The $500 deductible is subtracted from the amount payable, thus making the new amount payable $19,500.

The exhibit illustrates how the amount payable is determined. See the exhibit "Determination of Amount Payable."

Determination of Amount Payable

Item	Description	Claimed	Coverage Limits/ Issues	Amount Payable
Wind damage to building	Destroyed roof shingles and broken windows	$20,000	Within coverage limit	$20,000
Water damage to building	Repairs to first floor	$95,000	Excluded	$0
Water damage to maintenance equipment	A lawnmower, an electric hedge trimmer, and a vacuum cleaner stored on the first floor sustained damage	$750	Excluded	$0
Subtotal				$20,000
Effect of Policy Deductible			Loss recovery reduced by $500	($500)
Total Amount Payable				$19,500

[DA07843]

SUMMARY

The Loss Conditions and Additional Conditions sections of the BPP state the duties of the insured and the insurer after a loss has occurred, establish procedures for adjusting claims, explain methods for establishing the value of damaged property, outline requirements for coinsurance, and explain the interests of a mortgageholder (mortgagee).

The BPP contains four optional coverages: Agreed Value, Inflation Guard, Replacement Cost, and Extension of Replacement Cost to Personal Property of Others. Optional Coverages only apply when an appropriate notation is made on the declarations page.

The Commercial Property Conditions Form contains these conditions:

- Concealment, Misrepresentation, or Fraud
- Control of Property
- Insurance Under Two or More Coverages
- Legal Action Against Us
- Liberalization
- Transfer of Rights of Recovery Against Others to Us
- No Benefit to Bailee
- Other Insurance
- Policy Period, Coverage Territory

The Common Policy Conditions form is attached to every CPP or monoline policy written subject to ISO Commercial Lines Manual rules. The form contains these conditions: Cancellation; Changes; Examination of Your Books and Records; Inspections and Surveys; Premiums; and Transfer of Your Rights and Duties Under This Policy.

Hundreds of endorsements can be used to modify commercial property coverage. Examples of the exposures that can be covered by endorsement include building ordinance or law, spoilage, flood, and earthquake. The BPP can be supplemented in either of two ways to address the problem of fluctuating personal property values: the Peak Season Limit of Insurance endorsement and the Value Reporting Form.

Commercial property premiums are affected by the limit of insurance, the causes of loss covered, the applicable coinsurance percentage, deductible amounts, the inclusion of optional coverages, and the building's construction, occupancy, protection, external exposure, and location.

Just because damaged property qualifies as Covered Property does not mean that the loss is covered. The peril(s) causing the loss must also qualify as a Covered Cause of Loss. In this case, the property damaged directly by windstorm was covered, but the property damaged by flooding, even though it resulted from storm surge, was excluded.

ASSIGNMENT NOTE

1. "Few Homes Have Insurance Coverage for Earthquake or Tsunami, Although the U.S. Is At Risk for Both," Insurance Information Institute, March 23, 2011, www.iii.org/press_releases/few-homes-have-insurance-coverage-for-earthquake-or-tsunami-although-the-us-is-at-risk-for-both.htm (accessed July 11, 2011).

Direct Your Learning ▶▶

Business Income Insurance

Educational Objectives

After learning the content of this assignment, you should be able to:

▷ Describe the following aspects of the business income loss exposure:

- Measurement of business income loss

- Effect of business interruption on expenses

- Property and perils involved in business income losses

▷ Summarize the provisions of the Business Income and Extra Expense insuring agreements in the ISO business income coverage (BIC) forms.

▷ Explain how each of the Additional Coverages and the Coverage Extension supplement the business income coverage (BIC) forms.

▷ Summarize the Limits of Insurance, Loss Conditions, and Additional Condition (Coinsurance) of the business income coverage (BIC) forms.

▷ Explain how the optional coverages each modify the business income coverage (BIC) forms.

▷ Given a case, determine whether, and for what amount, a described loss would be covered either by the Business Income (and Extra Expense) Coverage Form or the Business Income (Without Extra Expense) Coverage Form.

Business Income Insurance

BUSINESS INCOME LOSS EXPOSURES

Commercial property coverage forms are tailored to insure buildings and personal property against damage by covered perils. However, the loss in value of the property and the expense of restoring it are not the only losses that a business may sustain.

Almost all of a commercial firm's property is acquired because of the income that it will generate or facilitate. This income can be lost when property is damaged or destroyed.

To evaluate the coverage needs an organization faces and determine how business income policy provisions are applied, an insurance practitioner should first understand how business income losses are measured, how a business interruption affects expenses, and the property and perils that business income losses can involve.

Measurement of Business Income Losses

Simply described, **business income insurance** covers the reduction in an organization's income when operations are interrupted by damage to property caused by a covered peril. The exact insurance recovery, of course, is determined by the terms and conditions of the policy. Because the severity of a business income loss is directly related to the length of time required to restore the property, business income coverage is considered a "time element" coverage. It is also called a "business interruption" coverage, because the loss of business income results from the interruption of the insured's business.

Business income losses are measured in terms of **net income**, which is the difference between revenues (such as money received for goods or services) and expenses (such as money paid for merchandise, rent, and insurance). It can be expressed by the formula:

$$\text{Revenues} - \text{Expenses} = \text{Net income}$$

Profit is net income that results when revenues exceed expenses. **Net loss** is the net income that results when expenses exceed revenues. For accounting purposes, the amount of a net loss appears in parentheses or is preceded by a minus sign (−).

Business income insurance covers the reduction in a firm's net income caused by accidental property damage. This reduction can be calculated by sub-

---

Business income insurance
Insurance that covers the reduction in an organization's income when operations are interrupted by damage to property caused by a covered peril.

Net income
The difference between revenues (such as money received for goods or services) and expenses (such as money paid for merchandise, rent, and insurance).

Profit
Net income that results when revenues exceed expenses.

Net loss
Net income that results when expenses exceed revenues.

tracting the amount of net income that a firm actually earned in a period of interruption from the amount of net income that the firm could reasonably have been expected to earn during the same period.

The following simplified example illustrates these concepts. Locksey Hardware Store suffered a partial fire loss and was closed for three months until the building could be repaired and the personal property replaced. During the three-month interruption, Locksey's revenue was reduced to nil, some ordinary expenses (payroll, electricity, and so on) were temporarily reduced or eliminated, and Locksey incurred some additional expenses (such as overtime labor and express freight on merchandise) to reopen the store as soon as possible. See the exhibit "Locksey's Revenue, Expenses, and Profit."

Locksey's Revenue, Expenses, and Profit

	Expected	Actual
Revenue	$300,000	$ 0
Expenses	240,000	120,000
Net profit (or loss)	$ 60,000	($120,000)

[DA02477]

The "Expected" column shows the revenue, expenses, and profit that Locksey could reasonably have expected during the three-month period, had no business interruption occurred. The "Actual" column shows its actual revenue, expenses, and net loss (indicated by parentheses) during the three-month period of interruption.

Locksey's business income loss is the $180,000 difference between the $60,000 profit it expected and the $120,000 net loss it actually experienced during the period of interruption.Locksey's loss can also be calculated by adding the $60,000 net income it would have earned to the $120,000 expenses that it actually incurred during the period.

For the sake of simplicity, this example assumes that Locksey's revenue returned to its normal level as soon as it reopened, which is seldom the case. In reality, Locksey's business income loss could have continued for several months after the store reopened.

Effect of Business Interruption on Expenses

During a business interruption, some of the organization's expenses (called **continuing expenses**) will continue, and other expenses (called **noncontinuing expenses**) will not continue. A business can also incur extra expenses during a business interruption. All changes in expenses must be considered when measuring a business income loss.

Continuing expenses
Expenses that continue to be incurred during a business interruption.

Noncontinuing expenses
Expenses that will not continue during a business interruption.

Continuing Expenses

If business is interrupted for only a short time, payroll of key employees, debt repayments, taxes, insurance, and many other expenses will continue during the interruption. If a longer interruption of business occurs, many expenses can be reduced or eliminated. Workers can be laid off, taxes are reduced (because of reduced income), and insurance premiums are smaller. It is often difficult to predict which expenses will continue and which will not.

Any reduction in expenses during a business interruption lessens the severity of the resulting business income loss. Nevertheless, continuing expenses can be, and ordinarily are, a significant part of business income losses. If, for example, an organization generates no revenue during a business interruption, its business income loss will be its lost profit for the period of interruption, plus the continuing expenses for that period, plus any extra expenses. In many cases, a company's continuing expenses exceed the profit that the company would have earned during the period.

Extra Expenses

Extra expenses are expenses, in addition to ordinary expenses, that an organization incurs to mitigate the effects of a business interruption. These are examples of extra expenses:

- In order to reopen an assembly line that had been shut down because of an explosion, a factory owner pays the additional costs of overtime labor and overnight air shipment of repair parts.

- After sustaining fire damage to its warehouse, a wholesale distributor rents a similar warehouse and continues its operations within two weeks instead of shutting down entirely for several months.

- To continue classes while an elementary school building is rebuilt following hurricane damage, a school district rents mobile classrooms and situates them on the school's playground.

Extra expense measures often pay for themselves. For example, the extra cost of overtime labor and air freight of needed parts may have been considerably less than the income that would have been lost had such measures not been taken. Such measures actually reduce the business income loss, and most organizations will readily undertake measures that reduce loss.

Some organizations will incur extra expenses even when such expenditures exceed any reduction in the business income loss. For example, after a property loss occurs, a hospital might incur substantial extra expenses to maintain essential services for its patients even though such expenses increase its business income loss. The decision to incur such extra expenses depends on the organization's objectives. For some organizations, maintaining continuous service to customers may be more important than reducing the business income loss.

Extra expenses

Expenses, in addition to ordinary expenses, that an organization incurs to mitigate the effects of a business interruption.

Property and Perils Involved in Business Income Losses

Business income losses typically result from physical damage to the affected organization's own buildings or personal property. However, a tenant's operations can be interrupted by damage to the building in which the tenant is located even though the part of the building the tenant occupies has not been damaged. For example, an explosion that debilitates heating, air conditioning, and ventilating equipment makes offices in sealed high-rise buildings uninhabitable in very hot or very cold weather, even though the offices themselves are not damaged.

In some cases, a physical loss at one location can cause a business interruption elsewhere. For example, a business may have to close because of damage to off-premises property that provides utilities such as electricity, water, or communications. Alternatively, one business may depend on another business as a major customer or as a key supplier. A business may be dependent simply because it is near a key facility or "magnet" property that attracts customers to the site (such as a major department store in a shopping mall). Damage to these kinds of properties could cause a business income loss at a location where no physical damage occurred.

The causes of loss for business income losses associated with property exposures are typically the same as those for physical damage losses. Thus, a fire or a windstorm that damages property may also cause a business income loss. A business income loss can also result when there has been no physical damage to buildings or personal property. For example, the closing of a road or a labor strike can cause a business income loss. However, such risks are generally not insurable. Any number of other events that are not covered by business income insurance can reduce an organization's net income. Prudent organizations use risk management techniques to avoid or lessen business income loss exposures that cannot be transferred by insurance. In order for business income insurance to apply, this must occur:

- An interruption of operations …
- caused by property damage from a covered peril …
- to property at locations or situations described in the policy …
- resulting in a loss of business income and/or extra expense.

If any of these conditions are not met, there is no coverage under business income coverage.

BIC INSURING AGREEMENTS

A producer, underwriter, or risk management professional must understand what each business income coverage form covers in order to recommend the correct form to an insured who has business income that may be lost if a covered peril occurs.

Insurance for most business income exposures can be provided under either of the two Insurance Services Office (ISO) coverage forms for providing business income coverage:

- The Business Income (and Extra Expense) Coverage Form covers both business income and extra expense losses (even if the extra expenses do not reduce the business income loss).
- The Business Income (Without Extra Expense) Coverage Form covers business income loss but covers extra expenses only to the extent that they reduce the business income loss.

The Business Income insuring agreement is found in both of these forms and the Extra Expense insuring agreement is found only in the Business Income (and Extra Expense) Coverage Form. Either BIC form can be included in a commercial property coverage part, with or without another commercial property coverage form such as the Building and Personal Property Coverage Form. The causes of loss included in business income coverage can be designated by either the same causes of loss form that applies to other coverage forms or by a different causes of loss form that applies only to business income coverage.

Because the two ISO business income forms are similar in all respects except extra expense coverage, this section applies equally to both forms unless otherwise specified. The abbreviation "BIC" is used to refer to both forms. The phrases "BIC and extra expense" and "BIC without extra expense" are used to distinguish between the two forms.

Business Income Insuring Agreement

The BIC allows an insured to choose any one of these three options for business income coverage:

- Business income including rental value
- Business income other than rental value
- Rental value only

The option chosen by the insured should always be clearly indicated on the declarations page.

The first option covers both loss of rental value and loss of other business income. An insured that owns and operates out of a multi-tenant office building that it rents in part to other tenants might choose this. If the building became physically damaged and unable to be occupied, the insurer would pay for both the insured's loss of rental income from tenants and the insured's loss of business income from its own business.

The second option covers business income other than rental value. A business that has no rental income to lose might choose this.

The third option is less expensive, but it covers rental value only. This option might be purchased by a landlord whose only income is derived from renting property to others.

The insurer agrees to pay the actual loss of business income sustained by the named insured because of the necessary "suspension" of the named insured's "operations" during the "period of restoration." (The BIC definition of these terms is discussed in subsequent paragraphs.) The suspension must result from direct physical loss or damage to real or personal property caused by a covered cause of loss and occurring at the "premises" described in the declarations.

If the insured is a tenant, the definition of premises is broadened to include "any area within the building or on the site…if that area services, or is used to gain access to, the described premises." Thus, if fire damages the elevator motors in the basement of a building, a tenant on the thirtieth floor would be covered for any resulting business income loss even if no damage occurs above the first floor.

The BIC defines business income as the sum of these two items:

- Net profit or loss that would have been earned or incurred if the suspension had not occurred
- Normal operating expenses, including payroll, that continue during the suspension

The amount of profit or loss that would have been earned or incurred if the suspension had not occurred must be estimated based on past and prospective performance of the business.

The continuing expenses can be determined during the suspension. These expenses may include salaries of key employees, property taxes, and interest expenses.

The terms "operations," "period of restoration," and "suspension" are defined in the BIC's Definitions section. The "operations" of the insured are (1) the business activities of the insured that occur at the premises described in the declarations or (2) in the case of rental value coverage, the "tenantability" (suitability for occupancy) of the described premises.

The "period of restoration" is the period during which business income loss is covered under the BIC forms. For business income coverage, it begins seventy-two hours after the physical loss occurs and ends when the property is (or should have been) restored to use with reasonable speed. With regard to extra expense coverage, it begins immediately after the physical loss occurs. In both cases, the period of restoration ends on the date when the property should be restored with reasonable speed and similar quality or when the business is resumed at a new, permanent location. Thus, for business income coverage, there is no coverage for the first three days following the physical loss. The seventy-two hour deductible can be reduced to twenty-four hours or eliminated entirely by endorsement for an additional premium.

The period of restoration does not include any additional time that might be required to repair or reconstruct the building in order to comply with any building code or law, unless the policy has been specifically endorsed to cover such additional time. The period of restoration also does not include any increased period required by ordinance or law to respond to or assess the effects of pollutants.

"Suspension" means the slowdown or cessation of business activities or, in the case of rental value coverage, that a part of the premises is rendered untenantable (unfit for occupancy).

Whichever cause of loss form applies to the BIC determines what qualifies as a covered cause of loss for purposes of business income coverage. All of the provisions in the causes of loss form apply to business income claims, including a set of exclusions that apply only to business income and/or extra expense losses.

In summary, these are the key requirements for a business income claim to be covered in the BIC:

- Actual loss of business income you sustain
- Due to the necessary suspension of your operations
- During the period of restoration
- Caused by direct physical loss of or damage to property at the described premises
- Loss or damage caused by a covered cause of loss

Apply Your Knowledge

Department Store (DS) is insured under a commercial package policy that includes the Business Income (and Extra Expense) Coverage Form. For each of the loss scenarios described, determine whether the circumstances of the loss satisfy the conditions imposed by the Business Income insuring agreement in DS's Business Income (and Extra Expense) Coverage Form.

DS sustained an actual loss of business income at the described store premises as a result of decreased shopper traffic for several months while nearby streets were blocked off as part of a subway construction project.

Feedback: No. The circumstances of the loss do not meet the conditions of the Business Income insuring agreement because there was no direct physical loss to property at the described premises by a Covered Cause of Loss.

DS sustained an actual loss of business income while the second floor of the described store was necessarily shut down for repairs after a fire (a Covered Cause of Loss) caused physical loss to that floor. Although sales continued on the ground and first floors of the store, DS's net income was reduced by approximately 30 percent until the second floor was restored to use.

Feedback: Yes. The circumstances of the loss meet all the conditions of the Business Income insuring agreement:

- DS sustained an actual loss of business income.
- The loss of business income was due to the necessary suspension of DS's operations. (Partial interruption qualifies as "suspension.")
- DS incurred loss of business income during the period of restoration (before the property was restored).
- The suspension of DS's operations was caused by direct physical loss or damage to property at the described premises.
- The loss or damage was caused by a Covered Cause of Loss.

Extra Expense Insuring Agreement

The BIC and extra expense coverage form contains a second insuring agreement—Extra Expense. The Extra Expense insuring agreement provides coverage for expenses that the named insured incurs to avoid or minimize the suspension of operations. Examples of such extra expenses include the costs to move to a temporary location, increased rent at the temporary location, rental of substitute equipment (furniture, fixtures, or machinery), and the cost of substitute services such as for data processing.

The BIC and extra expense coverage form covers such expenses in full, subject to the policy limit. With the exception of extra expense to repair or replace property, these expenses are not limited to the amount by which they reduce the extra expense loss; coverage applies even if the business income loss is not reduced at all.

Even with the BIC and extra expense coverage form, extra expenses to repair or replace property are treated differently. Such expenses are covered only to the extent that they actually reduce the business income loss. For example, a business owner may pay a contractor at an overtime rate to work around the clock to repair damaged property so that the business can reopen promptly. The additional cost paid to do so would be payable as extra expense, but only to the extent that it actually reduced the business income loss. Thus, if reopening earlier reduced the business income loss by $20,000, the insurer would pay the overtime charges up to that amount (and subject to the limit of insurance).

BIC ADDITIONAL COVERAGES AND COVERAGE EXTENSION

The Business Income Coverage (BIC) forms include additional coverages and a coverage extension that supplement the basic insuring agreement(s) in ways that are often vital to insureds recovering from business income losses.

Each version of the BIC form contains four additional coverages and one coverage extension to insure several sources of business income loss that would not otherwise be covered. The Business Income (Without Extra Expense) Coverage Form contains one more additional coverage, Expenses to Reduce Loss. The additional coverages and extension are shown in the exhibit. See the exhibit "BIC Insuring Agreements, Additional Coverages, and Coverage Extension."

BIC Insuring Agreements, Additional Coverages, and Coverage Extension

	Business Income (and Extra Expense) Coverage Form	Business Income (Without Extra Expense) Coverage Form
Insuring Agreement(s)	• Business Income • Extra Expense	• Business Income
Additional Coverages	• Civil Authority • Alterations and New Buildings • Extended Business Income • Interruption of Computer Operations	• Expenses to Reduce Loss • Civil Authority • Alterations and New Buildings • Extended Business Income • Interruption of Computer Operations
Coverage Extension	• Newly Acquired Locations	• Newly Acquired Locations

[DA02479]

Expenses to Reduce Loss

Instead of containing an Extra Expense insuring agreement, the BIC without extra expense form contains an additional coverage titled Expenses to Reduce Loss. This addition covers necessary expenses incurred by the named insured to reduce business income loss, other than the cost of extinguishing a fire.

Thus, the insured can incur the same types of expenses that are covered under the BIC and extra expense form, but they are covered only to the extent that they reduce business income loss.

A danger of the BIC without extra expense form is that the insured may incur extra expenses other than the reduction in business income loss. A large, uninsured extra expense loss can therefore result.

The BIC and extra expense form greatly reduces this possibility. Because the rate for the BIC and extra expense form is not much greater than the rate for the BIC without extra expense form, many businesses opt for the broader coverage form.

Civil Authority

In almost all cases, coverage under the BIC is related to damage to property at the insured's premises. However, Civil Authority additional coverage insures loss of business income that results when damage is to property other than the insured's and when access to the insured's premises is prohibited by civil authority. The insured's premises must be within one mile of the damaged property and access to the insured's premises must be denied by the civil authority because of a dangerous physical condition or to enable the civil authority unimpeded access to the damaged property. For example, fire damage to another building may make it unsafe for customers to go to the insured's premises.

If damage to the other premises resulted from a cause of loss covered by the insured's policy, the resulting income loss at the insured's premises would be covered for the period of suspension, beginning seventy-two hours after the time of the action by civil authority, up to a maximum of four consecutive weeks after the time of the action. The maximum period of coverage can be increased to 60, 90, or 180 days by endorsement. If the seventy-two hour period in the definition of "period of restoration" is reduced or eliminated in the BIC, the endorsement makes the same change in the Civil Authority additional coverage.

Apply Your Knowledge

Jennifer's shoe store has coverage under the BIC. A tenant situated a few doors away from Jennifer's store in the same shopping center had a fire that weakened the roof supports for part of the building. The civil authorities prohibited access to Jennifer's store because they were concerned that the building's roof could collapse. It took three-and-a-half weeks (twenty-four days) before the civil authorities allowed Jennifer's customers to visit her store again. Does Jennifer have a covered business income claim? Explain.

Feedback: Yes, the Civil Authority additional coverage insures losses that occur somewhere other than at the insured's premises. Jennifer's premises is within one mile of the damaged property. Access was denied by the civil authority because of a dangerous physical condition—the threat of the roof collapsing—and the time period of the prohibited access was less than the coverage's allotted four consecutive weeks and access was denied beyond the seventy-two hour waiting period.

Alterations and New Buildings

In most cases, business income losses result from the interruption of operations that are already underway. However, the BIC form also provides coverage for loss of income resulting from a delay in starting operations, if the delay results from damage at the described premises by a covered cause of loss to one of these:

- New buildings or structures, either completed or under construction
- Alterations or additions to existing buildings
- Machinery, equipment, supplies, or building materials located on or within 100 feet of the described premises (provided they are used in the construction, alterations, or additions or are incidental to the occupancy of new buildings)

The period of restoration for losses to new or altered buildings begins on the date that operations would have begun had the damage not occurred. The BIC and extra expense form specifically states that this additional coverage includes necessary extra expenses.

Extended Business Income

Business income coverage ceases when the period of restoration ends—that is, on the date when the property at the described premises should be repaired, rebuilt, or replaced with reasonable speed and similar quality. However, all of the insured business's former customers may not return immediately upon restoration, especially if the interruption has been long.

The Extended Business Income (EBI) additional coverage addresses this possibility by extending the regular business income coverage to include business income losses that continue after the period of restoration ends. The coverage begins when the damaged property has been restored and ends when the insured's business returns to normal, subject to a maximum of thirty days. For example, if a restaurant is closed because of fire damage, its regular customers will patronize other restaurants. Time will be needed for the insured's income to return to normal levels even after the physical repairs are completed.

Interruption of Computer Operations

A coverage restriction found in each of the BIC forms, titled Additional Limitation—Interruption of Computer Operations, states that no coverage applies when a suspension of operations is caused by destruction or corruption of, or any other loss or damage to, electronic data. An exception to this restriction is provided under the additional coverage Interruption of Computer Operations.

The additional coverage provides $2,500 of coverage for loss of business income or extra expense when business operations are suspended because of an interruption of computer operations resulting from the destruction or corruption of electronic data caused by a covered cause of loss. The $2,500 is an aggregate limit for all losses sustained in any one policy year that applies in addition to the regular limit of insurance. Most insurers are not willing to increase this limit.

The $2,500 limit is not a meaningful amount of coverage for most insureds covered by commercial package policies, because losses can easily exceed that amount. Inland marine and cyber risk coverages are available to provide greater coverage.

Newly Acquired Locations

The BIC forms' only coverage extension expands coverage to property at premises acquired during the policy period) if a coinsurance of 50 percent or more is shown in the declarations. Titled Newly Acquired Locations, this optional coverage for insureds does not include property at fairs or exhibitions.

The coverage at any newly acquired location is limited to $100,000. This is an additional amount of insurance above the limit stated in the declarations and is not subject to the Coinsurance condition. An additional premium is charged for the automatic coverage from the date of acquisition of the new property.

The Newly Acquired Locations coverage terminates on the earliest of (1) the expiration date of the policy, (2) the date on which the insured reports the acquisition to the insurer, or (3) thirty days after the date of acquisition. This extension is intended to provide temporary protection until the insured obtains permanent coverage.

BIC LIMIT OF INSURANCE AND CONDITIONS

The sometimes overlooked Limits of Insurance, Loss Conditions, and Additional Condition (Coinsurance) sections of the business income coverage (BIC) forms can be crucial in determining how much will be paid for a business income loss.

The Limits of Insurance, Loss Conditions, and Additional Condition (Coinsurance) sections of the Insurance Services Office (ISO) BIC forms contain policy provisions that guide both the insured and insurer when determining the amount payable for a business income loss. The Loss Conditions, in particular, also address these issues:

- Appraisal
- Duties in the Event of Loss
- Loss Determination
- Loss Payment

Limits of Insurance

The limit of insurance stated in the declarations is the maximum amount the insurer will pay for loss in any one occurrence.

Any amounts payable under these coverages of the BIC do not increase the limit of insurance:

- Extra Expense (in the Business Income [and Extra Expense] Coverage Form only)
- Expenses to Reduce Loss (in the Business Income [Without Extra Expense] Coverage Form only)
- Civil Authority
- Alterations and New Buildings
- Extended Business Income

The Interruption of Computer Operations additional coverage and the Newly Acquired Locations coverage extension are payable subject to their own limits. Any amounts the insurer pays for these two coverages do not reduce the limit of insurance shown in the declarations. Limits of insurance for business income can be written on either a specific or blanket basis. If they are written on a specific basis, a specific limit is set for each building insured. If they are written on a blanket basis, the limit applies to all buildings at one location or to all buildings at multiple locations. Writing coverage on a blanket basis can help a business with interdependent locations, with which a loss at one building could affect income at another building. For example, if a warehouse is damaged, it may be unable to supply goods to be sold at another building.

Loss Conditions

The Loss Conditions provide a forum to resolve disputes over amounts to be paid, require an insured to mitigate a loss, identify factors to apply when determining the amount of business income loss, and require prompt payment once an amount is agreed upon.

Appraisal

The Appraisal condition allows either the insured or the insurer to demand an appraisal of a loss if the insured and the insurer disagree on the amount of loss, but not in disputes as to coverage. The condition also describes the appraisal procedure to be followed in such cases.

Duties in the Event of Loss

The duties of the insured after loss—such as giving the insurer prompt notice of loss, protecting covered property from further loss, and cooperating with the insurer—are similar to the duties specified in the ISO Building and

Personal Property Coverage Form, also known as the BPP. The BIC imposes one additional duty on any insured that intends to continue its business: to resume operations, in whole or in part, as quickly as possible.

Loss Determination

The amount of a business income loss can never be known precisely, but business income loss is determined on the basis of these items:

- Net income of the business before the loss occurred
- Probable net income of the business if no loss had occurred
- Operating expenses that must continue during the period of restoration to permit the insured to resume operations with the quality of service that existed prior to loss
- Other relevant sources of information

Not all expenses terminate when a business's operations are suspended. Continuous expenses include payroll and, depending on the insured's circumstances, utilities, rental payments, taxes, interest payable on loans, and similar items. Other relevant sources of information may include the insured's financial and accounting records, bills, invoices, notes, deeds, liens, and contracts.

The BIC states that the amount of loss will not be based on the net income that might have been earned as a result of an increase in business due to favorable business conditions caused by the effect of the covered cause of loss. This change was motivated by questions that arose following Hurricane Andrew in 1992. Insurers believed that the proper measure of damages for a hotel, for example, would be the room rentals that the hotel would normally have earned had the hurricane not occurred. The policy wording change makes it clear that the increase in business resulting from a catastrophe will not be included when estimating the likely net income.

Loss Payment

The insurer agrees to pay for a covered loss within thirty days after the date on which the amount of loss is agreed to (or an appraisal award is made). The insured must have complied with all policy conditions, including filing a sworn statement of loss.

If the insured does not resume operations as quickly as possible, the insurer pays the loss based on the length of time it would have taken the insured to do so. If the insured does not resume operations at all (many businesses do not reopen after a serious fire or other damage), the period of restoration is based on the time it would have taken to resume operations as quickly as possible.

Additional Condition: Coinsurance

The BIC forms contain an additional condition establishing a coinsurance provision. The BIC coinsurance percentage may be 50, 60, 70, 80, 90, 100, or

125 percent. The policy may also be written with no coinsurance provision. The BIC loss payment calculation is:

$$\text{Loss payment} = \left(\frac{\text{Amount of insurance carried}}{\text{Amount of insurance required}} \right) \times \text{Loss amount}$$

The numerator of the fraction in this calculation is the amount of insurance carried. The denominator is the amount of insurance required; it is determined by multiplying the coinsurance percentage by the sum of the insured's net income (whether profit or loss) plus all operating expenses (less certain expenses specified in the form) that would have been incurred in the absence of a loss for the twelve-month period beginning at the inception or latest anniversary date of the policy.

Although the procedure is similar to that used with the BPP, the coinsurance basis used for business income insurance is significantly different. For other property coverages, the coinsurance basis is the same as the property covered. That is, if a building is the covered property, the coinsurance basis is either the replacement cost or the actual cash value of the building (depending on which valuation basis the policy provides). This is not the case with business income insurance. The item covered in business income insurance is net income plus continuing operating expenses; the coinsurance basis is the projected net income and all operating expenses except for certain deductible items.

Another difference between the item covered and the coinsurance basis is the period of time used in computing values. For coverage purposes, the time covered is the period of restoration plus thirty days of extended business income. For coinsurance purposes, coverage includes the estimated net income and expenses for one year, starting with the policy inception or anniversary. This makes calculating the amount of insurance needed to satisfy coinsurance more complicated for business income than for other property coverages.

To assist insureds in making the necessary calculations, ISO publishes a Business Income Report/Work Sheet. Completing this form requires a significant level of financial sophistication. Therefore, some small businesses prefer options that eliminate the coinsurance requirement.

The variety of coinsurance percentages from which the insured may choose reflects the fact that the maximum foreseeable loss for a given insured seldom equals the projected net income and operating expenses for twelve months. To be properly protected, insureds should carry, at minimum, an amount of insurance equal to their **probable maximum loss (PML)**.

For some insureds, PML may constitute only a small fraction of the coinsurance basis. For example, a retail store operating in an area that contains numerous empty stores may be able to relocate and be fully operational within three months if its present location is totally destroyed. In contrast, a manufacturer that depends on sophisticated, special-order machinery might be shut

Probable maximum loss (PML)
The largest loss that an insured is likely to sustain.

down for eighteen months or more while waiting for replacement equipment if it sustains extensive damage to key equipment.

The retail store might need an amount of insurance equal to less than half its coinsurance basis and could thus choose 50 percent coinsurance; the manufacturer might need an amount of insurance much greater than its coinsurance basis. It could select 125 percent coinsurance, which would reduce the rate, because rates are lower when higher coinsurance percentages are selected.

 Reality Check

Effect of Coinsurance Penalty

This hypothetical example shows how an insured's failure to comply with the BIC Coinsurance condition can result in an insufficient loss recovery, even when the amount of loss is less than the limit of insurance.

Karen operates a retail store. Her store is insured under a Commercial Package Policy that includes the BIC. She selected a coinsurance percentage of 80 percent and an amount of $200,000 for coverage of her business income losses. The sum of her store's net income plus all operating expenses that would be incurred in the absence of a loss for the twelve-month period beginning at the inception or latest anniversary date of the policy is $400,000. This amount, the coinsurance basis, is twice the amount of the insurance coverage she bought. So Karen was substantially underinsured when she had a fire at her store. She lost $100,000 in business income as a result of the fire.

Applying the coinsurance formula to determine how much the insurer will pay her, the $400,000 coinsurance basis is multiplied by 80 percent. The result is $320,000, which is the minimum amount of coverage she should have bought to avoid a coinsurance penalty. The $200,000 amount of insurance she did buy is divided by the $320,000 amount she should have bought. The result is 0.625, which is multiplied by the $100,000 business income loss. That result is $62,500, which is the amount Karen's insurer will pay for her $100,000 loss, despite the $200,000 of coverage she purchased.

The difference between $100,000 and $62,500 is $37,500. That amount is the coinsurance penalty assessed against the loss as a result of purchasing an inadequate amount of coverage. Options are available to Karen and other insureds to omit or suspend the Coinsurance condition, thereby avoiding coinsurance penalties.

[DA07853]

BIC OPTIONAL COVERAGES

Optional coverages that can be activated in the business income coverage (BIC) forms allow the insured to obtain significant coverage enhancements.

The BIC includes four optional coverages that modify the basic coverage:

- Maximum Period of Indemnity
- Monthly Limit of Indemnity
- Business Income Agreed Value
- Extended Period of Indemnity

The first three optional coverages eliminate or suspend the Coinsurance condition, and the fourth optional coverage covers loss of business income that continues after the Extended Business Income additional coverage ends.

Maximum Period of Indemnity

The Maximum Period of Indemnity optional coverage negates the Coinsurance condition while limiting loss payment to the lesser of (1) the amount of loss sustained during the 120 days following the start of restoration or (2) the policy limit. The Maximum Period of Indemnity is not an additional coverage: It is a restriction of the period of restoration provided by the BIC, which, from the insured's point of view, has the advantage of avoiding any coinsurance penalty.

The period of restoration begins seventy-two hours after the time of direct physical loss. Therefore, an effective three-day deductible applies to these optional coverages in the same way that it applies to the standard BIC. (The seventy-two-hour period can be reduced to twenty-four hours or eliminated by endorsement.)

The coinsurance condition does not apply at any location to which the maximum period of indemnity is applicable. Therefore, this optional coverage should be used only when the insured is certain that any suspension of operations will last no more than four months.

Monthly Limit of Indemnity

Activated by inserting a fraction in the appropriate space in the declarations, the Monthly Limit of Indemnity optional coverage negates the Coinsurance condition while limiting the amount recoverable during any month of business interruption to the noted fraction of the insurance amount. This optional coverage applies only to business income coverage. Therefore, in the Business Income (and Extra Expense) Coverage Form, this optional coverage does not limit recovery for extra expense.

The Coinsurance condition does not apply to any location at which the monthly limit of indemnity is applicable. But this optional coverage is sometimes chosen because the insured does not want to disclose financial information to prove compliance with the Coinsurance condition or because the Coinsurance condition requires more insurance than the insured deems necessary.

✓ **Reality Check**

Example of Applying the Monthly Limit of Indemnity Optional Coverage

This hypothetical example shows how the Monthly Limit of Indemnity optional coverage would limit payment of a business income loss.

If the fraction shown in the declarations is 1/4 and the policy limit is $100,000, the maximum amount the insured could recover for any business income loss during any period of thirty consecutive days is $25,000. The claim payment would be the lesser of the actual loss sustained or $25,000 for the applicable thirty-day period. So if the business is suspended for three months following the start of the restoration period, and the actual loss of income is $30,000 for each of those months, the claim payment is only $25,000 per month, or a total of $75,000.

[DA07851]

Business Income Agreed Value

The Business Income Agreed Value optional coverage suspends the Coinsurance condition as long as the insured carries an amount of business income insurance that is equal to the value agreed on by the policyholder and the insurer. An insurer that is willing to provide this coverage—which, like the Maximum Period of Indemnity coverage, helps the insured avoid a potential coinsurance penalty—must take two steps to activate it.

First, the insurer must secure from the insured a completed business income report/worksheet showing this information:

- The insured's actual data for the most recent twelve-month accounting period before the date of the worksheet
- Estimated data for the twelve months immediately following inception of the coverage

Second, the insurer must enter the agreed value into the declarations. The agreed value must be at least equal to the product obtained by multiplying the coinsurance percentage shown in the declarations by the estimated net income and operating expenses shown on the worksheet for the twelve months following the inception of the optional coverage.

The agreed value is effective for a period of twelve months or until the policy expires, whichever comes first. The insured must submit a new worksheet to the insurer every twelve months for the agreed value coverage to remain in effect.

The Coinsurance condition is suspended while this optional coverage is in place. However, during this period, the insured must carry an amount of insurance at least equal to the agreed value if losses are to be paid in full. The Coinsurance condition is automatically reinstated if the agreed value coverage lapses. This could happen, for example, if the insured renews a policy but does not submit a new worksheet.

 **Reality Check**

Example of Applying the Business Income Agreed Value Optional Coverage

This hypothetical example illustrates the operation of the Business Income Agreed Value optional coverage.

ABC Corporation has a BIC with an agreed value of $200,000. If ABC carries insurance of $200,000 or more, its covered losses will be paid in full, without any possibility of a coinsurance penalty, up to the amount of insurance. However, if ABC carries only $150,000 of insurance, the Coinsurance condition will be reinstated and, consequently, only three-fourths of its covered losses will be paid (calculated as $150,000/$200,000 = 0.75).

[DA07852]

Extended Period of Indemnity

The Extended Period of Indemnity optional coverage extends the duration of the Extended Business Income (EBI) additional coverage to include business income losses that continue for more than thirty days after the property is restored. The period of indemnity can be extended up to 730 days, or two years. The actual number of days selected depends on the insured's estimate of the amount of time it would take for revenues to return to normal after the property is restored.

Many insureds, such as restaurants and clothing stores, depend on strong customer relationships and repeat business and would be unlikely to return to normal income levels within thirty days of reopening after a severe loss. For such insureds, this optional coverage can be highly attractive.

DETERMINING WHETHER THE BIC FORM COVERS A LOSS

Knowing how to apply business income coverage to the facts of a case is an important skill. This case study will help you make the transition from knowing policy language to applying policy language to losses to determine whether coverage applies. As you progress through this case study, you can check your understanding of the coverage provided by answering the Knowledge to Action questions.

Case Facts

Given the facts presented by the case, will the business income loss be covered? If so, what amount will the insurer pay for the claim? When answering the questions in this case-based activity, consider only the information provided as part of this case.

Fancy Wear Boutique (FWB), a retail clothing store in Chicago, is insured under a commercial package policy that includes the Business Income (and Extra Expense) Coverage Form, the Causes of Loss—Special Form, the Commercial Property Conditions, and the Common Policy Conditions (as well as other forms that are not relevant to this case).

The Commercial Property Coverage Part Declarations Page describes the insured premises at the address of the store building owned by FWB and shows a $1 million Business Income limit of insurance for the location, subject to option (2), Business Income Other Than "Rental Value." The declarations also show that FWB had purchased the Business Income Agreed Value optional coverage and that the value agreed to by the insurer and FWB was $1 million. None of the other optional coverages of the Business Income (and Extra Expense) Coverage Form are in effect. Moreover, no endorsements apply to FWB's Business Income (and Extra Expense) Coverage Form or Causes of Loss—Special Form. The one-year policy period shown in the declarations began on January 1, 20X1.

On April 1, 20X1, FWB suffered a total direct physical loss to its store building and contents when a tornado touched down on FWB's premises but did not cause widespread damage in the immediate area. Replacement of the building and its contents was accomplished with reasonable speed and required one year. During this period of restoration, both the revenues and normal operating expenses that FWB expected to experience were reduced as shown in the table. The resulting loss of business income that FWB sustained during the period of restoration was $680,000. The business income loss for the first seventy-two hours following the physical loss totaled $4,000. See the exhibit "FWB's Expected and Actual Revenues, Expenses, Net Income."

FWB's Expected and Actual Revenues, Expenses, Net Income

	Expected	Actual
Revenues	$2,000,000	$1,000,000
Expenses	750,000	430,000
Net Income	$1,250,000	$570,000

Business income loss = $1,250,000 − $570,000

= $680,000

[DA07918]

To keep its business operating during the period of restoration, FWB rented and moved into a nearby building one month after the tornado occurred and continued operating the boutique at this location for the duration of the restoration period. During this period, FWB incurred additional costs totaling $34,000 ($20,000 for rent, $3,000 for moving expenses, $5,000 for leased equipment, and $6,000 for additional advertising expenses). FWB would not have incurred any of these expenses had the tornado damage not occurred.

After the period of restoration ended and FWB resumed operations at the insured premises, the boutique continued to sustain loss of business income for sixty days, in these amounts:

- First period of thirty days after reopening: $15,000
- Second period of thirty days after reopening: $10,000

All loss of business income that occurred after FWB reopened its store resulted from changes in customers' shopping behavior during FWB's year-long suspension of normal operations while temporarily relocated. The additional loss of business income did not result from unfavorable business conditions caused by the impact of the tornado in FWB's area. Moreover, there was nothing more that FWB could reasonably have done to restore its normal business income level any sooner than it did.

FWB and the insurer agreed on all loss determinations, and FWB fulfilled all its post-loss duties under the policy.

Necessary Reference Materials

To determine whether FWB's policy provides coverage for business income loss incurred as a result of the tornado, you need copies of the policy forms, and the declarations pages themselves. There are no endorsements that affect Business Income coverage, but if there were, they would need to be reviewed to see how they affect the Business Income (and Extra Expense) Coverage Form.

You will need to have copies of the following forms available for your reference while working on this coverage case:

- Business Income (and Extra Expense) Coverage Form (CP 00 30 06 07)
- Causes of Loss—Special Form (CP 10 30 06 07)
- Commercial Property Conditions (CP 00 90 07 88)

Determination of Coverage

When examining the policy forms to determine whether coverage applies to the losses, you can apply the four steps of the DICE method. This involves analyzing the policy declarations, insuring agreement, conditions, and exclusions and determining whether any information found at each step precludes coverage at the time of the loss. You should also examine other categories of policy provisions such as the insured's duties, general provisions, endorsements (if applicable), and terms defined in the policy in relation to the declarations, insuring agreements, conditions, and exclusions.

DICE Analysis Step 1: Declarations

The first DICE step is to review the declarations pages to determine whether it covers the person or the property at the time of the loss.

Action Task: Review the declarations in FWB's policy. See the exhibit "Excerpt from FWB's Declarations Page."

A basic requirement, expressed in the Policy and Coverage Territory provision in the Commercial Property Conditions, is that the loss or damage must commence during the policy period shown in the declarations and must commence within the coverage territory in order for coverage to apply. The facts of FWB's claim satisfy this requirement because the business income loss commenced on April 1, 20X1, which is within the policy period stated in the declarations; and the loss commenced at the described premises, which is within the coverage territory. Even though the business income and extra expense loss continued for several months after the policy period ended, FWB's claim for the entire business income and extra expense claim would be covered under the policy in effect at the time the loss commenced. This result is supported by this sentence in the policy definition of period of restoration: "The expiration date of this policy will not cut short the 'period of restoration.'"

DICE Analysis Step 2: Insuring Agreement

The second DICE step is to review the insuring agreement to determine whether it is applicable to the described loss. The Business Income (and Extra Expense) Coverage form has two insuring agreements—one for the business income and a second for extra expense. You should determine what part of the loss is covered under the Business Income insuring agreement and what part is covered under the Extra Expense insuring agreement.

To be covered under the Business Income insuring agreement, a loss must be an actual loss of business income as defined and must meet several requirements imposed by the Business Income insuring agreement.

FWB sustained a $680,000 loss of business income, as defined in the Business Income insuring agreement. Because the claim is for business income other than rental income, the loss falls within option (2), Business Income Other Than "Rental Value," shown in the declarations. (A claim for loss of rental income, for example, would not be covered under FWB's business income

Excerpt from FWB's Declarations Page

COMMERCIAL PROPERTY
CP DS 00 10 00

COMMERCIAL PROPERTY COVERAGE PART
DECLARATIONS PAGE

POLICY NO. 00123456   EFFECTIVE DATE 01 / 01 / 20X1   ☐ "X" If Supplemental
                                                              Declarations Is Attached

NAMED INSURED Fancy Wear Boutique

DESCRIPTION OF PREMISES

Prem. No.	Bldg. No.	Location, Construction And Occupancy
001	001	1234 Main St., Chicago, IL Joisted Masonry Clothing or Wearing Apparel Store

COVERAGES PROVIDED Insurance At The Described Premises Applies Only For Coverages For Which A Limit Of Insurance Is Shown

Prem. No.	Bldg. No.	Coverage	Limit Of Insurance	Covered Causes Of Loss	Coinsurance*	Rates
001	001	Building	600,000	Special	80%	See Sched.
		Your Business Personal Property	700,000	Special		
		Personal Property of Others	50,000	Special		
		Business income/Extra Expense	1,000,000	Special		
		Option (2) Business Income Other Than Rental Value				
		Business Income Agreed Value optional coverage	1,000,000			

CP DS 00 10 00   Copyright, Insurance Services Office, Inc., 1999   Page 1 of 1 ☐

[DA07919]

coverage.) Furthermore, the circumstances of the claim meet the other applicable requirements imposed by the insuring agreement:

- The actual loss of FWB's business income was due to the necessary suspension of FWB's operations.
- The suspension was caused by direct physical loss of or damage to property (in this case, building and contents) at the premises described in the declarations and for which a Business Income limit of insurance is shown.
- The loss or damage was caused by a Covered Cause of Loss (in this case, tornado, a type of windstorm that is not excluded by the Causes of Loss—Special Form and is therefore covered).

The Business Income insuring agreement states that the insurer will pay actual loss of Business Income only during the "period of restoration." According to the policy definition of this term, the period of restoration, for purposes of Business Income coverage (as opposed to Extra Expense coverage), begins "seventy-two hours after the time of direct physical loss or damage." Because FWB sustained $4,000 of business income loss during those first seventy-two hours (three days), that sum will be deducted from the covered amount of business income loss.

For expenses to be covered under the Extra Expense insuring agreement, the circumstances of the claim must meet the requirements imposed by that agreement. The requirements of the insuring agreement are satisfied by these case facts:

- FWB incurred $34,000 in additional costs during the period of restoration to continue its operations at a substitute store.
- FWB would not have incurred these costs if there had been no direct physical loss or damage or if the loss or damage had not been caused by or resulted from a Covered Cause of Loss (in this case, tornado).

Knowledge to Action

Do any additional coverages or coverage extensions apply?

Feedback: Yes, but the only additional coverage or coverage extension of the Business Income (and Extra Expense) Coverage Form that applies to FWB's claim is the Extended Business Income (EBI) additional coverage. EBI applies to the claim because FWB continued to sustain loss of Business Income after its property was replaced and operations resumed. Moreover, as explained in the case facts, the additional loss of business income did not result from "unfavorable business conditions caused by the impact of the Covered Cause of Loss in the area where the described premises are located."

Although EBI applies to FWB's claim, it is limited to the thirty consecutive days immediately following the date the property was replaced and operations resumed. FWB could have lengthened this thirty-day period by purchasing the Extended Period of Indemnity optional coverage, but chose not to obtain that optional coverage.

DICE Analysis Step 3: Conditions

The third DICE step is to review the policy conditions to determine whether they preclude coverage at the time of the loss.

Numerous policy conditions are associated with FWB's business income and extra expense coverage. In addition to the conditions contained in the Business Income (and Extra Expense) Coverage Form, the Commercial Property Conditions and Common Policy Conditions also apply. In investigating the loss, the insurer must ascertain that the insured and the insurer have performed their respective duties imposed by these conditions and that the circumstances of the loss satisfy any other applicable conditions.

As stated in the case facts, the insurer determined that FWB performed all the duties required by the Duties in the Event of Loss condition. Because the insurer and FWB agreed on the determination of the amount of Business Income loss and the amount of Extra Expense incurred, the Appraisal condition was not applicable.

Also, because FWB has a $1 million limit, which satisfies the requirement in the Business Income Agreed Value optional coverage that FWB has purchased, the Coinsurance condition is suspended and therefore there is no possibility of a coinsurance penalty that would reduce the recovery amount. No other conditions had any negative effect on coverage.

Due to FWB complying with all the terms of the coverage part, once the insurer and FWB agree on the amount of loss, the insurer must pay the claim within thirty days after receiving FWB's sworn proof of loss.

Knowledge to Action

Of the following conditions required of the insured, FWB, which are found only as a condition of business income coverage?

a. Timely reporting of claim to the insurer

b. Cooperating with the insurer in investigation of claim

c. Providing a sworn proof of loss statement to the insurer

d. Resuming operations, in whole or in part, as quickly as possible

Feedback: d. Resuming operations is a condition that is unique to business income coverage.

DICE Analysis Step 4: Exclusions

The fourth DICE step is to review the policy exclusions to determine whether they exclude or limit coverage of the loss. The case facts presented provide no indication that any exclusion applies.

Determination of Amounts Payable

Now that you have completed the DICE analysis, you can determine the amounts payable. This involves analyzing the limit(s) of insurance available to pay for the loss and any deductibles that apply. It also involves determining whether more than one policy provides coverage for the same loss. FWB has no other policy that would cover this business income loss and therefore the Other Insurance provisions do not need to be considered.

The full amount of business income loss sustained during the period of restoration ($680,000) is covered, minus the amount sustained during the first three days after the physical loss occurred ($4,000), which results in the covered amount of $676,000 of business income loss.

All of FWB's $34,000 in additional costs are covered as extra expense. The period of restoration for Extra Expense coverage begins immediately after the direct physical loss occurs; there is no deductible for loss sustained during the first seventy-two hours, as in the case of business income coverage.

Only the $15,000 of business income loss sustained during the first thirty days following resumption of operations is insured under the EBI coverage extension. The additional $10,000 of business income loss sustained after the initial thirty-day period is not covered. FWB could have covered the additional income loss by purchasing the Extended Period of Indemnity optional coverage. See the exhibit "Amounts Payable to FWB."

Amounts Payable to FWB

Type of Loss	Amount of Loss Covered
Business Income	$676,000
Extra Expense	34,000
EBI	15,000
Total	$725,000

[DA07920]

The limit of insurance for FWB's Business Income (and Extra Expense) Coverage Form is $1 million, which is the maximum amount payable for loss in any one occurrence. Because the covered amount of FWB's losses is

$725,000, the limit of insurance does not reduce the amount payable. As discussed in connection with Step 3, the Business Income Agreed Value optional coverage is in effect, suspending the Coinsurance condition and therefore eliminating any possibility of a coinsurance penalty that would reduce the amount payable.

Knowledge to Action

If FWB had purchased the Maximum Period of Indemnity optional coverage instead of Business Income Agreed Value, how would that have affected the amount payable for this loss?

Feedback: Purchasing the Maximum Period of Indemnity optional coverage would have limited FWB's recovery to the amount of business income loss and extra expenses incurred during the 120 days (approximately four months) immediately following the beginning of the period of restoration. Given that FWB's period of restoration lasted for one year, the Maximum Period of Indemnity optional coverage would have left FWB seriously underinsured for this loss.

SUMMARY

A business income loss can sometimes be more devastating for an insured than the associated property loss. A business income loss is measured as the reduction in the insured's net income—the difference between expected net income had no loss occurred and actual net income after the loss. The causes of loss are often the same as for direct property losses.

Using either the Business Income (and Extra Expense) Coverage Form or the Business Income (Without Extra Expense) Coverage Form, most business income exposures can be insured. The Business Income insuring agreement is found in both of these forms, while the Extra Expense insuring agreement is found only in the Business Income (and Extra Expense) Coverage Form.

The basic coverage provided by the BIC form is supplemented by these additional coverages and one coverage extension:

- Expenses to Reduce Loss (BIC without extra expense only)
- Civil Authority
- Alterations and New Buildings
- Extended Business Income
- Interruption of Computer Operations
- Newly Acquired Locations

The amount payable by an insurer for a business income loss is determined in part by the BIC's Limits of Insurance, Loss Conditions, and Additional

Condition (Coinsurance) sections. In particular, purchasing a limit of insurance that satisfies the BIC Coinsurance condition can help ensure an adequate recovery for business income losses.

The BIC includes four optional coverages that can be used to prevent application of a coinsurance penalty or to prolong business income coverage beyond the period of restoration.

The four optional coverages include:

* Maximum Period of Indemnity
* Monthly Limit of Indemnity
* Business Income Agreed Value
* Extended Period of Indemnity

You should now be able to apply policy language to business income losses to determine whether the losses are covered and the amount for which they are covered.

Direct Your Learning ▶▶

10

Workers Compensation and Employers Liability Insurance

Educational Objectives

After learning the content of this assignment, you should be able to:

▷ Explain how the development of the workers compensation system in the United States has affected employees' rights to sue their employers for occupational injury.

▷ Explain how the following issues affect the eligibility of individuals for coverage under workers compensation statutes:

- Distinction between employee and independent contractor

- Status as a statutory employee

- Temporary employees and leased employees

▷ Describe the criteria for a compensable workers compensation injury and the benefits provided.

▷ Describe the various methods employers can use to demonstrate their financial security to pay workers compensation benefits.

▷ Identify the circumstances that can make an employee eligible for benefits under the workers compensation statutes of multiple states.

▷ Describe the legal remedy for occupational injury provided by certain federal statutes and the type(s) of employees eligible for each remedy.

▷ Explain how the Workers Compensation and Employers Liability Insurance Policy enables an insured as employer to fulfill state workers compensation obligations.

▷ Describe the purpose and the provisions of each of the following workers compensation coverage options:

- Voluntary Compensation and Employers Liability Coverage Endorsement

- Foreign voluntary compensation coverage

10

Educational Objectives, continued

- Longshore and Harbor Workers' Compensation Act Coverage Endorsement
- Maritime Coverage Endorsement
- Waiver of Our Right to Recover From Others Endorsement
- Alternate Employer Endorsement

▷ Describe the purpose and operation of workers compensation experience rating.

▷ Explain whether the Workers Compensation and Employers Liability (WC&EL) Insurance Policy and related endorsements would cover a described claim.

Workers Compensation and Employers Liability Insurance

10

DEVELOPMENT OF WORKERS COMPENSATION STATUTES

The legal system in the United States generally permits any person who has suffered injury or loss as a result of another person's negligent or wrongful act or omission to sue the other party for damages. Workers compensation statutes enacted in the early 1900s fundamentally altered employees' rights to sue their employers for occupational injury. However, these laws did not eliminate employees' rights to sue their employers for occupational injury in all instances.

Workers compensation statutes (laws passed by legislative bodies) provide defined benefits to employees or their dependents for occupational injuries. In this context, "occupational injury" means either injury or disease arising out of and in the course of the injured person's employment.

Among the factors that influenced the development of the workers compensation system in the U.S. and affected employees' rights to sue were conditions that existed preceding the enactment of the workers compensation statutes, the environment that began to develop as workers compensation statutes were enacted in individual states, and the fact that tort suits (an employee suit against the employer) were still permitted in some instances.

Conditions Preceding the Workers Compensation System

Before the enactment of workers compensation statutes, employees could sue their employers for occupational injury allegedly resulting from their employers' negligent acts or omissions. However, in the early years of the industrial age, most employee lawsuits against employers were unsuccessful.

Employers were protected against employee suits by three common-law defenses:

- The assumption-of-risk defense prevented injured employees from recovering damages for occupational injuries resulting from risks or dangers to which the employees knowingly and voluntarily exposed themselves.
- The contributory negligence defense prevented injured employees from recovering damages for occupational injuries resulting in part from the employees' own negligence.
- The fellow-servant rule prevented injured employees from recovering damages for occupational injuries caused by the negligence of fellow employees.

By the early 1900s, a number of state legislatures had enacted employers liability statutes that restricted the assumption-of-risk defense, applied comparative negligence instead of contributory negligence, or restricted or eliminated the fellow-servant rule. Moreover, some courts rejected the assumption-of-risk defense if the employer had violated safety rules. But these efforts had a negligible effect on injured employees' ability to win judgments against their employers.

In addition to overcoming the defenses available to employers, injured workers faced a number of other problems:

- Employees bringing suit would usually be fired.
- Co-workers, often the only witnesses to an accident, were reluctant to testify against the employer.
- A lawsuit could take years to resolve.
- Even if employees won their suits, court awards were often inadequate.

In essence, the legal system was not meeting employees' needs for prompt and adequate compensation for their occupational injuries.

Enactment of Workers Compensation Statutes

The first workers compensation statutes were enacted in Europe in the late 1800s. These statutes balanced the interests of employer and employee.

Employees gave up their existing legal remedy: the right to sue their employers for workplace injuries resulting from employer negligence. Employers became obligated to respond to employee injuries in accordance with the terms of the applicable statutes. The statutes provided relative certainty about the amount of benefits to be paid for specified injuries.

Beginning in 1902, individual states in the U.S. began to enact workers compensation statutes. These early statutes, because they made the employer's participation compulsory, were declared unconstitutional by the Supreme Court as a deprivation of property without due process. Accordingly, the states began passing elective laws. Elective laws gave employers the choice of participating in workers compensation, but employers that chose not to participate were denied the common-law defenses that had previously protected them.

In 1917, the Supreme Court ruled that New York's compulsory workers compensation law was a legitimate exercise of the state's police power to protect the health and well-being of its inhabitants.[1] All fifty states, the District of Columbia, Puerto Rico, Guam, and the U.S. Virgin Islands now have workers compensation laws. Except for the Texas statute, all state workers compensation statutes are now effectively compulsory.[2] All of the Canadian provinces and territories also have workers compensation laws.

The U.S. workers compensation system has these specific goals:

- Promptly paying adequate income and medical benefits, according to a fixed and predetermined schedule, to injured employees or their dependents regardless of fault

- Eliminating the delays and costs of litigation to the employee and to society

- Establishing a guarantee of benefit payment, secured by insurance

- Promoting industrial safety and hygiene

Workers compensation statutes were intended to cure the defects of the common law and employers liability statutes and to present simple and rational provisions. The relief provided was to be certain and immediate.

Injury schedules attempted to make payments largely automatic, resulting in few occasions when adversarial proceedings would be required. The remedial and beneficial purpose of workers compensation laws is often cited as a justification for extending coverage in close or doubtful cases. This attitude has the support of legal scholars of workers compensation and is adhered to in practice by compensation hearing officers and judges.

Tort Suits Still Permitted in Some Instances

Receiving the benefits provided by the applicable workers compensation statute is frequently called an employee's exclusive remedy or sole remedy for occupational injury, meaning that the employee cannot also sue the employer.

However, workers compensation laws do not prohibit employees from suing their employers for occupational injury in every instance. When workers are outside the scope of the relevant workers compensation statute, they retain the right to sue their employers under tort principles. For example, some statutes exempt domestic employees, who therefore retain the right to sue their employers for occupational injury.

In some situations, even an employee who is covered by a workers compensation statute may be able to sue. For example, suit may be permitted if a worker's injuries were intentionally caused by the employer or resulted from the employer's performing in some capacity other than as employer (such as the manufacturer of a product that injures an employee while at work). These and other situations in which employees can sue their employers for occupational injury are associated with employers liability insurance.

In addition, some workers compensation laws state that if an employer fails to provide financial security for its workers compensation obligations (through insurance or a qualifying self-insurance plan, for example), its employees may exercise their common-law rights to sue the employer for occupational injuries, and the employer is barred from asserting its common-law defenses.

STATE WORKERS COMPENSATION STATUTES: PERSONS AND EMPLOYMENTS COVERED

Individual states' workers compensation statutes must address issues regarding eligibility.

Most workers compensation statutes are compulsory with regard to all private and public employments (other than employment by the federal government), subject to some exceptions that vary by state. For example, many statutes exempt domestic employees or casual (incidental) employees. Some statutes exempt farm workers or any employer with fewer than a stated number of employees—generally three, four, or five. Many statutes permit sole proprietors, partners, or corporate officers to reject coverage. Various other exemptions can be found under particular statutes. Employees not covered by the statute retain their common-law rights of action against their employers.

In addition to the exemptions specifically stated in each statute, these issues are also important in determining the persons for whom an employer might be required to provide workers compensation benefits:

- Distinction between employee and independent contractor
- Statutory employees
- Temporary employees and leased employees

Distinction Between Employee and Independent Contractor

Generally, an employer's legal obligations under the applicable workers compensation statute extend to employees only, not to independent contractors.

The essential distinction between employees and independent contractors is that the employer has the right to control and direct the activities of an employee, not only as to the result to be accomplished but also as to the methods and means by which the result is obtained.

Distinguishing between employee and independent contractor status can sometimes be difficult. Because the legislative intent expressed in most workers compensation statutes is to protect employees, courts and boards deciding workers compensation cases presume that an employer-employee relationship exists unless the facts clearly establish that the worker is an independent contractor.

The distinction is also important for tax purposes because an employer pays Social Security and Medicare taxes and withholds income taxes for employees but not for independent contractors. To assist employers, the Internal Revenue Service (IRS) has created a list of factors to consider in deciding whether an individual is an employee or an independent contractor. Furthermore, because the purposes of the workers compensation statutes and the United States tax code are different, courts might hold that a certain situation creates an independent contractor relationship for tax purposes but an employment relationship for workers compensation purposes. See the exhibit "IRS Factors for Determining Whether a Worker Is an Employee or an Independent Contractor."

Some states have a stricter definition of what constitutes an independent contractor. For example, a portion of the Wisconsin workers compensation statute states that a worker will be considered an employee unless all of the conditions set out in the law are met. See the exhibit "Definition of Independent Contractor Under the Wisconsin Statute."

Statutory Employees

Another important issue in determining the persons for whom an employer might be required to provide workers compensation benefits is whether the employee might be considered a statutory employee of the employer. Even when a person or an organization qualifies as an independent contractor, the workers compensation statutes of many states contain an important exception to the general rule that an employer's obligations under the statute do not extend to independent contractors. These statutes consider the employees of independent contractors to be employees of the principal (the entity hiring the independent contractor) if the independent contractor has not maintained workers compensation insurance covering its employees. The term **"statutory employee"** is used to describe such an employee.

Thus, if an employee of an uninsured independent contractor sustains a compensable injury (that is, an injury that is covered by the applicable workers compensation statute), the principal can be held liable to provide workers compensation benefits to the injured employee. However, after paying benefits to a statutory employee, the principal ordinarily has the right to seek reimbursement from the independent contractor.

A principal's obligation to provide workers compensation benefits to statutory employees also applies to a general contractor that has hired a subcontractor. That is, the employees of an uninsured subcontractor can become statutory employees of the general contractor.

Statutory employee

An independent contractor's employee who, because the independent contractor has not maintained workers compensation insurance, is considered to be an employee of the principal employing the independent contractor.

IRS Factors for Determining Whether a Worker Is an Employee or an Independent Contractor

In any employee-independent contractor determination, all information that provides evidence of the degree of control and the degree of independence must be considered. Facts that provide evidence of the degree of control and independence fall into three categories: behavioral control, financial control, and the type of relationship of the parties.

1. **Behavioral control.** Facts that show whether the business has a right to direct and control how the worker does the task for which the worker is hired include the type and degree of:

   - *Instructions that the business gives to the worker.* An employee is generally subject to the business's instructions about when, where, and how to work.

   - *Training that the business gives to the worker.* An employee may be trained to perform services in a particular manner. Independent contractors ordinarily use their own methods.

2. **Financial control.** Facts that show whether the business has a right to control the business aspects of the worker's job include:

   - *The extent to which the worker has unreimbursed business expenses.* Independent contractors are more likely to have unreimbursed expenses than are employees.

   - *The extent of the worker's investment.* An independent contractor often has a significant investment in the facilities he or she uses in performing services for someone else.

   - *The extent to which the worker makes his or her services available to the relevant market.* An independent contractor is generally free to seek out business opportunities.

   - *How the business pays the worker.* An employee is generally guaranteed a regular wage amount for an hourly, weekly, or other period of time. An independent contractor is usually paid by a flat fee for the job. However, it is common in some professions, such as law, to pay independent contractors hourly.

   - *The extent to which the worker can realize a profit or loss.* An independent contractor can make a profit or loss.

3. **Type of relationship.** Facts that show the parties' type of relationship include:

   - *Written contracts describing the relationship the parties intended to create.*

   - *Whether or not the business provides the worker with employee-type benefits, such as insurance, a pension plan, vacation pay, or sick pay.*

   - *The permanency of the relationship.* Engaging a worker with the expectation that the relationship will continue indefinitely, rather than for a specific project or period, is generally considered evidence of an intent to create an employer-employee relationship.

   - *The extent to which services performed by the worker are a key aspect of the regular business of the company.* If a worker provides services that are a key aspect of the employer's regular business activity, it is more likely that the employer will have the right to direct and control the worker's activities.

Source: "Employee or Independent Contractor?," IRS Publication 15-A, 2010 Edition, pp. 6–7, www.irs.gov/pub/irs-pdf/p15a.pdf (accessed December 8, 2010). [DA04860]

Because of the provisions regarding statutory employees, a principal that hires independent contractors should obtain certificates of insurance from its independent contractors before they begin working for the principal.

Definition of Independent Contractor Under the Wisconsin Statute

The Wisconsin workers compensation statute specifies that to be classified as an independent contractor, a person must meet all of the following conditions:

- He or she maintains a separate office or other facility.

- He or she has a federal employment identification number or has filed business or self-employment income tax returns with the IRS for the work or services in the previous year.

- He or she operates under contract to perform specific services for specific amounts of money and controls the means of performing the services.

- He or she incurs the main expenses related to the service or work performed.

- He or she is liable for failure to complete the work or services.

- He or she receives compensation under contract on a commission, per job, or competitive bid basis.

- He or she may realize a profit or suffer a loss.

- He or she has continuing or recurring business liabilities or obligations.

- The success or failure of his or her business depends on the relationship of business receipts to expenditures.

Source: Wisconsin Workers Compensation Act Section 107.07(8). [DA04861]

If the principal does not have evidence that its contractors carry workers compensation insurance, the principal's workers compensation insurer is entitled to charge a premium (determined when auditing the insured's records) for the work the independent contractor performed. Moreover, because a certificate of insurance does not guarantee that the insurance will be in effect after the certificate was issued, the principal should also maintain valid workers compensation insurance in case the contractor does not have insurance when a loss actually occurs.

Temporary Employees and Leased Employees

A third important issue in determining the persons for whom an employer might be required to provide workers compensation benefits is whether the employee is a temporary or leased employee, as opposed to a regular employee.

Many employers use either temporary employees or leased employees (or both) in addition to their regular employees. Temporary employees and leased employees differ from one another. Temporary employees are hired for short-term assignments to cope with peak workloads or to replace an employee who is on sick leave or vacation. Temporary employees are considered to be regular employees of the providing firm, not of the firm using the temporary employees' services. Accordingly, the providing firm is responsible for obtaining workers compensation insurance for these employees.

Leased employees, in contrast, may appear to be regular employees. They work continuously for the same firm and are subject to control by the firm just as they would be if they were the firm's regular employees. Technically, however, they are co-employees of the leasing contractor, sometimes called a professional employer organization (PEO), and of the client company.

Sometimes a firm will transfer all of its employees to the PEO and then lease them back. The PEO is responsible for all payroll taxes, employee benefits, and workers compensation coverage. Generally, a separate workers compensation policy is written showing the names of the PEO and the client company, although the requirements imposed by law vary by state.

WORKERS COMPENSATION CRITERIA AND BENEFITS

Workers compensation statutes were enacted to allow injured employees to receive prompt medical attention and funds for lost wages. Employees who receive workers compensation benefits return to work more rapidly than those who did not.

Historically, the purpose of workers compensation statues has been to provide benefits only for occupational injury—that is an employee's bodily injury arising from employment. The most prevalent occupational injuries are those caused by industrial accidents. Court decisions and changes in law have broadened workers compensation coverage to include some, but not all, occupational diseases. The medical, disability, rehabilitation, and death benefits coverages provided under workers compensation are standard nationwide. The amounts of compensation, requirements for compensation, methods of benefit calculation, and time frames for compensation, however, vary by state.

Qualifying Criteria for a Workers Compensation Injury

While workers compensation statutes and regulations vary by state regarding the elements required for an injury to be compensable, normally the injury elements must meet three criteria:

- Accidental—The injury must be due to an accident. Courts have defined "accident" as an injurious occurrence that is unforeseen and unintended.

- Arising from employment—The origin and/or cause of the injury must be reasonably connected to the risks of the employment type.

- In the course of employment—The time, place, and circumstances of the injury must be within the employment scope.

The injuries described in the exhibit originate in the workplace but may not embody all of the elements required to qualify the injured party for workers compensation. See the exhibit "How Injuries Qualify for Workers Compensation Benefits."

How Injuries Qualify for Workers Compensation Benefits

Employee Injury	Result of Injury	Does Injury Qualify Employee for Workers Compensation?
Employee Sam cuts his arm working on the production line.	He requires fifteen stitches and misses twelve days of work.	Sam's injury is accidental, is due to his job on the production line, and occurred at his place of employment. Therefore, his injuries qualify him for workers compensation benefits.
Employee Sue claims that she contracted a cold from her co-worker, with whom she shares a cubicle.	Sue requires a doctor's visit and medication, and misses three days of work.	Sue's cold is not accidental. It also is not connected to the specific risks of her employment, and being in her place of work is not the only manner in which she could have acquired the cold. Thus, Sue's condition does not qualify her for workers compensation.
Employee Steve is hit by an auto while walking back from lunch with his coworkers at a diner three blocks from the office.	His leg is broken, resulting in surgery and causing him to miss two months of work.	Steve's broken leg is accidental. Although he was having lunch with coworkers, Steve's employer did not exercise authority over Steve's lunchtime. When the employer does not exercise authority, lunchtime injuries are not considered to have arisen from employment or in the course of employment. Therefore, Steve's injury does not qualify him for workers compensation.

[DA06711]

Originally, for an injury to qualify for workers compensation benefits, it not only had to arise out of and in the course of employment, but it also had to be specific in time, place, and cause. Also, compensability was generally limited to physical injuries. Advances in science and technology and the growth of the service industry led to a broadening of the elements for compensability. Today, injuries that are not specific to date or time and that are not necessarily physical can qualify for workers compensation benefits. Because such injuries may take months or years to manifest, most state workers compensation statutes accommodate an extended period for filing a claim. See the exhibit "Workers Compensation: Compensable Versus Noncompensable Injuries."

Workers Compensation: Compensable Versus Noncompensable Injuries

Condition	Examples	Compensable?
Specified occupational diseases	Pneumoconiosis, the fibrous inflammation or chronic hardening of lung tissue caused by prolonged inhalation of dust. Black lung is a form of pneumoconiosis, as are asbestosis (caused by inhaling asbestos particles) and silicosis (caused by inhaling silica dust).	Yes.
Allergic reactions	Latex sensitivity.	Yes, in many states.
Cumulative trauma injuries	Carpal tunnel syndrome Hernias in the stomach, abdomen, and groin areas from repeated stress and strain frequently caused by heavy lifting.	Yes.
Mental injuries	Mental injuries substantially caused by work-related factors and greater-than-normal work stress:	
	• Mental illness caused by physical trauma (physical-mental)	All states cover physical-mental injuries.
	• Physical symptoms resulting from mental causes that are job related, such as unusual job-related tension and stress that result in a heart attack (mental-physical)	Some states cover mental-physical injuries.
	• Mental injuries unaccompanied by any physical manifestation, such as witnessing a fellow employee being seriously injured (mental-mental)	Some states cover mental-mental injuries.
Intentionally self-inflicted injuries	Nonaccidental injuries.	No.
Certain accidental injuries	Injuries resulting from certain causes, such as intoxication or willful failure to use a safety appliance or observe safety regulations.	No.

[DA06712]

For an injury to be considered compensable, it must arise "out of and in the course of employment." However, not all states use this precise wording in their workers compensation statutes. Depending on the state, the applicable wording may read "in the course and resulting from," "in the course of," or "arising out of or in the course of employment."

At one time the phrase "arising out of and in the course of employment" was stringently applied in determining an injury's eligibility for workers compensation coverage. The injury had to have been caused by a risk specific to the employment. For example, if a worker was badly burned after spilling hot coffee on her lap as she was typing, the injury would not have been considered compensable because hot coffee exists elsewhere besides the workplace. Today, most courts hold that an injury is compensable if it arises out of "increased risks" posed by employment. In the hot coffee case, the worker's performance of a job function in connection with the coffee constitutes increased risk.

"Arising out of employment" refers to the origin or the cause of the injury. That is, to be compensable, the injury must arise out of some risk reasonably incidental to the injured person's employment.

"In the course of employment" requires two elements:

- The employee must have been doing something for which he or she was employed.
- The employer must have set the time and place of employment.

When the employer has not set the time and place of work, the employee is usually considered to be in the course of employment when the time and place is required as part of the employment. Employees who work at home as a matter of personal convenience are usually not considered to be in the course of their employment if injured at home, unless it can be proven that they are injured while specifically engaged in the work for which they are employed.

Some states have adopted a positional risk doctrine, which specifies that an injury is considered to have arisen out of a worker's employment if the injury would not have occurred but for the fact that the conditions and obligations of the employment placed the claimant in the position where he or she was injured. For example, in a state that has adopted the positional risk doctrine, the injury an employee receives when an out-of-control car crashes through the employer's storefront would be compensable.

A general rule is that employees are not compensated for injuries that occur while commuting to and from work. There are exceptions to this rule. One is when an employee is conducting a work-related function during the travel to and from work. For example, if an employee stops at the post office to pick up the office mail prior to coming into work each day, the period during which the employee deviates from the route that would take her directly from home to the office would be considered time covered by workers compensation. Another exception to this general rule is travel on the employer's premises. While an employee is on premises owned, leased, or controlled by the employer, the coming and going rule does not apply. For example, if workers park on the company lot behind a manufacturing plant, workers compensation coverage applies once a worker drives onto the lot. Other exceptions are for employees traveling to accomplish an errand they were sent on by their employer and for employees who travel for business purposes.

Many states have enacted second injury funds as part of the workers compensation system. See the exhibit "Second Injury Funds."

Second Injury Funds

Defined—A state-operated or mandated fund that pays a portion of the workers compensation benefits of an injured employee whose disability is aggravated by a prior disability. In most cases, the initial injury does not have to be work related. It can result from injury, birth defect, or even a debilitating illness.

Purpose—To encourage the employment of employees with disabilities. New York created the first Second Injury Fund in 1916 to encourage the employment of employees with disabilities. By the 1940s, all states had them, partly as a result of the National Model Code to encourage the hiring of World War II veterans.

Benefits Given—Depending on the state. For example, may pay the excess over what the award would have been for an employee with no prior disability or assume payments once the amount reaches a certain level; may apply to permanent disability or apply to all medical and disability benefits; may make payments directly to the injured employee or reimburse them to the insurer or self-insured employer.

Method of Funding—In general, the states assess employers and/or insurers yearly a percentage of losses paid or premiums written the previous year. The percentage can vary depending on the financial needs of the fund.

Current Environment—Beginning in the 1950s, second injury funds began to include more types of injuries and enhance the benefits. Costs began to greatly increase. The passage of the Americans with Disabilities Act (ADA) in 1990, some argue, eliminated the need for second injury funds. As a result, only about thirty states currently have them.

[DA06663]

Benefits Provided

Workers compensation statutes provide employees with specified benefits that are to be paid promptly when a compensable injury occurs. This ensures that the injured worker receives the necessary and proper medical care and has funds to continue to meet daily living expenses when unable to work due to the injury. Workers compensation benefits are intended to assist in the employee's recovery and to allow him or her to return to work as a productive member of society. The benefits provided fall into four categories:

- Medical benefits
- Disability benefits

- Rehabilitation benefits
- Death benefits

Medical Benefits

For medical care to be covered, it must meet three criteria:

- It must be related to the injury.
- It must be reasonable in the amount of care given and the amount charged.
- It must be necessary to cure or relieve the injury.

In many states, workers compensation statutes establish payment amounts according to a fee schedule, and approved medical providers must accept the amounts specified in the fee schedule as full compensation.

The scope of covered medical care is broad. It includes physician fees, emergency room fees, hospital care, diagnostic testing, nursing care, medications, psychological treatments, physical therapy, home health aides, prosthetic devices, travel expenses to and from care treatment locations, and so forth. Coverage for medical expenses begins immediately.

State statutes differ on whether injured workers have the right to select their care provider. In some states, the choice may be limited to medical practitioners shown on a list provided by the employer. In others, workers with compensable injuries may be restricted to practitioners within a managed care organization for treatment of their work-related injuries. A managed care organization seeks to manage healthcare efficiently, usually by contracting with a network of approved healthcare providers.

The employer (and therefore its workers compensation insurer) generally has the right to have the injured worker examined by an independent medical examiner (IME) of its choice. An IME is a healthcare provider who has agreed to evaluate an injured worker for a fee and who is not involved in the injured worker's treatment.

The cost of medical care has steadily increased both in absolute dollars and as a percentage of total workers compensation losses. According to the National Council on Compensation Insurance (NCCI), of the total workers compensation losses in 1982, 60 percent consisted of indemnity-related expenses and 40 percent consisted of medical-related expenses. By 2008, only 40 percent consisted of indemnity-related expenses, while 60 percent consisted of medical-related expenses, a complete reversal.

Disability Benefits

Disability benefits provide compensation for an employee's loss of earned income or earning capacity resulting from a compensable injury. Four types are provided:

- Temporary total disability (TTD)
- Permanent total disability (PTD)
- Temporary partial disability (TPD)
- Permanent partial disability (PPD)

In virtually all states, disability benefits are payable to disabled employees only after a waiting period that usually ranges from three to seven days after the injury. In most states, benefits are retroactive to the date of the injury if the injured employee is unable to work for a specified period, which can be as brief as five days or as long as six weeks.

Temporary total disability (TTD) occurs when an injured employee is unable to perform any job duties for a period of time but is expected to return to full job duties after recovering.

Temporary total disability (TTD)

A disability caused by a work-related injury or disease that temporarily renders an injured worker unable to perform any job duties for a period of time.

The benefit for temporary total disability is calculated as a percentage (typically 66.67 percent) of the employee's average weekly wage, subject to maximum and minimum amounts that vary by state. Regardless of the employee's actual work week, benefits are paid at the rate of one-seventh of the average weekly wage for each day. Most states permit the employee to collect the temporary total disability benefit for the duration of the disability. Some states, however, limit the number of weeks or the total dollar amount payable.

Permanent total disability (PTD) occurs when an employee's injuries are such that he or she will never be able to return to gainful employment. PTD cases constitute a small percentage of all disability cases but account for a disproportionately large percentage of the total cost of indemnity benefits.

Permanent total disability (PTD)

A disability caused by a work-related injury or disease that renders an injured employee unable to ever return to gainful employment.

The PTD benefit is similar to TTD—a percentage of the employee's average weekly wage, subject to weekly maximums and minimums. Under most state workers compensation statutes, PTD benefits are payable for life or for the duration of the disability. Some states limit PTD to a specified number of weeks or to a dollar amount.

Temporary partial disability (TPD)

A disability caused by a work-related injury or disease that temporarily limits the extent to which a worker can perform job duties; the worker is eventually able to return to full duties and hours.

Temporary partial disability (TPD) occurs when an injured employee is able to continue working, at reduced efficiency, but is expected to recover and return to full duties and hours. The benefit payable is usually a percentage (typically 66.67 percent) of the difference between the weekly wage that the employee would have earned had no injury occurred and the weekly wage that the employee actually earned during the recovery period, subject to minimums and maximums.

Insurers and employers have found that encouraging employees to return to work on a light-duty basis is an important risk control measure that benefits both the employer and the employee. The employer benefits because it continues to derive production from the employee, while the employee benefits because he or she can continue to work with less physically demanding duties, a reduced workload, or an abbreviated workday.

Permanent partial disability (PPD) occurs when the injured employee, although permanently disabled, has lost only certain functioning. Thus, an employee with a permanent partial disability is able to work, but at reduced efficiency.

In theory, PPD benefits compensate an injured worker for the possible decrease in his or her future earnings. The degree of permanent partial disability is not measurable until the maximum medical improvement (MMI) has been reached. Therefore, an injured employee may receive TTD benefits starting at the time of the injury (after satisfying any waiting period) and then receive a PPD benefit when it is determined that a certain degree of disability is permanent.

Most states calculate the benefit for PPD according to a schedule that allots a certain number of weeks of benefits to loss of use of a particular bodily member, such as a hand, a foot, an eye, and so forth. The number of weeks is multiplied by the weekly TTD benefit. Partial loss of use of a bodily member generally results in an allowance equal to a percentage of total loss of use. For example, if total loss of use of one hand resulted in a 150-week benefit, a 20 percent loss of use of one hand would result in a 30-week benefit. When a PPD results from a cause (such as a back injury) other than one of the scheduled injuries, the benefit is calculated as either a percentage of the actual wage loss or as a percentage of total disability. Employers liability for permanent partial scheduled injuries does not continue indefinitely, but is fixed and limited by the calculated benefit and duration.

Permanent partial disability (PPD)
A disability caused by a work-related injury or disease that impairs the injured employee's earning capacity for life, but the employee is able to work at reduced efficiency.

Rehabilitation Benefits

Rehabilitation benefits include both physical and vocational rehabilitation services. Rehabilitation reduces the seriousness and, therefore, the cost of disabling injuries. Although considered an integral part of complete medical treatment, rehabilitation may include such services as vocational training or training to drive a specially equipped car.

Although a few states do not include specific rehabilitation provisions in their workers compensation statutes, rehabilitation is allowed and provided in all states even if unspecified in the statute. In some states, an employee's failure to accept rehabilitation services can result in a reduction or loss of disability benefits.

Many insurers conduct rehabilitation programs for disabled workers, often providing rehabilitation benefits that go well beyond those required by the statute. Conducting these programs often reduces the ultimate loss costs because rehabilitated employees are able to seek gainful employment.

Death Benefits

If an employee's death results from an accident or an occupational disease immediately or subsequently arising out of and in the course of employment, workers compensation statutes provide death benefits. These consist of income replacement to the deceased employee's surviving spouse and dependents and a burial allowance.

The amounts payable as death benefits vary by state. In over half the states, income replacement benefits to dependents are limited in time. Both the amount and the duration of the weekly benefit typically depend on whether the deceased employee has minor children. Benefits may also be limited or terminated if the surviving spouse remarries. As is true for permanent total disability benefits, about one-fourth of states adjust death benefits annually to match all or part of the increase in prices or wages. The maximum burial allowance varies by state from $3,000 to $15,000.

Work-related fatalities have decreased overall because of a greater emphasis on safety and the shift in employment from manufacturing to service industries. However, death benefits still account for a small percentage of total workers compensation benefits paid.

WORKERS COMPENSATION: METHODS OF DEMONSTRATING FINANCIAL SECURITY

Most workers compensation statutes require employers to demonstrate security, or financial ability, to pay any claims for which an employer is responsible under the statute.

An employer that fails to demonstrate financial security in compliance with workers compensation statutes is subject to severe penalties, which can include fines against the employer, imprisonment of company officers, civil penalties (such as a 50 percent increase in compensation payments to employees), prohibition of the employer to conduct business until the security requirement is met, and allowing injured employees to sue the employer without the employer's common-law defenses being available.

These are some of the methods of demonstrating security under workers compensation statutes:

- Obtaining insurance from the voluntary market
- Obtaining insurance from an assigned risk plan
- Obtaining insurance from a state fund

- Having a qualified self-insurance plan
- Participating in a self-insured group

Insurance From the Voluntary Market

An employer can meet its obligations under the workers compensation statute of a particular state by purchasing workers compensation insurance from any private insurer that is licensed to write workers compensation coverage in that state. Private insurers are collectively called the "voluntary market" because they insure only those applicants (apart from assigned risk placements) that they willingly accept in accordance with their underwriting guidelines. In return for the premium received from the policyholder, the insurer agrees to pay the benefits and assume most administrative duties required by the applicable workers compensation statute.

Insurance From an Assigned Risk Plan

Many states have created assigned risk plans to make workers compensation insurance available to employers that cannot obtain such insurance in the voluntary market. Typically, employers cannot obtain coverage in the voluntary market because they have poor workers compensation loss experience. In addition, a newly formed company might be rejected by the voluntary market because it has insufficient loss experience.

In either case, an employer rejected by insurers in the voluntary market can apply to the assigned risk plan in the appropriate state to obtain coverage. The plan then assigns the employer to an insurer licensed to write workers compensation insurance in the state. That insurer must then provide coverage for the assigned employer for a specific period. The amount of workers compensation business assigned to each licensed insurer is in proportion to the insurer's share of the voluntary workers compensation market. For example, an insurer writing 10 percent of the total premiums in the state's voluntary workers compensation market would be assigned 10 percent of the business insured through the assigned risk plan.

The workers compensation insurance rates for companies insured in assigned risk plans are usually substantially higher than the voluntary market rates for comparable classifications. Therefore, many companies that find themselves insured in the assigned risk plan take measures to leave the assigned risk plan and enter the voluntary market. These measures usually consist of implementing or improving risk control programs so that the organization's operations, and eventually its loss experience, will meet the underwriting standards of insurers in the voluntary market.

Insurance From a State Fund

Insurers called "state funds" provide workers compensation insurance in about half of the states. A **state fund** is a workers compensation insurer that is set up by the state in which it operates either as an agency of the state government or, in some cases, as a mutual or not-for-profit insurer. The term "territorial fund" is used to describe comparable insurers in Puerto Rico and the United States Virgin Islands.

State fund

A workers compensation insurer that is set up by the state in which it operates either as an agency of the state government or as a mutual or not-for-profit insurer.

In most cases, a state fund operates only in its home state. However, to meet the insurance needs of insureds with multistate operations, some state funds have created subsidiaries that operate in neighboring states. Other state funds use fronting arrangements with private insurers to provide their customers with workers compensation insurance in other states. In such a fronting arrangement, the private ("fronting") insurer issues a policy in its name but the state fund agrees to reimburse the fronting insurer for losses it pays under the policy.

State funds operate in essentially the same way as most other insurers. They are subject, for the most part, to the same regulatory requirements regarding surplus and reserves as are private insurers. The most significant difference is that a state fund accepts any good-faith applicant for workers compensation insurance in the state. Consequently, no assigned risk plan is necessary in the states that have state funds.

Competitive fund

A state fund that sells workers compensation insurance in competition with private insurers.

Most states that have state funds permit other licensed insurers to sell workers compensation insurance in competition with the state fund, which is therefore called a **competitive fund**. An employer in these states can purchase insurance from either the state fund or another insurer licensed in the state.

The exhibit shows the states that have competitive funds. Most new competitive state funds are organized as private insurers called employers' mutual insurance companies. A state fund that is called an employers' mutual insurance company is authorized to operate as a domestic mutual insurer but with continued oversight by the state. Often the state pledges to ensure the company's ability to maintain an adequate surplus to meet all foreseeable conditions. Although employers' mutuals can be characterized as private insurers, they are not part of the voluntary market. In addition, because they are state funds, employers' mutuals must accept all good-faith applicants.

Monopolistic state fund (exclusive state fund)

A facility, owned and operated by a state government, that provides workers compensation insurance and that does not permit any other insurers to sell workers compensation insurance in that state.

A few states authorize only the state fund to write workers compensation insurance. Because no other insurer is licensed to write workers compensation coverage in these states, the state funds have no competition and are therefore called **monopolistic funds** or exclusive funds. The exhibit shows the states and other jurisdictions that have monopolistic state funds. See the exhibit "Types of State or Territorial Funds by Jurisdiction."

Types of State or Territorial Funds by Jurisdiction	
Competitive Funds	Arizona, California, Colorado, Hawaii, Idaho, Kentucky, Louisiana, Maine, Maryland, Minnesota, Missouri, Montana, New Mexico, New York, Oklahoma, Oregon, Pennsylvania, Rhode Island, South Carolina, Texas, Utah
Monopolistic	Ohio, North Dakota, Puerto Rico, U.S. Virgin Islands, Washington, Wyoming, and each Canadian province

[DA04866]

Self-Insurance Plans

With a few exceptions, all states and territories allow employers to self-insure their workers compensation losses if they demonstrate the financial capacity to do so by meeting certain requirements.

To qualify as a self-insurer, an employer must post a surety bond or other collateral with the workers compensation administrative agency of the state to guarantee the security of benefit payments. In addition, most states require evidence of an ability to administer the benefit payments and services mandated by the law. Therefore, self-insurance is usually practical only for large employers that have the financial and personnel resources to meet state requirements.

Even if state law does not require it, many self-insurers purchase excess insurance (also called stop-loss coverage) to cover loss in excess of the amounts that they actually wish to retain. Two types of excess insurance that are commonly written in conjunction with self-insured workers compensation programs are specific excess and aggregate excess.

Self-Insured Groups

In searching for more economical ways for employers to insure their obligations under workers compensation laws, many states have authorized the formation of self-insured groups. **Self-insured groups**, also called pools and trusts, consist of employers in the same industry that jointly (as a whole) and severally (individually) guarantee payment of workers compensation benefits to the employees of the group's members.

Because no insurer is involved in this type of arrangement, the group retains an administrator to run the day-to-day operations and a third-party administrator (TPA) to manage claim administration. Sometimes one firm provides both services. Self-insured groups almost always also purchase excess insurance to protect their members against losses that exceed the desired retention level.

Self-insured group (pool or trust)

A group of employers in the same industry that jointly (as a whole) and severally (individually) guarantee payment of workers compensation benefits to the employees of the group's members. A not-for-profit association or corporation is typically formed to which they pay premiums for self-insurance purposes.

Before joining a self-insured group, an organization must understand the financial risks of such groups. If the group's assets are insufficient to cover its liabilities, all members of the group (including those members that had no claims at all) are subject to an assessment to fund the shortage. This approach is in sharp contrast to insurance from a private insurer. If a private insurer becomes insolvent, each of its policyholders is responsible only for its own losses. In the case of a self-insured group, a member can be assessed for a shortage resulting from claims of other members, investment losses, misman-agement, or any other cause.

Moreover, because group members are jointly and severally liable, a member can be held individually responsible for the entire deficit, not just its propor-tionate share. This member would then have the right to seek reimbursement from the other group members.

Unlike licensed private insurers, self-insured groups generally are not covered by state guaranty funds. Consequently, if a self-insured group becomes insol-vent, its members have no recourse to the state guaranty funds that become available when a private insurer goes insolvent.

EMPLOYEE'S ELIGIBILITY FOR BENEFITS UNDER MULTIPLE STATUTES

The workers compensation statutes of each state in the United States must address the issue of an employee's eligibility for benefits under multiple states' statutes, as well as the employment circumstances required for eligibility in that state.

In any given case of an employment-related injury, the workers compensation statutes of two or more states may apply if the circumstances of employment occur in different states.

Depending on the statute in the state involved, any of these circumstances of employment could provide a basis for an injured employee to choose the statute that applies to a particular incident:

- Place of injury
- Place of hire
- Place of employment
- Location of the employer
- Residence of the employee
- Whether the employee and the employer have agreed to abide by the workers compensation statute of a particular state

In circumstances where multiple states' statutes apply, an employee will gener-ally choose the statute that provides the most advantageous benefits. See the exhibit "Workers Compensation Multistate Example."

Workers Compensation Multistate Example

An employee who lives in State A agrees to work for an employer domiciled in State B and the employee is injured while working in State C. The workers compensation laws of all three states might apply, and, if so, the employee can select among the applicable state laws. The employee cannot receive duplicate benefits but can select the state law with the most advantageous benefits.

[DA06665]

To some degree, workers compensation statutes address this situation by including an **extraterritorial provision**. This provision enables an employee, who incurs an injury while temporarily working in a state other than the state where the employee was hired, and who chooses to apply the laws of the home state, to obtain workers compensation benefits. See the exhibit "Workers Compensation Extraterritorial Example."

Extraterritorial provision
A provision of a workers compensation statute that extends protection to an employee who is injured while temporarily working in a state other than the state of hire.

Workers Compensation Extraterritorial Example

A roofing contractor domiciled in State A contracts work in State B and sends its regular employees there to work. An employee who lives and regularly works in State A is injured while temporarily working in State B. The extraterritorial provision in the State A's workers compensation law entitles the employee to benefits under State A's law. Even though the accident occurred in State B and State B is not listed in the insured's policy declarations, coverage is provided by the insurer covering State A locations.

[DA06666]

Many states have reciprocal agreements with other states that permit the extraterritorial coverage of the home state policy to meet the coverage requirements of another state for injured employees temporarily working in the second state. Typically, this coverage extension applies for six months or less after employment begins in the reciprocating state. See the exhibit "Workers Compensation Reciprocal Agreement Example."

Workers Compensation Reciprocal Agreement Example

In the roofing contractor extraterritorial example, if States A and B have a reciprocal agreement and the injury occurs within the statutory time limit, the injured worker could choose to apply the workers compensation law from State B. Because of the reciprocal agreement, the State A insurer would pay benefits based on the State B workers compensation law.

[DA06667]

Not all states participate in reciprocal agreements, and some states place restrictions on the extraterritorial coverage. See the exhibit "Workers Compensation No Reciprocal Agreement Example."

Workers Compensation No Reciprocal Agreement Example

In the roofing contractor extraterritorial example, assume, instead, that States A and B do not have a reciprocal agreement and State B is not listed in the State A insurer's policy. If the injured worker chooses to apply the workers compensation law from State B, the State A insurer would not be required to pay benefits based on the State B statutes. If other restrictions in the law apply, the State A insurer may not be required to pay any benefits to the employee. The roofing contractor could be uninsured for this loss, but still liable for the injuries of its employee.

[DA06668]

REMEDIES FOR OCCUPATIONAL INJURY UNDER FEDERAL LAW

Workers compensation statutes provide defined benefits to employees or their dependents for occupational injuries. Federal law provides various other legal remedies for occupational injury of certain employees.

In addition to workers compensation statutes, various federal laws provide remedies for occupational injury of employees who may or may not be covered by workers compensation statutes. In this context, "occupational injury" means either injury or disease arising out of and in the course of the injured person's employment. These federal laws fall into three categories.

The first category consists of statutes that provide for no-fault benefits in the same manner as state workers compensation laws. This category includes these statutes, which apply to groups such as federal employees and maritime employees:

- Longshore and Harbor Workers' Compensation Act
- Defense Base Act
- War Hazards Compensation Act
- Outer Continental Shelf Lands Act
- Nonappropriated Fund Instrumentalities Act
- Federal Black Lung Benefits Act
- Federal Employees' Compensation Act

The second category consists of statutes that give certain employees the right to sue their employers for occupational injury allegedly caused by their employers' negligence. This category includes these statutes, which apply to groups such as employees of interstate railroads and crew members of vessels:

- Migrant and Seasonal Agricultural Worker Protection Act
- Federal Employers' Liability Act
- Jones Act
- Death on the High Seas Act

The third category includes aspects of general maritime law that provide remedies for crew members of vessels.

To insure the obligation to provide the benefits or pay the damages allowed under these laws, an employer can, in most cases, add various endorsements to the standard Workers Compensation and Employers Liability Insurance Policy.

Federal Compensation Statutes

Some federal statutes follow essentially the same approach as state workers compensation statutes. They eliminate the employee's right to sue the employer for occupational injury and instead obligate the employer to pay stipulated medical, disability, and death benefits. See the exhibit "Summary of Federal Compensation Statutes."

Longshore and Harbor Workers' Compensation Act

The United States Longshore and Harbor Workers' Compensation Act (LHWCA) provides for the payment of benefits for employment-related accidental injury, occupational disease, or death of a covered maritime employee. Although its provisions are similar to state workers compensation statutes, benefits under LHWCA are generally more liberal.

The Supreme Court has ruled that coverage under the LHWCA is meant to supplement, rather than supplant, coverage for injuries that might also be covered under a state workers compensation statute. Thus, some injured employees may be able to seek coverage under both a state workers compensation statute and the LHWCA, although double recovery is generally not allowed. Because of concurrent jurisdiction (overlapping of state and federal authority) and other ambiguities between state workers compensation statutes and the LHWCA, employers may need to obtain insurance for both loss exposures.

To be covered under the LHWCA, a claimant must satisfy both a situs (location) test and a status test. The **situs test** requires that the claimant's location at the time of injury be on navigable waters or certain adjoining areas. The term "navigable waters" is generally understood to mean any waters that, by themselves or by uniting with other waters, form a continuous highway over which commerce may be carried out with other states or foreign countries.

Situs test

A test that a claimant must satisfy to be covered under the U.S. Longshore and Harbor Workers' Compensation Act; it requires that, at the time of injury, the claimant must have been on navigable waters or on adjoining areas such as piers, wharves, dry docks, terminals, building ways, marine railways, or other areas customarily used in loading, unloading, repairing, dismantling, or building vessels.

Summary of Federal Compensation Statutes

Name of Statute	Employees Subject to Statute	Nature of Remedy
Longshore and Harbor Workers' Compensation Act (LHWCA)	Maritime employees, with some exceptions (such as the master or crew of a vessel)	Eligible employees are entitled to benefits defined by the LHWCA.
Defense Base Act	(1) Civilian employees at U.S. military bases acquired from foreign governments (2) Civilian employees working overseas under contracts with agencies of the U.S. government	Eligible employees are entitled to the same types of benefits defined by the LHWCA, but the minimum compensation rates of the LHWCA do not apply.
War Hazards Compensation Act	Same employees covered by Defense Base Act, while in a war zone and injured by a war-risk hazard	Eligible employees can collect the same benefit as under the Defense Base Act for injury occurring at any time; injury need not occur in the course of employment.
Outer Continental Shelf Lands Act	Employees on fixed offshore drilling and production platforms on the Outer Continental Shelf of the U.S.	Eligible employees are entitled to the same benefits as defined by the LHWCA.
Nonappropriated Fund Instrumentalities Act	Civilian employees of "non-appropriated fund instrumentalities" on U.S. military bases, such as stores and theaters	Eligible employees are entitled to the same benefits as defined by the LHWCA.
Federal Black Lung Benefits Act	Coal miners who have suffered or are suffering from black lung disease and were or are employed in one or more underground coal mines for ten years or more	Eligible employees are entitled to collect disability and death benefits as defined by statute.
Federal Employees' Compensation Act	Nonmilitary employees of the U.S. government	Eligible employees are entitled to collect benefits as defined by the statute.

[DA04867]

A strict reading of the LHWCA would appear to limit situs to injuries occurring within U.S. territorial waters, leaving those injured on the high seas, even when traveling between U.S. ports, uncovered. However, the courts have held that the purpose of the LHWCA favors a liberal construction that extends coverage under the LHWCA to the high seas, as long as the injury does not occur in foreign territorial waters (waters under the jurisdiction of a country other than the U.S.).

A 1972 amendment to the LHWCA introduced the **status test**, which focuses on the employee's overall occupation. Covered employees must be engaged in maritime employment, broadly interpreted to include activities that form an integral part of the loading and unloading of shipborne containers. Any employment that involves any part of the process of the five types of maritime activity specifically mentioned in the LHWCA—loading, unloading, repairing, building, or dismantling vessels—will satisfy the status test. However, to be covered under the act, an injury to a maritime employee must also occur at a covered situs. A traditional maritime employee who is injured while at a nonmaritime location is excluded from coverage under the LHWCA.

Status test

A test that a claimant must satisfy to be covered under the U.S. Longshore and Harbor Workers' Compensation Act; it requires that, at the time of injury, the claimant must have been engaged in maritime employment.

The LHWCA specifically excludes several types of employees, including masters or crew members of vessels; persons engaged to load, unload, or repair small vessels less than eighteen tons net (a measurement of cubic volume inside a vessel); and officers or employees of the U.S., U.S. government agencies, state governments, foreign governments, or subdivisions of such governments.

In addition, the law excludes several types of employees from receiving LHWCA benefits if they are covered under a state workers compensation law. They include clerical and security workers; employees in retail operations; marina employees not engaged in construction-related activities; people conducting temporary business on a maritime employer's premises; agricultural workers; and workers engaged in building, repairing, or dismantling recreational vessels less than sixty-five feet long.

Because these classes of employees qualify for LHWCA coverage if they are not subject to coverage under a state workers compensation law, it is important for organizations whose employees could be eligible for LHWCA benefits to have both types of coverage in place. LHWCA coverage can be added by endorsement to the standard Workers Compensation and Employers Liability Insurance Policy.

Defense Base Act

When first established in 1941, the main purpose of the Defense Base Act (DBA) was to apply LHWCA benefits to civilians working on military bases outside the U.S. The act was amended to include civilian employees of contractors performing services outside the U.S. under almost any contract with an agency of the U.S. government in support of U.S. foreign policy. More specifically, all of these categories of civilian employees working outside the

U.S. (including either U.S. citizens or foreign nationals) are covered under the DBA:

- Those working on a military base or reservation
- Those engaged in U.S. government-funded public works business
- Those engaged in a public works or military contract with a foreign government that has been deemed necessary to U.S. national security
- Those providing services funded by the U.S. government outside the realm of regular military issue or channels
- Employees of subcontractors of a prime contractor providing any of the services described in the preceding items

The DBA is an exclusive remedy; it supersedes any otherwise applicable state workers compensation laws. Like the LHWCA, the DBA specifically excludes vessel masters or crew members. To cope with unusual circumstances, the law allows the Secretary of Labor, on recommendation of the head of any U.S. department or agency, to make the provisions of the DBA inapplicable to a particular contract or classification of employee.

War Hazards Compensation Act

The War Hazards Compensation Act (WHCA) was enacted to supplement the DBA and shift to the U.S. government the costs of compensation for civilians who are injured by a war-risk hazard while working in a war zone. The WHCA provides benefits for covered employees regardless of whether they are in the course of employment at the time of injury. Thus, employees who qualify have protection equal to that provided by the DBA twenty-four hours a day, seven days a week, for any war hazard arising during a war or armed military conflict in which the U.S. is engaged. The WHCA does not cover injuries that occur independently of the conflict in a war zone.

If an insurer pays a claim under the DBA that may have arisen out of a war hazard, the insurer can file for reimbursement from the Division of Federal Employees' Compensation, a part of the U.S. Department of Labor. A key provision of the WHCA is that no reimbursement is allowed if the DBA insurer has charged additional premium for the war hazard.

Outer Continental Shelf Lands Act

The Outer Continental Shelf Lands Act (OCSLA) extends the benefits of the LHWCA to employees engaged in exploration for and development of natural resources on the outer continental shelf of the U.S. The act defines the outer continental shelf as the submerged lands of the U.S. adjacent to the coast but outside the area of a particular state's territorial boundaries. The territorial boundaries of Florida and Texas extend to ten nautical miles from their coastlines, and those of all other coastal states extend to three nautical miles from their coastlines.

Workers situated on offshore drilling and production platforms are examples of employees subject to the OCSLA. As in the LHWCA, the term "employee" does not include vessel masters or crew members or officers or employees of the U.S., states or foreign governments, or their agencies or subdivisions.

Nonappropriated Fund Instrumentalities Act

The Nonappropriated Fund Instrumentalities Act extends LHWCA benefits to civilian employees of the U.S. government. These employees are ineligible for coverage under the Federal Employees' Compensation Act because their salaries and other benefits are paid with funds generated from earnings rather than funds appropriated to the armed services by Congress. They primarily work at facilities on domestic military bases, such as stores (called post exchanges or PXs), restaurants, daycare centers, and movie theaters. U.S. citizens and permanent residents of the U.S. or its territories or possessions are covered for such employment outside the U.S.

Federal Black Lung Benefits Act

The Federal Black Lung Benefits Act was passed as Title IV of the Federal Coal Mine Health and Safety Act of 1969. The larger act was extensively revised and renamed the Federal Mine Safety and Health Act of 1977; however, Title IV remained a part of it. Title IV provides disability and death benefits for coal miners.

If a miner who is suffering from black lung disease (pneumoconiosis) has been employed in one or more underground coal mines for ten or more years, Title IV creates a rebuttable presumption that the miner's disease arose out of such employment. If a miner so employed has died from a respiratory disease, Title IV also creates a rebuttable presumption that death was due to this disease.

A rebuttable presumption is "[a]n inference drawn from certain facts that establish a prima facie case, which may be overcome by the introduction of contrary evidence" (*Black's Law Dictionary*, 9th ed.). In other words, these provisions of Title IV shift the usual burden of proof so that the miner does not have to prove that the disease resulted from mine employment. However, the employer has the right to present evidence that overcomes the presumption.

If a miner who has suffered from a chronic dust disease of the lung, based on certain specified medical evidence as defined in the law, becomes permanently disabled or dies, the law creates an irrebuttable presumption that the disability or death is due to this disease. An irrebuttable presumption is a "presumption that cannot be overcome by any additional evidence or argument" (*Black's Law Dictionary*, 9th ed.). Thus, the employer cannot present evidence that overcomes the presumption just described.

Federal Employees' Compensation Act

The Federal Employees' Compensation Act (FECA) provides benefits similar to those mandated by state workers compensation statutes to civilian employees of the U.S. government for occupational injury sustained while performing their duties. (Members of the military are covered by other legislation.)

Federal employees receive coverage regardless of the length of time on the job or the type of position held. Probationary, temporary, and term employees are covered on the same basis as permanent employees. Part-time, seasonal, and intermittent employees are also covered. FECA is administered by the Office of Workers' Compensation Programs (OWCP), U.S. Department of Labor. The federal government retains (self-insures) losses under FECA. The costs are paid from the Employees' Compensation Fund, which OWCP administers. Each agency reimburses the Fund each year for the amounts paid to its employees in compensation benefits during the previous year.

Federal Statutes That Permit Employees to Sue

Four federal statutes, rather than setting up separate compensation systems, give certain classes of employees the right to sue their employers for occupational injury. Before these laws were passed, many workers not covered by workers compensation, such as agricultural or dock workers, could recover damages for occupational injury only if they could prove that the employer was grossly negligent. See the exhibit "Federal Statutes That Permit Employees to Sue."

Federal Statutes That Permit Employees to Sue

Name of Statute	Employees Subject to Statute	Nature of Remedy
Migrant and Seasonal Agricultural Worker Protection Act	Migrant and seasonal farm workers	If not covered by workers compensation insurance, eligible employees can sue their employers for negligence.
Federal Employers' Liability Act	Employees of interstate railroads	Eligible employees can sue their employers for negligence
Jones Act	Members of a vessel's crew	Eligible employees can sue their employers for negligence.
Death on the High Seas Act	Members of a vessel's crew	Survivors of eligible employees may sue crew members' employers for death occurring beyond a marine league from the shore of any U.S. state or territory.

[DA04868]

Migrant and Seasonal Agricultural Worker Protection Act

The Migrant and Seasonal Agricultural Worker Protection Act provides various rights to migrant and seasonal agricultural workers, including the right to sue their employers for occupational injury under defined circumstances.

The act defines a migrant worker as a person employed in agricultural work of a seasonal or other temporary nature who is required to be absent overnight from his or her permanent place of residence. Seasonal agricultural workers differ from migrant workers only in that they are not required to be absent overnight from their permanent place of residence.

Many workers compensation statutes exempt agricultural workers and, as a result, in some states, only a small proportion of farm employers purchase workers compensation insurance. The act recognizes the right of those workers who are not covered under workers compensation to sue their employers for occupational injury.

Federal Employers' Liability Act

The Federal Employers' Liability Act (FELA) applies to employees of interstate railroads and employees of intrastate railroads that connect to interstate railroads by way of sidings or interchanges. FELA defines the right of eligible employees to sue their employers in federal court for damages resulting from occupational injury caused in whole or in part by the negligence of the employer or its agents or employees.

If an eligible employee dies as a result of an occupational injury, the employee's personal representative (the person appointed to manage the deceased employee's legal affairs) can bring a wrongful death action against the employer on behalf of the employee's surviving spouse and family members.

For claims brought under FELA, the law eliminates several traditional employer defenses. Traditionally, a plaintiff's contributory negligence of any degree could defeat a negligence suit. FELA instead applies a comparative negligence standard under which the employee's contributory negligence reduces the amount, but does not completely bar, the employee's recovery. FELA also eliminates assumption of risk as a defense against suits subject to FELA. Finally, FELA makes the employer liable for the negligence of all its officers, agents, and other employees, thus eliminating the fellow-servant rule.

Jones Act

The Merchant Marine Act of 1920, commonly called the Jones Act, gives injured crew members of a vessel the same right to sue their employers as FELA gives to railroad employees. Thus, an injured crew member may recover damages if the injury was caused in whole or in part by the negligence of the employer or its agents or employees, and the personal representative of a deceased employee may bring a wrongful death action against the employer on behalf of the employee's surviving family members.

Death on the High Seas Act

The Death on the High Seas Act (DOHSA) provides an additional remedy for survivors of deceased crew members and others who die at sea. Survivors can sue for damages resulting from a crew member's death "caused by wrongful act, neglect or default occurring on the high seas beyond a marine league [three nautical miles] from the shore" of any U.S. state or territory. DOHSA also permits crew members' survivors to sue for death resulting from the unseaworthiness of the vessel. The damages recoverable under DOHSA are essentially the same as those recoverable under FELA and the Jones Act. See the exhibit "Remedies Under General Maritime Law."

Remedies Under General Maritime Law

In addition to remedies provided by the Jones Act and DOHSA, three remedies for injured crew members or the survivors of deceased crew members are based on general maritime law rather than on statutes.

General maritime law is a branch of the federal common law, consisting of precedents and doctrines developed through federal case law in maritime litigation. Because crew members are not subject to state workers compensation laws or the LHWCA, their common-law right to sue for occupational injuries has not been eliminated as it has for most other types of employees.

Crew members have these remedies under general maritime law:

- Maintenance and cure—An employer is legally obligated to pay the costs of providing maintenance and cure for any person who is injured or who becomes ill while serving as a member of the vessel's crew. "Maintenance" includes the costs of lodging and food for the crew member until maximum medical cure is achieved; "cure" covers the costs of medical care. The employer may assert several defenses: that the crew member intentionally concealed the illness or injury at the inception of employment; that the illness or injury was a result of the crew member's own willful misbehavior, deliberate act, or indiscretion; or that the crew member inexcusably delayed reporting the injury or illness, impairing the vessel owner's ability to assert a defense.

- Vessel owner's warranty of seaworthiness—The vessel owner is liable for damages resulting from injuries sustained by crew members because of the vessel's unseaworthiness or a failure to supply and keep the vessel's appurtenances, gear, and equipment in proper working order. Proof of the existence of the unseaworthy condition is sufficient to create legal liability; the injured crew member does not have to prove fault or negligence on the part of the vessel owner.

- Liability for death under the Moragne remedy—The "Moragne remedy" (defined by the U.S. Supreme Court in *Moragne v. States Marine Lines, Inc.*[3]) provides for recovery for deaths occurring within territorial waters or on the high seas that are caused by either negligence or unseaworthiness of the vessel. Deaths of noncrew members can also fall under the Moragne remedy but not under the warranty of seaworthiness.

[DA06587]

NEED FOR WORKERS COMPENSATION AND EMPLOYERS LIABILITY INSURANCE

Employers will typically address workers compensation statutory obligations and employers liability loss exposures through a combination of risk control and insurance (unless the employer qualifies as a self-insurer).

In most states, **workers compensation insurance** is provided under a standard form known as the Workers Compensation and Employers Liability Insurance Policy (WC&EL policy). The same policy form can be used in various states because the applicable workers compensation laws are incorporated by WC&EL policy reference in the policy.

The WC&EL policy form was developed and filed in most states by the National Council on Compensation Insurance (NCCI), an insurance advisory organization for insurers writing workers compensation insurance. The WC&EL policy combines coverage for both of these:

- The insured's obligation to pay benefits required by a workers compensation law
- The insured's legal liability to pay damages because of occupational injury to the insured's employees as a result of a claim or suit based on legal grounds other than a workers compensation law or a similar law

Instead of a Declarations Page, the WC&EL policy begins with an Information page. The WC&EL policy form is relatively short compared to the CGL or Commercial Auto policy forms, with six pages that include a brief General Section and these six parts:

- Part One—Workers Compensation Insurance
- Part Two—Employers Liability Insurance
- Part Three—Other States Insurance
- Part Four—Your Duties If Injury Occurs
- Part Five—Premium
- Part Six—Conditions

The coverage provided by workers compensation laws is extensive, and generally workers compensation is considered, at least in theory, to be the exclusive remedy for injuries. However, depending on the law in effect, an employer can be held liable in several types of claims other than workers compensation, such as third party over, consequential injury to others, and dual capacity. Because these types of claims do not seek workers compensation benefits, they are not covered by workers compensation insurance. The CGL policy excludes liability coverage for employee's injuries. To fill this coverage gap, employers need employers liability insurance.

Workers compensation insurance

Insurance that provides coverage for benefits an employer is obligated to pay under workers compensation laws.

Information Page

The Information Page of the Workers Compensation and Employers Liability Insurance Policy (WC 00 00 01 A) is equivalent to the declarations page of other policies. It is divided into four major sections, called "Items." See the exhibit "WC&EL Information Page."

Item 1 provides essential information about the insured, including the insured's name and mailing address, the insured's type of legal entity, and the workplaces other than the insured's mailing address.

Item 2 shows the coverage period. Coverage begins and ends at 12:01 a.m. at the mailing address of the insured given in Item 1.

Item 3 summarizes the coverage provided by the policy under parts A-D:

- 3.A Workers Compensation Insurance—Lists benefits required by the workers compensation law of the state or states specifically listed that will be paid in the event of an injury to an employee. The states listed should be only those states in which the insured has ongoing operations and in which the insurer is licensed to write workers compensation coverage.

- 3.B Employers Liability Insurance—Shows the limits of liability under employers liability coverage for bodily injury by accident and by disease.

- 3.C Other States Insurance—Indicates that workers compensation coverage will be extended automatically to the additional states listed if the insured expands its operations to jurisdictions other than those listed in 3.A.

- 3.D Endorsements—Lists any endorsements attached to the policy.

Item 4 contains the information necessary to calculate the estimated policy premium. It includes a description of the classification(s) and the corresponding code number assigned to the types of employees working in the insured's business, which are taken from the applicable workers compensation manual. Another column contains the insured's estimate of what the remuneration (payroll) will be for the period covered by the policy. The estimated payroll is shown beside each classification.

The next column shows the rate applicable to each classification. Usually, the rate is expressed in dollars of premium per $100 of payroll. The last column shows the estimated premium determined by multiplying the estimated payroll by the rate for each classification.

Experience modification factor

A factor that tailors manual rates to an insured's experience based on the insured's payroll and loss record of certain prior years.

(Estimated annual remuneration divided by $100) × Rate per $100 of remuneration = Estimated annual premium

The Estimated Annual Premium is then multiplied by an experience modification applied to those insureds that meet premium eligibility requirements. Each employer is assigned an **experience modification factor** based upon the last three complete years of that employer's loss history.

WC&EL Information Page

WORKERS COMPENSATION AND EMPLOYERS LIABILITY INSURANCE POLICY

INFORMATION PAGE

Insurer:

```
P O L I C Y   N O .
| | | | | | | | | | | | | | | | | | | |
```

1. The Insured: AMR Corporation   ___ Individual   ___ Partnership
   Mailing address: 2000 Industrial Highway   X Corporation or _____
                    Workingtown, PA 19000

   Other workplaces not shown above:

2. The policy period is from   10/1/20X1   to   10/1/20X2   at the insured's mailing address.

3. A. Workers Compensation Insurance: Part One of the policy applies to the Workers Compensation Law of the states
      listed here: PA

   B. Employers Liability Insurance: Part Two of the policy applies to work in each state listed in Item 3.A. The limits of
      our liability under Part Two are:

      Bodily Injury by Accident $ __100,000__   each accident
      Bodily Injury by Disease $ __500,000__   policy limit
      Bodily Injury by Disease $ __100,000__   each employee

   C. Other States Insurance: Part Three of the policy applies to the states, if any, listed here:

      All except those listed in Item 3.A and ND, OH, WA, and, WY

   D. This policy includes these endorsements and schedules:

      See Schedule

4. The premium for this policy will be determined by our Manuals of Rules, Classifications, Rates and Rating Plans.
   All information required below is subject to verification and change by audit.

Classifications	Code No.	Premium Basis Total Estimated Annual Remuneration	Rate Per $100 of Remuneration	Estimated Annual Premium
Sheet Metal Shop	0454	300,000	11.53	34,590
Clerical Office	0953	275,000	.49	1,348
		Experience Modification of 1.382 Applied		13,728
		Estimated Premium Discount		(4,869)
		Total Estimated Annual Premium $		44,797

Minimum Premium $ 1,273   Expense Constant $ 140

Countersigned by _____A. M. Abel_____
                            (authorized representative)

WC 00 00 01 A

After the experience modification is applied, any estimated premium discounts are deducted to arrive at the total estimated annual premium. All endorsements and schedules attached to the policy at inception are listed on the Information Page or in a schedule attached to the policy.

Part One—Workers Compensation Insurance

Part One of the WC&EL policy provides workers compensation insurance, which covers the insured's obligation as an employer to pay all compensation and other benefits required by the workers compensation law of any state listed in Item 3.A. of the Information Page.

The policy definition of "workers compensation law" is "the workers' or workmen's compensation law and occupational disease law of each state or territory named in Item 3.A. of the Information Page." The definition includes any amendments to the law that are in effect during the policy period, but does not include any provisions of a law that relate to nonoccupational disability benefits. Moreover, the definition is limited to state laws and therefore excludes federal laws such as the U.S. Longshore and Harbor Workers' Compensation Act (LHWCA). The WC&EL policy can be extended by endorsement to cover an employer's obligations under federal compensation laws.

The policy definition of "state" means any of the fifty states or the District of Columbia. Coverage can be provided for the workers compensation law of a U.S. territory by naming the territory in Item 3 on the Information Page. Workers compensation coverage applies to bodily injury caused by accident or disease. To be covered by the policy, an accident must occur during the policy period, but in the case of occupational disease claims, the last exposure to conditions causing or aggravating disease in the employment of the insured must occur during the policy period.

Similarly, Part One contains no outright exclusions but pays claims in accordance with the provisions of the applicable workers compensation law. For example, if the law excludes a certain class of employees (such as farm workers), the insurer has no obligation to pay workers compensation benefits to an employee in that class.

All workers compensation laws covered by the policy become part of the insurance contract, as though they were written into the policy, and employees are entitled to the benefits defined by those laws. If the policy and the applicable workers compensation law conflict, the policy will conform to the law.

Covered Locations

The policy covers all of the insured's workplaces listed in Items 1 or 4 of the Information Page, as well as all the insured's workplaces in states listed in Item 3.A., unless the insured has other insurance or is self-insured for such workplaces.

Workers compensation statutes typically contain extraterritoriality provisions that cover accidents occurring in other states when employees are working outside the home state temporarily. When an out-of-state injury is covered by the extraterritorial provision under the home state's workers compensation law, the employer's WC&EL policy will cover the injury even if the state in which the injury occurred is not listed in the policy. See the exhibit "Workers Compensation—Extraterritorial Provision."

Workers Compensation—Extraterritorial Provision

XYZ plumbing is located in State A, and its WC&EL policy shows only State A in Item 3.A. of the Information Page. XYZ accepts a small residential job in State B, and an XYZ employee is injured while working at that job site. State A's workers compensation statute has an extraterritoriality provision, which applies to the injury that occurred in State B. XYZ's insurer will therefore pay the benefits in accordance with State A's laws, even though State B is not listed in the policy.

[DA06673]

Insurer's Duty to Defend

In some cases, employees who have been denied workers compensation benefits will sue their employers for the benefits to which they believe they are entitled. For example, an employee might sue after being denied benefits on the grounds that the employee's injury did not arise out of and in the course of employment. The WC&EL policy expresses the insurer's right and duty to defend the insured against any claim, proceeding, or suit for benefits payable by the policy. The insurer also agrees to pay additional costs as part of any claim, proceeding, or suit that the insurer defends.

Payments the Insured Must Make

In some cases, the insurer, because of the insured's misconduct, may have to make workers compensation payments in excess of the benefits ordinarily provided by the workers compensation law. Under such circumstances, the policy provides that the insured will reimburse the insurer for the difference between the benefits actually paid and the benefits that are ordinarily payable. The policy cites examples of situations in which extra benefits might be required:

- The insured engages in serious and willful misconduct.
- The insured knowingly hires an employee in violation of law.
- The insured fails to comply with a health or safety law or regulation.
- The insured discharges, coerces, or otherwise discriminates against an employee in violation of the workers compensation law.

Other Provisions

The insurer's subrogation rights are reaffirmed in the Recovery From Others provision. When the insurer pays workers compensation benefits on an insured's behalf, any right of recovery the insured or the injured employee may have against a third party becomes the right of the insurer.

The policy also recognizes legal requirements that directly obligate the insurer to pay workers compensation benefits to any injured employee or, in the event of death, to the employee's dependents. Because the policy is primarily for the benefit of employees and their dependents, they have a direct right of action against the insurer. Moreover, for the employee's protection, the policy provides that the insurer's obligations will not be affected by the employer's failure to comply with the policy requirements.

Part Two—Employers Liability Insurance

Part Two of the WC&EL policy is structured like a traditional liability policy, containing an insuring agreement in which the insurer agrees to pay damages on the insured's behalf, subject to any exclusions and other provisions that apply. **Employers liability insurance** covers an employer against its common-law liability for occupational injury to employees.

Employers liability insurance

Insurance that protects an employer against employee injury claims that are not covered by workers compensation laws.

Need for Employers Liability Insurance

Under a variety of circumstances, some employees and some employers are not subject to a workers compensation statute. For example, some statutes exclude agricultural workers and domestic servants, and other statutes do not apply to employers with fewer than a specified number of employees. When an employee or employer is excluded or exempt from workers compensation, an injured employee can ordinarily sue the employer for occupational injury under common-law principles. Generally, such claims are covered by employers liability insurance, subject to certain provisions. The CGL policy excludes coverage for liability resulting from injury to an employee of the insured. The employers liability section of the WC&EL policy describes four types of claims that are covered by employers liability insurance. These demonstrate the need for employers liability insurance:

- Third-party-over claims—Refer to a person or an organization other than the employer or the employee. If an employee of the insured sues a third party (such as a machine manufacturer) for an occupational injury, the third party can sue the employer. The suit might allege, for example, that the employer was negligent in maintaining the defective machine and that the employer must therefore indemnify the manufacturer for all or part of the damages the manufacturer had to pay to the employee.
- Claims for care and loss of services—Damages that the spouse of an injured or a deceased person can obtain from the liable party, also known as loss of consortium.

- Claims for consequential bodily injury—Suffered by family members of an injured employee as a consequence of injury to the employee. For example, AIDS contracted by the spouse of a healthcare worker who contracted AIDS as a result of negligence imputed to the worker's employer.

- Dual-capacity claims—Occur when an injured employee sues his or her employer for damages resulting from the employer having acted in some capacity other than as an employer. Typically, these involve products liability. For example, the employee, while working, might be injured by a product manufactured by the employer. In essence, the employee sues the employer in its capacity as a manufacturer rather than in its capacity as an employer. The CGL coverage form excludes dual-capacity claims.

Employers Liability Insuring Agreement

The insurer agrees to pay damages that the insured becomes legally obligated to pay because of bodily injury by accident or disease to an employee. The bodily injury must arise out of and in the course of employment, and the legal obligation must not be covered under a state or federal workers compensation or disability benefits law. The insurer also agrees to defend the insured against claims or suits seeking covered damages.

Another requirement is that the employment out of which the injury arises must be necessary or incidental to the insured's work in a state or territory listed in Item 3.A. of the Information Page. This coverage is subject to these provisions that indicate what must occur during the policy period in order for coverage to be triggered under the particular policy:

- For bodily injury caused by accident, the policy that is in effect when the injury occurs is the policy that applies.

- For bodily injury caused by disease, the policy that is in effect on the employee's last day of last exposure to the conditions causing or aggravating the injury is the policy that applies.

Employers Liability Exclusions

Employers liability insurance is subject to several exclusions, which prevent overlapping coverage with other forms of insurance and eliminate coverage not intended by the insurer.

In keeping with the basic purpose of employers liability coverage, several exclusions are aimed at eliminating coverage for claims that would be covered under these various statutes:

- Any workers compensation and occupational disease benefits law
- LHWCA
- The Federal Employers' Liability Act
- The Migrant and Seasonal Agricultural Worker Protection Act
- Any other federal workers compensation or occupational disease law

Various endorsements are available for extending the policy to cover excluded liabilities. Employers liability also excludes bodily injury that occurs outside the United States, its territories or possessions, and Canada. However, this exclusion does not apply to injury to a resident or citizen of the U.S. or Canada who is temporarily outside the locations listed.

Also excluded is liability assumed under a contract—even if the insured has assumed another party's liability for injury to the insured's own employee. The CGL coverage form covers liability assumed under an insured contract, even if the liability assumed is for injury to an employee of the insured.

Employers liability insurance also excludes these items:

- Punitive or exemplary damages for injury or death of any illegally employed person
- Bodily injury to employees employed in violation of the law with the knowledge of the insured or any executive officers of the insured
- Bodily injury intentionally caused by the insured
- Damages arising out of employment practices, including (but not limited to) demotion, evaluation, harassment, discrimination, and termination
- Fines or penalties imposed for violation of federal or state law

Limits of Liability

Unlike workers compensation coverage, employers liability coverage is subject to three monetary limits of liability stated on the information page:

- The bodily injury by accident limit is the most that the insurer will pay for bodily injury resulting from any one accident, regardless of the number of employees injured.
- The bodily injury by disease—policy limit is the most that the insurer will pay for all bodily injury by disease, regardless of the number of employees who sustain disease.
- The bodily injury by disease—each employee limit is the most that the insurer will pay for bodily injury by disease to any one employee.

Defense costs, as well as supplementary payments similar to those covered under the CGL coverage form, are covered in addition to the limits of liability. See the exhibit "State Monopolistic Workers Compensation Funds."

Part Three—Other States Insurance

Other states insurance

Insurance that automatically extends coverage to the insured's operations in any state listed in Item 3.C. of the WC&EL Information Page.

In some cases, after policy inception, an employer will begin operations in a state not listed in Item 3.A. To provide coverage for obligations under workers compensation laws of states other than those listed in Item 3.A., the WC&EL policy contains a feature known as **other states insurance**, incorporated within the policy as Part Three.

State Monopolistic Workers Compensation Funds

State workers compensation statute establishes the workers compensation insurance mechanism for those employers with employees covered by the state's workers compensation regulations. The state does not allow insurance companies to provide the workers compensation insurance. Because the state is the only source of workers compensation coverage, this type of compensation fund is considered monopolistic.

There are four monopolistic states: North Dakota, Ohio, Washington, and Wyoming. Employers liability coverage is not provided by these funds, but can be provided by insurance companies. This is commonly known as stopgap insurance.

[DA06674]

To activate other states insurance, the names of one or more states must be shown in Item 3.C. of the Information Page. When a state is listed in Item 3.C., the policy will cover the named insured's obligations under the workers compensation law of that state just as if that state were listed in Item 3.A.

For example, an injured employee may be able to qualify for benefits under the workers compensation laws of more than one state. Depending on the provisions of the laws involved, an employee who was hired in State A but who is currently working in State B might qualify for benefits under the workers compensation law of either state, giving the employee the option of choosing the law that will provide better benefits.

If the insured has operations in a particular state on the effective date of the policy but that state is not listed in Item 3.A., the insured must notify the insurer within thirty days or else no coverage will apply for that state. When operations do not exist in additional states on the effective date of the policy but could be extended into other states at a future point in time, those particular states should be listed in Item 3.C.

The WC&EL policy does not require that the injury occur in a state listed in Item 3.A. or 3.C. Because workers compensation coverage is restricted to paying benefits required by the workers compensation laws of those states shown in the policy, the policy could cover injury occurring anywhere as long as the insured is required to pay benefits by the workers compensation law of a state listed in the policy.

Part Four—Your Duties If Injury Occurs

Part Four of the WC&EL policy explains the duties of the insured that apply any time an injury may be covered by the WC&EL policy. Even if there is some question about whether an injury arose out of and in the course of employment, the insured should perform these duties as expressed by the WC&EL policy:[4]

1. Provide for immediate medical and other services required by the workers compensation law

2. Provide the insurer with the names and addresses of the injured persons and of witnesses, and other information as needed

3. Promptly provide all notices, demands, and legal papers related to the injury, claim, proceeding, or suit

4. Cooperate with and assist the insurer, as they request, in the investigation, settlement or defense of any claim, proceeding, or suit

5. Do nothing after an injury occurs that would interfere with the insurer's right to recover from others

6. Do not voluntarily make payments, assume obligations or incur expenses, except at the insured's own cost

Once the insured has notified the insurer of the injury and provided the required information, the WC&EL insurer can begin to investigate and determine whether the injury is covered.

Part Five—Premium

Part Five of the WC&EL policy explains premium determination procedures, establishing the role of insurer manuals in determining premium and stipulating that the manuals and the premium may change during the policy period. The policy establishes that the classifications and rates shown on the Information Page may change if they do not accurately describe the work covered by the policy.

Part Five defines payroll as the most common premium basis and states that the remuneration of executive officers and the payroll of employees of uninsured contractors and subcontractors are included. The Audit provision explains the insurer's right to examine and audit the insured's books and records at any time during the policy period and within three years after expiration insofar as such books and records relate to the policy. The insured must keep records of the information needed to compute the policy premium and provide such records to the insurer when requested.

Part Six—Conditions

The policy conditions in Part Six of the WC&EL policy limit or define the rights and obligations of the parties to the insurance contract:

*   Inspection—The insurer has the right, but is not obligated, to inspect a policyholder's workplaces and operations to determine that safe practices are used and proper precautions taken for the safety of employees, and to recommend changes. When such services are performed, this does not

constitute an undertaking to warrant that any workplaces, operations, machinery, or equipment inspected are safe or healthful.

- Long-Term Policy—If the policy period is longer than one year and sixteen days, each year is considered separate as far as policy provisions are concerned, and premium is computed in accordance with the manual rules and rates in effect for that year. An exception is a three-year fixed-rate policy that would carry an endorsement modifying this provision.

- Transfer of Your Rights and Duties—The named insured's rights and duties under the policy cannot be transferred, or assigned, to another party unless the insurer provides its written consent.

- Cancellation—The insurer's cancellation rights are outlined, and the insurer is subject in all cases to any requirements of the applicable workers compensation law. Unless subject to a different requirement under the applicable statute, the insurer must provide at least ten days' written notice before cancellation becomes effective; the insured need only give advance written notice of cancellation.

- Sole Representative—The first named insured acts on behalf of all insureds for premium payment, refund, cancellation, and other rights and duties under the policy.

ENDORSEMENTS TO THE WC&EL POLICY

The Workers Compensation and Employers Liability Insurance (WC&EL) Policy is the standard form used for providing coverage for an employer's obligations under the workers compensation statutes of most states. Various endorsements can be used to modify the WC&EL policy to cover liability under various federal statutes.

Several situations require modification of standard Workers Compensation and Employers Liability Insurance (WC&EL) Policy provisions through an appropriate endorsement. All of these endorsements are filed by the National Council on Compensation Insurance, Inc. (NCCI):

- Voluntary Compensation and Employers Liability Coverage Endorsement
- Foreign voluntary compensation coverage
- Longshore and Harbor Workers' Compensation Act Coverage Endorsement
- Maritime Coverage Endorsement
- Waiver of Our Right to Recover From Others Endorsement
- Alternate Employer Endorsement

Voluntary Compensation and Employers Liability Coverage Endorsement

The workers compensation statutes of most states exempt some types of employment from statutory workers compensation benefits. The most commonly exempted employments are farm, domestic, and casual labor. In some states, the statute does not apply to employers with fewer than a certain minimum number of employees. Even when exempt persons are not entitled to workers compensation benefits by law, the same benefits can be extended to them by voluntary action.

Voluntary Compensation and Employers Liability Coverage Endorsement

Endorsement that amends the WC&EL policy to cover employees who are not subject to a workers compensation statute.

The **Voluntary Compensation and Employers Liability Coverage Endorsement** (WC 00 03 11 A) amends the WC&EL policy to include an additional coverage called voluntary compensation. The additional coverage obligates the insurer to pay, on behalf of the insured, an amount equal to the compensation benefits that would be payable to such employees if they were subject to the workers compensation law designated in the endorsement.

The voluntary compensation endorsement states that if an employee entitled to payment under the endorsement brings a suit under the common law, the coverage provided by the endorsement reverts to employers liability insurance. The insurer will defend the insured against the employee's suit and pay any settlement awarded, subject to the stipulated limits of liability.

Brokers and risk managers for large firms often recommend adding the voluntary compensation endorsement to all workers compensation policies. Their reasoning is that these firms want workers compensation and employers liability coverage to apply to all of their employees, but a particular employee, in some circumstances, might not be covered by the workers compensation law.

For example, the firm might hire an employee in a state where it has no other employees. If the state does not require workers compensation insurance for employers with fewer than three employees in that state, voluntary compensation would fill the gap and provide workers compensation benefits for that employee even though he or she was not covered by the applicable law. See the exhibit "Workers Compensation for Volunteers."

Foreign Voluntary Compensation Coverage

WC&EL coverage applies differently to employees outside the United States, depending on whether they are temporarily outside the U.S. or their regular place of employment is outside the U.S.

Employees Temporarily Outside the U.S.

Employees who are temporarily outside the U.S. are generally covered by the extraterritorial provision of the workers compensation statute of the state in which they regularly work, provided they have not been out of the U.S. for

Workers Compensation for Volunteers

Both for-profit and not-for-profit organizations may want to provide workers compensation-type coverage for their volunteer workers. Certain volunteers, such as volunteer firefighters, police officers, and emergency medical personnel who perform services for political subdivisions, can or must be covered for workers compensation benefits under some state workers compensation statutes. Some statutes also permit workers compensation coverage for volunteer emergency medical personnel of organizations that are separate from political subdivisions.

However, true volunteers who are not compensated for their services do not, strictly speaking, come under the Voluntary Compensation and Employers Liability Coverage Endorsement unless the state's workers compensation law specifically includes them. Nevertheless, some insurers use the endorsement for nonmandated coverage, make a charge based on what the payroll would be for employees performing the same functions, and pay any claims that occur. An alternative approach is to purchase accidental death and dismemberment coverage for volunteers.

[DA06705]

longer than the time limit specified in the statute. That time limit can be as much as six months in some states but as little as thirty days in others.

In addition to time-limited coverage, firms with employees outside the U.S. must also consider that workers compensation laws in the U.S. do not provide coverage for transporting ill or deceased employees home, or coverage for disease that is prevalent in a particular country that an employee contracts as a consequence of his or her employment—for example, malaria in tropical countries.

Many insurers offer foreign voluntary workers compensation coverage, either as an endorsement to the insured's workers compensation policy or as part of a separate foreign insurance policy. **Foreign voluntary workers compensation coverage** provides "home-state" coverage or, for U.S. employees who are working outside the country with no time limit, coverage equal to that required by the Defense Base Act or the Longshore and Harbor Workers' Compensation Act (LHWCA). These endorsements often include coverage for repatriation expense and endemic disease.

Employees Regularly Outside the U.S.

Coverage for employee injuries and occupational disease can be very different outside the U.S. Only a few countries have workers compensation laws comparable to those found in the U.S. For example, in Canada, each province has a government-monopoly workers compensation law similar to monopolistic states in the U.S. In almost all other industrialized countries, employees are treated for on-the-job injuries and occupational disease under the nation's medical insurance program, and disability benefits for employment-related conditions are provided by the social insurance that applies to all other disabilities.

Foreign voluntary workers compensation coverage

Coverage that insures employees who are working outside the U.S. and who are not subject to a workers compensation law for benefits equal to those provided under either the workers compensation statute of a specified state or a specified federal compensation act.

Although no workers compensation insurance as such is available in those countries, in most cases, employees retain the right to sue their employers, and, therefore, employers need employers liability insurance.

LHWCA Coverage Endorsement

The U.S. Longshore and Harbor Workers' Compensation Act (LHWCA) follows the same principles as the state workers compensation statutes. In some instances, an employer may be simultaneously subject to both the LHWCA and a state workers compensation law. Both of these exposures may be insured, but they must be covered and rated separately.

United States Longshore and Harbor Workers' Compensation Act Endorsement

An endorsement that amends the Workers Compensation and Employers Liability Insurance Policy to cover the insured's obligations under the U.S. Longshore and Harbor Workers' Compensation Act.

The LHWCA exposure can be covered by adding the **United States Longshore and Harbor Workers' Compensation Act Endorsement** (WC 00 01 06 A) to the WC&EL policy. The endorsement amends the definition of workers compensation law to include the LHWCA with respect to operations in any state designated in the endorsement's schedule. The LHWCA coverage endorsement does not cover the insured's obligations under any other compensation statutes, including even those that extend LHWCA benefits to various classes of employees, such as the Defense Base Act or the Outer Continental Shelf Lands Act. Separate coverage endorsements to the WC&EL policy are available for covering an employer's obligations under those statutes.

Maritime Coverage Endorsement

Employers of the crew members of a vessel normally cover their liabilities for occupational injuries of crew members through a type of marine insurance called protection and indemnity (P&I). P&I, which covers a variety of liability loss exposures of shipowners, may or may not include coverage for the shipowner's liability for death or injury to crew members. An alternative way of covering an employer's liability for injury or death of crew members is by endorsing the standard WC&EL policy with the **Maritime Coverage Endorsement** (WC 00 02 01 A). The endorsement changes how insurance is provided by Part Two (Employers Liability Insurance) of the workers compensation and employers liability insurance policy to those employers required to provide maritime benefits under the Jones Act.

Maritime Coverage Endorsement

Endorsement that amends the Workers Compensation and Employers Liability Insurance Policy to cover an employers liability for injury or death of crew members.

Because the Maritime Coverage Endorsement may provide a narrower scope of coverage than crew coverage under a P&I policy, the endorsement is more likely to be used by employers who have minor or incidental crew exposures than by shipowners who have regular crews. For example, a building contractor might undertake a project on navigable waters that could involve Jones Act liability for some employees. Such a contractor might also need LHWCA coverage.

The Maritime Coverage Endorsement modifies only the Employers Liability section of the WC&EL policy. The endorsement extends the Employers

Liability section to cover bodily injury by accident or disease arising out of employment necessary or incidental to the maritime work described in the endorsement schedule.

Several important restrictions apply under the Maritime Coverage Endorsement:

- The bodily injury must occur within the territorial limits of, or in the operation of a vessel sailing directly between the ports of, the continental U.S., Alaska, Hawaii, or Canada. Therefore, the endorsement provides no coverage for injury occurring between other places, such as an injury occurring on a voyage from a U.S. port to a Mexican port.

- The endorsement does not cover bodily injury covered by a P&I policy issued to the insured or for the insured's benefit, even if the P&I policy does not apply because of another insurance clause, a deductible, or a similar provision. When an insured carries both a P&I policy and the Maritime Coverage Endorsement, coverage must be carefully arranged to avoid an unintended coverage gap.

- The Maritime Coverage Endorsement does not cover the insured's duty to provide maintenance and cure (lodging and food for a sick or injured crew member during his or her medical care and medical care until maximum medical care is achieved). However, standard WC&EL manual rules allow this exclusion to be deleted for an additional premium.

An additional endorsement for covering crew members is the Voluntary Compensation Maritime Coverage Endorsement (WC 00 02 03). This endorsement obligates the insurer to pay benefits to crew members in the same manner as the Voluntary Compensation and Employers Liability Coverage Endorsement.

Waiver of Our Right to Recover From Others Endorsement

Both Part One, Workers Compensation Insurance, and Part Two, Employers Liability Insurance, contain a Recovery From Others provision that affirms the insurer's subrogation rights to recover from anyone liable for a covered injury. This is a valuable right for the insurer.

When they enter into contracts (particularly construction contracts) with others, insureds are sometimes contractually required to obtain a waiver of the insurer's subrogation rights. To accommodate this requirement, the **Waiver of Our Right to Recover From Others Endorsement** (WC 00 03 13) provides that the insurer will not enforce its right to recover against organizations listed in the endorsement's schedule when the insured is performing work under a contract that requires a waiver. Insurers usually charge additional premium for providing this waiver. In a few states, contractual waiver of subrogation is prohibited by statute, rendering the endorsement invalid.

Waiver of Our Right to Recover From Others Endorsement

The endorsement in which a workers compensation insurer agrees not to enforce its right of subrogation against any organization listed in the endorsement's schedule.

Alternate Employer Endorsement

In some cases, more than one entity can be regarded as the employer of a given worker. This situation can arise in the case of employees provided by either temporary help agencies or employment leasing firms. Temporary help agencies provide workers to client companies to help them meet temporary staffing needs. Employment leasing firms, also known as professional employer organizations (PEOs), provide workers to their client companies for longer periods. The temporary help agency or PEO assumes legal responsibility as an employer, including payroll administration and human resource functions.

However, the client company has day-to-day control of the temporary or leased employees and may therefore also be considered an employer. The handling of workers compensation insurance for such situations varies by state. To help employers avoid the need for duplicate insurance, some states permit the **Alternate Employer Endorsement** (WC 00 03 01A) to be added to one WC&EL policy covering both the temporary help agency (or PEO) and the client company. The endorsement extends workers compensation and employers liability coverage to the insured and to the other party named in the endorsement. It usually is added to the WC&EL policy of the PEO for the benefit of the client company.

Alternate Employer Endorsement

The endorsement that extends workers compensation and employers liability coverage to an additional organization named in the endorsement.

Other Coverage Endorsements

Other NCCI coverage endorsements are available for insuring an employer's obligations for occupational injury or illness under these statutes:

- Defense Base Act (WC 00 01 01A)
- Outer Continental Shelf Lands Act (WC 00 01 09B)
- Nonappropriated Fund Instrumentalities Act (WC 00 01 08A)
- Federal Employers' Liability Act (WC 00 01 04A)
- Migrant and Seasonal Agricultural Worker Protection Act (WC 00 01 11)
- Federal Coal Mine Health and Safety Act (WC 00 01 02)

These endorsements, together with the LHWCA and Maritime Coverage Endorsements, can be difficult for small insureds to obtain in the voluntary market. Often, such insureds must use assigned risk plans or state funds to obtain coverage. Because of the operation of assigned risk plans, some insurers may be required to issue policies for which they do not have any spread of risk. To overcome this problem, the NCCI administers the National Workers Compensation Reinsurance Pool. The pool provides reinsurance on coverage provided under these specialty endorsements, as well as standard workers compensation coverage.

WORKERS COMPENSATION EXPERIENCE RATING

Experience rating plans encourage using risk control to the greatest extent practicable to prevent or reduce workers compensation losses.

Because insurance does not pay for lost production, retraining a replacement worker, lost executive and supervisory time, and other indirect costs, safety experts estimate that the indirect costs of a worker's injury can be four or more times the direct costs that are covered by insurance.

Federal Occupational Safety and Health Administration (OSHA) regulations and similar state regulations mandate a certain level of safety in working conditions. Adhering to the applicable safety regulations not only conforms with mandatory compliance, but also allows an employer to save indirect costs that would otherwise be incurred when employees are injured. An employer also may save costs related to workers compensation by improving its experience rating, which modifies its workers compensation coverage rate for a policy period based on its actual loss experience during prior policy periods.

Experience Rating Plans

An **experience rating plan**, in addition to federal and state mandates and incentives, can motivate employers to eliminate or mitigate industrial accidents. Experience rating can reduce workers compensation rates as much as 70 percent for insureds with excellent loss experience and increase rates up to 350 percent for those with poor experience.

Linking premiums to an insured's actual loss experience is more common and more formalized in workers compensation insurance than in many other types of insurance. One reason for this is that claim frequency is higher in workers compensation than in most other types of commercial insurance. Higher claim frequency means that loss experience is more statistically meaningful. Moreover, even though workers compensation insurance rates are developed for a variety of classifications, no two insureds have identical operations even within the same classification, and rates are usually uniform for each classification throughout a state despite territorial differences in medical costs, differing work environments, and so forth. Basing rates on an insured's actual loss experience provides a way of recognizing these differences.

A commonly used way to link an insured's premiums to the insured's actual loss experience is experience rating. In most states, experience rating is mandatory for all insureds whose workers compensation insurance premiums exceed a particular amount (which varies by state). Another approach to basing premiums on the insured's actual loss experience is retrospective rating, which determines the premium for a policy period based on the insured's actual loss experience during that same policy period.

Experience rating plan

A rating plan that increases or reduces the premium for a future period based on the insured's own loss experience for a period in the recent past.

Experience rating uses a formula that compares an insured's actual losses with the losses expected for an average insured in the same classification and adjusts future rates up or down based on the result. The experience rating plan used in most states was developed by The National Council on Compensation Insurance, Inc. (NCCI). The experience rating plans used in non-NCCI and monopolistic states are similar to the NCCI plan. The result of the formula is a number called the experience modification factor, or simply the "experience mod," which is multiplied by the manual rate(s) for the insured's classification(s).

Because experience rating plans depend on statistically meaningful data to appropriately estimate losses, such plans have certain characteristics:

- They apply only to employers whose average premiums for prior periods exceed a certain amount—The premium eligibility level varies by state. A common eligibility level is an average of $5,000 in premium for more than two years, or $10,000 total premium for two years or less. Employers with premiums too low to qualify for experience rating may benefit from merit rating or premium incentive plans. These rating plans, which are easier to administer than experience rating, consider loss experience over the preceding year or two and provide flat-rate discounts or surcharges based on the insured's loss experience.

- They use three years' experience as the basis for the modification—This reduces the fluctuations that would occur if only one year's experience were used. Because the data must be collected before policy renewal and accurately evaluating recent accidents is difficult, the most recently expired one-year policy period is omitted and the three prior one-year policy periods are used. Therefore, an experience-rated premium effective January 1, 2011, would be based on the insured's loss experience in the policy periods for 2007, 2008, and 2009.

- They do not depend entirely on the insured's own loss experience—Credibility factors dictate how much weight is given to the insured's own loss experience. The insured's loss experience and payrolls are compared to industry average losses and payrolls for similar businesses.

- They give more weight to small losses than to large losses because small losses occur more frequently than large losses—Because of their greater frequency, small losses are more credible than large losses for predicting future losses.

- They cap the maximum surcharge that can be applied.

Calculating Experience Modifications

The rating organizations or workers compensation bureaus in most states maintain premium and loss information for eligible insureds and calculate and publish the experience modifications that are used in rating workers compensation policies. The estimated annual premiums are then multiplied by the experience modification factors, as shown in the basic illustration.

Each employer is assigned an experience modification factor based on the last three complete years of its lost history. See the exhibit "Example—Workers Compensation Experience Modification."

Example—Workers Compensation Experience Modification

Estimated Annual Premium	Experience Modification Factor	New Estimated Premium
$20,000	0.75	$15,000
$20,000	1.00	$20,000
$20,000	1.50	$30,000

[DA06732]

When an entity's losses reflect the expected losses for its type of industry, the entity's experience modification will be 1.00. If the entity's losses are better than the industry by 25 percent, its experience modification will be 0.75. If the entity's losses are worse than the industry by 50 percent, its experience modification will be 1.50. An entity's experience modification directly affects its premium amount. Better loss control with fewer losses results in a lower premium and significant savings. After the experience modification is applied, any estimated premium discounts are deducted to arrive at the total estimated annual premium.

Accuracy of Experience Modification Calculations

For an organization to ensure that it receives an accurate experience modification factor, proper data entry, record keeping, and claim reviews must be maintained. Possible sources of errors in an experience modification calculation include these:

- Using incorrect classification codes or payroll allocations
- Failing to include all payroll data when calculating expected losses
- Incorrectly reporting loss reserves
- Failing to remove the reserves for closed claims from the rating data
- Failing to revise claim values to reflect subrogation recoveries, second injury fund recoveries, and loss apportionment among different insurers

Numerous firms specialize in analyzing experience modification calculations on a contingent-fee basis. Such firms are paid only if they find errors that produce a reduction for the insured. Contingent fees may be as high as 50 percent of the insured's savings. Insureds, their advisers, and insurers should carefully review experience modification calculations for errors.

WORKERS COMPENSATION AND EMPLOYERS LIABILITY COVERAGE CASE STUDY

Workers compensation insurance offers employers protection for the obligations prescribed by mandated employee benefits—namely, medical and disability benefits that arise from work-related injuries.

A workers compensation insurance contract is written broadly because it applies to those obligations that are outlined in a relevant workers compensation law. The workers compensation policy indicates it will pay the benefits required by law. The policy contains no limitations but rather subscribes to the legal requirements in each covered jurisdiction.

Case Facts

Innovative Counters is a corporation located in Marblehead, New York. This twenty-year old company has eighty-five employees with an annual payroll of $3.5 million. Though its corporate headquarters and operations are located in Marblehead, Innovative Counters does jobs in nearby states on occasion. It is considered a regional company and has an established reputation for quality countertop installations in commercial and residential applications. It uses various countertop materials, including granite, marble, tile, and concrete.

Marblehead Mutual provides Innovative with workers compensation coverage as evidenced in the declarations page. Over the course of one year, four separate incidents occurred. An insurance professional would review these situations to determine whether coverage is provided. See the exhibit "Innovative Counters Declarations."

In November, approximately two months prior to policy inception, Innovative Counters opened a permanent sales office in Pennsylvania. Ron, a salesperson, and his assistant work out of this newly established office, which was established due to an increase of customers in the area. This was a very busy year for Innovative Counters, and it neglected to contact its producer or insurer regarding this new location and inadvertently omitted it on the renewal application.

In early January, Ron injured his knee when he tripped on the carpeting in the office. Medical expenses were $48,000 and disability expenses were $12,000 for the injury. Ron filed a workers compensation claim under Innovative's workers compensation policy.

In February, while on a job in New Jersey, Len, another Innovative employee, injured his back in the process of installing a bathroom countertop in a customer's home. Len pursued workers compensation benefits under New Jersey law (and its associated menu of benefits), rather than that of Innovative's home state of New York.

Innovative Counters Declarations

WORKERS COMPENSATION AND EMPLOYERS LIABILITY INSURANCE POLICY

INFORMATION PAGE

Insurer: Marblehead Mutual

P O L I C Y   N O .
M|M|1|2|3|4|												

1. **The Insured:**   Innovative Counters
    Mailing address: P.O. Box 1234
    Marblehead, NY

    ___ Individual   ___ Partnership
    X Corporation or   _____

    Other workplaces not shown above:

2. **The policy period is from**   1/1/20XX   **to**   1/1/20XX   **at the insured's mailing address.**

3. A. **Workers Compensation Insurance: Part One of the policy applies to the Workers Compensation Law of the states listed here:**   NY

    B. **Employers Liability Insurance: Part Two of the policy applies to work in each state listed in Item 3.A. The limits of our liability under Part Two are:**

Bodily Injury by Accident	$ 500,000	each accident
Bodily Injury by Disease	$ 500,000	policy limit
Bodily Injury by Disease	$ 500,000	each employee

    C. **Other States Insurance: Part Three of the policy applies to the states, if any, listed here:**

    All except those listed in Item 3A and ND, OH, WA, WV, WY and OR

    D. **This policy includes these endorsements and schedules:**

    See listing of endorsements — Extension of information page

4. **The premium for this policy will be determined by our Manuals of Rules, Classifications, Rates and Rating Plans. All information required below is subject to verification and change by audit.**

Classifications	Code No.	Premium Basis Total Estimated Annual Remuneration	Rate Per $100 of Remuneration	Estimated Annual Premium

See schedule of operations — Extension of information page

Total Estimated Annual Premium $	54,980
Minimum Premium $ 600 **Expense Constant $**	175

Countersigned by _____ R. Jones _____

WC 00 00 01 A
© 1987 National Council on Compensation Insurance.
      © 1991 National Council on Compensation Insurance, Inc. All rights reserved. Reprinted with permission.

In April, an Innovative employee named Sally strained her shoulder while lifting a box of paper. She pursued workers compensation benefits from Innovative Counters, because the injury occurred in its office. Sally is one of two employees in the accounting department at the New York headquarters location who are leased from Argot Accountants—an employee leasing firm located in Pennsylvania. Under Argot Accountants' workers compensation policy, there is an alternate employer endorsement that names Innovative Counters as an insured.

Then, in late August, Mary, an administrative assistant at Innovative Counters' New York office, was chasing her pet dog at home when she tripped and hit her head against the corner of the granite countertop. She suffered a severe laceration and required medical attention and time off from work.

Mary lives in a residential community of about 150 homes located ten miles from Marblehead. Several years ago, when the houses were originally built, Innovative Counters was the subcontractor that provided the countertops in the kitchens of these homes. Although Mary felt the trip was her responsibility, the injury that she sustained would not have been as severe if the corner of the countertop had been properly beveled. After discussing the matter with legal counsel, she brought suit against Innovative Counters for $100,000 for her injury.

Case Analysis Tools

To determine whether the workers compensation policy applies to these situations, an insurance professional should review Innovative Counters' declarations page as well as the insuring agreement, and any applicable conditions and exclusions.

Determination of Coverage

The insurance professional will first review the declarations page of the policy to determine whether each incident occurred during the policy period. He or she will then review the policies to determine whether the incident triggers coverage under the WC&EL insuring agreement. The third step is to determine whether all policy conditions have been met, and the fourth step involves reviewing all policy exclusions to determine whether coverage is precluded for the incident. The insurance professional will follow this process for each of the reported incidents.

The January incident resulting in Ron's injury occurred in a permanent location that had not been reported to the insurer when the policy went into effect. The insurer is within its rights, therefore, to deny coverage to Innovative Counters for this claim. Although not providing appropriate notification was an innocent mistake, the insuring agreement under Part 3—Other States Insurance stipulates that if operations have begun in a state that is not already outlined in item 3.A. at the inception of the policy, no coverage will apply unless the insurer is notified within thirty days.

The states of operation of a business are paramount points of discussion in drafting policies. Upon inception of a policy, it is critical that states within which operations are expected to be performed are duly noted within item 3.A. on the declarations page. Although the workers compensation policy is designed to provide broad coverage, omissions in items 3.A. and 3.C. can result in lack of coverage for injuries to workers. See the exhibit "WC&EL Declarations, Item 3."

WC&EL Declarations, Item 3

3. A. **Workers Compensation Insurance: Part One of the policy applies to the Workers Compensation Law of the states listed here:**   NY

    B. **Employers Liability Insurance: Part Two of the policy applies to work in each state listed in Item 3.A. The limits of our liability under Part Two are:**

Bodily Injury by Accident	$ _500,000_	each accident
Bodily Injury by Disease	$ _500,000_	policy limit
Bodily Injury by Disease	$ _500,000_	each employee

    C. **Other States Insurance: Part Three of the policy applies to the states, if any, listed here:**

All except those listed in Item 3A and ND, OH, WA, WV, WY and OR

With regard to the February incident involving Len, the loss did occur during the policy period. Furthermore, Len was an employee and was injured in a work-related accident. Len, however, is asserting that his workers compensation benefits should be paid in accordance with the New Jersey statute. Employees may elect to choose which jurisdiction applies in the interest of obtaining the most attractive benefits.

In reviewing the declarations page, under item 3.A., workers compensation coverage is shown applicable to the state of New York. Item 3.C., Other States Insurance, indicates that the policy applies to all states except those listed. Because New Jersey is not listed as an exception, an insurance professional should review the Other States' Insurance provision to confirm that the New Jersey statute would pay benefits for Len's injury.

PART THREE

OTHER STATES INSURANCE

A. How This Insurance Applies

1. This other states insurance applies only if one or more states are shown in Item 3.C. of the Information Page.

2. If you begin work in any one of those states after the effective date of this policy and are not insured or are not self-insured for such work, all provisions of the policy will apply as though that state were listed in Item 3.A. of the Information Page.

3. We will reimburse you for the benefits required by the workers compensation law of that state if we are not permitted to pay the benefits directly to persons entitled to them.

4. If you have work on the effective date of this policy in any state not listed in Item 3.A. of the Information Page, coverage will not be afforded for that state unless we are notified within thirty days.

B. Notice

Tell us at once if you begin work in any state listed in Item 3.C. of the Information Page.[5]

Unlike the permanent sales office in Pennsylvania, the New Jersey job was a short-lived one and started after the effective date of the policy. Part 3—Other States Insurance clarifies that coverage will apply since the work did not begin until after the effective date of the policy (and there is no other applicable workers compensation insurance). Further, the insuring agreement affirms that states listed under item 3.C., which include New Jersey, apply as though they were listed under item 3.A. Therefore, the benefits under New Jersey law would apply under Innovative Counters' workers compensation policy.

The next incident to be reviewed is the April injury to Sally in the accounting department. Because Sally is a leased employee and the leasing firm's policy includes the Alternate Employer Endorsement, an insurance professional would begin by reviewing that form. See the exhibit "Sample Alternate Employer Endorsement."

Because the Alternate Employer's Endorsement lists Innovative Counters as the alternate employer, Sally's injuries will be covered under Argot Accountants' policy. Even though these leased employees were working within the purview of Innovative Counters, this endorsement stipulates that workers compensation and employers liability benefits will be provided by Argot Accountants.

When a company uses leased workers, the workers compensation coverage may be provided either by the leasing company or by their client. This fact warrants careful construction of the agreement between the parties and the addition of the proper endorsements to each workers compensation policy.

Based on Sally's incident, an insurance professional might recommend that Innovative Counters add the Employee Leasing Client Exclusion to its workers compensation policy. This endorsement will eliminate any coverage questions for similar incidents in the future. This endorsement, however, is not available in all states.

The final incident involves Mary's injury at home in August. By investigating the insuring agreements under the WC&EL policy, an insurance professional would determine an injury must result from an employment-related accident. This was not the case, as Mary was at home outside of regular work hours.

Sample Alternate Employer Endorsement

WORKERS COMPENSATION AND EMPLOYERS LIABILITY INSURANCE POLICY   WC 00 03 01 A

ALTERNATE EMPLOYER ENDORSEMENT

This endorsement applies only with respect to bodily injury to your employees while in the course of special or temporary employment by the alternate employer in the state named in Item 2 of the Schedule. Part One (Workers Compensation Insurance) and Part Two (Employers Liability Insurance) will apply as though the alternate employer is insured. If an entry is shown in Item 3 of the Schedule the insurance afforded by this endorsement applies only to work you perform under the contract or at the project named in the Schedule.

Under Part One (Workers Compensation Insurance) we will reimburse the alternate employer for the benefits required by the workers compensation law if we are not permitted to pay the benefits directly to the persons entitled to them.

The insurance afforded by this endorsement is not intended to satisfy the alternate employer's duty to secure its obligations under the workers compensation law. We will not file evidence of this insurance on behalf of the alternate employer with any government agency.

We will not ask any other insurer of the alternate employer to share with us a loss covered by this endorsement.

Premium will be charged for your employees while in the course of special or temporary employment by the alternate employer.

The policy may be canceled according to its terms without sending notice to the alternate employer.

Part Four (Your Duties If Injury Occurs) applies to you and the alternate employer. The alternate employer will recognize our right to defend under Parts One and Two and our right to inspect under Part Six.

Schedule

1. **Alternate Employer**   Innovative Counters   **Address**

2. **State of Special or Temporary Employment**   New York

3. **Contract or Project**

This endorsement changes the policy to which it is attached and is effective on the date issued unless otherwise stated.

(The information below is required only when this endorsement is issued subsequent to preparation of the policy.)

Endorsement Effective   Policy No.   Endorsement No.
Insured   Premium $

Insurance Company   Marblehead Mutual   Countersigned by_____

WC 00 03 01 A
                Sample of an Alternate Employer Endoresement

This is not, therefore, an employment-related matter and is not covered under the WC&EL policy. This action is a products liability claim under Innovative Counters' general liability policy.

If Mary had tripped in the kitchen at work and struck her head on a counter that had been installed by Innovative Counters, the claim would have been a work-related incident and such a tort action (which would have been brought against Innovative Counters as a product manufacturer) would have been covered under the employers liability coverage within the workers compensation policy.

Determination of Amounts Payable

Workers compensation insurance is not subject to any specific limit. Rather, benefits are paid in accordance with each state's workers compensation laws. Employers liability insurance, however, does have limits of insurance for those tort actions that may be brought. See the exhibit "WC&EL Insurance Policy—General Section C. and Part One B."

One of the more important considerations concerning these limits is that they, at a minimum, satisfy underlying limit requirements under an umbrella liability policy. Defense costs are also covered in addition to the limits under employers liability coverage.

Correct Answers

Employee/Month	
Ron/January	Not covered because the Pennsylvania operation was not reported to the insurer within thirty days of its inception.
Len/February	Covered under other states endorsement. New Jersey statutory benefits will be paid.
Sally/April	Not covered under Innovative Counters' WC&EL policy. Covered under Argot Accountants' WC&EL policy's Alternate Employer Endorsement.
Mary/August	Not covered under Innovative Counters' WC&EL policy, as it is not a work-related incident. Claim will be submitted under Innovative Counters' general liability policy.

[DA06795]

WC&EL Insurance Policy—General Section C. and Part One B

WORKERS COMPENSATION AND EMPLOYERS LIABILITY INSURANCE POLICY   WC 00 00 00 A

1st Reprint   *Effective April 1, 1992*   **Standard**

WORKERS COMPENSATION AND EMPLOYERS LIABILITY INSURANCE POLICY

In return for the payment of the premium and subject to all terms of this policy, we agree with you as follows:

GENERAL SECTION

A. The Policy

This policy includes at its effective date the Information Page and all endorsements and schedules listed there. It is a contract of insurance between you (the employer named in Item 1 of the Information Page) and us (the insurer named on the Information Page). The only agreements relating to this insurance are stated in this policy. The terms of this policy may not be changed or waived except by endorsement issued by us to be part of this policy.

B. Who is Insured

You are insured if you are an employer named in Item 1 of the Information Page. If that employer is a partnership, and if you are one of its partners, you are insured, but only in your capacity as an employer of the partnership's employees.

C. Workers Compensation Law

Workers Compensation Law means the workers or workmen's compensation law and occupational disease law of each state or territory named in Item 3.A. of the Information Page. It includes any amendments to that law which are in effect during the policy period. It does not include any federal workers or workmen's compensation law, any federal occupational disease law or the provisions of any law that provide nonoccupational disability benefits.

D. State

State means any state of the United States of America, and the District of Columbia.

E. Locations

This policy covers all of your workplaces listed in Items 1 or 4 of the Information Page; and it covers all other workplaces in Item 3.A. states unless you have other insurance or are self-insured for such workplaces.

PART ONE
WORKERS COMPENSATION INSURANCE

A. How This Insurance Applies

This workers compensation insurance applies to bodily injury by accident or bodily injury by disease. Bodily injury includes resulting death.

1. Bodily injury by accident must occur during the policy period.
2. Bodily injury by disease must be caused or aggravated by the conditions of your employment. The employee's last day of last exposure to the conditions causing or aggravating such bodily injury by disease must occur during the policy period.

B. We Will Pay

We will pay promptly when due the benefits required of you by the workers compensation law.

C. We Will Defend

We have the right and duty to defend at our expense any claim, proceeding or suit against you for benefits payable by this insurance. We have the right to investigate and settle these claims, proceedings or suits.

We have no duty to defend a claim, proceeding or suit that is not covered by this insurance.

D. We Will Also Pay

We will also pay these costs, in addition to other amounts payable under this insurance, as part of any claim, proceeding or suit we defend:

1. reasonable expenses incurred at our request, but not loss of earnings;
2. premiums for bonds to release attachments and for appeal bonds in bond amounts up to the amount payable under this insurance;
3. litigation costs taxed against you;
4. interest on a judgment as required by law until we offer the amount due under this insurance; and
5. expenses we incur.

E. Other Insurance

We will not pay more than our share of benefits and costs covered by this insurance and other

1 of 6

SUMMARY

Workers compensation statutes were enacted as an alternative to a tort system that did not satisfactorily address work-related injuries.

These issues are important in determining the persons for whom an employer might be required to provide workers compensation benefits:

- Distinction between employee and independent contractor
- Status as statutory employees
- Temporary employees and leased employees

Employees seeking workers compensation benefits must show that they suffered an injury arising out of and in the course of employment. Most state workers compensation statutes require that the injury be accidental. State workers compensation statutes cover occupational disease arising out of and in the course of employment. Workers compensation statutes provide medical benefits, disability benefits, rehabilitation benefits, and death benefits.

These are some methods of demonstrating security under workers compensation statutes:

- Obtaining insurance from the voluntary market
- Obtaining insurance from an assigned risk plan
- Obtaining insurance from a state fund
- Having a qualified self-insurance plan
- Participating in a self-insured group

The workers compensation statutes of two or more states may apply to an employee's injury, depending on various employment circumstances, including the place of injury, the place of hire, the place of employment, the location of the employer, and the residence of the employee. Extraterritorial and reciprocal agreements included in states' statutes determine whether an insurer is required to pay workers compensation benefits when statutes from more than one state may apply.

Various legal remedies for occupational injury are available under federal law for certain employees who may or may not also be covered by state workers compensation statutes. Some federal compensation statutes eliminate the employee's right to sue the employer for occupational injury and instead obligate the employer to pay stipulated medical, disability, and death benefits. Others permit employees to sue their employers for occupational injuries.

The Workers Compensation and Employers Liability (WC&EL) policy combines coverage for the insured's obligation to pay benefits required by a workers compensation law and the insured's legal liability to pay damages because of occupational injury to its employees due to a claim or suit based on legal grounds other than workers compensation or a similar law.

The WC&EL policy form has an Information Page that is equivalent to the declarations page of other policies and consists of six parts.

A number of situations require modification of standard WC&EL policy provisions by adding an appropriate endorsement to the policy, including these:

- Voluntary Compensation and Employers Liability Coverage Endorsement
- Foreign voluntary compensation coverage
- Longshore and Harbor Workers' Compensation Act Coverage Endorsement (LHWCA)
- Maritime Coverage Endorsement
- Waiver of Our Right to Recover From Others Endorsement
- Alternate Employer Endorsement

Experience rating modifies an insured's workers compensation coverage rate for a policy period based on the insured's actual loss experience during prior policy periods. The experience rating formula compares an insured's actual losses with the losses expected for an average insured in the same classification. The result of the formula is the experience modification factor, which is multiplied by the manual rate(s) for the insured's classification(s). Experience modification factor calculations may be subject to error and, therefore, should be carefully verified.

When determining whether the WC&EL policy applies to a loss, the insurance professional reviews the declarations page, as well as the insuring agreement and any conditions or exclusions that would modify the coverage.

ASSIGNMENT NOTES

1. *New York Central Railroad Co. v. White*, 243 U.S. 188.
2. To check the current status and features of workers compensation statutes, see U.S. Chamber of Commerce, Analysis of Workers' Compensation Laws, published annually.
3. 398 U.S. 375, 1970 AMC 967 (1970)
4. National Council on Compensation Insurance, Inc., 1991.
5. © 1991 National Council on Compensation Insurance, Inc. All rights reserved. Reprinted with permission.

11

Management Liability Loss Exposures and Insurance

Educational Objectives

After learning the content of this assignment, you should be able to:

▷ Describe the liability loss exposures of a corporation's directors and officers, with specific reference to their responsibilities and duties and the types of suits that may be made against them.

▷ Describe the provisions of directors and officers (D&O) liability policies.

▷ Describe the purpose and distinguishing features of each of the specialty directors and officers (D&O) coverages discussed.

▷ Describe the major types of claims associated with employment practices liability (EPL) loss exposures.

▷ Describe the provisions of employment practices liability (EPL) policies and the additional services that EPL insurers provide to their insureds.

▷ Describe the legal foundations for fiduciary liability loss exposures, with specific reference to the Employee Retirement Income Security Act (ERISA) and the duties of employee benefit plan fiduciaries.

▷ Describe the provisions of fiduciary liability policies.

▷ Indicate whether a described claim would be covered under a typical directors and officers (D&O) liability policy, a typical employment practices liability (EPL) policy, or a typical fiduciary liability policy.

Management Liability Loss Exposures and Insurance

11

DIRECTORS AND OFFICERS LIABILITY LOSS EXPOSURES

Both large and small corporations invite outstanding business, academic, and social leaders to join their boards to provide the benefit of their experience, advice, and contacts. The risk of being sued based on participation as a board member is a serious concern both for the prospective directors and the corporations.

It is important for risk managers and insurance professionals to be able to identify and analyze directors and officers (D&O) liability loss exposures. This requires an understanding of the role of directors and officers in corporations and the types of suits made against them. Because these suits can have wide-ranging consequences for corporations, as well as for the directors and officers who serve on their boards, risk control should be a key aspect in the management of these exposures.

Corporations and the Role of Directors and Officers

A corporation is owned by its stockholders but controlled by its board of directors. The directors (sometimes called trustees) may be major stockholders and executive officers of the corporation, but directors also usually include outside business or social leaders who often have little financial stake in the corporation. A corporation's directors are elected by its stockholders in accordance with the corporation's bylaws (the rules by which a corporation governs itself).

The board of directors establishes corporate policy, makes major business and financial decisions, and appoints the corporation's executive officers (such as the chief executive officer, president, secretary, and treasurer) to manage the corporation's daily operations. The executive officers are not necessarily the only employees who are officers of the corporation. The corporation's bylaws may specify that employees above a certain rank or holding certain positions are also considered to be officers of the corporation.

Other types of entities have similar directors and officers. These other types of entities include public bodies, not-for-profit organizations, trusts, limited liability companies, and limited partnerships. Although the titles of the officials may differ, their duties are very similar to those of corporate directors and officers.

Major Responsibilities and Duties of Directors and Officers

When directors and officers fail to fulfill their responsibilities and duties as required under the law, they can be held liable for losses that result. The major responsibilities of corporate directors include these:

- Establishing the corporation's basic goals and broad policies
- Electing or appointing the corporate officers, advising them, approving their actions, and auditing their performance
- Safeguarding and approving changes in the corporation's assets
- Approving important financial matters and ensuring that proper annual and interim reports are given to stockholders
- Delegating special powers to others to sign contracts, open bank accounts, sign checks, issue stock, obtain loans, and conduct any activities that may require board approval
- Maintaining, revising, and enforcing the corporate charter and bylaws
- Perpetuating a competent board by conducting regular elections and filling interim vacancies with qualified persons
- Fulfilling their fiduciary duties to the corporation and its stockholders

Fiduciary duty
The duty to act in the best interests of another.

The fiduciary relationship is the most important aspect of the corporation in analyzing D&O liability loss exposures. In addition to performing specific functions, directors and officers occupy a position of trust for stockholders, the board of directors, and the general public. Breach of **fiduciary duty** is a common basis for claims against directors and officers. Directors' and officers' fiduciary duties include the duty of care, the duty of loyalty, the duty of disclosure, and the duty of obedience.

Duty of Care

Directors and officers have the duty of care (also called the duty of diligence) when performing their corporate functions. They are considered to have met their duty of care if they meet these standards:

- Act in good faith and in a manner they reasonably believe to be in the corporation's best interests
- Discharge their responsibilities with informed judgment and a degree of care that a person in a similar position would believe to be reasonable under similar circumstances

Business judgment rule
A legal rule that provides that a director will not be personally liable for a decision involving business judgment, provided the director made an informed decision and acted in good faith.

In applying the concept of the general duty to exercise reasonable care, courts have held that directors and officers are not guarantors of the enterprise's profitability. Nor are directors required to have special business skills. Instead, courts grant directors broad discretion under the **business judgment rule**. Directors and officers are not liable for honest mistakes of judgment even if the result is a financial loss, provided they acted reasonably.

However, directors and officers can face claims that their actions do not fall within the protection of the business judgment rule. For example, a claimant might allege that the directors did not use reasonable care in making a decision that resulted in a financial loss to the corporation, that they did not use reasonable care in reviewing financial statements, and other similar allegations.

Directors and officers have a duty to keep themselves informed of the facts and other matters required to make prudent business decisions. At a minimum, directors and officers have a duty to attend board meetings and meetings of the committees on which they serve. Many large, for-profit corporations pay their directors substantial fees to participate in board and committee meetings.

Duty of Loyalty

Directors and officers have the general duty of undivided loyalty to the corporations they serve. Accordingly, directors and officers cannot usurp business opportunities that properly belong to the corporation. For the same reason, directors and officers cannot own or operate businesses that compete with the corporation.

Because directors (and sometimes officers) obtain their positions by the vote or consent of the stockholders, they also owe a duty of loyalty to the stockholders. Under the common law and the Securities and Exchange Act of 1934, no director or officer (or any other person) may use "insider information" to buy or sell stock of the corporation, whether the information was obtained directly or from others.

Moreover, section 16(b) of the Securities and Exchange Act of 1934 requires directors and officers of a corporation to disgorge back to the company any profit realized from sale of the corporation's stock within six months of its purchase, whether or not they had insider information.

Duty of Disclosure

Directors and officers have the general duty to disclose material facts to all persons who have a right to know such facts and would not otherwise be able to obtain them. For example, directors and officers have a duty to make public disclosures of facts that are material to stockholders, bondholders, and potential investors in the securities of the corporation.

However, there are certain matters that directors and officers must keep confidential. Normally, directors are not authorized to act as spokespersons for the corporation. In addition, directors and officers must refrain from discussing confidential or market-sensitive matters with others, including family members and colleagues.

Duty of Obedience

Some authorities include a duty of obedience (that is, obedience to the law) in the list of duties of directors and officers. Directors and officers are required to perform their duties according to federal and state law as well as the terms of the corporate charter.

Types of Suits Made Against Directors and Officers

When various stakeholders in a corporation believe they have suffered financial or other types of harm, they may take legal action against the corporation's directors or officers. The activities of an organization that may give rise to a perception of harm are varied. A typical example is a suit by investors when a corporation's stock price drops significantly. Another example is a suit against a charity that sells an old building used to house the homeless and replaces it with a modern facility. Persons who believe that the old building was adequate might sue the directors for wasting the charity's assets.

Suits made against directors and officers are generally classified as either derivative suits or nonderivative suits. Another type of suit is a class action suit.

Derivative Suits

A derivative suit is a lawsuit brought by one or more shareholders in the name of the corporation. Any damages recovered go directly to the corporation, not to the plaintiff-stockholder(s). However, successful plaintiffs are often awarded the expenses incurred in bringing the suit, including attorney fees. To be successful, the plaintiff-stockholders normally must establish that the defendants' conduct was outside the permissible boundaries of sound management practice, including the business judgment rule.

Nonderivative Suits

Nonderivative suits against directors and officers are not made in the name of the corporation. Customers, competitors, employees, creditors, governmental entities, or other persons outside the corporation may initiate such suits. Stockholders who suffer harm may also bring nonderivative suits in their own names as opposed to suing in the corporation's name.

Nonderivative suits typically name specific directors or officers and the corporate entity as co-defendants. The plaintiff must show that an injury or injustice resulted from wrongful acts or omissions of directors and/or officers. Examples are suits for violations of legislative statutes; failure to fulfill legal duties; and intentional, unfair, or harmful conduct.

These are examples of common allegations made against directors and officers in nonderivative suits:

- Providing false or inadequate disclosure in connection with stock issuance
- Making or permitting false entries in the corporate books and records

- Preparing and signing false documents filed with regulatory authorities
- Failing to correct inaccurate statements within a prospectus issued by the corporation
- Failing to review annual financial statements and monitor corporate affairs
- Missing an opportunity for expansion, acquisition, or sale of the corporation

Class Actions

A class action (or class action lawsuit) is a lawsuit in which one person or a small group of people represents the interests of an entire class of people in litigation. Many class actions against directors and officers are based on wrongful acts related to securities. A typical securities class action lawsuit commonly makes one or more of these allegations:

- The corporation's public statements (usually either in the corporation's communications with securities analysts or in its periodic reports to stockholders or to the Securities and Exchange Commission) contained material misrepresentations or omissions.
- The alleged misrepresentations or omissions artificially inflated the corporation's stock price.
- While the stock price was artificially inflated, insiders profitably sold their personal holdings in the corporation's stock. Following the completion of insider sales, the corporation's stock price dropped sharply.

The Class-Action Fairness Act of 2005 expanded federal jurisdiction over class actions with additional oversight of attorney fees in this type of suit.

Indemnification of Directors and Officers

Under the common law, corporate directors and officers who have successfully defended against a derivative suit have the right to indemnification from the corporation to reimburse them for expenses they have paid to defend against the suit. However, defense costs and the amount of time required to prepare an adequate defense can be devastating. Accordingly, corporations in many situations make payment to settle claims against their directors and officers. The result is that the suit is terminated with no determination of wrongdoing. In such situations, the common law is not clear whether directors and officers are entitled to indemnification. The rationale is that a wrongdoing insider cannot justifiably be reimbursed by the same party that the wrongdoer's misconduct harmed. Some early cases even denied indemnification for successful defense because the expenditure of corporate funds would not benefit the corporation and would therefore be **ultra vires**.

As a result of the confusion surrounding directors' and officers' common-law right to corporate indemnification, state legislatures enacted statutes granting

Ultra vires
An act of a corporation that exceeds its chartered powers.

directors and officers the right to indemnification. Some of the statutes permit indemnification, while others require it. Some of the indemnification statutes are "exclusive" in that they authorize indemnification only to the extent provided by the statute. Other statutes permit directors and officers to benefit from any of the rights to which they may be entitled under any bylaw, agreement, vote of stockholders, or otherwise.

Determining what rules apply is a matter for competent legal advice. As added protection for directors and officers, some authorities recommend that indemnification wording in corporate charters and bylaws require indemnification, not just permit it, and require corporations to reimburse directors and officers for defense costs as they are incurred rather than when the case is resolved.

In most states, for indemnification to be allowed, the corporation must have adopted some form of contractual provision that sets guidelines for reimbursement. This provision—which can be incorporated in the bylaws, a corporate resolution, or another written agreement, such as an employment contract—can obligate the corporation to indemnify the corporate official as long as the requisite standard of conduct is in accord with the statute. Under the laws of some states, corporations can adopt provisions that indemnification will be denied only when the director's or officer's act or omission constitutes gross negligence or willful misconduct.

A related problem for directors and officers is funding defense costs before settlement. Indemnification is retrospective—that is, it occurs after the suit has been concluded. Defense costs can amount to hundreds of thousands, even millions, of dollars. Directors and officers generally want and need advances to cover these expenses before settlement. Most statutes provide that corporations may include provisions for advancing expenses.

Such advances are generally paid subject to the agreement that they will be refunded by the director or officer ultimately found not to be entitled to indemnification. However, agreements to refund advances can be difficult or impossible to enforce. Moreover, a provision of the Sarbanes-Oxley Act of 2002 prohibits corporations from making most kinds of loans to officers or directors. Some authorities view advancing defense costs as a prohibited loan under Sarbanes-Oxley.

Controlling D&O Liability Loss Exposures

Claims against corporate directors and officers can create significant defense and settlement costs. Perhaps even more serious consequences are the amounts of time that key executives must devote to defending against the claims and the potential loss of reputation for the corporation. Although D&O liability insurance can transfer some of the financial risk of these suits, it cannot restore a corporation's reputation. Loss of a corporation's reputation can damage customer relationships, hinder access to the capital markets, and make it difficult to attract highly qualified executives. Therefore, risk control should be a central part of the management of D&O loss exposures. See the exhibit "Risk Control for D&O Liability Exposures."

Risk Control for D&O Liability Exposures

These are potential pillars for a risk control program for an organization's D&O liability loss exposures:

- Adhering to the requirements of the Sarbanes-Oxley Public Company Reform and Investor Protection Act of 2002 (Sarbanes-Oxley)

- Establishing the independence of a corporation's board of directors

- Providing opportunities that encourage open, clear, and concise communication among directors and officers

- Ensuring that directors and officers fully understand the organization's operations, corporate charter and bylaws, and securities and antitrust laws

[DA06612]

DIRECTORS AND OFFICERS LIABILITY INSURANCE

Directors and officers (D&O) liability insurance fills a coverage gap that is left by CGL and commercial auto policies.

The directors and officers of a corporation are insured persons with respect to their duties as such under the Commercial General Liability (CGL) Coverage Form and Business Auto Coverage Form of Insurance Services Office, Inc. (ISO). Directors and officers are specifically listed in the Who Is an Insured section of the CGL coverage form. The Business Auto Coverage Form does not specifically mention directors and officers, but it provides coverage for anyone liable for an insured's conduct to the extent of that liability, which would include directors and officers.

The CGL coverage form and Business Auto Coverage Form cover claims for bodily injury and property damage, and the CGL also covers personal and advertising injury liability. However, a corporation's directors and officers can be held liable for wrongful acts or omissions causing harm that does not qualify as bodily injury, property damage, personal injury, or advertising injury. The purpose of **directors and officers (D&O) liability insurance** is to provide coverage for claims alleging such harm.

To protect its directors and officers against such claims and to finance its indemnification agreements with its directors and officers, a corporation typically buys a D&O liability policy. Qualified individuals will ordinarily refuse

Directors and officers (D&O) liability insurance

Insurance that covers a corporation's directors and officers against liability for their wrongful acts covered by the policy and also covers the sums that the insured corporation is required or permitted by law to pay to the directors and officers as indemnification.

to serve on a board of directors unless they are satisfied that they are covered by adequate D&O liability coverage.

D&O liability policies are not standardized. Although the lack of standardization complicates the task of analyzing D&O policies, it enables insurers to tailor coverage to a client's needs. In D&O insurance, different policies can offer different coverage options, and insurers are more willing and able to modify their policies to meet customers' needs.

Analyzing D&O liability insurance involves sound knowledge of these components:

- Insuring agreements
- Claims-made provisions
- Persons and organizations insured
- Exclusions
- Other D&O policy provisions

Insuring Agreements

Most D&O liability policies have two insuring agreements, usually labeled Coverage A and Coverage B. Coverage A is direct coverage for the directors and officers, and Coverage B is indemnification coverage for the corporation. Some policies provide coverage for the corporation itself, called entity coverage or Coverage C.

A typical D&O liability policy is a claims-made form. Policy wording indicates that it covers loss as a result of any claim that is first made against the directors and officers during the policy period (or a discovery period, if applicable) for a wrongful act.

Coverage A and Coverage B

Coverage A and Coverage B, sometimes called Side A and Side B, insure different entities for the same types of claims:

- Coverage A insures the individual directors and officers. This coverage is sometimes captioned "Individual Coverage," "Direct Coverage," or "Directors and Officers Coverage." Coverage A indemnifies the corporation's directors and officers for covered claims only when such indemnification is not required by law, is not permitted by law, or is financially prohibited because of lack of funds or bankruptcy.

- Coverage B insures the corporation for the amounts that it is lawfully permitted or required to pay to defend or settle claims against the directors or officers. Coverage B is commonly captioned "Corporate Reimbursement Coverage" or "Indemnification Coverage."

To avoid stacking of coverage, Coverage A is limited to losses for which the corporation does not or cannot provide indemnification to the directors or officers. Therefore, if a director is held liable for a loss caused by a covered wrongful act and the corporation is lawfully able to indemnify the director, the loss will be paid under Coverage B. If the corporation cannot indemnify the director for any reason (for example, because the corporation is in receivership or liquidation, or its assets are frozen), the director's loss is payable to the director under Coverage A. Many D&O policies provide that the corporate provisions for the indemnification of directors and officers will be presumed to be as broad as those permitted by law.

 Reality Check

Toyota Motor Corp. Recall and D&O Liability

An auto manufacturer's recall of more than 200 million autos because of a dangerous defect would not normally prompt concerns about directors and officers (D&O) liability. However, a class action lawsuit filed against Toyota Motor Corp. alleging that the price of the manufacturer's stock was inflated because shareholders were not advised of the issues leading to the recall changes the focus to D&O liability. Michael A. Hamilton, partner and chairman of the National Insurance Coverage Group, offers this take on the situation:

"What is interesting here is that the suit is not alleging mismanagement or negligence, but that the company knew of the problem and intentionally ignored it in the name of safety and profits," said Hamilton, who added that many policies carry an exclusion against intentional conduct or intentional fraudulent acts.

"Carriers may have to pay for the defense of corporations in these types of cases, but if there is a finding of fraud, insurers are typically not liable for indemnification," Hamilton said. "Companies can get the defense, but it stops there. Insurers aren't going to pick up the tab once fraud has been determined."[1]

Hamilton goes on to consider the "claims-made" nature of most D&O policies and speculates about whether the company directors and officers were aware of the potential claims within the policy period (or the time frames outlined in the policy for disclosure). If they were aware of the potential claims, then the D&O insurers would not be responsible for providing coverage or for defending these lawsuits.

Hamilton notes the intentional conduct exclusion and the claims-made provisions, which are two D&O issues that commonly result in legal action and court determinations that often vary by state and by individual policy provisions. He mentions that if fraud is determined—a criminal act—only defense coverage for D&O would be available. Hamilton also notes the international fraudulent acts exclusion, which could become another D&O coverage issue in the emerging global economy.

[DA06737]

A D&O liability policy is ordinarily subject to an each loss limit of liability and an aggregate limit of liability. The each loss limit is the most that the insurer will pay for any one loss under Coverage A or Coverage B or both. The aggregate limit is the most the insurer will pay for all claims first made during the policy period or the extended reporting period (unless the extended reporting provision provides an additional aggregate limit).

Entity Coverage (Coverage C)

Many D&O liability policies may contain a third insuring agreement or endorsement that provides entity coverage. Entity coverage, also called Coverage C, makes the corporation itself (the "entity") an insured for claims made against it because of wrongful acts covered by the policy. Without entity coverage, a D&O liability policy (under Coverage B) covers the corporation only for indemnification of its directors or officers. It does not cover any loss attributable to the entity's wrongful acts.

Under the traditional type of D&O liability policy, providing only Coverage A and Coverage B, a lawsuit naming both the corporation and its directors and officers could result in conflicts about how much the corporation should contribute to the settlement. To avoid these conflicts and increase the protection provided by the policy, D&O insurers added entity coverage for the corporation itself. Entity coverage for large, publicly traded corporations is typically restricted to insuring claims for mismanaging securities.

Entity coverage can defeat the benefits intended for directors and officers. Because the limits of a D&O policy are shared by all insureds, covering the entity as an insured can erode the limits available to protect the directors and officers. Even worse, if the entity declares bankruptcy—an event that can precipitate a flood of D&O claims—the bankruptcy courts sometimes hold that the policy is an asset of the corporation and that no coverage is available under the policy for directors and officers until all claims against the corporation have been settled. Depending on its cancellation and change in control provisions, a policy may cease to provide protection for new occurrences once bankruptcy begins—or coverage may be canceled. Careful wording of provisions can help to secure the protection for directors and officers. This can be accomplished by including language specific to bankruptcy—such as priority of payments (who gets paid first), and specifications in the "insured" definition and in "insured-versus-insured" provisions—and by avoiding cancellation and "change in control" provisions that result in cancellation or disruption of benefits when the policy is transferred to a bankruptcy receiver.[2]

Recent producer-recommended practices are to create an executive liability program that includes a D&O policy with separate Side A limits and a difference in conditions (DIC) provision, an employment liability policy, and fiduciary liability insurance. The DIC provision provides primary coverage with fewer restrictions for Side A and with a limit that applies even before the D&O coverage is exhausted. The fiduciary liability insurance provides protection against alleged mismanagement of employee benefit plans.[3]

Definition of "Claim"

Because D&O policies are almost without exception written on a claims-made basis, the definition of "claim" is extremely important. A representative definition of claim from a D&O policy includes any of these actions taken against a director or an officer for a wrongful act:

- A written demand for monetary or nonmonetary relief
- A civil proceeding commenced by serving a complaint or similar pleading
- A formal administrative or regulatory proceeding commenced by filing a notice of charges, formal investigative order, or similar document

Not all definitions of claim are as inclusive. Some are limited to written demands for monetary damages and civil proceedings commenced against the insured. Criminal proceedings are often not included in the definition of claim. Even when criminal proceedings are included, coverage is limited to defense costs because public policy bars insurers from covering criminal penalties. A few policies define claim more broadly—for example, including arbitration proceedings as well as civil, administrative, or regulatory investigations.

Definition of "Loss"

D&O liability policies typically agree to pay for the amount of loss the individual directors and officers sustain because of a claim (Coverage A) or to reimburse the corporation for its loss when it indemnifies the directors and officers (Coverage B). The term "loss" is typically defined to include all damages that the directors and officers become legally obligated to pay, subject to certain exclusions and limitations.

Most important, D&O policies normally define loss to include defense costs. As a result, the per loss limit of liability and the annual aggregate limit apply to the sum of damages and defense costs combined. This contrasts with the CGL policy and many other liability policies, which cover defense costs in addition to the limits of liability. Insurers have placed D&O defense costs within limits because of the extremely high costs that can be incurred in defending against D&O claims. Insureds must select limits for a D&O policy that include defense costs within limits rather than in addition to limits. The definition of loss typically excludes certain costs such as taxes, criminal or civil fines or penalties, punitive or exemplary damages, or the multiplied portion of any damages (such as treble damages awarded under the Sherman Antitrust Act).

Some insurers provide coverage for punitive damages. Because many states prohibit insurers from providing such coverage, some insurers include a "most-favorable-jurisdiction" provision stating that coverage for punitive damages will be determined based on the law of the most favorable jurisdiction that can apply to policy interpretation.

Definition of "Wrongful Act"

The definition of "wrongful act" in a D&O policy is usually very broad but is limited by exclusions and other limitations expressed elsewhere in the policy. This is a representative D&O policy definition of wrongful act:

> Any error, misstatement, misleading statement, act, omission, neglect or breach of duty actually or allegedly committed or attempted by the directors and officers, individually or collectively, in their respective capacities as such, or any matter claimed against them solely by reason of their status as directors and officers.

The definition often includes a provision stating that all claims arising out of the same or any related wrongful act will be treated as a single claim—that is, all related claims will be subject to the limit of insurance, and the limit will not apply separately to each claim. This is a common provision, but in some D&O policies, it is contained in the limit of liability provision or in another provision other than the definition of wrongful act. Although the grouping together of related claims means that only one limit of insurance is available to the insured, the provision can also mean that only one deductible applies.

Claims-Made Provisions

Claims-made coverage trigger

The event that triggers coverage under a claims-made coverage form; the first making of a claim against any insured during either the policy period or an extended reporting period.

Most D&O policies have a **claims-made coverage trigger**. D&O loss exposures pose particular problems that are handled much better under claims-made rather than under occurrence-based policies. These are examples of such problems:

- Making errors in the corporation's financial statements is a common source of D&O claims. If a D&O policy were written on an occurrence basis, questions would arise about when the error occurred. Did the error occur when the corrected statement was issued; in prior years, when the directors issued inaccurate statements; or in all of the years?

- For claims alleging mismanagement, did the mismanagement occur in each of the years that the director served on the board or in just some of them?

- When claims allege that the board approved excessive compensation to the CEO, is each of several possible approvals of the excessive compensation a separate occurrence, or is it all one occurrence?

Numerous other types of claims would give rise to similar problems. Policy wording might address some of these problems in an occurrence-based policy, but claims-made is a much better solution for an insurer. The claims-made policy that is in effect when claim is first made for a wrongful act is the policy that applies to all related claims arising out of the wrongful act.

The claims-made approach avoids the possibility of multiple years' policies being triggered for claims resulting from a series of related wrongful acts. When covered under a claims-made policy, insureds must consider that only one policy will apply when determining appropriate limits of insurance.

The claims-made features of D&O policies (and other management liability policies) differ from the characteristics of the ISO claims-made general liability forms in their extended reporting periods, their retroactive date provisions and prior acts coverage, and the reporting of known wrongful acts.

Extended Reporting Periods

Extended reporting period provisions, commonly called tail coverage in D&O policies, function the same basic way as such provisions in other claims-made liability forms. These variations can apply to tail coverage:

- Thirty- to sixty-day automatic tail coverage
- Option to add one to five years of coverage after automatic tail
- Possible separate limit of liability for tail coverage: liability limit may be greater for tail coverage, less for tail coverage, or the same as coverage during the policy period for tail coverage

Even brief automatic tail coverage is beneficial in a claims-made D&O policy. For example, a claim for a wrongful act committed during the policy period might not be made until after the policy period ends. If the claim is first made during the automatic extended reporting period, the claim will be covered. Without this automatic tail, the claim would not be covered under the expiring policy. Optional tail coverage should be purchased only when the renewal policy will not cover claims for wrongful acts that occurred during the expiring policy period.

The optional tail coverage is usually available on a bilateral basis, meaning that the insured may purchase the optional tail when either the insured or the insurer decides not to renew the expiring policy. In some cases, however, the optional tail is available only if the insurer decides not to renew the policy.

Retroactive Date Provisions and Prior Acts Coverage

A few D&O policies require that a wrongful act must have occurred after the beginning of the policy period or after a retroactive date indicated in the policy. However, many D&O policies cover claims made during the policy period for wrongful acts that occurred either during the policy period or at any time before the policy period—often called prior acts coverage. This coverage is subject to a warranty, made in the insurance application, that none of the directors or officers knows of any circumstances that might result in a claim.

Prior acts coverage can also be provided when the policy contains a retroactive date provision that precedes the current policy's inception date. In this provision, only prior acts that occurred after the retroactive date would be covered. This measure of "no known or reasonably expected claims" eliminates the insured's need to repeat a listing of potential claims (included in the original application) when the policy renews. It also limits the insured's retained loss exposure to events occurring before the inception of the first policy issued by the insurer. When the insured changes insurers, claims arising from the potential claims listed in the application are excluded in the new policy.

Reporting of Known Wrongful Acts

Many D&O policies contain a discovery provision for wrongful acts that occur after the policy period. Under this provision, if the insured becomes aware of a wrongful act that is reasonably expected to result in a covered claim and provides written information on the act to the insurer during the policy period, then any subsequent claim arising out of that wrongful act will be covered. This provision is independent of any tail coverage. If the insured changes insurers, a report to the former insurer of events that may result in a claim may enable the insured to obtain coverage under the previous policy for a claim that would be excluded by the replacement policy.

Persons and Organizations Insured

The insureds under Coverage A are the individual directors and officers, generally defined to include any persons who were, now are, or shall become duly elected or appointed directors or officers of the insured corporation. In the event of the death, incapacity, or bankruptcy of an insured, coverage is usually provided for any claim against his or her estate, heirs, legal representatives, or assigns.

The entities insured for Coverage B are the insured corporation or corporations named in the declarations. Depending on the policy, coverage may be automatically extended to unnamed subsidiaries of the named insured.

D&O policies often provide automatic coverage for new entities resulting from mergers or acquisitions by the insured corporation. However, if the change involves an increase in assets above a certain percentage, sometimes as little as 10 percent, the named insured may be required to notify the insurer and pay an additional premium.

If an insured corporation is acquired by another organization, the named insured should check its policy to determine whether coverage is provided for new entities and whether the insurer must be notified in order to extend coverage to the new entities. Coverage can generally be continued until policy expiration, but only for wrongful acts taking place before the acquisition occurred.

Although the D&O policy does not cover any actual or alleged wrongful act of a director's or an officer's spouse or domestic partner, when collecting judgments against directors and officers, claimants often seek to attach the directors' and officers' marital assets. Consequently, many policies provide "spousal" or "marital" coverage for claims against the spouse of any director or officer arising solely out of that person's capacity as the spouse of an insured person.

Exclusions

Exclusions can vary considerably by policy. Typical D&O exclusions fall into these categories:

- Loss exposures better covered by other insurance
- Claims covered or reported under prior policies
- Failure to effect or maintain insurance
- Insured-versus-insured exclusion
- Loss exposures that are difficult to insure

Loss exposures that are better covered by other insurance policies are often excluded in D&O policies. D&O policies commonly exclude these types of claims: bodily injury, property damage, personal injury, advertising injury, and fiduciary liability under the Employee Retirement Income Security Act (ERISA) and similar laws; mental anguish and emotional distress, particularly when not associated with bodily injury; injury associated with employment practices (although some D&O policies designed for small firms, not-for-profits, and public entities cover employment practices liability); and pollution. D&O policies often exclude claims covered or reported under prior policies to avoid arguments as to whether a related claim can be covered under the current policy.

Some D&O policies exclude coverage for liability resulting from the failure to obtain or maintain adequate insurance for the corporation. For example, the directors might negligently decide that the corporation should retain its products liability losses. Subsequently, unexpected products liability losses cause the corporation to experience severe financial problems. For example, a D&O policy with this exclusion would not protect the directors against a stockholder suit alleging that they negligently failed to authorize the purchase of products liability insurance. Insurers often delete this exclusion after examining the corporation's insurance program.

D&O policies typically exclude insured-versus-insured claims, such as one director's suit against another director, or a director's suit against the insured firm. This exclusion is often subject to exceptions that allow coverage for claims such as these:

- A derivative action brought on behalf of the insured corporation by one or more persons who are not insured directors or officers
- A claim brought by an insured director or officer for wrongful termination of the director or officer
- An action in which an insured director or officer seeks indemnity or contribution from another director or officer for a claim covered under the policy
- Actions against directors or officers made by bankruptcy trustees in the event of the firm's insolvency—knowledgeable insurance practitioners allow this exception

D&O policies exclude coverage for wrongful acts that are difficult to insure, require special underwriting, or are uninsurable. For example, D&O policies exclude acts resulting in personal profit or advantage to which a director or an officer is not legally entitled, because this exposure would be difficult to insure and would require special underwriting.

Also excluded in D&O policies are fraudulent or dishonest acts that are uninsurable. These exclusions may apply only when acts are determined to be fraudulent or dishonest by judgment or other final adjudication that is adverse to the director or officer. This qualification of the exclusion resulted in insurers paying the defense costs of defendants in the corporate scandals of the 1990s. Until the cases were finally adjudicated, the exclusion did not apply. Many such cases are dismissed with no decision. Consequently, some insurers changed the wording of this exclusion to apply when the director has "in fact" acted fraudulently or dishonestly. Other insurers omitted the modifying language entirely to include all fraudulent or dishonest acts of directors or officers. See the exhibit "Notable Securities Acts Affected by D&O Insurance."

Notable Securities Acts Affected by D&O Insurance

The Securities Act of 1933—Often called the "truth in securities" law, it requires that investors receive financial and other significant information concerning securities being offered for public sale, and it prohibits deceit, misrepresentation, and other fraud in the sale of securities.

The Securities Exchange Act of 1934—created the Securities and Exchange Commission (SEC). The act gives the SEC broad regulatory authority over all aspects of the securities industry. It identifies and prohibits certain types of conduct in the markets and provides the SEC with disciplinary powers over regulated entities and persons associated with them. The SEC requires periodic reporting of information by publicly traded corporations. The Sarbanes-Oxley Act is an amendment to the 1934 act.

[DA06738]

D&O policies often exclude violations of securities acts because they are difficult to insure and require special underwriting. The D&O policies covering large public corporations often omit exclusions relating to securities laws because a policy with these exclusions would not provide coverage for most class-action securities law claims. However, coverage for profits on sales of the corporation's stock that directors or officers held for less than six months is almost always excluded. These types of stock transactions, called "short-swing" sales, are outlawed by the Securities Exchange Act of 1934. Defense coverage is usually provided if the charges are successfully defended.

Other D&O Policy Provisions

Many of the other provisions commonly found in D&O policies are similar to those in most other liability policies. However, there can be some important differences in provisions including those that address duty to defend, allocation of loss, consent to settle claims, severability of interests, deductibles and coinsurance, insured's duties to report claims, and arbitration.

Duty to Defend

Large corporations often prefer the right to control their own defense in D&O actions. Under a D&O policy, the insured typically selects and pays the defense lawyers and pays the other defense expenses. The insurer's consent to incur expenses and settle claims is usually required if the insured wishes to be reimbursed by the insurer for defense expenses for covered claims. A few policies give the insurer the option to assume the defense. Conversely, some policies that initially give the insurer the duty to defend permit the insured to take over the defense.

When the insured is responsible for defense, some policies do not address the issue of when the insured will be reimbursed. An insurer could contend that no payment is due to the insured until the claim has been finally settled. However, D&O cases can require years to resolve and can involve substantial defense expenses. Consequently, most policies require the insurer to make payments for defense expenses as they are incurred, to the extent that the expenses are covered under the policy. This provision complicates the allocation of loss expenses between covered and noncovered elements of the loss.

Allocation of Loss

In many suits against directors and officers, the plaintiff's allegations include acts not covered by the D&O policy, especially when the policy does not include entity coverage. Lawsuits on issues involving securities almost always include directors, officers, and the corporation as defendants, but even when entity coverage is included, suits frequently involve charges that the policy may not cover. Loss expenses must be allocated between covered and noncovered elements of the loss.

Courts have consistently held that the insurer must defend the entire claim as long as any part of it potentially falls within the policy's coverage because an insurer's duty to defend is broader than its duty to indemnify, when a policy contains duty-to-defend wording.

Because most D&O claims are settled before trial, insurers face difficulties recovering the defense costs that pertain to elements of the claim that were not covered under a duty-to-defend policy. Insurers are in a better position to assert that not all defense costs are covered by the policy when defense is controlled by the insured.

To prevent disputes over whether the insurer was entitled to reimbursement from the insured for defense costs, provisions that detail the handling of defense costs are often included in D&O policies.

Consent to Settle Claims

Because professional or business reputations might be at stake in claims against directors and officers, many D&O policies give the named insured the right to participate in the decision to settle a claim.

Some D&O policies contain an absolute consent-to-settle provision stating that the insurer cannot settle a claim without the insured's consent. In such a policy, if the insured does not consent to a proposed settlement that is acceptable to the claimant, the insurer, at its expense, must continue to defend the insured and pay any judgment that the court awards until the limit of its coverage has been exhausted. To avoid substantial defense expenses in these cases, some D&O policies provide that the insured must take over the defense and pay any further defense expenses, plus the part of any judgment or settlement that exceeds the amount for which the insurer could have settled the claim. This provision is sometimes informally called a "hammer clause" because the insured usually feels compelled or "hammered" to agree to the proposed settlement.

To lessen the harshness of the hammer clause, some policies provide that the insured and the insurer will share the additional defense and settlement costs that ensue when an insured refuses to consent to a settlement (a modified hammer clause). For example, the insurer's liability for such claim will not exceed the amount for which such claim could have been settled plus 70 percent of any amount in excess of the recommended settlement offer.

Severability of Interests

Some D&O insurers have either narrowed their severability of interests provisions or eliminated them entirely. D&O policies often provide that misrepresentations in the application will not defeat coverage for directors and officers who did not sign the application and were unaware of the true facts; hence, coverage is provided for innocent directors or officers. Furthermore, most D&O policies provide that certain excluded wrongful acts (such as fraud or willful violation of the law) will not be imputed to any other director or officer when determining whether the exclusion applies to directors and officers who did not participate in and did not have any knowledge of the wrongful act. For example, some insurers make severability inapplicable when the person signing the insurance application was aware of misstatements in the application. Other insurers impute the knowledge of a corporation's CEO and CFO to all insureds. Still other insurers provide some severability for Side A coverage, but not for Side B and entity coverage.

Deductibles and Coinsurance

D&O liability insurance is almost always subject to a deductible, also called a retention. D&O deductibles generally apply to both defense costs and judgments or settlements. The deductibles can vary substantially depending on the insured's size and risk management philosophy and the insurer's marketing and underwriting strategies.

D&O deductibles can be structured in different ways. In one policy, a deductible might apply only to Coverage B for corporate reimbursement claims. In another policy, separate deductibles, for different amounts, might apply to Coverage A and Coverage B. When separate deductibles apply, the deductible applicable to Coverage A (individual directors and officers) is often lower (sometimes significantly) than the deductible applicable to Coverage B.

The Coverage A deductible may apply separately to each individual against whom claim is made. When that is the case, an aggregate deductible typically applies as well. For example, a $10,000 deductible may apply to each director or officer involved in a loss, up to an aggregate deductible of $50,000 for the total loss, regardless of how many directors or officers might be involved.

Substantial deductibles often apply to Coverage B, with a small or no deductible applicable to Coverage A. To circumvent insured corporations from avoiding application of the Coverage B deductible by electing not to indemnify directors as allowed by the applicable law, D&O policies typically provide that the coverage will apply based on the presumption that the corporation has indemnified the directors to the fullest extent permitted by law unless financial impairment, such as bankruptcy, prevents the company from indemnifying them.

In addition to deductibles, a once-popular D&O coinsurance provision is included in some D&O policies. This provision resembles a percentage deductible rather than the coinsurance provision found in property insurance policies. Under a D&O coinsurance provision, the insured is responsible for paying a certain percentage of the loss. For example, if the policy contains a 95 percent coinsurance provision, the insured retains 5 percent of the loss above the deductible.

Insured's Duties to Report Claims

Most D&O policies require written notice of a claim either immediately, as soon as practicable, or as soon as possible. In practice, there is usually little difference in the insured's duty under these three different wordings. Courts generally interpret the requirement for immediate notice to mean as soon as practicable under the circumstances. However, some D&O policies include a requirement that the claim be reported within a specified number of days (such as thirty) after receipt of claim or within a specified number of days after policy expiration.

Arbitration

Recent D&O policy conditions include a binding arbitration provision for disputes between the insured and the insurer. Arbitration is less time-consuming and less expensive than judicial proceedings, and arbitrators can be chosen from a panel of individuals who have specialized expertise in a particular field.

SPECIALTY DIRECTORS AND OFFICERS (D&O) COVERAGES

Numerous specialty D&O coverages are available. Some are occupation-specific policies such as those written for school boards, municipalities, and not-for-profit organizations. Others provide coverage to meet specific needs, such as coverage for outside directors or separate coverage for directors and officers.

Occupation-Specific D&O Policies

A number of insurers have created specialty policies for specific fields, such as school boards, municipalities, and not-for-profit organizations. These policies often have names that do not clearly indicate that they provide D&O coverage. For example, policies for school boards are sometimes titled Educators' Legal Liability, Educators' Professional Liability, or School Board Legal Liability. Policies for municipalities are often titled Public Officials' Legal Liability or Public Officials' Errors and Omissions Liability. Policies for not-for-profit organizations might be titled Not-for-Profit D&O Liability or Nonprofit Management Liability.

These policies are more likely to include employment practices liability coverage and sometimes include certain professional liability coverages. They also often include coverages that are peculiar to the particular occupation. For example, some school board policies include coverage for special education due process hearings. Similarly, policies for municipalities may include coverage for defense costs to defend against actions seeking injunctions.

Outside Directors Liability Policies

D&O policies do not automatically cover liability arising out of the insured directors' or officers' services as directors of organizations that are not affiliated with the insured corporation. Coverage is limited to acts or omission as directors or officers of the insured corporation specified in the policy. Some D&O policies use a policy exclusion to accomplish the same effect.

Sometimes a corporation encourages or requests its directors or officers to serve as outside directors for an unaffiliated organization. For example, the corporation may encourage directors and officers to serve on the board of a local not-for-profit organization to demonstrate good corporate citizenship. In such cases, the corporation may want to provide D&O coverage for its directors while serving the unaffiliated organization, which may either have no D&O coverage or have D&O coverage with limits or policy terms that the outside director deems to be inadequate.

There are two approaches to covering outside directors. One approach is to cover outside directors in the insured corporation's D&O policy. Although a typical D&O policy does not cover the insured corporation's own directors or officers while serving as outside directors for other organizations, such outside directorships can be covered by adding a coverage extension or endorsement to the policy. The other approach is to obtain a separate policy, called an **outside directors liability policy**. The advantage of this approach is that claims payable under the separate policy will not reduce the aggregate limit of liability under the insured corporation's regular D&O policy.

To be covered, the director's service to the outside organization must be with the knowledge and/or direction of the corporation. Moreover, the outside directors' coverage is almost always excess to any D&O coverage available to the outside entity or any indemnification available from the outside entity itself.

Outside directors liability policy
A policy covering the liability of a corporation's directors while they serve as outside directors for another corporation.

Separate Coverage for Directors and Officers

For any of these reasons, directors and officers may find themselves without D&O coverage that they thought they had:

- The cost of defending the claim has depleted policy limits.
- The policy aggregate limits are used up in defending and paying other claims.
- A court freezes the corporation's D&O policy as part of bankruptcy proceedings.
- An insurer rescinds a policy because of material misstatements.

Another concern for directors and officers is the insured-versus-insured exclusion. The exclusion is intended to eliminate coverage for possibly collusive losses. The insured-versus-insured exclusion can pose a problem for directors and officers when bankruptcy trustees sue the directors and officers for mismanaging the bankrupt company.

Some courts have held that the trustees stand in the place of the company and that therefore the directors and officers are not covered for the claim by virtue of the insured-versus-insured exclusion. Other courts have reasoned that the trustee was pursuing a claim on behalf of the stockholders and therefore the D&O policy did provide coverage. No director wants to be forced to sue to establish coverage.

Side A-Only Coverage

To provide an added level of protection for directors and officers, several insurers offer separate coverage for directors and officers. These coverages include Side A-only coverage and coverage for independent directors.

As its name implies, **Side A-only coverage** provides only Coverage A. Side A-only coverage is not a substitute for normal D&O coverage, because it does not include any reimbursement coverage for the corporation when the corporation indemnifies the directors or officers, nor does it include any entity

Side A-only coverage
Directors and officers liability insurance that covers only the individual liability of the insured directors and officers.

coverage. Coverage in a Side A-only policy can be provided for all directors and officers or only for the specific directors and officers named in the policy.

Although some insurers offer Side A-only coverage on a primary basis, the coverage often applies as excess over any other insurance and any indemnification payments by the corporation, whether insured or not. Some Side A-only policies are pure excess and do not "drop down" to take the place of the underlying coverage if it is rescinded. Other Side A-only policies provide for drop down and even include coverage for loss exposures not included in the corporation's D&O policy, such as libel and slander and some pollution claims.

With a properly worded drop-down provision, the Side A-only policy can respond if the corporation's D&O policy becomes frozen by a bankruptcy court. In contrast, a Side A-only policy written on a pure excess basis might not respond in this situation, because the underlying insurance has not been exhausted. Side A-only policies are advantageous to directors in bankruptcy coverage disputes because the corporation is not an insured, and so the policy is not regarded as a corporate asset that can be frozen by the bankruptcy court.

Enhanced Side-A Only DIC

Some insurers have introduced policies called "Enhanced Side A-Only," "Side A-only DIC," or just "DIC" policies. (The acronym "DIC" is borrowed from property insurance terminology and stands for "difference in conditions.") In addition to providing excess coverage, these policies have broader wording or fewer exclusions than some Side A-only policies, such as in these examples:

- No Employee Retirement Income Security Act (ERISA) exclusion
- No previous litigation exclusion
- No pollution exclusion
- No exclusion for some violations of the Securities Exchange Act of 1934
- A more limited insured-versus-insured exclusion
- A more limited exclusion of bodily injury and property damage claims
- A broader definition of what constitutes a claim

Most of these policies provide that coverage will be as broad as the underlying policy and will apply if the underlying carrier wrongfully refuses to indemnify or is financially unable to perform. As might be expected, not every policy provides all these advantages.[4]

Independent Directors

Independent directors are those that are not otherwise affiliated with the corporation they serve. That is, they are not corporate officers, nor do they have a preexisting business relationship with the corporation (such as being its accountant). In some cases, independent directors may insist on having their own D&O coverage with insurance limits that will not be diluted by claims against other directors or the corporation. The corporation can fulfill this type of request by obtaining an additional D&O policy, called an **independent directors liability policy**, that insures only the independent director(s) named in the policy.

Independent directors liability policy

A D&O liability policy that insures only the independent director(s) named in the policy.

The coverage under an independent directors liability policy is triggered when the corporation does not indemnify the named director for a loss or the corporation's D&O policy is inadequate, invalid, or nonexistent. Some insurers include a provision making these policies nonrescindable except in the event of nonpayment of premiums.

Nonrescindable means that the insurer waives, in advance, its rights to seek rescission, except that such policies may still exclude coverage for a claim if the underlying policy is rescinded as a result of an act, error, or omission by the person insured in the independent directors policy. Nonrescindable coverage will drop down and become primary in the event that the primary coverage is rescinded.

An independent directors liability policy can be written for a specified independent director for any one or a combination of all the boards of directors that the director serves on. Alternatively, the policy can be written to cover all of the independent directors of a particular company solely for board activities for that company. Premiums for independent directors liability policies may be paid by the company, the director may be reimbursed by the company, or the director may personally incur the expense.

EMPLOYMENT PRACTICES LIABILITY LOSS EXPOSURES

Legislation has greatly expanded the basis for employment-related discrimination claims.

Employers face employment practices liability (EPL) loss exposures under a variety of federal and state laws. The first significant law in this area was the Civil Rights Act of 1964, which prohibits discrimination by employers. The act was amended in 1991 to include additional recoveries and to allow jury trial in discrimination cases.

Many states and even some local governments have employment-related laws that are broader than the federal laws. Although these laws can create EPL loss exposures, not all violations of them are covered by EPL insurance. In fact, EPL policies specifically exclude violations of some of these laws. Nevertheless, risk managers must be alert to the loss exposures created by these laws and develop strategies for handling both insurable and uninsurable loss exposures. See the exhibit "Laws Affecting Employment Practices Liability (EPL) Loss Exposures."

Laws Affecting Employment Practices Liability (EPL) Loss Exposures

Name of Statute	What the Statute Does
Title VII of the Civil Rights Act of 1964	Prohibits discrimination by employers based on color, race, religion, sex, or national origin. In 1978, the law was amended to bar discrimination on the basis of pregnancy, childbirth, or related medical conditions. The law applies to all employers with fifteen or more employees.
Civil Rights Act of 1991	Amends Title VII of the Civil Rights Act of 1964. Depending on the size of the employer, the law authorizes damage awards up to $300,000 in lawsuits for intentional gender discrimination and racial discrimination in employment and allows a claimant the right to demand a jury trial.
Age Discrimination in Employment Act (ADEA)	Prohibits discrimination against individuals age forty or older based solely on their age. ADEA applies to employers with twenty or more employees. Amended in 1990 by the Older Workers Benefit Protection Act (OWBPA), which prohibits employers from denying benefits to older employees.
Americans with Disabilities Act (ADA)	Prohibits discrimination against disabled persons and requires an employer to make reasonable accommodations in the workplace for disabled employees. This law currently applies to employers with fifteen or more employees.
Family and Medical Leave Act (FMLA)	Requires that all employers with fifty or more employees provide up to twelve weeks of unpaid leave in any twelve-month period to care for a newborn, adopted, or fostered child or to care for themselves or a child, spouse, or parent with a serious illness. Amended in 1998 by the National Defense Authorization Act to provide new military family leave entitlements.
Fair Labor Standards Act (FLSA)	Establishes minimum wage and overtime rates and regulates the employment of children. This law applies to employers with at least two employees engaged in interstate commerce and a business volume of over $500,000 per year.
Worker Adjustment and Retraining Notification Act (WARN)	Requires employers to provide notice sixty days in advance of covered plant closings and mass layoffs.
Consolidated Omnibus Budget Reconciliation Act (COBRA)	Gives workers and their families who lose their health benefits the right to choose to continue group health benefits provided by their group health plan for limited periods of time under certain circumstances.
Employee Retirement Income Security Act (ERISA)	Sets minimum standards for most voluntarily established pension and benefit plans.

[DA04876]

These are the major types of EPL claims:

- Discrimination claims
- Wrongful termination claims
- Sexual harassment claims
- Retaliation claims
- Other types of EPL claims

These classifications are not mutually exclusive. An employee may allege that a particular situation involves more than one employment-related offense.

Discrimination Claims

Discrimination does not have to be intentional to be unlawful. Many firms that do not consciously discriminate against individuals based on race, sex, religion, or other grounds nevertheless run afoul of the antidiscrimination rules developed to implement federal and local laws. Problems may arise because of the differences between overt discrimination, disparate treatment, and disparate impact:[5]

- Overt discrimination (also called intentional discrimination) is a specific, observable action that discriminates against a person or class of persons. An example of overt discrimination is refusal to interview job applicants of a certain race.

- Disparate treatment (also called unequal or differential treatment) is unfavorable or unfair treatment of someone in comparison to how similar individuals are treated. Disparate treatment occurs, for example, if female employees are regularly reprimanded for returning late from lunch but male employees who also return late are not.

- Disparate impact (also called discrimination by effect or adverse impact) is the application of personnel policies to all applicants or employees that have the effect of denying employment or advancement to members of protected classes. For example, requiring that all employees be more than five feet, ten inches tall will have a disparate impact because many more men than women exceed that height. Such a requirement eliminates more women than men from the pool of eligible employees. Unless the requirement is necessary for performance of the job, it is a violation of the law.

Wrongful Termination Claims

Wrongful termination of employment accounts for the majority of cases of alleged wrongful employment practices. Wrongful termination includes "constructive discharge." Constructive discharge means employees who resign because of unendurable conditions can, if allegations are proved, be treated as if their employment had been terminated by the employer. See the exhibit "Equal Employment Opportunity Commission."

Equal Employment Opportunity Commission

The Equal Employment Opportunity Commission (EEOC) is an independent commission that plays an important role in workplace discrimination claims.

The EEOC was created by the Civil Rights Act of 1964. Originally its function was to define acts of employment discrimination and to attempt to mitigate their effects by education and conciliation. In 1972, Congress gave the EEOC authority to sue nongovernmental employers, unions, and employment agencies. The EEOC could file suits based on pattern or practice, and Title VII coverage was expanded to include the federal government and state and local governments, as well as educational institutions.

Persons who believe that their employment rights have been violated may file charges of discrimination with the EEOC. In addition, an individual, organization, or agency may file a charge on behalf of another person to protect the aggrieved person's identity. If the charge also involves a state or local law, the EEOC "dual files" with the state or local agency, and vice versa.

The EEOC notifies the employer when a charge of discrimination has been filed against it with the EEOC. The EEOC can investigate and determine whether reasonable cause exists to believe discrimination occurred. The employer may opt to resolve a charge through mediation or settlement. The EEOC can ask for copies of personnel policies, the complainant's personnel files, the personnel files of other individuals, and other relevant information. An EEOC investigator is allowed to conduct interviews of nonmanagement-level employees without the employer's presence or permission.

The charge may be dismissed by the EEOC if it believes no basis exists for proceeding with further investigation. Employees do not have to submit a complaint to the EEOC to sue their employers, and dismissal of a complaint by the EEOC is not a bar to a suit by the employee.

[DA04877]

Many wrongful termination claims involve charges of discrimination, but it is possible to bring them for reasons other than discrimination. Traditionally, the legal doctrine of "employment at will" has allowed employers or employees to terminate the private employment relationship with or without cause at any time.

Several states base an exception to employment at will on the theory of implied contract. Under this theory, an employer's oral or written representations to employees regarding job security or disciplinary procedures are held to create a contract of employment even though no written contract exists.

When this doctrine was first established, many courts held that statements in employee handbooks could create an implied contract, absent any clear and express statements reinforcing employment-at-will status.[6] In a typical case, an employee cited an employee handbook provision stating the employees would be discharged only for "just cause." The court found that such wording created an implied contract that the employee would not be arbitrarily fired.[7]

Most employers have modified the wording in their employee handbooks to avoid these types of claims.

Courts in a minority of states hold that employment at will is subject to a covenant of good faith. Under this doctrine, just cause for discharge is required even when the employer has made no specific promise to limit discharges to just-cause circumstances. Terminations made in bad faith or motivated by malice are also prohibited.[8]

Sexual Harassment Claims

The basis for sexual harassment EPL claims developed mainly in the last decades of the twentieth century. In 1980, the Equal Employment Opportunity Commission (EEOC) issued its "Guidelines on Discrimination Because of Sex," which defines sexual harassment as "unwelcome sexual advances…when submission to such conduct is made either explicitly or implicitly a term or condition of an individual's employment."

Some sexual harassment claims are based on the allegation that the employer created a hostile work environment. A hostile work environment exists when an employee is subjected to sexual harassment that is so severe or pervasive that it alters the conditions of his or her employment and creates an abusive working environment.

To prevail in a claim of hostile work environment, an employee generally must prove all of these facts:

* The employee is a member of a protected class.
* The employee was subjected to unwelcome harassment based on the protected characteristic.
* The harassment affected a term or condition of employment.
* The employer knew or should have known about the harassment and failed to take prompt remedial action.

Claims of hostile work environment initially were recognized in the context of sex discrimination, but they have since been recognized in other contexts, such as discrimination because of race or disability. Isolated incidents are insufficient to establish a hostile work environment. In determining whether a workplace is a hostile work environment, courts consider such relevant factors as the frequency of the discriminatory conduct, its severity, and whether it unreasonably interferes with the employee's work performance. See the exhibit "Controlling Employment Practices Liability (EPL) Loss Exposures."

Retaliation Claims

EPL claims can arise from an employer's alleged retaliation for an employee's legitimate act. The number of retaliation claims filed each year with the EEOC has steadily increased since the mid-1990s. In the first decade of the

Controlling Employment Practices Liability (EPL) Loss Exposures

Organizations can take actions such as these to reduce the frequency and severity of potential EPL claims:

- Establish hiring practices that comply with standards set forth by federal, state, and local regulations and laws.

- Word employee handbooks clearly and concisely to document the company's policies and procedures, including employment-at-will status.

- Provide all employees with a formal policy regarding sexual harassment and discrimination, and document their receipt. Review the policy and update it as needed.

- Permanently post and distribute all EEOC documents, as well as state and local compliance documents.

- Conduct employee performance reviews at least annually, and initiate interim reviews to correct unacceptable behavior.

- Follow a carefully documented termination procedure, and exercise special care when handling terminations.

- Conduct exit interviews and carefully document them.

- Promptly investigate all allegations of harassment or discrimination.

Joseph G. Jarret, "Reducing Employment Practices Liability," Risk Management, September 2003, p. 20. [DA06675]

twenty-first century, the most common grounds for discrimination claims were retaliation and racial discrimination, followed by gender discrimination.[9]

Retaliation claims may be combined with claims of discrimination based on race, gender, age, or another protected classification. Retaliation claims are also brought by employees who, for example, allege that they were discharged because they filed a workers compensation claim; testified against the employer in a legislative or court hearing; or were "whistleblowers," who are protected by many federal and state laws.

Other Types of EPL Claims

In recent years, employees have made EPL claims that do not fall within the context of discrimination, wrongful termination, sexual harassment, or retaliation.

For example, costly litigation has ensued after firms have closed plants or otherwise discharged large numbers of employees at one time. In 1988, Congress enacted the Worker Adjustment and Retraining Notification Act (WARN) to mitigate some of the effects of mass layoffs.

Another example is class action lawsuits on behalf of employees who allege that they did not receive overtime compensation. Such claims have resulted in substantial awards. The majority of the claims involve improperly categorizing employees as "exempt" rather than "nonexempt." An exempt employee, such as a supervisory or management-level employee, is not entitled to overtime wages, whereas an employer must pay overtime wages to nonexempt employees.

Employee claims have also arisen from objectionable e-mail or Web site material sent by other employees.

 Reality Check

Discrimination Cases Related to Overtime Pay

In recent years, numerous class action lawsuits have been filed by pharmaceutical company sales representatives demanding overtime pay. The plaintiffs allege that they are misclassified as sales personnel when they do not actually make sales. Under the Federal Fair Labor Standards Act, sales personnel are classified as exempt employees—that is, salaried employees who are not entitled to overtime pay. The plaintiffs allege the nature of their work entitles them to overtime pay.

In a 2010 case,* an appeals court found for the plaintiffs. The court said the representatives do not sell drugs to physicians but provide them with information about the benefits of particular drugs and encourage them to prescribe those products. The court concluded, "[W]here the employee promotes a pharmaceutical product to a physician but can transfer to the physician nothing more than free samples and cannot lawfully transfer ownership of any quantity of the drug in exchange of anything of value, cannot lawfully take an order for its purchase, and cannot lawfully even obtain from the physician a binding commitment to prescribe it, we conclude that…the employee has not in any sense, within the meaning of the statute or the regulations, made a sale."

---

* In re Novartis Wage and Hour Litigation, 611 F.3d 141 (2010). [DA06676]

EMPLOYMENT PRACTICES LIABILITY INSURANCE

When employment practices liability (EPL) claims first started to surface, few insureds had specific EPL policies. Insurers asserted that EPL claims were excluded by the employers liability exclusion in the commercial general liability (CGL) policy or by the fact that the claims did not allege bodily injury. Courts generally accepted those arguments, but insurers were unsuccessful in some cases.

Coverage for **employment practices liability (EPL) insurance** includes indemnity and defense costs. Both Insurance Services Office (ISO) and American Association of Insurance Services (AAIS) offer EPL forms to their

Employment practices liability (EPL) insurance

Insurance that covers an organization, its directors and officers, and its employees against claims alleging damages because of wrongful employment practices such as sexual harassment, wrongful termination, and unlawful discrimination.

member companies. Despite the availability of ISO and AAIS forms, most EPL policies are written on independently developed forms with crucial differences in wording.

EPL policies resemble directors and officers liability (D&O) policies. In fact, EPL coverage is often included in D&O policies for small businesses, not-for-profit organizations, and governmental entities. Because companies both small and large can have EPL exposures, coverage can be written as a separate policy, included in a D&O liability policy, or added to a businessowners policy (BOP) as an endorsement.

EPL policies barely existed more than twenty years ago and as they developed in the area of management liability insurance, some of their policy provisions were modeled on those found in D&O policies. Other policy provisions, because of EPL loss exposures, differ in these specific areas:

- Insuring agreement
- Exclusions
- Persons and organizations insured
- D&O/EPL combination policies
- Added coverages and services

Background

The outcome of court cases involving employment liability has prompted the evolution of EPL coverage provisions, along with the development of EPL policies. In one case, the court ruled that sexual harassment by a co-employee did not arise out of and in the course of employment, and was therefore not excluded by the CGL.[10] In another case, the court held that the insurer had a duty to defend even if it had no ultimate duty to indemnify.[11] That was a worrisome result for insurers because EPL cases are expensive to defend. In the previously noted case n which the co-employee's behavior was not excluded by the CGL policy, the final award was $4,000, but the cost to defend was over $100,000.

ISO responded by developing a specific endorsement eliminating employment-related practices coverage to clarify that the CGL policy would not cover EPL claims. Although the endorsement is optional, many insurers attach it to every CGL policy they write.

Disputes arose about coverage under workers compensation policies, prompting the National Council on Compensation Insurance, Inc. (NCCI) to expand the wording of the employment practices exclusion in the Employers Liability section of the standard Workers Compensation and Employers Liability Insurance Policy. Insurance and risk management professionals now recognize that most insureds need specific EPL insurance, either as a separate policy or as part of a D&O liability policy, to obtain coverage for these loss exposures.

Insuring Agreement

EPL policies typically agree to pay, on behalf of the insured, loss resulting from claims first made during the policy period for a wrongful act—wording very similar to the insuring agreement of a D&O policy. The definitions of the terms "loss" and "claim" include the same variations as they do in D&O policies. However, the EPL policy definition of wrongful act differs from the D&O policy definition, and the wording varies by insurer. Some insurers use the term "wrongful employment practice or injury" instead of wrongful act, but the definitions are similar.

EPL policies define wrongful act either broadly, in general terms—a "broad form" approach, or by listing specific types of acts—a "named perils" approach. The definition of employee also determines coverage in EPL policies.

Broad Form Definition of Wrongful Acts

The broad form approach to defining wrongful acts covers employment-related claims with either a general description and no specific listing of offenses or with some examples of offenses followed by "or similar acts" or like wording.

When the terms are not defined, the coverage for these offenses is defined in the laws of the jurisdiction governing the claim. To ensure that their coverage is as broad as most named perils EPL policies, broad form EPL policies usually include a list of other offenses that are covered, such as wrongful treatment of an employee, retaliation, invasion of privacy, and other torts related to the employment relationship.

Named Perils Definition of Wrongful Acts

When the named perils approach to defining wrongful acts is used, the definition can range from brief listings of a few offenses to exhaustive lists that appear to provide coverage equal to the broad forms. Some EPL policies define numerous wrongful act offenses, while other EPL policies define only a few offenses, such as discrimination, wrongful termination, and sexual harassment. Limited language in EPL policies can result in disputes over invasion of privacy, retaliation, coercion, and other offenses as covered wrongful acts. Therefore, insureds, risk managers, and producers should carefully examine the provisions that each insurer offers and determine whether the provisions meet the particular employer's needs.

These offenses are among many that may be included in the definition of wrongful act:

- Wrongful refusal to employ
- Wrongful termination, whether active or constructive
- Wrongful demotion, reassignment, discipline, or failure to promote
- Wrongful negative evaluation

- Breach of employment contract
- Employment-related retaliatory action
- Workplace harassment; unwelcome sexual advances; or other verbal, visual, or physical conduct of a sexual nature
- Employment-related libel, slander, invasion of privacy, defamation, or humiliation
- Employment discrimination of any kind in violation of federal, state, or local law

Definition of Employee

The definition of employee determines EPL coverage because coverage is linked to employment status. Definitions of employee vary. They can include any natural person who was, now is, or will become a full-time, part-time, seasonal, or temporary employee of the insured. Some policies include leased employees in the definition of employee—a crucial detail for employers that lease all or part of their staff from an employee leasing firm.

EPL policies treat independent contractors in different ways. An EPL policy that does not specifically mention independent contractors would likely provide no coverage for claims made by independent contractors. Some EPL policies specifically exclude claims made by independent contractors. A few EPL policies specifically cover independent contractors' claims by including individual independent contractors or employees of contracting firms in the definition of employee or through an endorsement.

Many firms hire individuals who are classified as independent contractors but who work steadily for the insured and are exposed to many of the same situations that may lead to EPL claims, just as if they were employees. For example, an independent contractor working in an office as a computer programmer might be sexually harassed by one of the insured's regular employees. These firms need EPL coverage; hence, any policy language regarding independent contractors or the lack of such language deserves careful attention.

Exclusions

Exclusions also vary among different insurers' EPL policies. EPL policy exclusions might eliminate coverage for any of these:

- Claims arising out of circumstances reported under a prior EPL policy.
- Deliberate fraud or intentional violation of statutes, rules, or regulations. However, in many EPL policies, this exclusion applies only to the insured actually found responsible for the act through appropriate legal process, as in D&O policies.
- Liability assumed under a contract or an agreement, other than an employment contract, but coverage is provided to the extent that the insured would have been liable without such contract or agreement.

- Bodily injury or property damage other than emotional distress, mental anguish, or humiliation.

- Actual or alleged violation of the Employee Retirement Income Security Act (ERISA), Fair Labor Standards Act (FLSA) (except the Equal Pay Act), the National Labor Relations Act, Worker Adjustment and Retraining Notification Act (WARN), Consolidated Omnibus Budget Reconciliation Act (COBRA), and the Occupational Safety and Health Act (OSHA).

- Obligations under workers compensation, disability benefits, unemployment compensation, social security, and similar laws.

- Costs incurred to provide accommodations required by the Americans with Disabilities Act (ADA) or any similar federal, state, or local statute.

Some EPL policies exclude claim awards that include back pay or cover back pay awards for certain types of claims, such as discrimination. Back pay is income that the employee lost before a judgment was awarded or a settlement was made. Other EPL policies specifically cover claim awards of back pay and front pay. Front pay is income a plaintiff would have earned between the time of judgment and reinstatement or (if the employee is not reinstated) an award to compensate the employee for lost future income.

Typically, both front pay and back pay are claimed in wrongful termination actions, in actions for failure to accommodate in accordance with ADA, and in actions based on other offenses. For example, an injured police officer who alleged that his department failed to reassign him to work that he was capable of performing was awarded back pay, with interest, totaling almost $150,000 and front pay of $76,000.[12]

Some policies do not address back pay or front pay because they are typically included in payable damages whether they are specifically mentioned or not, unless the policy excludes such payments.

Persons and Organizations Insured

Unlike many D&O policies, stand-alone EPL policies always include the named employer as an insured. This is a potential gap when EPL coverage is included in a D&O policy that does not otherwise provide entity coverage. Such a D&O/EPL combination policy should be amended to include the employer as an insured with respect to EPL claims. Typically, past and present directors, officers, partners, members of a limited liability company, and so forth are all included as insureds in the definition of who is insured.

Employees and former employees are frequently included as insureds, although some policies do not provide coverage for former employees, particularly when EPL coverage is made a part of a D&O policy. Coverage is frequently expanded in policies for not-for-profit organizations and governmental entities to include committee members and volunteers.

EPL policies generally cover newly formed or acquired organizations under certain circumstances. Such coverage may be limited in time, such as ninety days from the date of formation or acquisition. The coverage may be limited for the newly formed or acquired organizations such as covering employees below a specified number (for example, the number of additional employees may not exceed 25 percent of the number of current employees).

D&O/EPL Combination Policies

If a D&O policy has no specific exclusion of employment practices, the policy will provide some coverage for EPL claims. However, even without a specific EPL exclusion, D&O policies do not cover claims against persons who are not directors or officers, and they do not cover the corporation unless the policy includes entity coverage. In addition, standard exclusions in a D&O policy may eliminate coverage for claims that can be covered by an EPL policy, such as claims by one insured against another or claims alleging breach of contract, libel, or slander. However, some insurers specifically include EPL coverage provisions in their D&O policies.

Small, closely held companies, not-for-profit organizations, and public entities can often obtain policies that combine EPL coverage with a D&O policy. The two principal advantages to these combination policies are lower cost and avoidance of conflicts about which policy applies to a particular claim. As an alternative solution, an insured can purchase separate EPL and D&O policies from the same insurer.

The disadvantages of D&O/EPL combination policies, however, can outweigh their advantages. EPL coverage in D&O policies is sometimes not as broad as that found in stand-alone EPL policies. Even when the coverage is as broad, only one set of limits may be provided for both coverages. Consequently, EPL claims can reduce or exhaust the aggregate limit applicable to D&O claims, and vice versa.

Some insurers provide separate aggregate limits for each coverage or provide an option to purchase reinstated aggregate limits if the original limits are exhausted. In addition, in the event of bankruptcy, the court may freeze the policy, leaving defendants in EPL cases without coverage. An insured must evaluate the options and compare the costs and coverages provided.

Added Coverages and Services

Some EPL insurers offer additional coverages and services. Additional coverages include third-party discrimination coverage, workplace violence coverage, and coverage for reputation management costs. The most commonly added service is assistance in controlling EPL loss exposures.

Third-Party Discrimination Coverage

In 1993, six black Secret Service agents ordered food at a Maryland Denny's. Compared with the service of food orders for their white colleagues, they waited so long for their service that they filed a class-action racial bias lawsuit for service denial, which settled for more than $54 million. Denny's worked closely with a civil rights group to restore its reputation.[13]

This case focused insureds and insurers on the loss exposure posed by discrimination claims made by third parties, as opposed to employees or applicants for employment. Policies that cover only third-party discrimination claims are available. Alternatively, some insurers endorse their EPL policies to cover third-party discrimination claims.

Customers, suppliers, independent contractors, or any other nonemployees who interact with the firm can all make third-party discrimination claims. The coverage generally applies to harassment or discrimination, and in most cases premiums increase by 10 to 15 percent, although the loss exposures facing some insureds may warrant much larger increases.

Workplace Violence Coverage

Based on preliminary counts for 2009, homicides are one of the third leading causes of death in the workplace (ranking equally with people falling to a lower level of a structure) and the second leading cause of death for women. Around 520 employees died in workplace violence incidents in 2009, and thousands more were injured.[14] Workers compensation insurance covers most of the direct costs, although some state courts hold that some workplace violence, such as a rejected lover entering the workplace and shooting an employee, does not arise out of and in the course of employment and is therefore not covered by workers compensation.[15] If the incident is not covered by the applicable workers compensation law, the employers liability section of the workers compensation policy might then apply, but in either case the indirect costs, such as lost productivity, increased security costs, and loss of reputation, are not covered.

To close some of these coverage gaps, a few insurers have introduced specialty workplace violence coverage either as a separate coverage or as an endorsement to an EPL policy. Such coverage can indemnify the insured for the costs of obtaining independent consulting services to help cope with the turmoil resulting from a workplace violence incident and public relations assistance to minimize the damage to the firm's reputation. It may also cover some of the resulting business income loss, and it often provides death and dismemberment benefits. The exact coverages provided differ among insurers and, in general, separate policies provide broader coverage than the EPL endorsements.

Reputation Management Costs

Workplace violence is not the only occurrence that can damage an organization's reputation. Being named as a defendant in an employment discrimination or harassment suit often results in headlines that are a public relations nightmare for management.

Some insurers offer separate policies or coverage as part of their EPL policies to minimize or repair damage to the insured's reputation resulting from such EPL claims. Such a policy could stipulate that coverage is triggered when a governmental agency commences proceedings or the insured is named in a class action or another lawsuit based on wrongful employment practices.

Once triggered, the coverage could apply to the expense to retain an approved public relations firm, crisis management firm, or law firm to counsel the insured on how to mitigate the damage to its reputation. Some insurers provide such coverage for mass layoffs resulting from plant closings, product discontinuance, and so forth.

EPL Risk Control Services

Some insurers offer comprehensive risk control services to their EPL insureds. These services are usually aimed at small to medium-sized firms. Larger firms generally have in-house risk control capabilities or can outsource their EPL risk control services.

The EPL risk control services that insurers offer include training programs that help insureds understand their human resources management responsibilities and show insureds how to create and maintain a workplace environment that will avoid employment practices violations.

These are other services available from insurers:

- Specimen employee handbooks
- Review of existing handbooks
- Telephone access to experienced attorneys or consultants to discuss a particular problem, such as a complaint from an employee
- Confidential EPL audits
- Consultants to help the insured prepare its response and to represent the insured at hearings before the Equal Employment Opportunity Commission (EEOC) or similar state or local agencies

Some of these services are provided without additional charge as part of the insurance transaction. Other services are provided at discounted hourly rates.

Risk control services are an important feature of EPL insurance. Available risk control services are one factor prospective insureds should weigh in selecting an EPL insurer. Insurers benefit from providing these services through improved loss ratios for small to medium-sized insureds that might not have in-house skills to properly manage EPL loss exposures.

FIDUCIARY LIABILITY LOSS EXPOSURES

Fiduciary liability loss exposures arise mainly out of the possibility that beneficiaries of an employee benefit plan (such as active employees or retirees) may make a claim against the plan officials (or fiduciaries) for breach of their fiduciary duties.

Fiduciary liability claims, once rare, are no longer either rare, nor are they insignificant. Under defined contribution retirement plans, such as profit-sharing and 401(k) plans, the size of an employee's benefit depends on the plan's earnings. In some cases, employee retirement plans that were heavily invested in company stock lost millions of dollars in value, and aggrieved plan participants filed class action fiduciary liability lawsuits against the fiduciaries of these plans.

Several topics are important for those who seek to identify and analyze fiduciary liability loss exposures:

- The Employee Retirement Income Security Act (ERISA)
- The duties and liabilities of employee benefit plan fiduciaries
- The Health Insurance Portability and Accountability Act of 1996 (HIPAA)

The exhibit contains examples of how three different companies had to deal with a fiduciary breach of responsibility. See the exhibit "Fiduciary Liability Claims."

Fiduciary Liability Claims

One of the first cases in the new era of fiduciary liability claims was a class action against Rite-Aid Corp. The class bringing suit was composed of employees who participated in Rite-Aid's defined contribution retirement plans. Attorneys for the class charged that corporate executives knew that the outlook for Rite-Aid's stock was below average but nevertheless invested a portion of the plan's assets in the company's stock. In 2001, Rite-Aid settled with its employees for $67.7 million.[16]

In 2004, insurers paid $85 million under two of Enron's fiduciary liability policies to settle fiduciary liability claims against Enron's board of directors and members of administrative committees. The claims alleged that the directors and administrators imprudently approved or failed to prevent investing in Enron's own stock.[17]

Later that year, MCI, part of WorldCom, settled similar claims with its employees for $46.8 million, with insurers paying about half of the settlement. Former WorldCom CEO Bernard Ebbers contributed an additional $4 million to the settlement.[18] Insurers were inundated with similar claims involving other firms.

[DA04881]

ERISA

ERISA is the federal law that governs retirement and other benefit plans. It was enacted in response to abuses and underfunding in many benefit plans uncovered by congressional hearings following the insolvency of several leading corporations.

ERISA applies, with only a few exceptions, to everyone involved with the employee benefit plans of employers engaged in interstate commerce or subject to federal minimum wage law. (Federal, state, and local governmental bodies are specifically exempted from ERISA. Religious organizations are exempt from some of the provisions of the law.)

Despite the word "retirement" in the official title of the act, ERISA applies to all types and sizes of employee benefit plans. Plans subject to ERISA range from a customized retirement plan for thousands of employees, having its own trustees, actuaries, and investment advisers, to a group health insurance policy for a small business. The latter plan is basically only a contract between the employer and the insurer. An employee benefit does not have to be called a plan, or declared to be a plan, or filed with or approved by anyone, for it to be a plan subject to ERISA. It only has to be some kind of agreement or arrangement made in advance to provide employee benefits.

Violators of ERISA are subject to penalties such as fines and loss of favorable tax status. Of particular importance to insurance and risk management professionals are the duties and liabilities imposed on plan fiduciaries.

Duties and Liabilities of Employee Benefit Plan Fiduciaries

A fiduciary duty can be defined in general terms as the duty to act for someone else's benefit. Under ERISA, practically anyone whose role in employee benefits involves discretionary control or judgment in the design, administration, funding, or management of a benefit plan or in the management of its assets is a fiduciary.

Each fiduciary of an employee benefit plan has the specific duties pertaining to the particular function that the fiduciary is performing under the plan and a general duty to act solely in the interest of plan participants, to abide by the relevant dictates of plan documents, and to avoid acting in ways that are expressly prohibited by ERISA.

Specific Duties

The duties of a plan fiduciary are comparable to those of a corporate director:

- Loyalty—A fiduciary's actions must be solely in the best interests of the plan and all of its participants and beneficiaries.

- Prudence—A fiduciary must carry out his or her duties with the care, skill, prudence, and diligence of a prudent person familiar with such matters. ERISA spells out the "prudent person" rule: a fiduciary must act with the care, diligence, and skill that would be exercised by a reasonably prudent person in the same or similar circumstances. For instance, a fiduciary who undertakes activities requiring specialized skills, such as investment of plan assets, will be held to the standard of care applicable to professional persons who perform such activities.

- Diversification—A fiduciary must ensure that the plan's investments are sufficiently diversified to minimize the risk of large losses.

- Adherence—A fiduciary must act according to the plan documents and applicable law. If the plan document is not in compliance with the law, the fiduciaries must follow the law and bring the plan document into compliance.

Standards and Liability

These duties imply a relatively high standard of care. The duty of loyalty may present difficult issues for fiduciaries who also are officers, directors, or employees of the employer that sponsors the plan. They cannot take the potential effect on the employer into consideration when making a decision as a prudent independent fiduciary.

If a fiduciary breaches a duty and the breach causes loss to a benefit plan, the fiduciary is personally liable to the plan for the full amount of the loss. Additionally, the guilty fiduciary might also be subject to a fine and an action for monetary damages brought by an aggrieved plan participant. A fiduciary may be liable for the breach of a duty by another fiduciary if the first fiduciary knowingly participates in the breach, conceals it, or makes no attempt to correct it.

An employer may be held vicariously liable for breaches of fiduciary duty committed by its employees or agents. The vicariously liable employer might be able to recover its share of the damages from the employee or agent.

Related to fiduciary liability loss exposures are the loss exposures arising from negligent counseling or administering in connection with employee benefit plans.

HIPAA

ERISA was amended by the Health Insurance Portability and Accountability Act of 1996 (HIPAA). Plans sponsored by employers with more than fifty employees are subject to HIPAA. In brief, HIPAA accomplishes four major objectives:

- Sets standards for health insurance "portability" by providing credit against preexisting condition exclusion periods for prior health coverage
- Limits exclusions for preexisting medical conditions
- Prohibits discrimination in enrollment and in premiums charged to employees and their dependents based on health-related factors
- Improves disclosure about group health plans

Of particular concern from an insurance point of view, HIPAA calls for the protection of employee medical information and subjects the employer and fiduciaries to penalties for failure to comply.

FIDUCIARY LIABILITY INSURANCE

Fiduciary liability claims, once rare, are no longer insignificant. Under defined contribution retirement plans, such as profit-sharing and 401(k) plans, the size of an employee's benefit depends on the plan's earnings. Significant declines in a plan's investment earnings can lead to class action fiduciary liability lawsuits against the plans' fiduciaries by plan participants.

The Employee Retirement Income Security Act (ERISA) governs retirement and other benefit plans. It was enacted in response to abuses and underfunding in many benefit plans uncovered by Congressional hearings following the insolvency of several leading corporations.

ERISA, among other provisions, imposes fiduciary status on those involved in the management and administration of employee benefit plans. Each fiduciary of an employee benefit plan has specific duties pertaining to his or her function, and has a duty to act solely in the interest of plan participants, to abide by the relevant dictates of plan documents, and to avoid acting in ways that are expressly prohibited by ERISA.

Fiduciary duties involve a relatively high standard of care. Liability loss exposures arise from the potential for participants and beneficiaries of benefit plans to allege financial or other types of harm, such as loss of privacy, as a result of a breach of fiduciary duty.

The appropriate type of insurance for fiduciary liability loss exposures is **fiduciary liability insurance**. See the exhibit "Fiduciary Liability Loss Exposures."

Fiduciary liability insurance
Insurance that covers the fiduciaries of an employee benefit plan against liability claims alleging breach of their fiduciary duties involving discretionary judgment.

Fiduciary Liability Loss Exposures

Fiduciary Duties	Fiduciary Liability Loss Exposures
Any person involved in the design, administration, funding, or management of a benefit plan or its assets has these fiduciary duties: • Loyalty—A fiduciary's actions must be solely in the best interests of the plan and all of its participants and beneficiaries. • Prudence—A fiduciary must carry out his or her duties with the care, skill, and diligence of a prudent person familiar with such matters. For example, a fiduciary who invests plan assets will be held to the standard of care of professionals who perform investment activities. • Diversification—A fiduciary must ensure that the plan's investments are sufficiently diversified to minimize the risk of large losses. • Adherence—A fiduciary must act according to the plan documents and applicable law. If a plan document is not in compliance with the law, the fiduciary must bring the plan document into compliance with the law.	• Breach of fiduciary duty resulting in financial loss or other harm to a benefit plan or beneficiary • Vicarious liability for breaches of fiduciary duty by an employee or agent • Negligent counseling in connection with an employee benefit plan • Negligent administrating of an employee benefit plan

[DA06714]

Fiduciary Liability Policies

In most ways, fiduciary liability policies closely resemble directors and officers (D&O) and employment practices liability (EPL) policies:

• Coverage, normally on a claims-made basis, applies to loss resulting from a claim for a wrongful act first reported during the policy period or an extended reporting period.

• Options for extended reporting periods are comparable to those for D&O policies.

- Defense coverage can be on either a duty-to-defend or reimbursement basis, and the same approaches to consent-to-settle clauses are generally found in fiduciary liability policies.
- Covered defense expenses are usually included within the overall limit instead of being payable in addition to the limit.

A fiduciary liability policy is generally subject to a deductible, or retention, which applies to both defense costs and damages paid on behalf of the insured. Policies written for insureds with smaller sized exposures, however, are often not subject to any deductible.

Persons and Organizations Insured

The named insured in a fiduciary liability policy is the sponsor organization, because it is sponsoring employee benefits plans for its employees. These are the persons and organizations typically insured under a fiduciary liability policy:

- The sponsor organization and its subsidiaries
- The insured plans
- Anyone who is, was, or becomes a director, officer, or employee of any insured, but only in his or her capacity as a fiduciary or trustee of an insured plan
- Anyone administering an insured plan

The term "insured plan" is usually defined to mean (1) any ERISA employee benefit plan operated by the insured or jointly by the insured and a labor organization for the benefit of the sponsor's employees and (2) any other employee benefit plan sponsored solely by the insured for the benefit of its employees.

Unless the policy is specifically endorsed, multi-employer plans are usually not covered. The plans must have existed as of the policy inception date and be noted in the application submitted to the insurer.

Fiduciary liability policies typically provide automatic coverage for an insured's new plans and newly acquired or created subsidiaries for a short period, such as the earlier of ninety days or policy expiration. For coverage to extend beyond that period, the insured must notify the insurer and pay any additional premium required. However, many policies provide that if the new plan or new subsidiary is smaller than a certain size, no notice is required for coverage to continue for the new plan or subsidiary until policy expiration.

Definition of Wrongful Act

Because coverage applies to loss resulting from a claim for a wrongful act, fiduciary liability policies define the types of wrongful acts that are covered.

The definition of wrongful act in a fiduciary liability policy usually includes these elements:

- Breach of the responsibilities, obligations, or duties imposed on fiduciaries of an insured plan by ERISA or by the common or statutory law of the United States or another jurisdiction
- Any other matter claimed against insureds solely because of their service as fiduciaries of any insured plan
- A negligent act, error, or omission solely in the administration of any insured plan

The coverage for negligent acts, errors, or omissions in fiduciary liability policies may duplicate the employee benefits liability (EBL) coverage frequently included by endorsement to commercial general liability policies. If an insured has EBL coverage under both its CGL policy and its fiduciary liability policy, it is important to check the Other Insurance provisions of both to be sure that they will not create a conflict in the event of a claim covered by both policies.

Exclusions

Many, but not all, exclusions in fiduciary liability policies are similar to exclusions found in D&O and EPL policies. These are some examples of fiduciary liability policy exclusions that differ from those in D&O and EPL policies:

- The exclusion of obligations under workers compensation, disability benefits, unemployment, or similar law usually contains an exception that covers claims arising under the Consolidated Omnibus Budget Reconciliation Act (COBRA).
- The exclusion of fines and penalties often contains an exception that will cover certain penalties imposed by ERISA.
- Fiduciary liability policies typically exclude any loss resulting from an insured's failure to collect required employee contributions or to properly fund the plan.

Exclusions similar to those found in most D&O and EPL policies exclude criminal or fraudulent acts, personal profit-taking, and claims made for acts that occurred before any retroactive period.

Like D&O and EPL policies, some fiduciary liability policies provide that no knowledge or information possessed by any insured person shall be imputed to any other insured person for purposes of applying the exclusions. Other fiduciary liability policies provide that in applying the exclusions, knowledge, or information possessed by any officer, director, or trustee of the insured or insured plan is imputed to the insured organization or insured plan.

Health Insurance Portability and Accountability Act of 1996 Endorsements

ERISA was amended by the Health Insurance Portability and Accountability Act of 1996 (HIPAA), to which employers with more than fifty employees are subject. HIPAA accomplishes four major objectives:

- It sets standards for health insurance "portability" by reducing exclusionary periods in employers' group health plans for preexisting conditions for those individuals who had health coverage ("creditable coverage") with a previous employer or another health plan.
- It limits exclusions for preexisting medical conditions.
- It prohibits discrimination in enrollment and in premiums charged to employees and their dependents based on health-related factors.
- It improves disclosure about group health plans.

Of particular concern from an insurance point of view, HIPAA calls for the protection of employee medical information and penalizes the employer and fiduciaries for failure to comply.

Fiduciary liability insurers have responded to HIPAA in various ways. For example, some insurers have developed HIPAA coverage endorsements that broaden the definition of sponsored plans to include those subject to HIPAA. Other insurers have added breach of duties imposed by HIPAA to the policy definition of wrongful act.

HIPAA allows for both civil fines and criminal penalties. The criminal penalties that can be imposed under HIPAA are not insurable. However, some insurers offer endorsements to cover the civil fines that HIPAA can impose if an employer does not properly protect employee medical information. Coverage for civil fines for unintentionally violating HIPAA privacy rules is generally limited to $25,000, which is the maximum annual civil fine that can be imposed under HIPAA for each calendar year for each provision that is violated.

Other Coverage

The fidelity bond (employee dishonesty) coverage required by ERISA for employee benefit plan fiduciaries and employee benefits liability (EBL) coverage are two other types of insurance that provide coverage similar to some of the provisions in fiduciary liability insurance policies.

EBL coverage can be added by endorsement to an employer's CGL insurance policy. This endorsement will provide coverage for administrative errors or omissions, such as an employer inadvertently neglecting to add a new employee to a group health insurance plan. The coverage provided by this endorsement may be sufficient for some small employers whose employee benefit plans are managed and administered by agents who have their own fiduciary liability insurance coverage.

ERISA requires all fiduciaries to be bonded. Organizations that administer or manage benefit plans purchase fiduciary bonds for all plan trustees and administrators to protect the plan against dishonesty by the fiduciaries. Fiduciary bonds provide coverage only in the event of dishonesty, such as a plan trustee appropriating plan funds for personal use. These bonds do not provide coverage for any other breach of fiduciary duty or for administrative errors.

MANAGEMENT LIABILITY CASE STUDY

Management liability policies provide coverage for damages other than bodily injury and property damage, typically covered by other policies. Damages such as financial losses can be complex, and determining coverage for such losses under management liability policies can also be complex.

Case studies provide students with an opportunity to apply knowledge about insurance and risk management to the types of situations that insurance and risk management professionals encounter in their work.

After reviewing the case studies relating to management liability, the student will determine whether coverage exists for the corporation or its directors and officers, whether the relevant policy covers the loss, whether any exclusions or other conditions apply, and the amount payable if there is coverage.

Case Facts

John had an idea for a men's health product. His biology background, enthusiasm for fitness, and entrepreneurial mindset led him to pursue this idea. He experimented with different formulas of organic herbs and vitamins in the basement of his home. He then offered his product to a group of men at his fitness club and conducted an informal study. The result was a positive response.

Mass production followed, and his company, Vita-Men, grew. He decided to expand and needed additional capital. In 2000, a public offering of stock took place to raise $2.5 million. John retained 50 percent ownership of the company.

From its origins in 1977, the company experienced consistent sales growth. However, the drive for continuing growth and the increase in the company's employee population generated problems in addition to revenue.

Scenario 1

To continue Vita-Men's growth, the company's management team decided to expand into products for women. The company invested significant capital into this new market. It decided to offer several different types of products in addition to its signature herbal vitamin capsules. Vita-Men doubled its production capacity in anticipation of increased demand.

Among various marketing issues, one involved branding. One management group believed that the existing Vita-Men brand should be used for the new women's products. This group believed that marketing efforts would benefit from consistency, brand recognition, and consumer product knowledge. Another management team thought that products needed to be rebranded to be marketed successfully to women. The decision was made to use the existing Vita-Men brand and to use labeling and advertising to target women.

Unfortunately, the expansion into the women's consumer market failed. The company lost $1.7 million for the fiscal year, and the earnings per share (EPS) of the stock dropped 40 percent.

A group of shareholders filed a derivative lawsuit against the company's directors and officers for their decision to invest such a large amount of the company's working capital in an unproved venture into a new market. Among other allegations, the complaint included lack of due diligence for the new enterprise. The suit demanded that $1.7 million be paid to the corporation.

As part of its retirement plan options, the company offered corporate stock, along with three mutual fund options, to employees participating in its 401(k) plan. The company's chief financial officer (CFO) administered the 401(k) plan. With the significant drop in stock value, employees experienced a reduction in their retirement assets. These employees asserted a complaint under the ERISA (Employee Retirement Income Security Act) statute. This complaint included, among other allegations, a failure to uphold a high degree of care in employee benefit plans. The employees lost a combined total of $840,000 in the value of their 401(k) plans.

Scenario 2

As Vita-Men's employee population grew from five to 500, the company's health insurance costs also increased. Vance was hired as the director of benefits and was charged by John and Vita-Men's board of directors with lowering the company's health insurance costs. Vance learned from the company's health insurer that a majority of the employees were overweight and did not participate in regular exercise programs.

Vance sponsored various health incentives, including an on-site gym with free membership. However, the rate of participation was low. Health costs continued to climb. Vance then decided on a new incentive program. All employees were asked to join the gym. At the end of the year, an athletic event was held in which employees ran through a course. At the end of the course, employees were required to strike a bell with a forty-pound mallet. The ringing of the bell would signal successful completion of the program. Any employee who completed the program, ran the course, and rang the bell received a bonus of 1 percent of his or her annual salary.

All the employees participated in the program. However, while 78 percent of the men finished and rang the bell, only 30 percent of the women succeeded in finishing the course and ringing the bell. Of the total of 300 women employees, 210 did not receive a bonus.

The 210 women who did not receive a bonus filed a complaint with the Equal Employment Opportunity Commission (EEOC) and a subsequent class action suit. The women alleged that the athletic event unfairly discriminated against women. The total bonus amount for which the group was eligible—but did not receive—was $187,000.

Determine whether there is coverage under one of Vita-Men's management liability policies for the claims in these cases.

Case Analysis Tools

Vita-Men's insurance program includes directors and officers (D&O) liability insurance, employment practices liability (EPL) insurance, and fiduciary liability insurance. See the exhibit "Management Liability Insurance Policies."

Management Liability Insurance Policies

Directors and Officers Liability Insurance	Employment Practices Liability Insurance	Fiduciary Liability Insurance
$1 million Limit of Liability (including defense costs)	$1 million Limit of Liability (including defense costs)	$1 million Limit of Liability (including defense costs)
Retroactive Date: 10/1/20XX	Retroactive Date: 10/1/20XX	Retroactive Date: 10/1/20XX

Retentions: $0   Coverage A
                    $25,000   Coverage B
                    $25,000   Coverage C
	Retentions: $25,000	Retentions: $5,000

Exclusions include but are not limited to: • Failure to maintain insurance • Fraud or dishonesty (subject to adjudication) • Pollution • Bodily injury or property damage • ERISA • Insured versus insured • Employment-related actions		

[DA06774]

All three of these management liability policies are claims-made coverage forms. All of the claims were made during the policy reporting period for occurrences after the policy retroactive date. No prior claims were made or paid under any of these policies for this policy period.

Determination of Coverage

A coverage determination will be made for each case by deciding whether there is coverage for the corporation and/or the director or officer, whether one of the relevant policies covers the loss, and whether any conditions or exclusions apply to the loss.

Scenario 1

The company suffered a significant financial loss. The stock price declined significantly after the company reported a 40 percent reduction in EPS. Shareholders were justifiably concerned about the failure of the new product launch and the company's financial position. However, both Vita-Men's management and its D&O insurer believed that the business judgment rule applied to this situation. The company's actions were made in good faith and within the authority and power of the organization. There was no evidence that the company's management did not exercise reasonable care or that they assumed unnecessary or highly speculative risk.

The claim representative for the D&O insurer believed that Vita-Men's decision to launch a product line for women was reasonable. The company had been successful for many years in marketing this product to men, and it had done marketing surveys indicating a strong demand among women for similar products. The decision to launch the new line under the same brand name may not have been the best choice, but it was not a reckless or an unreasonable one. The claim representative decided to deny the claim.

However, the loss sustained by the employees in their retirement plans was a different matter. The company's corporate attorney and the claim representative for the fiduciary liability insurer believed that the company would be liable for employee losses in their 401(k) plans. A fiduciary duty is the highest standard of duty implied by law. Employees were excited about the new product launch, and few of them realized the risks involved. Management made no efforts to communicate these risks to the employees. Therefore, the fiduciary liability insurer agreed to pay the amount of the employees' loss after applying the self-insured retention (SIR).

Scenario 2

Vita-Men's corporate counsel promptly reported the EEOC claim and subsequent class action lawsuit to the insurer for the company's EPL policy.

The employer was the named insured on the EPL policy. One of the wrongful acts covered by the policy is discrimination. Although there was no intent on the part of Vance or Vita-Men to discriminate against female employees, different types of discrimination are recognized by law. In addition to overt discrimination, disparate treatment and disparate impact can both constitute discrimination.

Vita-Men's corporate counsel discussed with the EEOC that nothing inherent in the athletic event prevented women from successfully completing it. In fact, ninety women did successfully complete it. However, the EEOC's opinion was that the challenge of lifting a heavy mallet to ring a bell after completing a strenuous exercise course was something that the company should have weighed more carefully before requiring it of the female employees.

The insurer's claim representative, after consulting with defense counsel, believed that the chances of prevailing in court were not good. The claim representative reviewed the policy, and there were no conditions or exclusions that would exclude coverage. The costs of defending the suit would be significant, and defense costs are covered by the EPL policy. The women and their attorney were willing to settle the claim. They agreed on a settlement of $60,000, to be divided among the women, plus attorneys' fees of $50,000.

Determination of Amounts Payable

Scenario 1

Vita-Men's D&O policy has a limit of $1 million, with no self-insured retention (SIR) for Coverage A. Although the insurer denied the claim, there will be litigation costs. Defense costs are covered in the policy, and the insurer will pay them.

Regarding the employees' claim, the fiduciary liability limit is $1 million, with a $5,000 SIR. The insurer will pay the amount of losses claimed—$840,000— minus the SIR of $5,000, for a total payable of $835,000.

Scenario 2

The limit of Vita-Men's EPL policy is $1 million, with a $25,000 SIR. The EPL insurer was able to settle the $187,000 claim for $60,000. The insurer will pay the $60,000 minus the $25,000 SIR, for a total payable of $35,000. See the exhibit "Coverage for Vita-Men's Management Liability Losses."

Coverage for Vita-Men's Management Liability Losses

Claim	Policy Coverage	Amount Claimed and Amount Payable by Insurer
Derivative shareholder lawsuit	D&O coverage denied—business judgment rule	$1.7 million claimed—claim not paid Defense costs paid
Employees' 401(k) plan losses	Fiduciary liability policy coverage accepted—fiduciary duty	$840,000 claimed—$835,000 paid by insurer after applying $5,000 SIR
Female employees' discrimination claim	EPL coverage accepted—discrimination is covered wrongful act	$187,000 claimed plus attorneys' fees; claim settled for $60,000—insurer paid $35,000 after applying $25,000 SIR

[DA06775]

SUMMARY

The directors and officers of a corporation have various responsibilities and duties. Various liability loss exposures occur from the exercise of these duties and responsibilities.

A corporation's directors and officers can be held liable for wrongful acts or omissions causing harm that does not qualify as bodily injury, property damage, personal injury, or advertising injury. The purpose of directors and officers (D&O) liability insurance is to provide coverage for claims alleging such harm.

D&O liability insurance covers such liability loss exposures of directors and officers, as well as the corporation for those sums that the corporation is lawfully permitted or required to pay to indemnify its directors or officers for defense or settlement costs arising out of claims made against the directors or officers.

Specialty D&O coverages include occupation-specific D&O policies, outside directors liability policies, and separate coverage for directors and officers.

Employers may be exposed to employment practices liability claims under state and federal laws. These claims may allege, for example, that the employer has wrongfully terminated the claimant's employment or illegally discriminated against the claimant, or that the claimant has been sexually harassed. A growing body of state and federal statutes, regulations, and court cases has more clearly defined unlawful employment practices and increased employers' exposure to such claims.

Employment practice liability (EPL) insurance includes indemnity and defense costs and is mostly written on independently developed forms with crucial differences in wording. It may be written as a separate policy, included in a D&O policy, or endorsed onto a businessowners policy. Some insurers offer comprehensive risk control services to their EPL insureds. These services are usually aimed at small to medium-sized firms. Larger firms generally have in-house risk control capabilities or can outsource their EPL risk control services.

Benefit plans offered by nongovernmental entities are subject to ERISA, which, among other provisions, imposes fiduciary status on those involved in the management and administration of employee benefit plans.

ERISA imposes fiduciary status on those involved in the management and administration of employee benefit plans. Fiduciary liability insurance covers the fiduciaries of an employee benefit plan against liability claims alleging breach of their fiduciary duties or other wrongful acts.

Management liability losses can jeopardize an organization's solvency. Management liability loss exposures often arise when an organization is already vulnerable because of financial losses that may result in lawsuits. Therefore, it is important for organizations to have management liability insurance as a component of their risk management programs.

ASSIGNMENT NOTES

1. Chad Hemenway, "Primary Toyota Lawsuits Point Out D&O Exposure Issues," insurancenewsnet.com, March 23, 2010, http://insurancenewsnet.com/article.aspx?id=174204 (accessed October 12, 2010).

2. Steve Hunziker, "Hijacking D&O Coverage," *American Agent & Broker*, May 12, 2010, www.agentandbroker.com/Issues/2010/May-2010/Pages/Highjacking-DO-coverage.aspx (accessed November 19, 2010).

3. Monica M. Minkel, "Tailor an Executive Liability Program to Fit Your Client," *American Agent & Broker*, October 12, 2010, www.agentandbroker.com/Issues/2010/October-2010/Pages/Tailor-an-executive-liability-program-to-fit-your-client.aspx?page=1 (accessed November 19, 2010).

4. Gary N. Dubois, "Is Your Board Really Covered?" *Risk Management*, September 2004, pp. 34–36.

5. Equal Employment Opportunity Commission, "Shaping Employment Discrimination Law," www.eeoc.gov/EEOC/history/35th/1965-71/shaping.html (accessed November 12, 2010).

6. Charles J. Muhl, "The Employment-at-Will Doctrine: Three Major Exceptions," *Monthly Labor Review*, January 2001, p. 7–8, http://findarticles.com/p/articles/mi_m1153/is_1_124/ai_71704724/pg_5/ (accessed November 12, 2010).

7. *Toussaint v. Blue Cross and Blue Shield of Michigan*, 408 Mich. 579, 292 N.W.2d 880 (1980). Despite the date, this case continued to be frequently cited as a leading case relating to the implied-contract exception.

8. Muhl, "The Employment-at-Will Doctrine: Three Major Exceptions," p. 10.

9. Jeffrey O'Shaughnessy, "Small Firms Can Face Big EPL Exposures," *P&C National Underwriter*, March 29, 2010,www.property-casualty.com/Issues/2010 (accessed November 23, 2010).

10. *SCI Liquidating Corp. v. Hartford Insurance Co. et al.*, 272Ga. 293, 526 S.E.2d 555 (2000).

11. *David Kleis, Inc. v. Superior Court*, 37Cal. App.4th 1035.

12. The Center for an Accessible Society, "Denver Police Must Pay Back Pay for Failure to Reassign," July 2000, www.accessiblesociety.org/topics/ada/adadojstories.htm (accessed October 25, 2010).

13. Horovitz, Bruce, "2 Million Enjoy Free Breakfast at Denny's," *USA Today*, updated February 3, 2009, www.usatoday.com/money/industries/food/2009-02-03-dennys_N.htm (accessed November 9, 2010).

14. United States Department of Labor, Bureau of Labor Statistics, "2009 Census of Fatal Occupational Injuries (CFOI) Charts," 2010, www.bls.gov/iif/oshwc/cfoi/cfch0008.pdf (accessed October 10, 2010).

15. See, for example, *Beverly A. Cramer, Jeffrey P. Cramer, Susan Rae Cramer, Appellants v. TheWash House of Susquehanna, Inc., Respondent*, 690 S.W. 2d 804 (1985).

16. Len Strazewski, "Fiduciary Risk: A Sleeper Awakes," *Risk & Insurance*, August 2004, p. 38.

17. Groom Law Group, "Employer Stock/Enron Litigation Update," May 28, 2004, www.americanbenefitscouncil.org/documents/employer_enronupdate061704.pdf (accessed January 16, 2008).

18. "WorldCom Pension Settlement Reached," *Business Insurance*, July 12, 2004, p. 1.

Direct Your Learning ▶▶

12

Excess and Umbrella Liability Insurance

Educational Objectives

After learning the content of this assignment, you should be able to:

▷ Explain why organizations need excess and/or umbrella liability insurance.

▷ Describe the basic differences between excess liability insurance and umbrella liability insurance.

▷ Describe the different types of excess liability insurance and how each operates.

▷ Describe the following aspects of umbrella liability insurance: drop-down coverage, required underlying coverages, aggregate umbrella limits, insuring agreement, coverage triggers, exclusions, and conditions.

▷ Explain how excess and umbrella liability insurance can be used in a layered liability insurance program, and describe the problems that may occur.

▷ Given a described large loss involving underlying and excess or umbrella liability policies, calculate the amount that each policy would pay.

Excess and Umbrella Liability Insurance

12

NEED FOR EXCESS OR UMBRELLA LIABILITY COVERAGE

Excess liability insurance and umbrella liability insurance are similar types of coverage that organizations buy for a variety of reasons, including the need to increase the limits of their commercial general liability, commercial auto, employers liability, and other primary liability policies.

The need for excess or umbrella liability insurance is closely related to three basic issues involved in the use of liability insurance:

- Difficulty in estimating maximum possible loss (MPL) for liability loss exposures
- Layering of liability coverages
- Effect of aggregate limits

Difficulty in Estimating Maximum Possible Loss

Most property loss exposures have a reasonably clear MPL. For example, the MPL for a building that would cost $2 million to rebuild is $2 million; no loss to the building could exceed the amount of money necessary to rebuild it. There is no comparable way to estimate the MPL for most liability loss exposures.

Awards to injured persons can reach large totals. These are examples of amounts of damages juries in the United States have awarded for types of claims that are commonly covered under commercial liability policies:[1]

- $1.672 billion—Intellectual Property Liability
- $300 million—Products Liability
- $178 million—Breach of Fiduciary Liability

Although these verdicts are extreme examples, and may have subsequently been appealed or reduced, multimillion-dollar verdicts have become increasingly common. No million-dollar verdicts occurred in the U.S. before 1962, but, according to the 2007 edition of *Current Award Trends in Personal Injury*, in 2004 and 2005 in the U.S., 64 percent of products liability awards, 55 percent of medical professional awards, 13 percent of premises liability awards, and 5 percent of vehicular liability awards were for $1 million or more.[2] The possibility of a liability loss in excess of $1 million exists for virtually every organization, regardless of its size or the type of product or service that it offers.

Layering of Liability Coverages

Insurers that provide primary liability insurance are often unwilling to provide a limit greater than $1 million per occurrence. An insured that wants higher limits than are available from its primary insurers can do so only by obtaining additional policies. To achieve its desired limits, a business may need to purchase one or more excess or umbrella liability policies.

A primary liability policy and corresponding excess or umbrella liability policies are referred to as "layers" of insurance. The various layers of insurance applicable to a particular set of liability loss exposures can be depicted with the primary layer on the bottom and subsequent layers stacked above. The widely used term "underlying insurance" corresponds to this depiction. With reference to a particular excess or umbrella liability policy, **underlying insurance** is the insurance in a lower layer. See the exhibit "Layers of Liability Insurance."

Underlying insurance
Insurance that applies below an excess or umbrella liability policy.

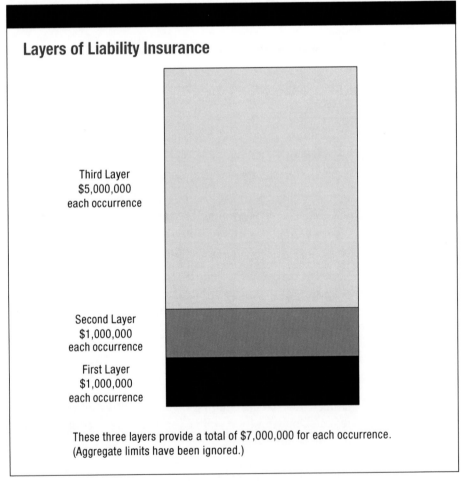

Layers of Liability Insurance

Third Layer
$5,000,000
each occurrence

Second Layer
$1,000,000
each occurrence

First Layer
$1,000,000
each occurrence

These three layers provide a total of $7,000,000 for each occurrence.
(Aggregate limits have been ignored.)

[DA05032]

Ordinarily, the coverage provided by the primary insurer must be exhausted before the next layer of insurance makes any payment. For example, assume that an insured has a commercial general liability (CGL) policy with a $1 million each occurrence limit (this is the primary coverage, or first layer) and an umbrella liability policy with a $5 million each occurrence limit (this is the second layer). If the insured became legally obligated to pay $1.8 million in damages for bodily injury to a third party, the primary insurer would pay its $1 million limit, and the umbrella insurer would pay the remaining $800,000.

The primary layer in an insurance program is not always financed through insurance. Some organizations that are financially able to pay sizable losses out of their own funds prefer to retain (self-insure) the first layer. For example, a large business might decide to retain the first $500,000 of its liability losses and buy excess liability insurance to pay for losses exceeding $500,000.

Effect of Aggregate Limits

In addition to an each occurrence limit, one or more aggregate limits for the policy period often apply to a liability insurance policy. Even if an insured never sustains a loss that exceeds the each occurrence limit of one of its primary policies, the insured could have several liability losses during one policy year that could exhaust an aggregate limit, leaving a subsequent claim uninsured or underinsured.

For example, assume that an insured has a CGL policy with a $1 million each occurrence limit, a $2 million general aggregate limit, and a $2 million products-completed operations aggregate limit. If the insured has four products liability losses for $500,000 each during the policy period, the policy will pay nothing for other products liability losses that occur during the same policy period, even if no subsequent claim exceeds the each occurrence limit (because $500,000 × 4 = $2 million, the products-completed operations aggregate limit).

BASIC DIFFERENCES: EXCESS AND UMBRELLA LIABILITY POLICIES

Excess liability policies and umbrella liability policies can be used to insure liability loss exposures that are too severe to be adequately covered under primary liability policies.

This is the basic distinction between excess liability insurance and umbrella liability insurance:

- An **excess liability policy** is designed to provide excess limits of coverage above the limits of the underlying coverage. An excess liability policy therefore offers no broader protection than that provided by the underlying coverage. In fact, the excess liability coverage may be even more

Excess liability policy

A policy that covers liability claims in excess of the limits of an underlying policy or a stated retention amount.

restrictive than the underlying coverage. An excess liability policy, for example, may not provide defense coverage.

- An umbrella liability policy is a type of excess liability policy that not only provides additional limits (as excess liability policies do), but also provides coverage not available in the underlying coverages, subject to the insured's assumption of a self-insured retention, or retained limit. Most umbrella liability policies also provide defense coverage.

In the example in the exhibit, both the excess liability policy and the umbrella policy provide $1 million of additional liability coverage for the same losses covered by the underlying policies. In addition, the umbrella policy covers some losses not covered by the underlying insurance, subject to a self-insured retention of $25,000. See the exhibit "Excess Liability Policy Versus Umbrella Liability Policy."

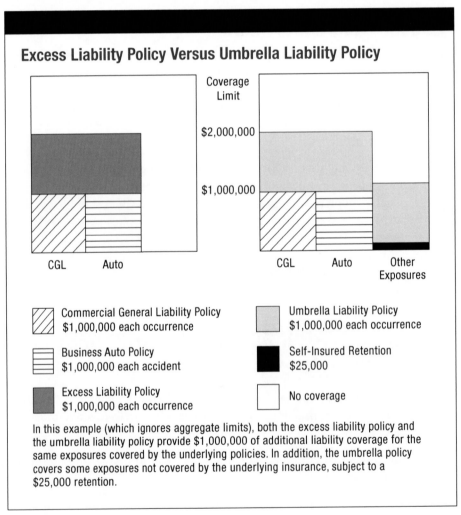

Excess Liability Policy Versus Umbrella Liability Policy

Commercial General Liability Policy
$1,000,000 each occurrence

Business Auto Policy
$1,000,000 each accident

Excess Liability Policy
$1,000,000 each occurrence

Umbrella Liability Policy
$1,000,000 each occurrence

Self-Insured Retention
$25,000

No coverage

In this example (which ignores aggregate limits), both the excess liability policy and the umbrella liability policy provide $1,000,000 of additional liability coverage for the same exposures covered by the underlying policies. In addition, the umbrella policy covers some exposures not covered by the underlying insurance, subject to a $25,000 retention.

[DA05033]

In actual practice, the distinction between excess and umbrella liability coverage is often unclear, especially because the courts and many in the insurance profession use the terms interchangeably. Moreover, many insurers providing excess and umbrella liability insurance do not use standardized policies. Rather, they develop their own policies, which vary considerably in the coverage that they offer and the format in which they are presented. What one insurer calls an excess liability policy may in reality be an umbrella policy, and what another insurer calls an umbrella policy may actually be an excess liability policy.

EXCESS LIABILITY INSURANCE

Organizations that need liability coverage beyond that provided by their commercial general liability policy may purchase excess liability insurance.

An excess liability insurance policy may take any of three basic forms:

- A following-form policy subject to the same provisions as the underlying policy
- A self-contained policy subject to its own provisions only
- A combination of these two types

In addition, when excess liability insurance applies above a retained primary layer instead of underlying insurance, two additional types of excess liability insurance—specific excess and aggregate excess—are often used, particularly in connection with self-insured workers compensation obligations.

Following-Form Excess Liability Policies

As illustrated in the exhibit, a following-form excess liability policy is an excess liability policy that covers a claim in excess of the underlying limits only if the loss is covered by the underlying insurance. A "true" following-form excess liability policy would state that, except for the policy limits, all of the provisions and conditions of the designated underlying policy are incorporated into and adopted by the excess liability policy, and it would contain no provisions conflicting with the underlying policy. See the exhibit "Application of Primary and Excess Liability Policies."

Although many excess liability policies are called following-form policies, most follow the provisions of the underlying policy only to the extent that the provisions of the underlying policy do not conflict with those of the excess liability policy. The result is that the coverage provided by an underlying policy and the coverage provided by a following-form excess liability policy are likely to differ. If the underlying policy would provide coverage for a loss that the excess liability policy would not cover, the provisions of the excess liability policy may take precedence when the loss reaches this layer, thus covering a narrower scope of events than the primary policy.

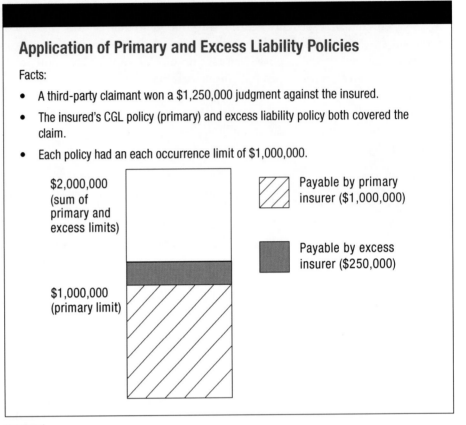

Application of Primary and Excess Liability Policies

Facts:

- A third-party claimant won a $1,250,000 judgment against the insured.
- The insured's CGL policy (primary) and excess liability policy both covered the claim.
- Each policy had an each occurrence limit of $1,000,000.

$2,000,000 (sum of primary and excess limits)

$1,000,000 (primary limit)

Payable by primary insurer ($1,000,000)

Payable by excess insurer ($250,000)

[DA05034]

Self-Contained Excess Liability Policies

Self-contained excess liability policy

An excess liability policy that is subject to its own provisions only and does not depend on the provisions of the underlying policies for determining the scope of its coverage.

A **self-contained excess liability policy** does not depend on the provisions of the underlying policies for determining the scope of the coverage (with one exception). Therefore, coverage gaps between the excess and underlying layer can occur. A self-contained excess liability policy applies to a loss that exceeds the limits of the underlying policy only if the loss is also covered under the provisions of the self-contained excess liability policy. For example, a self-contained excess liability policy may not cover injury within the products-completed operations hazard, even though the underlying policy does. In that case, the excess liability policy would not pay for a products liability claim, even though the claim was covered by the underlying policy and exceeded the each occurrence limit of the underlying policy.

One exception to the usual approach of a self-contained excess liability policy occurs when the excess liability policy provides coverage in excess of a reduced or an exhausted underlying aggregate limit. Some excess liability policies provide this coverage subject to their own provisions, but others specifically state that they will provide this coverage subject to the provisions of the underlying coverage. This approach can work to the insured's benefit when the excess liability policy contains exclusions or other restrictions that are not present in the underlying policy.

Combination Excess Liability Policies

An excess liability policy may combine the following-form and self-contained approaches by incorporating the provisions of the underlying policy and then modifying those provisions with additional conditions or exclusions in the excess liability policy.

One type of combination form is an excess liability policy that provides the broader coverages typically found in an umbrella liability policy, but without any obligation to "drop down" (provide primary coverage) when a claim is excluded by the primary policy but covered by the excess liability policy. A loss excluded under the primary policy may be covered under the excess policy to the extent it exceeds the primary policy limits. Because some insurers use the terms "excess liability" and "umbrella liability" interchangeably, insureds may not be aware that combination excess liability policies do not drop down (except to replace depleted aggregate limits).

One distinguishing feature of a true umbrella liability policy is a provision stating that the policy applies over a self-insured retention if the underlying policy does not cover a loss covered by the umbrella. In the absence of this provision, the policy is probably not a true umbrella liability policy.

Specific and Aggregate Excess Liability Insurance

Specific excess liability insurance and aggregate excess liability insurance are commonly used in connection with self-insured workers compensation plans. These types of policies are designed to apply over a self-insured layer instead of a primary layer of commercial insurance.

A specific excess liability policy requires the insured to retain a stipulated amount of loss from the first dollar for all losses resulting from each single occurrence. The insurer then pays losses from that occurrence in excess of the retention, up to the policy limit. For example, if the policy required a retention of $100,000, the insurer would pay all loss resulting from a single occurrence in excess of $100,000 up to the policy limit of $1 million.

An **aggregate excess liability policy** (also called a stop loss excess liability policy) requires the insured to retain a specified amount of loss from the first dollar during a specified period of time, usually one year. The insurer then pays, up to the policy limit, all losses for that period that exceed the retention. See the exhibit "Aggregate Excess Versus Specific Excess."

Aggregate, or stop loss, excess liability insurance policy

An excess liability policy that requires the insured to retain a specified amount of loss from the first dollar during a specified period of time, usually one year; the insurer then pays all loss for that period that exceeds the retention, up to the policy limit.

Aggregate Excess Versus Specific Excess

Aggregate Excess Liability Policy

$100,000 aggregate retention	$1,000,000 maximum limit
Losses from separate occurrences	$ 25,000
	75,000
	90,000
	35,000
Total losses	$225,000
Aggregate retention	100,000
Excess insurance will pay	$125,000

Specific Excess Liability Policy

$100,000 per occurrence retention	$1,000,000 maximum limit
Losses from separate occurrences	$ 25,000
	75,000
	90,000
	35,000
	$225,000

Because none of the losses exceeds the $100,000 per occurrence retention, the insured must retain all losses.

[DA05035]

Some policies combine the specific and aggregate excess approaches. Such policies provide the insured with the benefits of both approaches. For example, an insured may incur several moderate losses during a policy period, none of which exceeds the each occurrence retention. Under a specific excess liability policy, the insured would not be able to collect any insurance proceeds. With the combination aggregate excess and specific excess policy, if the total of losses for the policy period exceeded the aggregate retention, the insured could collect insurance proceeds for the amount of loss in excess of the aggregate retention. See the exhibit "Combination Aggregate Excess and Specific Excess Policy."

Combination Aggregate Excess and Specific Excess Policy

Aggregate Excess	Specific Excess	
$200,000 aggregate retention	$100,000 per occurrence retention	
$1,000,000 maximum limit	$1,000,000 maximum limit	
Losses from separate occurrences:		$ 25,000
		75,000
		90,000
		35,000
		$225,000

None of the losses exceeds the per occurrence retention. Therefore, the specific excess part of the policy would pay nothing. However, since total losses exceed the $200,000 aggregate retention, the aggregate excess part of the policy would pay $25,000.

[DA05036]

CHARACTERISTICS OF UMBRELLA LIABILITY INSURANCE

Umbrella liability coverage incorporates these components:

- Drop-down coverage
- Required underlying coverages
- Aggregate umbrella limits
- Insuring agreement
- Coverage triggers
- Exclusions
- Conditions

Drop-Down Coverage

To illustrate the first function of **drop-down coverage**, which may also be performed by an ordinary excess policy, assume that a manufacturer has these occurrence-basis policies:

- A CGL policy with an each occurrence limit of $1 million and a products-completed operations aggregate limit of $2 million
- An umbrella policy with an each occurrence limit of $5 million and an aggregate limit of $5 million

During one policy period, the primary CGL insurer pays products liability claims totaling $2 million, exhausting the aggregate limit. If the insured is

Drop-down coverage
Coverage provided by many umbrella liability policies for (1) claims not covered at all by the underlying policies and (2) claims that are not covered by an underlying policy only because the underlying policy's aggregate limits have been depleted.

sued by a consumer who alleges he was injured by the insured's product during the same policy period, the umbrella policy will "drop down" to defend the insured and/or pay damages (subject to the umbrella policy's limits) as if the umbrella policy were primary insurance. If subsequent products liability claims are made against the insured for injury that allegedly occurred during the policy period, the umbrella policy will defend or pay those claims also. The umbrella insurer's obligation to defend and pay ceases when its limits are exhausted.

As an example of the second aspect of drop-down coverage, assume that a manufacturer has a CGL policy and an umbrella liability policy. A products liability suit is brought against the manufacturer in a country not included in the CGL coverage territory. The CGL policy covers products liability worldwide, but only if the suit is first made in the United States or Canada. Therefore, in this case, the CGL policy does not apply. However, if the umbrella policy does not contain the same territorial restriction on products suits, it will drop down and handle the claim as though it were the primary policy.

Self-insured retention (SIR)

An amount that is deducted from claims that are payable under an umbrella liability policy and that are not covered at all by any primary policy.

When a claim covered by the umbrella policy is not covered at all by any primary policy, the drop-down coverage is usually subject to a **self-insured retention (SIR)**. If the retention shown in the umbrella policy is $25,000, for example, the umbrella policy will pay that part of the claim that exceeds $25,000, subject to the applicable limits of insurance (as illustrated in the exhibit). Retentions vary in amount, from as low as $500 for a very small business to $1 million or more for very large businesses. See the exhibit "Application of Umbrella Policy to a Claim Not Covered by Primary Policy."

Under the usual definition of SIR, the insured is responsible for adjusting and settling claims up to the SIR limit. In many policies, particularly those issued to small businesses, the retention does not apply to defense costs; such a provision is often referred to as "first-dollar defense coverage." In fact, many insurers no longer require any retention for small and mid-size insureds. In any event, the retention does not apply when the umbrella is paying in excess of a claim covered by the primary policy or dropping down to pay a claim because the primary policy's aggregate limit has been exhausted.

Required Underlying Coverages

Each insurer writing umbrella liability policies has its own requirements for the types and amounts of underlying insurance that the insured must have. For example, an umbrella insurer might require the insured to have these primary coverages and limits:

Commercial General Liability

- $1,000,000 each occurrence
- $2,000,000 general aggregate
- $2,000,000 products and completed operations aggregate

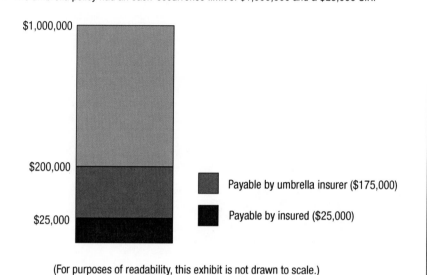

Application of Umbrella Policy to a Claim Not Covered by Primary Policy

Facts:

- A $200,000 claim was covered by the umbrella policy but not by any of the primary policies
- The umbrella policy had an each-occurrence limit of $1,000,000 and a $25,000 SIR.

$1,000,000

$200,000

$25,000

☐ Payable by umbrella insurer ($175,000)

■ Payable by insured ($25,000)

(For purposes of readability, this exhibit is not drawn to scale.)

[DA02677]

Business Auto Liability

- $1,000,000 combined single limit

Employers Liability

- $100,000 bodily injury each accident
- $100,000 bodily injury by disease each employee
- $500,000 disease aggregate

The umbrella limits apply in full in excess of each of the underlying coverages. Thus, if an insured with these underlying limits also carried a $10,000,000 umbrella policy, the total coverage available for one occurrence covered by the CGL policy and the umbrella would be $11,000,000 ($1,000,000 primary plus $10,000,000 umbrella), but the total coverage for one employers liability claim would be only $10,100,000 ($100,000 primary plus $10,000,000 umbrella). If the umbrella policy included a $25,000 retention for coverages on exposures not insured in the primary policies, the $10,000,000 coverage would apply above the $25,000 retention. See the exhibit "Interaction of Umbrella and Primary Liability Limits."

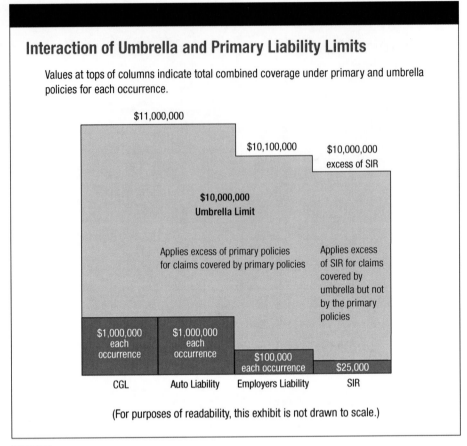

Interaction of Umbrella and Primary Liability Limits

Values at tops of columns indicate total combined coverage under primary and umbrella policies for each occurrence.

$11,000,000

$10,100,000

$10,000,000 excess of SIR

$10,000,000 Umbrella Limit

Applies excess of primary policies for claims covered by primary policies

Applies excess of SIR for claims covered by umbrella but not by the primary policies

$1,000,000 each occurrence

$1,000,000 each occurrence

$100,000 each occurrence

$25,000

CGL   Auto Liability   Employers Liability   SIR

(For purposes of readability, this exhibit is not drawn to scale.)

[DA02678]

Aggregate Umbrella Limits

The previous example ignores any aggregate limit in the umbrella policy. Almost all umbrella policies contain aggregate limits that operate like the aggregate limits in the primary insurance. In some cases, the aggregate limit applies to all claims under the umbrella; in other cases, the aggregate limit applies only to coverages that are subject to an aggregate in the underlying policies.

If the umbrella policy in the previous example included an aggregate limit, then the total available insurance would be reduced by payments on other claims payable by the umbrella policy. For example, assume that the umbrella policy described in the example had a $10 million each occurrence limit and a $10 million aggregate limit. Assuming also that no other claims had been paid by either policy, if a $3 million premises liability claim was paid ($1 million by the primary policy and $2 million by the umbrella), only $9 million would be available for the next covered claim—$1 million (the balance of the underlying aggregate) from the primary policy and $8 million (the balance of the umbrella aggregate) from the umbrella.

Insuring Agreement

Many umbrella liability policies contain one comprehensive insuring agreement instead of several specific ones. A common approach is for the insurer to promise to pay the amount in excess of the underlying limit that the insured becomes legally obligated to pay as damages for bodily injury, property damage, personal injury, or advertising injury arising out of an occurrence to which the policy applies, subject to the umbrella policy's limit.

The definitions of bodily injury, property damage, personal injury, and advertising injury in an umbrella policy may differ from those in the underlying policies. For example, bodily injury could be defined to include mental anguish.

Other umbrella policies use two insuring agreements, often referred to as "A" and "B." In effect, these policies combine an excess policy and an umbrella policy in one policy. Insuring agreement A is an excess coverage applying over the underlying policies. Insuring agreement B applies to occurrences for which coverage is available under the umbrella but not in the underlying policies. An umbrella form developed by the American Association of Insurance Services (AAIS) refers to coverages E and U, for excess and umbrella, instead of A and B.

Occurrence and Claims-Made Coverage Triggers

Umbrella policies usually have an occurrence (rather than claims-made) coverage trigger. However, the underlying primary policies sometimes include both occurrence and claims-made coverages (such as a claims-made CGL policy and an occurrence-basis auto liability policy).

Gaps in coverage can occur when the umbrella or excess policy has a different coverage trigger than the underlying coverage. To avoid this problem, some insurers provide both occurrence and claims-made coverage triggers in their umbrella policies. These policies provide that the trigger for the umbrella coverage will be the same as that used for the underlying coverage.

Exclusions

Like a CGL or an auto liability policy, an umbrella liability policy contains exclusions that restrict the broad coverage granted by the insuring agreement. Although the exclusions of umbrella policies resemble those found in underlying policies, there is usually some variation. In fact, when an umbrella policy provides broadened coverage, it is typically achieved by using exclusions in the umbrella policy that have narrower application than the exclusions of the underlying policies.

To illustrate, an umbrella policy might contain a watercraft exclusion that is stated not to apply to any watercraft, owned or nonowned, less than fifty feet long. In contrast, the watercraft exclusion of the underlying CGL coverage form is stated not to apply to nonowned watercraft less than twenty-six feet long. Consequently, the umbrella policy will provide drop-down coverage for owned boats less than fifty feet long and for nonowned boats between twenty-six and fifty feet long.

Another possibility is that the umbrella policy will contain an exclusion that does not exist in any of the underlying policies. For example, the umbrella policy may exclude claims for bodily injury arising from exposure to lead even though no such exclusion appears in the primary policy. In such a case, the umbrella policy provides narrower coverage than the underlying insurance for the particular exposure.

Conditions

The principal differences between the general conditions of primary liability policies and umbrella policies concern maintenance of underlying insurance and the coverage territory.

Maintenance of underlying insurance condition

An umbrella liability policy condition that obligates the insured to maintain all required underlying coverages in full force and effect during the policy period.

The **maintenance of underlying insurance condition** is an umbrella liability policy condition that obligates the insured to maintain all required underlying coverages in full force and effect during the policy period. The insured further agrees to notify the insurer promptly if any underlying policy is changed or replaced by a policy issued by another insurer.

If the underlying insurance is not maintained, the umbrella policy will apply as though the underlying insurance had been maintained. That is, a claim that would have been covered by an underlying policy, had it been kept in force, will only be covered for the amount that exceeds the limit of the underlying policy. The umbrella policy will not drop down to pay claims that would have been covered by the required underlying policy.

The maintenance of underlying insurance condition often requires that the underlying insurance remain in full force except for reduction in the aggregate limit due to payments of claims arising out of occurrences during the policy period. This constitutes a possible problem for insureds. If the underlying and umbrella policies are not concurrent (that is, they do not have the same inception and expiration dates), the aggregate limit in an underlying policy might be reduced by a claim occurring before the umbrella policy's inception date. In such a case, the insured would not be in compliance with the maintenance of underlying insurance condition and would have a gap in coverage for subsequent claims. If the policy periods of the primary and umbrella policies cannot be made concurrent, the insured should ask the umbrella insurer to endorse its policy to permit impairment of the aggregate limit in the underlying policy.

Most umbrella policies provide worldwide coverage, in contrast with the more limited coverage territories ordinarily found in primary policies. However, some umbrella policies require that suit be brought in the U.S. or Canada.

STRUCTURING A LIABILITY INSURANCE PROGRAM

Liability insurance is often arranged in layers. The primary (first) layer consists of one or more primary coverages (such as commercial general liability [CGL], business auto, and employers liability), with each occurrence limits typically ranging between $500,000 and $2 million. In some cases, principally with large organizations, the primary layer is self-insured (retained).

Working Layer and Buffer Layer

Many organizations have only one layer in excess of the primary. Typically, an organization in this category has an umbrella liability policy above its primary CGL, commercial auto, and employers liability coverages. It may also have one or more separate excess liability policies providing a second layer of coverage above other primary policies that are not covered by the umbrella policy. The primary and umbrella layers are generally referred to as the **working layers**, because they are the layers most often called on to pay claims.

In some cases, an insured must purchase a **buffer layer** of excess insurance between the primary layer and the umbrella policy. This approach is used when the umbrella insurer will not provide coverage unless the insured has underlying coverage limits higher than those that the primary insurer is willing to provide.

For example, an umbrella liability insurer may require minimum limits of $2 million per occurrence for the underlying CGL and auto liability coverages. One of the primary insurers, however, may be willing to provide limits of only $1 million. To qualify for the umbrella policy, the insured must obtain additional limits of $1 million.

This can be accomplished by purchasing an excess liability policy with its own limits of $1 million, which, when combined with the primary policy limits of $1 million, would provide the $2 million of underlying coverage required by the umbrella insurer. Insureds that must purchase buffer layer coverage should try to obtain a policy that follows the provisions of the underlying policy as closely as possible, and the policy periods should be concurrent.

Insureds that want higher limits of liability above the working layers usually do so through one or more additional layers of excess liability coverage. The number of layers varies, depending on the limits desired by the insured and the limits available from the prospective insurers. It is unusual to find a true umbrella policy in the higher layers of excess liability coverage. A multi-layered liability insurance program that includes a buffer layer policy is shown in the exhibit. See the exhibit "Layered Liability Insurance Program."

Working layers

The layers of coverage in an organization's insurance program that are most often called on to pay claims.

Buffer layer

A level of excess insurance coverage between a primary layer and an umbrella policy.

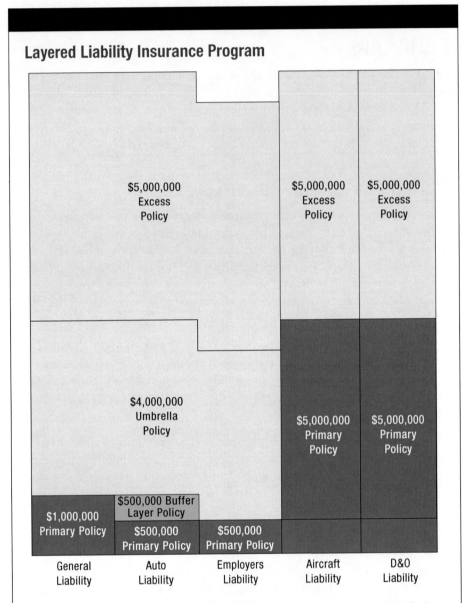

Layered Liability Insurance Program

$5,000,000 Excess Policy			$5,000,000 Excess Policy	$5,000,000 Excess Policy
$4,000,000 Umbrella Policy			$5,000,000 Primary Policy	$5,000,000 Primary Policy
$1,000,000 Primary Policy	$500,000 Buffer Layer Policy / $500,000 Primary Policy	$500,000 Primary Policy		
General Liability	Auto Liability	Employers Liability	Aircraft Liability	D&O Liability

For the sake of simplifying the presentation, this exhibit does not depict aggregate limits or umbrella drop-down coverage for claims not covered by the primary policies.

[DA05043]

Problems in Layering Coverage

Problems can occur when coverage is layered. The aggregate limits may vary with the umbrella and excess layers. The umbrella policy, for example, may be subject to a general aggregate limit and a products-completed operations aggregate limit, whereas some of the excess layers may be subject to a so-called basket aggregate limit, which applies to all coverages. Moreover, the excess liability policies may differ as to the insurer's obligations concerning defense.

Some excess liability policies may include coverage for defense costs (usually within policy limits), whereas others may not recognize such costs in determining whether underlying policy limits have been exhausted.

In addition, whenever excess liability layers are to apply over the first umbrella layer, the excess layers should follow the provisions of the umbrella policy exactly. However, excess liability policies are seldom true following-form policies in every aspect of coverage.

Even when an excess liability policy states that it is a following-form policy, it must be compared with the umbrella (or other underlying) policy to discover ways in which coverage under the excess liability policy is more restrictive than that provided by the underlying policy. Many excess liability policies contain wording similar to this:

> Except as otherwise provided by this policy, the insurance shall follow all of the terms, conditions, definitions, and exclusions of the underlying designated policies.

Adequacy of Excess Liability Limits

The layering of coverage allows many insureds the opportunity to secure high levels of protection. However, whether those limits are adequate is another matter. Consider a corporation with $1 million in assets. If it carries $1 million in liability insurance, a $2 million court judgment could cause bankruptcy. If it carries $2 million of liability insurance, a $3 million judgment could cause bankruptcy. Moreover, even a smaller uninsured verdict of, for example, $500,000 could bankrupt the firm or seriously impair its financial condition, particularly when the possibility of several such losses in a single year is acknowledged.

How should a risk manager determine the adequacy of liability insurance limits? Unfortunately, that question has no uniformly satisfactory answer. There is no monetary limit on the amount a jury might award.

Accordingly, risk managers of large corporations commonly buy the highest limits they can obtain and hope that those limits will be adequate. This approach neither guarantees that the available limits will be sufficient nor addresses the issue of whether the protection obtained was secured at reasonable prices. Even organizations that are willing and able to pay for high limits often do not believe that their limits are adequate. Some organizations feel the need for higher limits but are not willing or able to pay for them, and some find that higher limits are unavailable.

Given the problems of growing loss severity, insurance availability, and price, organizations must coordinate their insurance-buying decisions with careful consideration of all available alternatives. If an organization retains the small losses that are so costly to insure and instead spends its premium dollars to buy the high limits needed, and if it implements effective risk control, it should be in a much better position to obtain protection against catastrophic liability losses at feasible costs. In short, an organization can get the most risk management value from insurance only when it is properly combined with noninsurance techniques.

EXCESS OR UMBRELLA LIABILITY INSURANCE CASE STUDY

Commercial insurance programs are usually structured to include both primary and excess layers of coverage, and a large loss will typically trigger a response from one or more excess or umbrella policies.

This case study, involving a large loss for an organization, allows the student to develop a practical understanding of how an underlying policy and an umbrella policy would respond.

There are two key questions in this case:

- Is there coverage for the losses under one or both of the described policies?
- How much will each policy pay?

Case Facts

Eco-Shrubbery Landscaping was hired by the Nees to plant trees and shrubbery along the perimeter of their property. Jason, Eco-Shrubbery's foreman, neglected to check with the utility companies regarding the placement of underground lines before his crew began to dig.

While operating the backhoe, Ryan struck a gas line leading to the Patels' residence next to the Nee property. An explosion resulted from the ensuing gas leak. The explosion completely destroyed the Patels' house and contents, their dock, and their thirty-five-foot boat. The backhoe was also damaged. Fortunately, no one in the Patel family was home at the time of the explosion. It was also fortunate that none of Eco-Shrubbery's employees nor anyone in the Nee family was injured. Eco-Shrubbery had an Insurance Services Office (ISO) Commercial General Liability (CGL) policy (occurrence form) in effect with Liability Insurance Company (LIC) and an umbrella policy in effect with Umbrella Insurance Company (UIC). See the exhibit "Eco-Shrubbery's CGL and Umbrella Policy Limits."

Adam, the owner of Eco-Shrubbery, called his insurance agent, Marcos, from the scene of the explosion a few minutes after it occurred. Marcos met Adam at the scene. After Marcos quickly calculated a rough estimate of the likely damage to the Patels' property, he called both LIC and UIC. To control expenses, the claim representatives for LIC and UIC agreed to use the same field investigator to interview witnesses and photograph the accident scene and the damaged property. Both claim representatives agreed that Marcos could receive a copy of the report.

Eco-Shrubbery's CGL and Umbrella Policy Limits

	Policy	Limits
CGL	Each occurrence	$1,000,000
	General aggregate	$2,000,000
Umbrella	Each occurrence	$2,000,000
	Aggregate	$2,000,000
	Self-insured retention	$25,000

[DA06687]

Fletcher, the investigator, began his investigation the day of the accident. Two weeks later, he submitted his report to Allison, LIC's claim representative, and Craig, UIC's claim representative, with a copy to Marcos.

Fletcher included an estimate of the damages to the Patels' property based on his interviews with the Patels and expert appraisals. Fletcher confirmed that the house and its contents, dock, and boat were completely destroyed in the explosion, with no opportunity for repair. The only thing left of the house was the foundation. No objects were identifiable in the rubble. Fletcher photographed the damage and enclosed photos with his report. Fletcher also included receipts for a motel stay for the Patels and the lease for the house they located to rent. See the exhibit "Patel Property Damages."

Patel Property Damages

Item	Damage
House	$930,000
Dock	$18,000
Contents of house (including furnishings, art, jewelry, clothing, and personal articles)	$316,000
Boat (35 feet)	$107,000
House rental @ $3,500 per month for 1 year (estimated time to rebuild home)	$42,000
Hotel @ $95 per night for 7 nights	$665
Restaurant meals @ $60 per day for 7 days	$420
Total	$1,414,085

[DA06688]

Marcos held a conference call with Adam, Allison, and Craig after receiving Fletcher's report. All parties agreed on the next steps:

1. Allison would determine coverage under LIC's CGL policy.
2. Allison would next determine the amount payable by LIC under the policy for the covered damages.
3. Allison would submit her decision to the other parties.
4. Craig would then determine coverage under UIC's umbrella policy.
5. Craig would next determine the amount payable by UIC for the covered damages.
6. Craig would submit his decision to the other parties.

Coverage Under the CGL Policy

Allison reviewed Fletcher's report along with the CGL policy to determine which damages were covered under the policy.

Determination of Coverage

Allison first reviewed the policy declarations to determine that Eco-Shrubbery Landscaping was the named insured, that the CGL was an occurrence form, and that the accident occurred during the policy period.

She next reviewed the insuring agreement, which stated that the policy covered "property damage" that the insured was legally obligated to pay. Fletcher's investigation determined that the explosion was caused by the insured's negligence in digging without checking with utilities regarding underground lines and thus causing a leak in the gas line with the backhoe.

After determining the insured's liability and coverage for that liability under the CGL form, Allison then reviewed the items damaged, along with the policy's conditions and exclusions.

Allison first considered the property damage sustained by the insured, which consisted of the repair to the backhoe. Because of the exclusion for damage to the insured's own property, Eco-Shrubbery's repair costs were not covered.

Allison then turned her attention to the list of the Patels' property damage. She accepted coverage for the house, contents, and boat. She consulted the policy definition for property damage in analyzing coverage for the hotel, restaurant meals, and house rental. The policy defined property damage to include loss of use of damaged property and stated that the loss of use begins at the time of the occurrence. Therefore, Allison concluded that the Patels' hotel, restaurant, and house rental expenses were covered.

Determination of Amounts Payable

Allison then began calculations of the amount payable for the damages covered under the policy. She agreed that the amounts provided in Fletcher's report were reasonable for the covered damages. The total was $1,414,085.

The policy limits were $1 million per occurrence. Eco-Shrubbery had two smaller claims during the policy period totaling $78,000, but this reduction of the aggregate limits of $2 million would have no effect on this claim. Thus, the CGL policy would pay $1 million. Allison informed Craig, Marcos, Adam, and the Patels that LIC would pay policy limits for the damages the Patels sustained in this occurrence.

Coverage Under the Umbrella Policy

Craig then evaluated whether there was coverage under the umbrella policy for the damages that were not covered by the underlying CGL policy.

Determination of Coverage

Craig determined that the claim met the insuring agreement and conditions of the umbrella policy. The key condition of the umbrella policy was that the insured maintain primary insurance coverage, and Eco-Shrubbery Landscaping complied with that condition. Therefore, the umbrella policy would respond to claims that were not covered by the CGL policy because the underlying policy limits were depleted.

Determination of Amounts Payable

Craig verified that UIC had not paid for any of Eco-Shrubbery's losses during the policy period, and therefore the full $2 million aggregate limit was available. Craig first determined the amount payable by UIC for the Patels' damages that were not covered by the CGL policy because of the depletion of the underlying policy limits. The total damages were $1,414,085. After LIC paid policy limits of $1 million, the remainder was $414,085. Craig determined that UIC would pay $414,085. Craig submitted this decision to Allison, Marcos, Adam, and the Patels.

Coverage for Eco-Shrubbery Landscaping's Liability Loss

Damage	Coverage Under CGL Policy	Coverage Under Umbrella Policy
Eco-Shrubbery Landscaping's backhoe repair	Not covered due to exclusion for insured's property	Not covered due to exclusion for insured's property
Patels' damages	Coverage for the liability	Coverage for the liability excess over underlying policy limits
House and contents	Covered as property damage	Covered as property damage excess over underlying policy limits
Dock	Covered as property damage	Covered as property damage excess over underlying policy limits
Boat	Covered as property damage	Covered as property damage excess over underlying policy limits
Rental and restaurant expenses	Covered under definition of property damage that includes loss of use of damaged property	Covered as property damage excess over underlying policy limits
Amount payable	$1,000,000 (occurrence limit) payable by LIC	$414,085 payable by UIC

[DA06689]

SUMMARY

The maximum possible loss for liability loss exposures is difficult to estimate accurately. Organizations therefore generally want high limits of liability insurance. However, primary insurers typically offer limits of $1 million per occurrence. To obtain higher limits, organizations usually must obtain additional policies, which come in two basic types: excess liability policies and umbrella liability policies.

Excess and umbrella liability policies can be used to insure liability loss exposures that are too severe to be adequately covered under primary liability policies.

A true following-form excess liability policy covers excess losses subject to the same provisions in the referenced underlying policy. A self-contained excess liability policy is subject only to its own provisions. Some excess liability policies combine these two approaches. Specific excess liability policies and aggregate excess liability policies apply over a self-insured layer instead of a primary layer of commercial insurance. Policies that combine the specific and aggregate excess approaches provide the insured with the benefits of both approaches.

"Umbrella liability" describes excess insurance that is broader than ordinary excess liability policies.

Although ordinary policies may apply in excess of one or more underlying policies, an umbrella liability policy usually provides excess coverage over several primary policies (for example, commercial general liability, auto liability, and employers' liability).

Umbrella liability coverages have these characteristics:

- Drop-down coverage
- Required underlying coverages
- Aggregate umbrella limits
- Insuring agreement
- Coverage triggers
- Exclusions
- Conditions

Liability insurance is often arranged in layers. The primary (first) layer consists of one or more primary coverages (such as CGL, business auto, employers liability), with each occurrence limits typically ranging between $500,000 and $2 million.

Organizations may also have one or more separate excess liability policies providing a second layer of coverage above other primary policies that are not covered by the umbrella policy.

Excess or umbrella policies are important aspects of an organization's insurance program. Without the umbrella policy, the organization in this case would have been responsible for $414,085 that was not covered by the underlying policy, and financial hardship for the company, including bankruptcy, could have resulted. It is important for insurance and risk management professionals to consider excess and umbrella policies when designing or placing coverage as well as in determining coverage after a loss.

ASSIGNMENT NOTES

1. Verdictsearch Web site, "Top 100 of 2009," www.verdictsearch.com/index.jsp?do=top100 (accessed November 19, 2010).

2. Catherine Thomas, ed., *Current Award Trends in Personal Injury*, 46th ed. (Horsham, Pa.: LRP Publications, 2007), p. 44.

Direct Your Learning ▶▶

13

Cyber Risk and Terrorism Risk

Educational Objectives

After learning the content of this assignment, you should be able to:

▶ Explain how an organization can have cyber risk loss exposures in each of the following categories:

- Property

- Net income

- Liability

▶ Explain how organizations can control or finance their cyber risk exposures.

▶ Describe cyber risk insurance policies in terms of the following key elements:

- Insuring agreements

- Coverage triggers

- Exclusions

- Limits of insurance

- Coverage territory

▶ Describe the Terrorism Risk Insurance Act (TRIA) in terms of the following:

- Purpose and duration of TRIA

- Definition of certified acts of terrorism

- Lines of business to which TRIA applies

- Make-available provision and disclosure requirements

- Federal participation trigger

- Loss-sharing provisions and program cap

▶ Summarize the purpose and provisions of the terrorism endorsements developed by Insurance Services Office, Inc., and the National Council on Compensation Insurance, Inc.

▶▶

Cyber Risk and Terrorism Risk

13

CYBER RISK LOSS EXPOSURES

Organizations that use the Internet—for example, Web-based sales and services—as part of their daily operations may have more value residing in their databases than in their warehouses. Therefore, they must consider the risks presented to their electronic systems and electronic data as well as to those of their customers and suppliers.

A typical organization may rely on a computer network, electronic data, digital devices (for example, cell phones and personal digital assistants [PDAs]), and a Web site to conduct its business operations. Such technology-based systems can be damaged and their security unintentionally or intentionally compromised by the organization's employees or by customers and suppliers. Therefore, the use of such systems increases an organization's exposure to property, net income, and liability loss.

The high-tech risk posed to organizations that conduct their operations electronically and/or digitally is commonly known as "cyber risk." Additional terms for this type of risk and related loss exposures include e-commerce, cyber liability, Internet liability, cyber coverage (or insurance), and cyber security. The term cyber risk is a generic term that is generally accepted as the insurance industry standard. Cyber risk includes property, net income, and liability loss exposures.

Property

All organizations, not just those who routinely conduct online business transactions, should consider whether they have cyber risk property loss exposures. For example, a plumbing contracting business that is not involved in online sales or that does not have a Web site may believe it has no cyber risk property loss exposures. However, this may not be the case if the plumbing contractor has a computer network that supports its accounting, finance, and customer database. The data in such a network are exposed to multiple cyber risks, including computer viruses and corruption, which could severely impair the contractor's operations.

Property exposed to loss due to cyber risk typically falls into one or both of the two categories of personal property: **tangible property** and **intangible property**. The distinction between tangible property and intangible property is important because many commercial liability coverage forms define property damage to mean damage to tangible property and state that electronic

Tangible property
Property that has a physical form.

Intangible property
Property that has no physical form.

data are not tangible property for coverage purposes. Although commercial property forms typically do not distinguish between tangible and intangible property, they usually limit coverage for loss of electronic data to an amount that is insufficient for most insureds. Consequently, a number of specific cyber risk loss exposures are not adequately covered, or not covered at all, by basic commercial property and liability insurance policies.

Loss of or Damage to Tangible Property

In the context of cyber risk, tangible property exposed to loss or damage can include computer equipment and related media, such as software and computer hardware. Additionally, other types of tangible property, such as money and securities, may be exposed to theft resulting from cyber attack. Organizations should identify loss exposures from both viruses originating externally (for example, via incoming e-mail or by employees accessing an external Web site) and viruses originating internally (for example, by employee sabotage).

An organization's computer network and the software installed on it can be particularly vulnerable to cyber risk loss exposures such as network server damage and theft, as well as software damage or corruption. Additional tangible property cyber risk loss exposures include destruction of or damage to hardware (such as laptop computers or PDAs) because of security breaches and unauthorized use. Such exposures can significantly add to an organization's costs.

Loss of or Damage to Intangible Property

Although intangible property has no physical form, it can often be of substantial value to an organization. In the context of cyber risk, intangible property exposed to loss or damage can include electronic data (for example, confidential information such as Social Security and credit card numbers) and goodwill. Electronic data are particularly vulnerable to cyber loss exposures, such as corruption or virus contamination. For instance, consider a telemarketing organization that installs a software upgrade to its computer network. If the upgraded software contaminates the organization's data, the organization may be unable to perform its daily business operations because of the loss of its intangible property (the data).

Intellectual property

The product of human intelligence that has economic value.

Intangible property exposed to loss also can include **intellectual property**. For example, a trade secret is a practice, process, or other information used confidentially by an organization to maintain a competitive advantage in the marketplace. An unknown third party could obtain unauthorized access to an advertising firm's computer network and threaten to divulge the firm's trade secrets, a form of "cyber extortion."

Additional intangible cyber risk loss exposures include those resulting from trademark infringement, copyright infringement, or malicious code attack (software that, when installed on a computer system, produces harmful consequences such as "Trojan horses" or computer viruses). Intangible property loss exposures can significantly increase an organization's costs and harm its reputation.

Net Income

An organization can assess the potential extent of its cyber risk net income loss exposures by considering how it might be affected by a reduction in or cessation of its normal business operations as a consequence of a cyber loss. Such reductions in or cessations of normal business operations are commonly known as "business interruptions." Any possible business interruption that decreases revenues, increases expenses, or both should be considered by an organization when reviewing its cyber risk loss exposures.

Cyber risk net income loss exposures that result in business interruption can relate not only to the organization itself, but also to its key customers and suppliers. For example, an online toy retailer has a net income cyber loss exposure if it derives significant revenue from Internet sales. It may also lose income if a cyber loss (such as corrupted software that interrupts the toy manufacturing process) affects one of its key toy suppliers, thus reducing its inventory during its peak sales season.

Net income exposed to cyber risk loss can be discussed in terms of loss of business income (including contingent business income) and extra expenses. Both of these amounts can be affected should a cyber loss strike an organization.

Loss of Business Income (Including Contingent Business Income)

Loss of business income occurs when an organization's net income and normal operating expenses change as a result of a loss. In terms of cyber risk loss exposures, organizations typically examine potential losses that can occur to computer networks (hardware, software, data, and related media). For example, a denial-of-service attack can slow or block users' access to a Web site, e-mail address, or network by flooding an organization's network with requests for Web site pages or with numerous e-mail messages. For an organization that generates business income via its Web site, a denial-of-service attack can be very costly, directly affecting sales revenue.

An additional example of a cyber risk business income loss exposure is one in which a virus infects an organization's network, corrupting data and destroying software. An organization should routinely create a duplicate copy (backup) of its data. Although software can be replaced, at a cost, the organization will sustain a business income loss if it cannot conduct its normal operations during the period of restoration.

Cyber risk contingent business income loss exposures relate to an organization's income that is "contingent" (or dependent) on a location that is not owned or operated by the primary organization. For example, a key customer of an electronics components manufacturer typically places its orders to the components manufacturer through the Internet. If the key customer's computer network is attacked (for example, through a virus, a denial-of-service attack, or sabotage) and cannot be used to place orders, the resulting loss in revenue, if it cannot be replaced, is a contingent business income loss. Additionally, an organization that uses a Web-hosting company to manage its business Web site could suffer a contingent business income loss if the Web-hosting company's server is rendered inoperable for an extended time.

Similar cyber risk contingent business income exposures can apply to an organization's suppliers, utilities, and third-party outsourcers, including exposures related to the consequences of business interruption resulting from a utility's off-site power failure; failure of a third party to properly manage and secure data (possibly resulting in identity theft); Web site defacement; and abuse of wireless networks. All of these loss exposures can result in contingent business income losses.

Extra Expense

In addition to normal operating expenses, including payroll, that an organization has during a time of suspended or impaired business operations, it may also need to incur extra expenses (in excess of its normal expenses) to minimize the effects of the business interruption or continue its operations.

An organization may have cyber risk extra expense loss exposures if, as a consequence of a cyber loss, it has to purchase items such as software, hardware, or other electronic media or hire labor to recreate lost or stolen electronic data. For example, if a database is infected with a virus, the data may need to be restored or cleansed by technology specialists at an additional expense.

Liability

Organizations that maintain a presence in cyber space face increased cyber risk liability loss exposures. These exposures arise from activities such as using e-mail, maintaining Web sites, developing software, and conducting daily business operations (for example, sales and service) on the Internet.

The Federal Bureau of Investigation (FBI) reported that online crime complaints increased 22.3 percent from 2008 to 2009. The total loss linked to online fraud was $559.7 million in 2009, double the loss in 2008.[1] Because not all cyber crimes are reported and liability can result from noncriminal activity, actual liability losses are likely to be significantly higher. The categories of cyber risk liability loss exposures are bodily injury and property damage liability, personal and advertising injury liability, intellectual property liability, and errors and omissions (E&O) liability.

Bodily Injury and Property Damage Liability

Organizations engaging in technology-related activities, such as transmitting electronic data, maintaining information on or conducting business through Web sites, or designing and supporting software, must be on guard against the bodily injury and property damage loss exposures generated by these activities.

Cyber risk bodily injury liability loss exposures can occur because of an organization's software development. For example, a software developer develops a program for physicians and pharmacists regarding the potential adverse interactions of different prescription medications. Because of a formulary error in the program, physicians and pharmacists conclude that a particular combination of prescription drugs is safe when the combination actually produces a serious or fatal reaction in a number of patients. The patients and their families sue because of the bodily injury that resulted from the software error.

Another example of a cyber risk bodily injury loss exposure entails misinformation obtained from an organization's Web site. Some organizations do not exercise the same degree of care in monitoring information published on their online sites as they do with information published using traditional methods. For example, if an individual obtains information from a superstore retailer's Web site regarding common home health care treatment tips, but the information excludes or incorrectly states an important step, causing injury, the individual could sue the superstore for the resulting bodily injury.

Cyber risk property damage loss exposures can occur because of an organization's overall technology operations, including those related to software, hardware, electronic data, and other media. For example, an insurance industry software provider issues an updated version of its software to an insurance brokerage. However, because of a security failure that occurred when the software upgrade was developed and transmitted to the brokerage, upon installation, the upgrade renders the brokerage's computer network inoperable, causing significant property damage to the system. The insurance brokerage then sues the software provider for the property damage to the network.

Personal and Advertising Injury Liability

Organizations assess personal and advertising injury liability loss exposures as part of their general liability loss exposure analysis. Typical loss exposures include liability resulting from offenses such as malicious prosecution, slander, libel, defamation, disparagement, or false advertising. However, coverage for a number of personal and advertising injury liability loss exposures related to cyber risk is either limited or excluded by basic general liability coverage. These exposures should be addressed.

For example, consider an online stock market trading company that also offers discussion forums for its users. A user posing as an "insider" posts false information about the valuation of Company A and its stock, which eventually damages Company A's reputation as well as its market position. Company

A sues the trading company for defamation. Additionally, in an attempt to gain a competitive edge, the same trading company might disparage other online trading companies on its own Web site by making such statements as "Why use Company B if their Web site is always down?" or "You may think Company C costs less than us, but ask them about their service fees!" Company A's competition can sue for disparagement.

Organizations that conduct business on Web sites should be concerned about any personal and advertising injury liability arising from the consequences of advertisements of products for which the insured has assumed liability under contract or agreement. The organization is responsible for any loss exposures and related liability that is assumed by contract. Consider an online tire retailer that contracts to advertise and sell a particular manufacturer's tires. The online retailer advertises "Tires last for 50,000 miles!" However, in reality, the manufacturer's tires wear out after only 15,000 miles. Customers sue the online tire retailer for false advertising relating to the representations made about the manufacturer's tires.

Intellectual Property Liability

Cyber risk intellectual property liability loss exposures can affect an organization's copyrights, trademarks, patents, or trade secrets. For example, a copyright infringement loss exposure can occur when a major political blog site's owner posts on the blog copyrighted articles, in their entirety, from a well-known newspaper. If the site owner refuses to accede to the newspaper's demand that the blog stop posting the articles, the newspaper can sue the blog for copyright infringement.

Another example of a cyber risk intellectual property liability loss exposure relates to trademark infringement. A new social networking Web site could have as its logo a distinctive design that soon becomes very popular. However, if the logo is identical to one that belongs to a long-established real estate firm, that also does business on the Internet, the firm could sue the Web site owners for trademark infringement.

Errors and Omissions Liability

As organizations continue to expand their business operations into cyber space, whether they are manufacturing traditional products for sale online, developing software for retail sale, or maintaining computer networks, they should be aware of cyber risk E&O liability. E&O liability presents the possibility of considerable damage to the organization, not only financially but also to its reputation, market standing, and goodwill.

Organizations should consider the scope of their daily business operations and how their actions or failure to act could result in errors and omissions liability. For example, cyber risk E&O liability loss exposures can include design errors, manufacturing errors, or service errors. To illustrate, consider a high-tech company that specializes in software design and sells a software program to an

Internet-based company that offers music and video downloads for purchase. Because of a design error in the software company's program, thousands of customers were unable to complete the download process over a long holiday weekend, causing them to pay for music and video downloads they did not receive. The Internet music and video company holds the software design company liable for the design error in the software program and for the resulting damages caused by lost revenue.

Additional cyber risk E&O liability loss exposures can include loss resulting from errors relating to a company's product or the work it produces. For example, if a programmer creates a Web site for a retail client and neglects to include security safeguards to protect the site, the client could incur significant damages because of a business interruption if the Web site is hacked.

CONTROLLING AND FINANCING CYBER RISK LOSS EXPOSURES

Internet-related technology has created new opportunities for growth for all types of organizations; however, these opportunities increase organizations' vulnerability to cyber risk loss exposures from many sources, both internal and external. Theft of information and electronic data has now surpassed physical theft at global companies.[2]

Because cyber risk loss exposures have the potential to damage an organization's assets, reputation, market standing, and customer and supplier relationships, risk control measures for these exposures are essential for any organization.

Many organizations will also need risk financing for their cyber risk loss exposures. Typical commercial insurance policies often exclude or restrict coverage for cyber risk loss exposures.

It is important for risk management and insurance professionals to be aware that cyber risk is rapidly evolving. As technology becomes more widely used and more complex, cyber risk loss exposures increase in both frequency and severity. In response, new companies and products enter the insurance market to provide coverage.

Risk Control Measures for Cyber Risk

Specialized risk control measures are usually necessary for an organization to control cyber risk loss exposures involving property, net income, and liability. These risk control measures begin with an organization's determining the scope of its cyber risk loss exposures, often with assistance from a risk management or security specialist. A cyber risk security strategy should incorporate the organization's business objectives and available budget and should include an assessment of the appropriateness of the risk control measures for the loss exposures that are being addressed. Properly structured, a cyber risk security strategy can preserve an organization's resources, reduce the severity of losses that do occur, and hasten the organization's recovery from a cyber loss.

Specific risk control measures to prevent, deter, or mitigate cyber risk include these:

- Physical controls
- Procedural controls
- Personnel controls
- Managerial controls
- Investigation and prosecution of cyber crimes
- Post-cyber incident rapid recovery program

Physical Controls

Physical controls place barriers between cyber criminals and their targets. Organizations should provide basic physical protection, such as guards, locked doors, central security alarms, and automatic devices to detect intruders. Additionally, organizations can physically limit access to computer equipment and programs and can implement other administrative and managerial safeguards that control physical access to systems or to the computer network environment.

Cyber criminals may use tactics to which computer hardware and software are particularly vulnerable, such as damaging them through the magnetic disruption and interruption of electrical power. Therefore, surveillance should be used for highly sensitive areas where data are stored. Access to such areas should be controlled by requiring personnel to identify themselves with badges or through **biometrics**.

Biometrics
Biological identification of an individual using anatomy or physiology.

Procedural Controls

Procedural controls specify that tasks be performed in secure ways that prevent or reduce losses. In terms of cyber risk, procedural controls apply to how a computer system and all of its associated data are protected. Security policies should clearly state system authorization requirements for use of the system, levels of system access, and system response measures to unauthorized access.

Protection from hackers is a critical reason for organizations to create, implement, and regularly update procedural controls. Hackers have many motives for their attacks, including identity theft, extortion, destruction of competitive advantage, surveillance and reconnaissance, terrorism, political protest, and the satisfaction of defeating an organization's computer security system. If appropriate safeguards are not in place, organizations may never notice clandestine hacker intrusions that are designed to steal information. Other intrusions that use malicious software or codes (malware) are designed to deliberately and noticeably disrupt operations. Procedural controls that organizations use to thwart hackers include passwords, antivirus software, data encryption for stored data and data in transit, and firewalls.

Additionally, an organization can specify monitoring procedures in its procedural controls to prevent inappropriate access or use of its computers. For example, monitoring procedures may prohibit employees from using the organization's computers to access pornographic or other inappropriate Web sites, thereby eliminating activities that might expose the organization to a malware attack. Procedural controls may also be designed for network updates to ensure that new programs are tested before they are used to process actual data, possibly preventing an errors and omissions liability claim.

Other procedures can include establishment of a privacy policy and procedures for how, when, and under what terms an organization will allow material from other Web sites (such as hyperlinks or content) to appear on its own Web site. These policies and procedures could prevent claims for violation of privacy laws and for trademark or copyright infringement.

Personnel Controls

The attitudes, performance, and behavior of employees can leave an organization exposed to a cyber attack, regardless of whether the resulting loss or damage was intended. Some employees are inadvertently the source of cyber losses—for example, employees who download software from the Internet and unknowingly introduce a virus to the system. Others deliberately commit cyber crimes such as stealing intellectual property or committing identity theft. Disgruntled former employees with knowledge of or access to proprietary information are also potential sources of cyber losses.

Organizations can institute sound personnel controls to mitigate the cyber risk loss exposures presented by their employees. Personnel controls include such measures as preemployment screening, training, outlining unacceptable cyber behavior with associated consequences, and termination procedures that include revoking access and passwords.

Personnel controls can also extend to how the organization deals with its customers, suppliers, and neighbors. For example, a frustrated customer could become hostile and launch an electronic attack against the business by posting inflammatory information on public message boards and/or infecting the business's computer network with a virus or a **denial-of-service attack**. Consequently, the organization and its employees should try to maintain positive relationships with customers and other stakeholders and report any threat or suspicion of a cyber attack.

Denial-of-service attack

An attempt to overwhelm a computer system or network with excessive communications in order to deny users access.

Managerial Controls

Managerial controls reduce cyber loss exposures by establishing an environment that prevents cyber losses or assists in their detection. Managerial controls include centralizing responsibility for cyber security. Many organizations have a chief information officer (CIO) or a chief risk officer (CRO) whose responsibilities include overseeing all technological aspects of the organization's operations. Managerial controls also involve ensuring that systems and procedures that have been adopted are monitored and followed to control cyber loss exposures. This effort can include monitoring the cyber risk security plan and ensuring compliance with risk control measures such as the creation and storage of backup files and the segregation of responsibilities to prevent any individual from having control of the entire system or inappropriate system access.

Additionally, an organization should continually evaluate and revise its risk control measures. As quickly as risk control measures are instituted to combat cyber risk, the technology that cyber criminals use to overcome them evolves. Therefore, organizations must be prepared to update their techniques accordingly.

Investigation and Prosecution of Cyber Crimes

Often, organizations do not report cyber crimes to authorities because they fear negative publicity, worry that competitors could take advantage of an incident, or believe authorities cannot assist them in prosecuting cyber crimes. Although some initial negative publicity may result when an organization reveals that it has been attacked by a cyber criminal, the organization also may experience a public relations benefit by voluntarily releasing the news regarding a cyber crime, particularly if it is an innocent victim. The organization can describe the measures it is taking to prevent such an incident from recurring, thereby restoring consumer confidence and neutralizing any advantage competitors might gain from initial negative publicity. Additionally, many law enforcement agencies possess expertise in cyber crime and can help organizations control their loss exposures. Furthermore, organizations that vigilantly investigate and prosecute cyber criminals are less likely to be viewed as an "easy target" by cyber criminals.

Reporting certain types of cyber crimes may not be optional for some organizations. Most states now require organizations to disclose to authorities and affected individuals instances when data security breaches occur that expose personal information to identity theft or other types of cyber crime.

Post-Cyber Incident Rapid Recovery Program

A post-cyber incident rapid recovery program aids in reducing the severity of an organization's cyber losses and in restoring operational functionality as soon as possible. Implementing a rapid recovery program focuses on the organization's ability to preserve and sustain its net income in the event of a cyber loss.

Risk control measures the organization can use as part of a post-cyber incident rapid recovery program include maintaining full backups of the computer system—complete with an operational Web site, e-mail, and Internet links—

at an alternate location. Additionally, all vital legal and technical documents, as well as copies of computer storage media, should be secured in a fire-resistive, off-site repository, such as those operated by specialized data storage companies.

Contingency measures should be established to provide equipment, software, or any additional personnel that may be necessary to analyze, repair, cleanse, and restore lost or damaged data. Also, plans should be developed to address the effects on suppliers and customers.

A rapid recovery program should also include a public relations component so that, if necessary, the organization's public image, as well as customer and supplier relationships, can be preserved in the aftermath of a cyber loss. See the exhibit "Top Ten Most Effective Technologies To Use Against Cyber Criminals."

Top Ten Most Effective Technologies To Use Against Cyber Criminals

2007 Rank	Technology (2007 Percentage)
1	Stateful firewalls (firewalls that identify and monitor the state of network connections or communications crossing them) (82%)
2	Access controls (79%)
3	Electronic access controls (78%)
4	Application layer firewalls (72%)
5	Host-based anti-virus programs (70%)
6	Password complexity (70%)
7	Encryption (69%)
8	Heuristics-based spam filtering (filters with header or content sensitivity) (69%)
9	Network-based policy enforcement (68%)
10	Network-based anti-virus programs (65%)

Adapted from 2007 eCrime Watch Survey CSO Magazine, U.S. Secret Service, CERT®Program, Microsoft Corp.
[DA05048]

Risk Financing Measures for Cyber Risk

Organizations exposed to cyber risk must consider the financial consequences of a property, net income, or liability loss and whether they wish to transfer or retain those losses. Sources of risk financing can be arranged before (pre-loss financing) or after (post-loss financing) a loss occurs. Although an organization may have risk financing measures in place to address basic property, net income, and liability loss exposures, additional risk financing measures may be necessary to address cyber risk loss exposures. Risk financing measures include insurance, noninsurance risk transfer, and retention.

Insurance

Because the field of cyber risk is an emerging and dynamic one, many organizations are uncertain of the value of cyber risk insurance or even of its availability as a technique for dealing with cyber risk. Cyber risk insurance coverage forms are still evolving. However, insurance is an important technique for organizations to use to manage their property, net income, or liability losses and the costs of compliance (for example, notification of customers after a theft of computer data) as a consequence of cyber risk loss exposures.

The cost of cyber risk can be significant. Hackers increasingly focus on attaining "back door" access to organizations and obtaining proprietary information that they can use for quick financial gain. A survey of computer security professionals reports that the average loss from cyber crime was $350,424 in 2007.[3]

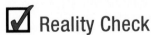 **Reality Check**

Cost of Data Breach

The cost of a data breach at an organization, whether or not the breach results in theft or damage, can be significant because of compliance with requirements to notify customers of the breach and other regulatory requirements. Even if no customer business is lost as a result of the notifications, the cost of the notifications and assistance to customers, such as monitoring their credit reports, can pose a risk to the bottom line of an organization.

For example, in one case, a January 2007 data breach at TJX Companies, the company paid, in addition to other large losses, $9.75 million to settle claims from forty-one state attorneys general relating to TJX's failure to adequately safeguard customers' financial information.

"Attorney General Martha Coakley Announces Multi-State Settlement with the TJX Companies, Inc., Over Massive Data Breach," Office of the Attorney General, Commonwealth of Massachusetts, June 23, 2009, www.mass.gov/?pageID=cagopressrelease&L=1&L0=Home&sid=Cago&b=pressrelease&f=2009_06_23_tjx_settlement&csid=Cago (accessed November 15, 2010). [DA06671]

One serious cyber loss could threaten any organization's financial position. Therefore, it is important for organizations to carefully consider insurance coverage as part of their cyber risk management programs.

Noninsurance Risk Transfer

Organizations can use noninsurance risk transfer as one means of risk financing. When entering into contracts or online agreements, organizations must ensure that the contractual language properly protects them from cyber risk loss exposures. A hold-harmless agreement, or indemnity agreement, is a type of noninsurance measure that organizations can use to receive reimbursement for cyber risk losses or to transfer their cyber risk loss exposures. For example, a Web site hosting company could sign a hold-harmless agreement promising to indemnify a customer, such as a retailer, for lost online sales if its server malfunctions. Another example is for an organization, through an indemnity agreement, to request to be named an additional insured under the indemnitor's insurance policy.

In addition to using hold-harmless agreements, many software firms also use liability disclaimers. While disclaimers do not transfer risk or act as risk financing, they can be used to limit the scope of liability. For example, organizations that collect their customers' personal information can post liability disclaimers and disclosure statements on their Web sites to fully inform customers of how their personal information may be used and the extent of the organization's liability should the information be illegally disclosed. They can also require electronic signatures from the customers to indicate consent.

Retention

An organization may use **retention** to finance its cyber risk loss exposures. One advantage of retention is that it encourages risk control. For example, when an organization pays the cost of its own losses, it may have a greater incentive to prevent and reduce them. A disadvantage associated with retention is that when an organization decides to retain its cyber risk loss exposures, the associated uncertainty of loss outcomes can negatively affect its financial position.

Should an organization decide to finance its losses by retaining rather than transferring them, it faces the possibility that retained losses will be more frequent or severe than expected. Because of this uncertainty, an organization should limit its retention for each individual loss to a severity level at which it can tolerate the potential variability in the sum of its retained losses. For example, a social networking Web site could purchase insurance for its third-party liability cyber risk loss exposures and decide to retain its first-party cyber risk loss exposures. Another organization could opt for both first-party and third-party coverage and strategically use deductibles when placing its coverage.

Retention

A risk financing technique by which losses are retained by generating funds within the organization to pay for the losses.

CYBER RISK INSURANCE POLICIES

Cyber risk insurance emerged as a specialized product category to meet the need for coverage that was not provided by traditional policies. Specialized cyber insurers, as well as traditional insurers, offer a variety of cyber risk insurance policies that can be customized to meet an organization's specific cyber risk loss exposures. Cyber risk insurance is one of the fastest growing lines of business. Written premiums for 2010 are estimated at $600 million, double the premiums written in 2006.[4]

Traditional commercial property and liability policies either exclude cyber risk loss exposures or provide limited coverage that is inadequate for most organizations. Meanwhile, the use of technology and related loss exposures continue to increase and create demand for insurance coverage. In 2009, e-commerce grew at a rate of 11 percent, compared to overall retail growth of 2.5 percent. Before the economic downturn in 2008, e-commerce was growing at an annual rate of 20 percent.[5] As technology continues to evolve with advances such as cloud computing, the loss exposures also evolve.

The lack of traditional insurance coverage and the expansion of the Internet provided an opportunity for new insurance products to meet the growing demand. An increasing number of insurers are entering the market. In addition to offering specialized cyber risk insurance policies, some insurers now offer Internet liability coverage in their management liability policies.[6]

The specific provisions of cyber risk insurance policies differ by insurer. Insurers typically offer policies containing first-party-only coverage (property and theft), third-party-only coverage (liability), or both in a combination policy format. Because first-party cyber risk losses can be difficult to assess and quantify, policies that offer first-party coverages have not been as widely available as those that include third-party coverages. Some insurers offer combination property and liability policies. Combination policies in particular allow insurers and organizations to match coverage with cyber risk loss exposures. Insurance and risk management professionals should understand the general aspects of cyber risk policies, including insuring agreements, coverage triggers, exclusions, limits of insurance, and coverage territory.

Insuring Agreements

The cyber risk coverage needs of organizations are as variable as the available coverage options. Therefore, some insurers allow their customers to supplement a basic product with the insuring agreements that are appropriate for them, while others allow for full policy customization using insuring agreements. Other insurers offer a standard package of insuring agreements or "modular policies" that include a particular range of coverage options.

Insuring agreements apply to various coverage areas. Their names can vary slightly from insurer to insurer. For example, "digital asset" coverage with one insurer may be known as "electronic data" coverage with another insurer.

Insuring agreements that are commonly found in cyber risk insurance policies fall into these categories:

- Electronic data protection
- Cyber extortion
- Cyber crime
- Notification or remediation
- Business interruption
- Network security liability
- Privacy liability
- Electronic media liability
- Technology errors and omissions liability
- Intellectual property liability
- Terrorism coverage

The insuring agreements discussed do not represent any single insurer's insuring agreements, either with regard to policy language or coverage. Rather, the discussion focuses on the types of coverage available. Careful review of an actual policy is required to determine the coverage provided by that particular policy.

Electronic Data Protection

An electronic data protection insuring agreement typically provides coverage for costs to recover or restore electronic data that have been altered, destroyed, deleted, or damaged. For instance, a computer virus attack can damage an insured's software and corrupt its associated data, requiring the insured to purchase and install replacement software and restore corrupted data.

Cyber Extortion

A cyber extortion insuring agreement provides coverage for expenses related to computer network kidnap and/or ransom events. For example, a hacker may covertly penetrate an organization's computer network and threaten to reveal specific details regarding the attack's execution unless the organization capitulates to his or her demands.

Cyber Crime

A cyber crime insuring agreement covers theft of money and securities and, depending on the insurer's form, intangible property. Cyber crime losses typically result from computer attack or computer fraud. For example, a cyber criminal could gain unauthorized access to an insured's computer network and, through fraudulent billing, divert funds from the insured's cash accounts.

Notification or Remediation

A notification or remediation insuring agreement provides coverage for expenses related to crisis management during and after a cyber risk loss (typically related to a security breach). Coverage can include crisis management-related expenses such as costs to notify customers of a security breach and costs to develop and execute a public relations campaign to manage any negative publicity surrounding the breach and to maintain the insured's reputation.

Business Interruption

A business interruption insuring agreement provides coverage for loss of business income, loss of contingent business income, and payment of extra expenses incurred as a consequence of a business interruption or suspension of the insured's computer system (or dependent system) due to cyber risk loss. Depending on the insuring agreement offered by the insurer, in some cases only business income coverage (without extra expense coverage) is provided. For example, if an online retailer's Web site is forced offline for several days during a peak sales period because of a denial-of-service attack, the business interruption insuring agreement can compensate the retailer for loss of business income.

Network Security Liability

A network security liability insuring agreement provides coverage for liability arising from security breaches to an insured's computer network. Examples of sources of network security liability losses include a situation in which a cyber criminal attempts to gain access to the insured's network for personal financial gain, a random **malware** transmission, and a denial-of-service attack. The resulting liability losses include, for example, damage to customers' data, customers' loss of use of services, or misappropriation of funds from customer accounts.

Malware
Malicious software, such as a virus, that is transmitted from one computer to another to exploit system vulnerabilities in the targeted computer.

Privacy Liability

A privacy liability insuring agreement provides coverage for liability arising from unauthorized disclosure or use of the private information of others or, depending on the insuring agreement, liability arising out of an insured's failure to comply with privacy provisions contained in laws such as the Health Insurance Portability and Accountability Act (HIPAA), the Gramm-Leach-Bliley Act (GLBA), or any anti-identity theft legislation. Actions typically are generated by a network security breach or unauthorized access to or use of information. For example, a bank employee could gain unauthorized access to the bank's customer database and obtain customers' Social Security numbers, generating a privacy liability. The employee could also reveal the Social Security numbers and other personal customer information to an accomplice, who could use the information to commit identity theft.

Electronic Media Liability

An electronic media liability insuring agreement provides coverage for liability arising from the insured's electronic content. Depending on the insuring agreement, the coverage can include e-mail communications; Web site content; and message board or discussion forum content that results in actual or alleged acts of defamation, disparagement, libel, slander, or false advertising. Electronic media liability also can be categorized as errors and omissions in the written or spoken word resulting in claims alleging financial loss or damage. For example, a company may post advertising on its Web site that makes certain claims about its product that are subsequently proved to be greatly exaggerated or simply untrue. In such a case, a competitor or customer can sue the company for false advertising under its electronic media liability coverage.

Technology Errors and Omissions Liability

A technology errors and omissions liability insuring agreement provides coverage for liability arising from any negligent act, error, or omission relating to an insured's products or services provided to others. For example, an information technology (IT) consultant may recommend that a customer test its network after performing a software update. The customer runs the test and the computer network crashes, causing the customer's business operations to be interrupted for a week. If the customer sued the consultant for loss of business income and recovery costs, the consultant could be protected against this suit by technology errors and omissions liability coverage. Depending on the insuring agreement, the coverage can also apply to the employees of the insured's independent contractors.

Intellectual Property Liability

An intellectual property liability insuring agreement provides an insured with coverage for any copyright, trade secrets, trademark, or patent infringement claims arising out of the use of the insured's protected ideas or works (or infringing on the protected ideas or works of another). For example, a Web site offers copyright-protected films available for viewing and downloading, for a fee. If some of the videos are not yet authorized for release by the film studios who own their distribution rights, the Web site owner may be sued for copyright infringement.

Terrorism Coverage

Cyber risk policies, like most other commercial insurance policies, are subject to the Terrorism Risk Insurance Act (TRIA) of 2002, as amended in 2005 and 2007. Therefore, an insurer writing cyber risk coverage must include coverage against "certified acts of terrorism" as defined in TRIA, unless the insured declines the coverage. TRIA does not prohibit the insurer from excluding terroristic acts other than "certified acts of terrorism."

Coverage Triggers

Cyber risk insurance policies are usually subject to a claims-made coverage trigger. A claim is typically made when the insured first becomes aware of facts that could cause a reasonable person to assume that a loss of a type covered by the policy has occurred. Because insuring agreements vary, so, too, can the claim-triggering events, which can include a denial-of-service attack, loss of data, or a computer virus attack.

As is typical with claims-made policies, coverage is usually available for prior acts, subject to a retroactive date found either in the base form or added by endorsement.

Some insurers that provide policies focusing more on media liability, intellectual property liability, and technology-related coverages may offer forms with an occurrence coverage trigger. Occurrence coverage triggers are also specified in the insuring agreements and can include any covered event that occurs during the policy period, such as liability arising out of Web site content errors and omissions or trademark infringement liability. Because there is typically a provision in these policies that the trigger for coverage is the date of publication of the content that allegedly violates a trademark, patent, or copyright, an occurrence coverage form usually is more appropriate than a claims-made policy.

Exclusions

Exclusions restrict and clarify the coverage available under cyber risk policies and can vary by specific insuring agreements, a group of insuring agreements, or by overall policies. Just as the types of cyber risk policies offered vary, so do the types of policy exclusions.

Some cyber risk policies contain exclusions that are commonly found in standard property-casualty insurance coverage forms. These standard exclusions, which can include exclusions for pollution, strikes, war and insurrection, civil commotion, and nuclear energy, are not specific to cyber risk loss exposures. Additional standard exclusions typically relate to perils such as fire, explosion, lightning, wind, earthquake, or flood; these perils relate to loss exposures that are otherwise insured under other property and liability policies.

As with the various cyber risk insuring agreements, the particular exclusions found in cyber risk coverage differ. Exclusions contained in cyber risk coverage forms should be examined closely and considered together with other policy provisions to determine how coverage is applied as well as to make accurate comparisons among insurers. Insurance and risk management professionals should note that the described exclusions are commonly found in cyber risk policies but are not standard exclusions; some insurers may not include them (thereby providing the otherwise-excluded coverage), while other insurers may add exclusions less commonly used. Additionally, the language of each insurer's exclusion provisions varies. Therefore, all or part of the coverage excluded by the provision may also vary. Cyber risk policy exclusions can be grouped for this discussion into these categories:[7]

- General insurance exclusions
- Product-related exclusions
- Service-related and security-related exclusions
- Cyber risk-related exclusions

General Insurance Exclusions

General insurance exclusions are those exclusions found in cyber risk policies that may also be found in other types of policies that provide professional insurance coverage or related errors and omissions-type coverage, such as management liability insurance or professional liability insurance. Examples of general exclusions include those applying to losses due to dishonest, fraudulent, criminal, or malicious acts; intentional acts; Securities and Exchange Commission (SEC) violations; unfair competition; and punitive damages.

Product-Related Exclusions

Product-related exclusions are found in cyber risk policies that apply to products produced by the insured and/or serviced and supported by the insured. Examples of product-related exclusions include those applying to losses due to product recall, defects in design, bodily injury and property damage, and breach of warranty.

For example, an insured organization could be an information technology consultant that designs computer networks. The insured designs and installs a network for a particular customer, and the network design is executed according to specifications. However, if a flaw in the design itself causes the network to malfunction after installation, any claim the customer presents for damages arising from the network design defect may be excluded under cyber risk policies.

Service-Related and Security-Related Exclusions

Service- and security-related exclusions are found in cyber risk policies that are typically purchased by technology services and support providers. Examples of service- and security-related exclusions are those relating to losses due to contractual liability, performance delay, security breach, failure to prevent a computer virus from spreading, and theft of data.

For example, many technology-based companies funded by venture capital firms are required to carry cyber risk insurance that includes computer network security coverage. However, some cyber risk policies may exclude claims for losses relating to unauthorized access to the network, electronic data theft, denial-of-service attacks, transmission of computer viruses, or unauthorized e-commerce transactions.

Cyber Risk-Related Exclusions

Cyber risk-related exclusions are found in the cyber risk policies typically purchased by technology-oriented organizations that have Web site ownership and/or operations as a primary focus of their business operations. Examples of cyber risk-related exclusions are those pertaining to losses related to personal injury, advertising injury, intellectual property (including patent and copyright infringement), and adverse effect on **goodwill**.

Goodwill

The value an organization has attained beyond the value of its tangible assets because of its favorable reputation.

For instance, an insured software distributor acquires another software distribution company and sells software licensed to the acquired company. The developer of the software could sue the insured for copyright infringement, claiming that the insured's continued sale of its software violates the original license agreement. However, some cyber risk policies exclude losses arising from copyright infringement.

Limits of Insurance

Several types of limits of insurance are available for cyber risk policies. The structure and application of the types of limits offered typically depend on whether the policy has an annual aggregate limit of insurance (also referred to as a policy aggregate limit or simply an annual aggregate). If a cyber risk policy does not have a policy annual aggregate, as in most package or modular policies, the insuring agreements work independently, each with its own limit of insurance.

For example, in the case of a modular policy without an annual aggregate, a $1 million limit of insurance applies to a cyber extortion insuring agreement (less any applicable deductible). A separate $3 million limit of insurance applies to electronic data protection. A total of $4 million in coverage is available between the two insuring agreements.

A policy aggregate limit of insurance is the maximum amount an insurer will pay during the policy period for the sum of all losses that occur. If a cyber risk policy is written with an annual aggregate, each of the policy's accompanying insuring agreements will have an insuring agreement aggregate limit of insurance. An insuring agreement aggregate limit of insurance is the maximum amount an insurer will pay for the sum of all losses that occur during the policy period relating to that specific insuring agreement. Insuring agreement aggregates are subject to the policy aggregate and as such reduce the policy aggregate in the event of loss.

Policy retentions and/or deductibles apply to each insuring agreement, per loss, and are often packaged with specific limits, particularly if the cyber risk policy is modular. Defense expenses are payable within the policy limits, thereby reducing the limit of insurance. Some insurers offer a blanket limit applicable to separate insuring agreements, which is helpful to an insured organization that is uncertain about where its maximum possible cyber risk loss exposure may exist. See the exhibit "Cyber Risk Policy Sample Limits of Insurance."

Cyber Risk Policy Sample Limits of Insurance

	Coverage Applies Y/N	Limit	Retention
Policy aggregate limit of insurance	Y	$3,000,000	
Electronic data protection	Y	$3,000,000	$25,000
Cyber extortion	Y	$3,000,000	$25,000
Network security liability	Y	$3,000,000	$25,000
Business interruption	Y	$5,000/hour	8 hours with $500,000 aggregate

[DA05049]

Coverage Territory

Cyber risk insurance policies usually differ from standard property-casualty coverage forms in terms of the scope of coverage territory stipulated in the policy provisions. Virtually all cyber risk insurers provide worldwide coverage. Some variations apply, contingent on whether a loss is a first-party loss or a third-party loss and in what geographic location a suit for damages is brought.

For example, some insurers provide worldwide coverage only if a suit is brought in the United States, its territories, Puerto Rico, or Canada. Others provide worldwide coverage if a suit is brought anywhere in the world, subject to certain conditions or restrictions, such as settlement provisions for first-party losses that are applicable only if a suit is brought in the U.S.

THE TERRORISM RISK INSURANCE ACT

The aftermath of the terrorist attacks of September 11, 2001, awoke the United States insurance industry to the catastrophic loss exposure posed by terrorist acts. Insurers responded by excluding terrorism losses from commercial property policies, especially for risks in central business districts. Most reinsurers subsequently announced that they would exclude terrorism coverage in their contracts.

The Terrorism Risk Insurance Act (TRIA) of 2002 was enacted to help alleviate the urban economic instability, lack of growth, and job loss that occurred after the September 11, 2001, terrorist attacks. TRIA created a backstop intended to satisfy market concerns over future terrorist acts by providing federal reinsurance for terrorism losses. This enabled insurers and reinsurers to offer coverage for acts of terrorism, allowing property owners to secure financing to resume construction projects that had been halted in the absence of such coverage.

Intended to expire at the end of 2005, TRIA was modified and extended two years by the Terrorism Risk Insurance Extension Act (TRIEA) of 2005. Before TRIEA expired, the Terrorism Risk Insurance Program Reauthorization Extension Act (TRIPRA) of 2007 further modified and extended TRIA. TRIPRA extended the program for seven additional years with certain changes. References to TRIA in the remainder of this material include the cumulative modifications of TRIEA and TRIPRA.

A review of TRIA provisions includes these general topics:

- Purpose and duration of TRIA
- Definition of certified acts of terrorism
- Lines of business to which TRIA applies
- Make-available provision and disclosure requirements
- Federal participation trigger
- Loss-sharing provisions and program cap

Purpose and Duration of TRIA

The potential costs of a terrorist attack are too unpredictable for insurers to properly price the exposure, and the continuing threat deters insurers from offering terrorism coverage, especially for policyholders that are perceived to be particularly at risk. Before the passage of TRIA, insurers generally would not accept the terrorism exposure or would do so only at a price that discouraged property owners from purchasing coverage in central business districts. The federal government postulated that private insurance market forces would eventually be able to manage the terrorism exposure. TRIA, with the modification provided by TRIEA, provided temporary relief for insurers through a federal reinsurance program. However, the period that the legislation allotted for insurers to find long-term solutions for the terrorism exposure ultimately proved insufficient.

The passage of TRIPRA extended the TRIA provisions for seven more years to allow time for the insurance industry and the government to develop alternate means to manage the terrorism exposure. TRIPRA is scheduled to expire on December 31, 2014.

Definition of Certified Acts of Terrorism

To qualify for reinsurance coverage under TRIA, an act of terrorism must be certified by the Secretary of the Treasury, in concurrence with the Secretary of State and the U.S. Attorney General. The Treasury Secretary cannot delegate this responsibility to any other party.

To be a "certified act of terrorism," an act must meet these requirements:

- It must be a violent act or an act that is dangerous to human life, property, or infrastructure.

- It must result in damage within the U.S. (including its territories and possessions and Puerto Rico; certain air carriers or vessels; or the premises of a U.S. mission).

- It must be committed by individual(s) in an effort to coerce the U.S. civilian population, to influence U.S. policy, or to affect U.S. government conduct by coercion.

- It must result in aggregate property-casualty insurance losses that meet or exceed $5 million.

An important change to the law in the 2007 extension expanded the program to include domestic terrorism as well as foreign acts of terrorism in the U.S. For example, a domestic terrorist attack such as the 1995 bombing of the Alfred P. Murrah Federal Building in Oklahoma City would currently be covered under TRIA.

Except for workers compensation coverage, an act may not be certified as an act of terrorism if it is committed in connection with a war that Congress has declared. Additionally, TRIA does not require that insurers offer coverage for nuclear, biological, chemical, or radiological (NBCR) acts of terrorism if the policy would not cover such losses if caused by a non-terrorism event (for example, because of a nuclear or pollution exclusion). Insurers cannot accurately estimate losses and price coverage for such attacks because of the unpredictability of their long-term effects. The TRIPRA modifications contain a requirement for further study of NBCR terrorism.

Lines of Business to Which TRIA Applies

TRIA applies to all commercial lines of business other than these, which it specifically excludes:

- Commercial auto
- Professional liability (other than directors and officers)
- Burglary and theft
- Farmowners multi-peril
- Crop
- Private mortgage
- Medical malpractice
- Financial guarantee
- Life and health
- Flood coverage provided under the National Flood Insurance Program (NFIP)
- Reinsurance
- Surety

Make-Available Provision and Disclosure Requirements

TRIA contains what is called a "make-available provision." This provision requires insurers to offer coverage for certified acts of terrorism on the same terms that the insurer offers non-terrorism coverage. In most instances, this means that the insurer is required to offer a policy without a terrorism-specific exclusion or limitation. Insurers must offer the coverage at the time of the initial offer, purchase, and renewal of insurance.

In conjunction with this make-available provision, insurers must provide clear and conspicuous disclosure to their policyholders of the premium for coverage for certified acts of terrorism. They must also clearly state that the aggregate liability of insurers and the federal government for damages from certified acts of terrorism will not exceed a $100 billion mandated annual cap. Insurers must advise their policyholders that if the aggregate cap is met, insurance coverage for acts of terrorism may be reduced.

Federal Participation Trigger

Under TRIA, the federal government will not make any payment for certified acts of terrorism until the aggregate industry insured losses in a single calendar year resulting from the certified act meet or exceed $100 million (the federal participation trigger). For example, although an event causing aggregate losses between $5 million and $100 million could be certified as an act of terrorism, insurers would not receive any federal reinsurance for losses from that event because its associated aggregate losses did not meet the $100 million trigger level.

Loss-Sharing Provisions and Program Cap

TRIA specifies loss-sharing provisions that define the responsibilities of insurers and the government. These provisions require insurers to meet a deductible before any federal reimbursement will occur. After the deductible is met, remaining losses up to an annual aggregate program cap are shared between the insurer and the federal government on a quota share (proportional) basis. The provisions include these:

- An insurer's deductible is 20 percent of its prior year's direct earned premiums.
- The insurer pays 15 percent of losses that exceed its deductible.
- The federal government pays 85 percent of losses that exceed the insurer's deductible.
- The annual aggregate program cap of $100 billion applies for insurer and government liability for payments under the program.

- The Treasury Secretary must develop a process for determining the allocation of pro rata shares of insured losses (below the cap) when the $100 billion program cap is exceeded.
- The insurance marketplace aggregate retention is $27.5 billion.

The 2007 passage of TRIPRA strengthened the $100 billion cap by eliminating wording in the original act stating that the aggregate applied until Congress acted otherwise regarding such losses. Furthermore, the Treasury Secretary must now notify Congress within fifteen days of an act of terrorism if insured losses are expected to exceed $100 billion.

An insurance marketplace aggregate retention amount combines all insurers' deductibles and quota share loss amounts. If the federal payments made for losses incurred in a calendar year ultimately are less than the insurance marketplace aggregate retention, insurers must begin mandatory recoupment of at least some part of the federal share of losses through policyholders' surcharges according to the time schedule described in TRIA. See the exhibit "TRIA Loss-Sharing Summary."

TRIA Loss-Sharing Summary

$100 Billion Program Cap	
Insurer's Share of Losses: 15%	Government's Share of Losses: 85%
Insurer Deductible: 20% of prior year's direct earned premium	
$100 Million Federal Participation Trigger	

[DA05050]

TERRORISM ENDORSEMENTS FOR COMMERCIAL PROPERTY AND LIABILITY FORMS

Insurance advisory organizations have developed various endorsements to help insurers provide coverage for terrorism-related losses in accordance with federal law.

Under the Terrorism Risk Insurance Act (TRIA), the federal government shares the financial responsibility for terrorism losses with the insurance industry (through federal reinsurance). Insurers that write the lines of business subject to TRIA are required to make coverage available for certified acts of terrorism on the same terms and conditions as coverages that apply to nonterrorism events.

To help insurers comply with TRIA, Insurance Services Office, Inc. (ISO) has developed multiple versions of specific types of terrorism endorsements to complement various commercial coverage forms. The National Council on Compensation Insurance (NCCI) offers endorsements that address TRIA-related issues in workers compensation policies. ISO and NCCI also have developed endorsements specifically for states that have special provisions that affect terrorism coverages.

Disclosure Endorsements

When insurers extend an offer to purchase insurance or to renew a policy, and at the time of purchase, TRIA requires them to inform policyholders about the costs and limitations of terrorism coverage through these three required disclosures:

- The portion of the policy premium that is attributed to certified acts of terrorism—Additionally, insurers must list (in an endorsement or in the policy declarations) the coverages to which that premium applies.
- The federal share of compensation for certified acts of terrorism under the program—After the insurer's deductible is met, the federal share is 85 percent of losses attributed to certified acts up to the program cap.
- The amount of the program cap ($100 billion)—This disclosure must explain that if the program cap is exceeded, the amount of coverage for certified losses may be reduced at the discretion of the Secretary of the Treasury.

ISO has developed disclosure endorsements applicable to the ISO lines of business to which TRIA coverage applies, and NCCI has developed disclosure endorsements for workers compensation. For the ISO lines of business, policyholders can decline certified acts of terrorism coverage, in which case other options may be offered by endorsement at the insurer's discretion.

Cap Endorsements

TRIA places a $100 billion program cap on annual aggregate insured losses paid by the federal government and all insurers for certified acts of terrorism. When a policyholder accepts certified acts of terrorism coverage, the ISO *Commercial Lines Manual* requires the insurer to attach a cap endorsement developed for the specific line of business and coverage provided.

This endorsement clearly describes certified acts of terrorism as defined in TRIA (as do most of the other terrorism endorsements) and informs the policyholder that the insurer's responsibility to pay losses for certified acts of terrorism will end if the program cap is reached. Additionally, the endorsement states that if the cap is exceeded, the Secretary of the Treasury will mandate calculation of pro rata shares of insured losses below the cap, which could reduce the policyholder's coverage. The program cap does not apply to any acts of terrorism that are not certified acts of terrorism.

Certified Acts Exclusion Endorsements

ISO's certified acts exclusion endorsements exclude coverage for certified acts of terrorism when the insured has declined the insurer's offer of TRIA coverage. These endorsements may be attached for each line of business and coverage to which TRIA applies. Acts of terrorism that are not certified under the federal program are not excluded by this endorsement; however, coverage of such acts would be subject to other exclusions or limitations in the policy.

Some states require that any policy insuring property loss caused by fire provide coverage that is at least equal to the coverage provided under a Standard Fire Policy (SFP). In these states, fire losses caused by terrorist action cannot be excluded. Certified acts exclusion endorsements contain an exception for these "SFP" states indicating that coverage is not excluded for direct loss or damage by fire to covered property when the fire results from a certified act of terrorism. The exception further states that these fire losses are limited by the program cap.

This SFP exception and its related schedule are for property coverages and are not included in certified acts exclusion endorsements developed for liability (only) policies.

NBCR Exclusion Endorsements

TRIA does not mandate coverage for losses from terrorist attacks that use nuclear, biological, chemical, or radiological materials (NBCR acts of terrorism) when such coverage is not provided in the base policy. Therefore, ISO has developed endorsements for excluding losses caused directly or indirectly by NBCR acts. These endorsements may be offered, at the insurer's option, only when the insured initially rejects certified acts of terrorism coverage.

Limitations Endorsements

If a policyholder initially declines certified acts of terrorism coverage, the insurer may offer more limited terrorism coverage amounts in return for a reduced premium. An insurer may accomplish this by writing the coverage for a sublimit that is lower than the limit applicable to other exposures. Such a sublimit could apply to a subsequent certified act of terrorism that occurs within an annual policy period if the limits are not exhausted by the prior act of terrorism. ISO has developed limitations endorsements for certified acts of terrorism that include a schedule of sublimits that apply to each coverage form, coverage part, or policy to which the endorsement is attached.

Aggregate Limit Endorsements

Aggregate limit TRIA endorsements are available for use with certain commercial liability coverage forms. These endorsements limit the insurer's exposure and provide limited liability coverage for certified acts for a reduced premium. The insurer may offer the aggregate limit endorsements only when the insured initially rejects certified acts of terrorism coverage.

When used with commercial general liability and farm liability coverage forms, the Certified Acts of Terrorism Aggregate Limit applies to bodily injury, property damage, personal and advertising injury, and medical payments arising out of certified acts of terrorism. When used with the Products/ Completed Operations Liability Coverage Form, the limit applies to bodily injury and property damage only.

When applicable to a particular policy, the Certified Acts of Terrorism Aggregate Limit is subject to the policy's general aggregate and products/ completed operations aggregate limit. Other policy limits, such as the each occurrence limit, continue to apply (to damages arising out of a certified act of terrorism) if and to the extent that the Certified Acts of Terrorism Aggregate Limit specified in the endorsement is not exhausted.

Punitive Damages Exclusion Endorsements

Insurers providing liability coverage for certified acts of terrorism may wish to exclude payment for terrorism-related punitive damages that result from civil actions. ISO has developed punitive damages exclusion endorsements for liability coverages when state laws permit such exclusions. These endorsements exclude coverage for punitive damages awarded against a policyholder that arise directly or indirectly out of certified acts of terrorism as defined by TRIA.

Other Acts Exclusion Endorsements

ISO also makes endorsements available for excluding acts of terrorism other than TRIA-certified acts of terrorism. These endorsements allow insurers to exclude noncertified acts of terrorism occurring outside the United States (including its territories and possessions and Puerto Rico). These endorsements are available only for use with commercial liability coverages, because those coverages insure some exposures outside the jurisdictional boundaries of TRIA.

These endorsements exclude other acts of terrorism committed outside the U.S. only when one or more of these situations exist:

- The total of all damages (including business interruption) to all types of property from terrorism exceeds $25 million (in U.S. dollars).
- Fifty or more people sustain serious physical injury or death.
- The act of terrorism involves the use, release, or escape of nuclear materials or results in nuclear reaction, radiation, or radioactive contamination.
- The act of terrorism is carried out by means of the dispersal or application of pathogenic or poisonous biological or chemical materials.
- Pathogenic or poisonous biological or chemical materials are released when one purpose of the terrorist act appears to be the release of such materials.

Auto Coverage Endorsements

TRIA does not apply to auto insurance, regardless of whether coverage is provided in a primary auto liability coverage form (such as the Business Auto Coverage Form) or included along with other liability coverages in a commercial umbrella or excess liability policy. (ISO has made terrorism exclusions available for use with primary commercial auto coverage forms, although these exclusions are not specifically related to TRIA.)

With respect to the ISO Commercial Liability Umbrella Coverage Part or Commercial Excess Liability Coverage Part, ISO has developed terrorism-related endorsements that address auto liability coverage. The basic purpose of these endorsements is to either cover or exclude acts of terrorism with respect to auto liability exposures, regardless of whether coverage for terrorism is provided or excluded for exposures other than auto.

Workers Compensation Endorsements

Workers compensation insurance is subject to TRIA. Therefore, insurers must include coverage for certified acts of terrorism in any workers compensation policies they write. Moreover, state workers compensation statutes prohibit insurers from excluding or limiting coverage for acts of terrorism (whether certified or not). Therefore, few terrorism-related endorsements are needed for workers compensation policies.

NCCI has developed endorsements to help insurers comply with the TRIA disclosure requirements and to inform policyholders about premiums related to acts of terrorism. The Terrorism Risk Insurance Program Reauthorization Act Endorsement defines certified acts of terrorism and discloses the portion of workers compensation premium that is attributed to certified acts, the federal share of compensation for certified acts under the program, and the amount of the program cap ($100 billion). In contrast to the ISO disclosure endorsements, this workers compensation endorsement states that an insured loss means any loss resulting from an act of terrorism, including an act of war, for purposes of workers compensation. This endorsement also describes the insurer's deductible under the program (20 percent of direct premium earned during the prior year).

SUMMARY

An organization's cyber risk loss exposures affect its property, net income, and liability. Property that can be affected by cyber risk loss exposures includes tangible property and intangible property. An organization's net income that can be affected by cyber risk loss exposures includes business income, contingent business income, and extra expenses. Liability that can be affected by cyber risk loss exposures includes bodily injury and property damage liability, personal and advertising injury liability, intellectual property liability, and E&O liability.

Organizations control their cyber risk loss exposures through the use of a variety of risk control and risk financing techniques. Risk control measures include physical controls, procedural controls, personnel controls, managerial controls, investigation and prosecution of cyber crimes, and a post-cyber incident rapid recovery program. Risk financing measures include insurance, noninsurance risk transfers, and retention. By using these risk control and risk financing measures, organizations can control cyber risk loss exposures involving property, net income, and liability.

Insurers offer a wide variety of cyber risk-related policies, and their insuring agreements apply to various coverage areas. Additionally, cyber risk policies contain coverage triggers, exclusions, limits of insurance, and coverage territory provisions that often vary. Risk management and insurance professionals should thoroughly review cyber risk policies to facilitate accurately interpreting and comparing cyber risk coverage.

TRIA provides federal financial backing for insurers to help cover the exposure from certified acts of terrorism. Unless extended by Congress, TRIA will expire on December 31, 2014. Various provisions of TRIA define certified acts of terrorism and describe the lines of business to which TRIA applies; make-available provisions and disclosure requirements; the federal participation trigger; and the loss-sharing provisions and program cap.

ISO and NCCI have developed numerous versions of terrorism endorsements to complement the various coverage forms filed by these organizations. General categories include disclosure, cap, certified acts exclusion, NBCR exclusion, limitations, aggregate limit, punitive damages exclusion, other acts exclusion, auto coverage, and workers compensation endorsements. These endorsements help insurers comply with TRIA and effectively serve their policyholders' needs.

ASSIGNMENT NOTES

1. Internet Crime Complaint Center, (IC3), a partnership between the FBI and the National White Collar Crime Center, "IC3 2009 Annual Report on Internet Crime,"www.ic3.gov/media/2010/100312.aspx (accessed November 3, 2010).

2. "Information Theft at Global Companies Surpasses All Other Forms of Fraud for First Time," Kroll Inc. news release, October 18, 2010,www.kroll.com/news/releases (accessed October 25, 2010).

3. Insurance Information Institute, "Cybercrimes Increase as Economy Falters," February 23, 2009,www.iii.org/press_releases/222564.html (accessed November 15, 2010).

4. Richard S. Betterley, "Cyber Risk and Privacy Insurance Market Survey 2010,"http://thebetterleyreport.wordpress.com/2010/06/21/cyber-risk-insurance-market-survey-2010-snips-from-our-latest-report/ (accessed November 18, 2010).

5. Geoffrey A. Fowler, "E-Commerce Growth Slows, But Still Outpaces Retail," Wall Street Journal, March 8, 2010, http://blogs.wsj.com/digits/2010/03/08/e-commerce-growth-slows-but-still-out-paces-retail (accessed November 18, 2010).

6. Betterley, "Cyber Risk and Privacy Insurance Market Survey 2010."

7. Categories for exclusions adapted from Richard S. Betterley, "Technology Errors & Omissions Market Survey—2008: Privacy Concerns Drive Product Enhancements and the Market," The Betterley Report, April 2008, p. 8.

Direct Your Learning ▶▶

14

Other Commercial Property Coverages

Educational Objectives

After learning the content of this assignment, you should be able to:

▶ Describe inland marine insurance in terms of these elements:

- The role of the Nationwide Marine Definition

- The distinction between filed and nonfiled classes of inland marine business

- The role of judgment rating

▶ Summarize the key provisions of each of these traditionally nonfiled classes of inland marine insurance:

- Contractors equipment

- Builders risk

- Transit

- Motor truck cargo liability

- Difference in conditions

- Electronic data processing (EDP) equipment

- Bailees

- Instrumentalities of transportation and communication

▶ Describe what is covered by each of the filed classes of inland marine insurance.

▶ Describe the basic characteristics of the ISO commercial crime program and financial institution bonds.

▶ Summarize the eight insuring agreements of the Commercial Crime Coverage Form in terms of these elements:

- Covered causes of loss

- Covered property

- Where coverage applies

14

Educational Objectives, continued

▸ Identify losses that the Commercial Crime Coverage Form excludes.

▸ Explain how the Commercial Crime Coverage Form's conditions address each of these issues:

- Interests insured

- Where coverage applies

- When coverage applies

- Claim-related duties and procedures

- Conditions applicable to Employee Theft only

▸ Summarize the guarantee provided by the particular types of surety bonds within the following bond classifications:

- Contract bonds

- License and permit bonds

- Public official bonds

- Court bonds

- Miscellaneous bonds

Other Commercial Property Coverages

OVERVIEW OF INLAND MARINE INSURANCE

A century ago, inland marine insurance developed as a way to cover emerging loss exposures linked to transportation. Today, inland marine insurance continues to be a source of flexible coverage solutions.

These concepts provide a foundation for understanding the types of inland marine insurance and why inland marine policy forms and rates are more flexible than those for most other types of insurance:

- Nationwide Marine Definition
- Distinction between filed and nonfiled classes of inland marine business
- Role of judgment rating

Nationwide Marine Definition

The term **inland marine insurance** was coined in the early 1900s, when United States insurers were restricted to writing one of three general kinds of insurance: fire insurance, casualty insurance, and **marine insurance**. Although fire insurers could insure buildings and their contents against fire and allied perils, they were not permitted to insure against most crime perils. In addition, they were generally not interested in providing fire and allied coverage on property in transit or on valuable property such as jewelry.

Marine insurers, however, were accustomed to covering ocean cargos of all types against many different causes of loss, including theft, while the property was either at sea or ashore. Consequently, they were willing to provide broad perils or "all-risks" coverage on the types of property that fire insurers avoided covering. The inventories of jewelry stores, property in the course of inland transit, and bridges were typical properties covered by marine insurers in the early 1900s. The insurance became known as inland marine insurance.

By the 1930s, inland marine insurance had grown to cover so many types of property that fire insurers believed that marine insurers were encroaching on their territory. To resolve the conflict, in 1933 the National Association of Insurance Commissioners (NAIC) adopted a **Nationwide Marine Definition**, a statement used mainly to determine whether a particular coverage is marine insurance (inland or ocean). The definition restricted the underwriting powers of marine insurers to specified types of property.

Inland marine insurance
Insurance that covers many different classes of property that typically involve an element of transportation.

Marine insurance
Insurance that, in the U.S., includes both ocean and inland marine coverage and in the rest of the world is limited to insurance for vessels and cargo.

Nationwide Marine Definition
Statement of the types of property that may be insured on inland marine and ocean marine insurance forms.

The enactment of legislation in the 1950s permitted a single insurer to offer fire, casualty, and marine coverages. Hence, the Nationwide Marine Definition was no longer needed for restrictive purposes. However, many states continue to use a similar, updated definition to determine whether a particular coverage is marine insurance (either inland or ocean) under their form and rate filing laws. Typically, commercial inland and ocean marine insurance is subject to less rate and form regulation than other lines of insurance. See the exhibit "Summary of Nationwide Marine Definition."

Summary of Nationwide Marine Definition

This summary lists many, but not all, types of coverage that can be classified as marine.

A. Imports

B. Exports

C. Domestic shipments

D. Bridges, tunnels, and other instrumentalities of transportation and communication, such as piers, wharves, docks, pipelines, power and telephone lines, radio and television towers and communication equipment, and outdoor cranes and loading equipment

E. Various types of property owned or used by individuals, such as jewelry, furs, musical instruments, silverware, coin collections, and stamp collections

F. Various types of property pertaining to a business, a profession, or an occupation, such as mobile equipment, builders risks, property in the custody of bailees, live animals, property at exhibitions, and electronic data processing equipment

[DA02503]

Filed and Nonfiled Classes of Business

A variety of inland marine policies cover many classes of business (such as contractors equipment, builders risk, motor truck cargo, and so forth). Insurance regulatory authorities have recognized this diversity by dividing inland marine classes of business into two categories: filed and nonfiled.

The filed classes are the classes of inland marine business for which the policy forms and/or rates must be filed with the state insurance department. Filed classes are characterized by a large number of potential insureds and reasonably homogeneous loss exposures. Examples of filed classes are policies that cover musical instruments and photographic equipment.

Insurance Services Office, Inc. (ISO) and the American Association of Insurance Services (AAIS) file forms and rates for these classes on behalf of their member companies. Many states, however, specify additional classes for which forms and rates must be filed.

Nonfiled classes are the classes of inland marine business for which neither policy forms nor rates must be filed with the state insurance department. The classes of inland marine insurance that are nonfiled vary by state. To avoid violating state laws that require the filing of insurance forms and/or rates, insurers must determine which classes of inland marine insurance can be written on a nonfiled basis in every state in which the insurer wishes to write those classes of business. The term "traditionally nonfiled classes" is sometimes used to denote those classes that are nonfiled in some states but not others.

Nonfiled classes are characterized by a relatively small number of potential insureds, diverse loss exposures, or both. The contractors equipment floater is an example of a class of inland marine insurance that has traditionally been nonfiled because of the diverse loss exposures that can be covered by this type of policy. (The term "floater" is often used to denote an inland marine policy that covers property moved between different locations, or, in other words, "floating" property.)

Many types of property may be covered ranging from simple hand tools and small power equipment to very large cranes and earthmovers. The property may be used in a variety of locations and climates such as in a desert, in a rain forest, or on the Arctic tundra. It may be used for many purposes, such as to build roads, buildings, pipelines, or other structures, or to remove snow or mow grass in public areas. Policies must be drafted, rates calculated, and underwriting keyed to all of these variables. In states where these policies do not need to be filed with state regulators, insurers can customize appropriate policy provisions and rates for individual insureds.

Role of Judgment Rating

Rating methods for the filed commercial inland marine forms are based on procedures contained in the ISO *Commercial Lines Manual* (CLM). The CLM does not contain rating methods for the traditionally nonfiled classes of inland marine insurance. However, many nonfiled inland marine policies are so widely written that both their coverage provisions and rates have become standardized to an extent. Motor truck cargo liability insurance, for example, is a common form of inland marine coverage with rates based on many years of loss experience. Insurers active in insuring truck shipments have developed their own manuals and rate schedules for this coverage.

In other cases, the property being insured under a nonfiled policy may be so unusual or the coverage terms so specialized that there is not enough previous loss information to give the insurer a statistically accurate idea of what the coverage should cost. What is a fair price for transporting a priceless painting from one museum to another for a special exhibit? How much should be charged for coverage on a one-of-a-kind piece of machinery that could be damaged as it is custom-fitted and installed in a new factory? How could an insurer rate coverage on a drawbridge?

When faced with such questions, inland marine underwriters must rely on their best judgment to set rates. Judgment rating is a rating method used by underwriters to rate one-of-a-kind risks. As opposed to manual rating (the method used to determine the premium for filed lines of insurance), judgment rating requires a thorough knowledge of the class of business for which coverage is being written. An underwriter might have to draw on expertise in any of several specialized fields—fine arts, heavy equipment, construction, or communications—to determine an adequate rate for the unique risks that are eligible for inland marine coverage. Realistically, rates are also influenced by market conditions.

NONFILED CLASSES OF INLAND MARINE INSURANCE

The largest classes of inland marine business (as measured by premiums written) are the traditionally nonfiled classes. Historically, each insurer has developed its own forms for these coverages, though both the American Association of Insurance Services (AAIS) and Insurance Services Office (ISO) offer advisory nonfiled forms for their affiliated insurers. Nonfiled forms can range from preprinted documents and endorsements used by most insureds to one-of-a-kind manuscript policies drafted for unusual risks.

Though there are many other classes of nonfiled inland marine insurance, these are significant examples:

- Contractors equipment
- Builders risk
- Transit
- Motor truck cargo liability
- Difference in conditions
- Electronic data processing equipment
- Bailees
- Instrumentalities of transportation and communication

Contractors Equipment

Contractors equipment floater
A policy that covers mobile equipment or tools while located anywhere in the coverage territory.

Contractors equipment typically represents the largest class of commercial inland marine business. The equipment used by contractors may include cranes, earthmovers, tractors, stone crushers, bulldozers, mobile asphalt plants, portable offices, and scaffolding. All such equipment can be covered under a **contractors equipment floater**.

This policy normally contains a schedule that lists each piece of equipment and its corresponding limit of insurance. A policy may also provide blanket coverage on unscheduled hand tools and miscellaneous equipment.

It is difficult, if not impossible, to maintain a current insurance schedule of all items when several hundred pieces of equipment are used by an insured. A large contractor may therefore obtain blanket coverage applying to all equipment, whether owned, rented, or borrowed by the contractor. A policy providing such blanket coverage is subject to an annual accounting of value of the insured equipment.

Coverage may be provided for named perils only or on an open perils basis, an approach that covers causes of loss that are not specifically excluded. When coverage is on a named perils basis, the perils commonly included are: fire, lightning, explosion, windstorm, hail, vandalism, theft, earthquake, flood, collision, overturn, and collapse of bridges and culverts.

Contractors equipment floaters frequently include rental reimbursement coverage, which pays the cost of renting substitute equipment when covered property has been put out of service by a covered cause of loss.

Builders Risk

Although an ISO Builders Risk Coverage Form can be issued as a component of a commercial property coverage part, buildings or other structures in the course of construction can also be insured under a nonfiled inland marine **builders risk policy**. The nonfiled approach is often preferred by both insureds and insurers because it allows more coverage and rating flexibility.

Inland marine builders risk policies typically cover the structure under construction, temporary structures at the building site, and building materials that have not yet become part of the building. Building materials are covered while on the insured location, in transit, or in storage at another location. Business income coverage may be provided as part of the policy.

Inland marine builders risk policies usually cover losses on an open perils basis, and many insurers provide coverage for losses usually excluded under standard commercial property forms, such as these:

- Flood
- Earthquake
- Theft of building materials that have not been installed

Many insurers that write inland marine builders risk policies offer an endorsement providing soft costs coverage. Soft costs coverage covers various incidental expenses that might result from a physical loss to a building project, such as additional interest, advertising expenses, or real estate taxes. Incidental expenses may also include additional costs and commissions incurred during lease renegotiation.

Builders risk policy
Policy that covers a building in the course of construction, including building materials and supplies while on or away from the building site.

Closely related to the builders risk policy is the installation floater, which covers a contractor's interest in building supplies or fixtures that the contractor has been hired to install. It does not cover the entire building, as in the case of a builders risk policy.

Transit

Transit insurance, also called transportation insurance, covers owners of property against damage to their property while in the course of transit by land, air, or water carriers. Shippers use this coverage because their property may be damaged in circumstances under which a carrier has no legal obligation to pay the shipper's loss.

Two basic types of transit insurance are available. The trip transit policy covers a particular shipment of goods specified in the policy. This kind of policy is purchased by occasional shippers. Designed for frequent shippers, the annual transit policy covers all shipments made or received by the insured throughout a one-year policy period.

Examples of property excluded in an annual transit policy include these:

- Contraband is not insurable as a matter of law and is therefore explicitly excluded by most insurance policies.

- Other types of property are commercially insurable but are especially attractive to thieves and therefore expensive to insure (for example, precious metals, furs, jewelry, and money and securities). Most annual transit policies exclude these items.

- Some insurers also exclude certain high-risk commodities such as electronics, tobacco products, alcoholic beverages, or fresh and frozen food.

If coverage for these items is wanted, and the insured is willing to pay an additional premium, the exclusions can be deleted or modified to provide coverage. Coverage may also be obtained under another policy, such as a jewelers or furriers block policy or a crime policy covering money and securities.

Most annual transit policies cover on an open perils basis. For example, flood and earthquake are not excluded.

Many annual transit policies cover only within the continental United States, Alaska, and Canada, including airborne shipments between those places. The continental U.S. does not include Hawaii, Puerto Rico, or any overseas possessions. Such wording precludes the insurer from having to cover air or water shipments to or from overseas locations. Overseas shipments by plane or ship (even between places within the coverage territory) are usually insured under ocean marine cargo policies.

Property covered under an annual transit policy is usually valued at the amount of invoice, including shipping charges, if the property is being transported between buyer and seller. If no invoice applies—such as when a company is shipping its own property between its own locations—the property may be valued at actual cash value.

Motor Truck Cargo Liability

A motor carrier (a trucking company) can be held liable for damage to the property it is transporting in certain circumstances. To cover this exposure, a motor carrier can purchase a **motor truck cargo liability policy**. This form of insurance applies only to cargo damage for which the motor carrier is legally liable. It is not direct property insurance for the benefit of the cargo owner.

Motor truck cargo liability policy

Policy that covers a trucker's liability for damage to cargo of others being transported by the trucker.

In addition to limiting coverage to losses for which the insured is legally liable, some policies also limit coverage to losses caused by specified perils. Other forms cover any loss for which the insured is liable as long as the loss is not subject to any of the exclusions expressed in the form.

The description of covered property usually encompasses most property accepted by the insured for transportation. However, as in transit policies, certain types of valuable property likely to be targeted by thieves are commonly excluded, such as precious metals, jewelry, and fine arts. Some policies exclude liquor and cigarettes, two other commodities that attract hijackers. A motor carrier that transports such commodities can usually have the exclusions deleted in return for an additional premium.

The property is covered only while in or on a land vehicle operated by the insured (including connecting carriers) or while located at the insured's terminal. Terminal coverage, however, is usually limited to a certain time period, such as seventy-two hours. The insurer will usually extend the duration of terminal coverage for an additional premium.

Difference in Conditions

A **difference in conditions (DIC) policy** can serve a variety of needs. Its basic purpose is to fill in gaps left by the insured's commercial property insurance. Originally, a DIC policy was intended to provide open perils coverage to insureds whose basic policy provided only named perils coverage. DIC policies are still used for that purpose, but with the widespread availability of the Causes of Loss—Special Form, which provides open perils coverage in commercial property policies, organizations now buy DIC policies for these reasons:

Difference in conditions (DIC) policy, or DIC insurance

Policy that covers on an "all-risks" basis to fill gaps in the insured's commercial property coverage, especially gaps in flood and earthquake coverage.

- To provide coverage for flood and earthquake exposures not covered by basic policies
- To provide excess limits over flood and earthquake coverages included in basic policies
- To cover loss exposures not covered in basic policies, such as property in transit or loss of business income resulting from theft or transit losses
- To cover property at overseas locations

DIC policies are a nonfiled class of inland marine insurance in most states. Thus, insurers have great flexibility in arranging the insurance to address the specific needs or exposures of their insureds.

Electronic Data Processing Equipment

An electronic data processing (EDP) equipment floater covers computer equipment, software, and electronic data owned by the insured, as well as similar property of others in the insured's care, custody, or control. "Electronic data processing equipment" basically means "computer equipment." Some insurers expand the term to include medical equipment, robotics, and even computerized gaming equipment such as slot machines. Although such equipment is covered as business personal property in commercial property forms, an inland marine EDP equipment floater can provide added benefits. Many EDP equipment floaters cover perils that are not usually covered in commercial property policies, such as mechanical or electrical breakdown. They may also insure covered property while it is in transit or at unlisted locations. Moreover, because EDP equipment is a nonfiled class of inland marine in many states, an EDP equipment floater can be tailored to meet the insured's individual needs.

The policy definition of "equipment" usually includes, but is not limited to, mainframe computers, servers, server racks or server "farms," display terminals, monitors, printers, imaging devices (optical scanners), disk drives and other storage devices, network components, and laptops and other portable devices. The term "data" includes both computer programs—which direct the processing of data—and data files—which store processed data, such as customer mailing lists. "Media," such as disks and tapes, are the materials used to store data.

An EDP policy usually includes coverage for extra expenses incurred as the result of covered loss. Business income coverage can often be added when the insured requests it. Coverage is usually on an open perils basis but without all the exclusions found in the Causes of Loss—Special Form. In addition, breakdown coverage can usually be added to an EDP policy. Subject to a separate deductible, breakdown coverage insures loss to equipment resulting from such perils as mechanical failure, electrical disturbance, and changes in temperature resulting from breakdown of air conditioning equipment.

Equipment and data are usually subject to separate valuation methods. Equipment may be valued at its actual cash value, replacement cost, or upgraded value. Upgraded value is the cost to replace the property with the latest, comparable, state-of-the-art equipment available. For data and media, property can be valued at the actual cost of reproduction or for an agreed dollar amount.

Bailees

Insurers use two basic approaches to insuring bailees for the property in their custody.

The first approach covers loss to customers' goods only if the insured bailee is legally liable for the loss. A common example of this type of coverage is a warehouse operator's legal liability policy, which covers warehouse operators against liability for damage to the property of others being stored in operators' warehouses.

The second approach covers damage to customers' goods, regardless of whether the insured bailee is legally liable for the loss. An inland marine policy that takes this approach is called a bailees' customers policy; this policy covers damage to customers' goods while in the possession of the insured, regardless of whether the insured is legally liable for the damage. Because this type of policy allows the bailee to pay customers' losses even when the bailee is not legally obligated to do so, it can preserve customer goodwill under circumstances in which a legal liability policy would not cover the loss. Bailees' customer policies are written for dry cleaners, laundries, furriers, tailors, upholsterers, and appliance repair shops, among others.

Instrumentalities of Transportation and Communication

Property essential to transportation or communication can be insured under an inland marine policy. The major types of properties in this class are bridges, tunnels, pipelines, and radio and television broadcasting equipment.

FILED CLASSES OF INLAND MARINE INSURANCE

Though an insurer may file its own inland marine rates, rules, and forms, Insurance Services Office (ISO) and the American Association of Insurance Services (AAIS) file inland marine coverage forms, endorsements, manual rules, and loss costs for several classes of commercial inland marine business. Insurers affiliated with ISO or AAIS can use these forms and endorsements to compose a commercial inland marine coverage part. The coverage part can be included in a commercial package policy or issued as a monoline policy that provides inland marine insurance only.

The ISO commercial inland marine coverage forms are briefly described in this section. These forms provide coverage on an open perils basis, meaning that they cover direct physical loss by any cause other than those that are specifically excluded. Valuation is typically on an actual cash value basis. However, ISO *Commercial Lines Manual* (CLM) rules permit the valuation clause to be modified to provide for any other basis of valuation to which the insurer and the insured might agree.

Commercial Articles

The Commercial Articles Coverage Form covers photographic equipment and musical instruments used commercially by photographers, motion picture producers, professional musicians, and others. It is not intended for dealers of these types of property. Coverage can be provided on a scheduled or blanket basis.

Camera and Musical Instrument Dealers

The Camera and Musical Instrument Dealers Coverage Form covers the stock in trade (inventory) of camera dealers or musical instrument dealers and similar property of others in the insured's care, custody, or control. Coverage can be provided by endorsement for other types of equipment while it is on the insured's premises.

Equipment Dealers

The Equipment Dealers Coverage Form covers the stock in trade of dealers that sell agricultural or construction equipment. The form also covers similar property of others in the insured's care, custody, or control. Coverage under a reporting form is available.

Physicians and Surgeons Equipment

The Physicians and Surgeons Equipment Coverage Form covers the professional equipment, materials, supplies, and books of physicians, surgeons, and dentists. It also covers the insured's office equipment and (if the insured is a tenant) improvements and betterments that the insured has made to a leased building.

These coverages can be added by endorsement:

- Office equipment while off premises for no more than thirty consecutive days
- Extra expenses following a covered loss
- Money and stamps on premises
- Personal effects of the insured or others while on premises
- Valuable records

Signs

The Signs Coverage Form covers neon, fluorescent, automatic, or mechanical signs. The covered signs must be scheduled with a limit of insurance shown for each item. This form (or a comparable commercial property endorsement) is used by many businesses because commercial property coverage forms severely limit coverage for signs.

Theatrical Property

The Theatrical Property Coverage Form covers stage scenery, costumes, and other personal property used in theatrical productions. It covers similar property of others in the insured's care as well as property owned by the insured. The insured must have used or must intend to use the property in a production stated in the declarations.

Film

The Film Coverage Form covers exposed motion picture film and magnetic tapes or videotapes, including related soundtracks or sound records. The amount of insurance reflects—and the form covers—the cost of reshooting the film if it is lost or damaged.

Floor Plan

The Floor Plan Coverage Form covers merchandise that is being held for sale and financed through a floor plan. The Floor Plan Coverage Form may be used to insure the dealer's interest in the merchandise, the lender's interest in it, or both. Coverage is written on a reporting form basis. The Nationwide Marine Definition includes policies covering floor plan merchandise, but only for merchandise other than automobiles. Therefore, floor plan insurance on automobiles is not handled as inland marine.

 Reality Check

Financing Merchandise Under a Floor Plan

Retailers (dealers) who offer certain types of high-priced merchandise often open a line of credit with a lender (a finance company or manufacturer) to obtain product inventory. This arrangement, called a floor plan, enables the dealer to display a number of models, colors, or options for products on its sales floor or lot, which encourages sales. Floor plan financing is often used for autos, recreational vehicles, manufactured homes, agricultural and construction equipment, and major home appliances.

Under a floor plan, the lender holds title to each item of merchandise (the collateral) until the dealer sells it. As property is sold, the dealer uses the proceeds to pay the lender for the merchandise, restoring that amount to the dealer's credit line, and the lender transfers the title to the buyer. When sales of floor plan merchandise are slower than expected, the lender can demand payment of interest and depreciation from the dealer for the collateral.

[DA07867]

Jewelers Block

The Jewelers Block Coverage Form covers the merchandise of retail jewelers, including similar property of others in the insured's care, custody, or control. It was designed to meet the needs of small retail jewelers. Depending on the nature of the insured's operations, this can be either a filed or nonfiled coverage. The filed coverage form covers damage to the insured's stock of jewelry, precious and semiprecious stones, watches, precious metals, and similar merchandise, along with other stock used in the insured's business.

Mail

The Mail Coverage Form is written for banks, trust companies, insurance companies, investment brokers, and other financial institutions that frequently ship securities and other valuable items through a government postal service. The form covers the insured against loss of securities (such as bonds, stock certificates, and certificates of deposit) and other negotiable instruments (such as bills of lading and warehouse receipts) while in transit by first-class mail, certified mail, express mail, or registered mail. Valuable items such as bullion, currency, and jewelry are covered property only if sent by registered mail.

Accounts Receivable

Many businesses would be unable to collect their accounts receivable (monies owed to them) if the records of those accounts were destroyed. This exposure can be significant, but it is easily overlooked.

The Accounts Receivable Coverage Form covers losses (including uncollectible accounts) due to destruction of the insured's records of accounts receivable. The insurer pays the amount of accounts receivable the insured is unable to collect because of the destruction of records. The form also covers the cost to reconstruct accounts receivable records, interest on loans made necessary by an inability to collect accounts receivable, and increased collection costs resulting from loss of records. Coverage may be written on either a reporting or nonreporting form.

Because many businesses keep backup (duplicate) copies of all their computer records, including records of accounts receivable, at a secure off-premises location, they do not buy accounts receivable insurance. However, insurers frequently include a certain amount of accounts receivable coverage in their package policies. An insured may use the inland marine form to obtain a higher coverage limit than the insurer is willing to include in a package policy.

Valuable Papers and Records

The Valuable Papers and Records Coverage Form covers printed or otherwise recorded items such as an architect's blueprints and plans, as well as the cost of necessary research to reconstruct the records. Irreplaceable records, such as original manuscripts or rare books, are scheduled with an agreed value shown for each item.

OVERVIEW OF COMMERCIAL CRIME INSURANCE

Organizations use various techniques to manage their loss exposures resulting from criminal acts such as robbery, burglary, and other forms of theft. Among these techniques are avoidance (for example, paying employees by check or direct deposit instead of in cash), risk control (for example, installing burglar alarms), and insurance.

Many types of insurance provide coverage against some property losses that result from criminal acts. Because crime loss exposures can vary significantly among policyholders and require special underwriting skills, insurers prefer to insure certain types of crime-related property loss under separate commercial crime insurance forms. These forms allow organizations to cover crime losses that are not insured under other insurance policies.

Briefly described, commercial crime insurance covers money, securities, and other property against a variety of criminal acts, such as employee theft, robbery, forgery, extortion, and computer fraud. Many insurers use Insurance Services Office's (ISO's) commercial crime forms. Financial institution bonds are used to meet the crime insurance needs of banks, insurance companies, and other types of financial institutions.

ISO Commercial Crime Program

The ISO commercial crime program includes crime coverage forms that can be added to a commercial package policy, as well as crime policy forms that can be written as monoline crime policies. The principal difference between the coverage forms and the policy forms is that the policy forms include the conditions contained in the ISO Common Policy Conditions form, thus eliminating the need to attach them to a monoline crime policy. Each coverage form and policy form comes in two versions: a discovery form and a loss sustained form.

The ISO commercial crime coverage forms and policy forms are designed for insuring any type of nongovernment commercial or not-for-profit entity other than a financial institution. A separate set of ISO government crime coverage forms and policy forms is used to insure government entities, such as states, counties, and public utilities.

The loss sustained version of the Commercial Crime Coverage Form is the most commonly used of the ISO crime forms. The other forms and policies provide similar coverages. See the exhibit "Crime Forms: Discovery Form Versus Loss Sustained Form."

Crime Forms: Discovery Form Versus Loss Sustained Form

Discovery Form	Loss Sustained Form
Form that covers losses discovered during the policy period even though they may have occurred before the policy period.	Form that covers losses actually sustained during the policy period and discovered no later than one year after policy expiration.

[DA07817]

Financial Institution Bonds

Few industries have crime loss exposures equal to those faced by banks and other financial institutions. A financial institution bond is an insurance policy that covers the crime loss exposures of financial institutions. Financial institution bonds were developed by the Surety and Fidelity Association of America (SFAA) and are called "bonds" because one of the key coverages that they provide is employee dishonesty insurance, which was traditionally called a "fidelity bond."

Although banks are the most common type of financial institution, other entities—such as savings and loan associations, credit unions, stockbrokers, finance companies, and insurance companies—are also eligible to be insured under financial institution bonds. Entities eligible for financial institution bonds are not eligible for the ISO commercial crime program.

The most widely used financial institution bond is Standard Form No. 24, used to insure banks and savings and loan associations. For many years, this form was called the "bankers blanket bond," a term still often used informally to refer to this coverage. The forms used for other types of financial institutions are similar to Form 24. ISO also publishes financial institution forms similar to the SFAA forms, and many of the insurers that specialize in financial institution coverage have developed their own forms.

COMMERCIAL CRIME INSURING AGREEMENTS

Insurance Services Office's (ISO's) Commercial Crime Coverage Form offers eight optional insuring agreements that enable organizations to customize crime coverage to meet their business needs.

The ISO Commercial Crime Coverage Form includes these eight insuring agreements:

- Employee Theft
- Forgery or Alteration
- Inside the Premises—Theft of Money and Securities
- Inside the Premises—Robbery or Safe Burglary of Other Property
- Outside the Premises
- Computer Fraud
- Funds Transfer Fraud
- Money Orders and Counterfeit Money

Insureds may select one or more of these insuring agreements and can add other crime coverages by endorsement.

Employee Theft

The insuring agreement covers an employer against theft of its property by its own employees. The scope of the coverage is determined by policy definitions of various terms. See the exhibit "Summary of Employee Theft Coverage."

Summary of Employee Theft Coverage

Cause of Loss	"Theft" committed by any "employee."
Property Covered	"Money," "securities," and "other property."
Where Coverage Applies	Covered territory is United States (including its territories and possessions), Puerto Rico, and Canada. Coverage also applies to loss caused by an employee who is temporarily outside the covered territory for not more than ninety consecutive days.

[DA02511]

The policy defines "theft" as the unlawful taking of "money," "securities," or "other property" to the deprivation of the insured. No police report or criminal conviction is required for coverage to apply. The Employee Theft insuring agreement also states that the term "theft" includes forgery—thereby clarifying that forgery committed by an employee is covered under this insuring agreement, not under the Forgery or Alteration insuring agreement.

The policy definition of "employee" is a natural person (not a corporation) who is currently employed by the insured or who was employed by the insured within the past thirty days; who is compensated by the insured by salary, wages, or commissions; and who is subject to the control and direction of the insured.

The policy defines these types of covered property:

- "Money" means currency, coins, and bank notes in current use with a face value, and travelers' checks, register checks, and money orders held for sale to the public.
- "Securities" means negotiable and nonnegotiable instruments or contracts representing money or other property, such as stocks, bonds, tokens, tickets, stamps, and evidences of debt issued in connection with credit cards other than cards issued by the insured.
- "Other property" means all other tangible property that has intrinsic value. Computer programs, electronic data, and other specified property is excluded. "Tangible" means "possible to touch." Copyrights, patents, intellectual property, and other intangible items are not covered property under the crime coverage form.

The Employee Theft insuring agreement extends the coverage territory to include loss caused by any employee while temporarily outside the regular policy territory (the United States, including its territories and possessions, Puerto Rico, and Canada) for up to ninety consecutive days.

Forgery or Alteration

This insuring agreement covers loss sustained for these reasons:

> "forgery" or alteration of checks, drafts, promissory notes, or similar written promises, orders or directions to pay a sum certain in "money" that are:
>
> (1) Made or drawn by or drawn upon you; or
>
> (2) Made or drawn by one acting as your agent;
>
> or that are purported to have been so made or drawn.[1]

The coverage pays losses of the insured or its representatives resulting from forgery or alteration of checks and similar instruments; it does not pay losses resulting from the insured's knowing acceptance of instruments that have been forged or altered by others. See the exhibit "Summary of Forgery or Alteration Coverage."

Forgery or alteration coverage does not apply to loss resulting from dishonest acts of the insured or of its partners, members, directors, trustees, representatives, or employees. Forgery committed against the insured by the insured's employees is covered under the Employee Theft insuring agreement, not under the Forgery or Alteration insuring agreement.

Summary of Forgery or Alteration Coverage

Causes of Loss	"Forgery" and alteration
Property Covered	Checks, drafts, promissory notes, or similar instruments made or drawn by the insured or the insured's agent
Where Coverage Applies	Worldwide

[DA07838]

Inside the Premises—Theft of Money and Securities

This insuring agreement covers money and securities inside the "premises" or "banking premises" against theft, disappearance, or destruction.

Under this insuring agreement, "premises" means the interior of any commercial building the named insured occupies. A "banking premises" is the interior of that portion of a building occupied by a banking institution or similar safe depository.

The insuring agreement extends coverage to apply to loss or damage to the premises if the insured is the owner or is liable for the damage, and to containers that hold covered property if damage is caused by safe burglary or attempted safe burglary.

The policy definition of theft includes any type of "unlawful taking" of covered property "to the deprivation of the insured." Hence, an insured loss (subject to exclusions) can be caused by burglary, robbery, observed or unobserved theft, or any other unlawful taking of money or securities. However, for this coverage to apply, the thief must be present inside the premises or the banking premises; thus, theft committed through a remote computer would not be covered.

Disappearance or destruction includes losses regardless of whether they are caused by unlawful acts. For example, coverage is provided for money and securities destroyed by fire, and disappearance of property is covered regardless of whether theft appears to be the cause. See the exhibit "Summary of Inside the Premises—Theft of Money and Securities Coverage."

Inside the Premises—Robbery or Safe Burglary of Other Property

The insuring agreement covers "other property" from actual or attempted "robbery" of a "custodian" and actual or attempted "safe burglary."

Summary of Inside the Premises—Theft of Money and Securities Coverage

	Basic Coverage	Extension for Damage to Premises	Extension for Containers
Covered Causes of Loss	"Theft," disappearance, destruction	Actual or attempted "theft" of "money" or "securities"	Actual or attempted "theft" or unlawful entry
Covered Property	"Money," "securities"	The "premises" or their exterior	Locked safe, vault, cash register, cash box, or cash drawer
Where Coverage Applies	Inside the "premises" or "banking premises" (The thief must be present inside the premises.)	At the "premises"	Inside the "premises"

[DA02514]

According to the policy definition, the unlawful taking of property is considered "robbery" if the person taking the property has caused or threatened to cause bodily harm to the person having care or custody of the property or if the custodian witnesses an obviously unlawful act (for example, seeing someone run out of the store with property for which he or she has not paid). See the exhibit "Summary of Inside the Premises—Robbery or Safe Burglary of Other Property Coverage."

Summary of Inside the Premises—Robbery or Safe Burglary of Other Property Coverage

	Basic Coverage	Extension for Damage to Premises	Extension for Containers
Covered Causes of Loss	Actual or attempted "robbery" of a "custodian" or "safe burglary"	Actual or attempted "robbery" or "safe burglary" of "other property"	Actual or attempted "robbery" or "safe burglary"
Covered Property	"Other property"	The "premises" or their exterior	Locked safe or vault
Where Coverage Applies	Inside the "premises"	At the "premises"	Inside the "premises"

[DA02521]

For robbery coverage to apply, the property must be inside the premises when taken from the named insured, the named insured's partners, or any employee who is a custodian as defined in the policy. A custodian may be a salesperson or cashier working inside the insured's store but cannot be a watchperson (hired exclusively to have care and custody of property inside the premises with no other duties) or janitor (a doorkeeper or person who cleans or maintains the premises).

The other covered peril, "safe burglary," is the unlawful taking of a safe or vault from inside the premises or of property from within a locked safe or vault by a person unlawfully entering the safe or vault as evidenced by marks of forcible entry. Coverage is only provided if a burglar leaves marks of forcible entry into the safe or vault. In an actual or attempted robbery or safe burglary, coverage extends for resulting damage to the premises and for loss of or damage to a locked safe or vault located inside the premises.

Outside the Premises

The insuring agreement covers money, securities, and other property while outside the premises and in the care and custody of either a "messenger" or an armored vehicle company. The policy defines "messenger" as the named insured, a relative of the named insured, any partner or member of the named insured, "or any 'employee' while having care and custody of property outside the 'premises.' "[2] For example, an employee who takes cash and checks to the bank for deposit in the insured's account is a messenger.

The perils insured against vary by the type of property involved in the loss. Money and securities are covered against theft, disappearance, or destruction. Other property is covered against actual or attempted robbery. See the exhibit "Summary of Outside the Premises Coverage."

Computer Fraud

The insuring agreement covers loss of money, securities, and other property resulting from the use of a computer to fraudulently transfer property from inside the premises or a banking premises to either a person (other than a messenger) or a place outside the premises.

The insuring agreement does not require the computers used to commit the fraud to be the property of the insured or located on the insured's premises. Coverage applies if a nonemployee uses his or her own computer to gain access to the insured's computer system and to transfer funds to his or her own account. The Computer Fraud insuring agreement does not cover computer-related theft committed by the insured's own employees. See the exhibit "Summary of Computer Fraud Coverage."

Summary of Outside the Premises Coverage

	Coverage for "Money" and "Securities"	Coverage for "Other Property"
Covered Causes of Loss	"Theft," disappearance, destruction	Actual or attempted "robbery"
Where Coverage Applies	Outside the "premises" while in care or custody of a "messenger" or an armored car company and inside the United States (including its territories and possessions), Puerto Rico, and Canada	Outside the "premises" while in care or custody of a "messenger" or an armored car company and inside the U.S. (including its territories and possessions), Puerto Rico, and Canada

[DA02522]

Summary of Computer Fraud Coverage

Covered Cause of Loss	Use of a computer to fraudulently cause a transfer of covered property
Covered Property	"Money," "securities," and "other property"
Where Coverage Applies	The property must be transferred from inside the "premises" or a "banking premises" to a person or place anywhere else in the world.

[DA02523]

Funds Transfer Fraud

Hundreds of billions of dollars move electronically between banks daily. The Funds Transfer Fraud insuring agreement covers loss of money and securities from the insured's account at a financial institution because of a "fraudulent instruction," as defined in the policy:

- Electronic, telephonic, telefacsimile, telegraphic, cable, or teletype instructions by someone without the insured's knowledge or consent

- Forged or altered written instructions, other than those covered in the Forgery or Alteration insuring agreement

- Instructions the insured receives that were purportedly prepared by an employee of the insured but were in fact prepared by someone else, without the insured's or the employee's knowledge or consent

Computer fraud is excluded from this coverage. See the exhibit "Summary of Funds Transfer Fraud Coverage."

Summary of Funds Transfer Fraud Coverage

Covered Cause of Loss	"Fraudulent instruction" directing a financial institution to transfer, pay, or deliver funds.
Covered Property	"Funds" defined to mean money and securities.
Where Coverage Applies	The financial institution must be located within the policy territory.

[DA02524]

Money Orders and Counterfeit Money

The insuring agreement covers loss from money orders that are not paid when presented and "counterfeit money" that the insured has accepted in good faith in exchange for merchandise, money, or services. See the exhibit "Summary of Money Orders and Counterfeit Money Coverage."

Summary of Money Orders and Counterfeit Money Coverage

Covered Cause of Loss	Good-faith acceptance of: (1) Money orders that are not paid upon presentation or (2) "Counterfeit money"
Covered Property	Money orders issued by any post office, express company, or bank; and "counterfeit money" paper currency acquired during the regular course of business
Where Coverage Applies	United States (including its territories and possessions), Puerto Rico, and Canada

[DA02525]

COMMERCIAL CRIME EXCLUSIONS

As with most insurance coverage forms, the Commercial Crime Coverage Form excludes losses that are best covered under other insurance, are not insurable, or are not anticipated in the policy rates.

In the Insurance Services Office (ISO) Commercial Crime Coverage Form, the basic crime insuring agreements are subject to several exclusions. The exclusions are divided into different groups depending on whether they apply to all insuring agreements or only to some insuring agreements.

Exclusions are presented in the coverage form and described in this section based on these groupings:

- General exclusions
- Exclusions applicable only to employee theft
- Exclusions applicable to inside the premises and outside the premises
- Exclusions applicable only to computer fraud
- Exclusion applicable only to funds transfer fraud

General Exclusions

Ten general exclusions are applicable to any of the crime insuring agreements:

- Acts Committed by You, Your Partners or Your Members—The exclusion eliminates coverage for loss resulting from theft or any other dishonest act committed by the named insured, the named insured's partners, or (if the named insured is a limited liability company) the named insured's members, whether acting alone or in collusion with other persons.
- Acts of Employees Learned of by You Prior to the Policy Period—The exclusion eliminates coverage for loss resulting from theft or any other dishonest act committed by an employee if the named insured, the named insured's partners, or the named insured's members, or any managers, officers, directors, or trustees not in collusion with the employee knew that the employee had committed theft or a dishonest act before the policy effective date. This exclusion prevents the insurer from having to cover employee theft committed by employees who are known, prior to the policy period, to have committed any type of dishonest act.
- Acts of Employees, Managers, Directors, Trustees or Representatives— The commercial crime form excludes theft or other dishonest acts committed by the named insured's employees, managers, directors, trustees, or authorized representatives. The exclusion applies whether such person was acting alone or in collusion with others and while such person was performing services for the named insured or otherwise. The exclusion states that it does not apply to loss covered under the Employee Theft insuring agreement.

- Confidential Information—The form excludes losses resulting from the unauthorized disclosure of confidential information such as patents, trade secrets, processing methods, or customer lists. Loss due to unauthorized use or disclosure of confidential nonpublic information, such as another person's or entity's financial, personal, or credit card information, is also excluded.

- Governmental Action—Like virtually any policy covering property loss, the commercial crime form excludes loss resulting from seizure or destruction of property by order of government authority.

- Indirect Loss—The form lists three examples of indirect loss that are not covered: (1) business income losses; (2) payment of damages for which the insured is legally liable (other than compensatory damages arising directly from a loss covered by the policy); and (3) expenses incurred in establishing either the existence or the amount of loss under the policy. The exclusion is not limited to just those three types of indirect loss; any indirect loss is excluded.

- Legal Fees, Costs and Expenses—The form excludes fees, costs, and expenses related to any legal action, except when covered under the Forgery and Alteration insuring agreement.

- Nuclear Hazard—Similar to the Nuclear Hazard exclusion in the commercial property causes of loss forms, the Nuclear Hazard exclusion in the commercial crime form excludes loss or damage caused by any nuclear reaction or radiation, or by any radioactive contamination.

- Pollution—This exclusion eliminates coverage for any loss or damage that in any way results from pollution, which the exclusion defines as "the discharge, dispersal, seepage, migration, release or escape of any solid, liquid, gaseous, or thermal irritant or contaminant." Pollution includes residuals of pollutants, such as smoke, vapor, fumes, and so forth, along with materials to be recycled, reconditioned or reclaimed.

- War and Military Action—This exclusion is identical to the War and Military Action exclusion in the commercial property causes of loss forms. The exclusion eliminates coverage for loss or damage resulting from war or civil war, whether declared or undeclared; warlike actions by a military force; or acts of rebellion or revolution, including governmental action to defend against such acts.

Exclusions Applicable Only to Employee Theft

This group of exclusions applies only to the Employee Theft insuring agreement:

- Inventory Shortages—The insurer will not pay for any loss that depends on inventory or profit-and-loss calculations to prove either the existence or the amount of the loss. An inventory shortage is the difference between a physical inventory and the inventory shown in the insured's books and records. An inventory shortage may occur for reasons other than employee theft. For example, there may have been bookkeeping or arithmetic errors, obsolete inventory may have been discarded, or samples may have been sent to customers but not deleted from the inventory records. Therefore, insurers will not accept an inventory calculation as proof that the insured has sustained an employee theft loss. However, if an insured establishes without inventory computations that it has sustained a loss, the form allows the insured to offer inventory records and actual physical count of inventory in support of the amount of loss claimed.

- Trading—An employer may sustain a large financial loss resulting from an employee's unauthorized trading in stocks, bonds, futures, commodities, or other similar items. Because employee theft coverage rates do not contemplate such losses, the form excludes loss resulting from trading, whether the trading occurs in the named insured's name or in a "genuine or fictitious account."

- Warehouse Receipts—The Warehouse Receipts exclusion eliminates coverage for "[l]oss resulting from fraudulent or dishonest signing, issuing, canceling or failing to cancel, a warehouse receipt or any papers connected with it." Such a loss may occur, for example, when an employee releases merchandise without canceling the receipt or issues a receipt without having received the merchandise. The customer could then make a claim for missing goods based on the erroneous receipts. Such claims would not be covered because of this exclusion.

Exclusions Applicable Only to Inside the Premises and Outside the Premises

These eight exclusions apply specifically to the Inside the Premises—Theft of Money and Securities, Inside the Premises—Robbery or Safe Burglary of Other Property, and Outside the Premises insuring agreements:

- Accounting or Arithmetical Errors or Omissions—The form excludes losses resulting from accounting or arithmetical errors or omissions. Although many losses of this type are within the policy deductible, some losses could be sizable. The exposure falls within the general category of business risks that should be addressed by loss control measures, with any losses retained by the business.

- Exchanges or Purchases—Loss due to giving or surrendering property in an exchange or purchase is excluded. Thus, a fraudulent transaction that involves the loss of money, securities, or other property is not covered. For example, the loss sustained when a purchaser pays with a forged cashier's check is excluded from coverage.

- Fire—The three insuring agreements do not cover loss or damage resulting from fire, regardless of its cause. However, the exclusion does not apply to fire damage to a safe or vault. The exclusion also does not apply (under Inside the Premises—Theft of Money and Securities) to money or securities damaged or destroyed by fire. Nearly all organizations have commercial property insurance to cover the fire losses that the crime form excludes; money, however, is not covered under commercial property coverage forms.

- Money Operated Devices—Loss of property from money operated devices (such as vending machines, amusement devices, or change machines) is not covered unless a continuous recording instrument inside the machine keeps track of the amount of money deposited. In the absence of a recording device, establishing the amount of the loss would be difficult or impossible.

- Motor Vehicles or Equipment and Accessories—The form excludes loss of or damage to motor vehicles, trailers, or semi-trailers, or for equipment and accessories attached to them. Theft of automobiles and related equipment can be insured under automobile physical damage coverage, and theft of mobile equipment can be insured under inland marine forms.

- Transfer or Surrender of Property—Loss of or damage to property after it has been transferred or surrendered to a person or place outside the premises or banking premises is excluded under several specified circumstances. For example, loss of property that the insured has voluntarily sent to an imposter on the basis of unauthorized instructions is excluded.

- Vandalism—Coverage extensions stated in the two inside the premises insuring agreements cover damage to the premises and their exterior and loss of or damage to various types of receptacles containing covered property, if directly caused by a covered peril. The Vandalism exclusion eliminates coverage for damage to those types of property by vandalism or malicious mischief. Commercial property forms normally include coverage for damage to such property by vandalism or malicious mischief, including building damage caused by the breaking in or exiting of burglars.

- Voluntary Parting With Title to or Possession of Property—The Voluntary Parting exclusion eliminates coverage when the insured or an agent of the insured is tricked into voluntarily surrendering property to a thief. For example, a business owner tells the firm's cashier that a bank messenger is to pick up money at a given time each day. If a wrongdoer impersonates the messenger and succeeds in getting the cashier to part with the money voluntarily, the loss would not be covered by Inside the Premises—Theft of Money and Securities.

Exclusions Applicable Only to Computer Fraud

These three exclusions apply only to the Computer Fraud insuring agreement:

- Credit Card Transactions—Loss resulting from the use or purported use of credit, debit, charge, access, convenience, identification, stored-value, or other cards or the information contained on such cards is excluded.

- Funds Transfer Fraud—Loss resulting from a fraudulent instruction directing a financial institution to transfer, pay, or deliver funds from the insured's accounts is excluded. This exclusion is intended to avoid duplication of coverage provided by the Funds Transfer Fraud insuring agreement.

- Inventory Shortages—A separate Inventory Shortages exclusion applies to computer fraud coverage. Unlike the general exclusion, this exclusion does not include the wording permitting the insured to use inventory records in support of the amount of loss claimed.

Exclusion Applicable Only to Funds Transfer Fraud

To avoid duplicating coverage provided by the Computer Fraud insuring agreement, the Funds Transfer Fraud insuring agreement excludes loss due to the use of a computer to transfer money, securities, or other property.

Apply Your Knowledge

Identify any exclusions of the Commercial Crime Coverage Form that would apply to these losses. In each case, the insured has purchased all of the insuring agreements under this coverage form.

Tom, an employee of the insured, commits an act that meets all of the requirements under the Employee Theft insuring agreement. The insurer's claim investigation reveals that Tom had been arrested for shoplifting before the policy period began. However, Tom's employer had no knowledge of Tom's prior dishonesty until it was revealed by the investigation. Would the Acts of Employees Learned of by You Prior to the Policy Period exclusion eliminate coverage for this loss?

Feedback: No. The exclusion applies only if the insured learned of the prior dishonest act before the beginning of the policy period. In this case, Tom's employer did not know about Tom's prior dishonest act before the policy period, so the exclusion does not apply.

Vandals set the insured's building on fire. In addition to damaging the building and its contents, the fire destroyed $5,000 of money that was in the insured's building. The loss of money meets all the requirements under the Inside the Premises—Theft of Money and Securities insuring agreement, which covers money and securities against theft, disappearance, or destruction. Would the Fire exclusion eliminate coverage for this loss?

Feedback: No. The Fire exclusion does not apply to loss of or damage to money or securities.

A thief broke into and stole money from vending machines located in a convenience store. The vending machines did not contain recording instruments to track the money that was deposited. The loss of money meets all the requirements under the Inside the Premises—Theft of Money and Securities insuring agreement. Would the Money Operated Devices exclusion eliminate coverage for this loss?

Feedback: Yes. The Money Operated Devices exclusion eliminates coverage from such devices that do not have a continuous recording instrument inside the machine to keep track of the amount of money deposited.

COMMERCIAL CRIME CONDITIONS

The Insurance Services Office (ISO) Commercial Crime Coverage Form includes numerous policy conditions that affect the application or extent of coverage provided.

As with all insurance policies, conditions are included in the ISO Commercial Crime Coverage Form that extend or eliminate coverage under various circumstances. Some conditions apply only to certain insuring agreements. Other conditions apply to all of the insuring agreements. The latter group, although listed alphabetically in the form, are presented here in logical order followed by two conditions that apply only to the Employee Theft insuring agreement.

Interests Insured

Several conditions help to clarify issues concerning the interests insured under a crime policy.

The Ownership of Property; Interests Covered condition states that the insurance applies only to property owned, leased, or held by the named insured regardless of whether the insured is legally liable for loss to such property. However, the insurance is for the insured's benefit only; any claim must be made by the insured. If the insured does not want to present a claim, the owner of the property cannot make a direct claim on the insurance. Coverage for theft by the insured's employee of client's property may be added by endorsement.

The Joint Insured condition appoints the first named insured as agent for all other insureds with regard to all transactions under the policy. It also provides that an employee of any insured is considered to be an employee of every insured and that knowledge possessed by any insured or any partner, officer, or limited liability company (LLC) member of any insured is considered to be known to all insureds.

If, during the policy period, the insured adds additional premises or employees other than by consolidation, merger, or acquisition, the Additional Premises or Employees condition states that policy coverage will be extended automatically. No notice is required, and no additional premium is charged for the remainder of the policy period. On renewal, the insured must give the insurer full information, and the renewal premium will reflect the revised exposure.

If the insured acquires additional employees or premises by consolidation, merger, or acquisition, the Consolidation—Merger or Acquisition condition states that coverage will be extended automatically for ninety days to the new employees or premises. If the insured wishes to extend coverage beyond ninety days, the insured must notify the insurer of the consolidation, merger, or acquisition promptly and pay the appropriate additional premium.

Where Coverage Applies

Many of the crime insuring agreements limit coverage to occurrences inside the premises described in the policy. When coverage is not restricted to the premises, the Territory condition defines the geographical scope of coverage. This condition limits coverage for all insuring agreements to acts committed or events occurring within the United States (including its territories and possessions), Puerto Rico, and Canada. The territorial provision for employee theft coverage is extended to include coverage for loss caused by employees temporarily outside the coverage territory for not more than ninety days. The territorial provisions for forgery or alteration and computer fraud are extended to cover loss resulting from occurrences taking place anywhere in the world.

When Coverage Applies

Three conditions are principally concerned with determining when a loss must occur in order to be covered under the loss sustained version of the Commercial Crime Coverage Form:

- Extended Period to Discover Loss
- Loss Sustained During Prior Insurance Issued by Us or Any Affiliate
- Loss Sustained During Prior Insurance Not Issued by Us or Any Affiliate

Extended Period to Discover Loss

Under the loss sustained form, the insurer will pay for loss that the named insured sustains through acts committed or events occurring during the policy period. Moreover, coverage applies only to acts discovered during the policy period or within one year after the policy is canceled. However, the discovery period terminates immediately as of the effective date of any other insurance that the insured obtains (from any insurer) that replaces coverage in whole or in part. See the exhibit "Discovery Form."

Loss Sustained During Prior Insurance Issued by Us or Any Affiliate

Some losses occurring before the current policy period of a loss sustained crime policy may be covered by the policy currently in effect. Under the Loss

Discovery Form

All of the ISO crime forms are available in loss sustained and discovery versions. The discovery form covers losses regardless of when they occurred if they are first discovered during the policy period or during the sixty-day discovery period that applies to most claims under the discovery form.

To limit the broad coverage for prior occurrences that discovery forms provide, the insurer may attach a retroactive date endorsement. This endorsement states that coverage is limited to losses the insured sustains through acts committed or events occurring after the retroactive date shown in the policy schedule. For coverage to apply, the loss must still be discovered during the policy period or the extended loss discovery period.

[DA07834]

Sustained During Prior Insurance Issued by Us or Any Affiliate condition, the insurer agrees to pay a loss that meets these criteria:

- The loss is discovered during the policy period shown in the declarations.
- The loss occurred while prior insurance, issued by the same insurer or an affiliated insurer, was in effect.
- The current insurance became effective when the prior insurance was canceled.
- The loss would have been covered by the present insurance if the insurance had been in force at the time of loss.

If these requirements are met, the current policy applies, but the most the insurer will pay is the amount recoverable under the prior insurance, if it had remained in effect.

The same condition also contains provisions for settling covered losses that occurred over more than one policy period. Such losses typically are associated with employee theft, in which an employee may have embezzled funds for years before the employer discovers the loss.

Coverage must be continuous; that is, the renewal policy must have commenced when the prior policy expired, but no limit of insurance accumulates from year to year. A policy in force for ten years with a $50,000 limit will pay a maximum of $50,000 for any one covered loss, not ten times $50,000. This is important to consider when selecting the amount of insurance for employee theft coverage. A dishonest employee often steals smaller amounts on numerous occasions over many years that can accumulate in significant losses.

This condition is found in the loss sustained form only; it is not needed in the discovery form because the discovery form covers loss, regardless of when it occurred, that is discovered during the current policy period.

Loss Sustained During Prior Insurance Not Issued by Us or Any Affiliate

If the prior insurance was not provided by the current insurer or an affiliate, the Loss Sustained During Prior Insurance Not Issued by Us or Any Affiliate condition applies. Under this condition, which is found in the loss sustained form but not in the discovery form, the insurer agrees to pay a loss that meets all of these criteria:

- The loss is discovered during the policy period shown in the declarations.
- The loss occurred while prior insurance, issued by another unaffiliated insurer, was in effect.
- The current insurance became effective when the prior insurance was canceled or terminated.
- The loss would have been covered by the present insurance if the insurance had been in force at the time of loss.

If these requirements are met, the insurer will pay the *lesser* of the amount recoverable under the present insurance or the prior insurance (if it had remained in effect).

 Reality Check

Loss Sustained During Prior Insurance Not Issued by Us

This hypothetical example illustrates why an insurer would be willing to cover a loss that occurred during the prior policy period of another insurer.

Joanie, the proprietor of an electronics store, was alarmed when her commercial crime insurer raised the premium on her loss sustained crime policy by 20 percent. She consulted Mark, her insurance agent, because she wanted to change insurers. However, she was concerned that she would not be covered for any crime loss that occurred when that policy was in effect but was not discovered until after the policy was canceled.

Mark explained that another insurer offers loss sustained coverage using ISO's Commercial Crime Coverage Form. He told Joanie that the form has a condition that would cover a loss sustained during prior insurance not issued by the new insurer if the loss met specified criteria.

After Mark explained the criteria and quoted Joanie a lower premium on the new crime policy, Joanie was surprised that the new insurer would be willing to cover such a loss. Mark explained that without the offer of such coverage, it would be nearly impossible to persuade an insured to switch to a new insurer. In effect, providing this coverage for a prior period is one of an insurer's costs of acquiring new policyholders.

[DA07835]

The essential difference between these two provisions concerns the available limits. If the loss is covered by both the current insurance and prior insurance issued by the same or an affiliated company, the highest limit in force under any of the policies covering the loss will be available to the insured. If the loss occurred under prior insurance issued by another insurer, recovery is limited to, at most, the applicable limit in the policy in effect at the time of the loss.

Claim-Related Duties and Procedures

Several conditions establish the duties and procedures to follow after a loss involving covered property.

The insured's duties stated in the Duties in the Event of Loss condition in a crime policy are essentially the same as such duties under other property policies. After discovering a loss or a situation that may result in a loss, the insured has these duties:

*   Notify the insurer as soon as possible and, except for employee theft and forgery and alteration losses, notify the police if the insured believes that the loss involves a violation of law

*   Submit to examination under oath if requested by the insurer

*   Produce all pertinent records for the insurer to examine

*   Submit a detailed, sworn proof of loss within 120 days

*   Cooperate with the insurer in its investigation of the loss

The Records condition in a crime policy requires the insured to keep sufficient records to enable the insurer to verify the amount of loss.

Under the Valuation—Settlement condition of a crime policy, the value of a covered loss is determined differently for each of the three categories of covered property:

*   Money is valued at its face value. If foreign money is lost, the insured has the option of receiving payment for the loss at the face value of the money or at its equivalent U.S. value on the date of the loss.

*   Securities are valued as of the close of business on the day the loss is discovered. In many cases, duplicate securities can be issued if the insured posts a bond. The insurer will pay the cost of the bond as part of the loss. The insurer has the option of paying the market value of lost securities or replacing them in kind. If securities are replaced, the insured must assign to the insurer all rights, title, and interest in the lost securities.

*   If property other than money and securities is lost or damaged, the insurer has the option of paying the replacement cost of the property, repairing the property, or replacing it. If the property is not promptly repaired or replaced as soon after the loss or damage as possible, the insurer will pay the loss on an actual cash value basis.

The Recoveries condition of a crime policy specifies how any subrogation or salvage recoveries will be divided between the insurer and the insured. First the insured is reimbursed for its covered loss that exceeded the limit of insurance. The remaining amount of the recovery is paid to the insurer until it has recovered all that it paid. Any remaining value is paid to the insured to reimburse it for the deductible amount and for any loss not covered by the insurance.

As with most insurance policies, the crime general provisions include a subrogation provision. Under the Transfer of Your Rights Against Others to Us condition, for any loss the insurer pays to the insured, the insured must transfer its rights of recovery against others to the insurer. Moreover, the insured must do nothing after loss to impair those rights. (The insured is permitted to waive its rights of action against other parties if the waiver is made before loss occurs.)

The Other Insurance condition is split into two parts: primary and excess.

If the insurance is written as primary, a loss will be shared on a pro rata by limits basis with other insurance subject to the same terms and conditions. If the other insurance is not subject to the same terms and conditions, the insurance will apply as excess coverage over any other insurance available to the insured to cover a loss. Often, the other policy will have a similar clause. When two or more policies cover a loss and all policies purport to be excess over other insurance, courts usually require the insurers to contribute on a pro rata basis if the insurers are unable to agree on a mutually acceptable method.

If the insurance is written on an excess basis, the insurer will only pay the amount of loss that exceeds the limit and deductible of the other insurance.

Conditions Applicable to Employee Theft Only

Two conditions apply only to the Employee Theft insuring agreement: the Termination as to Any Employee condition and the Employee Benefit Plans condition.

The first part of the Termination as to Any Employee condition automatically terminates employee theft coverage with respect to any employee who has committed a dishonest act as soon as the act is known to the insured or any partner, officer, or director not in collusion with the employee. Coverage on the employee is terminated regardless of whether the act was committed against the insured or others (before or after the employee was hired by the insured) and regardless of whether the employer learns of it before or after policy inception.

If the insured first learns of an employee's dishonest act after the employee has committed an employee theft, the loss will be covered (assuming no other exclusions apply), but coverage with respect to that employee for any further claims will be terminated.

If, in another situation, a claim investigation of an employee theft loss reveals that the insured knew about a prior dishonest act by the same employee, the current claim will not be covered, because coverage for that employee was automatically terminated when the insured learned of the prior dishonest act.

The second part of the Termination as to Any Employee condition gives the insurer the right to cancel coverage with respect to any employee by providing thirty days' advance notice to the insured.

The Employee Benefit Plans condition explains how employee theft coverage applies when the policy includes one or more employee benefit plans as insureds for the Employee Theft insuring agreement. This condition eliminates the need to attach the Employee Retirement Income Security Act of 1974 (ERISA) compliance endorsement to the policy to satisfy the ERISA fidelity bonding requirement. Employee theft coverage was traditionally called a fidelity bond, and the term "fidelity" is still used to refer to employee theft coverage.

Apply Your Knowledge

On August 5, Millright Foods canceled its crime insurance policy, which it had purchased from Insurer A. Millright then purchased a new crime policy from Insurer A's affiliate, Insurer B, which took effect on the cancellation date of Insurer A's policy. Insurer B's policy uses the ISO Commercial Crime Coverage Form. Four months after Insurer B's policy became effective and during its policy period, Millright discovered that one of its former managers, who left Millright's employment on July 15 of that year, had been embezzling funds over the previous three months. Insurer A denied coverage for the loss because the loss was not discovered until after Insurer A's policy was canceled.

How would the Loss Sustained During Prior Insurance Issued by Us or Any Affiliate condition in Insurer B's policy affect coverage for this loss?

Feedback: This condition specifies that the loss will be covered under Insurer B's policy if these requirements are met: the loss is discovered during the policy period shown in the declarations, the loss occurred while the affiliate's insurance was in effect, the current insurance became effective when the prior insurance was canceled, and the loss would have been covered by the present insurance if the insurance had been in force at the time of loss.

TYPES OF SURETY BONDS

Many types of surety bonds are needed to address a variety of surety bonding needs.

Surety bonds may be designed to comply not only with various contractual arrangements that arise between a **principal** and an **obligee**, but also with various legal and statutory requirements.

Obligee

The party to a surety bond that receives the surety's guarantee that the principal will fulfill an obligation or perform as promised.

Principal

The party to a surety bond whose obligation or performance the surety guarantees.

Suretyship

The obligation of one entity to answer for the debt, default, or miscarriage of performance of duties by another entity.

Contract bond

A surety bond guaranteeing the fulfillment of obligations under construction contracts or other types of contracts.

Surety

The party (usually an insurer) to a surety bond that guarantees to the obligee that the principal will fulfill an obligation or perform as required by the underlying contract, permit, or law.

Bid bond

A contract bond guaranteeing that a contractor bidding on a construction or supply contract will enter into the contract and will provide a performance bond if the bid is accepted.

Performance bond

A contract bond guaranteeing that a contractor's work will be completed according to plans and specifications.

Suretyship is usually conducted by insurers. Because surety bonds are used to provide a wide range of guarantees, many types exist. They fall into these categories:

- Contract bonds
- License and permit bonds
- Public official bonds
- Court bonds
- Miscellaneous bonds

Contract Bonds

Contract bonds are often required of an individual or organization (the principal) that is contractually obligated to perform work or a service for another individual or organization (the obligee). They serve two broad purposes:

- The **surety**'s willingness to furnish the bond is evidence that, in the surety's judgment, the principal is qualified to fulfill the terms of the contract.
- The surety guarantees that, even if the principal defaults, the obligations of the contract will be performed, or the surety will indemnify the obligee.

Contract bonds are frequently required by law; therefore, obligees are often government entities. However, private entities can also be obligees in such contracts. See the exhibit "Relationship Between Parties in a Contract Bond."

Contract bonds fall into several categories, each with unique characteristics:

- **Bid bond**—The obligee is usually the owner of a proposed construction project, although in some cases it may be a general contractor. If the principal (the bidder) fails to fulfill this obligation, the surety will pay the obligee the difference between the amount of the principal's bid and the bid finally accepted, plus any additional expenses incurred because of the contractor's default.
- **Performance bond**—The surety typically has several options if the principal has defaulted, including completing the contract using either the existing contractor or a replacement, having the obligee arrange for completion of the work and reimbursing the obligee for the additional costs, or paying damages. The surety has the right to seek reimbursement from the principal for any payments.

Relationship Between Parties in a Contract Bond

Owner, a fast-food chain, wants to build a new outlet and engages Contractor to construct a building. The building contract between Owner and Contractor can be illustrated in this way:

Contractor ▬▬▬▬▬▬▬ Owner

Building Contract

Owner wants assurance that if Contractor defaults, Owner will not lose money and the project will be completed as per agreement. Contractor goes to Surety to obtain a guarantee that will satisfy Owner. The three-party contractual situation, or surety bond, can be illustrated in this manner:

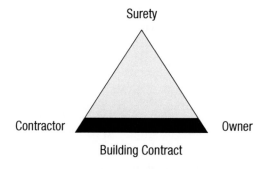

Surety

Contractor   Owner

Building Contract

[DA07774]

- **Payment bond**—This payment guarantee, also known as a labor and materials payment bond, is usually included in the contractor's performance bond but could be issued in a separate bond. It offers payment protection vital to private project owners because labor and material suppliers who go uncompensated can usually apply a mechanic's lien to the property. When a lien is placed on property, the owner does not have clear title to the property until all debts are settled.

- **Maintenance bond**—Some performance bonds automatically include this coverage without an additional charge for one year.

Contract bonds are also used to secure a variety of contracts other than construction contracts, such as those that deal with mechanical equipment rental with or without operators, transportation of school children, snow and garbage removal, or street cleaning.

Payment bond

A contract bond guaranteeing that the project will be free of liens.

Maintenance bond

A contract bond guaranteeing that the work will be free from defects in materials and workmanship for a specified period after the project is completed.

License and Permit Bonds

Cities, states, and other political subdivisions often require persons or organizations wanting to engage in a particular business or trade, such as auto dealers, liquor stores, or building contractors, to obtain a license. Similarly, a person or an organization wanting to exercise a particular privilege in connection with its business may be required to obtain a permit. Examples of activities that may require permits include food handling and use and disposal of chemicals that may cause pollution.

License and permit bonds vary in what they guarantee. Some bonds guarantee compliance with laws that apply to the licensed activity; some additionally guarantee the payment of damages to anyone who suffers a loss resulting from noncompliance with those laws.

Other such bonds apply to specific activities. For example, merchandising and dealer bonds guarantee that the principal will conduct merchandising activities according to law and account for any funds held in trust. Reclamation and environmental protection bonds guarantee that, after operations are complete, the principal will restore land to its original state and will clean up polluting spills or runoff.

Public Official Bonds

Public official bond

A commercial surety bond guaranteeing that a public official will perform his or her duties faithfully and honestly.

Certain types of public officials are required by law to have bonds that protect the public against the officials' failure to perform their duties faithfully and honestly. Officials required to obtain such **public official bonds** are those whose duties involve the handling of public funds, the seizure and disposition of property, the arrest or detention of persons, or any other duties that could result in violation of the rights of others. Among the public officials required to be bonded are treasurers, tax collectors, sheriffs and deputies, police officers, judges and court clerks, notaries public, insurance commissioners, and bank examiners.

Court Bonds

Court bonds

A classification of surety bonds guaranteeing that a person or an organization will faithfully perform certain duties prescribed by law or by a court or will demonstrate financial responsibility for the benefit of another until the final outcome of a court's decision.

Court bonds are often required by courts in connection with lawsuits. For example, if a defendant wants to appeal a court decision, the defendant must provide an appeal bond guaranteeing that the judgment will be paid if the appeal is unsuccessful.

Court bonds are also required in connection with disputes over the ownership of personal property. For example, Sean and Amy disagree about which one of them owns property in Sean's possession. Amy asks a court to compel Sean to return the property. The court will likely require both Sean and Amy to post court bonds until the case is decided. Sean's bond will guarantee that he will turn the property over to Amy if the case is decided in her favor. Amy's bond will guarantee that she will pay Sean any damages resulting from this action if it is decided in Sean's favor.

Court bonds also include fiduciary bonds, which guarantee the performance of persons appointed by a court to administer the property or interests of others. Principals of fiduciary bonds can include court-appointed guardians of minors or others, executors or administrators of estates, and receivers or trustees in bankruptcy proceedings.

Miscellaneous Bonds

Miscellaneous bonds are those that do not fit under other surety bond categories. These bonds often support private relationships and unique business needs. These examples illustrate the use of miscellaneous bonds:

- Lost securities bonds guarantee that an entity that issues replacements for lost securities will be indemnified for any financial loss that results from the duplication of the securities.

- Hazardous waste removal bonds guarantee federal or state governments that owners or operators of hazardous waste facilities will comply with laws for closure and post-closure care of the facilities.

- Credit enhancement financial guaranty bonds guarantee governmental entities that investors will be paid promised interest and that principal will be returned at maturity of debt instruments.

Apply Your Knowledge

Which type of bond (contract, license and permit, public official, court, or miscellaneous) may apply to each of the following scenarios?

a. A nuclear power plant stores spent nuclear fuel on its property.

b. A landscape designer is hired to landscape a housing development.

c. After Howard dies without a will, his nephew Sebastian is appointed to administer his estate.

d. A civic organization applies to the city for permission to stage a public fireworks display.

e. Marilyn is appointed treasurer of a school district.

Feedback: a. Miscellaneous (hazardous waste removal) bond; b. contract bond; c. court (fiduciary) bond; d. licensing and permit bond; and e. public official bond.

SUMMARY

Inland marine insurance provides a variety of flexible coverage solutions. Many states continue to use an updated NAIC Nationwide Marine Definition to differentiate marine insurance from other types of insurance for form and rate regulation. Inland marine business can be filed or nonfiled with state insurance departments, and underwriters use judgment rating for less common types of nonfiled, inland marine insurance.

ISO and AAIS file various forms on behalf of their members. However, the largest classes of inland marine insurance are, in many states, nonfiled and include contractors equipment, builders risk, transit, motor truck cargo liability, difference in conditions, and electronic data processing equipment.

Filed classes of inland marine insurance include coverage forms for commercial articles, camera and musical instrument dealers, equipment dealers, physicians and surgeons equipment, signs, theatrical property, film, floor plan merchandise, jewelers block, mail, accounts receivable, and valuable papers and records.

The ISO commercial crime program includes crime coverage forms that can be added to a commercial package policy and crime policy forms that can be written as monoline crime policies. ISO offers two versions of crime forms, the discovery form and the loss sustained form. Financial institution bonds provide employee dishonesty insurance and other crime coverages designed for banks, insurance companies, and other types of financial institutions.

Insureds can select from among the eight insuring agreements of the ISO Commercial Crime Coverage Form to tailor coverage for their businesses. These insuring agreements cover money, securities, and other property against a variety of covered perils, such as employee theft, forgery or alteration, robbery, safe burglary, theft, disappearance, destruction, computer fraud, funds transfer fraud, and good-faith acceptance of counterfeit money.

In the commercial crime form, the exclusions are divided into different groups depending on whether they apply to all insuring agreements or only to some insuring agreements.

The ISO Commercial Crime Coverage Form includes numerous policy conditions that extend or eliminate coverage under various circumstances. While some conditions apply only to particular insuring agreements, such as two that apply to Employee Theft, other conditions apply to all insuring agreements.

Surety bonds may be designed to comply not only with various contractual arrangements that arise between a principal and an obligee, but also with various legal and statutory requirements. Most surety bonds fall into these categories: contract bonds, license and permit bonds, public official bonds, court bonds, and miscellaneous bonds.

ASSIGNMENT NOTES

1. Copyright, ISO Properties, Inc., 2005.
2. Copyright, ISO Properties, Inc., 2005.

Index

Page numbers in boldface refer to pages where the word or phrase is defined.

C